FOUNDATIONS OF INTELLECTUAL PROPERTY

By

ROBERT P. MERGES
Wilson, Sonsini, Goodrich & Rosati Professor of Law
UC Berkeley
Professor of Law
UC Davis

JANE C. GINSBURG
Morton L. Janklow Professor
of Literary and Artistic Property Law
Columbia University

FOUNDATION PRESS

NEW YORK, NEW YORK

2004

THOMSON

™

WEST

© 2004 By FOUNDATION PRESS

       395 Hudson Street
       New York, NY 10014
       Phone Toll Free 1–877–888–1330
       Fax (212) 367–6799
       fdpress.com
Printed in the United States of America

ISBN 1–58778–754–7

 *TEXT IS PRINTED ON 10% POST CONSUMER RECYCLED PAPER*

RPM: This one is just for Jo

JCG: For George and Paul and Clara

*

PREFACE

This book is meant to provide a comprehensive yet concise collection of commentaries on the topic of intellectual property. Our goal has been to bring together the most influential writings on patent, copyright, trademark and design protection, beginning with early material from the seventeenth century and continuing into the contemporary law review literature. Because this literature continues to grow quickly, we decided on a "cutoff date" of the year 2000, however, so some very recent contributions of note will not be found among the excerpts. At the same time, each excerpt or group of excerpts is supplemented by extensive notes and questions, which typically include citations and extended discussions of more recent literature (up until our publication deadline of June, 2004).

The excerpts have been very heavily edited. Given our desire to provide a comprehensive overview, and because many of the articles we draw on are quite long, the excerpts set forth here are in many cases little more than a précis of the original. While we have tried very hard to capture the essential animating ideas of each excerpt, many of the nuances, elaborations, and qualifications (not to mention, footnotes) that often surround careful scholarly work are either barely discernable or else entirely missing from the excerpts in this book. For a full and detailed understanding of an author's argument, there is simply no substitute for consulting the original text.

Scholarship, though in many ways a solitary enterprise, takes place within a community. A book like this one brings this fact home with extra force. First, it reminds us that today's work builds on many labors from the past—that we are part of a scholarly enterprise stretching over time and space, connected by our interest, concern, and even passion for this branch of the law. Second, at a more prosaic level, a book like this requires the permission and consent of many authors and many publishers of legal scholarship. Without procedures and norms for granting permission, and in some cases arranging compensation, a book like this would be impossible. We take this opportunity to thank the many authors, law review staff members, and other publishers, who took time to answer our inquiries and grant us permission to works over which they hold copyrights.

Finally, and in some ways most importantly, each of the editors has a support system that makes it possible to work on projects such as this book. Here we record our debt to the people who support us.

Rob Merges would like to thank Roberta Romano of the Yale Law School for originally proposing this project, and patiently waiting several years for it to come to fruition, and also Steve Errick of Foundation Press for encouragement, enthusiasm, and editorial support. Merges also thanks Chris Swain, Kathleen Vanden Heuvel, and Susan Russell at Boalt Hall School of Law, U.C. Berkeley, for help in tracking down and digitizing various excerpts; and especially Carrie Armstrong-Ruport of the U.C. Davis Law School, for her cheerful, energetic help in formatting, editing, and typing many excerpts, all of which was absolutely indispensable to the completion of this project. And as always the Merges family, Jo, Robbie and James, was there to support, divert, indulge, and love in just the right proportions to see the project through.

Jane Ginsburg thanks Rob Merges for inviting her to participate in this project: the reacquaintance that a task of this kind requires with so many leading historical and contemporary commentaries has proved enriching and in some cases even surprising. Thanks also to Steve Errick for consistent and cheerful editorial support, and to Gabriel Soto of Columbia Law School for valued administrative assistance. Ginsburg is especially grateful to Hannah Shay Chanoine, Columbia Law School class of 2004, whose perseverance, intellectual generosity, and patient fulfillment of ever-evolving (not to say, occasionally contradictory) requests made editing the Copyright and Trademarks chapters of this book both possible and fun.

ABOUT THE AUTHORS

Robert P. Merges is Wilson Sonsini Goodrich & Rosati Professor of Law and Technology at U.C. Berkeley (Boalt Hall) School of Law, and Professor of Law, U.C. Davis Law School. He is also a co-Director of the Berkeley Center for Law and Technology. He is the co-author of leading casebooks on patent law and intellectual property, and has written numerous articles on the economics of intellectual property. Professor Merges has worked with government agencies such as the Department of Justice and the Federal Trade Commission on IP-related policy issues. He has also consulted with leading law firms and companies. He has a B.S. from Carnegie-Mellon University, a J.D. from Yale Law School, and graduate legal degrees from Columbia Law School.

Jane C. Ginsburg, Morton L. Janklow Professor of Literary and Artistic Property Law, and co-Director of the Kernochan Center for Law, Media and the Arts, has been a member of Columbia Law School faculty since 1987. She teaches Legal Methods, Copyright Law, and Trademarks Law, and is the author or co-author of Foundation Press casebooks in all three subjects. Professor Ginsburg has taught French and U.S. copyright law and U.S. legal methods at the University of Paris and other French universities. A Graduate of the University of Chicago (BA 1976, MA 1977), she received a JD in 1980 from Harvard, and a Doctorate of Law in 1995 from the University of Paris.

FOUNDATIONS OF LAW SERIES

ROBERTA ROMANO, General Editor

Foundations of Administrative Law
Edited by Peter H. Schuck, Yale Law School

Foundations of Contract Law
Edited by Richard Craswell, Stanford Law School and Alan Schwartz, Yale Law School

Foundations of Corporate Law
Edited by Roberta Romano, Yale Law School

Foundations of Criminal Law
Edited by Leo Katz, Michael S. Moore and Stephen J. Morse, all of the University of Pennsylvania Law School

Foundations of The Economic Approach to Law
Edited by Avery Wiener Katz, Columbia Law School

Foundations of Employment Discrimination Law
Edited by John Donohue, III, Stanford Law School

Foundations of Environmental Law and Policy
Edited by Richard L. Revesz, New York University Law School

Foundations of Intellectual Property
Edited by Robert P. Merges, University of California Berkeley and Davis Schools of Law and Jane C. Ginsburg, Columbia University School of Law

Foundations of International Income Taxation
Edited by Michael J. Graetz, Yale Law School

Foundations of Labor and Employment Law
Edited by Samuel Estreicher, New York University Law School and Stewart J. Schwab, Cornell Law School

Foundations of the Law and Ethics of Lawyering
Edited by George M. Cohen, University of Virginia School of Law and Susan P. Koniak, Boston University School of Law

Foundations of Tort Law
Edited by Saul Levmore, University of Chicago Law School

CONTENTS

CONTENTS

CONTENTS

FOUNDATIONS OF INTELLECTUAL PROPERTY

*

I

Patents

I. History and Basic Concepts

A. Basic Concepts

We begin our exploration of patent law with an excerpt from the writings of John Locke, whose seventeenth century treatises form one of the cornerstones of property rights theory. Historians and legal scholars have long recognized Locke's "labor theory" of property—set out in the following excerpt—as one of the foundations of intellectual property law. See, e.g., Adam Mossoff, "Rethinking the Development of Patents: An Intellectual History," 1550–1800, 52 *Hastings L.J.* 1255 (2001) (emphasizing influence of Locke's writing on various aspects of patent law).

Second Treatise on Government (1690)

JOHN LOCKE

Chapter V

Of Property

24.   Whether we consider natural reason, which tells us that men, being once born, have a right to their preservation, and consequently to meat and drink and such other things as Nature affords for their subsistence, or "revelation," which gives us an account of those grants God made of the world to Adam, and to Noah and his sons, it is very clear that God, as King David says (Psalm 115. 16), *"has given the earth to the children of men,"* given it to mankind in common. But, this being supposed, it seems to some a very great difficulty how any one should ever come to have a property in anything . . .

25.   God, who hath given the world to men in common, hath also given them reason to make use of it to the best advantage of life and convenience. The earth and all that is therein is given to men for the support and comfort of their being. And though all the fruits it naturally produces, and beasts it feeds, belong to mankind in common, as they are produced by the spontaneous hand of Nature, and nobody has originally a private dominion exclusive of the rest of mankind in any of them, as they are thus in their natural state, yet being given for the use of men, there must of necessity be a means to appropriate them some way or other before they can be of any use, or at all beneficial, to any particular

men. The fruit or venison which nourishes the wild Indian, who knows
no enclosure, and is still a tenant in common, must be his, and so his—
i.e., a part of him, that another can no longer have any right to it before
it can do him any good for the support of his life.

26.   Though the earth and all inferior creatures be common to all men,
yet every man has a "property" in his own "person." This nobody has
any right to but himself. The "labour" of his body and the "work" of his
hands, we may say, are properly his. Whatsoever, then, he removes out
of the state that Nature hath provided and left it in, he hath mixed his
labour with it, and joined to it something that is his own, and thereby
makes it his property. It being by him removed from the common state
Nature placed it in, it hath by this labour something annexed to it that
excludes the common right of other men. For this "labour" being the
unquestionable property of the labourer, no man but he can have a right
to what that is once joined to, at least where there is enough, and as
good left in common for others.

27.   He that is nourished by the acorns he picked up under an oak, or
the apples he gathered from the trees in the wood, has certainly
appropriated them to himself. Nobody can deny but the nourishment is
his. I ask, then, when did they begin to be his? when he digested? or
when he ate? or when he boiled? or when he brought them home? or
when he picked them up? And it is plain, if the first gathering made
them not his, nothing else could. That labour put a distinction between
them and common. That added something to them more than Nature,
the common mother of all, had done, and so they became his private
right. And will any one say he had no right to those acorns or apples he
thus appropriated because he had not the consent of all mankind to
make them his? Was it a robbery thus to assume to himself what
belonged to all in common? If such a consent as that was necessary, man
had starved, notwithstanding the plenty God had given him. We see in
commons, which remain so by compact, that it is the taking any part of
what is common, and removing it out of the state Nature leaves it in,
which begins the property, without which the common is of no use. And
the taking of this or that part does not depend on the express consent of
all the commoners. . . . The labour that was mine, removing them out of
that common state they were in, hath fixed my property in them.

28.   . . . Though the water running in the fountain be every one's, yet
who can doubt but that in the pitcher is his only who drew it out? His
labour hath taken it out of the hands of Nature where it was common,
and belonged equally to all her children, and hath thereby appropriated
it to himself.

29.   Thus this law of reason makes the deer that Indian's who hath
killed it; it is allowed to be his goods who hath bestowed his labour upon
it, though, before, it was the common right of every one. . . . And even
amongst us, the hare that any one is hunting is thought his who pursues
her during the chase. For being a beast that is still looked upon as
common, and no man's private possession, whoever has employed so
much labour about any of that kind as to find and pursue her has

thereby removed her from the state of Nature wherein she was common, and hath begun a property.

30. It will, perhaps, be objected to this, that if gathering the acorns or other fruits of the earth, etc., makes a right to them, then any one may engross as much as he will. To which I answer, Not so. The same law of Nature that does by this means give us property, does also bound that property too. *"God has given us all things richly."* Is the voice of reason confirmed by inspiration? But how far has He given it us—"to enjoy"? As much as any one can make use of to any advantage of life before it spoils, so much he may by his labour fix a property in. Whatever is beyond this is more than his share, and belongs to others. Nothing was made by God for man to spoil or destroy . . .

31. . . . As much land as a man tills, plants, improves, cultivates, and can use the product of, so much is his property. He by his labour does, as it were, enclose it from the common. Nor will it invalidate his right to say everybody else has an equal title to it, and therefore he cannot appropriate, he cannot enclose, without the consent of all his fellow-commoners, all mankind. God, when He gave the world in common to all mankind, commanded man also to labour, and the penury of his condition required it of him. God and his reason commanded him to subdue the earth—i.e., improve it for the benefit of life and therein lay out something upon it that was his own, his labour. He that, in obedience to this command of God, subdued, tilled, and sowed any part of it, thereby annexed to it something that was his property, which another had no title to, nor could without injury take from him.

32. Nor was this appropriation of any parcel of land, by improving it, any prejudice to any other man, since there was still enough and as good left, and more than the yet unprovided could use. So that, in effect, there was never the less left for others because of his enclosure for himself. For he that leaves as much as another can make use of does as good as take nothing at all. Nobody could think himself injured by the drinking of another man, though he took a good draught, who had a whole river of the same water left him to quench his thirst. And the case of land and water, where there is enough of both, is perfectly the same.

33. God gave the world to men in common, but since He gave it them for their benefit and the greatest conveniencies of life they were capable to draw from it, it cannot be supposed He meant it should always remain common and uncultivated. He gave it to the use of the industrious and rational (and labour was to be his title to it); not to the fancy or covetousness of the quarrelsome and contentious. He that had as good left for his improvement as was already taken up needed not complain, ought not to meddle with what was already improved by another's labour; if he did it is plain he desired the benefit of another's pains, which he had no right to, and not the ground which God had given him, in common with others, to labour on, and whereof there was as good left as that already possessed, and more than he knew what to do with, or his industry could reach to.

Notes and Questions

1. John Locke was born in Bristol, England on August 29, 1632. He attended Oxford University. In the early 1680s, his views on freedom of religion and the rights of citizens brought him into conflict with the British monarchy, and he took refuge in Holland. He returned in 1689, the year of Britain's "Glorious Revolution," and then began publishing his views more widely. Both his first and second Treatises on Government were published in 1690. He died in 1704.

2. In Paragraph 25, Locke lays the foundation for property as a means of *appropriating* what nature provides: "[Y]et being given for the use of men, there must of necessity be a means to appropriate [nature's products] some way or other before they can be of any use, or at all beneficial, to any particular men." For Locke, the need to appropriate follows strictly from the fact that the fruits of nature are given to man for his survival. How are the *physical* appropriations Locke discusses— picking up acorns or apples, for example—different from appropriating an idea, principle, concept or new technology? In what ways are they the same?

Scholars disagree about whether Locke's "natural law" approach to property works well, or even at all, in the realm of intellectual property. Compare James V. DeLong, "Defending Intellectual Property," *in Copy Fights: The Future of Intellectual Property in the Information Age* 17 (Adam Thierer & Clyde Wayne Crews Jr. ed., 2002) with Tom W. Bell, "Indelicate Imbalancing in Copyright and Patent Law," in *Copy Fights*, supra, at 4. For an argument that Locke's theory has little relevance to intellectual property and other intangible goods, see Jacqueline Lipton, "Information Property: Rights and Responsibilities," 56 *Fla. L. Rev.* 135, 179 (2004). For a nuanced view of these issues, ultimately concluding that copyright law in particular squares reasonably well with Lockean labor theory, see Richard Epstein, "Liberty Versus Property? Cracks in the Foundation of Copyright Law," 1 IPCentral Rev. No. 1 (April 8, 2004), available at www.ipcentral.info/review.

3. In Paragraph 26, Locke describes the first of several limits he sees as necessary to any system that allows humans to claim things as property:

> Whatsoever, then, he removes out of the state that Nature hath provided and left it in, he hath mixed his labour with it, and joined to it something that is his own, and thereby makes it his property.... [N]o man but he can have a right to what that is once joined to, **at least where there is enough, and as good left in common for others**.

The idea reappears in Paragraph 33. The highlighted phrase has been referred to as the "sufficiency proviso," see Jeremy Waldron, "Enough and As Good Left for Others," 29 *Phil. Q.* 319–28 (1979), or simply "the Lockean proviso," see Wendy Gordon, "A Property Right in Self–Expression: Equality and Individualism in the Natural Law of Intellectual Property," 102 *Yale L.J.* 1533, 1538 (1993).

What does it mean to leave "enough, and as good ... for others" in the realm of intellectual property? One view would be that so long as an appropriator claims only what is original to him or her, leaving all the ideas and information that existed before, this criterion would be satisfied. See, e.g., Jeremy Bentham, *Manual of Political Economy*, in 3 *The Works of Jeremy Bentham* 31, 71 (John Bowring ed., Edinburgh, William Tait 1843). Some have argued, however, that certain works are so important and foundational that others coming after their creation must have access to them for them to have "enough and as good." See, e.g., Wendy Gordon, 102 *Yale L. J.*, supra.

4. An additional limitation on the scope of property claims appears in Paragraph 30:

> As much as any one can make use of ***to any advantage of life before it spoils, so much he may by his labour fix a property in***. Whatever is beyond this is more than his share, and belongs to others. Nothing was made by God for man to spoil or destroy.

This has been referred to as the "spoilation limitation." See C.B. MacPherson, *The Political Theory of Possessive Individualism: Hobbes to Locke*, 233 (Oxford: Oxford University Press 1962). One scholar has also identified a third limitation on property in the writings of Locke, "the doctrine of charity." Jeremy Waldron, *God, Locke and Equality: Christian Foundations in Locke's Political Thought* 177 (Cambridge: Cambridge University Press, 2002). So Locke wrote, for example, that "Charity gives every man a title to so much out of another's plenty, as will keep him from extreme want, when he has no means to subsist otherwise." John Locke, *First Treatise on Government,* Chapter 4, Paragraph 42, reprinted in 5 *The Works of John Locke* (London: Thomas Tegg, 1823), avail. http://socserv.mcmaster.ca/econ/ugcm/3ll3/locke/government. pdf.

5. There are numerous challenges in translating Locke's basic concepts into practice. For example, under contemporary patent law, there are many cases where an independent inventor can be barred from using his or her own invention because another inventor patented the invention first. Why should the inventive labor of the second inventor be ignored in favor of another person whose effort happened to be expended earlier—sometimes just barely earlier? For a criticism of "natural rights" defenses of exclusive intellectual property rights along these lines, see R.A. Macfie, *The Patent Question under Free Trade* (2d ed.; London, 1864), p.8. Note that limited "prior user rights" are in place in the U.S. for inventions relating to "business methods." See 35 U.S.C. § 273; Robert P. Merges and John F. Duffy, *Patent Law and Policy* (3rd ed.) 172–173 (New York: Matthew Bender, 2002). For some recent arguments that patent law ought to incorporate a general prior user right—in the form of an "independent invention defense"—see Stephen M. Maurer & Suzanne Scotchmer, "The Independent Invention Defense in Intellectual Property," 69 *Economica* 535–547 (2002); John S. Liebovitz, "Note, Inventing a Nonexclusive Patent System," 111 *Yale L.J.* 2251 (2002).

Toward a Theory of Property Rights*

HAROLD DEMSETZ

When a transaction is concluded in the marketplace, two bundles of property rights are exchanged. A bundle of rights often attaches to a physical commodity or service, but it is the value of the rights that determines the value of what is exchanged. Questions addressed to the emergence and mix of the components of the bundle of rights are prior to those commonly asked by economists. Economists usually take the bundle of property rights as a datum and ask for an explanation of the forces determining the price and the number of units of a good to which these rights attach.

In this paper, I seek to fashion some of the elements of an economic theory of property rights. The paper is organized into three parts. The first part discusses briefly the concept and role of property rights in social systems. The second part offers some guidance for investigating the emergence of property rights. The third part sets forth some principles relevant to the coalescing of property rights into particular bundles and to the determination of the ownership structure that will be associated with these bundles.

Externality is an ambiguous concept. For the purposes of this paper, the concept includes external costs, external benefits, and pecuniary as well as nonpecuniary externalities. No harmful or beneficial effect is external to the world. Some person or persons always suffers or enjoy these effects. What converts a harmful or beneficial effect into an externality is that the cost of bringing the effect to bear on the decisions of one or more of the interacting persons is too high to make it worthwhile, and this is what the term shall mean here. "Internalizing" such effects refers to a process, usually a change in property rights, that enables these effects to bear (in greater degree) on all interacting persons.

A primary function of property rights is that of guiding incentives to achieve a greater internalization of externalities. Every cost and benefit associated with social independence is a potential externality. One condition is necessary to make costs and benefits externalities. The cost of a transaction in the rights between the parties (internalization) must exceed the gains from internalization. In general, transacting cost can be large relative to gains of "natural" difficulties in trading or they can be large because of legal reasons. In a lawful society the prohibition of voluntary negotiations makes the cost of transacting infinite. Some costs and benefits are not taken into account by users of resources whenever externalities exist, but allowing transactions increases the degree to which internalization takes place.

The Emergence of Property Rights

If the main allocative function of property rights is the internalization of beneficial and harmful effects, then the emergence of property

* Reprinted by permission from *The American Economic Review*, Vol. 57, No.2, Papers and Proceedings of the Seventy–Ninth Annual Meeting of the American Economic Association (May, 1967), 347–359, © 1967 The American Economics Association.

rights can be understood best by their association with the emergence of new or different beneficial and harmful effects.

Changes in knowledge result in changes in production functions, market values, and aspirations. New techniques, new ways of doing the same things, and doing new things—all invoke harmful and beneficial effects to which society has not been accustomed. It is my thesis in this part of the paper that the emergence of new property rights takes place in response to the desires of the interacting persons for adjustment to new benefit-cost possibilities.

The thesis can be restated in a slightly different fashion: property rights develop to internalize externalities when the gains of internalization become larger than the cost of internalization. Increased internalization, in the main, results from changes in economic values, changes which stem from the development of new technology and the opening of new markets, changes to which old property rights are poorly attuned. A proper interpretation of this assertion requires that account be taken of a community's preferences for private ownership. Some communities will have less well-developed private ownership systems and more highly developed state ownership systems. But, given a community's tastes in this regard, the emergence of new private or state-owned property rights will be in response to changes in technology and relative prices.

I do not mean to assert or to deny that the adjustments in property rights which take place need to be the result of a conscious endeavor to cope with new externality problems. These adjustments have arisen in Western societies largely as a result of gradual changes in social mores and in common law precedents. At each step of this adjustment process, it is unlikely that externalities per se were consciously related to the issue being resolved. These legal and moral experiments may be hit-and-miss procedures to some extent but in a society that weights the achievement of efficiency heavily, their viability in the long run will depend on how well they modify behavior to accommodate to the externalities associated with important changes in technology or market values.

A rigorous test of this assertion will require extensive and detailed empirical work. A broad range of examples can be cited that are consistent with it: the development of air rights, renters' rights, rules for liability in automobile accidents, etc. In this part of the discussion, I shall present one group of such examples in some detail. They deal with the development of private property rights in land among American Indians. These examples are broad ranging and come fairly close to what can be called convincing evidence in the field of anthropology.

The question of private ownership of land among aboriginals has held fascination for anthropologists. It has been one of the intellectual battlegrounds in the attempt to assess the "true Nature" of man constrained by the "artificialities" of civilization. In the process of carrying on this debate, information has been uncovered that bears directly on the thesis with which we are now concerned. What appears to be accepted as a classic treatment and a high point of this debate is Eleanor Leacock's memoir on *The Montagnes "Hunting Territory" and the Fur Trade*. Leacock's research followed that of Frank G. Speck who had discovered that the Indians of the Labrador Peninsula had a long-established tradition of property in land. This finding was at odds with what was known about the Indians of the American Southwest and it prompted Leacock's study of the Montagnes who inhabited large regions around Quebec.

Leacock clearly established the fact that a close relationship existed, both historically and geographically, between the development of private rights in land and the development of the commercial fur trade. The factual basis of this correlation has gone unchallenged. However, to my knowledge, no theory relating privacy of land to the fur trade has yet to be articulated. The factual material uncovered by Speck and Leacock fits the thesis of this paper well, and in doing so, it reveals clearly the role played by property right adjustments in taking account of what economists have often cited as an example of an externality—the overhunting of game.

Because of the lack of control over hunting by others, it is in no person's interest to invest in increasing or maintaining the stock of the game. Overly intensive hunting takes place. Thus a successful hunt is viewed as imposing external costs on subsequent hunters—costs that are not taken into account fully in the determination of the extent of hunting and of animal husbandry.

Before the fur trade became established, hunting was carried on primarily for purposes of food and the relatively few furs that were required for the hunter's family. The externality was clearly present. Hunting could be practiced freely and was carried on without assessing its impact on other hunters. But these external effects were of such small significance that it did not pay for anyone to take them into account. There did not exist anything resembling private ownership in land. And in the *Jesuit Relations*, particularly Le Jeune's record of the winter he spent with the Montagnes in 1633–34 and in the brief account given by Father Druilletes in 1647–48, Leacock finds no evidence of private land holdings. Both accounts indicate a socioeconomic organization in which private rights to land are not well developed.

We may safely surmise that the advent of the fur trade had two immediate consequences. First, the value of furs to the Indians was increased considerably. Second, and as a result, the scale of hunting activity rose sharply. Both consequences must have increased considerably the importance of the externalities associated with free hunting. The property right system began to change, and it changed specifically in the direction required to take account of the economic effects made important by the fur trade. The geographical or distributional evidence collected by Leacock indicates an unmistakable correlation between early centers of fur trade and the oldest and most complete development of the private hunting territory.

> By the beginning of the eighteenth century, we begin to have clear evidence that territorial hunting and trapping arrangements by the individual families were developing in the area around Quebec ... The earliest references to such arrangements in this region indicate a purely

temporary allotment of hunting territories. They [Algonkians and Iroquois] divide themselves into several bands in order to hunt more efficiently. It was their custom ... to appropriate pieces of land about two leagues square for each group to hunt exclusively. Ownership of beaver houses, however, had already become established, and when discovered, they were marked. A starving Indian could kill and eat another's beaver if he left the fur and the tail. [Leacock, The Montagne's Hunting Territory, at 15.]

The next step toward the hunting territory was probably a seasonal allotment system. An anonymous account written in 1723 states that the "principle of the Indians is to mark off the hunting ground selected by them by blazing the trees with their crests so that they may never encroach on each other ... By the middle of the century these allotted territories were relatively stabilized."

The principle that associates property right changes with the emergence of new and reevaluation of old harmful and beneficial effects suggests in this instance that the fur trade made it economic to encourage the husbanding of fur-bearing animals. Husbanding requires the ability to prevent poaching and this, in turn, suggests that socioeconomic changes in property in hunting land will take place. The chain of reasoning is consistent with the evidence cited above. Is it inconsistent with the absence of similar rights in property among the southwestern Indians?

Two factors suggest that the thesis is consistent with the absence of similar rights among the Indians of the southwestern plains. The first of these is that there were no plains animals of commercial importance comparable to the fur-bearing animals of the forest, at least not until cattle arrived with Europeans. The second factor is that animals of the plains are primarily grazing species whose habit is to wander over wide tracts of land. The value of establishing boundaries to private hunting territories is thus reduced by the relatively high cost of preventing the animals form moving to adjacent parcels. Hence both the value and cost of establishing private hunting lands in the Southwest are such that we would expect little development along these lines. The externality was just not worth taking into account.

The Coalescence and Ownership of Property Rights

I have argued that property rights arise when it becomes economic for those affected by externalities to internalize benefits and costs. But I have not yet examined the forces which will govern the particular form of right ownership. Several idealized forms of ownership must be distinguished at the outset. These are communal ownership, private ownership, and state ownership.

By communal ownership, I shall mean a right which can be exercised by all members of the community. Frequently the rights to till and to hunt the land have been communally owned. The right to walk a city sidewalk is communally owned. Communal ownership means that the community denies to the state or to individual citizens the right to interfere with any person's exercise of communally-owned rights. Private ownership implies that the community recognizes the right of the owner to exclude others from exercising the owner's private rights. State ownership implies that the state may exclude anyone from the use of a right as long as the state follows accepted political procedures for determining who may not use state-owned property. I shall not examine in detail the alternative of state ownership. The object of the analysis which follows is to discern some broad principles governing the development of property rights in communities oriented to private property.

It will be best to begin by considering a particularly useful example that focuses our attention to the problem of land ownership. Suppose that land is communally owned. Every person has the right to hunt, till, or mine the land. This form of ownership fails to concentrate the cost associated with any person's exercise of his communal right on that person. If a person seeks to maximize the value of his communal rights, he will tend to overhunt and overwork the land because some of the costs of his doing so are borne by others. The stock of game and richness of the soil will be diminished too quickly. It is conceivable that those who own these rights, i.e., every member of the community, can agree to curtail the rate at which they work the lands if negotiating and policing costs are zero. Each can agree to abridge his rights. It is obvious that the costs of reaching such an agreement will not be zero. What is not obvious is just how large these costs may be.

Negotiating costs will be large because it is difficult for many persons to reach a mutually satisfactory agreement, especially when each hold-out has the right to work the land as fast as he pleases. But, even if an agreement among all can be reached, we must yet take account of the costs of policing the agreement and these may be large, also. After such an agreement is reached, no one will privately own the right to work the land; all can work the land but at an agreed upon shorter workweek. Negotiating costs are increased even further because it is not possible under this system to bring the full expected benefits and expected costs of future generations to bear on current users.

If a single person owns land, he will attempt to maximize its present value by taking into account alternative future time streams of benefits and costs and selecting that one which he believes will maximize the present value of his privately-owned land rights. We all know that this means that he will attempt to take into account the supply and demand conditions that he thinks will exist after his death. It is very difficult to see how the existing communal owners can reach an agreement that takes account of these costs.

In effect, an owner of a private right to use land acts as a broker whose wealth depends on how well he takes into account the competing claims of the present and the future. But with communal rights there is no broker, and the claims of the present generation will be given an uneconomically large weight in determining the intensity with which the land is worked. Future generations might desire to pay present generations enough to change the present intensity of land usage. But they have no living agent to place their claims on the market. Under a communal property system, should a living person pay others to reduce the rate at which they work the land, he would not gain anything of value for his efforts. Communal property means that future generations must speak for themselves. No one has yet estimated the costs of carrying on such a conversation.

The land ownership example confronts us immediately with a great disadvantage of communal property. The effects of a person's activities on his neighbors and on subsequent generations will not be taken into account fully. Communal property results in great externalities. The full costs of the activities of an owner of a communal property right are not borne directly by him, nor can they be called to his attention easily by the willingness of others to pay him an appropriate sum. Communal property rules out a "pay-to-use-the-property" system and high negotiation and policing costs make ineffective a "pay-him-not-to-use-the-property" system.

The state, the courts, or the leaders of the community could attempt to internalize the external costs resulting from communal property by allowing private parcels owned by small groups of persons with similar interests. The logical groups in terms of similar interests, are, of course, the family and the individual. Continuing with our use of the land ownership example, let us initially distribute private titles to land randomly among existing individuals and, further, let the extent of land included in each title be randomly determined.

The resulting private ownership of land will internalize many of the external costs associated with communal ownership, for now an owner, by virtue of his power to exclude others, can generally count on realizing the rewards associated with husbanding the game and increasing the fertility of his land. This concentration of benefits and costs on owners creates incentives to utilize resources more efficiently.

Notes and Questions

1. Harold Demsetz was born in Chicago in 1930. He has taught economics at the University of Michigan, the University of Chicago, and UCLA, where he is now an emeritus Professor of Business Economics.

2. The central idea in this paper—that property rights evolve in response to changes in underlying economic conditions—is frequently referred to as the "Demsetz thesis." See Thomas W. Merrill, "The Demsetz Thesis and the Evolution of Property Rights," 31 *J. Leg. Stud.* (Part 2) S331–S338 (2002). Its impact has been immense:

> The point of departure for virtually all efforts to explain changes in property rights is Harold Demsetz's path-breaking article, "Toward a Theory of Property Rights." The article is still widely cited and reproduced, especially in first-year property courses in law schools.

Id., at S331.

The Demsetz thesis has natural appeal to students of intellectual property, who see in it a simple theory outlining the underlying reasons for the growth—in recent years, quite rapid growth—in the scope and strength of intellectual property rights. See Peter S. Menell, "Intellectual Property: General Theories," in *Encyclopedia of Law & Economics: Volume II* (2000) (Boudewijn Bouckaert and Gerrit de Geest (eds.)) (Cheltenham, UK: Edward Elgar); Robert P. Merges, "Intellectual Property Rights and the New Institutional Economics," 53 *Vand. L. Rev.* 1857 (2000).

3.   Economic historians have reexamined the "case study" of Labradorian Indians on which Demsetz based his theory. Their main conclusion is that whatever informal property rights existed in native lands were ineffective to prevent the serious depletion of native beaver stocks. See Ann M. Carlos and Frank D. Lewis, "Property Rights, Competition, and Depletion in the Eighteenth–Century Canadian Fur Trade: The Role of the European Market," 32 *Can. J. Econ.* 705–728 (1999). An earlier study concluded that the Beaver trade constituted a fairly small component of the Indians' overall economic activity. John C. McManus, "An Economic Analysis of Indian Behavior in the North American Fur Trade," 32 *J. Econ. Hist.* 36–53 (1967).

4.   A recent appreciative critique of Demsetz states the following:

> Demsetz' pioneering work moved property rights out of the deep background of economic theorizing, and into the foreground. Yet these early writings were quite stylized in one important respect: they assumed that changed conditions would automatically translate into revised property rights. For this reason, Demsetz' theory has aptly been described as "the naive theory of property rights." More recently, the theory has been restated in somewhat more sophisticated form, to emphasize that property rights are strengthened when there is *potential* for higher asset valuation. The Demsetz theory, particularly in revised form, does explain at a primitive level the repeated recalibrations of property rights that are now recognized as such an important component of economic growth.... What Demsetz omitted, of course, was politics. Only governments can grant property rights. Thus the translation of changed conditions into property rights takes place only through the mediation of political institutions. Demsetz had an excuse for ignoring politics: very few economists had much to say about the matter (in a scholarly fashion, anyway) until recently.

Robert P. Merges, "Intellectual Property Rights and the New Institutional Economics," 53 *Vand. L. Rev.* 1857, 1867–68. See also Saul Levmore, "Two Stories About the Evolution of Property Rights," 31 *J. Leg. Stud.* 421 (2002) (contrasting Demsetzian theory with rent-seeking theory).

B. History

Patents, Property Rights, and Economic History: The "Statute of Monopolies" Era in Great Britain*

DOUGLASS NORTH and ROBERT PAUL THOMAS

With the Tudors [during the sixteenth century], the English monarchy was at the zenith of its powers. Still, during the era of rising nation-states, Henry VII was confronted with the restriction that the king was expected to 'live on his own'. This king did manage to expand his revenues to meet the requirements of state-building in ingenious ways: by selling grants and privileges and by exacting an increasing number of fines and levies to augment his regular revenue sources. His successor, Henry VIII, added to his revenues by the confiscation of church lands. Yet the fact of the matter was that 'the most powerful dynasty ever to sit on England's throne was powerful only as long as it did not go outside the limits laid down by a nation'.[1] The confiscation of the monasteries' lands and possessions evidently did not extend beyond these bounds, but the king found that 'with nearly half the peers and at least four-fifths of the clergy against him, Henry had need of the House of Commons and he cultivated it with sedulous care'.[2] The rise of the House of Commons, which was dominated by the rising merchant class and landed gentry, was an integral part of Tudor political policy. This dynasty found it necessary to attempt to control parliament rather than to supplant it. The Tudors cannot be considered as other than as opportunistic in their dealing with property rights. They opposed enclosures, espoused monopolies and failed to recognize the gains that were available in extending the market. They sought revenues where they could, without regard to their effect upon economic efficiency.

The Stuarts inherited what the Tudors had sown. The Commons, by the beginning of the Stuart reign, was ready and able to assert itself. The controversy between the Stuarts and parliament is a familiar one. Its importance for our account is that in essence it was a dispute over fiscal matters.[3] The Crown, caught up in the expensive rivalry between nations, needed more revenues and parliament proved intractable. The Crown viewed the government as its prerogative, the parliament saw the Crown as circumscribed by the common law.

The early seventeenth-century history of English government is inextricably entwined with the life of Sir Edward Coke. It was Coke who

---

* Reprinted by permission from *The Rise of the Western World: A New Economic History* (Cambridge Univ. Press 1973), pp. 146–148, © 1973, Cambridge University Press.

1. W. C. Richardson, *Tudor Chamber Administration* (University of Louisiana Press, 1952), p. 5.

2. G. R. Elton, *The Tudor Revolution in Government* (Cambridge University Press, 1953), p. 4.

3. There is no room here to trace the background of the fiscal [crisis].... The classic source is F. C. Dietz, *English Public Finance*, 1558–1641 (*The Century Co.*, 1932).

insisted that common law was the supreme law of the land and repeatedly incurred the anger of James I; it was Coke who led the parliamentary
opposition in the 1620s; this group was responsible for securing the
common-law control over the development of commercial law; and finally
his leadership of the parliamentary opposition cemented the alliance of
parliament with the common law.

Coke's contribution was not confined simply to advocacy of the
supremacy of the common law; he also insisted that this law should
strike down those monopolistic special privileges associated with Crown
prerogative. The right of the Crown to grant special privileges for the
creation of markets and fairs had been exercised since the high Middle
Ages. In 1331, one John Kemp, a Flemish weaver, was given a patent to
undertake weaving, granting a protected market and exemption from the
legal apprenticeship requirements. The social justification for a patent
monopoly was that a skill should be new to the country and that there
should be sufficient uncertainty about techniques and markets to require
that, for success, the innovator be initially free from competitors. It
became increasingly clear during the last half of the sixteenth century
that the Crown was using such grants as court currency either to raise
money or to reward court favorites.

These awards cost the Crown nothing, but the wider effects were
often harmful when they interfered with existing manufactures or
blocked profitable expansion. In his writings, Coke not only attacked the
Crown's grants of monopolies but also the existence of exclusive trading
privileges. He regarded the Monopolies Act as a reaffirmation of the law
rather than an innovation. Coke described the case of *Darcy* v. *Allein,* in
which a patent monopoly of playing cards granted by the Crown was
challenged (and the holder of the exclusive franchise unsuccessfully
sought court action against the infringer of the patent), as a classic case
of monopoly, which should be and was eliminated, the common law
temporarily triumphing over the Crown.

Yet it would distort the picture to give undue prominence to an
individual in describing the growth of market freedom in England. Coke
mirrored the sentiments of a growing and powerful group of merchants
and traders, who were restive at the restrictions imposed on their
actions. The profitable opportunities in trade and commerce seemed
everywhere circumscribed by privileges, barriers to entry and mobility,
which had only to be removed to increase the scope and profitability of
enterprise and consequently to promote economic growth. The Statute of
Monopolies in 1624 did more than proscribe royal monopolies, it also
embodied in the law a patent system to encourage any true innovation.

Yet the detailed political history of the first forty-one years of the
seventeenth century, like that of the sixteenth century, provides, aside
from the Statute of Monopolies, little indication that a set of impersonal
and efficient property rights was emerging. Rather it is a piecemeal story
of the Stuart's fiscal crises and their efforts to recoup their fortunes by
desperate measures. There was the disastrous Cockayne scheme in 1614,
whose projectors promised James I £300,000 from reorganizing the cloth
trade. A series of patents were granted to overcome the smallness of

fiscal revenues in the early 1620s, and the tariff and monopoly privileges were the means by which Charles I attempted to meet his deficits in the 1630s.

The consequence of these policies for the economy was not only disruption of external trade in the face of efficient Dutch competition, but the arbitrary granting of property rights internally, which increased uncertainty. In this context, Coke and his successors reacted by attempting to place the creation of property rights beyond the royal whim; to embed existing property rights in a body of impersonal law guarded by the courts.

Notes and Questions

1. Douglass North, co-author of the book from which this excerpt was drawn, won the Nobel Prize for Economics in 1993 for his contributions on economic history, and particularly for his emphasis on institutions and economic growth. For an approachable overview of his work—which forms part of the "New Institutional Economics" school of thought—see Douglass C. North, *Institutions, Institutional Change, and Economic Performance* (Cambridge University Press 1990). North received undergraduate and graduate degrees from U.C. Berkeley. He is Spencer T. Olin Professor in Arts and Sciences at Washington University in Saint Louis. A brief autobiography may be found at http://www.nobel.se/eco nomics/laureates/1993/north-autobio.html.

2. The legal case discussed in the text, *Darcy v. Allen*, was dubbed "The Case of Monopolies" by the famous jurist Sir Edward Coke (1552–1634), whose report of the case (at 11 Co. Rep. 84b, 77 Eng. Rep. 1260 (1603)) is the primary source on its facts and holdings. It has been argued that, because Coke both argued the case and wrote its report, the report may not be a completely accurate statement of what really went on. For an in-depth discussion of the issues, arguments, and case reports in the case of *Darcy v. Allen*, see Jacob Corré, "The Argument, Decisions and Reports of *Darcy v. Allen*", 45 *Emory L.J.* 1261 (1996). Among other conclusions, Corré finds that "the opinion in *Darcy v. Allen* should not be viewed as a late-Tudor instance of the kind of explicit and concerted constitutional attack on the Crown that contributed so significantly to the Civil War forty years later." Id., at 1266. Corré argues that a more nuanced reading of the evidence surrounding the opinion reveals a host of less sweeping grounds on which the judges involved may well have decided the case.

3. For the British, the lesson of the Elizabethan era with respect to patents was that unregulated royal grants could too easily devolve into political rewards with no economic justification. Christine MacLeod, *Inventing the Industrial Revolution: The English Patent System*, 1660–1800 (Cambridge, England: Cambridge University Press 1988). When businesspeople make profits above what they would under normal, competitive conditions, economists call those supracompetitive profits "rents." The active pursuit of them—e.g., by petitioning the government—is called "rent-seeking." Thus Edward Darcy, the court favorite holding the royal privilege to sell trading cards in the case of *Darcy v.*

Allen, was almost surely a rent-seeker. See Anne O. Krueger, "The Political Economy of the Rent–Seeking Society," 64 *Am Econ. Rev.* 291– 303 (1974). Rent-seeking is a common practice with respect to all government largesse, and intellectual property rights are no exception. Most recently, petitioners seeking to overturn Congress' 1998 extension of the term of protection for U.S. copyrights argued that it was designed to favor a small number of copyright owners at the expense of the general public. See *Eldred v. Ashcroft*, 537 U.S. 186 (2003) (rejecting these arguments). See generally Michele Boldrin & David K. Levine, "The Case against Intellectual Property," 92 *American Economic Review* 209–212 (2002); Michele Boldrin and David K. Levine, *The Case Against Intellectual Monopoly* (Book Chapter draft), avail. http://levine.sscnet.ucla.edu/papers/ip.ch1.pdf, at p. 2 (describing James Watt's efforts to extend patent on his steam engine invention).

4. Douglass North is associated with a wide-ranging school of economics known as the New Institutional Economics. For background, see Thrainn Eggertsson, *Economic Behavior and Institutions: Principles of Neoinstitutional Economics* (Cambridge, England: Cambridge Univ. Press, 1990); James M. Buchanan and Gordon Tullock, *The Calculus of Consent* (Ann Arbor: Univ. of Michigan Press, 1962). For discussion of how the works of this school apply to the analysis of intellectual property rights, see Robert P. Merges, "Intellectual Property Rights and the New Institutional Economics," 53 *Vand. L. Rev.* 1857 (2000).

5. The anti-monopoly sentiment traditionally associated with Lord Coke was evidently shared by another great British jurist, William Blackstone (1723–1780). In volume 2 of his timeless *Commentaries on the Laws of England* (1765–1769), Blackstone, speaking mainly of copyright, notes that statutory protection for writings and inventions springs from the *Statute of Monopolies*, which provides that "a temporary property becomes vested in the patentee." (2 Blackstone, *Commentaries* 406 (1766; 1979 ed., Chicago: University of Chicago Press, 1979). But Blackstone makes quite clear the outgrowth of patents as a statutory exception to otherwise prohibited monopolies in a later book (4 Blackstone at 159):

> MONOPOLIES are much the same offence in other branches of trade, that engrossing is in provisions: being a licence or privilege allowed by the king for the sole buying and selling, making, working, or using, of any thing whatsoever; whereby the subject in general is restrained from that liberty of manufacturing or trading which he had before. These had been carried to an enormous height during the reign of queen Elizabeth; and were heavily complained of by sir Edward Coke [3 Inst. 181], in the beginning of the reign of king James the first: but were in great measure remedied by st[atute] 21 Jac. I. c. 3 [, i.e., the Statute of Monopolies], which declares such monopolies to be contrary to law and void; (except as to patents, not exceeding the grant of fourteen years, to the authors of new inventions;) and monopolists are punished with the forfeiture of treble damages and double costs, to those whom they attempt to disturb; and if they procure any action, brought against them for these damages, to

be stayed by any extrajudicial order, other than of the court wherein it is brought, they incur the penalties of [the offense of] praemunire [i.e., obeying a foreign authority, a form of treason].

Combinations also among victuallers or artificers, to raise the price of provisions, or any commodities, or the rate of labour, are in many cases severely punished by particular statutes; and, in general, by statute 2 & 3 Edw. VI. c. 15. with the forfeiture of 10 £, or twenty days imprisonment, with an allowance of only bread and water, for the first offence; 20 £, or the pillory, for the second; and 40 £, for the third, or else the pillory, loss of one ear, and perpetual infamy. In the same manner, by a constitution of the emperor Zeno, all monopolies and combinations to keep up the price of merchandize, provisions, or workmanship, were prohibited upon pain of forfeiture of goods and perpetual banishment.

Letter from Thomas Jefferson to Isaac McPherson, August 13, 1813

From *Writings of Thomas Jefferson*, vol. 6, H.A. Washington, Ed., 1854, pp. 180–181

[The background to this letter touches on an inventor whose invention and patent were very important in the early history of the American republic. Oliver Evans, among the most famous of early American inventors, had in 1791 patented a new design for a flour mill incorporating numerous machines powered by a central water power source. Thomas Jefferson, then Secretary of State, had passed on the validity of the patent, as required by the Patent Act of 1790. The patent was invalidated in an infringement suit in 1807 on the grounds of a technicality: Jefferson's office had provided a short description of the invention which was inadequate under the law. *Evans v. Chambers*, 8 F.Cas. 837 (C.C.D.Pa. 1807) (No. 4,555). Congress, spurred by Evans' repeated petitions, passed an Act providing special relief for Evans by extending his original patent (which had expired) for fourteen years—i.e., a complete additional patent term. The Act was duly signed into law—by President Jefferson. The Act caused significant consternation among flour millers of the day. See Edward C. Walterscheid, *To Promote the Progress of Useful Arts: American Patent Law and Administration 1798–1836* (Littleton, CO: Fred B. Rothman & Co. 1998), at 352–354. Isaac McPherson was very likely one of these millers, or perhaps a lawyer representing one or more of them. Although Thomas Jefferson was retired from political life when he wrote this letter in 1813 (his second term as President ended in 1809), his views were obviously seen as highly influential and worth having on the subject. Indeed, Jefferson himself apparently considered the letter important enough to authorize its almost immediate publication. See Walterscheid, *supra*, at 324 (describing publication of letter "[w]ith Jefferson's permission" in 1814). Perhaps, as intimated in the final paragraph here, he even wrote it as a public statement of his views.]

Thomas Jefferson To Isaac McPherson–Monticello, [Virginia] August 13, 1813

SIR,—

Your letter of August 3d asking information on the subject of Mr. Oliver Evans' exclusive right to the use of what he calls his Elevators, Conveyers, and Hopper-boys, has been duly received. My wish to see new inventions encouraged, and old ones brought again into useful notice, has made me regret the circumstances which have followed the expiration of his first patent. . . .

Your letter, however, points to a much broader question, whether what have received from Mr. Evans the new and proper name of Elevators, are of his invention. Because, if they are not, his patent gives him no right to obstruct others in the use of what they possessed before. I assume it is a Lemma, that it is the invention of the machine itself, which is to give a patent right, and not the application of it to any particular purpose, of which it is susceptible. If one person invents a knife convenient for pointing our pens, another cannot have a patent right for the same knife to point our pencils. . . . A string of buckets is invented and used for raising water, ore, & c., can a second have a patent right to the same machine for raising wheat, a third oats, a fourth rye, a fifth peas, & c? The question then whether such a string of buckets was invented first by Oliver Evans, is a mere question of fact in mathematical history. Now, turning to such books only as I happen to possess, I find abundant proof that this simple machinery has been in use from time immemorial. Doctor Shaw, who visited Egypt and the Barbary coast in the years 1727–8–9, in the margin of his map of Egypt, gives us the figure of what he calls a Persian wheel, which is a string of round cups or buckets hanging on a pully, over which they revolved, bringing up water from a well and delivering it into a trough above. He found this used at Cairo, in a well 264 feet deep, which the inhabitants believe to have been the work of the patriarch Joseph. Shaw's travels, 341, Oxford edition of 1738 in folio . . .

The screw of Archimedes is as ancient, at least, as the age of that mathematician, who died more than 2,000 years ago. Diodorus Siculus speaks of it, L. i., p. 21, and L. v., p. 217, of Stevens' edition of 1559, folio; and Vitruvius, xii. The cutting of its spiral worm into sections for conveying flour or grain, seems to have been an invention of Mr. Evans, and to be a fair subject of a patent right. But it cannot take away from others the use of Archimedes' screw with its perpetual spiral, for any purposes of which it is susceptible.

The hopper-boy [component of the Evans mill design, a mechanical device for raking and cooling just-ground flour] is an useful machine, and so far as I know, original.

It has been pretended by some, (and in England especially,) that inventors have a natural and exclusive right to their inventions, and not merely for their own lives, but inheritable to their heirs. But while it is a moot question whether the origin of any kind of property is derived from nature at all, it would be singular to admit a natural and even an hereditary right to inventors. It is agreed by those who have seriously considered the subject, that no individual has, of natural right, a sepa-rate property in an acre of land, for instance. By an universal law, indeed, whatever, whether fixed or movable, belongs to all men equally and in common, is the property for the moment of him who occupies it; but when he relinquishes the occupation, the property goes with it. Stable ownership is the gift of social law, and is given late in the progress of society. It would be curious then, if an idea, the fugitive fermentation of an individual brain, could, of natural right, be claimed in exclusive and stable property. If nature has made any one thing less susceptible than all others of exclusive property, it is the action of the thinking power called an idea, which an individual may exclusively possess as long as he keeps it to himself; but the moment it is divulged, it forces itself into the possession of every one, and the receiver cannot dispossess himself of it. Its peculiar character, too, is that no one possesses the less, because every other possesses the whole of it. He who receives an idea from me, receives instruction himself without lessening mine; as he who lights his taper at mine, receives light without darken-ing me. That ideas should freely spread from one to another over the globe, for the moral and mutual instruction of man, and improvement of his condition, seems to have been peculiarly and benevolently designed by nature, when she made them, like fire, expansible over all space, without lessening their density in any point, and like the air in which we breathe, move, and have our physical being, incapable of confinement or exclusive appropriation. Inventions then cannot, in nature, be a subject of property. Society may give an exclusive right to the profits arising from them, as an encouragement to men to pursue ideas which may produce utility, but this may or may not be done, according to the will and convenience of the society, without claim or complaint from any body. Accordingly, it is a fact, as far as I am informed, that England was, until we copied her, the only country on earth which ever, by a general law, gave a legal right to the exclusive use of an idea. In some other countries it is sometimes done, in a great case, and by a special and personal act, but, generally speaking, other nations have thought that these monopolies produce more embarrassment than advantage to soci-ety; and it may be observed that the nations which refuse monopolies of invention, are as fruitful as England in new and useful devices.

Considering the exclusive right to invention as given not of natural right, but for the benefit of society, I know well the difficulty of drawing a line between the things which are worth to the public the embarrass-ment of an exclusive patent, and those which are not. As a member of the patent board for several years, while the law authorized a board to grant or refuse patents, I saw with what slow progress a system of general rules could be matured. Some, however, were established by that board. One of these was, that a machine of which we were possessed, might be applied by every man to any use of which it is susceptible, and that this right ought not to be taken from him and given to a monopo-list, because the first perhaps had occasion so to apply it. Thus a screw for crushing plaster might be employed for crushing corn-cobs. And a chain-pump for raising water might be used for raising wheat: this being merely a change of application. Another rule was that a change of material should not give title to a patent. As the making a ploughshare of cast rather than of wrought iron; a comb of iron instead of horn or of ivory, or the connecting buckets by a band of leather rather than of hemp or iron. A third was that a mere change of form should give no right to a patent, as a high-quartered shoe instead of a low one; a round hat instead of a three-square; or a square bucket instead of a round one. But for this rule, all the changes of fashion in dress would have been under the tax of patentees.

These were among the rules which the uniform decisions of the board had already established, and under each of them Mr. Evans' patent would have been refused. First, because it was a mere change of application of the chain-pump, from raising water to raise wheat. Secondly, because the using a leathern instead of a hempen band, was a mere change of material; and thirdly, square buckets instead of round, are only a change of form, and the ancient forms, too, appear to have been indifferently square or round. But there were still abundance of cases which could not be brought under rule, until they should have presented themselves under all their aspects; and these investigations occupying more time of the members of the board than they could spare from higher duties, the whole was turned over to the judiciary, to be matured into a system, under which every one might know when his actions were safe and lawful. Instead of refusing a patent in the first instance, as the board was authorized to do, the patent now issues of course, subject to be declared void on such principles as should be established by the courts of law. This business, however, is but little analogous to their course of reading, since we might in vain turn over all the lubberly volumes of the law to find a single ray which would lighten the path of the mechanic or the mathematician. It is more within the information of a board of academical professors, and a previous refusal of patent would better guard our citizens against harrassment by law-suits. But England had given it to her judges, and the usual predominancy of her examples carried it to ours.

... I have thus, Sir, at your request, given you the facts and ideas which occur to me on this subject. I have done it without reserve, although I have not the pleasure of knowing you personally. In thus frankly committing myself to you, I trust you will feel it as a point of honor and candor, to make no use of my letter which might bring disquietude on myself. And particularly, I should be unwilling to be brought into any difference with Mr. Evans, whom, however, I believe too reasonable to take offence at an honest difference of opinion. I esteem him much, and sincerely wish him wealth and honor. I deem him a valuable citizen, of uncommon ingenuity and usefulness. And had I not esteemed still more the establishment of sound principles, I should now have been silent. If any of the matter I have offered can promote that object, I have no objection to its being so used; if it offers nothing new, it will of course not be used at all. I have gone with some minuteness into the mathematical history of the elevator, because it belongs to a branch of science in which, as I have before observed, it is not incumbent on lawyers to be learned; and it is possible, therefore, that some of the proofs I have quoted may have escaped on their former arguments. On the law of the subject I should not have touched, because more familiar to those who have already discussed it; but I wished to state my own view of it merely in justification of myself, my name and approbation being subscribed to the act. With these explanations, accept the assurance of my respect.

Th. Jefferson

Notes and Questions

1. Thomas Jefferson's refutation of the "natural rights" theory of intellectual property in this letter is perhaps its most influential aspect; this portion of the letter has been cited by many authorities, including the Supreme Court. See *Graham v. John Deere Co.*, 383 U.S. 1, 8–9 (1966). Jefferson states his position succinctly:

> Inventions then cannot, in nature, be a subject of property. Society may give an exclusive right to the profits arising from them, as an encouragement to men to pursue ideas which may produce utility, but this may or may not be done, according to the will and convenience of the society, without claim or complaint from any body.

This "utilitarian" view of intellectual property is widely held to be the intellectual foundation for U.S. intellectual property law. See, e.g., *Mazer v. Stein*, 347 U.S. 201, 219 (1954) ("The economic philosophy behind the clause empowering Congress to grant patents and copyrights is the conviction that encouragement of individual effort by personal gain is the best way to advance public welfare through the talents of authors and inventors in 'Science and useful Arts.' "); *Precision Instrument Mfg. Co. v. Automotive Maintenance Machinery Co.*, 324 U.S. 806, 816 (1945) ("A patent by its very nature is affected with a public interest. As recognized by the Constitution, it is a special privilege designed to serve the public purpose of promoting the 'Progress of Science and useful Arts.' "); William M. Landes and Richard A. Posner, *The Economic Structure of Intellectual Property Law* 10 (2003).

Nevertheless, certain features of U.S. law seem difficult to justify on purely utilitarian grounds—and indeed, appear to have some roots in a "natural rights" view of intellectual property. One example would be the "first to invent" priority rule in U.S. patent law. There is little doubt that a "first to file" priority rule is much less expensive to administer. And if we assume that the difference in incentive effects between the two rules is minimal, first to file might therefore be superior on utilitarian grounds. (Less costly, same advantages.) Thus the long adherence to first to invent may well have some basis in considerations of fairness or natural law Cf. Adam Mossoff, "Rethinking the Development of Patents: An Intellectual History," 1550–1800, 52 *Hastings L.J.* 1255 (2001) (describing overlooked natural law roots for various patent law doctrines).

2. Thomas Jefferson not only served as one of the first "patent examiners" in his role as Secretary of State under George Washington; he was also said to have been instrumental in initiating the Patent Act of 1793, which eliminated the examination system and instead called for the mere registration of patents (with validity to be sorted out later by the courts). The traditional account of Jefferson's centrality to the early patent system is set forth, and then criticized, in an article by patent system historian Edward Walterscheid:

> The mythology, however, has far outstripped the record. While Jefferson certainly influenced the administration of the first patent system under the Act of 1790, he did little or nothing to create that system, and bore little if any responsibility for the language of the patent statute. Jefferson did significantly influence certain language of the Act of 1793, but he did not draft it nor was he primarily responsible for its content. He was the driving force for the major change in the patent system brought about by that statute, i.e., the change from examination to registration. He later, though, strongly believed that the registration system was a mistake, although he would never admit that he was the one who brought it about. In particular, Jefferson came to rue the primacy of judicial interpretation which the registration system relied upon. Surprisingly, he seems never to have attempted, publicly or privately, to suggest modification or amendment of the Act of 1793, although he did indirectly seek to influence the judicial interpretation under that Act.

Edward C. Walterscheid, "Patents and The Jeffersonian Mythology," 29 *J. Marshall L. Rev.* 269, 311–312 (1990) (footnotes omitted). See also Edward C. Walterscheid, "The Use And Abuse Of History: The Supreme Court's Interpretation Of Thomas Jefferson's Influence On The Patent Law," 39 *IDEA* 195, 195 (1999) ("The [Supreme] Court has, in particular, overrated and over stressed Jefferson's ostensible influence on the early development and interpretation of the patent law through a selective use of the historical record.").

3.   Historians of technology have much greater praise for Evans' invention than Jefferson did. Consider for example the views of historian David Hounshell, who wrote that "it should be recalled that Evans's flour mill, especially its flour handling machinery, represented a brilliant synthesis of existing components . . ." David Hounshell, *From the American System to Mass Production*, 1800–1932 (Baltimore, MD: Johns Hopkins University Press, 1984), at p. 11. Hounshell cites other historical research crediting Evans as one of the important inspirations for Henry Ford's revolutionary Model T assembly line. Id. Another historian of technology focuses specifically on Thomas Jefferson's criticism of the Evans invention:

> Evans was particularly antagonized by Thomas Jefferson, who made a point of the well-known nature of the components Evans had used to design his automated mill. Jefferson said that he admired Evans but did not regard his mill as deserving a patent. In this he was wrong, because nearly all patented machines were composed of previously known components.

Brooke Hindle and Steven Lubar, *Engines of Change: The American Industrial Revolution 1790–1860* (Washington, D.C.: Smithsonian Institution Press, 1986), at 103. See also See Theodore R. Hazen, *The Hopper Boy of Oliver Evans*, 24 Old Mill News (Summer 1995), at pp. 8–9. Today, patent law typically recognizes that there may be patentable invention in the combination of existing elements into a new assembly. See e.g., *Lindemann Maschinenfabrik GMBH v. American Hoist & Derrick, Co.*, 730 F.2d 1452 (Fed. Cir. 1984), though as recently as the 1970s the requirement of "synergy" among old components in a new assembly was still sometimes mentioned. See Robert P. Merges and John F. Duffy, *Patent Law and Policy* 707–708 (3d ed.) (New York: Matthew Bender, 2002).

4. Jefferson was not the only member of the "Founding Generation" in the U.S. who expressed something less than enthusiasm over the idea of patents. Consider these remarks from Benjamin Franklin:

> [H]aving, in 1742, invented an open stove for the better warming of rooms, and at the same time saving fuel, as the fresh air admitted was warmed in entering, I made a present of the model to Mr. Robert Grace, one of my early friends, who, having an iron-furnace, found the casting of the plates for these stoves a profitable thing, as they were growing in demand. To promote that demand, I wrote and published a pamphlet, entitled "An Account of the new-invented Pennsylvania Fireplaces; wherein their Construction and Manner of Operation is particularly explained; their Advantages above every other Method of warming Rooms demonstrated; and all Objections that have been raised against the Use of them answered and obviated," etc. This pamphlet had a good effect. Gov'r. Thomas was so pleas'd with the construction of this stove, as described in it, that he offered to give me a patent for the sole vending of them for a term of years; but I declin'd it from a principle which has ever weighed with me on such occasions, viz., That, as we enjoy great advantages from the inventions of others, we should be glad of an opportunity to serve others by any invention of ours; and this we should do freely and generously.
>
> An ironmonger in London however, assuming a good deal of my pamphlet, and working it up into his own, and making some small changes in the machine, which rather hurt its operation, got a patent for it there, and made, as I was told, a little fortune by it. And this is not the only instance of patents taken out for my inventions by others, tho' not always with the same success, which I never contested, as having no desire of profiting by patents myself, and hating disputes. The use of these fireplaces in very many houses, both of this and the neighbouring colonies, has been, and is, a great saving of wood to the inhabitants.

The Autobiography of Benjamin Franklin, http://www.worldwide school.org/library/ books/hst/biography/TheAutobiographyofBenjamin Franklin/chap43.html.

The Patent Controversy in the Nineteenth Century*

FRITZ MACHLUP, EDITH PENROSE

The patent system has lately been subjected to investigation by committees of Congress, and reforms have been proposed to meet some of the most serious criticisms. In recent publications commenting on these discussions it has been suggested that opposition to the patent system is a new development. A writer of a "history of the patent monopoly" asserted that "there never has been, until the present time, any criticism of this type of exclusive privilege,"[4] and he attributed the allegedly new attitude to "modern witch-hunters," "hungry aspirants to public office," and by innuendo, to enemies of all private property.[5]

In actual fact, the controversy about the patent of invention is very old, and the chief opponents of the system have been among the chief proponents of free enterprise. Measured by number of publications and by its political repercussions—chiefly in England, France, Germany, Holland, and Switzerland—the controversy was at its height between 1850 and 1875. The opposition demanded not merely reform but abolition of the patent system. And for a few years it looked as if the abolitionist movement was going to be victorious.[6]

The patent controversy, as most seesaw battles, attracted at the time the widest public interest; frequent reports appeared in the daily press and in weekly magazines. That the whole story was later forgotten and now seems to be unknown even to experts in this field is probably due to the absence of any modern historical accounts of the debates that were carried on in the nineteenth century. It is the purpose of this article to give a systematic account of that patent controversy and to show that, despite all the changes in the economic scene, our thinking on the subject has hardly changed over the century.

I.

For a better understanding of "learned opinion" current at the outset of this controversy, it is advisable first to present a brief survey of the growth and spread of the patent system before 1850 and of its fortunes in the half century that followed.

The Growth of the Patent System Until 1850

Most writers on the origins of the patent system discuss almost exclusively the development of the use of patent grants in England under Elizabeth and James I. . . .

By the end of the eighteenth century three of the important countries of the world had statutory patent systems. In France the Constitu-

---

* Reprinted by permission from the *Journal of Economic History*, Volume 10, Issue 1 (May, 1950), 1–29, © 1950, Cambridge University Press.

4. Harold G. Fox, *Monopolies and Patents: A Study of the History and Future of the Patent Monopoly* (Toronto: University of Toronto Press, 1947), p. 178.

5. *Ibid.*, pp. 200, 204, 206.

6. "It is probable enough that the patent laws will be abolished ere long . . ."—*The Economist*, June 5, 1869, p. 656.

ing a patent was expensive, clumsy, and uncertain. Various groups were

tional Assembly had passed a patent law in 1791. In the United States of America Congress had passed the first patent law in 1793. Inventors could obtain as a matter of right—merely *de facto* in England but *de jure* in France and the United States—patent protection from competition in the exploitation of their inventions. During the next half century the patent system, in the sense of a system of inventor's protection regulated by statutory law, spread to other countries. Patent laws were enacted in Austria in 1810, Russia in 1812, Prussia in 1815, Belgium and the Netherlands in 1817, Spain in 1820, Bavaria in 1825, Sardinia in 1826, the Vatican State in 1833, Sweden in 1834, Württemberg in 1836, Portugal in 1837, and Saxonia in 1843.

The Rise of the Antipatent Movement

For two hundred years after the enactment of the Statute of Monopolies in England that patent law had not been brought up for consideration or amendment in the Parliament.[7] It was around 1827 that the subject of patent reform first began to claim the attention of the legislature, chiefly because of complaints that the procedure for obtaining a patent was expensive, clumsy, and uncertain. Various groups were formed to obtain a law more favorable to inventors, and considerable agitation was carried on in Parliament and in the press. This provoked a counterattack, not from those who favored the existing law, but from those who wished to see the patent system abolished entirely. In the latter camp were the influential London Economist, the Vice–President of the Board of Trade, some outstanding inventors of the time, members of Parliament, and representatives of manufacturing districts such as Manchester and Liverpool.

Select committees of Parliament and royal commissions investigated the operation of the patent system in 1851–1852, in 1862–1865, and again in 1869–1872. Some of the testimony before the commissions was so damaging to the repute of the patent system that leading statesmen in the two houses of Parliament proposed the complete abolition of patent protection. A patent-reform bill, drafted in the basis of the 1872 commission's report, provided for a reduction of patent protection to seven years, strictest examination of patent applications, forfeit of patents not worked after two years, and compulsory licensing of all patents. The bill was passed by the House of Lords.

In Germany a strong movement against the patent of invention began as a reaction not only to demands on the part of patent advocates for a strengthening of patent protection in the individual German states, but also to demands for the uniform patent legislation for all member states of the German Zollverein [i.e., customs union]. In the attacks on patent protectionism, free-trade arguments were used more than they were in England, and economists were almost unanimous in the condemnation of the system.[8] Trade associations and chambers of commerce

7. E. Wydham Hulme, "The History of the Patent System under the Prerogative and at Common Law," *Law Quarterly Review*, XII (1896), 141.

8. At the annual meeting of the Kongress deutscher Volkswirthe held in Dresden, September 1863, the following resolution was adopted "by an overwhelming majority": "Considering that patents hinder rather than further the progress of invention; that they

submitted reports recommending reform or abolition of the patent laws. The debate was carried on in books, pamphlets, journals, and in the daily press; in various societies of lawyers, engineers, and economists; and in the legislatures. Engineers, inventors, and would-be inventors, industrialists with a vested interest in patents, patent lawyers, and others who felt they stood to profit from the patent laws were wholehearted advocates of the system. They were opposed by commercial interests, by industrialists and inventors who felt their activities directly restricted, and by economists.

After several years of public discussion, the government of Prussia decided to oppose the adoption of a patent law by the North German Federation, and in December 1868 Chancellor Bismarck announced his objections to the principle of patent protection.

Switzerland was the only industrial country in Europe that had failed to adopt a patent system at this time. Several petitions to the government urging the institutions of a patent system had been rejected. On the basis of a statement issued by the faculty members of the Zurich Institute of Technology, the government continued to refute arguments of engineers who urged the adoption of a patent system. Having rejected previous proposals in 1849, 1851, 1854, and early 1863, the legislature in December 1863 renewed its opposition to the patent system with a reference to the fact that "political economists of greatest competence" had declared that the principle of patent protection was "pernicious and indefensible" (verderblich und vewerflich).[9]

In Holland the antipatent movement was even more than elsewhere linked with the free-trade movement. This does not mean that the controversy was mainly one of ideologies. As a matter of fact, the chief issues centered around the workability of the patent laws and the difficulties of reforming them in a way satisfactory to the parties concerned.[10] The debate ended with a victory for the abolitionists: in July 1869 the patent law was repealed.

The Victory of the Patent Advocates

At the end of the 1860s the cause of patent protection seemed completely lost. But the success of the anitpatent movement in Europe was not lasting. The advocates of the patent system organized a mighty counteroffensive. The techniques of propaganda employed in the years between 1867 and 1877 were quite remarkable for the time. New societies for patent protection were formed, resolutions were drafted and distributed to the daily press, speakers were delegated to professional

hamper the prompt general utilization of useful inventions; that on balance they cause more harm than benefit to the inventors themselves and, thus, are a highly deceptive form of compensation; the Congress of German Economists resolves: that patents of invention are injurious to common welfare."—Translated form "Bericht über die Verhandlungen des sechsten Kongresses deutscher Volkswirthezu Dresden am 14., 15., 16. und 17. September," *Vierteljahrschrift für Volkswirthschaft und Kulturgeschichte,* Erster Jahrgang (1863), III, 221.

9.   *Offiizielles Bundeblatt,* Jahrgang (1864), II, 510–11.

10.   Mr. Godefroi, leading member of the Liberal party, stated during the debate in the Dutch Parliament: "I am thoroughly persuaded that a good law of patents is an impossibility."—*Quoted in the British House of Commons Sessional Papers,* LXI, doc.41 (February 16, 1870).

and trade association meetings, floods of pamphlets and leaflets were released, articles were planted in trade journals and reproduced in daily papers, public competitions were announced with prizes for the best papers in defense of the patent system, petitions were submitted to governments and legislatures, international meetings were arranged, and compromises were made with groups inclined to endorse liberal patent reforms.

It is not contended here that propaganda alone succeeded in turning the tide. Several explanations of the rather sudden disappearance of the antipatent movement after 1873 have been offered, but the best is found in the simultaneous weakening of the free-trade movement in Europe in consequence if the severe depression in these years. The idea of patent protection regained its public appeal when, after the crisis if 1873, protectionists won out over the free traders.

Whatever the reasons for the silencing of the opposition to strong patent protection, the reversal of opinion is clearly evidenced by the actions of the legislatures in the various countries. In England the Patent Bill of 1874, which had been passed by the House of Lords, was withdrawn in the House of Commons. In Germany a uniform patent law for the entire Reich was adopted in 1877. Switzerland, more conservative than most other European countries, held out longer against the pressures of the patent advocates. In a referendum in 1882 the constitutional amendment required for the adoption of patent legislation was rejected, though only by a small majority. The people yielded eventually after strong external pressures had attached to the lack of a patent system the stigma of "piracy" and threatened the pirate nation with discrimination in commercial policy. A new referendum, in 1887, enabled the legislature to pass a patent law. Holland was the last bastion of "free trade in inventions": for forty-two years after 1869 no patents were granted. Only in 1910 was a new patent law adopted, which came into force in 1912.

II.

In the course of the patent controversy on the political scene, economists began to turn their special attention to the economic effects of patent protection. This does not mean that economists before 1850 had been silent on this subject. Some of them had given their views in their general discussions of monopolies, governmental policy, and competition.

Early Economic Opinion

Before the 1850s the voices of economists were far more often approving than critical of the patent system. This is particularly true of England, where the classical writers accepted the traditional philosophy expressed in the Statute of Monopolies of 1623: the temporary monopolies in the exploitation of innovations should be exempt from the general proscription. Jeremy Bentham went so far as to say that the exclusive privilege given to inventors "has nothing in common with monopolies which are so justly decried."[11] Although Adam Smith found that monop-

---

11. Jeremy Bentham, "Observation on Parts of the Declaration of Rights, as Proposed by Citizen Sieyes." First published in French, republished from the English MS. in *The Works of Jeremy Bentham*, ed. John Bowring (Edinburgh, 1843), II, 533.

olies in trade "deranged more or less the natural distribution of the
stock of society," which was "necessarily hurtful to the society in which
it takes place,"[12] he argued that a temporary monopoly granted to the
inventor of a new machine could be justified as a means of rewarding
risk and expense.[13] John Stuart Mill stated categorically that "the
condemnation of monopolies ought not to extend to patents . . .," and he
explained why he thought so.[14]

* * *

In France, Jean Baptiste Say agreed with the English classical
writers. "Who could reasonably complain about a merely apparent
privilege?" he asked. "It neither harms nor hinders any branch of
industry that was previously known. The costs are paid only by those
who do not mind paying them; their wants . . . are not less fully satisfied
than before."[15] Simonde de Sismondi, the dissenter, dissented on this
issue as on most others. In his view,

> the result of the privilege granted to an inventor is to give him a
> monopoly position in the market against the other producers in the
> country. As a consequence the consumers benefit very little from the
> invention, the inventor gains much, the other producers lose, and their
> workers fall into misery.

He wanted "all inventions immediately made known and immediately
subjected to imitation by all the competitors of the inventor." If the zeal
of inventors should thereby be cooled, this would be a most welcome
result, in Sismondi's opinion.[16] On the other extreme, there was in
France a large literature urging perpetual rights in intellectual products,
assignable and hereditary forever. Against the claims for such *majorats*
in ideas Proudhon wrote a satiric pamphlet.[17] But he did not object to
temporary protection, for he regarded the striving toward temporary
monopolies in industry as the most effective stimulus of progress.
Indeed, without the possibility of monopoly, society could not progress.
Thus, he found that the grant of temporary monopolies to inventors was
a "necessity" in our society.[18] The most prolific advocate of perpetual
patent protection was the Belgian, J.-B.-A.-M. Jobard, who between 1829
and 1852 published no less than forty-eight books, ranging from brief
pamphlets to five-hundred-page tomes, on the same subject. The *idée fixe*
which possessed him was that everyone had a permanent and inalienable

---

12.   Adam Smith, "Wealth of Nations" (*World's Classics*; London: Oxford University
Press 1928), Bk. IV, chap. VII. Part III, 244 (first published, 1776).

13.   *Ibid.*, Bk. V, chap. I, Part III, 388.

14.   John Stuart Mill, "Principles of Political Economy," ed. W.J. Ashley (London:
Longmans, Green & Co., 1909), Bk. V, chap. x, 932 (first published, 1848).

15.   Jean Baptiste Say, *Traité d'économie politique* (1st ed.; Paris, 1803), p. 263. *This
passage does not appear in some later editions.*

16.   J.-C.-L. Simonde de Sismondi, *Nouveaux principes d'économie politique ou de la
richesse dans ses rapport avec la population* (2d ed.; Paris, 1827), II 334–35.

17.   Pierre-Joseph Proudhon, *Les Majorats littéraires* (*Complete Works*; Paris 1868),
Vol. XVI.

18.   Pierre-Joseph Proudhon, *Système des contradictions economiques ou la philoso-
phie de la misère* (2d ed.; Paris, 1850), I, 235–42 (first published, 1846).

natural right to the sole disposal of himself and his work. For this right he coined the term "monautopoly," meaning a monopoly of oneself.

* * *

The strength in nineteenth-century Europe of the movements against privilege and monopoly and for free international trade was such that the ideological linking of patent protectionism with tariff protectionism and of patent monopoly with monopoly privileges in general tended to help the opponents and to weaken the defenders of the patent system. It was strategically essential for the latter to separate as far as possible the idea of patent protection from the monopoly issue and from the free-trade issues.[19] This was attempted by presenting the case of patent protection as one of natural law and private property, of man's right to live by his work and society's duty to secure him his fair share, and of society's interest in achieving swift industrial progress at the smallest possible cost. The arguments for patents, formulated in these terms and opposed and defended during the controversy of the nineteenth century, are still used today whenever the patent system is debated. Indeed, little if anything, has been said for or against the patent system in the twentieth century that was not said equally well in the nineteenth.

R.A. Macfie, the most vocal patent abolitionist in England and a severe critic of the theory of natural property rights in inventions, declared that if there were any "natural rights" in connection with inventions it would be the inventor's "right to use his own invention." But just this right, he argued, was frequently denied under the patent system: all too often an inventor would find himself barred from using his own idea because somebody else had obtained a patent on it; this might happen even if his idea were better than the patented one but was considered a version of it.[20] This point was stressed also by J.E.T. Rogers, professor at Oxford and London,[21] and by the French economist, Coquelin.[22]

As early as 1850 an editorial in the London *Economist* presented similar views as follows:

> Before ... [the inventors] can ... establish a right of property in their inventions, they ought to give up all the knowledge and assistance they have derived from the knowledge and inventions of others. That is impossible, and the impossibility shows that their minds and their inventions are, in fact parts of the great mental

19. Most authoritative support came from John Stuart Mill: "I have seen with real alarm several recent attempts, in quarters carrying some authority, to impugn the principle of patents altogether; attempts which if practically successful, would enthrone free stealing under the prostituted name of free trade, and make men of brains, still more than at present, the needy retainers and dependents of the men of money-bags." Mill, *Principles of Political Economy*, p. 932.

20. R.A. Macfie, *The Patent Question under Free Trade* (2d ed.; London, 1864), p.8.

21. "By a perfectly independent train of thought, another person may have discovered simultaneously exactly the same utility, but he has been last in the race [for the patent] and he must forego his natural privilege of labour...."—J.E.T. Rogers, "On the rationale and Working of the Patent Laws," *Journal of the Statistical Society of London*, XXVI (1863), 125.

22. Coquelin, "Brevets d'invention," *Dictionaire de l'economie politique*, 218.

whole of society, and that they have no right of property in their inventions, except that they can keep them to themselves if they please and own all the material objects in which they may realize their mental conception.[23]

[During] the third quarter of the nineteenth century, chiefly in Germany, the patent opposition was able to weaken the cause of patent protection partly by demolishing its shaky construction as a natural property right. German patent advocates found it expedient to abandon this position and retreat to stronger ones.

The Just Reward for the Inventor

* * *

The London *Economist*, under the editorship first of Sir James Wilson and later of Sir Walter Bagehot, championed this position, maintaining: " ... what the community requires is, that inventors be rewarded; that skillful men who contribute to the progress of society shall be well paid for their exertions. The Patent Laws are supported because it is erroneously supposed that they are means to this end."[24] J.E.T. Rogers wrote, in a letter reproduced by Macfie: "All that the opponents of the patent system do say is, that the present machinery gives the minimum advantage to the inventor and inflicts the maximum disadvantage on the public."[25] Prince–Smith was convinced that patents, "in so far as they are to secure rewards to inventors, are the worst and most deceptive form of reward, causing more often losses than profits even to the inventors."[26]

The alternatives most frequently recommended in lieu of patents were bonuses granted to inventors (a) by the government, (b) by professional associations financed through voluntary contributions by private industries, (c) by an intergovernmental agency, or (d) by an international association maintained through contributions from industries of all countries. Proposals along these lines were discussed in the professional journals and conferences almost everywhere.

The proposals for bonus systems of rewarding inventors did not receive great support. The chief objection was that their administration would give rise to partiality, arbitrariness, or even corruption—the dangers of all institutions giving discretionary power to administrators. Bentham had written, many years earlier: "An exclusive privilege is of all rewards the best proportioned, the most natural, and the least burdensome."[27] John Stuart Mill clung to this view. He was still convinced that

23. *The Economist* (London), December 28, 1850, p. 1434....

24. *The Economist*, July 26, 1851, p. 812.

25. Quoted in R.A. Macfie, ed., *Recent Discussions on the Abolition of Patents for Inventions in the United Kingdom, France, Germany, and the Netherlands* (London, 1869), p. viii. Mr. Rogers, however, was not in favor of governmental bonus systems either.— Rogers, "On the Rationale and Working of the Patent Laws," *Journal of the Statistical Society of London*, XXVI (1863), 127.

26. Prince-Smith, "Ueber Patente für Erfindungen," *Vierteljahrschrift für Volkswirthschaft und Kulturgeschichte*, Erster Jahrgang (1863), III, 161.

27. Jeremy Bentham, "A Manual of Political Economy," *Works*, ed. Bowring, III, 71 (date first published uncertain).

... an exclusive privilege, of temporary duration is preferable; because it leaves nothing to anyone's discretion; because the reward conferred by it depends upon the invention's being found useful, and the greater the usefulness, the greater the reward; and because it is paid by the very persons to whom the service is rendered, the consumers of the commodity.[28]

This became the standard argument in the defense of the patent system as the most adequate method of securing just rewards to inventors.

Mill's argument was, however, flatly contradicted by a large number of authorities, including Lord Stanley, the chairman of the royal commission that inquired into the patent system in 1863–1865. On the basis of these inquiries, which changed his earlier, favorable views on the patent system, Lord Stanley objected to the "principle of patents," because it was (1) almost impossible that the reward go to him who deserved it, (2) impossible that the rewards be in proportion to the services rendered, and (3) impossible to prevent great injury being inflicted upon others.[29]

If the patent system could not be credited with meeting the demands of distributive justice, it was still possible to defend it not on the ground of justice, but on the ground of its social usefulness.[30] Even if the system could not qualify as a method of meting out just rewards, it might still be the cheapest and most effective device to stimulate industrial progress. For many of the writers who stressed the justice of rewarding the inventor, the social usefulness of the system was merely incidental. But to others the social benefits were the paramount consideration, and their position, especially since the justice of the working results of the patent system was seriously questioned, became the one by which the system could be most persuasively supported.

The Best Incentive to Invent

Many writers tried to point to history as proof for or against the efficiency of the patent system as a lever of industrial progress. Continental writers were prone to take the rapid industrialization of England and the United States plus the fact that these nations had patent systems as sufficient grounds from which to infer a causal relation between patents and progress. On the other hand, there were some German and Swiss economists who attributed industrial progress in their countries to the absence of effective patent protection.[31] Rogers branded all attempted historical "proofs" as instances of "the fallacy of *post hoc ergo propter hoc.*"[32] Some writers held that patents may pro-

28. Mill, *Principle of Political Economy*, p. 932.

29. Speech of the Right Hon. Lord Stanley, M.P., House of Commons, May 28, 1868. Reproduced in Macfie, ed., *Recent Discussions on the Abolition of Patents for Inventions*, p. III.

30. " ... the practical failure of the law to secure a reward to the inventor and the frequent disproportion between the reward and the service rendered ... are points of no consequence so long as the public is generally a gainer by the law."—*The Economist*, June 5, 1869, p. 657. The editorial went on to say that the public was a heavy loser.

31. "German industry undoubtedly owes its present prosperous condition also to the fact that only a few patents have been granted in Germany...." Böhmert, *Die Erfindungspatente*, p. 48. Böhmert also suggested that England developed industrially *in spite* of her patent system but less than she would have without it.—*Ibid.*, p. 79.

32. Rogers, "On the Rationale and Working of the Patent Laws," *Journal of the Statistical Society of London*, XXVI (1863), 129.

mote technological innovation in earlier stages of industrial development while at more advanced stages they become retarding influences. With a relation between patents and progress as complex as this, most writers relied primarily on logical analysis.

The main thesis demonstrating the beneficial effects of patents rested on the following assertions: (1) industrial progress is desirable, (2) invention is a necessary condition of industrial progress, (3) not enough inventions will be made or used unless effective incentives are provided, (4) patents are the cheapest and most effective means of providing these incentives. The opponents of patents did not deny the first two propositions, but they rejected one or both of the others.

To say that patents are effective incentives to inventive activity is one thing; it is another to contend that they are necessary for inducing an adequate amount of such activity. For both assertions, usually not kept apart, scores of authorities can be quoted.

The counterclaim that patents were the cheapest means of providing effective incentives turned attention to the comparison between the social benefits and social costs of the patent system.

The majority of British economists obviously accepted Mill's endorsement of the social benefits of patents, which did not substantially qualify Bentham's opinion that the exclusive privilege of inventors "produces an infinite effect and costs nothing."[33] Nevertheless the reports of the British patent commissions pointed out that a heavy social cost of the operation of the patent laws was unavoidable. And a group of economists joined the opposition, so vocal on the Continent, claiming that the social costs of the patent systems were too high and the social net benefits negative.

To the extent that the stimulus of the patent system is effective, in the sense of causing people to do what they would not do otherwise, its effectiveness may consist chiefly in diverting existing activity into different, perhaps less productive, channels. This is one of the main contentions of the economists opposing the patent system. The diversion may be from ordinary productive pursuits into "inventing," or from innovation or research activities in one field to the same kind of activities in another field in which the results enjoy patent protection.

The sacrifice of the production that would otherwise have occurred through the alternative uses of the productive resources steered into different channels by the patent incentive must of course be considered a social cost of the patent system. But three other factors were counted among the cost: First, the cost of the bureaucracy administering the patent system: the court personnel, lawyers, agents, and others engaged in prosecuting patent applications and litigations. Second, the economic disadvantages connected with the extension of the monopoly power of certain firms, an extension that often goes far beyond the scope of an individual patent grant.[34] And, third, the social loss involved in the

33. Bentham, "A Manual of Political Economy," *Works*, ed. Bowring, III, 71.

34. "... a few great firms in any branch of business, buying up ... any new patent applicable to their business, and prepared to fight for it, could so hamper other competitors

temporary prevention of the use of the most efficient processes by most, if not all, other producers.

It was this social loss that some writers felt was the worst effect of the patent system, and they emphasized the obstacles that the system put in the way of improvement by others of patented inventions:

> The privileges granted to inventors by patent laws are prohibitions on other men, and the history of inventions accordingly teems with accounts of trifling improvements patented, that have put a stop, for a long period, to other similar and much greater improvements. It seems also with accounts of improvements carried into effect the instant some patents had expired. The privileges have stifled more inventions than they have promoted, and have caused more brilliant schemes to be put aside than the want of them could ever have induced men to conceal. Every patent is a prohibition against improvements in a particular direction, except by the patentee, for a certain number of years; and, however beneficial that may be to him who receives the privilege, the community cannot be benefited by it ... On all inventors it is especially a prohibition to exercise their faculties; and in proportion as they are more numerous than one, it is an impediment to the general advancement, with which it is the duty of the Legislature not to interfere, and which the claimers of privileges pretend at least to have at heart.[35]

It had been one of the strongest arguments of the patent advocates that the exclusive rights granted to inventors did not deprive others of anything they had had before and that the patent system, therefore, simulated invention at no cost to anybody, merely delaying the general use of the new inventions for a number of years. This argument was now sharply rejected. According to the patent opponents, the patent grants *did* deprive others of what they had had before: of the opportunity to evolve and use the same idea that the patentee has had. Where many people work simultaneously on the solution of technical problems posed by consumer demand and the current state of the arts, the patent granted to the one who first arrives at the solution deprives all the others of the chance to use their own, independent ideas and deprives society of the benefits that would flow from the more widespread use of these ideas.[36]

Very often the advocates as well as the opponents of patents discussed the economic effects of the system on the assumption that the inventor was also the owner of the firm using the patent. It was not overlooked, however, that most inventors are either "employed by a manufacturer or capitalist"[37] or must sell their patents to them for a

as to secure a practical monopoly." Speech of the Right Hon. Lord Stanley, M.P. in Macfie, ed. *Recent Discussions on the Abolition of Patents for Inventions*, p. 112.

35. *The Economist*, February 1, 1851, pp. 114–15.

36. " ... it commonly happened that half-a-dozen men who were competing ... were upon the track of the same discovery. Each of these ... would probably have hit upon the invention which was wanted, independently ... But the first who hit upon it, and who took out a patent for it, was thereby entitled to exclude the general public and competitors from the use of that which, if he had never existed, they would probably have hit upon within a few weeks."—Lord Stanley, in Macfie, ed., *Recent Discussions on the Abolition of Patents for Inventions*, p. 113.

37. *The Economist*, June 5, 1869, p. 656.

"pittance."[38] This separation and possible conflict of interests between the inventor and exploiter not merely added to the arguments against the "just-reward" theory but weighed heavily also against the theory that inventive activity requires a special incentive. If the inventors could not hope to reap the fruits of their work, the patent system could hardly be the incentive to their activity that it was represented to be. But another theory could be substituted for the weakened theory of the patent as an incentive to invent: a theory of the patent as an incentive to venture capital for the financing of the development and pioneer exploitation of inventions. It is hardly surprising, however, that the function of the patent as a stimulus to the inventor's financier was not given, in the period here examined, the full emphasis that it now has.[39]

The academic controversy about the patent of invention did not end in any "decision." But the political controversy, as we reported in the early pages of this article, ended with a victory for the patent advocates. On the Continent, especially Germany, this was a victory of the allied forces of protectionism: the acceptance of the idea of protection of industry against competition from abroad as well as from domestic imitators.

It is not surprising that, once the controversy in the legislatures was settled, economists returned to other questions. After the 1870s, the agenda of their professional meetings rarely included debates on the patent system. Only the old participants in the controversy continued to write about the topic that had been so heatedly discussed between 1850 and 1875. The "younger" economists were not interested. The controversy all but disappeared from the economic journals. Economists who wrote general treatises on economic theory and policy had, of course, to make passing references to the subject of patent protection. But, to judge from their usually brief remarks, most of them did not study the controversy that had been waged in pamphlets and journals; instead, they took the observations of the classical writers, J.S. Mill in particular, as their point of departure if not as their only authority.

When patent-reform plans came up for hearings before legislative committees in various countries, economists were usually not present, and lawyers and engineers appeared as the "experts" on the economic effects of the patent laws and their possible changes.

Notes and Questions

1. Fritz Machlup (1902–1983) was born in Austria and studied economics at the University of Vienna with several famous founding members of the "Austrian School" of economics, Ludwig von Mises and Friedrich

---

38. "No patent brings its holder any immediate pecuniary right. He can only sue people who infringe his patent, and the costliness of patent suits is such that he is seldom able to protect himself. To make the property worth anything, a capitalist must take it up; but the capitalist, in doing so, stipulates for the lion's share of the profit. Probably in the ninety-nine cases out of a hundred the reward was obtained by such spectators, and not inventors."—*The Spectator*, June 5, 1869. These observations reflect a House of Commons debate of May 28, 1869.

39. Nevertheless, it was said that patents "are not required as an inducement either to inventors or capitalists, and the reason of the law fails."—*The Economist*, June 5, 1869, p. 657.

Hayek. Machlup taught at the University of Buffalo, Princeton, and New York University, and wrote on topics ranging from industrial organization (industry structure and competition) to the economics of information. Edith Penrose (1914–1996) obtained a BA in economics from U.C. Berkeley. She worked in Switzerland during World War II, and is said to have assisted many Jews in escaping from Germany. She later became a professor of economics at the London School of Economics and INSEAD School of Business in France, among other places. See Michael H. Best and Elizabeth Garnsey, "Edith Penrose, 1914–1996," 109 *Econ. J.* 187–201 (1999). She is most remembered among economists for her book, *Theory of the Growth of the Firm* (Oxford, UK: Oxford University Press, 1959), which launched various productive strands of research in strategic management theory. See, e.g., David J. Teece, "Towards An Economic Theory Of The Multiproduct Firm," 3 *J. Econ. Beh. & Org.* 39–63 (1982); Nicolai J. Foss (ed.), *Resources, Firms and Strategies* (Oxford, UK: Oxford University Press, 1997). She also wrote a book on *The Economics of the International Patent System* (Baltimore, MD: Johns Hopkins Univ. Press, 1953). In the 1970s, her writings criticized the wealth gap between developed and developing countries; one paper in particular focused on the role played by patents in creating and sustaining this divergence. See Edith T. Penrose, "International Patenting and the Less Developed Countries," 83 *Econ. J.* 768–786 (1973).

2. Machlup and Penrose ("M & P") document the rapid dismantling of the "patent abolition" movement in the 1870s, and attribute it at least in part to the end of free trade sentiment. But note too their description of public education and lobbying efforts that were mounted at the time in defense of patents:

> New societies for patent protection were formed, resolutions were drafted and distributed to the daily press, speakers were delegated to professional and trade association meetings, floods of pamphlets and leaflets were released, articles were planted in trade journals and reproduced in daily papers, public competitions were announced with prizes for the best papers in defense of the patent system, petitions were submitted to governments and legislatures, international meetings were arranged, and compromises were made with groups inclined to endorse liberal patent reforms.

Although Machlup and Penrose do not describe the firms, institutions, and individuals who mounted this "counteroffensive," there were apparently a good number of them, and they were well-motivated to succeed. Revisiting the "Demsetz thesis" from the last reading, can you provide a hypothesis, based on that thesis, about why some people were motivated to fight to maintain their national patent systems?

3. For another assessment of the effects of the "antipatent" movement, see Eric Schiff, *Industrialization Without National Patents: The Netherlands, 1869–1912, Switzerland, 1850–1907* (Princeton, N.J.: Princeton University Press, 1971). Schiff notes the development of several large firms in "patent haven" countries—those that abolished their patent laws, as described by M & P—and the overall continued viability of those national economies where patents were abolished. Of course, Switzerland and the Netherlands were the exception and not the rule, and therefore firms based in those countries could learn techniques and borrow technologies from firms in other countries (which maintained their patent systems). This historical "experiment" would have been far more damning of the patent system if all the countries of the world, or at least Europe, had abolished their patent laws at the same time.

4. While the nineteenth century patent controversy raged in Europe, patents were never systematically questioned in the U.S. One explanation might be the Americans' fascination with new technologies, and perhaps, novelty in general. These themes formed the basis of a campaign speech by Abraham Lincoln in 1859; note that when Lincoln refers to "Old Fogy," he is probably referring to a particularly European character:

> We have all heard of Young America. He is the most *current* youth of the age. Some think him conceited, and arrogant; but has he not reason to entertain a rather extensive opinion of himself? Is he not the inventor and owner of the *present*, and sole hope of the *future?* ... The great difference between Young America and Old Fogy, is the result of *Discoveries, Inventions,* and *Improvements.* These, in turn, are the result of *observation, reflection* and *experiment.* ... I have already intimated my opinion that in the world's history, certain inventions and discoveries occurred, of peculiar value, on account of their great efficiency in facilitating all other inventions and discoveries. Of these were the arts of writing and of printing—the discovery of America, and the introduction of Patent-laws. The date of the first, as already stated, is unknown; but it certainly was as much as fifteen hundred years before the Christian era; the second—printing—came in 1436, or nearly three thousand years after the first. The others followed more rapidly—the discovery of America in 1492, and the first patent laws in 1624. When man was possessed of speech alone, the chances of invention, discovery, and improvement, were very limited; but by the introduction of each of these, they were greatly multiplied....
> In one word, by means of writing, the seeds of invention were more permanently preserved, and more widely sown.... Next came the Patent laws. These began in England in 1624; and, in this country, with the adoption of our constitution. Before then, any man might instantly use what another had invented; so that the inventor had no special advantage from his own invention. The patent system changed this; secured to the inventor, for a limited time, the exclusive use of his invention; and thereby added the fuel of *interest* to the *fire* of genius, in the discovery and production of new and useful things.

"Second Lecture on Discoveries and Inventions," Feb. 11, 1859, speech delivered at Illinois College, Jacksonville, Illinois (reprinted in *Abraham Lincoln: Speeches and Writings*, 1859–1865) (Don E. Fehrenbacher, ed.) (Library of America, 1989) (emphasis in original). The final phrase in the excerpt has become famous in patent circles; it was engraved over the entrance to the old Patent Office building in Washington, D.C.

The "American exceptionalism" of Lincoln's speech may reflect something more than national pride. One of the distinctive features of the early American economy was a distinct shortage of labor. The simple fact was that for many years after the War of Independence, the young United States faced the prospect of settling and developing a vast continent with very few people. Although economic historians debate the impact of this labor shortage on American patterns of invention and innovation, it was certainly a noteworthy feature of the American landscape. See H.J. Habakkuk, *American and British Technology in the Nineteenth Century: The Search for Labor Saving Inventions* (Cambridge, UK: Cambridge University Press, 1962). Habakkuk's thesis—that high wages and labor scarcity stimulated technological progress in the U.S. in the 1800s—is in some sense simply a special application of the general theory of John R. Hicks, set forth in *The Theory of Wages* 124–125 (London: Macmillan, 1932): "a change in the relative prices of the factors of production is itself a spur to invention, and to invention of a particular kind—directed to economizing the use of a factor which has become relatively expensive." If the Habakkuk thesis is correct, it may well explain why the U.S. avoided the "patent controversy" of the nineteenth century.

The Corporation as Inventor, Patent–Law Reform and Patent Monopoly*
DAVID F. NOBLE

> The patent system was established, I believe, to protect the lone inventor. In this it has not succeeded ... The patent system protects the institutions which favor invention.
>
> —E. F. W. Alexander

When he intimated his opinion of those particular inventions and discoveries which had most facilitated other inventions and discoveries, Abraham Lincoln included, along with the art of writing and printing and the discovery of America, "the introduction of patent laws." For it was these laws, he explained to his Springfield audience in 1860, that had "added the fuel of interest to the fire of genius," by conferring the protection of monopoly over an invention to the "true inventor" exclusively, thereby directly rewarding the inventive spirit. When Lincoln's oft-quoted words were inscribed in stone above the doors of the new Patent Office in 1932, however, they no longer conveyed either the intent or the *de facto* practice of the system administered therein. "In his day, Abraham Lincoln could well say that 'the patent system added the fuel of interest to the power of genius,' " one observer concluded after the hearings of the Senate Patent Committee in 1949. "Today it would be more correct to say that the patent adds another instrument of control to the well-stocked arsenal of monopoly interests ... it is the corporations, not their

* Reprinted from America By Design, 84–90 (1979), © Oxford University Press.

scientists, that are the beneficiaries of patent privileges." The mass of evidence of the corporate use of patents to circumvent antitrust laws which was collected in the testimony before the Temporary National Economic Commission in the early 1930s prompted another writer to concur. "It would require more than twenty years of Rip Van Winkle oblivion to events of this world," he wrote, "to miss the fact that the overwhelming proportion of significant inventions now come out of scientific laboratories, and that these ... are institutions which have largely if not wholly removed—by deliberate intent—the pecuniary reward for the inventor."

These latter-day critics were but echoing the warnings of those who had much earlier witnessed the transformation of the patent system. Within a half-century after Abraham Lincoln offered his glowing evaluation of it, the American patent system had undergone a dramatic change; rather than promoting invention through protection of the inventor, the patent system had come to protect and reward the monopolizer of inventors, the science-based industrial corporations. "It is well known that patents in the United States are bought up in large numbers for the purpose of suppressing competition," one commentator observed in the *Iron Trade Review* of 1915. He noted that the monopoly of an industry by means of patent control constituted a "monopoly of monopolies" and "a patent on the very industry" as a whole. Such control of patents, he warned, with the resultant capacity for direction and suppression of invention itself, "strangles the sciences and the useful arts, and contributes liberally to illegitimate commercial schemes." As it gave rise to "monopoly of monopolies," the patent system gradually fostered the corporate control of the process of invention itself and thus facilitated the commercially expedient retardation, as well as promotion, of invention.

Praising the admirable foresight of the Founding Fathers, Frederick Fish explained how they had "adopted a new theory that men are encouraged to invent by the certainty of reward; if the fire of genius is fed with the fuel of interest, the industries will take care of themselves." As a former president of AT & T and GE's chief patent counsel, Fish could declare with assurance that the industries had done so, and in ways never imagined by the framers of the Constitution: "as business units became larger, patent-owning corporations supplanted inventors in the exploitation of patents." The inventor, the original focus of the patent system, tended increasingly to "abandon" his patent in exchange for corporate security; he either sold or licensed his patent rights to industrial corporations or assigned them to the company of which he became an employee, bartering his genius for a salary. In addition, by means of patent control gained through purchase, consolidation, patent pools, and cross-licensing agreements, as well as by regulated patent production through systematic industrial research, the corporation steadily expanded their "monopoly of monopolies." Although the first patent pool, among manufacturers of sewing-machine parts, was established as early as 1856, it was not until the end of the century that corporations clearly became the dominant factor in patent exploitation. In 1885 twelve percent of patents were issued to corporations; by 1950 "at least three-fourths of patents [were] assigned to corporations." The change in the focus of the patent system, from the protection of the inventor to the protection of the corporation which either employed the inventor or purchased his patents, was succinctly phrased by E.F.W. Alexanderson, a Swedish immigrant who became one of GE's early leading research engineers. "The patent system was established, I believe," he said, "to protect the lone inventor. In this it has not succeeded ... the patent system protects the institutions which favor invention."

The growth of the corporations, and the intensification of their control through trusts, holding companies, mergers and consolidations, and the community of interest created by intercorporate shareholding and interlocking directorates generated a counterdevelopment within American society: the antitrust laws. The patent system which conferred legal monopolies to inventors came into increasing conflict with antimonopoly legislation as corporations replaced lone inventors as the primary holders of patents, and used patents to create monopolies. The conflict surfaced in court interpretations of the patent monopolies in light of the Sherman and after 1914, the Clayton antitrust acts. Section three of the latter explicitly declared the illegality of monopoly based upon sales regulation of patented machinery and products, and was largely a response to the monopoly held by the United Shoe Machinery Company. The interpretations of corporate patent practice varied form court to court, but the judicial history of patent monopolies falls roughly into three periods. Between the signing of the Constitution and the first decade of the twentieth century there was either disregard for, or approval of, monopolies based upon patents. For two decades thereafter there was a gradual tightening of restrictions, although as late as 1926, in an important precedent-setting case involving General Electric, the Supreme Court "emphasized the right of a patent owner to license manufacturers with restrictions as to price." In the third period, beginning "about 1940, indifference and leniency in general gave way to a more aggressive prosecution and court decisions and decrees which reflect[ed], as never before, the purpose of the Sherman Act." The period under examination here, that of 1900–1929, was one of comparatively little judicial restriction of corporate patent monopoly and the market control it made possible. The tremendous strides made along these lines in this period, in addition, were of such proportions as to render subsequent judicial and legislative efforts to check corporate monopoly through patent control too little too late.

The novel American patent system, designed to protect the inventor by granting him a monopoly over his creations, had by the turn of the century fostered the development of "institutions" that demanded a controlled promotion of the "progress of science and the useful arts," one that conformed to the exigencies of corporate stability and prosperity. The science-based industries, based upon patent monopolies from the outset, thus sought to redefine the patent system as yet another means to corporate ends. In particular they aimed to bend the system in ways which would enable them to circumvent the antitrust laws. Their efforts included intercorporate agreements, industrial research and regulated patent production, and reform of the patent-system apparatus. Edwin J.

Prindle, a mechanical engineer and patent lawyer, was active in all three areas.

In numerous articles Prindle outlined the means of securing patent monopolies to bypass the antitrust laws; methods of securing patents from inventors, and employee-inventors; and the legislative means of streamlining the patent system along corporate lines. An early member of the American Patent Law Association, which was founded in 1897, Prindle pursued a career which involved him in countless court cases in the defense of patent-holding corporations, and provided him with the opportunity of formulating, along with Frederick Fish and the other members of the National Research Council Committee on Patents, the bill which authorized the revamping of the Patent Office in the early 1920s. In a widely read series in *Engineering Magazine* in 1906, entitled "Patents as a Factor in a Manufacturing Business," Prindle clearly spelled out the possible uses of the patent system for purposes of corporate monopoly. In offering his suggestions, he indicated that they arose out of his own experience at the patent bar and as a practicing engineer, as well as from the successful experiences of the pioneers in such undertakings: Bell Telephone, GE, Westinghouse, and the United Shoe Machinery Company.

> Patents are the best and most effective means of controlling competition. They occasionally give absolute command of the market, enabling their owner to name the price without regard to cost of production ... Patents are the only legal form of absolute monopoly. In a recent court decision the court said, "within his domain, the patentee is czar ... cries of restraint of trade and impairment of the freedom of sales are unavailing, because for the promotion of the useful arts the constitution and statutes authorize this very monopoly."

> The power which a patentee has to dictate the conditions under which his monopoly may be exercised has been used to form trade agreements throughout practically entire industries, and if the purpose of the combination is primarily to secure benefit from the patent monopoly, the combination is legitimate. Under such combinations there can be effective agreements as to prices to be maintained ...; the output for each member of the combination can be specified and enforced ... and many other benefits which were sought to be secured by trade combinations made by simple agreements can be added. Such trade combinations under patents are the only valid and enforceable trade combinations that can be made in the United States.

Prindle proceeded to outline methods of prolonging monopolies and expanding them through ownership of auxiliary patents. "If a patent can't be secured on a product," he suggested that "it should be secured on processes for making the product." And "if none of these ways is feasible, it should be considered whether or not the product cannot be tied up in some way with a patent on some other product, process, or machine." As a patent lawyer, Prindle understood that "a patent is valid only when granted in the name of the inventor," and he emphasized the importance, for corporations, of securing the patent rights of their employees. He alluded to a long series of cases in which corporations were successful in their attempts to gain control of patented inventions of their employees because they had failed to contract with them specifically for such privileges. He thus strongly argued that

> It is desirable to have a contract with every employee who is at all likely to make inventions which relate to the business of the employer ... the courts will sustain such contracts, even though they contain no further provision for return for the inventions than the payment of the ordinary salary....

Prindle was aware that he was deliberately subverting the intent of the patent system. In citing cases where employees had refused to give up "their rights" guaranteed by the Constitution, he emphasized the importance of using "psychology" to obtain the patent rights of employees, acknowledging thereby that "rights" were in fact being lost, and that at least some employees were fully aware of it. "The difficulty of inducing the employees to sign such a contract," he noted, "will be reduced if the officers of the company will set the example by signing such a contract." Quite clearly, Prindle understood that what he was proposing—the compulsory signing of employment contracts which automatically assigned employee patent rights to the employer—amounted to confiscation, and something that neither he nor his readers would have liked to have happen to them. Prindle thus acknowledged that the signing of the contract by the officer to set a "reasonable" example was in fact reasonable for the officer alone, since for him it was "a mere matter of form, as [he] is frequently a man who is either not inventive or one who is glad to take his returns in the form of dividends from the stock." For corporate employees in the science-based industries, however, this matter of form would become standard and compulsory procedure.

Notes and Questions

1. David Noble is a Professor of History at York University in Ontario, Canada. He is the author of *The Religion of Technology: The Divinity of Man and the Spirit of Invention* (New York: Penguin Publishing, 1999), and has been an outspoken critic of internet-based coursework in higher education. See "Digital Diploma Mills," avail. at http://www.first monday.dk/issues/issue3_1/noble/.

2. The process that Noble describes might be called "the corporatization" of patent law. As large-scale industrial research and development groups began to form in the late nineteenth century, corporate inventors and their patent lawyers began to call for changes in the patent system to better reflect the emerging reality.

> In 1885, only 12 percent of patents were issued to corporations. Slightly more than one hundred years later, the proportions had completely reversed: by 1998, only 12.5 percent of patents were issued to independent inventors. These two statistics define the end points of a process that, more than any other single factor, drove changes in patent law over the past one hundred years. As the twentieth century progressed, inventions were more and more likely to be the product of large-scale corporate R & D rather than of the lone workshop tinkerer. The newer form of corporate R & D not only brought more hands into the inven-

tive process, but also made available large pools of concentrated capital, and freed corporate inventors from the onerous task of constantly raising new money to finance research.... The rise of corporate inventorship spurred a rapid rise in the volume of patents during the early part of the century. In response, the Patent Office modernized its operations along a number of important dimensions. At the urging of industry, the Office raised salaries and hired a large number of new examiners. And with the increase in the volume of patents came the need to more quickly and accurately search the "prior art," and hence the development of modern patent classification.The same period saw a growing professionalization in the ranks of the patent examiners, including the founding of important professional organizations. The quiet but effective administrative revolution culminated in the Lampert Patent Office Bill of 1922, which both required qualifications and salaries for examiners, and generally streamlined Patent Office procedures. By this time, Congress and industry, working together, had largely brought the Patent Office up to date with the faster-paced world of corporate research.

Robert P. Merges, "One Hundred Years of Solicitude: Intellectual Property Law 1900–2000," 88 *Cal. L. Rev.* 2187, 2215–2216 (2000) (footnotes omitted). See also see Leonard S. Reich, *The Making of American Industrial Research: Science and Business at GE and Bell*, 1876–1926 (New York, N.Y.: Cambridge Univ. Press 1985); David C. Mowery & Nathan Rosenberg, *Paths of Innovation: Technological Change in 20th Century America* (New York, N.Y.: Cambridge Univ. Press 1998), especially Chapter 2, "The Institutionalization of Innovation," pp. 11–46. For a good description of the era of "independent inventors" (1870–1920), see Thomas P. Hughes, *American Genesis* 13–52 (New York, N.Y.: Viking Penguin 1989). For a more popular account, replete with details on the vicissitudes of fund-raising, see L. Sprague de Camp, *The Heroic Age of American Invention* (New York, N.Y.: Doubleday 1961).

3. The notion that the patent system was designed for the self-employed sole inventor might be thought of as a sort of "patent populism." One aspect of this view is that the patent system has been and continues to be diverted from its roots by large, powerful corporations. This form of populism is a consistent strain in patent discourse. See, e.g., Jay Dratler, Jr., "Incentives for People: The Forgotten Purpose of the Patent System," 16 *Harv. J. Legis.* 129 (1979). It continues to inform policy debates and even Congressional activity. See Symposium, "Early Patent Publication: A Boon or Bane? A Discussion on the Legal and Economic Effects of Publishing Patent Applications after Eighteen Months of Filing," 16 *Cardozo Arts & Ent. L.J.* 601, 604 (1998) (proposed bill to require publication of patent applications eighteen months after filing "exposes a growing fault line in the patent community" between large corporations, which support the proposal, and small inventors who oppose it); Reiko Watase, Note, "The American Inventors Protection Act of 1999: An Analysis of the New Eighteen–Month Publication Provision," 20 *Cardozo Arts & Ent. L.J.* 649, 668 (2002) (describing small inventors' objections to 18–month publication during Congressional hearings).

4. For an in-depth description of caselaw from the "corporatization" era of American research, see Catherine L. Fisk, "Removing the 'Fuel of Interest' from the 'Fire of Genius': Law and the Employee–Inventor," 1830–1930, 65 *U. Chi. L. Rev.* 1127, 1132–1133 (1998):

> There are three overlapping conceptual stages in the development of the law respecting the inventions of the employee-inventor. The first was the period between roughly 1840 and the mid–1880s, when the inventor's status as an employee was irrelevant to ownership of inventions, and the shop right was a variation on equitable estoppel.... [in the form of] a license that existed only through the employee's acquiescence. In many cases the existence of an employment relationship was irrelevant to the court's analysis. The second period began in the 1880s, when courts began to attend more to the nature and existence of the employment relationship when deciding ownership of inventions. In this period, the employer could claim a shop right, and even outright ownership of an employee's invention, based on the employment relationship. Courts more frequently concluded that the employer had hired the employee to invent and thus had bought, through wages or salary, the products of the employee's inventive efforts ... The third period, which began at the turn of the century, is marked by the dominance of contract as the method of analyzing invention ownership. The development of a body of law of employment contracts, covering all aspects of the employment relationship, made it much easier for courts to conclude that employers could and did validly contract to own their employees' inventions.

Later in the article, Fisk recaps her earlier analysis, emphasizing the role of social class and social class perceptions in these legal changes:

> If the judges perceived the inventive employee as a man like Eli Whitney or Thomas Edison, they found it hard to treat him like a servant. However, once employer lawyers disabused judges of the inventor-hero image in favor of the modern vision of inventive employees working in a big, employer-financed laboratory, the law began to change. It would be a vast oversimplification to suggest that Taylorism and the change in the cultural perception of invention from the inventor-hero to Bell Labs were the only catalysts of change. The influence did not go in one direction from culture to law; rather it went from culture to law and then back again. Legal categories also affected cultural conceptions. The Patent Office's bureaucratic insistence on the existence of an individual inventor no doubt influenced the way that employers and employees perceived who had been the inventor in fact. Moreover, the rise of contract in the late nineteenth century certainly changed the way employers did business with their workforce. Additionally, the spread of the corporate form of business ownership emphasized for courts the

corporate, or collective, nature of work and idea ownership. This is an area where law and culture cross-fertilized one another in their creation of and reaction to social class. If a judge could not see an inventive man as part of the working class, the judge vastly increased the employee's chances of becoming an entrepreneur if he was not one already. Once judges began to see inventive employees as employees first and inventors second, it became much harder for the employee to capitalize on his ideas.

Id., at 1198.

Patents and Free Enterprise (Temporary National Economic Committee, Monograph No. 31) (76th Congress 3d Session Senate Committee Print (1941))

WALTON HAMILTON

As current opinion has it, the patent and the invention are to each other as incentive and achievement. Yet, it is usage, grooved into thought and grounded into the law, which makes inevitable the connection between them. It was not to prod the sluggish industrial arts along their way that the grant of royal favor came into being, and the trade-ways had managed somehow to advance before the King's prerogative in their progressive cause.

The patent, as an encouragement of technical advance, came slowly into being. The King's pleasure is as venerable as his authority; it had from olden times often been invoked to bestow office, issue a pardon, guard privilege against trespass, and even to create the right of taxation. In due time it appeared a suitable instrument for an increase in the wealth of the realm. Britain was situated on the rim of Christendom; its useful arts were few and primitive by comparison with Flanders and Florence. If fame and power were to come to the commonwealth, the trades of Merry England must be quickened and multiplied. In 1331, a certain John Kempe, a weaver by calling, just out of the Low Countries, was promised the King's protection in return for teaching his art to Englishmen. The grant was not exclusive; a like protection was specifically promised to others who would bring their crafts from overseas. The instance contained its implication which ripened into a policy. A kindred privilege was presently extended to some clock-makers from Delft. As the patent moved into its industrial office, again groups of skilled artisans were lured to the humid little island; and a country made up of sheep runs was headed toward its destiny as shopkeeper to the world.

The "letters" granted to John Kempe were little more than a passport. They conferred upon him the privilege of entry and the right to ply his trade. But no monopoly of his craft and no immunity to authority was granted. He came into a country possessed of its own usages: as denizen and artisan he was expected to abide by the customs of the town and the law of the land. At the time industry was still under the control of the guilds; they set standards, solemnly passed ordinances, provided for the government of their trades, punished breaches of discipline—and the patentee was expected to conform to the rule of his mystery. The liberties granted were manufacturing, not commercial, in character; the purpose was to promote new arts, not to vest interests in old ones.

* * *

Thus, as late as the middle of the 1790's, the patent against the premium system was not yet a closed question. Letters patent had been thoroughly discredited in the great movements by which the monarchy was curbed, men were secured in their rights, and colonies became separate states. Its use, even for so limited and so public a purpose, carried its hazards; it might break its bondage to the commonwealth and become a sanction for privilege. But the purchase of the inventor's rights and the immediate release of device or process to all who could make use of it was likewise open to attack. It was not possible to tell in advance what arts would prove useful or how useful they would prove. The premium system threatened to be prodigal with public funds; the patent system threw all risks upon those who asked for favors. It was not the command of the Constitution, but sheer expediency, which dictated the eventual choice.

There was a call for action; and, as so often happens, the choice was made long before the battle of words had reached a decision. In a speech to Congress on January 8, 1790, George Washington, who had presided over the Convention, urged: "I cannot forbear intimating to you the expediency of giving effectual encouragement, as well to the introduction of new and useful inventions from abroad, as to the exertions of skill and genius in producing them at home." In response to this suggestion—and to the pressure of inventors seeking private bills of monopoly—Congress passed the first patent statute.

* * *

From the forties—and increasingly after the Civil War—great corporate estates appear in the national economy. As truly as the demesne of old, each of these demands its legal titles, its sanctions, the protection of its territories, the expansion of its frontiers, its armament of attack and defense. It is a task of no small magnitude to keep a corporate estate going. To enlarge the realm and increase its power calls for zeal, ingenuity, acquisitive skills, the large strategy. In such an activity a grant of patent—a letter reciting an exclusive right which emanates from the Government itself—is a counter of consequence. It is at once a privilege, a legal warrant, a shield against attack—a versatile thing whose reach is as broad as the courts will allow and whose possibilities only imaginative use can fully explore. In three distinct ways it operated to make secure the frontiers of corporate estates—and to restrict and modify individual enterprise.

The first was that the inventor passed into the background. He was accorded an exclusive license in respect to method, process, design, or machine. But unless he had funds with which to venture, he was in no position to exploit his grant. And, since machines were required to make other machines, he became beholden to the financier for the opportunity to make the most of his discovery. At first the situation was met with an expediency. A partnership was formed between the man of talent and the man of money; or the inventor arranged with some concern to make and vend the article and took a percentage of the profits. But eventually a clear-cut division of function was established. The inventor assigned his rights to a corporation: his claims were liquidated in a contract: the assignee came into full possession and was entitled to all the return the novelty could be made to yield.

The second was that the field for individual talent was restricted. The free lance inventor could no longer roam at will wherever his curiosity led him. As an estate was blocked off by patents, there was no longer a ready access to its arts. The insiders alone had a real chance to play with its mechanisms, to experiment with its processes, to suggest its next steps. If the process hedged off was superior to any alternative open, the independent had an empty and indefeasible right to tinker. If from time to time the mystery, protected by law, could be refreshed with infusions of novelty, the domain might be closed against the stranger almost indefinitely. His only chance would be to take a new road, stumble upon a fundamental discovery, or project the technique from a new base. Even here opportunity is not for all. A radical shift comes as often as not from a transfer of a process from one industry to another— all under proper corporate auspices.

As in 1790 the first patent act was passed, all industry was virgin territory. By 1840 a number of corporate estates had been staked out within the public domain. The old-fashioned inventor had no passport to enter the domains of iron and steel, agricultural implements, machine tools, and telegraphy. The established concern wanted no help from outside in the development of its technology. In the half century stretch to 1890 the great discoveries came in fields not yet subject to proscriptive right. Individual initiative found expression through Edison in electricity, Westinghouse in air-brakes, Eastman in photography, Ford in the motorcar, the Wright brothers in aeronautics. As in turn these were closed off, the man of talent had to accept the affluence of wage slavery, or from his garret seek to penetrate uncharted country.

The third was that the nature of the invention was transformed. As the machine process was developed, it became an intricate affair broken down into many specialties. The concern of the individual was not with the whole technology, but with an aspect of it. This narrowed for the inventor the field of knowledge and the chance at experimentation. His creative gifts moved from a spatial to an interstitial orbit and his inventions tended to become refinements upon an accepted discipline. Advances were likely to appear within confined areas and to be of an esoteric character. Only in rare instances did they exhibit the indispensability which marks the pioneer discovery. The step forward was under strict control; it must not depart too far lest it fail easily to be assimilated into the going art. It must not visit obsolescence upon equipment or carry a threat to the financial structure.

Such changes came about slowly enough; an array of facts marked their direction before their trend could be clearly seen. It remained for an act of Congress to bring drift into focus, to make the patentee consciously aware of the possibilities in his grant, and to provoke into growth a novel scheme of usages. A spirit of unrest gathered momentum during the eighties. Little fellows were crushed, trades were barricaded against those who desired to enter, prices were made to carry all the traffic would bear, the doors of opportunity seemed to be closing, the public took legislative notice of the situation. In response the Fifty-first Congress went in for trust-busting; passed the Sherman bill; and outlawed every contract, combination and conspiracy in restraint of trade. The law of the land was invoked to break down barriers, to remove obstacles from the channels of commerce, to make competition the rule for industry.

It was not the purpose of Congress to amend the patent law. Not even the hint of such an intent appears in the debates. Yet, although their text was in nowise amended, the usages which had grown up to give protection to the inventor were completely remade. In the injunction that all men must compete and let the market do justice among them, the Government took offensive. Gentlemen, to whom restraints were dear, looked around for an adequate defense against such an attack and discovered in the patent a weapon deftly suited to their purpose. The writ came from the Government; it conveyed an exclusive right to all it covered. It was hoped that the privilege decreed for the invention might be conveyed into an immunity for the business; that exemption from law could be pushed along marketing channels so far as the contagion could be made to carry. The patent was a counter to be played for all it could be made worth. The passage of the Sherman Act created a situation whose implications business proceeded to make explicit in trade practice. Placing the point invited the counterpoint.

An ancient usage cleared the way for the new strategy; the inventor assigned his rights to a corporation. In the act there is nothing novel; a contract between parties passes title along and the law recognizes the change in ownership—and that is all. In the economy the transaction extends far beyond its legal form; it falls little short of a transfer of the invention from one culture to another. It lifts the patent out of the province in which it is supposed to operate, separates it from the objectives it is supposed to serve, strips away the world of the idea and custom which impinges upon it. It sets the grant down in a universe of business, makes it a counter in the acquisitive game, subjects it to the discipline of money-making. A radical change in its character attends the journey of the instrument to a new habitat.

Nor could the integrity of the invention withstand the change in climate. It remained a device capable of being put to industrial work; it became a technique to be enlisted in the pursuit of gain. Whether it was used, held in reserve, or laid away in moth balls was no longer to be dependent upon its intrinsic merits; instead its employment was to wait upon the existence of corporate policy. As with the invention, so too, with the progress of the art. A patent was a counter of consequence; but its limited term made periodic renewal necessary. As patents lived out their span of years, others must be had to replace them. Improvements were necessary; and to make secure its realm, the corporation created a research agency.

The conduct of research became a response to corporate policy. One held, for the duration of his patents, as a tenant of the Government itself. If a few basic patents could be kept alive, the estate was in perpetuity. Yet an excess of zeal in the pursuit of invention was to be avoided. More novelty might be turned up than the going concern could easily assimilate; a jeopardy to an interest already vested was to be avoided. Next steps become imperative; and they must be of such a kind as to maintain an advantage over the competitor who had access only to technology upon which patents had expired. But a strong presumption was set down against the radical innovation. In every instance judgment turned, not upon the up-to-date or backward state of the art, but upon such considerations as estimated expense, threat to investment, the protection of old and the conquest of new markets. In a word the corporate office of invention was severely defined.

As the corporation became master to his profession, the inventor passed into its service. As he accepts a pecuniary allegiance, a vestige of his own status is reserved to him; the device or process which he contrives is initially his property; he applies for a patent and it is issued in his name. But there the cloak of a nominal independence is put off; he is an employee, he works for a salary, his contract obligates him to sign away his rights. He is no longer free to roam at will where the urge of curiosity leads; his talents are pent within the corporate field; his tasks fall within the ambit of its operations. He may look ahead, explore, and propose; but it is for the executives to decide how his capacities are to be employed, the lines along which his researches are to extend. His quest after knowledge is strictly subject to business direction. He is devoid of authority over the making, vending, and using of his machines. In instances he may receive a bonus graduated to the sales of the things he has contrived. But in the usual case the connection between the reward to the inventor and the returns from the invention is completely broken. Like a lawyer or an engineer he receives as much as, and no more than, the market value of his services. The research technician, who has succeeded the solo inventor, has become a hired specialist creating monopolistic credits which after corporate endorsement are put into circulation.

But if the inventor has fallen into bondage, the rivalry between corporate estates continues. Like nations intent upon the game of power politics, they seek to maintain and to expand their dominions. Each has its arsenal of weapons with which to ward off, buy off, eliminate, or sterilize with a dictated truce all who may challenge or impede. In the fray not one, but a number of patents, may be hurled at the enemy. The conflict is strenuous, the field for maneuver wide. The protagonist must vary his attack, seize his openings, capitalize all breaks. Victory is to the strong and the resourceful. Firms of inferior financial strength hesitate before going into such a struggle. The patents they hold may be of high value, but frequently they prefer such validation as a process of bargaining may give to the hazards of a resort to court. A grant of intrinsic value is a card with which to buy entrance into a patent pool. Another, a mere nuisance which it would cost a struggle to abate, often serves quite as well. The accords between large corporations and lesser firms often reflect relative strength of the parties. And the validity accorded or denied to patents, in whose name the arrangements emerge, are little more than the rhetoric of justification.

As invention is harnessed to acquisitive ends, the defense must be secure, the attack ever ready. Its armament must be adequate to any campaign and equal to any emergency. The first requisite is to fence in its industrial preserves. But technology is a voluminous and intricate affair; its processes cross, overlap, intermingle. As scientists serve many interests, private claims come into frequent dispute; norms, knowledge, understanding are not beyond peradventure. The business firm, however conservative its research attitude, is very much concerned over the number of its patents, and seeks for every aspect of its productive process the coverage of a legal umbrella . . .

In business, as in war, a vigorous offense is the best defense. A portfolio of patents provides sanctions which, if the staying power is not lacking, will last out a long campaign. Not the least among the weapons which it has called into being is the infringement suit. It has become accepted practice for a concern to harass its competitors with threats; and, if threats do not deter, to take to law. In 1894, for instance, the Eastman Kodak Co. [made an] initial move to secure a preliminary injunction against the manufacture and sale of its rival's products. In the struggle, the temporary stay was the trump card, and the ultimate outcome almost irrelevant. Although the injunction was eventually lifted and the aggressor adjudged to have been the real infringer, the mischief had been done, and Boston Camera was persuaded to transfer its ownership to Eastman Kodak [See U.S. v. Eastman Kodak Co., 226 *Fed.* 62 (1915), pp. 68, 69.] A repetition, with variations, of this ruthless strategy had its effect; within 4 years it had won for Eastman a virtual monopoly of the field of photography it had staked out for itself.

* * *

It is a far cry from 1787 to 1941, and the signing of the Constitution and the report of the Temporary National Economic Committee lie worlds apart. Over the decades the usages of American democracy have traveled fast and far. But none have gone farther or moved faster than the cluster of usages which make up the patent system. The ultimate reference, "to promote the progress of science and the useful arts" persists—somewhat obscured by a judicial gloss written over the original text. The relevant statutes have departed little form the original act of Congress; in the variety of provisions which amendment has put into place there is little that would have taxed the eighteenth century understanding. Yet the patent-system-in-action is an affair that was never designed and which only an elaborate explanation could make clear to the gentlemen who on an historic occasion gathered at Philadelphia.

To insist that the patent has strayed form its original office is not to condemn. An institution, even an American institution, is not immune to the law of growth. As circumstance takes its course, adaptation is the price of survival; to speak of its changing identity is only to say that a thing lives. The grant, as the Fathers knew it, is gone beyond recall. Their useful arts and their economy are not our useful arts and our economy; and an instrument whose office it is to mediate between them could not retain its original nature. The quarrel is not that there has been departure—that was inevitable. It is rather that change has been guided by no conscious policy. As private interests harnessed patent to their own service, the Government remained inactive. As a stream of decisions enveloped the sanction in novel usages, a guiding purpose remained off-stage.

If at the moment "the patent question" seems monumental, long years of neglect have made it so. As issues were ignored, they were postponed; as the industrial system took its tumultuous course, they accumulated into a mighty docket. It is now much too late for the occasional stitch in time by court and Congress. The problem demands a series of attacks upon a number of levels. The machinery of issue needs to be modernized. A resort to law needs to become a more certain and efficient instrument of justice. The terms of the grant need to be brought into accord with the conditions out of which inventions currently spring. The rank growth of custom, by which sanctions are held in bondage to vested interests, needs to be trimmed away or subdued to the public interest. And a conscious policy needs to appoint for the patent its proper place in the national economy. Although ways and means present numerous alternatives, the direction is clear. All that needs to be done cannot be done at once. Knowledge, analysis, intelligent prescription must determine the pace at which a reform running far behind schedule can hasten on its way.

* * *

* * * It is evident that a patent not in use does not promote the development of technology. Its idleness may cause no public loss; a dozen other techniques may lead to the same end. Or its suppression may arrest the progress of an industrial art. In such a case, there should be power to invoke the courts to cancel the instrument—lease, assignment, license, patent—by which the invention is laid upon the shelf. Some cases will call for severe remedies. If the patentee squats upon the public domain in the path of industrial progress, some public body should have power to compel a license. Such an authority is in strict accord with the theory of free enterprise. It was in vogue in a number of colonies at the time of the Constitution was drawn up. By the Fathers, the power to compel license was not regarded as an invasion of the exclusive right of author or inventor. At that time private claims encroached little upon the fund of common knowledge. Now, access to an up-to-date technology is essential to entrance into the majority of industries. If at that time the common good reserved such a power to the Government, its necessity would appear far more obvious now.

It is said, however, that the compulsory license will discourage scientific progress; that the new method, if not put to use, will become available to competitors. Inventions will fall into the hands of manufacturers content to use them for what they are—whereas the up-and-coming concern will hold them back until they are perfected. Thus, the requirement will undermine the value of patents whose industrial application has not yet been perfected. It will destroy the bargaining power of the small inventor who is not in a position to exploit his discovery; for, if he does not like the terms offered him, the large manufacturer can extract a compulsory license from the little fellow.

The reasons advanced have cogency in some industries; in others they are at sharp variance with the facts. Administrative discretion in a case by case approach is the proper way to apply a general statute of diverse situations. A statute flexible enough to meet the demands of unlike industries must wait upon a more detailed inquiry. But the demands for national defense call for an immediate answer to specific needs. An item in the catalog of armament must be produced in quantity. All available capacity must be turned to account and quality cannot be sacrificed. Firms which produce for the Government must have full access to the latest and most efficient technical processes. And, since nations now fight each other with economies as well as armies, the necessity extends to commodities not ordinarily thought of as military supplies. It may be that power to compel the necessary licenses can now be spelled out from provisions already upon the statute books. If not, this deficit in national defense needs at once to be repaired by legislation.

Notes and Questions

1. Walton Hale Hamilton (1881–1958) was an economist, educator, and attorney; a prolific contributor to economic and legal periodicals; and a specialist in what would now be termed regulatory economics; he was also active in the New Deal. He taught economics at University of Michigan (1910–1914), University of Chicago (1914–1915), Amherst College (1915–1923), and Robert Brookings Graduate School (1923–1928); and was a professor of law at Yale University (1928–1948). He worked at the National Recovery Administration Board (1934–1935); was special assistant to the U.S. Attorney General (1938–1945); and practiced law in Washington, D.C. (1948–1958).

The Temporary National Economic Committee (TNEC) was established in 1938, one of a host of Depression-era federal initiatives aimed at understanding problems of the American economy and recommending solutions. TNEC's primary objective was to investigate the causes of economic concentration in the U.S. economy; as patents were largely thought to be a major contributor to economic concentration, TNEC quickly "drew the patent system into the ambit of its investigations." Stefan Riesenfeld, "The New United States Patent Act in the Light of Comparative Law," 102 *U. Pa. L. Rev.* 291, 291 (1954). On TNEC generally, see Charles R. Geisst, *Wall Street—A History* (Oxford, UK: Oxford Univ. Press, 1999).

C. Economics

An Economic Review of the Patent System (U.S. Senate, Committee on the Judiciary Study No. 15, 1958)
FRITZ MACHLUP

I. Introduction

Patent, the adjective, means "open," and patent the noun, is the customary abbreviation of "open letter." The official name is "letters

patent," a literal translation of the Latin "litterae patentes." Letters
patent are official documents by which certain rights, privileges, ranks,
or titles are conferred. Among the better known of such "open letters"
are patents of appointment (of officers, military, judicial, colonial),
patents of nobility, patents of precedence, patents of land conveyance,
patents of monopoly, patents of invention. Patents of invention confer
the right to exclude others from using a particular invention. When the
term "patent" is used without qualification, it nowadays refers usually
to inventors' rights. Similarly, the French "brevet," delivered from the
Latin "litterae breves" (brief letters), is a document granting a right or
privilege, and usually stands for "brevet d'invention."

Defined more accurately, a patent confers the right to secure the
enforcement power of the state in excluding unauthorized persons, for a
specified number of years, from making commercial use of a clearly
defined invention. Patents of invention are commonly classed with other
laws or measures for the protection of so-called "intellectual property"
or "industrial property." This class includes the protection of exclusivity
for copyrights, trademarks, trade names, artistic designs and industrial
designs besides technical inventions; other types of "products of intellectual labor" have at various times been proposed as worthy of public
protection. It has seemed "unjust" to many, for example, that the
inventor of a new gadget should be protected and perhaps, become rich,
while the savant who discovered the principle on which the invention is
based should be without protection and without material reward for his
services to society. Yet, proposals to extend government protection of
"intellectual property" to scientific discoveries have everywhere been
rejected as impractical and undesirable.

II.   Historical Survey

A. *Early History (Before 1624)*

The oldest examples of grants of exclusive rights by kings and rulers
to private inventors and innovators to practice their new arts or skills go
back to the 14th century. Probably the first "patent law," in the sense of
a general promise of exclusive rights to inventors, was enacted in 1474
by the Republic of Venice. In the 16th century patents were widely used
by the German princes, some of whom had a well-reasoned policy of
granting privileges on the basis of a careful consideration of the utility
and novelty of the inventions and, also, of the burden which would be
imposed on the country by excluding others from the use of these
inventions and by enabling the patentees to charge higher prices.

Some of the exclusive privileges were on new inventions; others on
skilled crafts imported from abroad. Some of the privileges were for
limited periods; others forever. (For example, the canton of Bern in
Switzerland granted in 1577 to inventor Zobell a "permanent exclusive
privilege.") Some of the privileges granted protection against imitation
and therefore, competition, and thus created monopoly rights. Others,
however, granted protection from the restrictive regulations of guilds,
and thus were designed to reduce existing monopoly positions and to

increase competition. In view of the latter type of privilege, patents have occasionally been credited with liberating industry from restrictive regulations by guilds and local authorities and with aiding the industrial revolution in England. In France, the persecution of innovators by guilds of craftsmen continued far into the 18th century. (For example, in 1726, the weavers' guild threatened design printers with severe punishment, including death.) Royal patent privileges were sometimes conferred, not to grant exclusive rights, but to grant permission to do what was prohibited under existing rules.

III. Institutional Facts and Problems

A. *Conditions, Procedures, and Limits of Patent Protection*

* * *

The question who is to judge the patentability of an invention and at what stage of the game, have received different answers and different procedures have been adopted in different countries. Under the registration system the validity of a registered patent is examined only if an interested party attacks it in the courts and asks that the patent be invalidated. Under the examination system a patent is issued only after the Patent Office has carefully examined the patentability of the invention. This examination may include so-called "interference proceedings," when the Office finds that two or more pending applications seem to claim, partly or wholly, the same invention, so that the priority of one invention has to be established. The so-called "Aufgebotssystem," or examination-plus-opposition system, provides for an interval of time after publication of the specifications examined and accepted by the official examiner and before the issuance of the patent, in order to enable interested persons to oppose the patent grant. In such proceedings the grounds of the opposition, such as "prior use" or "prior patent grant," are heard and examined by the Patent Office. The registration system is administratively the cheapest but may burden the economy with the cost of exclusive rights being exercised for many inventions which, upon examination, would have been found unpatentable. In favor of the examination system it has been said that it avoids a mass of worthless, conflicting, and probably invalid patents, onerous to the public as well as to bona fide owners of valid patents; that it prevents the fraudulent practice of registering and selling patents similar to the claims being patented by others; and that it drastically reduces the extent of court litigation. The latter advantage, however, may not be realized if Patent Office and courts apply different standards of patentability.

IV. Economic Theory

* * *

B. *The Chief Arguments for Patent Protection*

The four best-known positions on which advocates of patent protection for inventors have rested their case may be characterized as the "natural-law" thesis, the "reward-by-monopoly" thesis, the "monopoly-profit-incentive" thesis, and the "exchange-for-secrets" thesis.

The "natural-law" thesis assumes that man has a natural property right in his own ideas. Appropriation of his ideas by others, that is, their unauthorized use, must be condemned as stealing. Society is morally obligated to recognize and protect this property right. Property is, in essence, exclusive. Hence, enforcement of exclusivity in the use of a patented invention is the only appropriate way for society to recognize this property right.

The "reward-by-monopoly" thesis assumes that justice requires that a man receive reward for his services in proportion to their usefulness to society, and that, where needed, society must intervene to secure him such reward. Inventors render useful services, and the most appropriate way to secure them commensurate rewards is by means of temporary monopolies in the form of exclusive patent rights in their inventions.

The "monopoly-profit-incentive" thesis assumes that industrial progress is desirable, that inventions and their industrial exploitation are necessary for such progress, but that inventions and/or their exploitation will not be obtained on sufficient measure if inventors and capitalists can hope only for such profits as the competitive exploitation of all technical knowledge will permit. To make it worthwhile for inventors and their capitalist backers to make their efforts and risk their money, society must intervene to increase their profit expectations. The simplest, cheapest, and most effective way for society to hold out these incentives is to grant temporary monopolies in the form of exclusive patent rights in inventions.

The "exchange-for-secrets" thesis presumes a bargain between inventor and society, the former surrendering the possession of secret knowledge in exchange for the protection of a temporary exclusivity in its industrial use. The presupposition again is that industrial progress at a sustained rate is desirable but cannot be obtained if inventors and innovating entrepreneurs keep inventions secret; in this case, the new technology may only much later become available for general use; indeed, technological secrets may die with their inventors and forever be lost to society. Hence, it is in the interest of society to bargain with the inventor and make him disclose his secret for the use of future generations. This can best be done by offering him exclusive patent rights in return for public disclosure of the invention.

* * *

C. Discussion of These Arguments: Economic Opinion 1850–73

* * *

In contrast to property in material things, so-called intellectual property is neither control of a thing nor of an idea but rather "control of a market" for things embodying an idea. A material thing must "belong" to somebody who can determine how it has to be used; it would be necessary to take it away from its possessor before it could be used by somebody else; by contrast, "an idea can belong to an unlimited number of persons" and its use by some does not prevent its use by others. And so on. It is interesting that some French lawyers conceded that they preferred to speak of "natural property rights" chiefly for propaganda purposes, especially because some of the alternative concepts, such as "monopoly right" or "privilege," were so unpopular.

The "reward-by-monopoly" thesis was strongly supported by English economists who, though opposed to all other kinds of monopoly, held that a temporary monopoly grant to inventors would be a just reward. Some opponents denied the need for reward: "Geniuses, just as stars, must shine without pay." Moreover, "nearly all useful inventions depend less on any individual than on the progress of society" and there was no need to "reward him who might be lucky enough to be the first to hit on the thing required." Others recognized the inventor's moral right to be rewarded, but held that the reward would come without government intervention. The headstart of the first user of a new invention would, as a rule, suffice to enable him to earn enough to cover a reward for the inventor. Some economists, who concede that competition worked too speedily in wiping out the innovators' profits, proposed that inventors be rewarded by prizes or bonuses according to the social value of their inventions. They regarded patents as "the worst and most deceptive form of reward, causing more often losses than profits even to the inventors." The contention that a reward in the form of a temporary monopoly would avoid bureaucratic discretion, would be commensurate to the usefulness of the invention, and would be paid by its beneficiary, namely, the consumers, was countered by the charge that under the patent system the rewards rarely go to those who deserve them, are never in proportion to the services rendered, and are always combined with great injury and injustice to others.

The "monopoly-profit-incentive" thesis is independent of the question whether or not a reward to inventors is called for in the name of justice. To be sure, the hope for a "just" reward may serve as an incentive, but often it will not be sufficiently attractive, and either more or something else may be needed to promote technological progress: a bait rather than a just reward. The profit expectations connected with the hope for a patent monopoly may induce inventive talents to exert their efforts, and venturous capitalists to risk their money, in research, experimentation, development, and pioneer plants; in order to be effective, the hoped-for-gains from the hoped-for-monopoly may have to be a multiple of the expenses incurred since few would want to risk the loss of their entire stakes unless they had a good chance of getting back much more than they put up; the possible gains must be in the nature of a first prize in a lottery or a jackpot in a game of chance. A series of counter-arguments have been advanced against this thesis; that no pecuniary incentive, indeed no incentive at all, is needed to spur on those who love to contrive and to innovate; that "the seeds of invention exist, as it were, in the air, ready to germinate whenever suitable conditions arise, and no legislative interference is needed to insure their growth in the proper season"; that, if some spur should be desirable, honors and prizes would be preferable; that, is profit incentives should be required, the profits to be made thanks to the headstart of the innovator and the natural lagging behind of imitators would suffice; that incentives, if effective, work only through diverting productive activity into different channels, for example, from ordinary productive pursuits into research and development, and from research in unprotected fields to research in fields in which the results enjoy patent protection; and, finally, that the obstacles and hindrances which patent protection puts in the way of competitive enterprise involve a social cost in excess of any benefits derived form the system.

The "exchange-for-secrets" thesis is independent of the question whether or not there would be enough new inventions without the monopoly-profit incentive; the point is that they would be kept secret and that society can obtain the substantial social benefit of disclosure only by offering patent protection in exchange for publication.

The patent constitutes a genuine contract between society and inventor; if society grants him a temporary guaranty, he discloses the secret which he could have guarded; quid pro quo, this is the very principle of equity.

The most frequent answer to this has been that society would lose little or nothing if some inventors tried to guard their secrets, because few producers could succeed in doing so for very long and, moreover, similar ideas are usually developed by several people within a short time, if not simultaneously. The most cogent objection rested on a simple reflection: An inventor who, optimistically, thinks he need not fear that others would either find out his secret or come independently upon the same idea, will not go to the expense and trouble of taking a patent; he will disclose only what he fears cannot be kept secret. Another kind of counter-argument tried to show that, at one stage at least, the patent system might promote rather than reduce secrecy; since patents are granted only on inventions developed to a stage at which they can be reduced to practical us, the system encouraged secrecy in the developmental stage of inventions whereas, if there are no patents to be obtained, earlier publication of ideas might hasten technological advance on all fronts. The only support for this argument was an analogy from basic research, namely, the pure scientists' urge to publish as early as possible.

F. Competitive Research, Waste, and Serendipity

Not only is research in general competitive with other economic activities, but research on particular problems and in particular fields is competitive with research on other problems and in other fields. This needs to be mentioned chiefly because in recent years another concept of "competitive research" has received increased attention: different firms and different research teams competing with one another in finding solutions to the same research problem in the same field.

Competition among rival firms which takes the form of a race between their research teams—a race, ultimately, to the patent office—may have various objectives: (a) To be the first to find a patentable solution to a problem posed by the needs and preferences of the customers—a better product—or by the technological needs and hopes of the producers—better machines, tools, processes; (b) after a competitor has found such a solution and has obtained exclusive patent rights in its exploitation, to find an alternative solution to the same problem in order to be able to compete with him in the same market—in other words, to "invent around" the competitor's patent; and (c) after having found and patented the first solution, to find and patent all possible alternative solutions, even inferior ones, in order to "block" competitor's efforts to "invent around" the first patent.

These forms of "competitive research" were described and discussed by antipatent economists during the patent controversy of the 19th century. Concerning the first form, there was complaint that other inventors who discovered practically simultaneously "the same utility," but were not the first in the race to the patent office, had to forego their "natural privilege of labor" and were barred from using their own inventions. The fact that there was competition in making new inventions was found to be healthy. But that he who lost the race to the patent office should be barred from using his own invention, and should have to search for a substitute invention, was found to be absurd.

What may appear absurd to a disinterested observer, or unjust and unfair to one who lost the right to use the fruit of his own labor and investment, must to an economist appear as sheer economic waste. Of course, one may regard this as an incidental expense of an otherwise beneficial institution, an unfortunate byproduct, an item of social cost, which, perhaps, is unavoidable and must be tolerated in view of the social advantages of the system as a whole. However, from merely defending the need of "inventing around a patent" as a minor item of waste, the discussion has recently proceeded to eulogize it as one of the advantages of the system, indeed as one of its "justifications."

The advantage is seen in the additional "encouragement" to research. If the competitors were given licenses under the patent of the firm that won the race, they would have to pay royalties but would not be compelled to "invent around" it. Exclusivity, however, forces some of them to search for a "substitute invention." But why should this be regarded as an advantage? The idea is probably that, if industrial research is desirable, more research is more desirable, and that it does not matter what kind of knowledge the research effort is supposed to yield. From an economic point of view, research is costly since it absorbs particularly scarce resources which could produce other valuable things. The production of the knowledge of how to do in a somewhat different way what we have already learned to do in a satisfactory way would hardly be given highest priority in a national allocation of resources.

This same, or a still lower, evaluation must be accorded to the third form of "competitive research"—inventive effort for the purpose of obtaining patents on all possible alternatives of an existing patented invention just in order to "block" a rival from "inventing around" that patent. In this case inventive talent is wasted on a project which, even (or especially) if it succeeds exactly in achieving its objective, cannot possibly be as valuable as would be other tasks to which the talent might be assigned. When thousands of potential inventions are waiting to be made—inventions which might be of great benefit to society—how can one seriously justify the assignment of a research force to search for inventions that are not intended for use at all—but merely for satisfying a dog-in-a-manger ambition?

There is, however, another "justification" for this kind of "competitive research": it can be summarized in the colorful word "serendipity." This means "the faculty of making happy and unexpected discoveries by accident." The idea is that the research teams engaged in "inventing around patents," or in inventing to obtain patents to "block" other people's efforts to "invent around patents," might by sheer accident hit upon something really useful. In other words, the work of these research forces is justified by the possibility or probability that they might find something which they did not set out to find.

There is no doubt that these happy accidents occur again and again. But can one reasonably let an effort to produce something without social value take the credit for accidental byproducts that happen to be useful? Can one reasonably assert that research not oriented toward important objectives is more likely to yield useful results than are research efforts that are so oriented? Is it easier to find the important by seeking the unimportant?

There is good historical evidence for the truth in the old saying that "necessity is the mother of invention." The continental blockade on the Napoleonic War led to the development of beet sugar; the blockade in World War I led to the process of obtaining nitrogen from air; the U-boat blockade in World War II led to the invention of atabrine as a substitute for quinine; etc., etc. Does it follow that it would be a good idea to institute more blockades? Perhaps the necessity of seeking substitutes would help us find many fine things; "serendipity" might yield splendid results.

If the Nation had masses of unemployed scientists and a scarcity of research problems, a strong case could be made for encouraging research of any kind; even an assignment to duplicate inventions made in the past might yield accidental inventions of great usefulness. But the situation is different: there is a scarcity of imaginative scientists and there is no scarcity of unsolved problems. The use of scarce research resources for seeking alternative solutions to satisfactorily solved problems can hardly be justified under the circumstances—no matter how well serendipity works.

J.   The Cost and Value of Additional Inventions

The analysis of the "increment of invention" attributable to the operation of the patent system, or to certain changes in the patent system, can only be highly speculative, because no experimental tests can be devised to isolate the effects of patent protection form all other changes that are going on in the economy.

May we "dream up" some experimental testing of the differences between a world with patents and one without patents? Let us duplicate our world, so that we have two worlds identical in every respect, except that one shall have a patent system and the other shall not; and then let us observe, for 50 years or so, these identical twin worlds and see what happens. And let us also have identical twin worlds of the years 1700, 1750, 1800, 1850, and 1900, one of the twins always with and the other without a patent system. It is conceivable that such "experiments" would yield trustworthy results, especially if we were able to repeat them and control some of the other factors that might make a difference to the rate of technological progress. It is also conceivable that the findings would be somewhat inconsistent: For example, the worlds of 1700 and 1750 might show superior progress in the specimen equipped with patent systems; the worlds of 1800 might show no differences in the rates of progress; and the worlds of more recent vintage might show faster progress in the specimen without patents. Such findings would be in accord with the hunches of some writers of the late 19th century, who hypothesized that the patent system may have been useful in kindling the spirit of inventive ambition, but is unnecessary or harmful once industrial inventiveness is sufficiently developed. Yet there is no use imagining the findings of the imaginary experiments. There are not real experiments that can answer our questions and we have to fall back on speculative analysis, inferring conclusions from assumptions which, on the basis of common experience ("casual empiricism"), seem to be the most plausible.

One may be fussy and contend that it makes no sense to speak of an "increment of invention" (attributable to the patent system) because inventions can be neither counted nor weighed nor measured in any practical way. Perfectly true. Inventions can often be subdivided or fused, and hence counting is arbitrary; and even if one agrees on some system of counting, one must realize that there are highly important and altogether nugatory inventions, and that it would be silly to give them equal weight. Yet, when all this is said and done, one will still have to concede that it is not meaningless to say that some times have been more productive of new inventions than others, and that some conditions may be more conducive to inventive success than others; and what can this mean if it does not mean "more" inventions? If more people are put to work on industrial research and development, more inventions, important as well as trifling ones, will be produced. The exact meaning of the "more"—of the increment—may be in doubt. But we need not be so fussy, and may be satisfied with something less exact. Incidentally, since we are going to use the concept of the "quantity" or "amount" of invention only in a speculative analysis, we may proceed as if we were able to give an exact meaning to the concept.

The bulk of technological advances, especially the millions of small improvements in production techniques which probably account for a large part of the increases in labor productivity, have nothing to do with patent protection. This can probably be tested by examining the types of technological change made over recent years in many different industries. Thus, only some part (of unknown size) if all increases in productivity is derived from patented inventions. Of these inventions, some might *never* come into being without the patent incentive; others might come *later*; and the rest might come in any case and at the *same time*, with or without patents. This means that the patent system is not to be credited with all patented technology, but only with that technology obtained "only with patents" and that obtained "earlier with patents."

O. Concluding Remarks

* * *

If one does not know whether a system "as a whole" (in contrast to certain features of it) is good or bad, the safest "policy conclusion" is to "muddle through"—either with it, if one has long lived with it, or without it, if one has lived without it, If we did not have a patent system, it would be irresponsible, on the basis of our present knowledge of its economic consequences, to recommend instituting one. But since we have had a patent system for a long time, it would be irresponsible, on the basis of our present knowledge, to recommend abolishing it. This last statement refers to a country such as the United States of America—not to a small country and not a predominantly nonindustrial country, where a different weight of argument might well suggest another conclusion.

While the student of the economics of the patent system must, provisionally, disqualify himself in the question if the effects of the system *as a whole* on a large industrial economy, he need not disqualify himself as a judge of proposed *changes* in the existing system. While economic analysis does not yet provide a sufficiently firm basis for choosing between "all or nothing," it does provide a sufficiently firm basis for decisions about "a little more or a little less" of various ingredients of the patent system. Factual data of various kinds may be needed even before some of these decisions can be made with confidence. But a team of well-trained economic researchers and analysts should be able to obtain enough information to reach competent conclusions on questions of patent reform. The kind of analysis that could form the framework for such research has been indicated in the present study.

Notes and Comments

1. For biographical information on Fritz Machlup, see Note 1, page 34, supra.

2. Machlup's description of the efforts of late medieval trade guilds to suppress innovation were long the standard description of guild activities in that era. But the idea that guilds were merely "cartels" designed to limit competition in various trades has given way in recent years. Now economic historians have identified many pro-innovation features of guilds. See, e.g., Stephen R. Epstein, "Craft Guilds, Apprenticeship, and Technological Change in Preindustrial Europe." 58 *Journal of Economic History* 684–713 (1998). In particular, in a world with weak central states and poorly defined property rights over information, guilds provided a "protective circle" within which members could develop and share new techniques. In this view, guild rules preventing outsider access were designed to protect the trade secrets of the group. And the elaborate regulation of the length and training of apprentices served to insure that this knowledge would be passed on and preserved. See Patrick McCray, *Glassmaking in Renaissance Venice: The Fragile Craft* (Aldershot, U.K, 1999: Ashgate Publishing).

3. After exploring early roots, Machlup takes the then-current state of patent law as a given, and does not explore in depth the evolution or growth of this body of law over time. For an argument that the state of intellectual property law generally has grown up over time without a central, guiding theme, and therefore resembles animals whose attributes reflect their unguided, episodic evolution, see Paul A David, "Intellectual Property and the Panda's Thumb: Patents, Copyrights and Trade Secrets in Economic Theory and History," in *Global Dimensions of Intellectual Property Rights in Science and Technology* (Michael B. Wallerstein, Mary Ellen Mogee & Roberta A. Schoen, eds. 1993) (Washington, DC: Nat'l Academy Press), at 21:

> So, it would be really quite remarkable if the evolution of legal institutions concerning patents, copyrights, and trade secrets had somehow resulted in a set of instruments optimally designed to serve either public policy purposes or the private economic interests of individuals and firms seeking such protections.

Appropriating the Returns from Industrial Research and Development*

RICHARD C. LEVIN
ALVIN K. KLEVORICK
RICHARD R. NELSON
SIDNEY G. WINTER

To have the incentive to undertake research and development, a firm must be able to appropriate returns sufficient to make the investment worthwhile. The benefits consumers derive from an innovation, however, are increased if competitors can imitate and improve on the innovation to ensure its availability on favorable terms. Patent law seeks to resolve this tension between incentives for innovation and widespread diffusion of benefits. A patent confers, in theory, perfect appropriability (monopoly of the invention) for a limited time in return for a public disclosure that ensures, again in theory, widespread diffusion of benefits when the patent expires.

Previous investigations of the system suggest that patents do not always work in practice as they do in theory.[1] On the one hand, appropriability is not perfect. Many patents can be circumvented; others provide little protection because of stringent legal requirements for proof that they are valid or that they are being infringed. On the other hand, public disclosure does not always ensure ultimate diffusion of an invention on competitive terms. For example, investments to establish the brand name of a patented product may outlive the patent itself. And patents may not always be necessary. Studies of the aircraft and semiconductor industries have shown that gaining lead time and exploiting learning curve advantages are the primary methods of appropriating

---

* Reprinted by permission from *Brookings Papers on Economic Activity*, 3, 1987, © 1987 The Brookings Institution.

1. F. M. Scherer and others, *Patents and the Corporation: A Report on Industrial Technology under Changing Public Policy*, 2d ed. (privately published, 1959); and C.T. Taylor and Z. A. Silberston, *The Economic Impact of the Patent System: A Study of the British Experience* (Cambridge University Press, 1973).

returns. Other studies have emphasized the importance of complementary investments in marketing and customer service.[3]

Evidence on the nature and strength of conditions for appropriability and on the working of the patent system is, however, scattered and unsystematic. Because imperfect appropriability may lead to underinvestment in new technology, and because technological progress is a primary source of economic growth, it would be useful to have a more comprehensive empirical understanding of appropriability, in particular, to identify those industries and technologies in which patents are effective in preventing competitive imitation of a new process or product. It would also be desirable to know where patents can be profitably licensed. Where patents are not effective, it would be useful to understand why they are not and whether other mechanisms are.

This paper describes the results of an inquiry into appropriability conditions in more than one hundred manufacturing industries. We discuss how this information has been and might be used to cast light on important issues in the economics of innovation and public policy. Our data, derived from a survey of high-level R & D executives, are informed opinions about an industry's technological and economic environment rather than quantitative measures of inputs and outputs.

Questionnaire Design and Survey Methods

The content of our questionnaire was shaped with guidance from the conceptual literature on technological change, empirical literature on the economic impact of the patent system, the work of Mansfield and his associates on imitation costs, and numerous case studies.[14] The questionnaire was aimed at high-level R & D managers with knowledge of both the relevant technology and market conditions. To check the interpretability of the questions and the likely validity and reliability of the responses, we pretested the questionnaire with twelve managers representing diverse businesses.

To understand how appropriability differs across industries, we asked each respondent to report typical experiences or central tendencies within a particular industry. Respondents were thus treated as informed observers of a line of business rather than as representatives of a single

3. The importance of lead time and learning curve advantages is documented in Almarin Phillips, *Technology and Market Structure: A Study of the Aircraft Industry* (Lexington Books, 1970); and John E. Tilton, *International Diffusion of Technology: The Case of Semiconductors* (Brookings, 1971) For the importance of marketing and customer service, see Marie–Therese Flaherty, "Field Research on the Link between Technological Innovation and Growth Evidence form International Semiconductor Industry," working paper 84–83 (Harvard University, Graduate School of Business Administration, no date).

14. Among the sources of ideas for the questions are Paul Allan David, *Technical Choice, Innovation and Economic Growth: Essays on American and British Experience in the Nineteenth Century* (Cambridge University Press, 1975); Richard R. Nelson and Sidney G. Winter, "In Search of Useful Theory of Innovation," *Research Policy*, vol. 6 (Winter 1977), pp. 36–76; Nathan Rosenberg, "Science, Invention and Economic Growth," *Economic Journal*, vol. 84 (March 1974), pp. 90–108; and Devandra Sahal, *Patterns of Technological Innovation* (Addison–Wesley, 1981). For empirical literature on the economic effects of the patent system, see Scherer and others, *Patents and the Corporation*; and Taylor and Silberston, *The Economic Impact of the Patent System*. For imitation costs, see Edwin Mansfield, Mark Schwartz, and Samuel Wagner, "Imitation Costs and Patents: An Empirical Study," *Economic Journal*, vol. 91 (December 1981), pp. 907–18.

firm, an approach that encouraged cooperation (they were not placed in the position of possibly divulging practices or policies of their own firms), but led inevitably to heterogeneity in the responses within a given industry.

Methodological Issues

Given our interest in identifying differences in the appropriability of R & D, it is reassuring that analysis of variance confirmed the presence of significant interindustry variation in the responses to most question-naire items. There was, however, also substantial intraindustry variation in the responses.

There are several potential sources of intraindustry heterogeneity in the responses to any given question. First, the lines of business as defined by the FTC may be objectively heterogeneous in their products and technologies. For example, if two firms classified as manufacturer of industrial inorganic chemicals produce different products using different technologies, they might differ markedly in their perception of the effectiveness of patents or the time required for imitation in their "industry." To eliminate this source of heterogeneity, we asked respondents to identify two major innovations—a process and a product—within their industries during the past ten to fifteen years. For most industries with ten or more respondents, more than half the respondents agreed on at least one such innovation. We thus believe it unlikely that overly aggregated industry definition was a major source of interindustry heterogeneity.

Patents and Other Means of Appropriation

The picture is striking. For new processes ..., patents were general-ly rated the least effective of the mechanisms of appropriation: only 20 percent of the lines of business surveyed rated process patent effective-ness in excess of 4.0 [on a 7–point scale]. Eighty percent scored the effectiveness of lead time and learning curve advantages on new process-es in excess of 4.3 Secrecy, though not considered as effective as lead time and learning advantages, was still considered more effective than patents in protecting processes.

Patents for products were typically considered more effective than those for processes, and secrecy was considered less effective in protect-ing products than processes. Generally, lead time, learning curves, and sales or service efforts were regarded as substantially more effective than patents in protecting products. Eighty percent of the sample businesses rated the effectiveness of sales and service efforts above 5.0, but only 20 percent considered product patents this effective.

The tendency to regard secrecy as more effective than process patents but less effective than product patents probably reflects the greater ease and desirability of maintaining secrecy about process tech-nology. Firms may sometimes refrain from patenting processes to avoid disclosing either the fact or the details of an innovation. But firms have every incentive to advertise the advantages of new or improved products and to get them into the hands of customers, thereby facilitating direct observation of the product and the technology it embodies. Maintaining secrecy about product innovations is thus likely to be both difficult and undesirable.

Respondents also tended to regard patents to prevent duplication as more effective than patents to secure royalty income. This finding was consistent with the view that licensing arrangements are beset with transactional difficulties.

Only 3 of 130 lines of business rated process patents higher than five on a seven-point scale of effectiveness in preventing duplication. Two of these were concrete and primary copper; the other had only a single respondent. Only 5 of 130 industries rated product patents to prevent duplication higher than six points. Two of these were singletons; the other three were drugs, pesticides, and industrial organic chemicals. Twenty other lines rated product patents between five and six. Of those with more than two responses, almost all fell neatly into chemical products (including inorganic chemicals, plastic materials, synthetic fibers, synthetic rubber, and glass) or relatively uncomplicated mechanical equipment (air and gas compressors, power-driven hand tools, and oilfield machinery). The only anomalies were roasted coffee and products of steel rolling and finishing mills.

The data on the eighteen most heavily sampled industries help to establish the robustness of our conclusion about the limited effectiveness of patents as a means of appropriation. In none did a majority of respondents rate patents—either to prevent duplication or to secure royalty income—as more effective than the most highly rated of the other four means of appropriating returns from new processes, although in drugs and petroleum refining a majority regarded process patents as at least the equal of the most effective alternative mechanism of appropriation. In only one industry, drugs, were product patents regarded by a majority of respondents as strictly more effective than other means of appropriation.

The most probable explanation for the robust finding that patents are particularly effective in chemical industries is that comparatively clear standards can be applied to assess a chemical patent's validity and to defend against infringement. The uniqueness of a specific molecule is more easily demonstrated than the novelty of, for example, a new component of a complex electrical or mechanical system. Similarly, it is easy to determine whether an allegedly infringing molecule is physically identical to a patented molecule; it is more difficult to determine whether comparable components of two complex systems "do the same work in substantially the same way." To the extent that very simple mechanical inventions approximate molecules in their discreteness and easy differentiability, it is understandable that industries producing such machinery rank just after chemical industries in the perceived effectiveness of patent protection.

The perceived ineffectiveness of patents in most industries raises the question of why firms use them. Further work is needed here, but we offer some speculations informed by the comments of our pretest subjects and by several survey respondents at a conference we held to report preliminary findings. These executives identified two motives for patent-

ing that have little connection with appropriating returns form investment. One is to measure the performance of R & D employees, which is a
significant problem because these worker are typically engaged in team
production. Legal standards for identifying inventors on a patent applications are, however, reasonably rigorous. The second motive is to gain
access to certain foreign markets. Some developing countries require, as
a condition of entry, that U.S. firms license technology to a host-country
firm, and some patents are filed primarily to permit such licensing.

* * *

Limitations on Effectiveness of Patents

To understand why patent protection might be weak in some industries, we asked respondents to rate the importance of possible limitations
on patent effectiveness.... The ability of competitors to "invent
around" both process and product patents was rated higher than five on
a seven-point scale of importance by 60 percent of the responding
industries. Only one other constraint—the lack of ready patentability for
new processes—was rated this important by more than 20 percent.
Limitations on patents were generally considered more severe for processes than for products, which was consistent with our finding that
product patents tend to be more effective than process patents. In
particular, the lack of patentability was more serious for processes than
for products, and so was the disclosure of information through patent
documents.

The responses concerning limits on patent effectiveness may illuminate and focus policy discussion. In recent years there has been considerable interest in making patent protection more effective. One initiative
has been to make the legal requirements for a valid patent claim less
stringent. Another has been to vacate court decrees that compel licensing. Our data identified industries in which stringent requirements for
patent validity or compulsory licensing were perceived as important
limitations on the usefulness of patents in appropriating returns.

Respondents from twenty-two lines of business, mostly in the food
processing and fabricated metals sectors, considered the likely inability
to withstand challenges to validity as significantly limiting the effectiveness of process patents (scoring the importance higher than five on a
seven-point scale); for fourteen of these industries the mean response
was six or higher on the scale. This group and the nineteen industries
citing invalidity as a constraint on the effectiveness of product patents
(again assigning a score higher than five) overlapped considerably.
Further investigation would be required to determine just why these two
sectors appear to have difficulty establishing valid claims. Perhaps
because they are mature industries, opportunities may be limited or
novelty may be difficult to achieve or simply difficult to prove.

* * *

The choice between obtaining a patent and maintaining secrecy may
be influenced by the extent to which the disclosures made in the patent
document facilitate inventing around the patent. Our data provided

some support for this theory. The effectiveness of secrecy was positively correlated with the extent to which disclosures limited the effectiveness of patents. The link was stronger for product patents than for process patents. But patent disclosures represented a substantial limitation on the effectiveness of product patents for only 4 of the 130 industries (scoring as high as six on the scale), and only 16 regarded process disclosures as comparably important. In only one line of business of those with five or more respondents—metal cutting machine tools—did disclosures constrain so substantially the effectiveness of both process and product patents.

Cost and Time Required for Imitation

* * *

Patents tend to raise imitation costs and time for each category of innovation. These increases can be regarded as alternative indicators of the relative effectiveness of patents in different industries.

To explore this point further, we coded the individual responses to the imitation costs and time questions on a six-point interval scale, calculated the individual and industry mean increases in costs and time associated with the presence of patents, and correlated these, respectively, with individual and industry mean responses to our questions on the effectiveness of patents in preventing duplication. For each category of innovation, the reported effectiveness of patents was positively correlated with the increase in duplication costs and time associated with patents, although the correlations tended to be stronger for products than for processes. We also found some evidence, at the level of the individual respondent, that patent effectiveness was associated with the absolute level of duplication costs for patented processes and products. We found a much stronger association, however, between reported patent effectiveness and the amount of time required to duplicate both patented process and product innovations.

These broad-brush patterns of association conceal some striking anomalies. For particular categories of innovation, at least two and as many as fourteen industries reported that patents actually reduced the costs or time required for duplication. A partial explanation is that a disproportionate number of these industries also reported that disclosure of information through patent documents was a significant limitation on patent effectiveness.

A second anomaly is that, despite the positive correlation between patent effectiveness and the costs of imitating patented products, in several industries patents were relatively ineffective and duplication costs were nonetheless very high, whether or not the innovation was patented. Among these were guided missiles and several types of industrial machinery (food products machinery, electric weldings apparatus, and speed changers, drives, and gears). In these instances the relative complexity of the products presumably makes reverse engineering inherently costly despite relatively weak patent protection.

It is interesting to compare our findings with those of Edwin Mansfield, Mark Schwartz, and Samuel Wagner, who studied the effects of patents on imitation costs in three industries.[41] They concluded that patents generally raised imitation costs by 30 percentage points in drugs, 20 points in chemicals, and 7 points in electronics. To render our data comparable, we evaluated each respondent's answer at the mean of the relevant range and computed crude industry average imitation costs for each type of innovation. Our results were consistent with those of Mansfield, Schwartz, and Wagner. We found that patents raise imitation costs by 40 percentage points for both major and typical new drugs, by 30 points for major new chemical products, and by 25 points for typical chemical products. In electronics, our results differed somewhat for semiconductors, computers, and communications equipment, but the range was 7 to 15 percentage points for major products and 7 to 10 for typical products.[43]

* * *

Remarks on Policy

Our findings suggested some general principles relevant to policies that affect the incentive to engage in innovative activity.

A first principle is that the patent system and related institutions to protect intellectual property should be understood as social structures that *improve* the appropriability of returns from innovation. They are not the only nor necessarily the primary barriers that prevent general access to what would otherwise be pure public goods. Lead time accrues naturally to the innovator, even in the absence of any deliberate effort to enhance its protective effect. Secrecy, leaning advantages, and sales and service efforts can provide additional protection, though they require the innovator's deliberate effort. The survey confirmed that these other means of appropriation are typically more important than the patent system. Hence in examining a proposed adjustment of the patent system or related institutions, it is important to recognize that the incremental effect of the policy change depends on the protection other mechanisms provide.

The survey results also confirmed substantial interindustry variation in the level of appropriability and in the mechanisms that provide it. From this follows our second major principle, which is that the incremental effects of policy changes should be assessed at the industry level. For example, in the aircraft industry, where other mechanisms provide considerable appropriability, lengthening the life of patents would tend

41. Mansfield, Schwartz, and Wagner, *Imitation Costs and Patents.*

43. Our results on the time required to duplicate a rival's new products or processes were also roughly consistent with recent findings of Edwin Mansfield. In all but one of the ten industries he surveyed, the median respondent indicated that six to twelve months usually elapsed before the nature and operation of a new product were known to a firm's rivals. Effective duplication, as we have defined it, should take as long or longer. . . . The median and modal industries require one to three years to duplicate a major innovation or a typical patented innovation. A typical unpatented innovation, however, is more often duplicated within six to twelve months. *See* "How Rapidly Does New Industrial Technology Leak Out?" *Journal of Industrial Economics*, vol. 34 (December 1985), pp. 217–24.

to have little effect on incentives for innovation. In the drug industry the effect of a longer lifetime would matter more.

Finally, improving the protection of intellectual property is not necessarily socially beneficial. Empirical work has so far indicated a positive cross-sectional relationship between strong appropriability, as measured by variables constructed from our survey, and innovative performance. But the social cost-benefit calculation is not straightforward. Stronger appropriability will not yield more innovation in all contexts and, where it does, innovation may come at excessive cost.

* * *

Notes and Questions

1. Richard Levin received a B.A. from Stanford and his Ph.D. in economics from Yale, where he taught for many years. He is now President of Yale University. Alvin Klevorick received his B.A. degree from Amherst and his Ph.D. from the economics department at Princeton. He has taught at Yale University since 1967. Richard R. Nelson received his bachelor's degree from Oberlin College and his Ph.D. in economics from Yale. He has taught at Carnegie Institute of Technology (Carnegie–Mellon University) and Yale, among other places, and is now Professor of International and Public Affairs, Economics, and Business at Columbia University. Sidney Winter is a professor at the Wharton School of Business, University of Pennsylvania. He received his Ph.D. in economics from Yale University, and a bachelor's degree from Swarthmore College.

2. This study is a very-widely cited source of empirical information concerning the usefulness of patents in various industries. See, e.g., Richard T. Rapp, "How Economists See Competition Problems In High-Technology Industries," in "Antitrust/Intellectual Property Claims in High Technology Markets, American Law Institute—American Bar Association Continuing Legal Education," Jan. 26, 1995, C137 *ALI–ABA* 139, at 147 n. 18 ("The best studies of this subject [i.e., industry-preferred appropriability mechanisms], which were led by Richard Levin [et al.] ...").

3. More recent studies have confirmed many of the basic findings of this study, and extended them in some interesting directions. See, e.g., Wesley M. Cohen, Richard R. Nelson, and John P. Walsh, "Protecting Their Intellectual Assets: Appropriability Conditions and Why U.S. Manufacturing Firms Patent (or Not)," *National Bureau of Economic Research Working Paper* 7552 (2000).

4. One recent article builds on this study to show that patents are used in many cases not to appropriate R & D investments, but as "signals" regarding firm capabilities to investors, competitors, and the like. See Clarisa Long, "Patent Signals," 69 *U. Chi. L. Rev.* 625 (2002). If patents are used primarily to indicate technological prowess to various "audiences," does that suggest any changes in policy? Does it make patents less valuable to society?

II. *Establishing and Asserting Patent Rights*

A. Patentable Subject Matter

The Patentability of Algorithms*

DONALD CHISUM

I. Introduction

New and useful algorithms, including mathematical algorithms, should constitute subject matter eligible for patent protection. Yet, the current state of the law is that "mathematical" algorithms "as such" or "in the abstract" do not constitute patentable subject matter[1]—at least not in theory.

In this Article, I hope to demonstrate the weakness of the second, descriptive statement and the soundness of the first, normative statement. My case consists of the following (nonalgorithmic) line of analysis. First, prior to the Supreme Court's decision in *Gottschalk v. Benson* [409 U.S. 63 (1972)] in 1972, the lower courts had, for appropriate reasons, rejected earlier doctrine on the nonpatentability of so-called mental steps and established a firm basis for the patenting of algorithmic ideas. Second, the *Benson* decision, which held that mathematical algorithms could not be patented, was poorly reasoned and stemmed from an antipatent judicial bias that cannot be reconciled with the basic elements of the patent system established by Congress. Third, the awkward distinctions and seemingly irreconcilable results of the case law since *Benson*, including the Supreme Court's decisions in *Parker v. Flook* [437 U.S. 584 (1978)] and *Diamond v. Diehr* [450 U.S. 175 (1981)] are a product of the analytical and normative weakness of *Benson* itself. Finally, an examination of the policy implications of extending patent protection to new algorithms will show that such extension will not harm the creation and dissemination of knowledge in computer science and other areas of technology and will in fact provide much needed additional incentives for investment in computer software development.

* * *

III. The Bull in the China Closet: The Supreme Court's *Benson* Decision

A. Benson–Tabbot BCD-to-Binary Conversion

---

* Reprinted by permission from 47 U. Pitt. L. Rev. 959 (1985–1986), © 1986 University of Pittsburgh Law Review.

1. As will be discussed below, the primary source for this rule of nonpatentability is the Supreme Court's 1972 *Benson* decision. The rule was softened but not fundamentally altered by the Court's 1981 decision in Diamond v. Diehr, 450 U.S. 175 (1981).

On October 9, 1963, Gary Benson and Arthur Tabbot filed a patent application disclosing and claiming a method of converting numerical information in data processing systems. The method related to the conversion of "binary coded decimals" to pure binary numbers. The binary number system should be well understood by all of us in this computer saturated era. A binary coded decimal (BCD) is an intermediate step between decimal numerals and binary numerals. BCD numerals involve substituting for the decimal numbers (0–9) their individual binary equivalents. A decimal "21" is converted to "10 01" in BCD and from there to "10101" in binary.

The *Benson* case focused on two claims in the Benson–Tabbot application. Application claim number 8 was for the method as carried out on a piece of hardware (a reentrant shift register). Application claim number 13 was more generally stated as a "data processing method" with no reference to hardware. A person can easily carry out the method of claim 13 using pencil and paper by following the specified steps. All such a person needs to know are the meanings of the terms in the stated algorithm (such as "most significant decimal digit representation") and how to perform elementary operations (such as adding a binary 1 or 0 to a binary number and "testing" (*i.e.*, discriminating whether there is a 0 or 1 at a particular specified number position). Carrying out the operation—even with pencil and paper—is a very "mechanical" (*i.e.*, machine-like) operation. No "thinking" or judgment is required other than concentration on carefully following the instructions for the discrete operations prescribed by the algorithm.

B.   The Definition of an Algorithm

At this point it is appropriate to consider what an "algorithm" is since the method claimed in *Benson* clearly was such a thing.[2]

Prior to the holding in *Benson*, there was no patent law definition of an "algorithm" and indeed, but for the nonpatentability rule in *Benson*, there would be no need for such a definition. The literature on mathematics and computer science offers a number of definitions of an algorithm that differ in wording but are for the most part consistent. Some authors describe an algorithm simply, broadly and informally, such as "a recipe or specific set of rules or directions for performing a task," or "a set of formal directions for obtaining the required solution."
* * *

These definitions come close to equating an algorithm with a "process" in the patent law sense of a sequence of specifically defined

2. As to the origin of the term "algorithm," see 1 D. KNUTH, THE ART OF COMPUTER PROGRAMMING: FUNDAMENTAL ALGORITHMS 1 (2d ed. 1973):

The word did not appear in *Webster's New World Dictionary* as late as 1957; we find only the older form "algorism" with its ancient meaning, i.e. the process of doing arithmetic using Arabic numerals. In the middle ages, abacists computed on the abacus and algorists computed by algorism. Following the middle ages, the origin of this word was in doubt. . . . Finally, historians of mathematics found the true origin of the word algorism: it comes from the name of a famous Persian textbook author, Abu Ja'far Mohammed ibn Mûsâ al-Khow arizm (c. 825). . . . Khowârizm is today the small Soviet city of Khiva. . . . Gradually the form and meaning of "algorism" became corrupted; as explained by the Oxford English Dictionary, the word was "erroneously refashioned" by "learned confusion" with the word *arithmetic*.

operations to accomplish a useful result. One author attempts to differentiate algorithms from other concepts of problem solving (such as
recipe, process, method, technique, procedure, routine) by listing five
"important features" of an algorithm:

1) Finiteness. An algorithm must always terminate after a finite
   number of steps

2) Definiteness. Each step of an algorithm must be precisely defined; the actions to be carried out must be rigorously and
   unambiguously specified for each case ...

3) Input. An algorithm has zero or more inputs, i.e., quantities
   which are given to it initially before the algorithm begins. These
   inputs are taken from specified sets of objects ...

4) Output. An algorithm has one or more outputs, i.e., quantities
   which have a specified relation to the inputs ...

5) Effectiveness. An algorithm is also generally expected to be
   effective. This means that all of the operations to be performed in
   the algorithm must be sufficiently basic that they can in principle
   be done exactly and in a finite length of time by a man using
   pencil and paper. Many algorithms appear to have another feature—recursiveness: one or more of the steps entails going back
   and repeating one or more of the prior steps.

In *Benson*, the Supreme Court recited a definition of an algorithm in
the course of describing the Benson–Tabbot method:

A procedure for solving a given type of mathematical problem is
known as an "algorithm." The procedures set forth in the present
claims are of that kind; that is to say, they are a generalized
formulation for programs to solve mathematical problems of converting one form of numerical representation to another. From the
generic formulation, programs may be developed as specific applications.[3]

The Court erred both in implying that algorithms relate only to
mathematical problems and in characterizing the method involved in
Benson as directed to "mathematical" problems. It is true that algorithms are often devised to solve problems of a mathematical nature. But
algorithms may also be devised to solve all sorts of nonmathematical
problems. The method at issue in *Benson* meets all of the above definitions of an algorithm (including the five "features"). But is the method
one for solving a "mathematical problem" as the Court states? It would
seem that a conversion of decimal numbers to binary-coded numbers to
binary numbers is a "mathematical" problem only in a very loose sense.
It is more properly described as a translation problem—comparable to
converting temperature values from Fahrenheit to Celsius. The algorithm involves some arithmetic steps (such as adding in binary form), but
the problem solved is not a mathematical one (such as finding the
greatest common divisor of two numbers or a trigonometric function).
The imprecision of the Court in characterizing the algorithm before it in

3. Gottschalk v. Benson, 409 U.S. at 65.

Benson created uncertainty as to the scope of the exclusionary rule that it upholds.

C. Unraveling the Confusion in the Benson Opinion

The Supreme Court in *Benson* held unanimously that the two claims of Benson and Tabbot did not constitute proper subject matter for a patent (no matter how useful or new the claimed invention may have been). The reasoning in *Benson* is monstrously bad. Such a charge should and can be backed up by paragraph-by-paragraph, line-by-line examination of the opinion, the authorities upon which it relies, and the policy justifications that it recites.

After describing the procedural posture of the case, the actions of the lower tribunals, and the nature of the Benson–Tabbot claimed invention, the opinion offers thirteen paragraphs of reasoning. The bulk of this reasoning consists of recitation of statements from prior Supreme Court decisions dating back to the mid–19th century.

After quoting ... three cases, *Benson* offers a dogmatic statement: "Phenomena of nature, though just discovered, mental processes, and abstract intellectual concepts are not patentable, as they are the basic tools of scientific and technological work."[4] This statement makes three assertions—two explicit and one implicit. The explicit assertions are that (1) natural phenomena, mental processes, and abstract intellectual concepts are to be lumped together as unpatentable subject matter, and (2) the reason for such unpatentability is that all are "basic tools" of technological work. The implicit assertion is that an algorithm (such as that claimed by Benson and Tabbot) is a phenomenon of nature, mental process or abstract intellectual concept. None of the three assertions will bear up fully under analysis.

First, a mathematical or other algorithm is neither a phenomenon of nature nor an abstract concept. The Benson–Tabbot algorithm is very much a construction of the human mind. One cannot perceive an algorithm in nature. The algorithm does not describe natural phenomena (or natural relationships). Indeed, it does not describe anything other than a series of operations to be performed by a machine or possibly by a human being. It is certainly not analogous to the formulae at issue in *McKay Radio,* which did describe relationships relating to radio wave phenomenon. Neither is the algorithm fairly described as an "abstract intellectual" concept (such as "all persons are created equal" or "for every action there is an equal and opposite reaction"). Algorithms are by definition highly specific rather than abstract.

Second, there is no basis for lumping together phenomena of nature and abstract concepts with "mental steps." A process consisting partially or wholly of "mental steps" does not exist in nature and can be quite specific. The Court's reference to "mental processes" is disturbingly terse. Arguably, the Benson–Tabbot algorithm as stated in claim 13 (though not in the machine claim 8) did involve "mental processes" if the claim is construed as covering human and not just machine imple-

---

4. 409 U.S. at 67.

mentation. The Court did not cite the long line of lower court cases on the mental steps doctrine.

Third, the unpatentability of "phenomena of nature" is not so clear and self-evident as the Court in *Benson* would have us believe. The primary Supreme Court decision on the patentability of natural phenomena is that quoted in the same Benson paragraph as the above statement—*Funk Brothers Seed Co. v. Kalo Inoculant Co.* [333 U.S. 127 (1948)].

In *Funk Brothers*, the subject matter was various bacteria of the genus Rhizobium, which enable leguminous plants to fix nitrogen. A major problem was that different species of the genus were only effective for different plants. Manufacturers of bacterial inoculants sold only single specie inoculants because the different species produced an inhibitory effect on each other. The patentee discovered that certain strains of certain species were noninhibitive to each other. This discovery enabled the production of a mixed culture, which would eliminate the necessity of selecting and using a variety of inoculants. The patent contained claims to (1) the process (or method) of making mixed cultures, and (2) the product consisting of such mixed cultures. Only the product claims were at issue in *Funk Brothers*. The Court held the claims invalid, reasoning that (1) the property of noninhibition was a natural phenomenon that could not be patented, and (2) given that phenomenon, the making of a mixed culture "fell short of invention" (*i.e.*, was obvious)—it was no more than convenient packaging.

There are serious analytical shortcomings in this line of reasoning, which are exposed in the powerful concurring opinion of Justice Frankfurter. Whatever the shortcomings, *Funk Brothers* did concern a discovered natural phenomenon and a patent claim for a product that was so broadly worded as to cover any inoculant that took advantage of that phenomenon. The vice of the patent claim at issue in *Funk Brothers* (if there was one) was undue breadth—the patentee claimed more than he had invented and disclosed.

Finally, the *Benson* "basic tools" rationale—that phenomena of nature, mental processes, and abstract intellectual concepts should not be patentable because they "are the basic tools of scientific and technology work"—is superficially attractive. However, on further analysis, it is either wrong as a factual matter or inconsistent with the established manner in which the patent system operates. The "basic tools" of research are those matters within the body of accumulated human knowledge relating to particular fields of technology. Any process or structure within that body of knowledge cannot be patented, not because it does not qualify as patentable subject matter, but simply because it is not new and unobvious. Patents are regularly allowed for processes and structures that have primary and even sole utility in research, including chemical processes, electrical apparatus, and optical instruments. Literally, a microscope is a "basic tool" for scientific work, but surely no one would assert that a new type of microscope lay beyond the scope of the patent system.

If the trio of "unpatentables" are in fact properly excluded from the patent system, it is for distinct reasons and not their "tool" status. If natural phenomena are excludable, it may simply be because they are not "new" as the patent statutes require. Abstract concepts are excludable because of the disclosure and clear claiming requirements of the patent statutes.

2. *Abstract and Sweeping Scope—Unknown End Uses*

The second paragraph of the analytical portion of the *Benson* opinion poses an argument for unpatentability based on the alleged abstract nature of the algorithm and the sweeping scope of its potential use.

> Here the "process" claim is so abstract and sweeping as to cover both known and unknown uses of the BCD to pure binary conversion. The end use may (1) vary from the operation of a train to verification of drivers' licenses to researching the law books for precedents and (2) be performed through any existing machinery or future-devised machinery or without any apparatus.[5]

As to "uses," the algorithm as claimed probably has a fairly limited scope in terms of *direct* uses. It is most likely primarily useful for creating programs for a particular type of machine—a digital computer. But even if the potential direct uses are vast and not fully known at the time the patent is applied for, it is unclear why this should matter. Generally, in our patent system, an inventor must find one specific practical utility for a new product or process. However, once patentability is established, the patent will cover all uses of the claimed patent—including those that were not or could not have been conceived of by the inventor. This occurs fairly commonly with inventions such as chemical compounds and materials.

But, in any case, the Court's focus was on *end* uses. It is even less clear why the focus should be on end uses. Why should it matter that a computer made more efficient by use of a better algorithm in its programming has a vast array of uses? To use an analogy, a new type of ignition system may have direct use primarily in automobiles, trucks and buses. One doubts whether the Supreme Court or any one else could deny that a claim to such a device constitutes patentable subject matter simply because the potential "end uses" of motor vehicles are vast.

As to the usability of the algorithm on "any existing ... or future-devised machinery or without any apparatus," that would seem to be the whole point of allowing patents on processes and methods.

8. Benson *in Historical Perspective: A Vestige of Another Era*

Perhaps the best way to view *Benson* is as a vestige of another era in terms of the attitude of the United States Supreme Court toward the patent system. Throughout the 1930s and 1940s the Supreme Court heard a large number of appeals in patent cases. The pattern of results (most patents were held either invalid or noninfringed)[6] and the lan-

---

   5. *Gottschalk,* 409 U.S. at 68.

   6. The pattern led Justice Jackson to complain, with considerable justification, in a dissent that "the only patent that is valid is one which this Court has not been able to get

guage in the opinions showed a marked hostility toward patent rights on the part of many of the Justices on the Court during that period, most particularly William O. Douglas, author of the *Benson* opinion. Statements in two of the opinions of the Court written by Justice Douglas during that era were repudiated by Congress in the Patent Act of 1952.

During the 1950s and 1960s, the Supreme Court heard relatively few patent appeals. The 1966 *Graham* trilogy is the foundational case interpreting the nonobviousness requirement of section 103 of the Patent Act and has been widely accepted as a balanced explanation of that key provision of patent law. Benson is one of a handful of other Supreme Court decisions that carry forward the older attitude of suspicion toward the patent system. Eight years after Benson came the watershed 1980 decision, *Diamond v. Chakrabarty*, holding that genetically-altered micro-organisms constitute patentable subject matter. The pattern of Supreme Court decisions since *Chakrabarty* on patents and other areas of intellectual property law is clearly one of greater receptiveness towards the Congressionally-established systems of protecting inventions, writings, and marketing symbols.

V.   The Policy Implications of Patenting Algorithms

Discussions in the legal literature of the patentability of computer software, programs, or algorithms often include analyses of the policy implications of allowing patent protection on such subject matter. Much of this analysis is at a high level of generality. Any excursion into policy should focus on the factors pertinent to the issue at hand—which is, given the statutory framework of patent protection for applied technology generally, are there any good reasons for excluding as a matter of law all useful innovations of a certain type or in a particular field of technology?

A.   *The Burden of Proof*

. . . The patent system is a given. It was established by statute in 1790 and has been maintained by Congress ever since. This represents a policy determination by Congress that in fact the public interest is served by offering limited periods of exclusive rights in disclosed innovations in the useful arts. The statutory scheme includes within its subject matter the category of "processes" in a broad sense. In the *Flook* decision, the Supreme Court admitted that a mathematical algorithm came within the normal definition of a process. Given that literal inclusion of algorithms within the patent system, the burden of proof on the excludibility of algorithms in a judicial or administrative forum should shift to the side that seeks such exclusion. The burden of proof should be carried only by a demonstration that (1) the evident policies of the statutory patent system prescribe that the word "process" be given a special nonliteral meaning that excludes algorithms or (2) the constitutional provision that authorizes Congress to establish a patent system places algorithms outside the permissible scope of such a system.

its hands." Jungerson v. Ostby & Barton Co., 335 U.S. 560, 572 (1949) (Jackson, J., dissenting).

*B. The Case for Not Legislatively Excluding Algorithms from the Patent
System*

If we move the question of the excludability of algorithms from the
patent system to the legislative arena, where policy considerations can be
given free rein, there are still good reasons for not "reinventing the
wheel" and deciding whether the patent system is economically viable as
applied to mathematical algorithm inventions. If the patent system is
maintained for most areas of technology but excluded for one area, the
inevitable result will be less investment in research and development in
that area and more investment in other areas which offer the prospect of
effective patent protection. No one argues that computer software is or
should be a disfavored technology.

This Article is a legal study and is not based on any systematic
research into the rate of investment in software technology or other facts
that would be pertinent to the legislative question of the impact that the
incentives of the patent system has upon the creation and utilization of
software technology. But it may be beneficial to use a classic technique
of trial lawyers—posing a question to an expert and calling for an
opinion based on a hypothetical set of facts.

Assume that a study of the production and utilization of computer
technology, both software and hardware, resulted in the following findings:

1. The continuing trend is for hardware technology, including
semiconductor technology (*e.g.*, processor and memory chips) and
peripheral devices (*e.g.*, mass storage and interfacing devices), to
become more powerful and cheaper.

2. While the powerful new hardware has tremendous potential for
satisfying human needs, that potential can only be realized by
production of suitable programming (software).

3. The continuing trend is for software technology to become more
complex and more expensive to produce, the primary reason being
that such production continues to use intensively highly skilled
labor.

4. The production of software entails at least two stages. One is the
conceptualization of the basic method for solving the problems at
hand (*i.e.*, the generation of algorithms). The other is the preparation of detailed instructions to implement the method on a computer
(*i.e.*, the preparation of computer programs and detailed code based
on the algorithms).

5. Algorithm generation is qualitative in nature and may entail
either the application of known techniques or the formulation of
distinctly new and superior techniques. Better algorithms enable
computers to be used more efficiently and effectively.

6. Program preparation is quantitative in nature and entails a
large amount of intellectual work that follows known techniques.

7. Both algorithm generation and program preparation are expensive, but in different ways and for different reasons. In the qualita-

tive, algorithm-generation stage, much time is likely to be devoted to efforts that turn out to be nonproductive. There is no guarantee that superior techniques will in fact be produced. In the implementation, program preparation stage, the results are more predictable; the expense factor is simply a function of the amount of time that must be devoted to achieving those results.

8.   Once software in the form of a computer program is produced and publicly distributed, it may be copied and utilized easily by others in a number of ways. One way is the copying of the detailed instructions. Such copying eliminates the need to duplicate the entire expense of the program preparation stage. Such copying normally results in a program that closely resembles the copied program in terms of means and results. Another way is to utilize one or more of the underlying algorithms in the program. The algorithms may be used without any close copying of the detailed instructions of the source program and indeed can be used to prepare entirely new programs that achieve different results in different ways.

Assuming that these are the facts (and I strongly suspect that these "hypothetical" findings closely track reality), then the "expert opinion" must be that exclusion from the patent system of algorithms useful in computer programming cannot be justified. The pattern of production of algorithms and computer programs is the same as the production of other products and services. The lure of patent protection attracts greater investment in the research stage, whether it be in the exploration for a new chemical process or compound or in the generation of algorithms. Since patents may properly be granted only for new innovations, the result will be the disclosure through the publication of patents of new and superior technology. The trend in hardware technology seems to guarantee an almost perpetual shortage of needed software. Hence incentives to increase the general level of investment in software generation are perfectly appropriate....

Establishing that the *benefits* of the patent system apply as well to software technology as to other areas of technology is only half the case. Inquiry must made into whether the *burdens* of the patent system will be especially onerous as to algorithms so as to justify excluding them from the system. That granting patents on algorithms will tend to raise the price of software products using such algorithms and thereby to restrict their utilization proves nothing. The patent system presumably has that effect in all areas of technology to which it applies.

Two points about the special impact of allowing patents on algorithms useful in computer programming warrant discussion. The first aspect arises from the manner in which algorithms are used. In and of itself, an algorithm is not a directly vendible commodity or process, as might be the case with a pharmaceutical composition subject to patent protection. However, a new and more efficient algorithm for solving a logical or mathematical problem can be used to create a useful and vendible product, such as a computer program embedded in a media. In fact, a valuable algorithm, such as that at issue in *Benson*, will normally be useful in creating a wide variety of programs. Of course, many, indeed probably most, structures and processes that are traditionally subject to patent protection are mere building blocks and require further development in order to create a commercially marketable product. What distinguishes algorithms is that the products constructed from them will almost inevitably be subject to an additional independent intellectual property right—to wit, a copyright on the actual computer program. In other areas of technology, use of a basic patented invention may lead to further intellectual property rights—patents on improvements, trade secrets, and the like—but not as inevitably as with algorithms.

These two characteristics—that algorithms are building blocks for constructing directly useful products and that the resulting products are subject to an independent intellectual property right in the producer— mean that the *burden* of patent protection on algorithms will, if anything, be *less* than patent protection on other technological developments. These two characteristics mean that licensing of the patent rather than exclusive control will normally be the most feasible strategy for optimizing revenue. The patent owner will often not have the resources to develop all the possible programs in which a new algorithm will be useful. Potential licensees will have a positive attitude toward patent licensing because they will use the granted privilege to create a work that is independently protectable against misappropriation by third persons and indeed against misappropriation by the patent licensor. There is every reason to believe that algorithm patents will be extensively licensed at reasonable royalty rates.

Notes and Questions

1. Donald Chisum is a Professor of Law at Santa Clara University; before moving to Santa Clara, he taught for many years at the University of Washington. In 1978, he wrote the first contemporary treatise on patent law, which has now grown to 14 volumes and which is constantly being updated. He received undergraduate and law degrees from Stanford.

2. Professor Chisum's views have largely carried the day in the courts. See, e.g., State Street Bank and Trust Co. v. Signature Financial Group, Inc., 149 F.3d 1368 (Fed. Cir. 1998). Some see this as the inevitable triumph of consistency and good policy. See Richard S. Gruner, "Better Living Through Software: Promoting Information Processing Advances Through Patent Incentives," 74 *St. John's L. Rev.* 977 (2000). There are still those who argue that software patents are a bad idea, however. See Jay Dratler, Jr., "Does Lord Darcy Yet Live? The Case Against Software and Business–Method Patents," 43 *Santa Clara L. Rev.* 823 (2003).

3. Professor Chisum states that algorithms are "highly specific," as part of his refutation of the Benson court's concern with over-broad patents in this area. But Chisum argues earlier that "algorithm" is simply a synonym for "process," and processes can be far from specific. Was Chisum perhaps influenced by the fact that most high-level software engineering algorithms sought to be patented in the 1980s were tied fairly closely to a limited class of computing environments? Was he perhaps assuming that this was the essential nature of computer algorithms? Subsequent developments have shown that claim drafters are quite capable of crafting claims that abstract away from particular machines and programming languages; does this perhaps lend some credibility to the concerns expressed by Justice Douglas in the Benson case?

4. Professor Chisum is quite skeptical of the Supreme Court's reading of prior case law regarding patentable subject matter, which the Court consolidates into the notion that "basic tools" of research cannot be patented. Chisum responds by stating that the phrase "basic tools" is equivalent to "accumulated knowledge," and that therefore this material is not patentable because it is already known, i.e., in the prior art. Is this a fair analysis of the Supreme Court's concern? Is Chisum arguing, in effect, that the categories of "basic tool" and "patentable invention" are somehow mutually exclusive? Chisum notes in the article that the prospective breadth of an invention is not considered a bar to patentability in other areas, such as mechanical devices and chemical compounds. Yet consider: a new and important invention of very broad applicability may be so potentially fundamental to so many technological developments that the social cost of granting property rights might be quite high. Perhaps one role for § 101 of the Patent Act is to restrict the grant of a property right under these circumstances. (Even if you agree, does it follow that it is therefore necessary to preclude patents for software? Are all software inventions—even a program consisting of a few lines of computer code that performs a simple task—inherently so far-reaching that the Patent Act should consider them unpatentable?)

5. The article argues that software patents will not stand in the way of the industry's development; "licensing . . . rather than exclusive control will normally be the most feasible strategy for optimizing revenue." This stems in part, Chisum argues, from the fact that licensees have significant leverage in the form of copyright in their own code. For an argument that property rights may lead to more efficient production of software by creating the conditions for a market in software code, see Mark Lemley and David O'Brien, "Encouraging Software Reuse," 49 *Stanford Law Review* 255 (1997). For a comparative analysis of the U.S. and Japanese software industries, which makes the point that better-developed property rights in the U.S. facilitated the emergence of "off the rack" software products, see Robert P. Merges, "A Comparative Look at Intellectual Property Rights in the Software Industry," in *The International Computer Software Industry: A Comparative Study of Industry Evolution and Structure* (Oxford Univ. Press 1996) (David Mowery, ed.), pp. 272–303. One recent commentary suggests that if we are going to have software patents, we ought to be very careful to pay attention to the limits on their scope, to better facilitate the way innovation takes place in the software industry. Mark A. Lemley and Julie E. Cohen, *Patent Scope and Innovation in The Software Industry*, 89 Cal. L. Rev. 1 (2001).

Benson Revisited: The Case against Patent Protection for Algorithms and Other Computer Program–Related Inventions*

PAMELA SAMUELSON

For most of the past twenty-five years, it was widely believed that computer program-related inventions were rarely, if ever, patentable. The 1972 Supreme Court decision, Gottschalk v. Benson, in which the Court ruled that a computer program algorithm is not patentable,[1] contributed significantly to this view. This decision also seemed to call into question the patentability of other computer program innovations. Two subsequent Supreme Court decisions, Parker v. Flook[2] in 1978 and Diamond v. Diehr[3] in 1981, reaffirmed the Benson ruling on the unpatentability of algorithms. Even though the Supreme Court did conclude that Diehr's invention was patentable, the Diehr decision was regarded as a very limited one for many years. It is limited in that it affirms only that patents can issue for traditionally patentable industrial processes which include a computer program as an element.

Despite the consistency in the Supreme Court's rulings against the patenting of algorithms, the Patent Office is now issuing patents for a wide variety of non-industrial computer program-related inventions and even seems to be issuing patents for computer program algorithms. Some patent lawyers argue that this change is consistent with Diehr, which they read to hold that only claims for "unapplied'" algorithms are unpatentable. Professor Donald Chisum, the prominent patent scholar, attacks the Supreme Court case law more directly by calling for Benson to be overruled and for patent law to embrace the patentability of algorithms and other computer program-related inventions.[4]

The purpose of this article is to restate the case against patent protection for algorithms and many other computer program-related inventions in order to clarify the legal and public policy debates on this important subject. The author finds a substantial basis in patent law for Benson's ruling that computer program algorithms are unpatentable and for rejection of patents for many other program-related innovations. Both the appellate court case law on program patentability and the recently issued Patent Office guidelines lack a sound theoretical basis and rely heavily on indefensible distinctions. This article explains the basis for these assertions and analyzes recent appellate court decisions

---

* Reprinted by permission from 39 Emory Law Journal 1025 (1990), © 1990 Emory Law Journal.

   1. 409 U.S. 63 (1972). The legal issue before the Court in Benson, and in most of the subsequent cases on the patentability of computer program-related inventions, was whether the claimed invention (in Benson, an algorithm for converting binary coded decimals to pure binary form) was a "process'" that was patentable under the patent statute. See 35 U.S.C. § 101 (1988).

   2. 437 U.S. 584 (1978)....

   3. 450 U.S. 175 (1981)....

   4. See Chisum, The Patentability of Algorithms, 47 U.Pitt.L.Rev. 959, 971 (1986). Professor Chisum's thesis is discussed and criticized [later in this article]. [Chisum's article is also excerpted in this volume.—Eds.]

that have created a contradictory line of decisions on program-related patentability. These decisions have brought the debate about patentability of program-related inventions around full circle to where it began more than twenty years ago: The appellate court that reviews the Patent Office's decisions has come to adopt the Patent Office's first rationale for rejecting claims for program-related inventions, but has not acknowledged that it has done so.

In order to have a clear view of where the law now stands on the patentability of computer program innovations, therefore, it is necessary to go back to its historical roots.... [T]his article reviews the terms of the debate over computer program patentability in the years before the Supreme Court decision in Benson.... [It] discusses the Benson case and how and why the Supreme Court's decision changed the nature of the debate over the patentability of program innovations [, and then] ... reviews the myriad ways in which the Court of Customs and Patent Appeals (CCPA) evolved in its interpretation of Benson in the years before the Supreme Court's Diehr decision. [It also] analyzes the Diehr decision, asks whether some of the recently issued program algorithm patents are consistent with Diehr, and analyzes Professor Chisum's argument in favor of granting patents to algorithms and overruling Benson. [Finally, this article] discusses recent case law that raises serious doubts about the patentability of data-processing innovations. This part also establishes the link between patentability questions raised by claims for "mathematical algorithms' " and claims for algorithms for processing other kinds of data. The unusual nature of computer programs is to blame for the complex problems that computer program innovations present for the patent system.

Professor Chisum correctly states that the pre-Benson case law eliminated doctrinal barriers to the patentability of computer program algorithms. This article questions whether the CCPA did so for appropriate reasons and with considered judgment about the consequences likely to flow from this action. While Professor Chisum is also correct that the Supreme Court poorly articulated its rationale in Benson, this article argues that there is a more substantial basis in patent law for the Court's decision than Professor Chisum perceives. Unlike Professor Chisum, the author does not see evidence of an " 'antipatent judicial bias' " in Benson. Indeed, as she reads Benson, the Court was keeping an open mind about the patentability of computer program-related inventions.

Professor Chisum also rightly observes that the post-Benson case law is replete with awkward distinctions and results that are difficult to reconcile. This article has, however, shown that much of the muddle in the post-Benson decisions was a muddle of the CCPA's own making. That which was not the CCPA's doing was due more to the inability of legal decisionmakers to grasp the nature of computer program innovations than to the reasoning in the Benson decision.

Computer scientist Allen Newell responded to the Chisum article by commenting:

Chisum may well be right that the Benson case has brought on much analytic confusion in the software patent area. He may also be right in supposing that, if Benson had only been decided differently, the specific confusion that occurred in its aftermath would not have materialized. It seems to be his view that a different holding in Benson would have brought about analytic sweetness and light.

My point is precisely to the contrary. Regardless how the Benson case was decided ... confusion would have ensued. The confusions that bedevil algorithms and patentability arise from the basic conceptual models that we use to think about algorithms and their use. That is why I have entitled my remarks, "The Models Are Broken, The Models Are Broken.' "[5]

This author joins Professor Newell in questioning whether the model of invention with which the traditional patent system has operated might be " 'broken' " when applied to algorithms and computer programs.

While Professor Chisum discusses some policy reasons for giving patent or patent-like protection to computer program algorithms, he understates the even stronger countervailing policy arguments which are explored at length [later in this Article]. Even if policy reasons were to favor the patenting of program algorithms, it may be more appropriate for such a decision to be made by Congress than by an appellate court or an administrative agency like the Patent Office because the patenting of computer program algorithms represents a significant departure from patent tradition.

To judge whether Benson should be overruled, either legislatively or by judicial decision, one needs a clear notion of what kinds of "processes' " would, in a new regime, be considered patentable. The Supreme Court thus far has not been persuaded to extend its interpretation of patentable processes beyond the traditional transformation of matter standard. Although Professor Chisum criticizes this restriction as unwarranted, it is fair to ask what alternative definition of patentable subject matter Professor Chisum offers. Because Professor Chisum holds up the CCPA's decision in In re Musgrave [431 F.2d 882 (CCPA 1970)] as "the highwater mark of rationality' " concerning what is patentable subject matter, it is appropriate to revisit the Musgrave decision.

However, Professor Chisum's main argument in favor of the patentability of computer program algorithms like the Benson algorithm rests on the fact that, like other patentable processes, program algorithms define a sequence of operations that accomplishes a useful result. From this, he argues that the post-Benson case law distinction between "mathematical' " and " 'nonmathematical' " algorithms is artificial.

---

5. [Allen Newell, "The Models are Broken, The Models are Broken," 47 U. Pitt. L. Rev. 1023 (1986).] Professor Newell asserts that these conceptual problems do not derive from the nature of algorithms themselves, but only from the efforts to create legal distinctions between "mathematical" and "nonmathematical" algorithms, between "numerical" and "nonnumerical" algorithms, or between "algorithms" and "mental steps," all of which he finds to be "doomed to failure." Id. at 1024–25. In this respect, Newell and Chisum seem to be in agreement, for Chisum would repudiate the mental process limitation on patentability in general, and not just as it applies to algorithms.

While Chisum's argument has some appeal, it ignores important distinctions traditionally made by patent law. Some algorithms, like those for making steel, have their primary instantiation in the processing of raw materials in a steel plant. Computer program algorithms, such as Benson's method for converting binary coded decimals to pure binary form, have their primary instantiation in computer programs written to implement them. Still other algorithms, such as ones for performing statistical analyses on data, for analyzing the sentence structure in Balzac's novels, or for ordering names and telephone numbers, may have their primary instantiation in written texts. Patentability has traditionally been judged by the nature of the primary instantiation anticipated by the procedure. Instantiation in the text of written works has traditionally been regarded as outside the bounds of the patent system.

As reflected in the popular press, the current "controversy" over software patents has nothing whatsoever to do with the fine points of the court decisions, doctrinal analysis, and Patent Office practice on which this article has mainly concentrated. Rather, the issue has a more legislative tone, as though the patentability of computer programs and algorithms is an open issue about which it would be appropriate to ask if patents are "good" or "bad" for the industry and for society. Predictions that patents may be harmful to the software industry, computer science, mathematics, or society as a whole have been quite frequent, even from some of the most well-known people in the software and computer science fields . . .

Patent lawyers tend to respond to such concerns by saying that, although this may be an interesting social policy issue, the reality is that the legal system has already established a rule in favor of software patents. Court decisions have upheld the patentability of program-related inventions. There are many issued patents now, there will be many more in future years, and all are presumed to be valid. It would take congressional action to alter what has become the status quo, and that is not likely to happen.

This article argues that the legal foundation on which the current belief in the patentability of all program-related inventions rests is not as solid as many patent lawyers would like to believe. The CCPA decisions upholding software patents are hardly models of enlightened clarity and well-explicated principles. Indeed, the only principle which seems to have guided that court's deliberations over the years is one of upholding the patentability of as many program-related inventions as possible while still appearing to show some respect for the Supreme Court's decisions. Both the CCPA decisions and the Patent Office's current more generous attitude toward software patents go beyond what the Supreme Court approved in the Diehr case. As a result, the legal debate over the patentability of computer program-related inventions may not be as settled as some patent lawyers claim.

Although the author's study of the computer program patent cases has caused her to be critical of these decisions and of Professor Chisum's argument for overturning Benson, it is primarily because of the widespread concerns about the ill effects of patents from within the industry and the technical community that she has pursued this study questioning patent protection for computer program-related inventions.

... [M]any mathematicians, computer scientists, and others in the software development community assert that computer program algorithms ought not to be protected by intellectual property law because they are, as the Supreme Court first said eighteen years ago, basic intellectual tools of science and mathematics. Algorithmic advances have been extremely important to growth in the field of computer science, one of the most fecund fields during the latter part of the twentieth century, and it has grown without patent protection. As Professor Newell observes, if we want to be sure that fundamental theoretical discoveries of computer science are available to be used, tested, and built upon by others, it may be more sensible to withhold patent protection for algorithms than to grant them.

Accepting an expansive realm for software patents requires ignoring that many in the software industry itself are strongly opposed to patents for software innovations. This warning of harm should be of concern to us all. The point that innovation in the software field has developed rapidly without the aid of patents should not be forgotten. If those in the industry who now seek patents could show that conditions have changed so much that what would once have been harmful would now be beneficial, then there might be more reason to expand the existing patent realm without this showing.

Absent this showing, either copyright alone or a fourth alternative should be adopted: the construction of a new law for the protection of computer programs and the innovations they embody. If it is true that computer programs are too much of a machine to fit comfortably in the copyright system and too much of a writing to fit comfortably in the patent system, it would be better to create a new law for the protection of computer programs than to stretch existing legal categories past their breaking points.

Many agree that patent law may be unsuited for the protection of program innovations. For example, Professor Newell argues that the conceptual model on which the patent system is built is "broken" and that a new model must be constructed—one that is attentive to the nature of programs and of the " 'inventables' " which computers permit people to create and utilize ... [A] sui generis law for computer programs might include the following features:

1) Certain coverage for minimally "original" program source and object code from the moment of fixation in either form;

2) An exclusive right to transform source into object code, and an exclusive right to control certain unauthorized copying and distribution of source or object code;

3) Protection for object code such that if an unauthorized person mechanically transformed that code into an object code which was not identical to the protected code, but was proven to be merely a "scrambled" version of it, infringement would be found;

4) Protection for source code that would protect against direct translation of that code from one programming language to another programming language in a related class of languages;

5) A duration of protection limitation that would commence upon the first commercial or other public distribution of the code and would last no more than twenty years;

6) A mandatory notice of assertion of protection of the program code which would include the year of the first commercial or public distribution of the code;

7) A copyright-like registration process (low cost, fast, minimal review) for program code; and

8) A right on the part of lawful possessors of the protected code to modify and copy it in order to make it useful to themselves.

Notes and Questions

1. Pamela Samuelson graduated from the University of Hawaii and Yale Law School. She is a Professor in the School of Information Management and Systems, and in the School of Law, at the University of California, Berkeley. She previously taught at the University of Pittsburgh School of Law. She was named a MacArthur Fellow in 1997.

2. There is now at least some empirical support for some of the arguments Professor Samuelson makes in the preceding excerpt. See, e.g., James Bessen and Robert M. Hunt, "An Empirical Look at Software Patents," working paper, August 2003, avail. at www.researchoninnovation.org/swpat.pdf. Bessen and Hunt find that (1) software patents became cheaper to acquire, on average, than other patents during the 1990s, leading some firms to acquire a large number of them; and (2) for firms that acquire them, an increase in the number of patents obtained did not increase expenditures for research and development (R & D), but actually *decreased* those expenditures. That is, software patents were found to be a substitute for doing more R & D, rather than a complement.

3. Professor Samuelson states that if "fundamental theoretical discoveries of computer science are available to be used, tested, and built upon by others, it may be more sensible to withhold patent protection for algorithms than to grant them." Compare this to the arguments in the preceding excerpt, from Donald Chisum. What is the chief point of dispute between the two scholars? Why is Chisum less concerned that broad patents will interfere with the dissemination and use of "fundamental discoveries"? Certain other areas of science and technology have experienced the presence of both fundamental patents and rapid, widespread growth; biotechnology comes to mind. Is software different? Note that at least some broad, pioneering patents in biotechnology are held by universities. Does this perhaps explain the liberal licensing of these patents? Would a private firm have different incentives? Would it behave differently?

4. For an exploration of an intellectual property regime where property rights are available, but interfere less with the dynamics of the software

industry, see Pamela Samuelson, Randall Davis, Mitchell D. Kapor, and
J.H. Reichman, "A Manifesto Concerning the Legal Protection of Computer Software," 94 *Colum. L. Rev.* 2308 (1994), excerpted infra, p. 355.

The Patenting of the Liberal Professions*

JOHN R. THOMAS

The regime of patents has traditionally been nothing if not humble. Its
plodding acquisition procedures and formal enforcement analyses historically confined themselves to the artifacts of the Industrial Revolution
and their immediate successors. The painstakingly catalogued Patent
Office classification scheme betrayed the sense, shared if not easily
articulated by the patent bar, of the sorts of inventions that could be the
subject of a patent and those that could not.

Times have changed in patent law. Inventors from diverse disciplines, animated by a lenient judiciary and elevated to proprietors by the
Patent Office, have offered the patent system a bold new vision. The
sheer range of recently issued patents suggests that few restraints bound
the sorts of subject matter that may be appropriated via the patent
system. As we read with amusement patent instruments claiming methods for swinging a golf club, treating cancer or administering a mort-
gage, we come to realize that the patent law seems poised to embrace the
broadest reaches of human experience.

The recent opinion in *State Street Bank & Trust Co. v. Signature
Financial Group, Inc.*[1] suggests that the United States Court of Appeals
for the Federal Circuit will pass an approving glance upon much of this
Patent Office work product, if called upon to do so. In *State Street*, the
plaintiff held a patent for a data processing system consisting of software
for managing a stock mutual fund. The Federal Circuit not only held
that data transformation through a series of mathematical calculations
presented patentable technique, but also took the opportunity to obliterate the venerable proscription on patenting so-called "methods of doing
business." Keenly aware of the *State Street* holding, applicants have
besieged the Patent Office with applications ranging from financial
software to Internet-based business models.

State Street presents the latest in a series of cases testing the
boundaries of the "useful Arts," the constitutional expression of subject
matter appropriate for patenting. Embodying the current understanding
of this term to mean the "technological arts," the patent statute further
refined patentable subject matter to include processes, machines, manufactures and compositions of matter. The first of these terms appears the
most troubling, particularly in light of its circular statutory definition as
a "process, art or method." For without more, the scope of the statutory
term "process" appears co-extensive with nearly any possible endeavor,

---

* Reprinted by permission from 40 B.C. L. Rev. 1139 (1999), © 1999 Boston College
Law Review.

1. 149 F.3d 1368 (Fed. Cir. 1998), *cert. denied*, 119 S. Ct. 851 (1999).

as almost any imaginable function can be articulated in a series of steps in the fashion of a patent instrument.

[T]his Article explores the broad ramifications of the *State Street* opinion. The Patent Office's willingness to consider business method applications means that fewer constraints bar the grant of patents on other utilitarian processes. Disconnected from any physical apparatus, such patents will set forth not so much technical artifacts, but a broad category of proprietary modes of analysis, techniques and protocols from disciplines ranging from the social sciences to the law. Yet surely the constitutional directive that patents apply to the "useful Arts," as well as our long-held sense of the reach of the patent system, must somehow cabin the extent of patentable subject matter. We have come to this place, this Article reasons, because of our near-total engagement with the artificial. Identifying the ontic dimension of technology has perplexed not only the courts, but epistemologists and the most accomplished of technological observers as well.

Resolving to develop an articulation of those aspects of human endeavor we may fairly call technological, [this Article] invokes contemporary thought about technology. Turning to the technological commentary of Robert McGinn, Paul W. DeVore and Carl Mitcham, this Article develops a typology of traits that distinguish technology from other forms of human activity. This Article concludes that technological activities are concerned with the production or transformation of artifacts through the systematic manipulation of physical forces. Bounded by interaction with the external environment, technological activities expend resources and knowledge in order to fabricate or modify products, or to develop procedural systems for so doing. Furthermore, technology presents a form of rational and systematic knowledge, oriented towards efficiency and capable of being assessed through objective criteria.

This Article continues ... by considering how we can move from a catalogue of characteristics to an essentialist, legally apt definition of the technological. Recent experience concerning methods of medical treatment suggests one technique: amendment of the Patent Act to create particularized patent-free spheres of activity. This Article concludes that due to the obligations of the TRIPS Agreement, the intellectual property component of the World Trade Organization treaty, such efforts are unlikely to succeed. Given the TRIPS Agreement mandate that patent rights be enjoyable without discrimination as to the field of technology, even the recent amendment concerning medical methods appears suspect.

This Article finds a more favorable solution in the standard of industrial application. Long a part of many foreign laws and fully compatible with the TRIPS Agreement, the standards developed under the industrial application requirement bear a striking resemblance to contemporary thought about the scope of technological activities. By restricting patentable advances to the repeatable production or transformation of material objects and excluding subject matter founded upon the aesthetic, social observation or personal skill, the industrial application requirement would restore a sense of patentable subject matter that matches our sensibilities.

* * *

B.   *Toward a Refined View of Technology*

As a central aspect of modern life, technology has attracted a justifiable amount of concern and commentary. Yet divergence concerning the scope of this phenomenon has often hindered discourse. The fields of engineering, epistemology, sociology, anthropology and phenomenology have lent "technology" meanings that range from artifacts, to knowledge, to sociotechnical systems of manufacture and use. Despite the ubiquity of technology, no recognized taxonomy of technological characteristics exists.

* * *

A review of commentators such as [philosophers of technology] McGinn, DeVore and Mitcham illustrates that we can achieve a structured definition of technology. Although embedded in social systems, technology is an endeavor that both intuition and sustained analysis would distinguish from other aspects of human society. In brief, technology may be characterized as knowledge that is applied toward material enterprise, guided by an orientation to the external environment and the necessity of design.

[Thomas notes the limits of "piecemeal legislation," such as specific exclusions of medical process patents from patent protection.]

* * *

A second method of limiting the scope of patent eligibility to the technological would be for Congress to add an essentialist definition into our patent statute. In this regard, we can receive guidance from two of the world's great patent statutes: the European Patent Convention and the Japanese Patent Act. Each of these laws requires that inventions be susceptible to so-called "industrial application" in order to qualify for or receive patent protection. Concise, proven and compatible with the TRIPS Agreement, the industrial applicability requirement provides an apt way to limit the patent system to what we understand to be technological.

The requirement that potential patents have an industrial application has long been part of German patent law. As originally conceived, patentable technologies were limited to those which involved the treatment or processing of raw materials through mechanical or chemical means. The requirement has been more recently held to require a "technical rule for the control of natural forces,"[2] or, stated somewhat differently, "a teaching for systematic activity using controllable natural forces for the attainment of a causally predictable result."[3]

   2. *A.E.K. v. Federal Patent Office*, 15 Int'l Rev. Indus. Prop. & Copyright L. 82, 83 (1984) (reporting the September 21, 1982, opinion of the Swiss Supreme Court).
   3. Gert Kolle, *The Patentable Invention in the European Patent Convention*, 5 Int'l Rev. Indus. Prop. & Copyright L. 140, 146 (1974).

Currently, the European Patent Convention presents the most fulsome articulation of the industrial applicability standard. Article 52 of the European Patent Convention stipulates that the following shall not be considered patentable inventions: "(a) discoveries, scientific theories and mathematical methods; (b) aesthetic creations; (c) schemes, rules and methods for performing mental acts, playing games or doing business, and programs for computers; (d) presentations of information." Article 57 of the European Patent Convention goes on to provide that "an invention shall be considered as susceptible of industrial application if it can be made or used in any kind of industry, including agriculture." In its Examination Guidelines, the European Patent Office describes Article 57 as a reinforcing provision that excludes from patentability few inventions not set forth in Article 52.

That Article 52 expressly excludes "programs for computers" may seem implausible to many, especially those familiar with the *European Patent Office Gazette*. In fact, the European Patent Office has drawn a distinction between computer software per se and its application towards the resolution of technical problems, excluding from patentability only the former class of inventions. . . .

The Japanese Patent Office has also issued extensive guidelines on the industrial application requirement. That agency views the requirement of industrial application as complementing the Japanese Patent Act's definition of a statutory invention—that is, the "creation of technical ideas utilizing natural laws." Inventions claiming discoveries or natural laws, personal skill, the simple presentation of information, aesthetic creations and matter contrary to natural laws are all considered non-statutory.

Conclusion

There is much to commend the adoption of the standard of industrial application in the United States patent law. Our patent law should comport with our perception of what technology is, not defy it. Restoring a patentability standard firmly grounded in industrial applicability, rather than equating technology with anything artificial, would enable us to maintain the integrity of our current patent system. Moreover, it would enable us to respect the boundary between the whole expression of our humanity and that small part of it that is properly called technological. However central to contemporary life and worthy of nurturing through the patent system, technology is but one manifestation of the human experience.

Notes and Questions

1. Jay Thomas received a B.S. from Carnegie Mellon University; a J.D. from the University of Michigan, and an LL.M. degree from George Washington, where he served on the faculty for several years. He is currently a Professor at Georgetown Law School.

2. The "industrial application" standard preferred by Thomas has much to recommend it, as Thomas notes, most importantly that it comports well with commonsense notions of what "technology" is. But recall the history of software patent doctrine in the U.S. reviewed in earlier excerpts from Donald Chisum and Pamela Samuelson. At various times, U.S. courts have attempted to restrain software patents by limiting them to applications in the "industrial arts." But the courts became dissatisfied with a narrow definition of "industry," as cases such as *State Street Bank* make clear. Why, they seem to ask, should a programmer working for a steel manufacturing company be a potential patentee, while a programmer working on Wall Street is not? If they both face an equal challenge, and both do a good job, how can the patent system discriminate between them? Does Thomas' discussion of the meaning of "technology" provide a satisfactory answer to this question?

3. Numerous commentators and various economic indicators suggest that the world economy is now undergoing a fundamental change. The nineteenth and twentieth century economy, characterized by the manufacturing of tangible goods, is giving way to an "information economy." The substrate of the economy is moving, as the saying goes, from "atoms to bits." If this is true, and if Thomas' proposal is accepted, the patent system will undoubtedly shrink in importance. The property rights it confers will be concentrated in the "low growth" areas of the economy. Is this a good result? Are patents tied so ineluctably to tangible aspects of industry that they should move aside in importance while the information economy takes off? For an interesting analysis of the differences between copyrights and patents which bears on this issue, see Clarisa Long, "Information Costs in Patent and Copyright," 90 *U. Va. L. Rev.* 465 (2004). If Thomas is correct about the historically-grounded meaning of the constitutional phrase "the useful arts," what does this say about the viability of an eighteenth century constitution to set the ground rules for commerce and industry in the twenty-first century?

4. A primary concern raised by the advent of business method patents centers on issues of patent quality. The increased volume of applications brought on by *State Street Bank*, together with widespread skepticism about certain individual patents issued early in the history of this new area, occasioned calls for patent system reform. See, e.g., Robert P. Merges, "As Many as Six Impossible Patents Before Breakfast: Property Rights for Business Concepts and Patent System Reform," 14 *Berkeley Tech. L.J.* 577 (1999). A subsequent empirical study, using quantitative proxies for patent quality (such as number and type of prior art citations) concludes that even these early internet business method patents are of no lower quality than other patents. John R. Allison, Emerson H. Tiller, "The Business Method Patent Myth," 18 *Berkeley Tech. L.J.* 987 (2003).

5. For a discussion of international treaty implications of business method patents, see Vincent Chiappetta, "Trip–Ping Over Business Method Patents," 37 *Vand. J. Transnat'l L.* 181 (2004). For an argument concerning the constitutionality of these patents, see Malla Pollock, "The Multiple Unconstitutionality of Business Method Patents: Common Sense, Congressional Consideration, and Constitutional History," 28 *Rutgers Computer & Tech. L.J.* 61 (2002).

B. Requirements for Patentability

Laying the Ghost of the "Invention" Requirement*

HONORABLE GILES S. RICH

The Subject

I am going to discuss § 103 of Title 35 United States Code, the 1952 Patent Act, the unobviousness provision, because it is the heart of the patent system and the justification of patent grants. Why do I say that? For two reason: *First*, it is Section 103 which brings about statutory *compliance with the Constitutional limitation* on the power of Congress to create a patent system, assuming novelty of the invention, of course, which is also necessary. (35 USC 101 and 102.) *Second*, it is the provision which assures that the patent grant of exclusive right is *not in conflict with the anti-monopoly policy* brought to this country from England by the colonists, long before our antitrust statutes, and that patent rights do not conflict with the policy of those statutes, which is to prevent odious monopolies and unreasonable restraints of trade.

Both compliance with the Constitution and avoidance of conflict with antimonopoly principles involve the same considerations: promoting progress in the technological arts while not interfering with the free use of technology which is fairly in the public domain. As I hope to make clear, Section 103 assures this result by allowing exclusive rights to inventors only when their inventions would not have been obvious to the ordinary workers in the field, preserving inviolate the common fund of technical knowledge which is obvious to the workers in the art. A time-limited exclusive right to subject matter which was neither known, nor obvious from what was known, *takes nothing from the public which it had before*. As a necessary corollary, the disclosure in a valid patent gives to the public knowledge it did not possess, actually or potentially, and thereby makes for progress.

It is worth remembering, furthermore, that we had a statutory patent system in this country for a century before we had a statute against monopoly. Antitrust law, therefore, should be so construed as to maintain a viable patent system. The 1952 Patent Act did several things to draw the line between patent rights and established anti-monopoly principles. The enactment of § 103 was one of those things.[1]

I have written on this subject before and discussed it in innumerable opinions, as have my colleagues—long before the question got to the Supreme Court in 1966. In 1964 I wrote that I was discussing this

* Reprinted with permission from the APLA Quarterly Journal, Vol. I, No. 1 1972, pp. 26–45, © 1972 American Intellectual Property Law Ass'n ... Substance delivered as a speech to Los Angeles Patent Law Association, Sept. 18, 1072; San Francisco Patent Law Association, Sept. 20, 1972; New Jersey and Philadelphia Patent Law Associations and Patent Section N.J. State Bar, October 12, 1972.

1. "The Vague Concept of 'Invention' as replaced by § 103 of the 1952 Patent Act," IDEA, Vol. 8 Conf. Number 1964, p. 136.

subject because it was "the one I think causes the most trouble, the clarification of which I therefore believe would do the most good."

In 1966, I felt that the Supreme Court had quite successfully clarified it. I am discussing it again because I and many others see that confusion remains rampant in the courts and has arisen even in the Supreme Court, which fact is creating even more confusion in the lower courts. It all seems so unnecessary and it is damaging to the patent system and discouraging to inventors, to whom we owe much, and that is bad for the country. It is even more discouraging to those who risk the investment to perfect and commercialize the inventions the inventors made and thus give the benefit of them to the public. Lawyers may thrive on confusion but businessmen like to know where they are at. Confusion in the law costs them money. That cost they pass on to the public.

So, once again, I address myself to the problem I think causes the most trouble in the sincere hope it may do some good.

I am not discussing Section 103 theoretically or on the basis of research into its "legislative history," as a young law clerk would do today, twenty years after its enactment. I am doing it as one of its authors and, I believe, as the originator of one of its principal features. I hope a little of what I say will be remembered, because we who wrote it are gradually becoming an extinct species.

Of course, there are legal philosophers who would say it makes no difference what the authors intended, that Section 103 means what the courts say it means. Well, that is unhappily true. But what the courts are saying is conflicting and often wrong. While I live I shall therefore continue to tell the world what Section 103 was intended to mean and intended to do. Judge Learned Hand knew in 1955. My court found out in 1956 and has consistently acted on that knowledge for sixteen years. The Patent Office has changed its practice accordingly. The Supreme Court found out in 1966 and approved. Yet today ... opinions continue to issue in most circuits showing misunderstanding, confusion, and inconsistency. We have been in a state of transition in thinking for twenty years now, since the Patent Act of 1952, and it is high time we had uniformity of interpretation. My hope is to promote it.

The History

I think the best approach to a discussion of § 103 is historical, to show what happened and why.

The gist of *Hotchkiss* v. *Greenwood* [52 U.S. 248 (1850)] is that the Supreme Court, like Jefferson, sensed that Congress had not included in the statute a necessary limitation on the grant of patents and added that condition itself. This was judicial legislation. The Court added a *condition* but, as it turned out, it was not much of a standard, because it was too vague. The condition, as refined and sharpened in Section 103, creates a statutory system under which all patents granted pursuant to statute do serve to promote the progress of useful arts because, being for unobvious subject matter, they necessarily add to the sum of useful knowledge.

In any event, for the century following *Hotchkiss* v. *Greenwood* we had what was called the "requirement for invention," which I emphasize, we have *not* had for the past 20 years. Instead we have Section 103.

The requirement for "invention" was at one and the same time a hard reality and a great mystery. Really, it was an absurdity. To be patentable, courts said, an invention had to involve "invention." If one asked for an explanation, the answer was, as the Supreme Court had pontifically announced in *McClain* v. *Ortmayer*, 141 U.S. 419, 427, in 1891, that "Invention cannot be defined." Only experienced patent lawyers, the Patent Office and judges knew what "invention" meant. You knew it by intuition, presumably from experience which, of course, judges passing on its presence or absence did not always have. The essence of being a patent lawyer or examiner—or a judge in a patent case—was to know an invention when you saw one yet there was no formal ordination. It was as easy as becoming a bird watcher. Judges, ex officio, were instant experts on the question.

As is usual with a doctrine derived from a court opinion, the doctrine persists and evolves while the facts of the case are forgotten. The words of the opinion of the first case are quoted in a second and embroidered upon, quoted again, and again reembroidered until after a century you have quite a body of so-called "law," or more properly *lore*, on the subject. Learned Hand, one of the great patent judges, summed it all up in 1955, saying to a Senate committee: "You could find nearly anything you liked if you went to the opinions. It was a subject on which judges loved to be rhetorical.... Patent lawyers ... like to quote all those things. There are lots of them." But, he said, "They never seemed to tend toward enlightenment."[2]

I think the height of absurdity appears in what is supposed to be our leading textbook, *Walker on Patents*, first Deller edition (1937, Vol. 1, p. 110): "An invention is the result of an inventive act." Various cases I could cite were equally mystical in explaining that patentable invention or just "invention" results from the exercise of the inventive effort. One leading New York lawyer who had the temerity to argue to the Supreme Court in 1941 that the statute required only novelty and utility, which was so, and that the courts could not require more, was rewarded with an opinion which drove patent lawyers up the wall saying that to be patentable an invention had to be the result of a "flash of creative genius." (*Cuno Eng. Corp.* v. *Automatic Devices Corp.*, 314 U.S. 84, 91.)

* * *

This kind of mystical reasoning left the judiciary free to indulge their personal whims about patentability. Notwithstanding what the Supreme Court has said, we went through periods of too much leniency and too much strictness, depending primarily, just as now, on what judges thought and the mood of the country.

In the depression and post-depression thirties and forties we were going through one of the strict periods. Pressure began to build up to

---

2. Hearings pursuant to S. Res. 92, 84th Cong., 1st Sess., on the American Patent System, Oct. 10–12, 1955, p. 113, conducted by Senator O'Mahoney, Chairman, Subcommittee on Patents, Trademarks and Copyrights of the Committee on the Judiciary.

curb the courts by statute. Some bills were introduced. Just at that time the congressional committee in charge of codifying the various titles of the U.S. Code decided it would be a good idea to codify Title 35, the patent law. That enterprise got under way through what was called the Coordinating Committee, a group of about 30 lawyers from private, corporate, and governmental practice, which worked with the House subcommittee. I was a member of the Coordinating Committee and of its small Drafting Committee.

* * *

In December 1950 the bar was far from unanimous in thinking that the statute should deal with the requirement for "invention," not even the members of the Committee agreed. There are always those who prefer the *status quo*, with which they have learned to live, no matter how ridiculous it may be. Now, it was very significant that what persuaded the Coordinating Committee to replace the case law with a statutory provision was the Supreme Court's opinion, and Mr. Justice Douglas' concurring opinion, published in the New York Times on the very day in 1950 the Committee was having a meeting, in the case of *The Great Atlantic & Pacific Tea Co.* v. *Supermarket Equipment Corp.*, 340 U.S. 147, 87 USPQ 303, (the "A & P" Case on the checkout counter). I am sure that it is the date because I remember reading the opinions aloud that day to the Drafting Committee. The *decision* may have been all right, but we considered what was said in the opinions to be typical of all that was wrong with the patent law's "invention" requirement. . . . It found no "unusual or surprising consequences" from the new checkout counter at bar; that each element of the combination did only what one would expect it to do (which is what the gears, jewels, and hands of your watch do, or the transistors, capacitors, inductances, resistors and wires of your radio do); and that though the invention was "a good idea" it just wasn't patentable. . . .

That reasoning is what clinched the decision to enact a statutory substitute that would make more sense, would apply to all kind of inventions, would restrict the courts in their arbitrary, *a priori* judgments on patentability, and that, above all, would serve as a uniform *standard of patentability*. And so we come to 35 USC § 103.

The Anatomy of Section 103

The first policy decision underlying Section 103 was to cut loose altogether from the century-old term "invention." It really *was* a term impossible to define, so we knew that any effort to define it would come to naught. Moreover, it was felt that so long as the term continued in use, the courts would annex to it the accretion of past interpretations, a feeling history has shown to be well founded.

So Section 103 speaks of a condition of *patentability* instead of "invention." The condition is *unobviousness*, but that is not all. The unobviousness is *as of a particular time* and *to a particular* legally fictitious, technical *person*, analogous to the "ordinary reasonable man" so well known to courts as a legal concept. To protect the inventor from hindsight reasoning, the time is specified to be *the time when the invention was made*. To prevent the use of too high a standard which would exclude inventors as a class and defeat the whole patent system the invention must have been obvious at that time to "a person having *ordinary* skill in the art to which said subject matter (i.e., *the* invention) pertains." But *what* must have been obvious is "*the subject matter as a whole.*" That, of course, is the invention as defined by each patent claim. If, for example, a *combination* is claimed, Section 103, requires that to invalidate the claim, it must be shown that the *combination* was obvious, not merely its components.

As compared to finding or not finding "invention," Section 103 was a whole new way of thinking and a clear *directive* to the courts to think that way. Some courts and some lawyers do not yet seem to realize that.

Section 103 in the Courts The "Codification" Question

Section 103 was sprung on a mentally unprepared world accustomed to thinking in terms of the requirement of "invention." After January 1, 1953, when the new patent act took effect, Courts by the dozen went merrily on in their old way invalidating patents for lack of "invention" and sustaining them because they found it. This I must blame in part on the lawyers who were also going merrily on in their old way, thinking and arguing on the basis of the old precedents. Some of them still do.

The first thing observable in the post-'53 cases was that many courts ignored Section 103 altogether, buying the argument that it was merely a "codification" of the old requirement, which they would therefore apply as they were accustomed to doing. They repeatedly held that no new test had been laid down. One of the troubles which hindsight now makes clear but which was far from obvious at the time is that even we who wrote Section 103 did not fully realize the magnitude of the change in thinking Section 103 required, at least we did not realize it sufficiently to do a good job of selling it.

But there was at the time another reason for not trying to sell it as a major change which those who were not working on the project probably do not realize. The revision of Title 35 *was* primarily a codification project by a House codification committee and to get it enacted promptly without a long debate it had to be kept noncontroversial. This had a profound effect on the way things were presented. It is not surprising therefore, to find the House and Senate reports accompanying the bill, which were written primarily by Mr. Federico and which are almost identical, presenting § 103 as placing in the statute a "condition" which, according to the reports, had "existed [in the law] for more than a hundred years" and as paraphrasing "language which has often been used in decisions of the courts" − which was literally true. There were thousands of opinions on patentability *some* of which, like *Hotchkiss*, had in them ideas very similar to those in Section 103. But *A & P* was not such an opinion. The reports also say that "the section is added to the statute for uniformity and definiteness." Such statements and others made it arguable that it was just a "codification." But what does that mean? What is a codification? Do you follow the statute or ignore it? If you ignore it, why have it?

Codification is a loose term. It has been defined as the collection, condensation, systematizing and *reconciling* of what is scattered or *contradictory.* Yes, Title 35 as a whole is a codification; but it is also specifically and officially described as a codification and *revision.* An example of strict codification of case law is Section 102(e) which put the rule of the *Milburn Case,* 270 U.S. 390 (1926), into the statute without change. An example of an outright change in prior law − revision −is Section 102(d) under which a foreign patent granted on an application filed more than a year before the U.S. application bars the U.S. patent only if it issues before the U.S. *application* is filed, whereas formerly it was a bar if issued before the U.S. *patent* issued. Section 271(a) is straight codification or restatement of existing case law which was entirely clear. But Section 271(b)-(d) is codification of another sort altogether. A controversy had been raging in the courts over contributory infringement and misuse and these paragraphs were designed to put an end to it and to overrule certain decisions. Section 103 was of a similar nature except that the situation was different. It was a new statement of an old requirement of the law which was utterly uncertain and indefinite. The statute undertook to remove ambiguity and provide definiteness. Calling that a "codification" proves nothing. . . .

Hopefully, that clears up the "codification" question. Whatever you call it, the purpose was to substitute Section 103 for the requirement of "invention" and for all prior case law, including the *A & P Case,* even though *some* cases contained the same principles. It was to be statutory, not case law in the future.

On the point of Section 103 being "codification" it is interesting to consider the last sentence of the section which says "Patentability shall not be negatived by the manner in which the invention was made." The specific intent of that sentence, which courts universally accepted without question, was to overrule the *Cuno* case dictum that a "flash of genius" was necessary. One cannot call that "codification."

. . . The very first judicial recognition of what was intended by Section 103 was Judge Learned Hand's opinion for the Second Circuit Court of Appeals in *Lyon v. Bausch & Lomb,* 244 F.2d 530, 106 USPQ 1, in 1955. He also understood the underlying reason for Section 103. He correctly stated in *Reiner v. I. Leon,* 285 F.2d 501, 128 USPQ 25 (1960), that it was "to change the slow but steady drift of judicial decision that had been hostile to patents . . ."

When I came to the CCPA in 1956, three and a half years after Section 103 came into effect, I found it being totally ignored. That is not too surprising. The court was dealing with office actions several years old rejecting claims for lack of "invention" and the appellants' briefs, like those of the Patent Office Solicitor's, were still couched in those terms. It was probably in my first conference that I suggested that for some time we had had a statute that had pat patentability on another basis which we should follow. . . .

Section 103 Reaches the Supreme Court

The Great Event, of course, was the Supreme Court's 1966 entry into the arena in "The Trilogy," generally identified by the title *Graham v. John Deere* and *Calmar v. Cook* and *United States v. Adams,* 383 U.S.

1, 39, 148 USPQ 459, 479. That was 13 years after the effective date of the 1952 Patent Act.

All things considered, Section 103 fared well in the *Trilogy* from the point of view of its authors. It was held to be a constitutional exercise of legislative power. It was accurately construed in those two now familiar sentences (383 U.S. at 17):

> "Under Section 103, the scope and content of the prior art are to be determined; differences between the prior art and the claims at issue are to be ascertained; and the level of ordinary skill in the pertinent art resolved. Against this background, the obviousness or nonobviousness of the subject matter is determined."

Except for the last step, determination of nonobviousness, which is a question of law and the ultimate determination of the court, these are factual inquiries, subject to proof by evidence. The first two, determination of the prior art and the differences from it which exist in the invention, are relatively easy to determine and prove with exactness. Level of ordinary skill is more difficult, more of a value judgment. Here is where judges have trouble and where they need help. Where do they get it? Well, maybe they will get some opinion testimony which isn't very persuasive; but the *best* evidence and the *most reliable* may be the *circumstantial* evidence.

"Secondary" or Circumstantial Considerations

If a man is observed coming away from the scene of a murder with a bloody knife or a smoking pistol, the evidence thereof may be more convincing than what he says. So it is if a competitor suddenly gives up his way of doing things, and switches to the invention or, as in the *Adams* case of the Trilogy, after pooh-poohing the invention and reporting that it won't work, the defendant adopts it and uses it successfully on a large scale. Well, what did the Supreme Court say about such evidence? It said (383 U.S. at 17–18):

> "Such secondary considerations as commercial success, long felt but unresolved needs, failure of others, etc., [please note the 'etc.'; these are but exemplars] might be utilized to give light to the circumstances surrounding the origin of the subject matter sought to be patented. As indicia of obviousness or nonobviousness, these inquiries may have relevancy."

Well of course they *do* have relevancy and the Supreme Court itself applied them in the *Adams Case*.

There is just one unfortunate word in that passage: "secondary." I don't think it should be given any weight though some courts seem to have done so, in effect, first deciding obviousness by visceral reaction and then saying that, having decided the issue, it is no longer necessary to consider the best evidence on the issue. This would be hard to explain except that in patent law there was an old rule which also made no sense that in determining "invention" one took commercial success into account only in *doubtful* cases, to tip the scales when they were otherwise evenly balance. I sense that courts or lawyers transported that old thinking into their dealing with Section 103. If commercial success and similar circumstantial evidence was considered only in doubtful cases in determining "invention," why not the same rule in determining nonobviousness?

I do not believe the Supreme Court intended to signify anything by the term "secondary." It could equally have said "other considerations." ... As a judge, if I were presented with a defense of obviousness and the evidence showed that the defendant, long knowing about a problem in his product or his manufacturing process for which he had found no solution, changed over to use his competitor's patented invention as soon as he heard of it, I would not call that evidence "secondary" and ignore it in considering his argument that it was an obvious invention. I would think as did Learned Hand (*Safety Car Heating and Lighting Co. v. General Electric Co.*, 155 F.2d 937, 939) in 1946 that:

> "In appraising an inventor's contribution to the art ... *the most reliable test* is to look at the situation before and after it appears ... Courts, made up of laymen as they must be, are likely either to underrate, or to overrate, the difficulties in making new and profitable discoveries in fields with which they cannot be familiar; and, so far as it is available, they had best appraise the originality involved by the *circumstances* which preceded, attended and succeeded the appearance of the invention.... We have repeatedly declared that in our judgment this approach is *more reliable* than a priori conclusions drawn from vaporous, and almost inevitably self-dependent general propositions." (My emphasis)

* * *

The most important question answered in *Graham* was whether Section 103 replaced "invention" as a test for patentability, so that it is legally dead. The answer is "Yes." ...

Notes and Questions

1. Giles S. Rich was born in 1904 and graduated from Harvard in 1926. He attended Columbia Law School, and practiced patent law in New York for 27 years. He then served on the Court of Customs and Patent Appeals, and later the Federal Circuit, for 45 years; he died, still in active service, in 1999 at the age of 95. In his many years on the patent bench, Judge Rich authored many influential opinions. He also taught as an adjunct professor at Columbia Law School and George Washington University Schools of Law. For a tribute, see Neil A. Smith, *Remembrances and Memorial: Judge Giles Sutherland Rich 1904–1999*, 14 Berkeley Tech. L.J. 9009 (1999), reprinted in 82 J. Pat. & Trademark Off. Soc'y 597 (2000).

2. Judge Rich notes that the characterization of the 1952 Act as a "codification" of established principles was required "to get it enacted promptly without a long debate," and to keep it "uncontroversial." This is no doubt a practical way to approach the Congressional role in lawmaking. It surely lends credence to the view that highly interested parties can be expected to spend resources to make sure that legislation furthers their economic interests. See Robert P. Merges, "Intellectual Property Rights and the New Institutional Economics," 53 *Vand. L. Rev.* 1857, 1868–1874 (2000) (describing application of the "political economy" literature to IP lawmaking). Is it surprising that individual members of Congress would take a close interest in the details of patent law? When these members sought reassurance from the drafters of the revision bill that became the 1952 Patent Act, was it accurate to say that the Act would be a codification when in fact several provisions were aimed explicitly at overturning recent Supreme Court opinions in the patent area? In what way might it be accurate to argue that Justice Douglas was one of the key influences on the 1952 Patent Act?

3. Compare Judge Rich's analysis of the relationship between the historical "invention" test and the statutory test of 35 USC § 103 with that in the following excerpt, written immediately in the wake of the Supreme Court's decision in *Graham v. John Deere*.

Graham v. John Deere Co.: New Standards for Patents*

EDMUND W. KITCH

In the 1964 Term, it was news of importance to the patent bar, though of little note elsewhere, that the Supreme Court had, for the first time in fifteen years, undertaken to review some patent cases turning on the issue of invention. The Court had granted certiorari to consider the effect of the standard of non-obviousness imposed by § 103 of the Patent Act of 1952 on theretofore judicially developed tests of invention.

The interest of the patent bar derived from a widespread concern that the Court might use § 103 as a basis for promulgating more rigorous standards of invention than had yet been utilized. Indeed, after the Court had granted certiorari in *Graham v. John Deere Co.*,[1] in order to resolve a conflict between the Fifth[2] and Eighth[3] Circuits, the Solicitor General had invited the Court "to consider pressing problems relating to the administration of the patent laws in a variety of contexts and in broad perspective." This language took on an ominous sound when the Court accepted the invitation and granted certiorari in *United States v. Adams*[4] and the twin cases of *Calmar, Inc. v. Cook Chemical Co.* and *Colgate-Palmolive Co. v. Cook Chemical Co.*[5]

The Court was inundated with a shower of amicus curiae briefs revealing an apprehension that the Court would utilize the new statutory language as a valve to cut down the flow of patents that pour forth from the Patent Office each year. The worry of the patent bar was perhaps expressed most frankly in an amicus brief filed by Professors Ernest Goldstein and Page Keeton of the University of Texas patroniz-

*Reprinted with permission from 1966 Sup. Ct. Rev. 293 (1966), © 1966, The University of Chicago Press.

1. 383 U.S. 1 (1996).

2. The Fifth Circuit had found the patent valid in Graham v. Cockshutt Farm Equip. Co., 256 F.2d 358 (5th Cir. 1958), and Jeoffrey Mfg. Inc.v. Graham, 219 F.2d 511 (5th Cir. 1955).

3. The Eighth Circuit had held the patent invalid. John Deere Co. v. Graham, 333 F.2d 529 (8th Cir. 1964).

4. 383 U.S. 39 (1966).

5. 383 U.S. 1 (1966).

ingly entitled "Brief Amicus Curiae in Support of 35 USC 103." Such a brief was necessary, wrote these self-appointed defenders of the statute, "because some writings by some Justices of this Court and the opinions by the Court of Appeals in this case, appear to put the practical operating life of the patent system at stake, and to put the whole socio-economic functioning of the entire patent system at issue."

The decisions that the Court has rendered may assuage this fear. They expressly purport to follow the earlier decisions and to turn toward neither leniency nor harshness. "We believe," wrote Mr. Justice Clark for the court, "that the revision [in 1952] was not intended by Congress to change the general level of patentable invention."[6] And, if actions speak louder than words, the Court held a patent valid for the first time in twenty-two years.[7] The opinions leave the impression that the decisions represent a mere ripple in the long stream of the law of invention and that the Court will now leave that complicated and hopelessly technical subject to the care of the courts of appeals for another fifteen years. But in fact the cases may, indeed, foreshadow an important doctrinal clarification of what has been a needlessly confused concept.

The petitioner in *Deere* eschewed the arguments offered by the amici curiae and asserted instead that "there can be no doubt that Congress has spoken and has defined for the first time a statutory requirement for patentable invention. The wording of the statute is clear and should be followed." In essence, he argued that the Court of Appeals for the Eighth Circuit had erroneously used a standard of invention that required proof of a new or different result in order to sustain the validity of the patent. The patent involved in *Deere* was on an improved clamp whose structure is difficult to describe but simple to understand from a diagram. The clamp was designed to provide a strong connection between the shank of a plow and the implement frame. The important feature of the clamp was that it permitted the shank to pivot upward when the plow point struck rocks, preventing damage. The patented clamp was an improvement on an earlier clamp that functioned in the same way and was also developed and patented by Graham. By having the shank pass under instead of over the pivot point and providing a rigid connection between the end of the shank and the clamp, Graham had designed a clamp that would perform better because of less wear and because it offered minutely greater freedom of movement along the whole length of the shank.

The Eighth Circuit had rejected this as a ground of patentability because "the inversion of the parts so as to allow the shank to flex downwardly away from the plate above it did not bring about a significantly new or different result." On this issue it differed from the Fifth Circuit, which had found the patent valid because of the rule "long recognized by this Court, that an improvement combination is patentable even though its constituent elements are singly revealed by the prior art, where, as here, it produces an old result in a cheaper and otherwise

6. 383 U.S. at 17.

7. United States v. Adams, 383 U.S. 39 (1966) (8–1). The Court last held a patent valid in Goodyear Tire & Rubber Co. v. Ray–O–Vac Co., 321 U.S. 275 (1944) (5–4).

more advantageous way.'"[8] A concern with the "result" as a test for invention has venerable origins in American patent law, but the petitioners in *Deere* argued with complete persuasiveness that "nowhere in [the] ... statute is there any requirement that to be patentable an invention must produce a new result." The Court agreed, concluding "that neither Circuit applied the correct test."[9]

By rejecting the "result test" of invention, the Court brought to an end a standard of patentability that has created confusion for far too many years. Even more important is the implication that in the future § 103 can be used to eliminate other historic tests of invention that have no rational relationship to the non-obviousness inquiry required by § 103. It is thus that the approach adopted by the Court in *Deere* may make it an important turning point in the history of American patent law. But to understand this possibility it is necessary first to understand the history.

The generally received history seems to be that the non-obviousness test of § 103 was articulated in the very first patentability case before the Supreme Court, *Hotchkins v. Greenwood*,[10] and has remained the test of invention ever since, with the possible exception of certain "hostile" Supreme Court decisions after 1930.[11] Thus, the Supreme Court concluded in *Deere* that § 103 "was intended to codify judicial precedents embracing the principle long ago announced by this Court in *Hotchkins*."[12] And at oral argument all counsel appeared to agree that the test of invention is the same today as it was a century ago.

The idea that the history of a test for invention has so stable a continuity, however, is simply misleading. The history of invention in American patent law only begins to make sense if it is first understood that there have been not one but three different tests which, during the twentieth century, have existed side by side in the decisions of one of those three tests and a rejection of the other two.

* * *

I. The Three Tests

The three distinct tests of patentability can be denominated, in the order of their historic development, the "novelty" test, the "genius" test, and the "non-obviousness" test. It is the thesis of this paper that only the last survives the decision in *Deere*.

8. 219 F.2d at 519.

9. 383 U.S. at 4.

10. 11 How. 248 (1851).

11. Discussion of this thesis generally centers on Great Atl. & Pac. Tea Co. v. Supermarket Equip. Corp., 340 U.S. 147 (1950), and Cuno Eng'r Corp. v. Automatic Devices Corp., 314 U.S. 84 (1941), as the most hostile. But under the non-obviousness test, the Supermarket case was clearly right on its face and Cuno arguably so. General Elec. Co. v. Jewel Incandescent Lamp Co., 326 U.S. 242 (1945), discussed below, appears to be the most hostile: wrong both on its facts and its law. But two Terms earlier the Court had held a doubtful patent valid. Goodyear Tire & Rubber Co. v. Ray–O Vac Co., 321 U.S. 275 (1944).

12. 383 U.S. at 3–4.

A. The Novelty Test

The novelty test focuses inquiry on a simple question: Is the device new? If the device is new, then is it patentable. This was the test of the Statute of Monopolies and of the American patent acts of 1793, 1836, and 1870.

In its simple, natural law form, the rationale can be stated as follows. In the specifications of his patent the inventor has given to society something that is, by definition, new, something that society did not have before. Because he has given this to society, it is only natural justice that society should give him the exclusive right to its commercial development.

If one prefers an economic justification to one based on "natural rights," an argument can also be made that the test of patentability should be "newness." In this view, the purpose of the patent system is not only to encourage invention but to encourage the production and marketing of new products. A new process or product that would be of marginal entrepreneurial interest when facing free entry might become an attractive investment proposition if the right to commercial development were exclusive.

* * *

In 1942, Judge Frank stated this rationale at some length:[13]

[T]here seems still to be room for some kind of patent monopoly which, through hope of rewards to be gained through such a monopoly, will induce venturesome investors to risk large sums needed to bring to the commercially useful stage those new ideas which require immense expenditures for that purpose ... [I]f we never needed, or do not now need, patents as bait for inventors, we may need them, in some instances, as a lure to investors.

B. The Genius Test

The genius test is an extension of the natural law argument for the novelty test. But it is based on a negative economic premise about patents. A patent monopoly is costly to the consumer and should not be granted without good reason. It is a reward that should be given only for worthy achievements, for the achievements of genius. The history of this test has been the unfolding of an effort to define this achievement, the true inventive act, as a certain kind of mental process.[14] One inevitable result of this approach has been the economically absurd conclusion that organized, plodding, group research does not produce patentable discoveries because a group does not have genius.[15] Section 103 of the 1952 Act provides that "patentability shall not be negatived by the manner in

---

13. Picard v. United Aircraft Corp., 128 F.2d 632, 642 (2d Cir. 1942) (concurring).

14. This effort received its fullest exposition in Robinson, *The Law of Patents for Useful Inventions* (1890).

15. Potts v. Coe, 145 F.2d 27, 28 (D.C. Cir. 1944) (Arnold, J.): "A discovery which is the result of step-by-step experimentation does not rise to the level of invention." *Cf.* Picard v. United Aircraft Corp., 128 F.2d 632, 636 (2d Cir. 1942) (Hand J.). Arnold went on to observe that "the research laboratory has gradually raised the level of industrial art until discoveries by ordinary skilled men, which would have seemed miraculous in the last century, are definitely predictable if money is available for organized research." 145 F.2d at 30. But why will the money be expended if it cannot be recovered by means of a patent monopoly?

which the invention was made, thereby eliminating the test of 'genius' from the patent law."

C. The Non–Obviousness Test

The non-obviousness test shares the economic premises of both the novelty and genius tests. With the novelty test it shares the premise that innovation should be encouraged. With the genius test it shares the premise that patent monopolies represent a substantial cost to the consumer. These two premises are accommodated by the basic principle on which the non-obviousness test is based: a patent should not be granted for an innovation unless the innovation would have been unlikely to have been developed absent the prospect of a patent. Unlike the novelty test, it does not view the inducement of investment in production and marketing facilities, after the innovation has been developed, as an appropriate function of the patent system. These are costs that must be borne by everyone who wishes to market the innovation and if, in the face of competition, investors do not find the innovation an attractive prospect, that is because there are better uses for their capital elsewhere, not because the competitive situation should be altered. The non-obviousness test makes an effort, necessarily an awkward one, to sort out those innovations that would not be developed absent a patent system. Through the years the test has been variously phrased, but the focus has always been on the question whether the innovation could have been achieved by one of ordinary skill in the art, or whether its achievement is of a greater degree of difficulty.

If an innovator must bear costs that need not be borne equally by his competitors (because they will have the advantage of his work) and that he cannot recoup, he will not make the expenditures to innovate. But in a competitive system some non-recurring costs can be recouped because the innovator has the advantage of the lead time inherent in his position. Even in the case of products that can be easily imitated the innovator has the advantage of the good will and additional experience inherent in the position of being first in the field. The argument that the innovator can reasonably expect to recoup his costs simply by being first has been seriously offered as an argument against any patent system at all.[16] The difficulty is that as a matter of empirical fact it is not known to what extent the position of innovator gives one an advantage in a competitive situation, nor is it possible to determine the magnitude of a particular innovator's costs to determine whether he can recoup them without an exclusive grant. But what the economic argument does underline is that much innovation will occur in a competitive system with no patent rights. Only the costlier kinds of innovation will be retarded by the absence of patents. That these innovations will probably be the socially and economically more important only underlines the importance of the patent system. But the central point is that not every innovation needs the patent system to induce its appearance. In fact in many cases, the desire to obtain a superior competitive position by being known as "advanced" and first on the market will induce the appear-

---

16. Plant, *The Economic Theory concerning Patents for Inventions*, Economica No. 1, 30, 43–44 (1934).

ance of the new product or process. An innovation obvious to one of ordinary skill in the art may indeed be new, in the sense that it did not exist before, and the costs may indeed be substantial is it takes a long time to perfect. But it is the implied judgment of the test that the cost of innovation of this order of difficulty can probably be recouped in a competitive situation while the costs of innovation of a greater difficulty cannot.

II. The History

These three tests, then, are the components of the history of the idea of invention in the patent law. But for the first eighty-five years there was one basic test, the test of novelty. The Act of 1793 provided that a patent should issue for the invention of any "machine, manufacture, or composition of matter" which was "new and useful." (The earlier Act of 1790 had provided that a patent should issue if the invention was "sufficiently useful and important." It has no significance in the history of the requirement of patentability.) The text of the Act of 1793 makes it clear that new as used in the Act means new and no more. But the drafters felt constrained to add that "simply changing the form or the proportions of any machine, or composition of matter, in any degree, shall not be deemed a discovery."

For the next eighty-two years American patent law followed the process of working out rules designed to prevent trivial advances from falling within the concept of patentable novelty. The problem was to distinguish between changes that were merely changes of form and changes that were changes of substance. "The sufficiency of the invention," Phillips wrote in 1837, "depends not upon the labor, skill, study, or expense applied or bestowed upon it, but upon its being diverse and distinguishable from what is familiar and well known, and also substantially and materially, not slightly and trivially so. This requisite of an invention is sometimes expressed to be a difference in principle." These distinctions have the ring of metaphysical debate and indeed the efforts of the courts to distinguish between the new and the really new were to lead them to distinctions that sound metaphysical and were meaningless. To quote Justice Story, "The doctrine of patents may truly be said to constitute the metaphysics of law."

The pressures that led to this line of developments are not difficult to identify. On the one hand, the courts were bound by the conceptual framework of a statute whose only requirement was that the invention be "new." On the other hand, they were confronted by a quickening pace of technological advance, particularly after the Civil War, that threatened to bring every commodity within a private patent grant.

* * *

The central influence on the development of the law of inventive novelty was nascent American legal scholarship. By the year 1850, American patent law had been the subject of three different treatises: Fessenden, Phillips, and Curtis. No other area received so much special attention, and the tradition of ponderous treatises on patent law extended into the first decade of this century before finally expiring. Reasons readily suggest themselves. First patent law, designed to induce technological innovation, had great appeal to scholars of a young country that prided itself on modernity and progress. Second, systematic English concern with the problem was relatively recent, and thus the Americans were less likely to be overawed in this area. Third, American patent law was a creature of statute and English cases could be dismissed as irrelevant. Fessenden, Phillips, and Curtis—together with the omniscient and omnipresent Story on circuit—laid the foundations.

* * *

IV. Commercial Success: The Cook Cases

The elimination of the inventive novelty tests cannot be effected by a simple declaration. Tests based on inventive novelty so permeate the patent cases that it is necessary to analyze each test in terms of its relation to non-obviousness. That much work remains to be done was revealed in the *Cook Chemical Co.*[17] cases, which turned on the role to be assigned to commercial success and long-felt need in a determination of non-obviousness. The patent was for a hold-down cap on the pump-type sprayers so familiar to every American housewife. Before the development of the patented cap, it had been necessary to distribute the fluids in bottles with regular caps and the sprayers separately attached to the package. After purchase, the customer had to remove the cap and put the sprayer on the bottle. The sprayer, thus exposed, was subject to loss and breakage. The patented cap holds the pump in retracted position and provides a seal effective against even low viscosity insecticides, making it possible to ship the fluids with the sprayer on the bottle forming a compact, break-resistant unit. The cap is, as the description should indicate, a simple device. The district court found it patentable on the basis of evidence that for at least five years the industry had been aware of the need for a sprayer that could be shipped on the bottle and that once the patented device was developed, it was a commercial success. Citing the *Barbed Wire Patent* case, the court concluded that "the last step is the one that wins and he who takes it when others could not, is entitled to patent protection."[18] The Court of Appeals affirmed, observing that "instantaneous industry, as well as public acceptance of the device in issue, confirms our belief invention was produced."

The Supreme Court held the patent invalid, answering that in this case factors such as commercial success and long-felt need did not "tip the scales of patentability." The Court added, however, that "such inquiries may lend a helping hand to the judiciary which, as Mr. Justice Frankfurter observed, is most ill-fitted to discharge the technological duties cast upon it by patent legislation. . . . They may also serve to 'guard against slipping into hindsight,' . . . and to resist the temptation to read into the prior art the teachings of the invention in issue."[19] . . .

17. Decided together with Graham v. John Deere Co., 383 U.S. 1 (1966).

18. 220 F. Supp. 414, 421 (W.D. Mo. 1963).

19. *Ibid.*, citing Marconi Wireless Co. v. United States, 320 U.S. 1, 60 (1943), and Monroe Auto Equip. Co. v. Heckethorn Mfg. & Supply Co., 332 F.2d 406, 412 (6th Cir. 1964).

But how is commercial success relevant to non-obviousness? The argument for commercial success is set out in a law review comment cited with apparent approval by the Court in *Cook*.[20]

The possibility of market success attendant upon the solution of an existing problem may induce innovators to attempt a solution. If in fact a product attains a high degree of commercial success, there is a basis for inferring that such attempts have been made and have failed. Thus the rationale is similar to that of long felt demand and is for the same reasons a legitimate test of invention.

This argument involves four inferences. First, that the commercial success is due to the innovation. Second, that if an improvement has in fact become commercially successful, it is likely that this potential commercial success was perceived before its development. Third, the potential commercial success having been perceived, it is likely that efforts were made to develop the improvement. Fourth, the efforts having been made by men of skill in the art, they failed because the patentee was the first to reduce his development to practice. Since men of skill in the art tried, but failed, the improvement is clearly non-obvious.

Each inference is weak. The commercial success might not be due to the innovation but rather, as the petitioners in *Cook* argued, "to sales promotion ability, manufacturing technique, ready access to markets, consumer appeal, design factors, and advertising budget." But given the commercial success of the innovation, why is it likely that the commercial potential was perceived in advance? And why is it likely that because the commercial potential was perceived, men of skill began work on the problems of that innovation as opposed to other potential improvements? And if men of skill start to work on the improvement, why does the fact that the patentee was first to perfect the improvement mean the others failed? Perhaps they were only a little slower. This seems a fragile thread on which to hang a conclusion of non-obviousness, particularly in a case where the patentee shows only commercial success but does not show that the commercial potential was perceived or that attempts actually were made that failed. How, then, does commercial success constitute a helping hand? The Court said that "these legal inferences or subtests do focus attention on economic and motivational rather than technical issues and are, therefore, more susceptible of judicial treatment than are the highly technical facts often present in patent litigation." Perhaps commercial success is a familiar distraction for judges confused by the facts.

It is not difficult to see why lawyers for patent owners are eager to introduce evidence of commercial success. By introducing evidence of commercial success the lawyer is telling the judge that his client's patent is very valuable and that if the judge holds the patent invalid he is destroying expectations of great value. This is not an argument without persuasiveness. The Supreme Court itself was once led to recognize an exclusive right simply because the plaintiff's right was valuable and he

20. Subtests of "Nonobviousness": A Nontechnical Approach to Patent Validity, 112 U.Pa.L.Rev. 1169, 1175 (1964).

had created it.[21] When Walker suggested to the courts that they should resolve borderline cases on the basis of commercial success, he was really saying "Decide all of the borderline cases where the patent is worth something in favor of the patentee, decide all the other borderline cases against the patentee." Since it is unlikely that patents that are not commercially successful will be brought to litigation, this amounts to a suggestion that borderline cases be decided in favor of patentees. In fact, if one is willing to infer from the litigation itself that the patent is valuable because it is worth litigating, and that since it is valuable it must be commercially successful, one ends up with the rule that all patents that are litigated should be held valid.[22]

If commercial success is a relevant "economic issue," then one can argue that it should be a factor weighing against patentability in borderline cases. Commercially successful patents are the ones that truly impose a monopoly tax on the market, and therefore courts should be even more cautious in holding them valid. Furthermore, it is in the area of innovations that quickly meet consumer acceptance that the innovator has the best chance of recovering his special costs without a patent monopoly. The chances of doing this in any particular case depend, of course, on the good-will advantages of being first and the speed with which potential competitors can enter. But the more quickly a substantial market can be developed and its profit returns enjoyed, the greater (as a general rule) would seem to be the advantages accruing to the innovator who enters the market first. He will not need extensive market development that will alert potential competitors before the profits begin. Thus, in the area of the commercially successful improvement quickly recognized by the market, a patent is less likely to be necessary to evoke the improvement. The argument assumes, of course, that the commercial potential is perceived in advance by the innovator so that it can affect his decision to develop the innovation. This is not necessarily so, but the same assumption is made by the traditional argument for commercial success as a factor favoring a finding of invention. At the very least, these two arguments should cancel each other and leave commercial success with no role to play in a non-obviousness inquiry.

* * *

VI. The Court's Responsibility

Deere, *Adams*, and *Cook* are hopeful signs that the courts will begin to work out the implications of the non-obviousness test that have been ignored. If the courts begin to face and solve these analytic issues, the administration of § 103 should be made easier. But the Supreme Court

21. See International News Service v. Associated Press, 248 U.S. 215 (1918). Use of commercial success as a basis for validity in patent cases reached its peak in Temco Elec. Motor Co. v. Apco Mfg. Co., 275 U.S. 319, 328 (1928), where the Court reversed a holding of invalidity because the patent's "usefulness was demonstrated by ten years' use in such large numbers and by such profitable business."

22. *Cf.* Diamond Rubber Co. v. Consolidated Rubber Tire Co., 220 U.S. 428, 441 (1911): "... the utility of a device may be attested by the litigation over it, as litigation 'shows and measures the existence of the public demand for its use.'" See also Eames v. Andrews, 122 U.S. 40, 47 (1887).

did not think the problem of § 103 was one for the courts at all. "[I]t must be remembered," said the Court, "that the primary responsibility for sifting out unpatentable material lies in the Patent Office. To wait litigation is—for all practical purposes—to debilitate the patent system. We have observed a notorious difference between the standards applied by the Patent Office and by the courts."[23] Although gentler in language, this criticism of the Patent Office is in the tradition of the attack on the office made by Mr. Justice Douglas in his concurring opinion in the *Supermarket Equipment Corp.* case.[24] This attack accuses the Patent Office of ruining the patent system because of its failure to apply the invention requirement with sufficient rigor. The problem with this statement is not that it is untrue but that it is unwise. The Court should be more sensitive to the roots of its power even in so small a matter. Can the Court seriously expect men who have dedicated themselves to the operation of the Patent Office and the patent system to respond warmly to the charge that they have debilitated the patent system? Yet the co-operation of these men is essential if there is going to be any change in Patent Office practice.

The usual complaint is that the Patent Office issues many patents that are invalid under § 103. This appears to be true, but how does it debilitate the system? The explanation offered is that each of the invalid patents issued is a "license to litigate" which can be used as a "threat" to "coerce" weaker competitors into submission.... But if the patents are invalid, how are they such an effective threat? The answer is that the defense of an infringement suit, even if the patent is held invalid, is expensive and that the patentee can always offer a settlement cheaper than the litigation costs. A leading patent lawyer has estimated the costs for each side in a patent infringement suit at a minimum of $50,000. Invalid patents, in the hands of unscrupulous and powerful men, are worth money. This debilitates the patent system because it makes patents the vehicles for suppression of competition rather than the reward for invention.

But why is it so expensive to defend a patent suit? The answer is twofold. First, there are endless procedural devices in the hands of a patent holder willing to use them. And, second, the factual issues in patent cases are made unnecessarily complex by the doctrinal difficulties of the invention requirement. These are not the fault of the Patent Office. If fault is the appropriate word, surely Congress and the Supreme Court might share the blame.

A determined patent holder is in a position to keep relitigating the validity of his patent against the infringing manufacturer and his cus-tomers. These suits can be brought in every part of the country. Motions under § 1404(a) for transfer and consolidation can be made, ruled on, and taken to the courts of appeals. The factual issues are "complicated" and summary judgment is seldom available. Discovery procedures can be used to increase the costs that a patent-infringement action inflicts on

23.   383 U.S. at 18.
24.   340 U.S. at 154.

the defendant. The Supreme Court must bear some responsibility for failing to keep these abuses in check.

For fifteen years the Supreme Court failed to take cases raising the issue of non-obviousness. Differences have arisen among the circuits, encouraging litigants to engage in complex maneuvering to get in the "right" court. It is traditionally said that the facts in patent cases are extremely complicated. This is not true. The facts in patent cases, as in any other class of cases, are sometimes complicated and sometimes simple. *Deere, Adams,* and *Cook* are examples of cases in which the facts themselves are simple and easily understood. But even simple facts become complicated if there are no controlling legal principles around which they can be organized. In a case as simple as *Deere* two circuits differed on the validity of the patent, not because they differed on the facts, but because they differed regarding the law. These failures of the Court are perhaps minor when one considers the heavy responsibilities that it has in other more important areas. But it ill becomes the Court, whose own performance in the area has suffered form lack of interest, to castigate the Patent Office for "debilitating" the patent system.

The Patent Office has remained insensitive to the requirement that invention must be shown for patentability because it applies the "inventive novelty" law that was in force prior to 1875. The basic question for a Patent Office examination is whether the device is new. The primary effort of the examiner is to have the claims narrowed so that they only read on what is new in the development. There seem to be two important reasons for this apparent disregard of the invention requirement. The first lies in the history of the Patent Office and the law. The Patent Office as presently organized has been an on-going institution since 1836. During the first thirty-nine years of its life, it quite appropriately applied the controlling law of inventive novelty. Since that time its internal traditions have perpetuated the approach. This tendency has been condoned by the Supreme Court, which never, until *Deere,* suggested that the inventive novelty approach was inconsistent with non-obviousness. The second reason is the organization of the Patent Office itself. Because of the heavy backlog of applications there is pressure on examiners to dispose of them. If an examiner approves the application, the matter is closed. If he denies it, the applicant has a right of appeal up through the Patent Office to the Court of Customs and Patent Appeals and now to the Supreme Court. Such an appeal places additional burdens on the office. At the very least, it is considered undesirable for an examiner to be reversed once an appeal is taken. In this situation even a conscientious examiner is unlikely to reject an application unless he is sure of his ground. A rejection for lack of novelty is relatively stable ground. If something is not new, it is hard for the applicant to argue that it is. But a rejection on grounds of non-obviousness is shakier because it may involve differences in judgment between the examiner and the review board.

It is even possible to argue that it is not the duty of the Patent Office to screen out non-obvious patents. Why should not the Patent Office concentrate on weeding out those applications that do not involve new developments? When a patent is granted on an innovation, it

assures that information about it is placed in the public record. At the
Patent Office stage in the proceedings it is difficult to predict whether
the patent will ever be important or the subject of controversy. The *ex
parte* proceeding of the Patent Office is not the best forum in which fully
to ventilate the validity issue. If the validity issue is determined nega-
tively, the information about the innovation is never placed on the public
record. Why should the resources necessary to make the non-obviousness
determination be expended unless the validity of the patent actually
matters? Once it matters, the courts can provide a forum in which the
validity issue can be litigated. Although this is not the system contemplated by the statute, it has long been the *de facto* system in American
patent law. And it would work, if the courts provided a reasonably
efficient and conclusive forum for the adjudication of validity. The
present statutory framework makes this difficult for the courts, but they
have not done their best to maximize their effectiveness even within this
framework.

　　Deere points in the direction of removing complicating doctrinal
irrelevancies and returning patent law to the relative simplicity of the
statute. It is a significant step toward the improvement of the patent
system if the courts are willing to insist that the inquiry be focused on
the statutory test of non-obviousness. It is perfectly possible for the
tradition-minded reader to interpret the opinions in *Deere, Adams*, and
Cook as simply continuing past doctrine. The myth of *Hotchkins v.
Greenwood* seems to be part of an even larger myth in patent law—the
myth that invention decisions differ only on the "facts" or the "attitude" of the court, but that they all embody the same law. The courts
ought not permit this myth to overtake *Deere*.

Notes and Questions

1.   Edmund Kitch graduated from Yale in 1961, and from the University of Chicago Law School in 1964. He taught at Indiana University and
the University of Chicago before moving to the University of Virginia
Law School, where he has taught since 1982.

2.   Kitch states at one point that the Supreme Court had not decided a
case in the "invention" or nonobviosness area in fifteen years. It has
now been almost forty; the *Deere* Trilogy is still the last word. For an
argument that the field will have to learn to live with minimal Supreme
Couort guidance, see Mark D. Janis, "Patent Law in the Age of the
Invisible Supreme Court," 2001 *U. Ill. L. Rev.* 387 (2001). For an
alternative view, noting the increasing frequency with which the Court
has addressed patent issues in recent years, see John F. Duffy, "The
Festo Decision and the Return of the Supreme Court to the Bar of
Patents," 2002 *Sup. Ct. Rev.* 273 (2002).

3.   Kitch pays special attention to the famous concurring opinion by
Judge Frank in the *Picard* case, which emphasizes the importance of
patents as an incentive to *develop inventions*, as opposed to inventing
them in the first place. For amplification of this view of patents, see
Robert P. Merges, "Uncertainty and the Standard of Patentability," 7
[Berkeley] High Tech. L.J. 1, 3 (1992) ("[As modeled,] [t]he patent

system is shown to have a stronger effect on the incentive to develop inventions as opposed to the incentive to invent."); F. Scott Kieff, "Property Rights and Property Rules for Commercializing Inventions," 85 *Minn. L. Rev.* 697 (2001).

4. Kitch states the ideal conceptual basis of the nonobviousness standard: it should separate out those inventions which would likely not be developed in the absence of a patent. This idea was first promulgated in 1949 by the sociologist S.C. Gilfillan in his book *The Sociology of Invention* (1935; reprinted Cambridge, MA: MIT Pres, 1963). In support of this notion, Kitch points to the fact that firms can often recoup R & D costs in ways other than through patents. Solid empirical support now backs up this claim; see the excerpt from Richard Levin, Richard Nelson, et al., later in this chapter. Kitch also indicates that "goodwill" accrues to an innovator, and permits some R & D costs to be recouped through reputational advantages. Cf., Gideon Parchomovsky and Peter Siegelman, "Towards an Integrated Theory of Intellectual Property," 88 *U. Va. L. Rev.* 1455 (2002) (describing how trademark and patent law can interact to enhance innovator profitability under some circumstances).

In this excerpt, Kitch grapples with the fundamental difference between how patent lawyers and economists view nonobviousness. Patent lawyers—exemplified by Judge Rich in his article "Laying the Ghost of the Invention Requirement" (excerpted earlier)—see this as a question of ascertaining some elusive technological quantum: to what degree is claim X technologically distinct from the sum of the prior art Y? Economists—including law and economics scholars such as Kitch—see it as a function of costs and benefits: how costly was research project X? How much benefit, Y, does it confer now that it is complete and shown to work? Legal doctrine tends to track the views of the patent lawyers, while serious theorizing about the issue tends to see it through the lens of economics. Some attempt has been made to bridge the gap, however. See, e.g., Robert P. Merges, "Uncertainty and the Standard of Patentability," 7 *[Berkeley] High Tech. L.J.* 1, 34 (1992) ("[Nonobviousness doctrine] presumes that there is a high social cost to granting patents that cover inventions that could have been made by any researcher with ordinary skill. The wisdom of this approach lies in its use of technical difficulty as a measure of social value.... [T]he easier an invention is to make, the greater the social cost involved in granting a patent to cover it.").

5. Kitch mentions the tradition of excellent patent treatises in the U.S. dating from early in the nineteenth century. One of the treatises Kitch speaks of was written by George Ticknor Curtis, who besides being a prominent Boston patent lawyer in the nineteenth century and brother of Supreme Court Justice Benjamin R. Curtis, was one of the lawyers who represented an escaped slave in the *Dred Scott* case. In one characteristic section of the second edition of his treatise on Patent Law, Curtis wrote of patents as representing a bargain or "contract" between society and an inventor. Note how a well-functioning nonobviousness requirement serves to insure the "adequacy of consideration" on the part of the inventor, in effect guaranteeing that what the inventor contributes is valuable enough to warrant the grant of a monopoly/property right:

[A] patent-right, under the modern law of England and America, differs essentially from one of the old English Monopolies. In those grants of the crown, the subject-matter of the exclusive privilege was quite as often a commodity of which the public were and long had been in possession, as it was any thing invented, discovered, or even imported by the patentee.

Nothing passed, in such cases, from the patentee to the public, in the nature of a consideration for the enormous privilege conferred upon him; but the public were robbed of something already belonging to them, namely, the right to make or deal in a particular commodity, for the benefit of the favored grantee of the crown. So broad is the distinction between these cases and that of the meritorious inventor or importer of something new and useful, that when Parliament, in the 21 James I, taking encouragement from the courts of law, prohibited the granting of exclusive privileges in trade, by the Statute of Monopolies, they introduced an exception in favor of "a letters-patent and grants of privilege for the term of one and twenty years or under, heretofore made, of the sole working or making of any manner of new manufacture, within this realm, to the first and true inventor or inventors of such manufactures, which others at the time of the making of such letters-patent and grants, did not use, so they be not contrary to law, nor mischievous to the state, by raising the prices of commodities at home, or hurt to trade, or generally inconvenient," & c.

Upon this exception, the law of England, concerning Patents for Useful Inventions, stands to this day.

The modern doctrine, in England, and undoubtedly the doctrine of our law, is, that in the grant of a patent right, a contract, or, as it has been said, a bargain, takes place between the public and the patentee. As far as the old cases on the subject of monopolies furnish, like other cases of grants by the crown, rules and analogies for the construction of this species of grant, so far the history of monopolies has a bearing upon this branch of jurisprudence. But it should always be remembered that in the grant of a patent privilege, as now understood, a contract takes place between the public and patentee, to be supported upon the ground of mutual considerations, and to be construed, in all its essential features of a bargain, like other contracts to which there are two parties, each having rights and interests involved in its stipulation.

George T. Curtis, Patent Law (3d ed. 1867), at 1–2. For a recent version of this idea, see Vincenzo Denicolò and Luigi Alberto Franzoni, "The Contract Theory of Patents," 23 *Int'l Rev. L. & Econ.* 365 (2003).

6. Kitch argues that commercial success is suspect evidence of nonobviousness, because it requires a long inferential trail to connect product sales volume with the technical superiority of a patented feature of the product. One point he makes is that multiple inventors might arrive at the same superior technical solution, but for non-patent-related reasons, a single product might record significant sales. Evidence of nearly simultaneous invention was sometimes cited in older cases following this scenario to support the view that the commercial success of a product did not prove the nonobviousness of a particular inventor's technical solution. See Robert P. Merges, "Commercial Success and Patent Standards: Economic Perspectives on Innovation," 76 *Cal. L. Rev.* 803, 816 n.41 (1988). For a Federal Circuit case rejecting this view, see Environmental Designs, Ltd. v. Union Oil Co., 713 F.2d 693, 698 n.7 (Fed. Cir. 1983), cert. denied, 464 U.S. 1043 (1984) (virtually simultaneous making of same invention does not preclude patentability).

7. Kitch's argument that, if anything, patents on commercially successful inventions ought to be invalidated *more often* finds an echo in a proposal to lessen the anticompetitive impact of patents by enforcing them less vigorously. See Ian Ayres and Paul Klemperer, "Limiting Patentees' Market Power Without Reducing Innovation Incentives: The Perverse Benefits of Uncertainty and Non–Injunctive Remedies," 97 *Mich. L. Rev.* 985 (1999).

8. Kitch's observations about the high cost of patent litigation, and the concomitant importance of weeding out undeserving patents prior to litigation, are closely related to newer proposals for improving "patent quality"; see the excerpts by Arti Rai, Mark Janis, and John Duffy in section III.D. of this Chapter, infra. At the same time, Kitch recognizes that the Patent Office and courts will necessarily apply different standards when determining nonobviousness, and states that the Patent Office might best stick to determining utility and novelty. For an article that pushes this idea even further, and champions a return to the 1793–1836 era in patent law by advocating a simple registration system, see F. Scott Kieff, "The Case for Registering Patents and the Law and Economics of Present Patent–Obtaining Rules," 45 *B.C. L. Rev.* 55 (2003).

C. Infringement

The Doctrine of Equivalents in Patent Law: Questions that *Pennwalt* Did Not Answer*

MARTIN J. ADELMAN
GARY L. FRANCIONE

* * *

The doctrine of equivalents is the primary (although not the exclusive) cause of the current uncertainty surrounding the scope of patent claims. This uncertainty has serious consequences. First, uncertainty about the scope of patent protection hinders both patent holders and potential defendants from assessing the possible outcome of litigation or from making other business decisions, such as the direction that research and development efforts should take. Second, a primary purpose of the protection of intellectual property is to encourage the production of

* Reprinted by permission from the University of Pennsylvania Law Review (January, 1989), © 1989, The University of Pennsylvania Law Review.

inventions, literary works, and the like. Patent law in particular provides a claiming system to put other potential inventors on notice of the precise boundaries of the invention so that they may 'design around' the patent.... The uncertainty generated by the doctrine of equivalents frustrates and chills the activities of these other inventors, who must be concerned about whether their efforts will be met by an infringement suit based on the amorphous doctrine of equivalents. Third, the doctrine permits abusive infringement actions claiming that the defendant infringes under the doctrine of equivalents and that a jury must decide the correctness of the claim. The imperative to settle under these circumstances is almost overpowering. Fourth, due process concerns are potentially raised to the extent that pervasive and systemic uncertainty generated by the doctrine of equivalents destroys the ability of patent claims to provide fair notice, so that they effectively provide no notice.

II.   Pennwalt: The Federal Circuit Adopts the Element-by-Element Approach

A.   *The Pennwalt Decision*

Pennwalt Corp. v. Durand–Wayland, Inc.[1] involved a patent on an apparatus that rapidly sorted items, such as fruit, by color, weight, or a combination of color and weight. The four claims-at-issue (1, 2, 10, and 18) in the Pennwalt patent were expressed in 'means-plus-function' language.[2]

Claims 1 and 2 described a sorter that transports items along a track with an electronic device that generates a signal proportional to the weight of the item. The device included the following means: reference signal means; signal comparison means (to compare the weight signals to the reference signals); clock means (to signal a change in the position of an item); position indicating means (to respond to the comparison signal means and the clock signal means for 'continuously indicating the position of an item to be sorted'); and discharge means (to respond to the position-indicating signal in order to discharge an item to be sorted at a predetermined position). Claims 10 and 18 described a multifunctional apparatus in which the item is transported along the weighing device and is also scanned optically in order to produce a signal proportional to the color of the item; the weighing device and color sensor are then combined and a signal is sent to discharge the item into the appropriate receptacle.

Pennwalt alleged that two sorters manufactured by Durand–Wayland infringed the Pennwalt patent. The specification of the Pennwalt sorter describes a " 'hard wired' network consisting of discrete electrical components which perform each step of the claims." The two Durand–Wayland sorters used computer software programs: The first sorter, the 'Microsizer,' had a central processing unit that used one of two possible

  1.   833 *F.2d* 931 (Fed. Cir. 1987) (in banc), cert. denied, 108 *S. Ct.* 1226 (1988).

  2.   See Pennwalt Corp. v. Durand–Wayland, Inc., 225 *U.S.P.Q.* (BNA) 558, 564–65 (N.D. Ga. 1984). A patent applicant is permitted to express an element in a claim for a combination as 'a means or step for performing a specified function.' 35 U.S.C. § 112, para. 6 (1982). For example, the legs of a chair could be described in 'means-plus-function' language as a means for keeping the seat of a chair a particular distance from the floor.

software programs to sort by weight alone; the second sorter used a third software program to sort by weight and color by employing both the 'Microsizer' and a color detection machine called a 'Microsorter.'

The district court, sitting without a jury, found the Pennwalt patent valid, but did not find that the accused devices infringed the patent.
* * *

[On appeal,] [t]he Federal Circuit ... [considered infringement under] the doctrine of equivalents. The majority appeared to base its decision on two separate grounds, which were blended in the opinion. First, the court held that analysis of infringement under the doctrine of equivalents required an element-by-element comparison in order to determine whether there was an equivalent for each element. This approach did not mean that the entire function/way/result test needed to be applied to each element; instead, the equivalent infringement could be found 'if an accused device performs substantially the same overall function or work, in substantially the same way, to obtain substantially the same overall result as the claimed invention.'[3]

In Pennwalt, as in most equivalents cases, there was no dispute that the accused device performed substantially the same overall function or work and achieved substantially the same overall result. In most cases, the issue is almost invariably whether the accused device performs the overall function in substantially the same way as the claimed invention. Under the element-by-element approach, each element of the claim is examined to determine whether it or its equivalent exists in the accused device. If there is no correspondence, the accused device will not be deemed to operate in substantially the same way as the claimed invention. There can be no infringement under the doctrine of equivalents under two conditions: if an element is missing completely from the accused device and there is no equivalent of the missing element or if an element has been changed in the accused device and the changed element does not operate in substantially the same way. If, as was the case in Pennwalt, a claim has functional elements and the accused device does not perform a particular function, then one must be able to point to something in the accused device that serves as an equivalent of that functional limitation.

The Federal Circuit held that the trial court had applied the proper standard concerning the doctrine of equivalents and that its finding of no infringement was not clearly erroneous. The court rejected Pennwalt's argument that the accused devices merely substituted computer technology for the hard-wired circuitry. Rather, the district court had found that the microprocessor in the accused devices was not programmed to perform certain functions. The Federal Circuit focused specifically on the district court's finding that the accused devices did not have any position-indicating means.

The majority agreed that the accused devices lacked the equivalent of the tracking function because the microprocessor in those devices could be, but was not, programmed to track position. In addition, the

3. Pennwalt, 833 *F.2d* at 934.

claimed device required that the position-indicating means be responsive to the signal from the comparison means, but the accused devices made no comparison of signals before the point at which the item to be sorted was discharged. The court found that the district court 'correctly rejected' Pennwalt's argument that the memory components of the accused devices, which involved the storage of data in queues and the use of pointers that moved synchronously with the movement of the conveyor cups, performed a function equivalent to that of the position-indicating means. The majority concluded that, because the accused devices did not involve later-developed technology that 'should be deemed within the scope of the claims to avoid pirating of an invention,' the doctrine of equivalents was not appropriate.[4]

In Pennwalt, the Federal Circuit tried to settle an important issue concerning the doctrine of equivalents. But the court's choice was, in many respects, not important. Whether the doctrine of equivalents is applied on an element-by-element basis or an entirety basis does not answer the key question: What is an 'equivalent'?

Language in Federal Circuit decisions suggests that the doctrine of equivalents cannot be used to encompass more than an "insubstantial change" or "minor modification"; ordinarily, however, the cases recite the standard function-way-result test, which gives no indication of what constitutes such a change. Until this question is answered, great uncertainty will surround the doctrine of equivalents, and the court's adoption of the element-by-element approach will do little to ameliorate the situation. This uncertainty will be exacerbated in light of the Pennwalt majority's willingness to allow the applicability of the doctrine of equivalents to be a factual issue in every case. A patent holder does not have to allege that there has been a "fraud on the patent" before the doctrine of equivalents applies. Rather, this amorphous standard applies in every case.

Pennwalt provides an excellent example of ... uncertainty. As a general matter, it would seem that if an element is missing from an accused device both literally and as an equivalent, there would be at least some danger that the 'way' prong of the equivalents test would be effectively elided. A determination that the accused device performs substantially the same overall function to achieve substantially the same overall result would lead inexorably to a conclusion that the accused device functions in substantially the same way when the claimed invention and the accused device are considered as wholes.

Moreover, the 'criteria' that the courts generally use to determine the application and scope of the doctrine of equivalents do not ameliorate this uncertainty. For example, although a finding of equivalents is a 'determination of fact' and '[p]roof can be made in any form,'[5] an important issue concerns whether 'persons reasonably skilled in the art would have known of the interchangeability of an ingredient not contained in the patent with one that was.'[6] This factor purports to

4. Id.
5. Graver Tank & Mfg. Co. v. Linde Air Prods. Co., 339 *U.S.* 605, 609 (1950).
6. Id. ...

establish an inquiry for the finder of fact to aid in determining whether the variation or change in the accused device falls within the permissible scope of equivalents. We argue, however, that this factor should be used to reject rather than support the application of the doctrine of equivalents.

* * *

A. Uses of the Doctrine of Equivalents

The justification for the doctrine of equivalents is that it would be unfair to deprive an inventor of the benefits of her invention when an infringer makes, uses, or sells a product or process that is not identical to, but is substantially similar to, the claimed invention. This justification raises a question: Why did the inventor not claim originally that item that she seeks to cover through the doctrine of equivalents? There are two plausible answers. First, the doctrine of equivalents is used in those instances in which the patent holder has inadvertently omitted to include a broader claim or, second, because of a technological development that occurs after the patent issues, it would have been impossible for the inventor to have obtained a claim that would cover the infringer's action due to the technical rules of patent law. Oddly, those two functions rely on theories that are to some degree opposite to each other.

Most frequently, patent holders use the doctrine of equivalents to rectify what is effectively a 'mistake' in the process of drafting and prosecuting the application in the PTO. The patent holder argues that the failure to include something in the claim was an oversight.

* * *

In such a situation, a patent holder may reasonably argue that what she is trying to capture through the doctrine of equivalents does not really exceed what the invention is. This same argument is made in any equivalents case in which the patent holder argues that those skilled in the art would, at the time of the patent application, have regarded the relevant element or elements in the accused device as interchangeable with the claimed invention.

The second primary use of the doctrine of equivalents involves new developments or technologies that come into existence after the patent issues. This second use involves a theoretical predicate that is opposite to the first use. The patent holder argues that those skilled in the art could not have regarded the relevant feature or features of the accused device as interchangeable with the claimed invention because the accused device is the product of new technology.

* * *

A modern example may be found in Hughes Aircraft Co. v. United States.[7] Hughes created a system for 'attitude control' of a satellite in order to orient the satellite in space. The Hughes invention taught an on-board sun sensor that transmitted [data] back to earth so that the ground crew could simulate the rotation of the satellite and calculate

---

7. 717 *F.2d* 1351 (Fed. Cir. 1983). [Editor's Note: see the notes following this excerpt for more discussion of this case.]

spin rate, sun angle, and ISA [i.e., instantaneous spin angle] position, which is 'the measure of where the satellite is in its spin cycle at any instant of time.' The ground crew would then send signals to the satellite that caused the satellite's jet valves to discharge pulses of gas that would reorient the satellite in space. The jets would fire synchronously upon receipt of the firing signals transmitted by the ground crew. The satellite was a 'dumb' satellite because all control information was relayed to the earth, and the jet on board the spacecraft fired promptly upon receiving a firing pulse from the earth. In the accused satellites, commonly known as store-and-execute satellites, sun pulses were transmitted to an on-board computer, which then calculated the spin rate of the satellite. The computer also 'knew' when it received sun pulses, so it could respond to signals that told it to fire the jet a certain number of seconds from the time it received a sun pulse indication. The information from the sun sensors was also sent to earth. The ground crew then sent a set of signals to the satellite. One signal told the computer how many times to fire the jet, and the second told the computer the number of seconds after receiving a sun pulse to wait before it fired the jet. The claims in suit were limited to the details of a 'dumb' satellite.

The Federal Circuit found that the doctrine of equivalents applied to the store-and-execute satellites because the development of new technology—advanced computers and digital communications techniques—made possible the replacement of certain functions of the ground crew by functions performed by the computer aboard the spacecraft. . . .

These two broad categories of uses of the doctrine of equivalents, error and new technology, are logically separate. The 'error' part of the doctrine relies on a theory of actual enablement, so that the patent actually enables those skilled in the art to make or use the variation that the patent holder seeks to encompass within the doctrine of equivalents. The patent holder is really arguing that the claimed invention, when understood by someone skilled in the art, would cover the accused device. The patentee could have obtained a claim that was specific to the accused device, because adding details concerning the device to the specification would not have constituted new matter. In the 'new technology' context, the patent cannot teach the actual enablement, which becomes possible only as the result of technological development. Thus, adding to the specification of the patent the details concerning the accused device would be new matter and hence impermissible. Under patent law rules, no claim could have been obtained to the specific embodiment of the accused device. Whether a broad claim that would cover both the original teachings and the new technology would be enabled would then depend on the predictable or not predictable nature of the art to which the invention pertains.

* * *

The difficulty with using the doctrine of equivalents to 'fix' mistakes is that the patent law already provides such a mechanism in the reissue procedure. To this extent the doctrine of equivalents is nothing more than the circumvention of a statutory procedure, and, more seriously, it is the circumvention of explicitly stated statutory protection for members of the public who may have relied on the original claims.

The reissue procedure, which allows the patent holder to return to the PTO in order to 'amend' a patent, was originally a judicial doctrine[8] that was codified in the patent statute in 1832.[9] The procedure was reaffirmed by Congress in the 1952 Act.[10] The reissue procedure is designed to deal with three situations. First, if the original claims are too broad and, therefore, invalid, the patent holder must seek to narrow the claims. This is called a narrowing reissue. Second, if the original claims are too narrow and, therefore, fail to provide to the inventor that which is actually enabled by the patent, the patent holder may seek to broaden the claims. This is called a broadening reissue. Third, if the patent contains 'a defective specification or drawing,' the patent holder may seek reissue to cure that defect.

* * *

Evidence that the use of the doctrine of equivalents is, most typically, an attempt to obtain a 'judicial' broadening reissue follows from a comparison of the reissue process and the doctrine of equivalents. The reissue process is explicitly limited to 'the invention disclosed in the original patent,' and the applicant cannot introduce any 'new matter.' When an applicant seeks to use the doctrine of equivalents based on the fact that those skilled in the art would view the element(s) in the accused device as interchangeable with that in the claimed invention, she is not trying to go beyond the scope of the original invention, but is arguing that the original patent actually enabled those skilled in the art to make or use the invention with the accused element. Similarly, the theory of a broadening reissue is that the reissue may not exceed the original invention. This theory does not suggest that an applicant meets the requirements of the reissue statute merely by demonstrating that the description and enablement provisions of section 112 are met. The reissue applicant must also show that the failure to include the broadened version of the claim was an error. Although a showing of error is not a requirement for invoking the doctrine of equivalents, the typical patent holder who relies on the doctrine of equivalents has unintentionally neglected to claim more broadly.

There are two reasons why patent holders are reluctant to use the reissue process instead of relying on the doctrine of equivalents. First, most patent holders who would seek to use the doctrine of equivalents want to broaden, not narrow, claims, and they would face the two-year limitation period for broadening reissues. Second, defendants subject to

---

8. A reissue was first sanctioned by the Supreme Court in 1832. See Grant v. Raymond, 31 *U.S.* (6 Pet.) 218 (1832). The Court had to decide whether 'to cancel a patent which had once been issued, and to grant a second patent for the same invention, with an amended specification.... Upon this question, there is not known a single case where the point has been expressly decided in the United States....' Id. at 236. The Court approved of the reissue, reasoning '[c]an it be supposed, that the law ever intended to punish their [patentees'] ignorance in drawing a very special legal paper, by a forfeiture of all the advantages of their invention?' Id.

9. See Act of July 3, 1832, ch. 162, § 3, 4 State 559.

10. See 35 U.S.C. §§ 251–252 (1982).

the use of the doctrine of equivalents would in many cases hold intervening rights under the reissue statute. As compelling as these reasons may seem from the perspective of the patent holder, they do not justify the use of the doctrine of equivalents when it circumvents the reissue procedure. The reissue procedure, which allows for amendment and reissue, accommodates the patent holder who has made a mistake in the scope of her claim. The use of the doctrine of equivalents to upset this statutorily crafted compromise cannot be justified.

This argument does not suggest that the reissue procedure is appropriate for every case, especially in light of the two-year limitation on broadening reissues. The solution, however, is for Congress to repeal the two-year limitation and treat broadening and narrowing reissues alike. The Federal Circuit has stated that '[t]he purpose of the law that a broadening reissue must be applied for within two years after patent grant is to set a limited time after which the public may rely on the scope of the claims of an issued patent.'[11] As long as the doctrine of intervening rights is enforced rigorously, however, the public will not be harmed by broadening reissues over the life of the patent. Moreover, whatever greater uncertainty would result from liberalizing the reissue rules would be more than offset by a decrease in the uncertainty engendered by use of the doctrine of equivalents.

Notes and Questions

1. Martin J. Adelman received B.A., M.S. and J.D. degrees from the University of Michigan. He taught at Wayne State University in Detroit, and is now a Professor of Law at George Washington University School of Law. He is also the author of a continuously updated treatise/commentary on patent law, Patent Law Perspectives. Gary L. Francione received a B.A. from the University of Rochester and M.A. and J.D. degrees from the University of Virginia. He taught at the University of Pennsylvania, and is now a Professor of Law at Rutgers–Newark School of Law.

2. Adelman and Francione argue that the doctrine of equivalents applies primarily in two situations: (1) "error" cases, where the patentee has made a mistake, and failed to claim a variant of an invention that could have and ought to have been claimed; and (2) "new technology" cases, where technological developments create an equivalent not known or contemplated at the time the patent issued. The Supreme Court addressed these issue in two important cases after the Adelman and Francione article was written: Warner–Jenkinson Co. v. Hilton Davis Chemical Co., 520 U.S. 17 (1997), which rejected the idea of abandoning the doctrine of equivalents altogether, and adopted the "element-by-element" approach of *Pennwalt* and subsequent Federal Circuit cases; and Festo Corp. v. Shoketsu Kinzoku Kogyo Kabushiki Co., Ltd., 535 U.S. 722 (2002), which reiterated the Court's support of the doctrine of equivalents, and rejected a highly restrictive approach to the related doctrine of prosecution history estoppel. Both cases stressed the importance of the "new technology" branch of the doctrine as described by

---

11. In re Fotland, 779 *F.2d* 31, 33 (Fed. Cir. 1985), cert. denied, 476 *U.S.* 1183 (1986).

Adelman and Francione, and both create a doctrinal framework that is largely unreceptive to the "error" branch.

3. Which of the two categories—error or new technology—do you think most important? Since patentees draft their own patents, why should courts save a drafter from a mistake? The "forseeability" test adopted by the Supreme Court in *Festo*, supra, follows the Federal Circuit's lead in leaving little room for a claim amendment which fails to include a specific infringing embodiment. As long as the embodiment was "foreseeable," the amendment will preclude coverage of the embodiment via the doctrine of equivalents. Does this place an undue burden on the patent drafter? How is the public benefited by this rule? "New technology" equivalents appear to be the paradigmatic "unforeseeable" embodiments. Coverage of these embodiments under the doctrine of equivalents is not sacrificed by a claim amendment drawn up when they were not yet in existence—i.e, unforeseeable. What policy does this rule advance? Why should a patentee be the beneficiary of a new technology he or she did not invent nor anticipate? These issues are well illustrated by the *Hughes Aircraft* case discussed by Adelman and Francione. For subsequent history of the *Hughes Aircraft* case, see the final Federal Circuit opinion (in a long line) at 140 F.3d 1470 (Fed. Cir. 1998), after vacatur and remand from the Supreme Court in the wake of *Warner-Jenkinson*, in which the court finally affirms a finding of infringement under the doctrine of equivalents.

4. Adelman and Francione emphasize the importance of "notice" to competitors, which militates against a broad doctrine of equivalents. This leads them to question the utility of the "interchangeability" test which formed a minor theme in the *Graver Tank* case from the Supreme Court in 1950. The Federal Circuit has followed this same reasoning in its doctrine of equivalents jurisprudence since the 1990s. The Supreme Court added impetus to this direction in emphasizing "foreseeability" in its *Festo* decision. In the same vein, Adelman and Francione are clearly skeptical about the value of using the doctrine of equivalents to correct inventor's "errors" when the inventor "could have obtained a claim that was specific to the accused device." They instructively compare their view, emphasizing the importance of "notice," with an alternative view which they denote "enablement." Under this view, if the patentee teaches the public how to build a class of embodiments, the patentee ought to have the opportunity to extend its property rights to the full range of embodiments taught—regardless of whether the claims include a particular embodiment or not. Does the Adelman and Francione position implicitly undervalue a patentee's overall contribution to the art, in favor of a "technical" emphasis on the specific claim language chosen during prosecution? For more on foreseeability, see Matthew J. Conigliaro, Andrew C. Greenberg and Mark A. Lemley, "Foreseeability in Patent Law," 16 *Berkeley Tech. L.J.* 1045 (2001).

5. Adelman and Francione's "reissue solution" to the doctrine of equivalents addresses the difficult conceptual problems of the doctrine of equivalents by resort to an administrative solution. In this it foreshadows more recent scholarship exploring the delicate interactions between the PTO and the courts. See infra, section III.D., "patent institutions."

One practical advantage of the doctrine of equivalents, as opposed to an administrative reissue proceeding, is speed: a court can rule on the equivalents issue relatively quickly, in the context of an overall patent litigation, whereas an administrative proceeding would require a stay of litigation and a potentially long PTO procedure.

A Theory of Claim Interpretation*

CRAIG ALLEN NARD

I. Introduction

Scholarly interest in theories of interpretation has increased dramatically over the last fifteen to twenty years, resulting in myriad scholarly publications. Interpretive theory is germane to almost all areas of the law, including patent law, a subject in which I have a particular interest. My interest, however, as reflected in this article is not in how courts interpret the patent code, although that is a subject worthy of exploration. Rather, my concern relates to what interpretive theories courts, particularly the United States Court of Appeals for the Federal Circuit, employ when interpreting patent claims.

The relationship between theories of interpretation (e.g., statutory or contract) and claim interpretation is important for at least three reasons. First, some judges on the Federal Circuit have analogized claim interpretation to statutory interpretation, while others have compared it to interpreting a contract; and, therefore, studying theories of interpretation can inform our understanding of how the court interprets patent claims. Second, in the words of one of the founding fathers of modern patent law, "the name of the game is the claim."[1] That is, the patent claim defines the proprietary boundaries of the invention, and determining where exactly these boundaries reside is often dispositive of such crucial issues as patent validity and infringement. Lastly, and perhaps most importantly, the manner in which the Federal Circuit interprets patent claims reflects the court's view of the proper scope of judicial power, which has implications for patent law's delicate incentive dynamic.

My goal in this article is to explore the proper scope of judicial power in patent law by focusing on the Federal Circuit's theories of claim interpretation. Specifically, I examine the court's claim interpretation jurisprudence in an attempt to discern whether there is a predominant interpretive school and whether this school is in accord with the patent code and post-patent innovation practice or what can be characterized as "improvement-theory" and "design-around theory." These two theories are concerned with the incentives for persons of ordinary skill in the art, namely competitors of the patent owner, to improve upon or design around the patented technology. Closely related to the relationship

* Reprinted by permission from 14 Harv. J. L. & Tech. 1 (2000), © 2000 Harvard Law and Technology Journal.

1. Giles S. Rich, Extent of the Protection and Interpretation of Claims—American Perspectives, 21 Int'l. Rev. Indus. Prop. & Copyright L. 497, 499 (1990).

between interpretive theory and post-innovation practice are the proper roles of the doctrine of equivalents and optimal claim scope. Indeed, the interpretive tools used by a court directly affect the extent of the patentee's property interest, and, therefore, where the patentee's competitors may and may not tread. Thus, claim interpretation theory lies at the heart of our patent system.

A study of the Federal Circuit's claim interpretation jurisprudence reveals two schools of interpretation. I characterize these approaches as (1) hypertextualism, which is the predominant interpretative theory; and (2) pragmatic textualism, which is gradually asserting itself. The hypertextualist judge has an expansive view of judicial power, characterizing claim interpretation as a question of law subject to de novo review. This highly formalistic approach stresses textual fidelity and internal textual coherence, but eschews extrinsic evidence as an interpretive tool, portraying its use as "rarely, if ever," proper. Although hypertextualism posits that expert testimony may be used if the intrinsic record is ambiguous, a hypertextualist judge rarely finds ambiguity. If ambiguity is found, expert testimony may be used to educate the judge in the relevant technology—not for the purpose of interpreting the ambiguous claim language.

On the other hand, the pragmatic textualist approach, while embracing the importance of textual fidelity and internal coherence, also emphasizes the relevance of extrinsic context and industry custom, of which patent law's "person having ordinary skill in the art" ("PHOSITA") is representative. This hypothetical artisan is one of the cynosures of our patent system and is valued by the pragmatic textualist as an interpretive tool because the artisan has knowledge of the underlying assumptions present in his technological community and is sensitive to the facts on the ground. Indeed, patents are written by and for persons having ordinary skill in the art, and to limit claim construction to the intrinsic record is, for the pragmatic textualist, a legal fiction largely detached from what Arthur Corbin referred to as the "undisputed contexts." Because the meaning of a word cannot be "divorced from the circumstances in which it is used," a pragmatic textualist approach would consider extrinsic evidence without a threshold determination of intrinsic ambiguity.

However, an interpretive theory, such as hypertextualism, that places too much emphasis on text is not without its problems. First, a legitimate theory of claim interpretation should embrace the technologic context and industry custom of which the claimed invention is a part. By characterizing claim interpretation as a question of law devoid of fact-finding and neglecting extrinsic context as an interpretive tool, the hypertextualist judge verges on abstraction and denies that language, particularly technical language, is, as Wittgenstein taught us, a "social enterprise" whose meaning is largely dependent on its context. Thus, hypertextualism ignores the insights of contemporary legal and hermeneutic philosophy, and, as importantly, disregards the centrality of patent law's artisan. Ignoring the role of the artisan is particularly problematic given the fact that innovation in "complex technologies is the work of organizational networks" and these "[n]etworks have proven especially capable of incorporating tacit knowledge into their learning processes." The hypertextualist divorces himself from these ramified networks by refusing to delve into their linguistic practices. This has significant implications for ex post innovation and the adjudication of claim scope. As the hypertextualist dismisses the very tools that enable one to discern accurately not only the patentee's inventive contribution to society, but also the contribution of the patentee's competitors, the separation between industry and court widens. Although researchers will no doubt continue to pursue their agendas, the question becomes at what costs in terms of wasteful rent-seeking behavior and unnecessary litigation?

Second, there are constitutional concerns with hypertextualism in that strict adherence to the patent's text ironically leads to a breakdown in separation of powers.... By refusing to consider the artisan's perspective, the Federal Circuit assigns meaning to a claim term without employing the congressionally mandated analytical framework set forth in Title 35. The irony is that although one would think that strict adherence to the patent's text would limit the exercise of judicial discretion, the judge, by turning a deaf ear to the skilled artisan, replaces the artisan and discerns claim meaning by examining the intrinsic record through her own eyes.

Lastly, the hypertextualists, in the name of certainty and uniformity, review claim interpretation de novo "without deference to the trial court's judgment." De novo review and the concomitant diminishment of the roles of the district court and extrinsic context were a natural outgrowth of the characterization of claim interpretation as a question of law. Although certainty is a laudable goal, there is a temporal dimension to the realization of certainty. Obviously, the earlier certainty is achieved in the litigation or business-planning process the better; yet, de novo review at the Federal Circuit level leads to dilatory certainty in claim meaning. Furthermore, hypertextualism ignores the district court's superior institutional position with respect to extrinsic evidence....

This article, therefore, is skeptical of hypertextualism as a theory of claim interpretation and argues that it ultimately cannot deliver on its promise of greater certainty and uniformity. As such, while both interpretive schools have as their lodestar the realization of certainty and uniformity, I argue that pragmatic textualism is the interpretive approach that can best realize these ends. To a large extent, Judges Rader, Newman, and Mayer are pragmatic textualists. Their opinions concerning claim interpretation demonstrate that they, "like other users of language, want to know its context, including assumptions shared by the speakers and the intended audience." Of course, the meaning that is ultimately given to the technical term must be consonant with the patent's text. This emphasis on textual internal coherence is central to pragmatic textualism, and the hypertextualists have correctly made this an essential part of their philosophy. However, "[t]extualism [certainly pragmatic textualism] is not literalism," and, unlike hypertextualism, which cabins itself within the four corners of the patent text, the pragmatic textualist is an instrumentalist who understands that "the meaning of a word is its use in the language." As Judge Easterbrook notes, "[m]eaning comes from the ring the words would have had to a skilled user of words ... thinking about the same problem."

In addition, the pragmatic textualists on the Federal Circuit are motivated by process considerations such as institutional competence. The question for them is not whether expert testimony is a question of law or fact; rather, having concluded that expert testimony (or other forms of extrinsic evidence) is useful and desirable when construing claim language, the pragmatic textualist asks: Is the trial judge or appellate judge better able to understand and incorporate expert testimony into the interpretive process? The pragmatic textualist appellate judge, well aware of his institutional limitations, opts for the former and would allow for a more deferential approach towards the district court's claim construction.

Pragmatic textualism strikes me as a judicious approach to claim interpretation. A judge who subscribes to this approach is grounded, self-aware, and empirically inclined. She has faith in the patent's text, but understands that the legitimacy of her faith depends upon her understanding of the technologic world around her, both in terms of discerning claim meaning and, once discerned, the effect the meaning will have on the technological community to which the invention belongs.

III.   Pragmatic Textualism: Through the Eyes of an Artisan

Because "[c]laims cannot be clear and unambiguous on their face," the Federal Circuit has stated that claims must be read "in the context of the patent."[2] It is over the interpretation of this battleground phrase—"in the context of the patent"—that hypertextualists and pragmatic textualists part company. When construing claim language, each camp examines the textual interrelationship among the claims, written description, and prosecution history, and each attaches varying degrees of emphasis to dictionaries. Indeed, this structural analysis of the intrinsic record is essential to claim construction. However, the hypertextualists limit their interpretive analysis to the intrinsic context because the patentee's "competitors are entitled to rely on the public record of the patent." Pragmatic textualists certainly agree with this proposition, but they have a broader view of the public record. They not only engage in a structural analysis of the intrinsic evidence, but also consider as equally authoritative the extrinsic context—namely, the underlying linguistic assumptions of the relevant technological community.

Thus, while the intrinsic context forms the structural interpretive foundation, contemporary hermeneutic and legal philosophy have taught us that meaning cannot be constructed solely from the text; rather, "meaning depends on both culture and context." That is, there is an inextricable bond between intrinsic and extrinsic context. The philosopher John Searle has referred to this extrinsic context as the "Background." According to Searle:

> ... The simplest argument for the thesis of the Background is that the literal meaning of any sentence can only determine its truth conditions or other conditions of satisfaction against a

2.   Markman, 52 F.3d at 979.

Background of capacities, dispositions, know-how, etc., which
are not themselves part of the semantic content of the sentence.

Indeed, several other notable thinkers such as Karl Llewellyn, Richard
Posner, Pierre Bourdieu, Cass Sunstein, [and] Stanley Fish have expressed the importance of culture and extrinsic context in discerning
meaning. Perhaps the most influential figure to do so was Ludwig
Wittgenstein in his Philosophical Investigations.[3] Wittgenstein's post-
Tractarian philosophy (after 1929) eschewed the demand for Platonic
certainty and a unified theory of language and posited that language is
best understood as a labyrinth of interconnected practices. That is, the
diversity and plurality of language make it impossible to discern a
universal linguistic algorithm. For Wittgenstein, the "philosophical concept of meaning has its place in a primitive idea of the way language
functions."[4]

B. *Pragmatic Textualism and the Useful Arts*

1. The Centrality of the Artisan

Upon reading Federal Circuit opinions written by both hypertextualists
and pragmatic textualists, one reads time and again that "the focus in
construing disputed terms in claim language is ... on the objective test
of what one of ordinary skill in the art at the time of the invention would
have understood the term to mean." Despite this language, the hypertextualist judge takes an expansive view of judicial power and positions
himself as both judge and artisan.

[T]he phrase "claim interpretation" is a misnomer. Understanding
the meaning of claim language usually does not entail interpretation;
rather, understanding the meaning of claim language is a result of
understanding how the language is used in practice. . . .

Patent law, perhaps more than any other area of the law, provides
the judge with access to the scientific method and the "prediction" and
"control" that accompany it. However, the hypertextualist judge ignores
this direct pipeline to the technological community and chooses instead
to engage in a de novo, acontextual interpretive analysis through a
mediating lens. This approach ... ineluctably leads to an opportunity for
judges to entertain their own background assumptions and biases, which
are themselves a form of extrinsic evidence.

Thus, much like Corbin's and Llewellyn's emphasis on custom and
trade usage in response to the Willistonian or classical contract model,
the pragmatic textualists on the Federal Circuit understand that meaning is derived from asking how persons of ordinary skill in the art
understand the claim language in question. The virtues of predictability
and certainty are achieved (or, at least, realized to a greater extent than
they would be under a hypertextualist approach) because technical
terms, through custom, training, and the cumulative nature of complex

---

3. [Ludwig Wittgenstein, Philosophical Investigations (G.E.M. Anscombe trans., 2d
ed. 1958).]

4. Wittgenstein, supra note [3], § 2.

technology, have acquired a common meaning that is shared by the artisans of the relevant technological community.

Notes and Comments

1. Craig Allen Nard received a B.A. from Washington and Jefferson College, a J.D. from Capital University Law School, and Ll.M. and JSD degrees from Columbia Law School, where he was the Julius Silver Fellow in Law, Science and Technology. He taught at Marquette University Law School, and now teaches at Case Western Reserve School of Law.

2. Which approach to claim interpretation makes more sense to you? Which do you think would be more predictable? More fair? Do you agree with Nard that context is the major determinant of meaning? Do you agree with Nard that the battle regarding claim interpretation is reminiscent of other disputes over interpretive approaches in various areas of law—constitutional and statutory interpretation, for example, or the "parol evidence rule" and contract interpretation? See generally William N. Eskridge, Jr. and Philip P. Frickey, *Statutory Interpretation as Practical Reasoning*, 42 Stan. L. Rev. 321 (1990); Eric A. Posner, The *Parol Evidence Rule, the Plain Meaning Rule, and the Principles of Contractual Interpretation*, 146 U. Pa. L. Rev. 533, 564 (1998).

3. Nard describes two basic approaches to claim construction: hypertextualist and pragmatic. A systematic empirical study of claim interpretation in the Federal Circuit divides claim interpretation methodology into two camps having substantial overlap with Nard's approaches: "proceduralist" and "holistic." See Polk Wagner and Lee Petherbridge, *Is the Federal Circuit Succeeding? An Empirical Assessment of Judicial Performance*, 152 U. Pa. L. Rev. 1105 (2004). Wagner and Petherbridge state that some features of the Nard approach do not lend themselves to empirical testing. Id., at 1131. Nevertheless, they come out strongly in favor of the view they characterize as "proceduralist," which seems closely akin to what Nard calls "hypertextualism." According to Wagner and Petherbridge, the judges Nard celebrates as most closely attuned to technological context are among the judges whose approach to claim interpretation varies the most from case to case. They also claim that as of 2004, when their article was published, the proceduralists were gaining ground in the struggle over interpretive approaches in the Federal Circuit.

4. Like the great contracts scholars he cites, Arthur Corbin and Karl Llewellyn, Nard celebrates the importance of custom and art-specific linguistic meanings. Recent scholarship, however, calls into question the assumption that individual trades (and hence, perhaps, individual technical arts) use language with monolithic consistency. See Lisa Bernstein, "The Questionable Empirical Basis of Article 2's Incorporation Strategy: A Preliminary Study," 66 *U.Chi.L.Rev.* 710 (1999).

5. Nard assumes the goal of patent claim interpretation is to get the meaning correct; he does not mention the cost of doing so, and assumes that whatever methodology produces the right result in a judicial proceeding is the proper approach to take. Do you agree? Is it important to

keep in mind that the "interpretive audience" for most patents is likely
to be primarily customers and competitors of the patentee, and that
patents rarely reach a court, let alone the rarified confines of a Federal
Circuit claim interpretation proceeding? Is this one way that patent
interpretation differs from contract interpretation, in which the parties
to the contract, and perhaps a court, are the only relevant "interpretive
audience"? Recall the discussion in the preceding excerpt by Adelman
and Francione regarding the importance of the "notice function" of
patent claims. Does this suggest a reason to perhaps give "hypertextualism" a more thorough hearing?

Contributory Infringement/Patent Misuse: Metaphysics and Metamorphosis*

SAMUEL ODDI

The doctrines of contributory infringement and patent misuse are said to
'rest on antithetical underpinnings.' As one doctrine expands the other
correlatively must contract. If 'philosophical' labels had to be attached to
these competing doctrines, contributory infringement could be labeled a
'pro-patent' doctrine—that is, expanding the scope of protection afforded
under a patent. On the other hand, patent misuse would be labeled as
'pro-competition' or 'anti-patent' doctrine narrowing the scope of protection afforded under the patent. The turbulent history of the clash of
these doctrines vividly illustrates their incompatibility.

From its humble beginning ..., contributory infringement, as the
patent law application of the tort doctrine of imposing joint and several
liability on tortfeasors acting in concert, had a rapid ascendency. The
doctrine was one of basic fairness enabling the patent owner to enforce
his patent against one who, strictly speaking, did not infringe the patent
but, rather, intentionally contributed to infringement by selling to the
infringer a necessary (albeit unpatented) element of the patented invention. Concerted action between the seller and the buyer of the element
was implied. Without this doctrine it was feared that (1) the patent
owner would be powerless to enforce his patent; and (2) it would be
practically impossible to enforce the patent against a multiplicity of
direct infringers.

At the apogee of the patent owner's rights under the doctrine of
contributory infringement, as seen in Heaton–Peninsular Button–Fastener Co. v. Eureka Speciality Co. (Button–Fastener case)[1] and Henry v.
A.B. Dick Co.,[2] the owner could condition the right to use his patented
invention upon the purchase of unpatented materials from him for use
with the patented invention—the classic 'tie-in.' These materials were to
be used in practicing the patented invention but did not need to be

* Reprinted by permission from 44 U. Pitt. L. Rev. 73 (1982); © 1982, University of
Pittsburgh Law Review.
    1. 77 F. 288 (6th Cir. 1896).
    2. 224 U.S. 1 (1912).

elements of the patented invention, and indeed, in theory could be entirely irrelevant to the invention. If a license was granted under a patent on condition that the licensee purchase unpatented materials only from, or with the authorization of, the patent owner, the licensee would directly infringe the patent if he purchased such materials from an unauthorized source. In so doing he would exceed the scope of his license. The unauthorized seller of the materials who had knowledge of the condition would be a contributory infringer.

With the twin-edged sword of direct infringement and contributory infringement, the patent owner could derive so-called monopoly profits not only from the patented invention itself but also from unpatented materials upon which he conditioned the use of his patented invention. So interpreted, the protection afforded under a patent was extensive and, of course, tended to suppress competition. On the other hand, such protection provided a strong incentive for inventive activity.

As might be expected with the rise of antitrust consciousness and the abuse of monopoly power, the extensive protection of the patent owner was short-lived. The doctrine of patent misuse was born, though, as in the case of contributory infringement, it was not at first so identified.... [P]atent misuse had its origins in Motion Picture Patents Co. v. Universal Film Manufacturing Co. (Motion Picture case).[3] The doctrine of patent misuse was first applied there to exclude a patent owner from conditioning the use of a patented invention upon the purchase of an unpatented article that was not an element of the patented invention. The rationale given for this result was that permitting such a restriction would extend the scope of the patent monopoly beyond the patented invention to encompass unpatented materials. The Motion Picture decision marked the beginning of the ascendency of patent misuse and the demise of contributory infringement....

The apogee of the patent misuse doctrine (and the correlative nadir of the contributory infringement doctrine) occurred when enforcement of a patent was refused against a contributory infringer who sold an element of a patented invention which had no other use but infringing the patented invention (a nonstaple element). Mercoid Corp. v. Mid–Continent Investment Co. (Mercoid I)[4] and Mercoid Corp. v. Minneapolis Honeywell Corp. (Mercoid II)[5] established that it was misuse for the patent owner to license others to sell the nonstaple element for use in the patented invention

At the persistent urging of the patent bar, contributory infringement was revitalized by the enactment of section 271 of the 1952 Patent Act. The full extent of the revitalization was not known until the decision of the United States Supreme Court in Dawson Chemical Co. v. Rohm & Haas Chemical Co.[6] in 1980.

3.   243 U.S. 502 (1917).
4.   320 U.S. 661, 665 (1944).
5.   320 U.S. 680, 684 (1944).
6.   448 U.S. 176 (1980).

If not metaphysical, the underlying philosophy of the majority at least appears clear and bears repeating: 'The policy of free competition runs deep in our law. . . . But the policy of stimulating inventions that underlies the entire patent system runs no less deep.'[7] . . .

As will be demonstrated below, Dawson is a paradoxical decision: the scope of patent protection is expanded on the one hand, while seemingly contracted on the other. Inventive activity is promoted with regard to at least one type of invention, but perhaps at the expense of retarding inventive activity with regard to other types of invention. At the heart of this paradox is the metamorphosis of the 'essential nonstaple' to the status of a patented invention.

II.   Contributory Infringement Misuse Interface Under Dawson

The facts in the Dawson case present a classic example of contributory infringement. The Wilson patent, owned by Rohm & Haas, covered a process of using a chemical compound (propanil) as an herbicide. Propanil itself was unpatented, and indeed unpatentable, because the chemical compound was known to others before the Wilson invention. The Wilson patent, however, claimed the 'new use' of propanil as an herbicide in the form of a process . . . Not only was the use of propanil as an herbicide a 'new use,' it was the only known use for propanil; thus, propanil was a 'nonstaple,' that is, in the negative language of section 271(c), 'not a staple article or commodity of commerce suitable for substantial non-infringing use.'

The conduct of the defendant Dawson Chemical was classically that of a contributory infringer. Having knowledge of the Rohm & Haas patent, Dawson sold propanil with instructions for its use as an herbicide with the intent that farmers purchasing the propanil would so use it to infringe the patent. Farmers who used the propanil purchased from Dawson to practice the patented method would thus be direct infringers of Rohm & Haas' patent under section 271(a). As might be expected, Rohm & Haas did not choose to sue individual farmers purchasing propanil from Dawson as direct infringers, but rather elected to sue Dawson as a contributory infringer under section 271(c). . . .

In defense of its continued selling of propanil for use as an herbicide, Dawson charged that Rohm & Haas was misusing its patent. Certainly, prior to the enactment of section 271 and after the Mercoid cases, Rohm & Haas' conduct would appear to present a classic example of patent misuse. Rohm & Haas itself did not practice the patented process of using propanil, but only sold the unpatented propanil. With every sale, Rohm & Haas granted an implied license to use the patented method to its purchasers. Farmers who purchased propanil from other suppliers, such as Dawson, did not receive an implied license under the patent and thus were direct infringers of the patented process. In fact, Rohm & Haas refused to license other suppliers, including Dawson, to sell propanil for use in the patented process. Rohm & Haas brought an action

---

7.   Id. at 221.

against Dawson for contributory infringement to enjoin sales of the unpatented propanil. Accordingly, Rohm & Haas sought to monopolize the market for unpatented propanil for use as an herbicide as taught by its process patent. The majority of the Supreme Court, after considering the case law prior to the enactment of section 271 and the legislative history of section 271, concludes: "By enacting §§ 271(c) and (d), Congress granted to patent holders a statutory right to control nonstaple goods that are capable only of infringing use in a patented invention, and that are essential to that invention's advance over prior art." Two conditions must therefore be met for a patent owner to exclude others from selling unpatented elements for use in the patented invention: (1) the unpatented element must be "nonstaple goods that are capable only of infringing use"; and (2) the goods must be "essential to that invention's advance over prior art."

Specifically with regard to Rohm & Haas' conduct and propanil the majority states: 'Respondent, to be sure, has licensed use of its patented process only in connection with purchases of propanil. But propanil is a *nonstaple* [emphasis by Court] product, and its herbicidal property is the heart of respondent's invention.' It thus appears clear that it is not the 'mere nonstaple' which affords patent owners a statutory right of control under paragraphs (c) and (d) of section 271. The nonstaple must in addition satisfy a quality standard ('essential to that invention's advance over the prior art' or 'heart of invention').

III.   Metamorphosis of the Nonstaple

A qualification should be made to the assertion that Dawson has transmuted the 'essential nonstaple' into a protected invention. To find contributory infringement under paragraph (c) of section 271 the seller must sell the element 'knowing the same to be especially made or especially adapted for use in infringement of such patent.' Paragraph (c) codified the common law principles of contributory infringement with regard to nonstaples. However, there was some disagreement over whether the seller need only know that the nonstaple was especially made or especially adapted for use in a particular way or combination or whether he must know of the patent and of the infringing use of the nonstaple. The latter view prevailed in Aro Mfg. Co., Inc. v. Convertible Top Replacement Co. (Aro II),[8] where the four dissenting justices were joined by Mr. Justice White in ruling that the seller must know that the combination for which the element sold was especially designed was both patented and infringed....

It is a general principle of American patent law that a patent owner is under no obligation either to use the patented invention himself or to authorize anyone else to use it.... Is there any justification for treating anything less than the patented invention itself as property? Should the patent owner whose patented invention includes a nonstaple be afforded the same property rights with respect to the nonstaple through the doctrine of contributory infringement, free from the restraining effects

8.   377 U.S. 476 (1964).

of the doctrine of patent misuse? Dawson appears to answer this question affirmatively, at least insofar as an 'essential nonstaple' is concerned.

The majority's analysis in Dawson of how the enactment of section 271 affected the doctrines of contributory infringement and patent misuse warrants careful consideration. The underlying premises of this analysis appear to be: (1) section 271(d) 'effectively confers' a power on the patent owner to exclude others from competing in 'essential nonstaples' used in the patented invention; (2) the power to demand royalties from a competitor to sell such nonstaples 'implies' the power to exclude competitors; and (3) since section 271(d)(2) exempts express licenses granted by the patent owner to competitors for the sale of nonstaples from a charge of patent misuse then, by analogy, it also exempts from such a charge implied licenses granted by the patent owner to his purchasers.

* * * The second premise of the majority, namely, that the power to license 'implies' the power to refuse to license, shows the metamorphosis of section 271(d) from a patent owner's shield against patent misuse in certain circumstances into a sword in the hands of a patent owner which enables him to exclude competition in unpatented nonstaples.

The impatience of the majority in dealing with the issue of the refusal to license is understandable, for once the conclusion is drawn based upon the logic that the power to license 'implies' the power to refuse, any controversy is ended. But such a conclusion also eliminates any distinction between the protections granted a patented invention and an unpatented 'essential nonstaple.' The shield of section 271(d) exempting certain conduct of the patent owner from the equitable defense of patent misuse is transmuted into a sword that empowers the patent owner to monopolize the market for unpatented 'essential nonstaples.' . . .

It is possible to formulate another solution, short of a reformulation of the court-made misuse doctrine. If misuse had been found for refusal to license the nonstaple and the injunction denied to the patent owner, thus permitting sales by competitors subject to the payment of royalties, a distinction would have been preserved between the property incidents of patented inventions and unpatented 'essential nonstaples.' The merits of this solution, as advocated by the dissenting justices in Dawson, in balancing the antithetical doctrines of contributory infringement and patent misuse can be debated. Some merit must, nonetheless, be attributed to any solution by which, in the words of Mr. Justice Cardozo, 'Consistency was preserved, logic received its tribute. . . .'[9]

Notes and Comments

1. Samuel Oddi received a B.S. in Electrical Engineering from Carnegie–Mellon University, a J.D., from the University of Pittsburgh School

---

9. B. Cardozo, The Nature of the Judicial Process 42 (1921).

of Law, and an Ll.M. from George Washington University School of Law. He taught at Northern Illinois University College of Law, and now teaches at the University of Akron School of Law.

2. The key issue in *Dawson*—the staple versus nonstaple nature of an unpatented component sold for use in a patented process—is important to the commercial prospects of some process patents. In Hodosh v. Block Drug Co., Inc., 833 F.2d 1575 (Fed. Cir. 1987), for example, the Federal Circuit confronted a process patent entitled "Method for Desensitizing Teeth." The preferred embodiment, and commercial product, was a form of toothpaste containing potassium nitrate. The accused infringer, which sold similar toothpaste, argued that potassium nitrate was a "staple article," and therefore there could be no infringement. The Federal Circuit disagreed, citing *Dawson* and noting that it is the entire product, and not just an ingredient, which must be a staple to escape infringement under *Dawson*.

3. Professor Oddi, siding with the dissent in *Dawson*, appears to endorse a "liability rule" entitlement for unpatented "essential nonstaples"—that is, he would require an infringer to pay royalties for sales of these items, but would not support granting an injunction against selling them. As he mentions, the Supreme Court has not endorsed such a "middle ground" solution in the area of patents. For a defense of strong property rights entitlements in this area, see Robert P. Merges, "Of Coase, Property Rules, and Intellectual Property," 94 *Colum. L. Rev.* 2655 (1994). For contrary views, see Pankaj Tandon, "Optimal Patents with Compulsory Licensing," 90 *J. Pol. Econ.* 470 (1982); Colleen Chien, "Cheap Drugs at What Price to Innovation: Does the Compulsory Licensing of Pharmaceuticals Hurt Innovation?," 18 *Berkeley Tech. L.J.* 853 (2003) (concluding, on the basis of empirical research concerning firms that have been subject to antitrust-related compulsory licensing decrees, that R & D in these firms has not declined, and that therefore fears concerning the harmful consequences of compulsory licenses may be unfounded). For creative proposals mixing both types of entitlements, see Abraham Bell and Gideon Parchomovsky, "Pliability Rules," 101 *Mich. L. Rev.* 1, 71–72 (2002); Martin J. Adelman, "Property Rights Theory and Patent–Antitrust: The Role of Compulsory Licensing," 52 *N.Y.U. L. Rev.* 977, 999 (1977) (proposing a compulsory licensing rule that once a patentee has issued more than one license, it is required to issue as many more as are requested).

4. A recent case centering on patent damages raised issues conceptually quite similar to those at issue in *Dawson*: may a patentee collect lost profit damages when an infringer's sales reduce the patentee's sales of products that are related to, but not actually covered by, the infringed patent? The Federal Circuit answered yes, over a spirited dissent by Judge Nies which sounds many of the same themes of the *Dawson* dissenters whose views are described by Professor Oddi. See Rite–Hite Corp. v. Kelley Co., 56 F.3d 1538 (Fed. Cir. 1995) (en banc).

D. Remedies

An Economic Analysis of Damages Rules in Intellectual Property Law*

ROGER D. BLAIR
THOMAS F. COTTER

Our principal thesis is that the optimal set of damages rules should preserve both the incentive structure of intellectual property law and the property-like character of intellectual property rights. As we demonstrate herein, in the absence of enforcement, information, and other transaction costs, these goals require at a minimum an award that renders the infringer no better off as a result of the infringement. As a first approximation, then, the optimal rule is to award the plaintiff the royalty to which the parties would have agreed prior to the infringement, in cases in which the infringer is a more efficient user of the subject property than is the plaintiff, or the defendant's profit attributable to the infringement in cases in which he is not. After eliminating the assumption of zero costs from the model, however, this rule must be modified in two crucial respects. First, to preserve the owner's incentive to create and to publish, in cases in which for whatever reason the rule fails to deter, the owner always should be able to recover her own lost profit resulting from the infringement. Second, in order to avoid having courts determine the value of intellectual property and to encourage the parties to engage in voluntary bargaining ex ante, the defendant always should be required to disgorge all of his profit attributable to the infringement, unless this would result in a double recovery. As a second approximation, then, the optimal rule is to award the plaintiff the greater of either her lost profits or the defendant's profit resulting from the infringement. On its face, this rule appears to provide the correct incentives for optimal use, inasmuch as lost profits will exceed the defendant's profit only when the plaintiff is a more efficient user than is the infringer, and vice versa.

As we also demonstrate, however, this second approximation may be subject to further modification in light of two additional factors that inject considerable uncertainty into the analysis. The first is that an award that merely renders the infringer no better off as a result of the infringement may be an ineffective deterrent, because only a portion of all possible infringements are susceptible of detection. This insight suggests that a substantial damages multiplier often may be necessary to achieve adequate deterrence. The second is that the standard of liability in intellectual property cases often is uncertain and that in some instances ... the infringer will have incurred substantial sunk costs by the time his infringement is detected. These facts suggest that, on occasion, the optimal award should be lower than the initial model would advise, in order to avoid the overdeterrence of marginally lawful conduct.

* Reprinted by permission from 39 Wm. & Mary L. Rev. 1585 (1997–1998), © 1998, William and Mary Law Review.

As a third approximation, then, the optimal rule is to award the prevailing plaintiff the greater of either a compensatory or restitutionary recovery, suitably enhanced or diminished in light of the competing interests in deterring infringements that otherwise may go undetected, and in discouraging would-be users from overcomplying with their legal obligations.

In a suit for patent infringement, the court may award the prevailing plaintiff injunctive relief, as well as "damages adequate to compensate for the infringement, but in no event less than a reasonable royalty for the use made of the invention by the infringer, together with interest and costs as fixed by the court." "Damages adequate to compensate for the infringement" may include an award of the plaintiff's lost profits attributable to the infringement, the amount of an established royalty, or a reasonable royalty. Significantly, the courts have interpreted the language quoted above as preventing them from awarding the plaintiff a restitutionary recovery consisting of the defendant's profits attributable to the infringement; as we shall demonstrate, patent law stands alone among the four branches of intellectual property law in forbidding a recovery of this nature under any circumstances. The court has the authority to "increase the damages up to three times the amount found or assessed," but normally it will exercise this discretion only in cases of willful infringement or bad faith litigation. The statute also permits the court to award attorneys' fees to the prevailing party "in exceptional cases," generally those in which either the defendant is found to have willfully infringed or the plaintiff obtained the patent by fraud or brought the action in bad faith. Finally, prejudgment interest usually is awarded to the prevailing plaintiff as a matter of course.

A substantial number of the law and economics scholars who have written on this subject appear to agree that it is generally preferable to protect intellectual property rights through the use of property, as opposed to liability, rules. As Merges has explained, in the context of a discussion of patents that is equally applicable to the other branches of intellectual property law:

> [A] property rule makes sense ... because: (1) there are only two parties to the transaction, and they can easily identify each other; (2) the costs of a transaction between the parties are otherwise low; and (3) a court setting the terms of the exchange would have a difficult time doing so quickly and cheaply, given the specialized nature of the assets and the varied and complex business environments in which the assets are deployed. Hence the parties are left to make their own deal.[1]

For these reasons, Merges and other scholars contend that compulsory licensing schemes, under which the owner of an intellectual property right must license users at some statutorily or judicially fixed rate, are less efficient than a system of property-like protection. Although recognizing that transaction costs and other bargaining obstacles may sometimes threaten to impede efficient transfers from going forward, these scholars suggest that the available methods for reducing these obstacles

---

1. [Robert Merges, Intellectual Property Rights and Bargaining Breakdown: The Case of Blocking Patents, 62 Tenn. L. Rev. 75, 78 (1994).]

within the framework of a property-rule system are more likely to induce the movement of rights to their highest-valued uses than would a liability-rule regime.

For purposes of this analysis, we shall assume that property rules are more likely than liability rules to encourage the efficient use of intellectual property. Developing a set of damages rules is, nevertheless, also necessary, as long as some infringements are likely to go undetected or unremedied for some period of time, to ensure that the purposes underlying the various bodies of intellectual property law are not frustrated. If a property-like entitlement structure is generally preferable, however, for the protection of intellectual property rights, then these damages rules should be largely ancillary to that structure; in other words, the rules should be designed so that the infringer is no better off than he would have been had he been enjoined from using the property ab initio. If this analysis is correct, then it suggests, for reasons explored below, that the standard measure of damages in intellectual property cases generally should be either the restitution of the infringer's profits or an award of compensatory damages, whichever is greater, subject to various context-specific adjustments. In the following Part, this model is developed further, and then [later in the Article] we attempt to discover whether the ways in which the actual rules differ from the model are consistent with an efficiency rationale.

III. A General Theory of Damages Rules

In this Part, we begin by modeling the incentive structure facing both the innovator and the potential infringer of the innovator's intellectual property. Applying the insights derived from this analysis, we then construct a simple model of optimal damages rules. . . .

A. *Preserving the Incentive to Create*

The decision to invest in the creation of intellectual property is often accompanied by uncertainty concerning matters such as the cost that will be incurred in attempting to produce the desired innovation; whether the attempt to produce will be successful; and, assuming that the attempt is successful, what the profit will be from the subsequent commercial exploitation of the innovation. In order to focus on what concerns us, however, let us assume initially that both the cost [C] and the profit [π] that will result if the creative venture is successful are known. Let P represent the probability of success ... At the initial stage, the potential creator's expected return E[R] ... may be [stated] as:

$$E[R] = P\pi - C,$$

i.e., the expected return equals the expected profit minus the cost of the creative effort.

Next, let us assume in addition that the profit to be derived from a successful creative effort is subject to uncertainty due to the possibility of infringement. If the expected value of the profit given a successful creative effort is below π, then the incentive to invest is reduced. To preserve the incentive to create intellectual property, then, it is important to devise damages rules that leave π unchanged. One way to accomplish this is to compensate the creator so that she is no worse off as a result of any infringement. Another way is to deter infringement, thereby preventing any deterioration in π in the first instance.

B. *Deterring Infringement*

[The authors demonstrate that it is necessary to reward a property right holder with a multiplier of actual damages if there is some chance the infringement will go undetected. This is the only way to deter infringement under these circumstances.]

* * *

[A detailed analysis shows that] if the infringer is a more efficient producer than the patentee, the short-term optimal result is for the infringer to use the work, either with or without the patentee's permission. To the extent that the incentive theory[2] is correct, however, permitting the infringer to use the patent without authorization will inhibit future inventors from investing in the creation or dissemination of similar information; to the extent that the prospect theory is correct, the infringer's unauthorized use threatens to inhibit the patentee from efficiently coordinating investment in invention improvements. The better result, then, if either theory is correct, is to require that the infringer pay for a license. In the alternative, if the patentee is the more efficient user of the invention, the optimal result is for the infringer to avoid using the patent altogether. This result will follow automatically because the potential infringer will not be able profitably to obtain a license from the patentee. (Moreover, since real-world transaction costs are never zero, this result should be optimal as well when the patentee and infringer are equally efficient users of the patented invention.) In the absence of enforceable patent rights, however, the infringer's incentive in either case would be to use the patent without compensation as long as the cost of appropriating it is less than or equal to the cost of negotiating for and purchasing a license, conditions that thus far have been assumed. The question therefore arises how to craft a set of damages rules that will encourage the would-be infringer to purchase a license in the first instance, and to avoid use altogether in the second.

The analysis above suggests that the answer to this question will vary, depending upon whether the would-be infringer is a more or less efficient user of the patented invention than is the patentee. If the would-be infringer is less efficient than, or as efficient as, the patentee— meaning that the former's marginal cost curve is greater than or equal to the latter's—then the minimal sanction necessary to induce him to refrain from use is the profit attributable to the infringement. Requiring the less-efficient user to disgorge his profit, in other words, should deter unauthorized use because the infringer is no better off as a result of the infringement. Alternatively, if the infringer is the more efficient user, then the minimal sanction necessary to deter infringement (and, concomitantly, to induce the user to seek a license) is not the entire profit attributable to the infringement, but rather only the amount of the royalty R that the parties would have agreed upon ex ante as a condition

[2. For a discussion of the incentive theory of patents, see the excerpt from Fritz Machlup, An Economic Review of the Patent System, *supra* p. 51; on the "prospect theory," see the excerpt that follows this one, Edmund Kitch's "Nature and Function of the Patent System."]

of the more efficient party's use. As noted above, this amount will be less than or equal to the profit attributable to the infringement. An award of the lost royalty, then, like an award of restitution in the preceding case, renders the would-be infringer no better off as a result of the infringement, and therefore should be sufficient to deter his unauthorized use.
* * *

To restate these conclusions as simply as possible, the analysis thus far suggests that courts should award the prevailing patentee either her own lost profit attributable to the infringement or the defendant's profit attributable thereto, whichever is greater, and in either case suitably enhanced or diminished as necessary for the purpose of achieving optimal deterrence.

The principal way in which patent damages rules depart from the model, as well as from the rules that govern in copyright and trademark law, is by not permitting the prevailing plaintiff to recover the infringer's profits attributable to the infringement. The reason usually cited for prohibiting restitutionary awards in patent cases is one of cost. In a report on the 1946 amendments to the Patent Act, for example, the House of Representatives Committee on Patents cited the difficulty of accurately determining the amount of profits attributable to an infringement, as well as the attendant cost and delay, as reasons for limiting the prevailing plaintiff to an award of compensatory damages. Our analysis ... suggests that, at least in theory, this reasoning is not altogether implausible. If these costs are high enough, they may outweigh any efficiency gains derived from permitting such a recovery and may overdeter potential users from making, using, or selling inventions that are lawful, albeit only slightly beyond the scope of the patent's claims.

We nevertheless are inclined to agree with Dam[2] that the flat prohibition of restitutionary awards in patent cases is unwarranted. Granted, the calculation of profits attributable to an infringement often will be a difficult task and very likely will involve some uncertainty in the estimation process. Awards of this nature nevertheless are permitted in cases involving design patents, trade secrets, copyrights, and trademarks; and it is not readily apparent why an award of profits should be substantially more difficult to assess in these types of cases than in utility patent litigation. More importantly, in cases in which the infringer is more efficient than the patentee, the alternative to awarding restitution is to award a reasonable royalty—i.e., "a hypothetical royalty resulting from arm's length negotiations between a willing licensor and a willing licensee." Any expectation that a court can more easily calculate this hypothetical figure than it can the profit attributable to the infringement strikes us as fatuous; indeed, as we suggested above, it is precisely because courts are likely to be incapable of accurately assessing the value of such hypothetical licenses that a restitutionary recovery seems preferable. In any event, as our analysis above indicates, in the typical case the upper limit of the hypothetical royalty will be the profit attributable to the infringement. Any hope that courts can avoid esti-

---

2. See [Kenneth Dam, "The Economic Underpinnings of Patent Law," 23 *J. Leg. Stud.* 247 (1994)] ..., at 256–57.

mating the latter, in the course of determining the amount of a reasonable royalty, therefore would seem doomed to failure.

The good news is that the formal prohibition on restitutionary awards may have little impact upon the courts' actual behavior. Although it is usually considered erroneous to award the prevailing plaintiff 100% of the profit attributable to the infringement, commentators sometimes accuse courts of doing so nonetheless sub silentio. The availability of enhanced damages for willful infringement also limits the effect of the no-restitution rule, to the extent that a plaintiff's actual damages suitably enhanced may exceed the amount of the defendant's profits. Our analysis nevertheless suggests that the no-restitution rule by itself makes little economic sense; and that we should take solace in the fact that, thus far at least, the courts and legislatures have chosen not to extend it into the other branches of intellectual property law.

Notes and Questions

1. Roger D. Blair received B.A, M.A. and Ph.D. degrees in economics, from Michigan State University, and teaches in the economics department at the University of Florida. Thomas F. Cotter received B.S., M.S., and J.D. degrees from the University of Wisconsin, and teaches at the University of Florida School of Law.

2. Blair and Cotter's article presaged an upturn in the level of sophistication concerning the computation of patent damages. This trend was influenced in part by the involvement of noted law and economics scholar-turned-Judge Frank Easterbrook in a case involving lost profits damages. See Grain Processing Corp. v. American Maize–Products Co., 893 F.Supp. 1386 (N.D. Ind. 1995) (Easterbrook, J., sitting by designation), aff'd in part, vacated in part, 108 F.2d 1392 (Fed. Cir. 1997), on remand, 979 F.Supp. 1233 (N.D. Ind. 1997) aff'd, 185 F.3d 1341 (Fed. Cir. 1999). For a sampling of commentary, see John W. Schlicher, "Measuring Patent Damages by The Market Value of Inventions—The Grain Processing, Rite–Hite, and Aro Rules," 82 *J. Pat. & Trademark Off. Soc'y*, 503 (2000); Liane M. Peterson, "Grain Processing and Crystal Semiconductor: Use of Economic Methods in Damage Calculations Will Accurately Compensate for Patent Infringement," 13 *Fed. Circuit B.J.* 41 (2003). For a good overview of the pre-*Grain Processing* cases, see Paul M. Janicke, "Contemporary Issues in Patent Damages," 42 *Am. U.L. Rev.* 691 (1993).

3. To what degree should patent damages deter infringers? Do you agree that restitutionary damages ought to be available in patent cases as they are in other areas of intellectual property? Why or why not?

4. A key issue with respect to lost profits damages is whether the patentee would have made any or all of the infringer's sales if the infringer had been barred from the market. From an economist's perspective, the key to answering this question is the "cross-elasticity of demand" between the infringer's and patentee's products. Blair and Cotter, in a subsequent article, address this issue squarely. Roger D. Blair & Thomas F. Cotter, "Rethinking Patent Damages," 10 *Tex. Intell. Prop. L.J.* 1, 19–20 (2001) (noting that "patent litigants rarely estimate the cross-elasticity of demand between the infringing product and the noninfringing alternative, despite the potential usefulness of this information in determining whether the infringement has cost the patentee any sales."). For expansion on these ideas, see Anna F. Kingsbury, "Market Definition in Intellectual Property Law: Should Intellectual Property Courts Use an Antitrust Approach to Market Definition?," 8 *Marq. Intell. Prop. L. Rev.* 63 (2004).

III.   *Limitations, Scope and Institutional Issues*

A.   Patent Scope

The Nature and Function of the Patent System*

EDMUND W. KITCH

This essay argues that the patent system performs a function not previously noted: to increase the output from resources used for technological innovation. Recognition of this function makes it no longer possible to maintain that the patent inevitably reduces the output of the technology it subjects to exclusive control, but it does make more understandable what have heretofore been puzzling features of the patent system and reintegrates the patent institution with the general theory of property rights.

These ideas first crystallized in response to Barzel's essay, "The Optimal Timing Innovations,"[1] where he points out that the exploitation of technological information has much in common with fisheries, public roads, and oil and water pools—all resources not subject to exclusive control. If the rule of first appropriation controls, there will be an inefficiently rapid depletion of the resource. Barzel suggested this problem could be solved if technological monopoly claims could be granted or auctioned off, giving their owner the exclusive right to develop the technological opportunity. What Barzel did not realize is that a patent system can be such a claim system and, indeed, that it is a more sensible system than an auction system would be.

In brief, the view of the patent system offered here conceives of the process of technological innovation as one in which resources are brought to bear upon an array of prospects, each with its own associated sets of probabilities of cost and returns. By a prospect I mean a particular opportunity to develop a known technological possibility. Each

* Reprinted by permission from 20 J. L. & Econ. 265 (1977), © 1977 The University of Chicago Press.

1.   Yoram Barzel, Optimal Timing of Innovations, 50 Rev. Econ. & Stat. 348 (1968).

prospect can be pursued by any number of firms. Not only can any level of resources be used to develop the prospect, but the activities of any one firm need not be disclosed to the others. This process can be undertaken efficiently only if there is a system that tends to assure efficient allocation of the resources among the prospects at an efficient rate and in an efficient amount; if management of each prospect is in the hands of the entity best equipped to manage it; and if information found by one entity is communicated to other firms at an efficient rate. The patent system achieves these ends by awarding exclusive and publicly recorded ownership of a prospect shortly after its discovery. The patent system so viewed is closely analogous to the American mineral claim system for public lands. For expositional convenience, this view of the patent system will be called the prospect theory.

The conventional view of the patent system as a device that enables an inventor to capture the returns from his investment in the invention will be called the reward theory. The reward theory is not questioned on its own terms. Rather, it is argued that the reward theory offers an incomplete view of the functions of the patent system.

Economists formulated and extensively discussed their view of the patent system in the nineteenth century. The occasional discussions found in current literature are all based upon the conceptual structure developed then, although there is wide variation in judgments about the costs and benefits of the system. The patent is a reward that enables the inventor to capture the returns from his investment in the invention, returns that would otherwise (absent secrecy) be subject to appropriation by others. The existence of the reward tends to make the amount of private investment in invention closer to the value of its social product.... Offsetting this benefit of the patent system is the fact that the patent subjects new technology to exclusive control and, assuming that the demand curve for the technology has a negative slope, adversely affects social welfare, *ceteris paribus*.

* * *

I.   PATENTS AS PROSPECTS

This section simultaneously argues three separate points. First, any patent system will have some prospect elements.[2] Second, the rules of a patent system can be adjusted so as to make the prospect function important. Third, the prospect function is a significant, if not the predominate, function of the American patent system as it has operated in fact. The argument focuses on the third point both because it encompasses and illustrates the first two and because it is the most difficult to sustain. The difficulty of making authoritative statements about the effects of a system as complex as the patent system is further complicated by the fact that the American patent system has changed over time. For instance, much of the antitrust law designed to confine the operation of the patent system to its "proper sphere" has been implicitly based upon the reward theory and may have affected the

---

2. The existence of a prospect element has been noted by Steven N. S. Cheung, Property Rights and Inventions: An Economic Inquiry 17 (mimeo May, 1977). He calls the rights "development rights."

ability of the system to perform the prospect function. Consequently, the pre-antitrust, nineteenth-century patent system was probably more of a prospect system than the twentieth-century system has been.

The importance of the prospect function in the American patent system is argued from three features of the system. The first is the scope accorded to patent claims, a scope that reaches well beyond what the reward function would require. Second, there are rules, such as the priority, time-bar, and patentability rules, which force an early patent application whether or not something of value (and hence a reward) has been found. And third, there is the fact that many technologically important patents have been issued long before commercial exploitation became possible. These same three points have played an important role in the antipatent arguments so recurrent in the economic literature, for each is troublesome under the reward theory.[3]

One reason the prospect function of the patent system may have been so long overlooked is that the "hornbook" rule is very misleading—the inventor may not claim more than he has invented, and the claim marks the outer bounds of his rights. We tend to think of an invention as the thing an inventor has made or accomplished, and the rule seems to imply the inventor is confined to that. But the rule is misleading, because the invention as claimed in the patent claims and the physical embodiment of the invention are two quite different things. "A claim is an abstraction and generalization of an indefinitely large number of concrete, physical objects." Thus to illustrate from a nineteenth-century case, an inventor could claim a process of separating fats into glycerine and stearic, margaric and oleic acids through the use of heat, pressure, and water at any temperature and in any apparatus that would work.[4] This is so even though the inventor himself had used only a few of the possible combinations that would work. Such a claim would cover the use of machinery later developed to carry out the process, even if that machinery were far superior to the first inventor's. . . .

The second important feature of the patent system which makes it function as a prospect system are rules which force and permit application early in the development process. The most important forcing rule is the priority accorded to those first to file. In most patent systems, the patent is simply awarded to the first to file. In the American system, the patent is awarded to the first inventor, a technical status almost always obtained by the first to file. The patent application need not disclose a device or process of any commercial value, only a version of the invention that will work. Thus, the applicant can proceed from the positive results to the patent office, and his failure to do so may cost him the patent.

The emphasis on early filing in the patent system is of great practical importance. Multiple inventions of the same thing are not rare.

---

3. The first because the patent exceeds the contribution of the inventor; the second because the choice of the patentee does not take into account the quality of his contribution, which may be less than that of the unsuccessful claimants; and the third because the patent may expire before the invention is worth very much.

4. Tilghman v. Proctor, 102 U.S. 707 (1880) . . .

When technological developments bring something into the realm of the possible, it may be known to many and many may search. If their resources are similar, they will arrive at the goal at about the same time. Therefore, each searcher must fear that he will be second.

The rules of the American system that force early application are extensive. The person who is the first to file is, in the event of a second claimant, accorded the same status of a senior party. Although he has no absolute right to the patent, he can be dislodged by the second to file (the "junior" party) only if the junior files not later than one year after the senior patent issues and can prove that he is the first inventor. This proof must be by the preponderance of the evidence, or if the junior party files after the senior party's patent has issued, beyond a reasonable doubt. The rules for establishing prior inventorship are quite demanding and rather metaphysical.

In addition, there are "time-bar" rules that make a patent invalid if the application is filed more than one year after a commercial use, or after a publication describing the invention. Since the commercial or publication may be by others, the bar is not within the inventor's control. And any move by him to make commercial use of the invention—for instance, a contract to sell output from a newly invented process—will activate the time bar.

These forcing rules, however, would be of little effect if a valid patent application had to disclose an invention in fully developed or commercially valuable form. It need not. The application need only disclose an invention that works. If the claim is for a battery, it must produce current—not much, not reliably, nor inexpensively. If the claim is for a copying process, the copies need not be legible, cheap, or useful, but they must in some sense be copies. Indeed, the application need not show that the inventor has actually made the invention work. If the instructions can later be followed and they work, the patent is good.

The combined effect of these rules is that whenever a technological innovation has been discovered, it is risky not to immediately seek a patent—even though the practical significance of the innovation may be but dimly perceived. Indeed, if the actual first discoverer is tardy, he may find someone else has the patent and he is not entitled to use his own discovery. These pressures to immediate application exist because the patent system does not require a finished, commercially relevant invention. It only requires something that works.

That many important inventions are patented early in their development serves only to illustrate how the prospect function operates in the context of specific technology. Many inventions, including many important ones, are patented in a commercially significant form, yet the patented form is trivial . . . compared to the later derived and improved versions. Each significant innovation affects related aspects of the technology with which it interacts. A new industrial process may make possible changes in other phases of the process, in the nature of input materials, in the training and compensation of the work force, or in the geographic location of plants. As its introduction lowers the cost of the output, that output becomes suitable for purposes not previously considered, and so on. Thus each innovation generates shifts in the matrix of technological possibilities, and the realization of the possibilities may have a significance that dwarfs the original invention considered alone. A review of the invention case studies reported by Jewkes, Sawyer, and Stillerman [The Sources of Invention (N.Y.: WW Norton Co., 1969)] shows that the first patentable invention frequently occurs years before the first significant commercial product.

* * *

II. THE PATENT AND THE MINERAL CLAIM:
AN INSTITUTIONAL ANALOGY

The mineral claim system that developed from custom, federal law, and judicial decision in the American West during the last half of the nineteenth century made it possible to pursue the two competing objectives of retaining government ownership of public lands while making it possible for private firms to efficiently find and extract the minerals they contained. In brief, the system that evolved permitted one who found mineralization on the public land to file a claim which gave him the exclusive right to develop the claim. The analogy [between this system and patent law] works in considerable detail.

1. The claimant for the mineral claim need not show that the mineralization is of commercial significance. The mineralization showing required was of surface mineralization which could be found without extensive excavation.[5] Similarly, the patent applicant need not show that his invention has commercial significance.

When oil became a commercially significant mineral in the West, it created substantial problems for the mineral claim system because its presence was not associated with the usual forms of surface mineralization. This meant that searchers had to make large investments in drilling before the exclusive right could be claimed. This problem was finally solved by a federal statute that made it possible for the federal government to grant exclusive mineral leases prior to drilling.[6]

2. Priority was awarded on the basis of the first to discover, stake, and file. The "near miss" lost, without regard to the quality of his efforts nor to the extent of his investment relative to the first claimant.

5. ... "To hold that, in order to constitute a discovery as the basis of the location, it must be demonstrated that the discovered deposit will, when worked, yield a profit, or that the lands containing it are, in the condition in which they are discovered, more valuable for mining than for any other purpose, would be to defeat the object and policy of the law.... No court has ever held that in order to entitle one to locate [that is, establish rights to] a mining claim ore of commercial value, in either quantity or quality, must first be discovered." Curtis H. Lindley, A Treatise on the American Law Relating to Mines and Mineral Lands Within the Public Land States and Territories 768–69 (3rd ed. 1914).

6. Mineral Leasing Act of 1920, 41 Stat. 437 (1920), (current version with 1976 amendments is at 30 U.S.C.A. § 181) (1977). The act applied to deposits of coal, phosphate, sodium, potassium, sulphur, oil, oil shale, and gas. The developments leading up to the 1920 Act are described in Rocky Mountain Mineral Law Foundation, The American Law of Mining I, 71–86 (1976). "The Placer Act proved to be a misfit so as far as oil locations were concerned. The mineral could be reached only at great depth and after tremendous expenditure of money. In line with earlier decisions applicable to mining of hard minerals, the courts held that an oil location was not perfected until actual discovery of oil through drilling." *Id.* at 75.

Similarly, the patent system makes no effort to assess the relative efforts of the claimants.

3. The mineral claim system restricts the area that can be claimed through rules that specify maximum boundaries in relation to the location of the mineralization. In the patent system, the applicant must limit his claims to his invention.

4. The mineral claim system has a set of rules on staking requirements and boundary description which forces the claimant to specifically identify the scope of his claim and distinguish it from the rest of the public domain. In the patent system, the applicant must delimit in "claims" his view of the legal scope of his invention in a separate portion of the document that becomes the patent. If his claims exceed his invention, they are invalid.

5. The mineral claim system has rules designed to eliminate claims that prove unpromising and return them to the public domain. In order to keep a mineral claim in force, the owner must each year perform a certain amount of work on the claim. If his evaluation of the value of the claim is less than the expense of his work, he will abandon it. This function is performed in the American patent system by the limited term and in other systems by additional requirements for maintenance payments.

6. The interests in a mineral claim can be transferred, both before and after the rights to the claim are established. The same rule applies in the patent system.

One of the functions of the mineral claim system on the public lands of the West was to create incentives for prospectors to pack their burros and walk off into the desert in search of mineralization. It is misleading to suggest, however, that this was the only, or indeed the principal, function of the system. Although the existence of the system tended to generate the socially optimum level of investment in prospecting, most would agree it is erroneous to suggest that its effect was to reduce the mineral output from lands made subject to exclusive ownership as the result of its operation.

This familiar result in the mining case is offered not as proof that the results of the patent system are the same, but as an analogy to assist the reader unfamiliar with the patent system in thinking about the prospect function. The mining case is usually seen as one with a horizontal demand curve for the mineral output—the standard competitive case. This model makes the efficiency results easy to see since there is no problem of monopoly constraint on production. Conversely, the patent case is always visualized as one of a demand curve with a negative slope and its attendant monopoly effects. In fact, the demand conditions faced by particular mines and particular patents vary widely. Demand conditions will depend upon the relationship of a mine's output to the total market supply, the market being defined in a way that takes into account the ore quality, mining cost, and geographic location of a mine. Many patents face competition from other processes or products. The question of whether the gains from unified control are greater than or less than the losses caused by the ability of the controlling entity to exercise market power is a question that could be examined in the case of each individual mine and each individual patent. A rule that changed the property rights in each individual case where the balance was adverse to society would entail heavy administrative costs and, because it would cast uncertainty over the ownership rights of the successful—and hence economically important—cases, would significantly undermine the functions of the property right system. In both cases the effect of the property rights on social welfare cannot be assessed without examining the demand conditions actually faced by owners of the rights and assessing the output increasing efficiency effects of the property system.

* * *

[A] patent "prospect" increases the efficiency with which investment in innovation can be managed. As already noted, Barzel pointed out that technological information is a resource which will not be efficiently used absent exclusive ownership. Barzel concentrated on the time dimension, but the result is well known and applies to all dimensions of the investment process. But unlike fisheries, public roads, and the other types of goods usually considered, technological information can be used without signaling that fact to another. Fishing boats can be detected, and one who is considering entry can take into account the magnitude of his competitor's activities. And if the fishery is depleted, that fact is likely to be immediately telegraphed by the absence of working boats. But in the area of technological innovation, it is possible for a firm working in secrecy to enter upon a "prospect," investigate it extensively, and depart without a trace. Subsequent investigation of the same prospect by other firms can neither build on the knowledge obtained by the first searcher nor determine the efficient level and strategy of search based upon his failure. Thus the potential gains from exclusive ownership are particularly large. No one is likely to make significant investments searching for ways to increase the commercial value of a patent unless he has made previous arrangements with the owner of the patent. This puts the patent owner in a position to coordinate the search for technological and market enhancement of the patent's value so that duplicative investments are not made and so that information is exchanged among the searchers.

Second, the patent owner has an incentive to make investments to maximize the value of the patent without fear that the fruits of the investment will produce unpatentable information appropriable by competitors. This is important only if the development of the patented inventions generally requires significant investments that lead to unpatented information a competitor can appropriate. Expenditures for such things as manufacturing plants that cannot be appropriated under basic property concepts by competitors need not concern us. In the case of many patents, extensive development is required before any commercial application is possible—for example the laser, the transistor, nylon, and xerography. The investments may be required simply to apply existing technology to the manufacture and design of the product and be so mechanical in their application as to be unpatentable. In any case, their patentability is impossible to predict in advance of their development. Nevertheless, they can be large and produce information as to product manufacture and design that would be appropriable by competitors absent the original patent.

Even in the case of an innovation patented in fully commercial form—as is the case with many relatively trivial patents—the firm must make significant investments to simply distribute and market the invention. But expenditures necessary to identify the market for the product and to persuade potential customers of its utility can easily be captured by competitive imitations. Absent a patent on the product, the incentives to provide information to purchasers about their need for a product as opposed to information about the particular characteristics of the seller's product are limited. The trademark law protects only the names and symbols identifying the seller's product; it confers no protection against imitators of the product itself. Thus competitors can ride on the demand for the product created by the first seller without incurring the expenses necessary to inform buyers of the advantages of the product. Only in the case of a patented product is a firm able to make the expenditures necessary to bring the advantages of the product to the attention of the customer without fear of competitive appropriation if the product proves successful. This aspect of the cost of introducing innovations is stressed here both because managements find that marketing is a major cost in innovation and to illustrate that even in the case where nothing remains but to make and sell the patented invention, there are significant costs whose return could be appropriated by competitors. Absent a patent, firms have less than the optimal incentive to invest in providing information about and techniques for using the new technology.

Third, a patent system lowers the cost for the owner of technological information of contracting with other firms possessing complementary information and resources. A firm that has a design for a new product or process needs to be able to obtain financing, knowledge about or use of complementary technology, specialized supplies, and access to markets. Unless the firm already possesses the needed inputs, it must enter into contracts. The practical difficulties of entering into contracts concerning trade secrets are spelled out in the applied legal literature. Disclosure of the secret imperils its value, yet the outsider cannot negotiate until he knows what the secret is. Disclosure under an obligation of confidence strengthens the discloser's legal position but may prove costly to the receiver, who must accept the obligation before he knows the secret. The patent creates a defined set of legal rights known to both parties at the outset of negotiations. And although the patent will seldom disclose the real value of the patent, the owner can disclose such information protected by the scope of the legal monopoly. Indeed, most know-how or trade-secret licensing take place within the framework of patent rights, the agreement involving both a license of the patent and an undertaking to disclose how to apply the technology efficiently. This reduced transaction cost increases the efficiency with which inventions can be developed.

Fourth, a patent system enables firms to signal each other, thus reducing the amount of duplicative investment in innovation. Once a patent has been issued, other firms can learn of the innovative work of the patent holder and redirect their work so as not to duplicate work already done. Indeed, the patent gives its owner an affirmative incentive to seek out firms and inform them of the new technology, even before issuance, if the most efficient and hence patent-value-optimizing way to exploit the invention is to license it. Under a regime of trade secrecy, the competitive firm might never learn of a competitor's processes and would not learn of the technology incorporated in a new product until it was marketed. During this period, the investments made in a search for technology already invented by others is wasted. This private incentive to disseminate information about the invention should be distinguished from the reward for disclosure theory traditionally discussed. That theory assumes that the disclosure effect of the patent system comes from the disclosure on the public record.

After a patent is issued, other firms have an incentive to invent substitute technologies even if the substitute technology is less efficient than the patented technology but can be produced more cheaply than the existing royalty rate. Even more efficient inventions should not, from a social point of view, be produced unless the cost of producing them is less than or equal to their saving over the existing technology, absent any royalty on that technology. . . .

Fifth, a patent system reduces the cost of maintaining control over technology. Under a trade secret system, the owner must control access to the technology and make specially tailored arrangements with those who must have access to it. These precautions can affect the cost of using a process or developing a product. Resources devoted to keeping the technology secret are saved, just as legal protection of property rights generally reduces the need for investment in self-help.

* * *

Industrial organization economists have tended to view the unification of control of patents that perform economically competing functions as a standard problem of horizontal merger. Where the market share of the unified patents is significant, they have tended to see a loss of competition in an important factor of production.

Introduction of the prospect function greatly complicates this problem. The prospects generated by the patent system are largely shaped by technological history. Ownership of different parts of what can be most efficiently exploited as one prospect may be in different hands. The only way to obtain the efficiency gains of a prospect may be to permit the parties to rearrange control of the various patents involved.

To return to the mineral claim analogy, a claim system may generate separate ownership rights in areas that upon further development turn out to be subject to the most efficient exploitation under unified control. For instance, a single main shaft may be sufficient for all mines, or the works of one mine may threaten the safety of another. Unification of control may provide the most efficient solution. Similarly, two patents may be so closely related that it makes sense to look for improvements to both at once, or, conversely, the search for improvements to one may carry the risk that that improvement will infringe the other.

Consider the situation in the cracking patents case. This technology developed without any single firm obtaining a dominant pioneering patent. Ownership of patents relating to numerous different but closely related cracking processes was dispersed in a large number of firms. Process innovations were occurring rapidly and all the firms were searching for improvements. If ownership of the patents was not unified, then each firm would have to shape its research program in relation to its patent position although that might not be the most efficient research strategy. Thus firm *A* would not look for improvements to the patented processes of firm *B*, and vice versa. These considerations did not escape the Court's notice. "An interchange of patented rights ... is frequently necessary if technical advancement is not to be blocked by threatened litigation."[7]

Notes and Questions

1. For biographical information on Edmund Kitch, see p. 110, supra.

2. One of the most-cited aspects of this article is Kitch's use of the "mining clam analogy." This analogy had been suggested earlier. See George E. Frost, "Legal Incidents of Non–Use of Patented Inventions Reconsidered," 14 *Geo. Wash. L. Rev.* 273, 279 n.24 (1946) ("An interesting analogy may be drawn between the law relating to patents for inventions and the mining law, an analogy which emphasizes the fact that patents are only one of the many situations where an exclusive grant is provided to encourage effort and capital investment."). But Kitch fleshed out the analogy, and drew attention to the underlying economic logic uniting the two fields. It is interesting that some recent research regarding holders of overlapping oil field development rights shows that multiple rightholders do not always reach efficient development agreements, and that various forms of governmental intervention may be more effective. See Steven N. Wiggins & Gary D. Libecap, "Oil Field Unitization: Contractual Failure in the Presence of Imperfect Information," 75 *Am. Econ. Rev.* 368 (1985); Gary D. Libecap, Contracting for Property Rights (Cambridge, England: Cambridge University Press, 1989).

3. In support of his argument that the U.S. patent system encourages early filing—and hence, the staking of early claims to prospects—Kitch recites a number of doctrines in U.S. patent law. There is no question that early filing is one of several goals at the heart of various doctrines. But there is also a counter-thrust, reflected particularly in the utility doctrine, against filing *too early*. For general economic discussion of this issue, see See Dean Lueck, "The Rule of First Possession and the Design of the Law," 38 *J.L. & Econ.* 393 (1995). For a discussion of this issue in the context of patents for genes and gene fragments, see Matthew Erramouspe, "Staking Patent Claims on The Human Blueprint: Rewards and Rent-Dissipating Races," 43 *UCLA L. Rev.* 961 (1996). Kitch also states that the U.S. "first to invent" rule almost always produces the same result as the "first to file" rule in other countries, and hence in effect reflects an early filing policy. A recent study calls into doubt

---

7. Standard Oil v. United States, 283 U.S. 163, 171 (1931).

whether the two priority rules really do produce the same outcome in most cases. See Mark Lemley and Colleen V. Chien, "Are the U.S. Priority Rules Really Necessary?," 54 *Hastings L.J.* 1299, 1309 (2003) ("[I]n ... 76 cases [studied in the article] ..., junior parties won 33 times (or 43%). Thus, it seems that when priority is actually adjudicated, the first to invent is quite frequently not the first to file."). Again, this does not contradict Kitch's point that early filing is a goal of the U.S. system; it merely points out that the system reflects other goals as well.

4. Kitch states: "The question of whether the gains from unified control are greater than or less than the losses caused by the ability of the controlling entity to exercise market power is a question that could be examined in the case of each individual mine and each individual patent." Numerous commentators have taken up the theme of the costs and benefits of "unified control." The excerpt that follows from Merges and Nelson is in part an extended critique and comment on the "unified control" theory. For other discussions of this issue, see Scott Kieff, "Property Rights and Property Rules for Commercializing Inventions", 85 *Minn. L. Rev.* 697, 707 n.47 (2001); John F. Duffy, "Rethinking the Prospect Theory of Patents," 71 *U. Chi. L. Rev.* 439 (2004).

5. Kitch identifies two sorts of follow-on costs that must be incurred to bring a new invention to market: (1) technological development costs, i.e., the costs of scaling up a product, making it manufacturable, etc.; and (2) marketing and information costs. Both, he says, justify the grant of a property right that compensates an inventor for more than the simple cost of invention—i.e., a broader right than would be required under a simple "reward for invention" theory. Yet more recent scholarship points out that, as an empirical matter, patents are in a fair number of cases not the most effective means by which firms recoup R & D investments. See the Levin, Nelson et al. excerpt in this volume, at p. 61. In addition, firms appear to be quite sophisticated about intermixing various "appropriability mechanisms", which suggests that there may be non-patent means for recouping the higher costs Kitch identifies. See, e.g., David J. Teece, "Profiting from Technological Innovation: Implications for Integration, Collaboration, Licensing and Public Policy," 15 *Res. Pol'y* 294 (1986).

6. Kitch points out that patents facilitate transactions as much as they encourage inventive effort. The seminal work in this respect is by Kenneth Arrow. See Kenneth Arrow, "Economic Welfare and the Allocation of Resources for Invention," in The Rate and Direction of Inventive Activity: Economic and Social Factors 609 (National Bureau of Economic Research) (Princeton, N.J.: Princeton University Press 1962). For a discussion of these issues from the point of view of the "boundaries of the firm," i.e., which transactions are organized by contract and which must be conducted inside a unified firm, see Ashish Arora and Robert P. Merges, "Specialized Supply Firms, Property Rights, and Firm Boundaries," 13 *Ind. & Corp. Change* 451 (2004); Dan L. Burk, "Intellectual Property and the Theory of the Firm," 71 *U. Chi. L. Rev.* 3 (2004).

On the Complex Economics of Patent Scope*
ROBERT P. MERGES
RICHARD R. NELSON

The economic significance of a patent depends on its scope: the broader the scope, the larger the number of competing products and processes that will infringe the patent. Many theoretical papers have tried to assess the effects of fine tuning various aspects of the patent system to make it more efficient. But only a few have focused on patent scope, even though scope decisions are subject to far more discretion than most of the aspects more intensively studied.

Furthermore, most theoretical writing on patents is directed toward issues that as a practical matter are considered largely settled. For example, several economists have explored the question of optimal patent duration. Their work did have a direct impact on the decision to extend patent terms on pharmaceuticals to compensate for regulatory lag. But despite the scholarly attention to patent duration, the term of most patents remains fixed.... Likewise, there has been considerable debate over the years on the merits of compulsory licensing of patents under some circumstances, yet the intellectual property community has repeatedly rejected the idea. Thus, while the literature continues to generate interesting questions about bedrock assumptions and practices, it has little bearing on the everyday operations of the patent system. This Article is an attempt to redress this deficiency by analyzing the economic effects of patent scope.

The Patent Office and the courts are constantly making patent scope decisions. The Patent Office does so when it determines the claims it will allow on a specific patent. The courts do so in litigation, where questions of patent infringement are decided. In the former context, the applicant wants to claim as much as she can, and the Patent Office must decide what claims are allowable. While decisions regarding what to allow are constrained by a number of legal principles, and by the invention itself, in many cases the Patent Office has considerable room for discretion. Within that discretionary zone, the Office must decide which claims should be admitted and which ones pruned back or rejected.

* * * Our own exploration of the economics of patent scope has led us to focus on very much the same kinds of issues as raised by [Professor Edmund] Kitch. We proceed as follows: We begin by considering the legal doctrines that define a patent's scope, then identify the room for discretion which often exists, and point out areas of consistency and inconsistency in current practice. Next, we develop an economic analysis that illuminates the central issues at stake in varying permissible patent scope. This analysis differs from standard economic models by moving beyond the two-dimensional analysis of incentives and deadweight loss.

Much of our discussion will center on the post-invention environment for development and subsequent improvements. By contrast, the

* Reprinted with permission from 90 Colum. L. Rev. 839, © 1990 Columbia Law Review, Robert Merges, and Richard Nelson.

work of [William] Nordhaus and others is concerned with conditions surrounding the initial invention. One way to describe our approach is to view it as a broadening of what counts as an incentive to invent or as a social cost of issuing patents. The concept of incentives, in our view, should embrace post-invention conditions favorable to the inventor, such as extension of an initial patent to cover subsequently-developed versions of the invention. Likewise, the notion of a patent's social costs should include its potential to reduce competition in the market for improvements to the patented technology.

Like Kitch, then, we see the important question as how patent scope decisions influence the development of a technology, both in the sense of an individual invention and that of a future line of improvements extending from it. However, contrary to what Kitch suggests, we do not presume that granting broad scope to an initial inventor induces more effective development and future invention. We regard this as an open question.

Our analysis differs from the existing literature on patents in a second way as well. This literature tends to assume that invention is the same in all technologies. In contrast, we develop several models of technical advance in industry, models that differ in terms of how various inventions are related to each other. These models are designed to highlight and capture the different ways in which technical advancement proceeds in different fields. One of our major objectives is to show that the issues at stake regarding patent scope depend on the nature of technology in an industry. This dependence includes two characteristics: the relationship between technical advances in the industry, and the extent to which firms license technologies to each other.

Theoretical argument alone, however, cannot resolve the question of whether technical advance proceeds more vigorously and effectively under competition or under a regime where one person or organization has a considerable amount of control over developments. Therefore we follow our theoretical analysis with an empirical-historical examination of the course of technical advance in several industries, guided by the various models we have developed. In each industry, critical rulings regarding the scope of important early patents significantly influenced the subsequent path of the technology. Our focus will be on those critical decisions and their consequences.

We conclude with an attempt to draw lessons regarding appropriate patent scope. Our basic conclusion is this: Without extensively reducing the pioneer's incentives, the law should attempt at the margin to favor a competitive environment for improvements, rather than an environment dominated by the pioneer firm. In many industries the efficiency gains from the pioneer's ability to coordinate are likely to be outweighed by the loss of competition for improvements to the basic invention. Throughout the article we suggest ways that patent doctrine can be applied to carry out this goal.

[After discussing the "reverse doctrine of equivalents," which explicitly considers the merits of an accused infringing device, the authors turn to a general analysis of patent infringement, particularly the doctrine of equivalents.]

At first blush, the technical merits of the allegedly infringing device might seem to be irrelevant where literal infringement is concerned. After all, a patent is the right to exclude; an astoundingly meritorious improvement, while no doubt deserving a patent of its own, ought not escape infringement. The improver can patent the improvement, but this should not affect the original patentee's rights.

This is an appealing argument. An economic rationale for improvement patents would stress their tendency to encourage bargaining between improvers and original patentees. To the extent the improver has a very significant cost-saving technology, it would be in the interest of the original patentee to cross-license with the improver, to gain access to the improved technology.

Unfortunately, the original patentee may use her patent as a "holdup" right, in an attempt to garner as much of the value of the improvement as possible. The chances of this being successful depend on the relative contributions of the original patented invention and the improvement to the "original plus improvement" combination. Where the original invention contributes most of the value, or where the original and improvement inventions contribute roughly equal value, issuing an improvement patent may be a reasonable solution. But where the original patent contributes very little value compared to the improvement, the holdup problem may be significant. That is, the holder of the original patent may use it to extract much of the value of the "original plus improvement" combination from the improver. The reverse doctrine of equivalents solves the problem by, in effect, excusing the improver from infringement liability—and therefore removing the original patentee's holdup right. Reverse equivalents, of course, did not evolve in explicit recognition of this problem. But the fear of the inefficient use of holdup power does provide a rational account of the doctrine and might even assist courts in applying it. Note too that the same rationale could be applied to analysis of infringement under the doctrine of equivalents; the more significant the technological advance represented by the allegedly infringing device, the less willing the courts should be to find it an equivalent of the patentee's device.

II. The Economics of the Patent System Revisited

A. *The Social Benefits and Costs of the Patent System*

In most analyses of the different aspects of the patent system, concern has centered on a simple tradeoff. The analysis has concentrated on how changing patent coverage affects the balance between incentives to the inventor and underuse of the invention due to patent monopolies....

However, other analyses of the effects of the patent system open up a much more complex set of issues. These studies recognize that at any time many actors may be in the invention game, and that the game may have many rounds. This broader orientation brings into view the question of how the lure or presence of a strong patent can influence the multiactor portfolio of inventive efforts. It also alerts the analyst to the possible effects of patents on the ability or desire of different parties to stay in the inventing competition over time, and on the efficiency of the inventive effort over the long run.

We believe that analysis of the effects of varying patent scope needs to recognize this dynamic multiactor context.... [One problem with prior articles is that they treat substitute technologies] as if they were already in existence or could be made so trivially. It is here that we find their analysis inadequate. Our concern is with the effects of patent scope decisions on whether or not, and if so how efficiently, these substitutes are created. More importantly, these papers for the most part ignore what we consider a critical set of "substitutes": subsequent inventions that not only substitute for the initial invention, but also improve on it in some way. Since some of the follow-on efforts of inventors could result in something not simply slightly different but significantly better than the patented technology, broad patents could discourage much useful research. Thus, these papers are not of much help in rationalizing and reforming those aspects of legal doctrine that apply to the economically significant class of improvement inventions.

The economic models that do try to encompass multiactor dynamics are quite stylized. In some, invention is analogized to fishing from a common pool. There are many competitive inventors, and the first to make an invention gets the patent on it. Each knows that as others catch (invent) there is less in the pool for her. The result is "overfishing": too many people seeking inventions at once. Other economists have modelled technical advance in terms of a multifirm "race to patent," in which many would-be inventors identify a particular goal, and the first to achieve the goal gets the patent. A good deal of variation has been introduced into these models, with different assumptions being made about such variables as the strength of patents and the costs and benefits of innovating versus imitating. Many of the implications of these models are sensitive to particular assumptions, but some are robust. In particular, under a wide range of assumptions, rivalrous inventive efforts generate a great deal of inefficiency.

Despite the drawbacks of these models, the authors of this paper regard that basic conclusion as persuasive. Not only does proprietary control of technology tend to cause "dead weight" costs due to restrictions on use. (We presume here that in general it is not possible to write licensing agreements to completely offset this problem, a matter to which we will return shortly.) Where invention is rivalrous, the process leading to invention is itself inefficient. With exclusive property rights, we pay both kinds of costs in exchange for the benefits of technical advance. But recognition of the costs of rivalrous inventive efforts leads one to speculate about how these costs might be mitigated. This question is the source of Edmund Kitch's prospect theory.

1. The Prospect Theory.—Edmund Kitch, in formulating his "prospect theory" of patent rights, moved beyond the static tradeoff model mentioned earlier and incorporated into his analysis some of the insights of the common pool models. * * *

Reacting to the inefficiencies highlighted by the fishing models, Kitch clearly has a preference for single-firm domination of a technological prospect. As Kitch recognizes, this can be achieved by licensing, where a number of firms hold patents on components of a key invention. Alternatively, one firm can hold a single dominant patent. In either case, the advantage seen by Kitch is that development is under the control of a single entity. Rivalry is avoided. Planning is possible.

We have trouble with the view that coordinated development is better than rivalrous. In principle it could be, but in practice it generally is not. Much of our case is empirical. But there are sound theoretical reasons for doubting the advantages of centralization.

For one thing, under rivalrous competition in invention and innovation there is a stick as well as a carrot. Block rivalry and one blocks or greatly diminishes the threatened costs of inaction. Kitch assumes a model of individual or firm behavior where if an action is profitable it will be taken, regardless of whether inaction would still allow the firm to meet its desired (but suboptimal) performance goals. Different models of behavior, like Simon's satisficing hypothesis, predict otherwise. As we shall see, there are many instances when a firm that thought it had control over a broad technology rested on its laurels until jogged to action by an outside threat.

More generally, the model of behavior Kitch is employing ignores the limits on cognitive capacity and the tendency to focus on past experience that are characteristics of other models and of organizational behavior as we know it. Once a firm develops and becomes competent in one part of a "prospect," it may be very hard for it to give much attention to other parts, even though in the eyes of others, there may be great promise there. Again, our empirical explorations show many examples of this. Consequently, one might expect that many independent inventors will generate a much wider and diverse set of explorations than when the development is under the control of one mind or organization.

This flags still another limitation of the "pool" or "mining" models. In these models the "fish" or the "minerals" are out there and known (with perhaps some uncertainty) to all parties. But with the technological "prospects," and perhaps even real life mineral prospects, no one knows for sure what possible inventions are in the technological pool. It is not even generally feasible to assign probabilities to possible outcomes on which all knowledgeable people will agree. Indeed different parties are almost certain to see the prospect differently. Because of this uncertainty, development of technology is critically different from other common pool problems. The real problem is not controlling overfishing, but preventing underfishing after exclusive rights have been granted. The only way to find out what works and what does not is to let a variety of minds try. If a property right on a basic invention covers a host of potential improvements, the property right holder can be expected to develop the basic invention and some of the improvements. But we would expect a single rightholder to under-develop—or even ignore totally—many of the potential improvements encompassed by their broad property right.

Of course, Kitch's notions about how a broad patent prospect can be worked out by the patent holder do not preclude involving many minds. However, we regard as fanciful the notion that wider talent can be brought in without real competition through selective licensing practices. A substantial literature documents the steep transaction costs of technology licensing,[8] and there is indirect evidence that these costs increase when major innovations are transferred.[9] Moreover, various studies have indicated that transaction costs tend to be very high if licenses are tailored to particular licensees. It is much simpler to grant roughly identical licenses to all who will pay a standard rate. In our own research, we have not found a single case where the holder of a broad patent used it effectively through tailored licensing to coordinate the R & D of others.

Undoubtedly our position is open to criticism. Rivalry no doubt causes waste. Yet we have little faith in the imagination and willingness of a "prospect" holder to develop that prospect as energetically or creatively as she would when engaged in competition. We are also skeptical about her ability to orchestrate development. Given the way humans and organizations think and behave, we believe we are much better off with considerable rivalry in invention than with too little.

B. Differences in Industrial Patterns of Technical Advance

We have noted earlier that, while most analyses of the effects of the patent system on invention assume implicitly that technical advance proceeds similarly in all industries, this assumption is mistaken: the pattern of technical advance varies significantly from field to field. One of the authors, Nelson, has concluded that at least four different generic models are needed. The first describes discrete invention. A second concerns "cumulative" technologies. Chemical technologies have special characteristics of their own. Finally, there are "science-based" technologies where technical advance is driven by developments in science outside the industry. In each of these models patent scope issues take on a special form. In any industry one or another of these models may be applicable at any given time, or appropriate characterization may require a mix. But the mix differs from industry to industry, and so too, therefore, the salient issues involving patent scope.

What we call the discrete invention model corresponds to much of the standard writing about invention. It assumes that an invention is

8. See, e.g., F. Contractor, International Technology Licensing: Compensation, Costs, and Negotiation 104–05 (1981) (transaction costs averaged over $100,000 for licensing deals studied); D. Teece, The Multinational Corporation and the Resource Cost of International Technology Transfer 44 (1976) (transfer costs constituted over 19% of total project costs in international projects studied)....

9. In addition to the studies by Teece and Contractor, this point is illustrated by the terms of a broad cross-licensing agreement between DuPont and Imperial Chemical Industries, Ltd., of Great Britain. The agreement provided for blanket licensing of all patents owned by the two companies (one of the reasons it was found to have masked a cartel, but "there was a clause allowing either party to remove a 'major invention' from the agreement altogether, so that they could make special terms." 2 W. Reader, Imperial Chemical Industries: A History 52–53 (1975).

discrete and well-defined, created through the inventor's insight and hard work. In the standard discussions it may be recognized that the original invention can be improved, or even that improvement or complementary advances may need to be made if the invention is to be of much use. The basic invention may be amenable to tailoring for different uses or customers. But it is implicit that the invention does not point the way to wide ranging subsequent technical advances. It does not define any broad prospect. There are many inventions that fit this model, and these may be of considerable economic and social value. Two examples are King Gillette's safety razor and the ball point pen.... [O]ther industries reveal a complex system with many components, subcomponents and parts, and technical advance may proceed on a number of different fronts at once. In these industries inventions may enhance some feature of a prior "dominant design," or they may be incorporated into subsequent inventions, or both.

There is much more at stake regarding allowed patent scope in these cumulative technologies than in those where inventions are discrete and stand separately. Particularly when the technology is in its early stages, the grant of a broad-gauged pioneer patent to one party may preclude other inventors from making use of their inventions without infringing the original patent. Two such examples are the Selden patent, which was used to control the development of automobiles, and Edison's successful attack on a broad patent covering light bulb filaments. Thus, a broad pioneer patent may give one party legal control over a large area. Alternatively, in multicomponent products, broad patents on different components held by several inventors may lead to a situation in which no one can or will advance the technology in the absence of a license from someone else. As we shall see, these are not just theoretical possibilities; they describe the development of several important technologies....

Technical advance in the chemical industries has some attributes that fit the discrete invention model, some that fit the cumulative technologies model, and some particular characteristics of its own. A new chemical product is in most cases a discrete entity, or it may encompass a particular class of products, like penicillin. But particular chemical product innovations seldom are the keystones to the development of large numbers of other chemicals. Although there are recognizable families of chemical products, the invention of one chemical species seldom gives more than general guidance in the development of other species. This is primarily a function of the complex and unpredictable relationship between chemical structure and function, most clearly evident in the pharmaceutical industry.

An invention in any of the three regimes described above may be assisted by recent developments in science. But technologies whose advance is predominantly driven by such developments, while rare, warrant special recognition. In these science-based technologies, of which modern biotechnology is a prominent example, research and development efforts attempt to exploit recent scientific developments. These scientific developments tend to narrow and focus perceived technological opportunities in the industry and concentrate the attention of inventors on the same things.

Such science-based technologies warrant analytic distinction for several reasons. In the first place, this is a context that engenders inventive races of the sort described earlier, particularly if it is anticipated that the first to apply a scientific finding will get a patent of considerable scope. Many are rushing toward the same objective that all see as feasible and several will get there, but only the first receives a patent. Second, new scientific and technological developments "in the air" open the possibility of a major advance over prior practice, and the contribution made by the individual or firm who first makes these possibilities operational may be relatively small. The invention may diverge from "prior art," in the sense of actual technological accomplishments, and sweep the market, yet still be only a successful application of knowledge that is apparent to the scientifically sophisticated. When this is a possibility, the patent system should be particularly careful in awarding patents of broad scope. Third, and this is where our focus will be, there is a real danger that allowing patent scope to be overbroad may enable the individual or firm who first came up with a particular practical application to control a broad array of improvements and applications.

We now turn to a more detailed discussion of these models of technical advance, with an eye toward what they can teach us about the effects of patent scope.

III.   Effects of Patent Scope in Various Industries

A.   *Cumulative Technologies*

We have asked two questions about the effects of broad patents on cumulative technologies. One concerns the consequences of "pioneer" patents. We wish to test the validity of the hypothesis that the granting of broad patents is likely to make subsequent invention and development more orderly and productive. The second question is how the presence of broad patents on components of a cumulative technology affects subsequent development.

One must keep in mind, however, what we are not testing. We do not ask whether any patent should have been granted in the following cases. We take it as axiomatic that some degree of patent protection is necessary and desirable. And we do not ask whether the scope of the patents discussed should have been limited to the precise embodiments the inventor had developed when the patents were filed. We accept that patents claiming the general inventive principle were justified; and we focus on the impact of broad scope on the environment for subsequent development and improvement.

1.   Electrical Lighting Industry.—The chain of reasoning in our critique of the prospect theory, and our view of the patent system, is consistent with most of the historical evidence on cumulative technologies. The early electrical illumination industry illustrates this most clearly.

Patents played a very important part in this industry from the beginning. In the field of incandescent lighting, Edison's early patent gave his company, later General Electric, a dominant position. But in certain other sectors, most notably arc lighting and the production of dynamos, efforts to establish dominance via a single broad patent failed. The contrast between these sectors, where entry was easy and competition for improvements was intense, and the incandescent lighting field is noteworthy for our purposes. Most importantly, the history of the early electrical industry supports the notion that broad pioneering patents can play a pivotal role in the evolution of industry structure.

No single patent better illustrates this than Edison's U.S. Patent 223,898, issued in 1880. This was "the basic patent in the early American incandescent-lamp industry," covering the use of a carbon filament as the source of light; it proved to have a profound effect on the industry until it expired.

Although the Edison General Electric Company had some difficulty establishing the validity of its basic patent, once it did the industry changed drastically. In 1891, U.S. Patent No. 223,898 was held valid and infringed by a competing design. General Electric officials then quickly obtained a series of injunctions that shut down a number of competitors. As the aptly-named industry historian Arthur Bright stated, "For twelve years after the issuance of the 223,898 patent competition had been possible; it suddenly became impossible." The company's market share grew from 40 to 75 percent; entry into the industry slowed from 26 new firms in 1892 to 8 in 1894, the last year of the patent's life; and the steady downward trend of lamp prices slowed until the patent expired.

More importantly for our purposes, the validation of Edison's broad patent slowed the pace of improvements considerably.

> Even as the courts were passing on the Edison lamp patent in 1891, the Edison General Electric Company.... [recognized that it] gradually had been slipping backward in its commercial position, particularly since 1886.... Its technological contributions were becoming relatively smaller than they had been during the early [eighteen] eighties.

Thus the broad Edison patent slowed down progress in the incandescent lighting field. The lesson, however, is not that this patent should not have been granted. It is rather a cautionary lesson: broad patents do have a significant impact on the development of a technology and hence on industry structure, and this should be reflected in those doctrines that collectively determine patent scope.

2. Automobiles and Airplanes.—We move now to two infamous cases regarding pioneer patents: the Selden patent in the development of automobile technology, and the Wright patent's influence on the growth of aircraft technology. As we have seen, the Selden patent claimed a basic automobile configuration, one using a light-weight internal combustion engine as the power source. The Wright patent was on a broadly defined airplane stabilization and steering system. In both of these cases, the holders of the pioneer patent engaged in extensive litigation against companies that did not recognize the patent, and the Wrights refused to license theirs. Our question is how the presence of these patents affected the evolution of the technologies.

The Selden patent had as its key claim the use of a light gasoline-powered internal combustion engine. This claim was extremely broad and covered a myriad of possible embodiments. Contrary to the prospect theory, however, neither Selden nor his assignee used the patent to orchestrate the efficient improvement of automobile technology; there was no policy of "developing the prospect." They were willing to license anyone who would acknowledge the validity of the patent and pay royalties; to this end they formed the Association of Licensed Automobile Manufacturers. But the Association's purpose was to collect royalties, and perhaps control competition in the industry, rather than to facilitate orderly technological development.

But did the presence of the Selden patent actually hinder technological progress in the industry? That is perhaps a bit more speculative. Law suits based on it surely did absorb considerable time and attention of people like Henry Ford, whose production methods revolutionized the industry. Perhaps more importantly smaller firms may have been put off by the threat of suit. At this early stage in the history of the technology, those that left the industry or chose not to enter may well have taken valuable improvements with them.

5. Licensing and Cumulative Technologies.—In many of the cases we have examined, licensing and industry consolidation emerged as solutions to patent blockages caused by patents. This would appear to have a bearing on our study. Does the consolidation of the radio industry in RCA, for example, support the position that development would have been more efficient had control been in the hands of one party from the beginning, in the form of one super-patent? Or does it imply that patent breadth was irrelevant—consolidation would have happened even with narrow patents?

The first possibility seems remote, and there is indirect evidence that the second is wrong as well. The fact that many inventors and firms made important advances in various components of radio technology indicates that no one firm had the inventive firepower to develop radio on its own. And there is no reason to believe that one firm could have orchestrated the development of the technology, since there was no way to know in advance which inventors would cultivate expertise in each component, or which inventor's approach would work. There were no "proven" experts in transmission or reception that a firm could have granted licenses to, for example; experts emerged only when their inventions turned out to work. And it would have been impossible to identify all the potential experts, since everyone was working on the various components simultaneously. In any event, the inventive scramble that in fact resulted, while by no means optimal, did result in the fairly rapid commercialization of a complex, multicomponent technology. It also resulted in a patent tangle, one that might have been lessened if some of the key patents had been narrower. But it is difficult to see how a single broad patent would have led to more rapid commercialization. The ex post consolidation, in other words, simply does not imply that a broad ex ante "prospect" would have been effective in this case.

As to the second objection to our analysis—that the radio industry would have consolidated regardless of patent breadth—two points seem relevant. First, narrower patents might have made consolidation unnecessary. If one or more firms could put together a complete radio system without infringing any patents, consolidation would not have been essential, at least for patent-related reasons. One candidate is General Electric: the only essential component for which patent blockage was a problem was the triode; if De Forest's patent had been narrower, or if inventor Edwin H. Armstrong had won his interference with De Forest, General Electric might have put together a noninfringing system.

Second, even if narrower patents would not have prevented the deadlock, they might have helped break it sooner. Perhaps without the value of a "holdup right" on an essential component of radio technology, the firms would have been content to contribute their patents to a pool and compete on the basis of improvements and price competition. Finally, even if this industry eventually consolidated into one firm, there is no promise that all industries will do so.

There is also no reason to assume that when blockages arise industries will always turn to the deadlock-breaking solutions we have seen, patent pooling and cross licensing. Though we saw the emergence of cross licensing among aircraft manufacturers, the impetus was wartime government pressure. In the case of the light bulb industry, the government stayed out; when the firms finally pooled technology, it was only to effectuate the operation of a cartel.

There is therefore no guarantee that pooling, cross licensing, or consolidation will always emerge to break an industry impasse. And without these solutions there is nothing to mitigate the effect of broad basic patents in cumulative technology industries. Earlier we saw that theory offered a number of reasons to be concerned about these patents. The historical evidence available is consistent with this theory. In most instances this evidence can be read as supportive of our concerns about the effects of broad patents on cumulative technology industries. . . .

V. Summary and Conclusions

* * *

In an earlier section of this essay, we suggested an important addition to conventional equivalency analysis. Once a court completes its assessment of the significance of the patented device, it should consider in addition the importance of the advance represented in the accused device. . . . The equivalents inquiry, even for a pioneer patent, should be centered around whether the improved structures of the accused device show major differences from the structures disclosed in the original specification. Specifically, the court should look for differences in the following areas:

- Materials;

- Changes in the number of components;

- Greatly improved efficiency in individual components;

- Increased efficiency in the way components work together, i.e., overall design improvements.

The same point should be borne in mind when a claim covers embodiments that turn out to be well beyond the teaching of the patent's disclosure. This is the case of so-called reverse equivalents. . . .

A more liberal use of reverse equivalents would be especially valuable when the allegedly infringing improvement embodies new technology not available when the patent was issued . . .

The essential point to grasp is that here, as with regular equivalents, courts have their only opportunity to review patent scope in light of later technological developments. They should make good use of the opportunity, with an eye toward preventing the kinds of blockage we have described.

2.   Chemical Industries.—As we saw in our review of the chemical industries, invention in this field has some of the features of discrete and some of cumulative technologies. For the reasons just described, the latter similarity leads us to counsel caution in the awarding of broad patents in this field. But there are two factors that mitigate our concerns somewhat. First is the relative rarity of very broad patents in the chemical field, primarily because of the unpredictability of chemical research.

Second is the very well established practice of licensing in these industries. Some of the examples we have explored bear this out. Because Ziegler was an academic scientist, he had to license his catalyst patents to make money on them. And even a huge chemical company like Imperial Chemical found it necessary to license several competing producers of polyethylene before a 1952 antitrust consent decree made licensing mandatory. The reason is probably the same as for bulk chemicals: no one producer could cover all the markets for applications of the products. There was also an incentive to cross-license; here as elsewhere competing firms embarked on a series of important process improvements. Even the holder of a basic product patent, such as Imperial Chemical with polyethylene, could probably not afford to ignore an economical improvement, even if that meant licensing the product patent to get it.

As described earlier, licensing by no means renders broad patents harmless. But it may indicate an attitude within these industries that reduces the potential blocking effect of a broad patent.

4.   Conclusions.—Our goal has been to show that scope doctrines can be used to approximate the "tailoring" function proposed by economists who model optimal patent length, with an eye toward retaining incentives for subsequent improvements.

Some readers may interpret the position we have detailed above as a reflection of an antipatent bias on our part. Not so. While it may seem at

first blush that any reduction in patent scope—indeed, any lessening of
the patentee's potential reward—may severely undercut the incentive to
invent, we do not believe this is the case. One must keep in mind that
the doctrinal modifications we have suggested will apply only to the
broader claims of a small number of patents, primarily those on pioneering breakthroughs. And even where our suggestions come into play, we
counsel sensitivity to the nature of technical advance in particular
industries. In this connection, we have discussed the limitations of the
prospect theory, insofar as it suggests a preference for broad scope across
industries.

Ultimately it is important to bear in mind that every potential
inventor is also a potential infringer. Thus a "strengthening" of property
rights will not always increase incentives to invent; it may do so for some
pioneers, but it will also greatly increase an improver's chances of
becoming enmeshed in litigation. Indeed this is the very heart of our
case. When a broad patent is granted or expanded via the doctrine of
equivalents, its scope diminishes incentives for others to stay in the
invention game, compared again with a patent whose claims are trimmed
more closely to the inventor's actual results. The same is true of a patent
granted unduly broad scope by the patent office. This would not be
undesirable if the evidence indicated that control of subsequent developments by one party made subsequent inventive effort more effective. But
the evidence, we think, points the other way.

Notes and Questions

1. Robert P. Merges received a B.S. degree from Carnegie–Mellon
University, a J.D. from Yale Law School, and Ll.M. and J.S.D. degrees
from Columbia Law School. He taught at Boston University School of
Law, and now is Wilson Sonsini Goodrich & Rosati Professor of Law at
U.C. Berkeley (Boalt Hall) School of Law, and Professor of Law at U.C.
Davis School of Law. For biographical information on Richard Nelson,
see p. 68, supra.

2. The authors challenge the prospect theory of Kitch on a number of
grounds, all of which center around the notion of a property right holder
as the most efficient coordinator of development avenues for a particular
technology. One aspect of the critique centers on the idea that "many
minds" may be superior to one (institutional) mind in the development
of something as complex as a pioneering technology. The authors cite the
early work of Nobel Prize-winning economist Herbert Simon for this
concept. See, e.g., Herbert A. Simon, Administrative Behavior 118–20
(4th ed. 1997) (describing notion of "satisficing" behavior). More recent
literature in law and economics engages similar themes, comparing a
more "behavioral" model of human behavior that is subject to inherent
mental judgment biases against the neoclassical model of rational maximizing behavior. See, e.g., Behavioral Law and Economics (Cass Sunstein, ed.) (Cambridge, England: Cambridge University Press, 2000);
Gregory Mitchell, "Taking Behavioralism Too Seriously? The Unwar-

ranted Pessimism of the New Behavioral Analysis of Law," 43 *Wm. & Mary L. Rev.* 1907 (2002).

3. For an argument that patent law ought to differentiate even more finely among inventive contexts than the four that Merges and Nelson call for, see Dan L. Burk & Mark A. Lemley, "Is Patent Law Technology-Specific?," 17 *Berkeley Tech. L.J.* 1155 (2002), and Mark A. Lemley and Dan L. Burk, "Policy Levers in Patent Law," 89 *U. Va. L. Rev.* 1575 (2003) (canvassing a wide variety of economic theories of patent law, including prospect theory, and a wide variety of patent doctrines, ranging from enablement to infringement to injunctions, and applying all this to a number of important industries, including biotechnology, chemistry/pharmaceuticals, software, and semiconductors). For a critique of some aspects of the Lemley–Burk approach, see R. Polk Wagner, "Of Patents and Path Dependency: A Comment on Burk and Lemley," 18 *Berkeley Tech. L.J.* 1341, 1342–43 (2003):

> [Burk and Lemley's] exposition makes a rather compelling case against precisely the sort of judicial ventures into technologically-specific innovation policy that they recommend. Instead, their examples of the ongoing struggle to adapt the patent law to technological changes illuminate the undesirability of entangling the patent doctrine in broad, policy-driven technological exceptionalism. As befits an expansive regulatory regime concerned with innovation policy, the patent law is inextricably intertwined with the process and details of technological development. As courts and commentators alike have long recognized, both a challenge and strength of our patent system is the ongoing effort to adapt the legal infrastructure to an ever-changing environment. The patent law—by explicit design—is technologically flexible, with significant adjustment points built into the system. That distinctions in treatment will exist between various technologies is both expected and unremarkable; rather than leveraging these differences for policy effect, the goal should be to embrace the flexibility while retaining the essential strengths of the unified patent system.

Wagner distinguishes between "micro-exceptionalism," the treatment of different inventions and technologies differently under standard patent law doctrines such as nonobviousness and disclosure requirements, and "macro-exceptionalism," the treatment of inventions from different *industries* using different standards. Id., at 1345–47. The former differentiates at the level of individual inventions, or at least areas of technology; the latter, industry-by-industry. Where do Merges and Nelson come down in this debate? If Wagner's critique is correct, does it suggest caution in implementing the Merges–Nelson proposals to differentiate patent scope depending on whether a patent is in a cumulative innovation industry, a science-based industry, or the like? To what extent does the "macro-exceptionalism" view depend on the idea that all invention in a given industry proceeds according to the same pattern? Is this justified?

Standing on the Shoulders of Giants: Cumulative Research and the Patent Law*

SUZANNE SCOTCHMER

Sir Isaac Newton himself acknowledged, "If I have seen far, it is by standing on the shoulders of giants." Most innovators stand on the shoulders of giants, and never more so than in the current evolution of high technologies, where almost all technical progress builds on a foundation provided by earlier innovators. For example, most molecular biologists use the basic technique for inserting genes into bacteria that was pioneered by Herbert Boyer and Stanley Cohen in the early 1970s, and many use a technique for causing bacteria to express human proteins that was pioneered at Grenentech. In pharmaceuticals, many drugs like insulin, antibiotics, and anti-clogging drugs have been progressively improved as later innovators bettered previous technologies. Computer text editors are similar to one another, as are computer spreadsheets, in large part because innovators have inspired each other. An early example of cumulative research was Eli Whitney's cotton gin, which was quickly modified and improved by other innovators who seriously curtailed his profit.

Most economics literature on patenting and patent races has looked at innovations in isolation, without focusing on the externalities or spillovers that early innovators confer on later innovators. But the cumulative nature of research poses problems for the optimal design of patent law that are not addressed by that perspective. The challenge is to reward early innovators fully for the technological foundation they provide to later innovators, but to reward later innovators adequately for their improvements and new products as well. This paper investigates the use of patent protection and cooperative agreements among firms to protect incentives for cumulative research.

Given that the length and breadth of patent protection cannot depend on the expected costs of an R & D project, the only way to ensure that firms undertake every research project that is efficient is to let the firms collect as revenue all the social value they create. Otherwise, some projects that are socially desirable will not be undertaken. If an innovation is a reduction in the cost of producing a good, then the social value is the saved costs. If the innovation is an improvement to a product, the social value is the difference in consumers' willingness to pay for the improved and unimproved products. When research firms collect all the social value as profit, households still benefit, but in their capacity as shareholders rather than as consumers.

But there are at least two problems with allowing research firms to collect all the social surplus as profit (or as much as possible). First, strong patent protection leads to socially inefficient monopoly pricing. Second, firms in a patent race may overinvest in research if the patent is worth more than the (minimum) cost of achieving it.... This problem is related to the problem of the commons: An increase in one firm's rate of

* Reprinted by permission from 5 Journal of Economic Perspectives 29 (1991), © 1991 American Economics Association.

investment transfers some probability of becoming the patent-holder from other firms to itself. Because of this transfer, all firms might overinvest. These points are well-recognized in the R & D literature.

When an initial innovation facilitates later ones, as is the case with basic research, another issue arises. Part of the first innovation's social value is the boost it gives to later innovators, which can take at least three forms. If the second generation could not be developed without the first, then the social value of the first innovation includes the incremental social surplus provided by second generation products. If the first innovation merely reduces the cost of achieving the second innovation, then the cost reduction is part of the social surplus provided by the first innovation. And if the first innovation accelerates development of the second, but at the same cost, then its social value includes the value of getting the second innovation sooner.

Because of these externalities provided to later innovators, developing the first innovation may be efficient even if its expected cost exceeds its value as a stand-alone product. First innovators will have correct incentives to invest only if they receive some of the social surplus provided by second generation products. But at the same time, enough profit must be left for the second innovators so that they will invest if investing is efficient. This essay asks how close patent incentives can come to accomplishing that goal.

A premise in much of what follows is that firms other than the first innovator should participate in development of second generation products. Since the first innovator might not have expertise in all applications, more second generation products are likely to arise if more researchers have incentives to consider them. In this view, contrary to the premise of much of the patent race literature, creativity is largely serendipitous. Not every R & D firm sees the same opportunities for new products.

However, outside research firms can integrate with initial patent-holders in at least two ways: the firms can form cooperative ventures to research and develop new products, and they can form licensing agreements after products have been developed and patents have been awarded. I will call these two types of contracts prior agreements and licenses, respectively. Prior agreements permit firms to share the costs, as well as the proceeds, of research. Licenses are negotiated after research costs are sunk and patents have been awarded. Both types of agreements can increase profit by improving efficiency and possibly by reducing product market competition. Although many authors have discussed cooperation in research, they have not focused, as I will, on how the breadth of patent protection and cooperation among research firms work together in protecting incentives to innovate. In this view of how incentives to innovate are protected, a key role of patent protection is that it sets bargaining positions for the prior agreements and licenses that will form, and therefore determines the division of profit in these contracts.

Patent Protection and Licensing

A system of property rights that might seem natural would be to protect the first innovator so broadly that licensing is required from all second generation innovators who use the initial technology, whether in research or in production. But such broad protection can lead to deficient incentives to develop second generation products. When the licensing agreement is negotiated after a patent has been granted, research costs have already been sunk. The bargaining surplus to be split between the first and second innovators at that time is the incremental market value of the second product, *not* net of research costs. A second innovator who cannot market the next generation product without a license has a very weak bargaining position. If the second innovator does not get all the surplus being bargained over, he will earn only a fraction of its social value, and this fraction may be less than the cost of developing it. Hence the incentive for an outside firm to develop second generation products can be too weak. Under such broad patent protection, the incentive for the first innovator to develop a second generation product will be stronger than for an outside firm (provided the first innovator has expertise to develop the new product, and thinks of it), since the first innovator will earn the entire incremental profit.

As well as offering deficient incentives for second innovators, broad patent protection might inefficiently inflate incentives for the first innovation. In licensing agreements, the first innovator will earn a share of the market value of each infringing later product. If the first innovation reduces the cost of achieving later innovations, but it is not the only possible vehicle to achieve them, the first innovator's share should not exceed the cost reduction. If it does, the first innovator will be overrewarded.

In what follows I explore two solutions to these defective incentives. The remainder of this section investigates what happens if the first innovator's patent protection is narrowed so that a different enough second generation product does not infringe and thus can be marketed without a license from the first innovator. In the following section, I investigate prior agreements in which second innovators can "sell" their ideas to the first innovator or integrate with the first innovator. Neither solution is perfect, as we shall see.

The inadequacies of narrowing patent protection are most easily exposed if we first suppose that first and second generation products do not compete in the market, although second generation build in the first generation technology; for example, many new pharmaceuticals that are therapies for different illnesses all build on a few basic techniques of bioengineering. Second innovators cannot have excessive incentive to invest, since they cannot earn more than consumers' willingness to pay in the markets they serve. Licensing from the first innovator would transfer away some of the second innovators' revenue and hence reduce their incentive to invest. To provide efficient incentives to the second innovator, society should protect the first innovation so narrowly that a new product never infringes and therefore second innovators never have to license. But such a scheme does not sufficiently reward the first innovator, since the first innovator does not profit from the cost reduction conferred on the second innovators.

The first innovator's incentive to invest becomes still weaker under narrow patent protection if the second generation product is a substitute for the first. Competition between the two patent-holders would erode their joint profit, transferring some of the social surplus of the combined innovations to consumers. As an example, suppose that the second generation product is a superior version of a drug, and that the two patent-holders compete on price. Then the second generation product will survive in the market and its price will equal the difference in consumer's willingness to pay for the two drugs plus the marginal cost of producing the drug. In this outcome, the second innovator earns as profit exactly the incremental social value of the newer drug, while the first innovator's profit falls to zero.

Such profit erosion could be mitigated if the antitrust authorities permitted collusive licensing among patent-holders who would otherwise compete. For example, licensing with per-unit royalties can lead to collusive outcomes, since the royalty raises the licensees' private production cost and therefore keeps the equilibrium price high. In ordinary antitrust law, collusion through licensing would violate the spirit of the Sherman Act and subsequent legislation. But where incentives to innovate are at stake and where later technology builds on an earlier technology, such collusion allows the first innovator to profit from the externality conferred on later innovators. Of course, firms would be tempted to exploit any leniency by the antitrust authorities in contexts where incentives to innovate are not at stake. This problem should not be minimized.

There is something quite general economists can say about the combined effects of patent law with licensing. No such policy can achieve fully efficient incentives, even if society permits collusive licensing between patent holders who would otherwise compete and the firms jointly collect all the social surplus as profit. This is essentially because of "double marginalization." To give the second innovator an incentive to invest whenever social benefits exceed R & D costs, the second innovator must earn the entire social surplus of his innovation. But to compensate the first innovator for the externality or spillover she provides, she too must earn part of this surplus. It is impossible to give the surplus to both parties.

When both first and second generation products are developed, the division of profit between the two innovators depends on the breadth of patent protection. To see this, assume that there is a random component to the outcome of a research project, so that when a research firm invests in a second generation product, it does not know whether its product will infringe the prior patent. The breadth of the prior patent determines the probability that the second generation product will infringe. If the second product turns out to infringe, the second innovator must license and this will force him to share the profit of the improvement with the first innovator. The second innovator is in a better position if its product turns out not to infringe, since the second innovator can profitably compete with the prior patent-holder in the market. Thus, if breadth of the first patent could be interpreted to depend on the expected costs and benefits of a second generation product, we could ensure that the second innovator's expected profit would be zero. If not, some second generation products will be stymied even though they would contribute positively to joint profit and to social welfare, and the second innovators who invest will typically make positive profit.

To summarize the "natural" system of property rights—requiring every later innovator to license any underlying technology—will on average give deficient incentives for outside firms to develop second generation products. This is because the second product infringes and therefore the second innovator must transfer some of the innovation's revenue to the first innovator by licensing. If the first innovator can be relied upon to develop all second generation products, this would not matter. Second, no system of narrower patent protection and licensing can give the right incentives to both the first innovator and other firms that develop improvements, even if collusive licensing among noninfringing products were allowed. The latter result depends on my premise that the breadth of an underlying patent cannot be separately tailored to the costs and benefits of each second generation product.

In the next section, I ask to what extent these inadequacies of patent protection and licensing can be overcome with prior agreements reached before some or all the patents have been obtained. Incentives with licensing are defective mainly because firms negotiate after all costs have been sunk and patents have been issued. A prior agreement integrates the potential second innovator into the firm of the first innovator before investing in the second innovation. Such prior agreements can indeed guarantee efficient investment in second generation products, but cannot perfectly solve the incentive problem unless the negotiation is before *all* costs are sunk, including the costs of the first innovator, or unless the first innovator has all the bargaining power.

Prior Agreements

Prior agreements among research firms are often called research joint ventures. Joint ventures presumably form to increase the joint profit of the members, but they do not necessarily increase social welfare, since the cooperation is among firms only and does not include consumers. Joint ventures increase profit both by providing incentives to the members to invest more efficiently, and by finding ways to transfer social surplus from consumers to firms. The greater efficiency might result form exploiting economies of scale, from sharing technological know-how, or from undoing the inefficiencies of a patent race.

One solution to the incentive problem would be to integrate all possible innovators into one firm before even the first innovator has invested. Then, provided the integrated firm gets most of the social surplus from the joint innovations, it should invest (close to) efficiently.

Although research firms do not know with certainty what projects they will think of after the first generation technology has been developed, they have expectations about the possible benefits and costs of such projects. Provided all researchers have similar expectations, an agreement negotiated before the first investment could ensure that the first innovation is undertaken if and only if efficient, where efficiency is defined relative to the prior judgments about costs and benefits. But the more serendipitous is the discovery of second generation products, and the more difficult it is to include all potential second innovators, the less feasible such an agreement seems. I therefore consider the more limited prospects when integration occurs after the first innovation. The difficulties in transferring profit to the first innovator are clearest if we assume that the innovators can jointly collect all the social surplus as profit, provided they do not compete in the market.

After the first patent has issued, a potential second innovator could approach the first patent-holder with an idea for an improvement or new product, and suggest that they share both the costs and proceeds of research. Such an agreement can increase joint profit by increasing investment in profitable second generation products and by preventing market compensation among firms that would otherwise own competing patents. If patent protection is broad, without this prior agreement the second innovator could have deficient incentive to invest, as explained above. With a prior agreement, the initial patent-holder can agree to share both the costs and the proceeds of the second innovation, and will do so whenever benefits exceed costs.

Prior agreements are a social improvement over licensing because they can improve incentives to invest in second generation products, whatever the breadth of patent protection. With licensing, the breadth of patent protection serves two purposes: It determines investment in second generation products and determines how the firms' joint expected profits will be divided. With prior agreements, the breadth of patent protection serves one purpose instead of two: The two innovators have an incentive to invest efficiently in second generation products whatever the breadth of patent protection. The breadth of protection determines only the bargaining positions, hence the division of profit.

Whether a prior agreement can provide efficient incentives for the first investment as well as the second depends on two factors: how much social surplus must be transferred from the second innovator to the first (how big the externality is), and the second innovator's bargaining power. A second innovator who has a strong bargaining position will earn positive profit in a prior agreement, thus limiting how much social surplus the first innovator can collect. The second innovator's bargaining position is strongest if there is a high probability the second innovation would not infringe and if the second generation product is itself patentable. The second innovator will also have a strong bargaining position if no other firm is capable of developing the second generation product.

Notes and Questions

1. Suzanne Scotchmer received a B.A. from the University of Washington, and M.A. and Ph.D. degrees in economics from Berkeley. She taught at Harvard University before moving to the University of California, Berkeley, where she teaches economics and public policy.

2. The ideas in this excerpt have proven to have very wide application. For just two examples, see Robin Feldman, "The Insufficiency of Antitrust Analysis for Patent Misuse," 55 *Hastings L.J.* 399, 435 (2003) (citing the Scotchmer article excerpted here for the proposition that patents often have important downstream effects, in context of argument that patent misuse can and should reach activities that do not run afoul of the antitrust law); Joseph Farrell and Philip J. Weiser, "Modularity, Vertical Integration, and Open Access Policies: Towards a Convergence of Antitrust and Regulation in The Internet Age," 17 *Harv. J.L. & Tech.* 85, 113 n.120 (2003) (in argument that facilitating follow-on development might be a structural problem with "closed" technical architectures, citing Scotchmer article as an exception insofar as it contemplates ex ante contracting with follow-on improvers). The problem of coordinating different inventions from potentially different firms at different times is clearly a common one, and the complexity and importance of the issues has captured the imagination of many.

3. One article discusses some of the potential problems—and proposes a legal solution—with the ex post bargaining Scotchmer discusses. See Robert P. Merges, "Intellectual Property Rights and Bargaining Breakdown: The Case Of Blocking Patents," 62 *Tenn. L. Rev.* 75, 75 (1994):

> The reverse doctrine [of equivalents] can be understood ... as a judicial response to the likelihood of a breakdown in bargaining between inventors who pioneer a new technology and those who later develop key improvements. Under this interpretation, the reverse doctrine serves as a judicial "safety valve," releasing pressure that builds up when pioneers and improvers fail to agree to a license.

The first excerpt in Section B. below, from Heller and Eisenberg, considers issues of bargaining breakdown and failed transactions generally on a more systemic level.

4. Can you see any obvious practical problems with the ex ante bargaining scenario described in the Scotchmer excerpt? How often will a pioneering firm be able to identify all the potential developers of improvements? How would a potential improver make a credible argument that they will achieve the improvement, and that it will possess characteristics the market will value, both of which are required for the ex ante negotiation to take place? Do these difficulties explain why many of the pioneer-improver transactions that do take place appear to be of the ex post variety? (On this, see James Bessen, "Holdup and Licensing of Cumulative Innovations With Private Information," 82 *Econ. Letters* 321, 322 (2004) (citing research showing that less than 10% of licenses occurred ex ante in one industry sector, in context of article suggesting the general impracticality of the ex ante licensing notion).

The Evolving Application of the Written Description Requirement to Biotechnological Inventions*

JANICE M. MUELLER

I. Introduction

The specification of a United States patent must provide:

> a written description of the invention, and of the manner and process of making and using it, in such full, clear, concise, and exact terms as to enable any person skilled in the art to which it pertains ... to make and use the same....

Though codified in the Patent Act of 1952, it was not until 1967 that the United States Court of Customs and Patent Appeals (CCPA) in In re Ruschig[1] first characterized this statutory language as requiring a "written description" of an invention, separate from and in addition to an "enabling" disclosure of how to make and use that invention. Since Ruschig, understanding and applying the written description requirement as a statutory criterion of separate purpose and function from the enablement requirement have proven difficult. Recent developments in the application of the written description requirement to biotechnological inventions illustrate the difficulties of maintaining a clear demarcation between the written description and enablement requirements.

At the forefront of the United States Court of Appeals for the Federal Circuit's evolving written description jurisprudence stands its recent and controversial invalidation of patents covering the pioneering recombinant DNA technology at issue in Regents of the University of California v. Eli Lilly and Co.[2] (Lilly). The Lilly decision establishes uniquely rigorous rules for the description of biotechnological subject matter that significantly contort written description doctrine away from its historic origins and policy grounding. The Lilly court's elevation of written description to an effective "super enablement" standard of uncertain scope and applicability will likely chill development in this critically important technological field and frustrate the United States patent system's policy goal of encouraging prompt disclosure of new inventions.

II. The Purpose and Development of the Written Description Requirement

A. The Historic "Notice" Function of the Written Description Requirement

* Reprinted with permission from 13 Berkeley Tech. L. J. 615 (1998), © 1998 Janice Mueller and the Berkeley Technology Law Journal.

1. 379 F.2d 990 (C.C.P.A. 1967).

2. 119 F.3d 1559 (Fed. Cir. 1997); see also A Bitter Battle Over Insulin Gene, 277 Science 1028, 1028 (1997) (describing suit as a "vicious fight [that] centers on a landmark discovery by [University of California at San Francisco] biologists at the dawn of the biotechnology era: the first successful cloning of the rat insulin gene") [hereinafter Bitter Battle].

The purpose and function of the written description requirement have changed over time as United States patent law has evolved from a central claiming system to the peripheral claiming system now in use. All United States patent statutes have required a "description" of the applicant's invention. * * *

The early Supreme Court case of Evans v. Eaton[3] interpreted this statutory language as containing two separate requirements, written description and enablement, with separate and distinct roles.

When Evans was decided in 1822, modern peripheral claiming practice had not yet evolved in the United States. Absent claims as we know them today, the written description provided notice to the public of the scope of exclusive rights asserted by an inventor.

The written description requirement had its modern "rebirth" in 1967, with the CCPA's decision in In re Ruschig. For the first time, the CCPA identified, within the language in section 112 of the Patent Act, a legal requirement for a written description that played a role different from that of enablement. The Ruschig court applied the written description requirement to a claim presented after the application was filed. In so doing, the court sought to ascertain if the application would disclose to one skilled in the art that the later-claimed invention was something that the applicant had "actually invented" as of the earlier application filing date. Thus, in Ruschig, the CCPA effectively transitioned the written description requirement from a superfluous, claim-like notice role into a convenient statutory descriptor for the general concept of "support" for claims not filed in an original application.

Though not expressly stated, the policy of concern to the Ruschig court appeared to be one of preventing the inventor from claiming, after-the-fact, more than she had a right to; the inventor would be limited to claiming that which she had identified as within the scope of her invention at the time of filing her original application. * * * Absent written description scrutiny, a later-presented claim not truly entitled to the earlier filing date of the application would be improperly examined against a smaller universe of prior art than is legally available.

III.   Application of the Written Description Requirement in Regents of the University of California v. Eli Lilly and Co.

Written description jurisprudence diverged from the principles discussed above when the Federal Circuit in July 1997 issued its decision in Lilly.

Generic claims 1, 2, 4, 6, and 7 of the [4,652,525] patent recited complementary DNA (cDNA) encoding vertebrate or mammalian insulin, while claim 5 specifically recited cDNA encoding human insulin. The '525 patent issued in 1987 from an application filed in 1977. As of the 1977 filing of the '525 patent, UC had determined and isolated the preproinsulin (PPI) and proinsulin (PI) cDNA sequences found in rats, but not in humans. Although UC included in the '525 patent a constructive or "prophetic" example describing a method that could be used to obtain the human insulin-encoding cDNA recited in claim 5, as well as

---

3.   20 U.S. (7 Wheat.) 356 (1822).

the amino acid sequences of human insulin A and B chains, UC did not actually isolate and sequence the human cDNA until nearly two years after the 1977 filing date.

* * * Lilly's decision to forego a challenge to the patent on enablement grounds is not surprising because UC's isolation of the rat insulin cDNA made the human insulin cDNA "relatively easy" to "fish out" thereafter.

* * * The Federal Circuit affirmed the district court's conclusion that all the asserted '525 patent claims were invalid for failure to comply with the written description requirement. The appellate court first analyzed species claim 5, which recited human insulin-encoding cDNA, and concluded that the '525 specification was fatally defective for failing to structurally describe the claimed cDNA. It then held that the human insulin-encoding cDNA of claim 5 was not adequately described, because the specification lacked a disclosure of that cDNA's "relevant structural or physical characteristics." The court specifically pointed to the absence in the specification of "sequence information indicating which nucleotides constitute human cDNA. . . ." Nor did UC's provision in example 6 of a process that could be used to isolate the human cDNA remedy the perceived deficiency of the disclosure: the court concluded that, "describing a method of preparing a cDNA or even describing the protein that the cDNA encodes, as the example does, does not necessarily describe the cDNA itself."[4]

The Lilly court thus demanded that the written description of a DNA invention meet a heightened "precise definition" test.

. . .

The Federal Circuit then turned to the generic vertebrate and mammalian insulin claims 1, 2, 4, 6, and 7 and concluded that they, like claim 5, were invalid as not supported by an adequate written description. The extent of the written description required to support claims 1, 2, 4, 6, and 7 mirrored, on the genus level, the court's pronouncement that a structural description must be provided to support a claim to a species of cDNA . . . . .

IV. Lilly's Heightened Written Description Standard Targeting Biotechnological Inventions Contravenes Precedent and Policy

The Lilly decision is a significant departure from prior written description cases in at least two respects. First, the Federal Circuit applied the written description requirement to claims originally filed with the application, rather than to claims presented or amended after the application filing date. In so doing, the court divorced the written description requirement from its role first envisioned in Ruschig and thirty years of subsequent case law development. In a case where enablement was never raised by the defendant, the Lilly court's application of the written description requirement to original application claims has created a new and undefined "super-enablement" standard for biotechnological inventions.

4. Id.

Second, the Lilly court ... [held] that the written description requirement is not satisfied for claims to a DNA absent an express disclosure in the specification of the nucleotide sequence of that DNA. This rule sets a significantly higher standard for the protection of biotechnological inventions than for other technological subject matter.

A. The Written Description Requirement Should Play No Role In the Analysis of Originally-Filed Claims Which Are Part of the Disclosure

* * *

In re Ruschig, the first case to recognize the written description requirement in the modern peripheral claiming era, enforced the requirement in the context of a claim to a specific chemical compound that was added to the appellant's application more than a year after its filing in order to provoke an interference.

1. Structure is not the only way to supply a written description of biotechnological subject matter

The requirement of explicit possession of the nucleotide sequences of the cDNAs claimed in Lilly is contrary to one of the earliest biotechnology decisions of the CCPA, In re Fisher.[5] ... Fisher establishes that disclosure of the physical structure of a biological compound is not required in order to provide sufficient written description support for claims thereto. More specifically, an inventor need not be able to define the amino acid sequence of a protein in order to provide adequate written description support for a later-presented claim to that sequence, if the inventor can at least functionally describe the protein.

V. Public Policy Does Not Favor Uniquely Rigorous Biotechnology Patentability Rules

In Lilly, the Federal Circuit has fashioned a newly heightened written description standard unique to biotechnological inventions, without meaningful explanation of policy concerns that would justify such a significant departure from earlier written description principles. Despite the fact that Lilly did not challenge the ability of UC's application to teach art workers how to isolate and sequence the claimed human, vertebrate, and mammalian cDNA, the Federal Circuit invalidated the claims because UC had not yet specified the nucleotide sequences of those cDNAs. In practical terms, Lilly may profoundly limit the scope of protection available for new gene inventions. Only those genes that can be precisely described by nucleotide sequence will be viable candidates for patenting; disclosure of function alone will no longer suffice.

Taken in tandem with recent developments in biotechnological enablement doctrine, the parallel "ratcheting up" of the written description requirement in Lilly signals the creation of a unique patent law jurisprudence for genetic engineering inventions. Unique patent law treatment, for biotechnology or any other particular technology, raises concern. Public policy favors uniform standards for all technologies. The development of uniquely stringent, biotech-specific patent law principles

---

5. 427 F.2d 833 (C.C.P.A. 1970).

cannot help but chill the development of new biotechnological products and processes. . . .

The Lilly decision also frustrates the policy of encouraging prompt filing of patent applications on new inventions, which in turn is thought to result in the more rapid disclosure to the public of new technical information. After Lilly, inventors can be expected to delay the filing of gene inventions until they have precisely determined the corresponding DNA sequences. They will be faced with a Hobson's choice of accepting a later priority date by delaying filing until written description compliance is certain, or filing sooner and risking invalidation for failure to meet a now-uncertain standard for adequate disclosure. In terms of obtaining broad generic claims, institutional patent applicants benefiting from greater resources for rapidly sequencing additional species of cDNA once a particular gene has been cloned will be at a decided advantage over independent entities or smaller firms without comparable resources.

Users of the patent system are justified in viewing the Lilly decision as reflecting an increasingly-widening gulf between the norms of the business and scientific community and those of the United States patent system. Persons skilled in the art of recombinant DNA technology were very likely to have understood that by making the rat insulin cDNA, the UC inventors conceptually possessed the human insulin cDNA (if not all mammalian cDNAs). But under the Lilly court's heightened "physical possession" standard for written description compliance, UC was denied any significant reward for its breakthrough contribution. Rather than awarding patent protection to the first to make it possible to clone a particular gene family, the written description standard of Lilly requires that the patent right go to the first firm to sequence a number of the genes (or, perhaps, even the first to correctly guess their sequence). The firm with the fastest or most accurate cloning and sequencing team will reap the benefits of an invention made possible by the pioneering research of others. The credibility of the patent system suffers as users come to recognize that it no longer reflects the realities of scientific contribution.

Notes and Questions

1. Janice Mueller received a B.S.Chem.E. from Virginia Polytechnic Institute, and J.D. from William Mitchell College of Law. She has taught at Suffolk University Law School and the John Marshall Law School, and now teaches at the University of Pittsburgh School of Law.

2. The issues Mueller discusses continue to occupy the Federal Circuit. Consider the important case of Enzo Biochem, Inc. v. Gen–Probe Inc., 285 F.3d 1013 (Fed. Cir.) ["Enzo I"] vacated by 296 F.3d 1316 (Fed. Cir.), republished at 323 F.3d 956 (Fed. Cir. 2002) ["Enzo II"]. The Federal Circuit in Enzo II backed down somewhat from a very restrictive application of the written description requirement in Enzo I. In a related opinion, Judge Rader of the Federal Circuit echoed some of the concerns identified in the Mueller excerpt. See 323 F.3d 956, 976 (Rader, J., dissenting from denial of motion for rehearing en banc):

The tortuous path of this case shows the perils of ignoring the statute and over thirty years of consistent written description case law.... Because the written description requirement as created and applied for thirty years does not apply to this case, I would grant en banc review and correct the rest of this court's misapplication of the description requirement.

See also id., at 983 (citing Mueller article and two other articles by academics critical of Federal Circuit written description law); Duane M. Linstrom, "Spontaneous Mutation: A Sudden Change in the Evolution of The Written Description Requirement as it Applies to Genetic Patents," 40 *San Diego L. Rev.* 947 (2003).

3. Contrast Mueller's point about the desirability of uniform standards across industries with the issues raised in the notes following the Merges and Nelson excerpt, on the topic of industry-and technology-specific rules in patent law. Which theory seems more convincing in the biotechnology context? Is the Federal Circuit's written description jurisprudence a good indication of the dissension that would result from an attempt to apply industry-specific rules, or does it suggest instead the advantages of explicitly addressing industry-level issues in crafting patent doctrine?

B. Transaction Costs

Can Patents Deter Innovation? The Anticommons in Biomedical Research*
MICHAEL A. HELLER
REBECCA S. EISENBERG

Thirty years ago in *Science*, Garrett Hardin introduced the metaphor "tragedy of the commons"[1] to help explain overpopulation, air pollution, and species extinction. People often overuse resources they own in common because they have no incentive to conserve. Today, Hardin's metaphor is central to debates in economics, law, and science and is a powerful justification for privatizing commons property. Although the metaphor highlights the cost of overuse when governments allow too many people to use a scarce resource, it overlooks the possibility of underuse when governments give too many people rights to exclude others. Privatization can solve one tragedy but cause another.

Since Hardin's article appeared, biomedical research has been moving from a commons model toward a privatization model. Under the commons model, the federal government sponsored premarket or "upstream" research and encouraged broad dissemination of results in the public domain. Unpatented biomedical discoveries were freely incorporated in "downstream" products for diagnosing and treating disease. In 1980, in an effort to promote commercial development of new technologies, Congress began encouraging universities and other institutions to

* Reprinted with permission from 280 Science 698 (May 1, 1998), © 1998 American Association for the Advancement of Science.

1. G. Hardin, *Science* **162**, 1243 (1968).

patent discoveries arising from federally supported research and development and to transfer their technology to the private sector. Supporters applaud the resulting increase in patent filings and private investment, whereas critics fear deterioration in the culture of upstream research. Building on Heller's theory of anticommons property,[2] this article identifies an unintended and paradoxical consequence of biomedical privatization: A proliferation of intellectual property rights upstream may be stifling life-saving innovations further downstream in the course of research and product development.

The Tragedy of the Anticommons

Anticommons property can best be understood as the mirror image of commons property. A resource is prone to overuse in a tragedy of the commons when too many owners each have a privilege to use a given resource and no one has a right to exclude another. By contrast, a resource is prone to underuse in a "tragedy of the anticommons" when multiple owners each have a right to exclude others from a scarce resource and no one has an effective privilege of use. In theory, in a world of costless transactions, people could always avoid commons or anticommons tragedies by trading their rights. In practice, however, avoiding tragedy requires overcoming transaction costs, strategic behaviors, and cognitive biases of participants, with success more likely within close-knit communities than among hostile strangers. Once an anticommons emerges, collecting rights into usable private property is often brutal and slow.

Privatization in postsocialist economies starkly illustrates how anticommons property can emerge and persist. One promise of the transition to a free market was that new entrepreneurs would fill stores that socialist rule had left bare. Yet after several years of reform, many privatized storefronts remained empty, while flimsy metal kiosks, stocked full of goods, mushroomed on the streets. Why did the new merchants not come in from the cold? One reason was that transition governments often failed to endow any individual with a bundle of rights that represents full ownership. Instead, fragmented rights were distributed to various socialist-era stakeholders, including private or quasi-private enterprises, workers' collectives, privatization agencies, and local, regional, and federal governments. No one could set up shop without first collecting rights from each of the other owners.

Privatization of upstream biomedical research in the United States may create anticommons property that is less visible than empty storefronts but even more economically and socially costly. In this setting, privatization takes the form of intellectual property claims to the sorts of research results that, in an earlier era, would have been made freely available in the public domain. Responding to a shift in U.S. government policy in the past two decades, research institutions such as the National Institutes of Health (NIH) and major universities have created technology transfer offices to patent and license their discoveries. At the same time, commercial biotechnology firms have emerged in research and development (R & D) niches somewhere between the proverbial "funda-

2. M. Heller, *Harvard Law Rev.* **111**, 621 (1998).

mental" research of academic laboratories and the targeted product development of pharmaceutical firms. Today, upstream research in the biomedical sciences is increasingly likely to be "private" in one or more senses of the term—supported by private funds, carried out in a private institution, or privately appropriated through patents, trade secrecy, or agreements that restrict the use of materials and data. . . .

The problem we identify is distinct from the routine underuse inherent in any well-functioning patent system. By conferring monopolies in discoveries, patents necessarily increase prices and restrict use—a cost society pays to motivate invention and disclosure. The tragedy of the anticommons refers to the more complex obstacles that arise when a user needs access to multiple patented inputs to create a single useful product. Each upstream patent allows its owner to set up another tollbooth on the road to product development, adding to the cost and slowing the pace of downstream biomedical innovation.

How a Biomedical Anticommons May Arise

Current examples in biomedical research demonstrate two mechanisms by which a government might inadvertently create an anticommons: either by creating too many concurrent fragments of intellectual property rights in potential future products or by permitting too many upstream patent owners to stack licenses on top of the future discoveries of downstream users.

Concurrent fragments. The anticommons model provides one way of understanding a widespread intuition that issuing patents on gene fragments makes little sense. Throughout the 1980s, patents on genes generally corresponded closely to foreseeable commercial products, such as therapeutic proteins or diagnostic tests for recognized genetic diseases. Then, in 1991, NIH pointed the way toward patenting anonymous gene fragments with its notorious patent applications on expressed sequence tags (ESTs). NIH subsequently abandoned these patent applications and now takes a more hostile position toward patenting ESTs and raw genomic DNA sequences. Meanwhile, private firms have stepped in where NIH left off, filing patent applications on newly identified DNA sequences, including gene fragments, before identifying a corresponding gene, protein, biological function, or potential commercial product. The Patent and Trademark Office (PTO), in examining these claims, could create or avoid an anticommons.

Although a database of gene fragments is a useful resource for discovery, defining property rights around isolated gene fragments seems at the outset unlikely to track socially useful bundles of property rights in future commercial products. Foreseeable commercial products, such as therapeutic proteins or genetic diagnostic tests, are more likely to require the use of multiple fragments. A proliferation of patents on individual fragments held by different owners seems inevitably to require costly future transactions to bundle licenses together before a firm can have an effective right to develop these products.

Patents on receptors useful for screening potential pharmaceutical products demonstrate another potential "concurrent fragment" anticommons in biomedical research. To learn as much as possible about the therapeutic effects and side effects of potential products at the preclinical stage, firms want to screen products against all known members of relevant receptor families. But if these receptors are patented and controlled by different owners, gathering the necessary licenses may be difficult or impossible. A recent search of the Lexis patent database disclosed more than 100 issued U.S. patents with the term "adrenergic receptor" in the claim language. Such a proliferation of claims presents a daunting bargaining challenge. Unable to procure a complete set of licenses, firms choose between diverting resources to less promising projects with fewer licensing obstacles or proceeding to animal and then clinical testing on the basis of incomplete information. More thorough in vitro screening could avoid premature clinical testing that exposes patients to unnecessary risks.

Long delays between the filing and issuance of biotechnology patents aggravate the problem of concurrent fragments. During this period of pendency, there is substantial uncertainty as to the scope of patent rights that will ultimately issue. Although U.S. patent law does not recognize enforceable rights in pending patent applications, firms and universities typically enter into license agreements before the issuance of patents, and firms raise capital on the basis of the inchoate rights preserved by patent filings. In effect, each potential patent creates a specter of rights that may be larger than the actual rights, if any, eventually conferred by the PTO. Worked into the calculations of both risk-taking investors and risk-averse product developers, these overlapping patent filings may compound the obstacles to developing new products.

Stacking licenses. The use of reach-through license agreements (RTLAs) on patented research tools illustrates another path by which an anticommons may emerge. As we use the term, an RTLA gives the owner of a patented invention, used in upstream stages of research, rights in subsequent downstream discoveries. Such rights may take the form of a royalty on sales that result from use of the upstream research tool, an exclusive or nonexclusive license on future discoveries, or an option to acquire such a license. In principle, RTLAs offer advantages to both patent holders and researchers. They permit researchers with limited funds to use patented research tools right away and defer payment until the research yields valuable results. Patent holders may also prefer a chance at larger payoffs from sales of downstream products rather than certain, but smaller, upfront fees. In practice, RTLAs may lead to an anticommons as upstream owners stack overlapping and inconsistent claims on potential downstream products. In effect, the use of RTLAs gives each upstream patent owner a continuing right to be present at the bargaining table as a research project moves downstream toward product development.

So far, RTLAs have had a mixed reception as a mechanism for licensing upstream biomedical research patents, but they appear to be becoming more prevalent. When Cetus Corporation initially proposed RTLAs on any products developed through the use of the polymerase chain reaction (PCR) in research, they met strong resistance from downstream users concerned with developing commercial products. Later, Hoffmann–La Roche acquired the rights to PCR and offered licenses that do not include reach-through obligations. The resulting pay-as-you-go approach increases the upfront cost of a license to use PCR, but it decreases the likelihood of an anticommons emerging. . . .

Transition or Tragedy?

Is a biomedical anticommons likely to endure once it emerges? Recent empirical literature suggests that communities of intellectual property owners who deal with each other on a recurring basis have sometimes developed institutions to reduce transaction costs of bundling multiple licenses.[3] For example, in the music industry, copyright collectives have evolved to facilitate licensing transactions so that broadcasters and other producers may readily obtain permission to use numerous copyrighted works held by different owners. Similarly, in the automobile, aircraft manufacturing, and synthetic rubber industries, patent pools have emerged, sometimes with the help of government, when licenses under multiple patent rights have been necessary to develop important new products. When the background legal rules threaten to waste resources, people often rearrange rights sensibly and create order through private arrangements. Perhaps some of the problems caused by proliferating upstream patent rights in biomedical research will recede as licensors and licensees gain experience with intellectual property rights and institutions evolve to help owners and users reach agreements. The short-term costs from delayed development of new treatments for disease may be worth incurring if fragmented privatization allows upstream research to pay its own way and helps to ensure its long-run viability. Patent barriers to product development may be a transitional phenomenon rather than an enduring tragedy.

On the other hand, there may be reasons to fear that a patent anticommons could prove more intractable in biomedical research than in other settings. Because patents matter more to the pharmaceutical and biotechnology industries than to other industries, firms in these industries may be less willing to participate in patent pools that undermine the gains from exclusivity. Moreover, the lack of substitutes for certain biomedical discoveries (such as patented genes or receptors) may increase the leverage of some patent holders, thereby aggravating hold-out problems. Rivals may not be able to invent around patents in research aimed at understanding the genetic bases of diseases as they occur in nature.

More generally, three structural concerns caution against uncritical reliance on markets and norms to avoid a biomedical anticommons tragedy: the transaction costs of rearranging entitlements, heterogeneous interests of owners, and cognitive biases among researchers.

Transaction costs of bundling rights. High transaction costs may be an enduring impediment to efficient bundling of intellectual property rights in biomedical research. First, many upstream patent owners are public institutions with limited resources for absorbing transaction costs and limited competence in fast-paced, market-oriented bargaining. Second,

3. R. Merges, *Calif. Law Rev.* **84**, 1293 (1996).

the rights involved cover a diverse set of techniques, reagents, DNA sequences, and instruments. Difficulties in comparing the values of these patents will likely impede development of a standard distribution scheme. Third, the heterogeneity of interests and resources among public and private patent owners may complicate the emergence of standard license terms, requiring costly case-by-case negotiations. Fourth, licensing transaction costs are likely to arise early in the course of R & D when the outcome of a project is uncertain, the potential gains are speculative, and it is not yet clear that the value of downstream products justifies the trouble of overcoming the anticommons.

Even when upstream owners see potential gains from cooperation and are motivated to devise mechanisms for reducing transaction costs, they may be deterred by other legal constraints, such as antitrust laws. Patent pools have been a target of antitrust scrutiny in the past, which may explain why few, if any, such pools exist today. Although antitrust law may be less hostile to patent pools today than it was in 1975 when a consent decree dismantled the aircraft patent pool, the antitrust climate changes from one administration to the next. Even a remote prospect of facing treble damages and an injunction may give firms pause about entering into such agreements.

Heterogeneous interests of rights holders. Intellectual property rights in upstream biomedical research belong to a large, diverse group of owners in the public and private sectors with divergent institutional agendas. Sometimes heterogeneity of interests can facilitate mutually agreeable allocations (you take the credit, I'll take the money), but in this setting, there are reasons to fear that owners will have conflicting agendas that make it difficult to reach agreement. For example, a politically accountable government agency such as NIH may further its public health mission by using its intellectual property rights to ensure widespread availability of new therapeutic products at reasonable prices. When NIH sought to establish its co-ownership of patent rights held by Burroughs–Wellcome on the use of azidothymidine (AZT) to treat the human immunodeficiency virus (HIV), its purpose was to lower the price of AZT and promote public health rather than simply to maximize its financial return. By contrast, a private firm is more likely to use intellectual property to maintain a lucrative product monopoly that rewards share-holders and funds future product development. When owners have conflicting goals and each can deploy its rights to block the strategies of the others, they may not be able to reach an agreement that leaves enough private value for downstream developers to bring products to the market.

A more subtle conflict in agendas arises between owners that pursue end-product development and those that focus primarily on upstream research. The goal of end-product development may be better served by making patented research tools widely available on a nonexclusive basis, whereas the goal of procuring upstream research funding may be better served by offering exclusive licenses to sponsors or research partners. Differences among patent owners in their tolerance for transaction costs may further complicate the emergence of informal licensing norms. Universities may be ill equipped to handle multiple transactions for acquiring licenses to use research tools. Delays in negotiating multiple agreements to use patented processes, reagents, and gene fragments could stifle the creative give-and-take of academic research. Yet academic researchers who fail to adopt new discoveries and instead rely on obsolete public domain technologies may find themselves losing grant competitions. Large corporations with substantial legal departments may have considerably greater resources for negotiating licenses on a case-by-case basis than public sector institutions or small start-up firms. This asymmetry may make it difficult to identify mutually advantageous cross-licensing arrangements. Patent owners are also likely to differ in the time frames they can tolerate for recouping current investments in transaction costs.

Owners are also likely to differ in their willingness and ability to infringe the patents of others, resulting in asymmetrical motivations to negotiate cross-licenses. Use of a patented invention in an academic laboratory or a small start-up firm may be inconspicuous, at least if not described in a publication or at a scientific meeting. Patent owners may be more reluctant to sue public sector investigators than they are to sue private firms. Differences in institutional cultures may make academic laboratories and biotechnology firms more tolerant of patent infringement than large pharmaceutical firms. Owners who do not feel vulnerable to infringement liability may be less motivated to enter into reasonable cross-licenses than owners who worry more about being sued.

Cognitive biases. People consistently overestimate the likelihood that very low probability events of high salience will occur. For example, many travelers overestimate the danger of an airplane crash relative to the hazards of other modes of transportation. We suspect that a similar bias is likely to cause owners of upstream biomedical research patents to overvalue their discoveries. Imagine that one of a set of 50 upstream inventions will likely be the key to identifying an important new drug, the rest of the set will have no practical use, and a downstream product developer is willing to pay $10 million for the set. Given the assumption that no owner knows ex ante which invention will be the key, a rational owner should be willing to sell her patent for the probabilistic value of $200,000. However, if each owner overestimates the likelihood that her patent will be the key, then each will demand more than the probabilistic value, the upstream owners collectively will demand more than the aggregate market value of their inputs, the downstream user will decline the offers, and the new drug will not be developed. Individuals trained in deterministic rather than probabilistic disciplines are particularly likely to succumb to this sort of error.

A related "attribution bias" suggests that people systematically overvalue their assets and disparage the claims of their opponents when in competition with others. We suspect that the attribution bias is pervasive among scientists because it is likely adaptive for the research enterprise as a whole. Overcommitment by individuals to particular research approaches ensures that no hypothesis is dismissed too quickly, and skepticism toward rivals' claims ensures that they are not too readily accepted. But this bias can interfere with clear-headed bargaining, leading owners to overvalue their own patents, undervalue others' patents, and reject reasonable offers. Institutional ownership could mitigate these biases, but technology transfer offices rely on scientists to evaluate their discoveries. When two or more patent owners each hope to dominate the product market, the history of biotechnology patent litigation suggests a likelihood that bargaining will fail.

Conclusion

Like the transition to free markets in postsocialist economies, the privatization of biomedical research offers both promises and risks. It promises to spur private investment but risks creating a tragedy of the anticommons through a proliferation of fragmented and overlapping intellectual property rights. An anticommons in biomedical research may be more likely to endure than in other areas of intellectual property because of the high transaction costs of bargaining, heterogeneous interests among owners, and cognitive biases of researchers. Privatization must be more carefully deployed if it is to serve the public goals of biomedical research. Policy-makers should seek to ensure coherent boundaries of upstream patents and to minimize restrictive licensing practices that interfere with downstream product development. Otherwise, more upstream rights may lead paradoxically to fewer useful products for improving human health.

Notes and Questions

1. Rebecca S. Eisenberg graduated from Stanford University and the U.C. Berkeley (Boalt Hall) School of Law. After a period in private law practice, she joined the faculty at the University of Michigan Law School where she is now Robert and Barabara Luciano Professor of Law. Michael Heller graduated from Harvard College and Stanford Law School. After teaching at the University of Michigan Law School he moved to Columbia Law School, where he is Lawrence A. Wien Professor of Real Estate Law.

2. The notion of an "anticommons" has captured the imagination of economic theorists who have fleshed out its basic structure in a number of articles. See, for example, James M. Buchanan and Young J. Yoon, "Symmetric Tragedies: Commons and Anticommons", 43 *J. L. & Econ.* 1 (2000); Francesco Parisi, Norbert Schulz, and Ben Depoorter, "Simultaneous and Sequential Anticommons," 17 *Eur. J. L. & Econ.* 175 (2004).

3. As the authors state, firms and universities have begun making "intellectual property claims to the sorts of research results that, in an earlier era, would have been made freely available in the public domain." Patents on these "upstream" research results or "research tools" have led to an important policy debate. This culminated in an official policy of the National Institutes of Health requiring grant recipients to promote the principles of free exchange of research tools. See Principles and Guidelines for Recipients of NIH Research Grants and Contracts on Obtaining and Disseminating Biomedical Research Resources: Final Notice, 64 Fed. Reg. 72,090 (Dec. 23, 1999). Others have proposed policies to soften the impact of research tool patents in various ways. See Natalie

M. Derzko, "In Search of a Compromised Solution to the Problem Arising from Patenting Biomedical Research Tools," 20 *Santa Clara Computer & High Tech. L.J.* 347, 347 (2004) ("certain users and uses of research tools should be exempted from patent infringement and limits should be imposed on amounts and types of royalties that a patent owner can collect from their research tool patents.")

Empirical research has demonstrated that to date, the "anticommons problem" in biomedical research has not had a significantly negative impact on the research enterprise. See John P. Walsh, Ashish Arora, and Wesley M. Cohen, "Effects of Research Tool Patents and Licensing on Biomedical Innovation," in Wesley M. Cohen and Stephen A. Merrill, eds, Patents in the Knowledge-Based Economy 285 (Washington, D.C: National Academies Press, 2003). Case studies of individual patented research tools back up this claim. See Heather Hamme Ramirez, "Defending the Privatization of Research Tools: An Examination of the 'Tragedy of the Anticommons' in Biotechnology Research and Development," 53 *Emory L.J.* 359, 377–78 (2004) (examples of Cohen–Boyer and PCR/Taq Polymerase patents as research tool patents that have been widely licensed and have accelerated, rather than retarded, biomedical research). This may be because the full force of patents in this area has yet to be felt, or perhaps because of the attention drawn to the problem by scientists in the field and the Heller and Eisenberg article itself.

4. Scholars continue to debate whether an anticommons is forming in the biotechnology industry, and if so, what to do about it. See, e.g., Richard A. Epstein, Steady the Course: Property Rights in Genetic Material 48–49 (Working Paper No 152 (2d Series), Olin Program in Law and Economics, University of Chicago Law School), online at http://www.law.uchicago.edu/Lawecon/index.html; Rochelle Cooper Dreyfuss, Varying the Course in Patenting Genetic Material: A Counter-proposal to Richard Epstein's Steady Course (Public Law Research Paper No. 59 NYU School of Law, Apr. 2003), online at http://papers.ssrn.com/id=394000.

5. If a policymaker sees the conditions of an anticommons taking place, what should he or she do about it? What normative steps does the theory suggest?

Contracting Into Liability Rules: Intellectual Property Rights and Collective Rights Organizations*

ROBERT P. MERGES

Today ... business people ... often ... encounter a tangled, twisted mass of IPRs, which criss-cross the established walkways of commerce.

* Reprinted by permission from 84 Calif. L. Rev. 1293 (1996), © 1996, California Law Review and Robert P. Merges.

Progress along this path does not come cheaply; rather, it requires numerous contracts with multiple, independent right holders.

In IPR systems around the world, a traditional solution to entanglements of this sort is to adopt a "middle path": the compulsory license. Legislation granting IPRs is conditioned, under this approach, with a statutory mandate that the rights must be licensed to all comers willing to pay the pre-set price.

Legislatively mandated licensing of this sort reduces transaction costs in two ways. First, contract terms are predetermined. This either eliminates haggling, or reduces it substantially. Second, compulsory licensing schemes often come equipped with built-in administrative support. This saves the parties the costs of record keeping, payment collection, and royalty disbursement.

Despite these savings, however, this Article counsels against compulsory licensing as a way to reduce transaction costs. The lesson learned in a number of industries is that privately established Collective Rights Organizations (CROs) will often emerge to break the transactional bottleneck. From patent pools to collective copyright licensing organizations such as ASCAP and BMI, IPR owners in various industries have demonstrated the workability of these private transactional mechanisms. Indeed, these case studies uncover two distinct advantages of CROs: expert tailoring and reduced political economy problems.

In a CRO, knowledgeable industry participants set the rules of exchange. These rules are not likely to be uniform, one-size-fits-all terms as in a statutory compulsory license; they often vary according to the broad features of the rights. Individual works covered by discrete IPRs are assigned to categories based on the members' knowledge and experience. Through this expert tailoring, CROs produce an intermediate level of contract detail, reflecting not only collective industry expertise but also the need for efficiency in carrying out a high volume of transactions.

An important component of expert tailoring, then, is the use of royalty rates as set by experts. But the statutory compulsory licenses often begin with rational royalty rates as well. What separates private CROs from compulsory licensing schemes is that the former have proven to be more flexible over time. ASCAP, for example, frequently adjusts the rates it charges radio and television stations. Statutes, on the other hand, are difficult to change. Because interested parties can often spend enough to veto a change in legislation, compulsory licenses in the IPR field are subject to "legislative lock-in." CROs avoid this problem.

To the extent these CROs outperform compulsory licenses in lowering transaction costs, they stand conventional entitlements theory on its head. The initially higher transaction costs of property rule entitlements actually serve a benign purpose: they lead individual IPR holders to form CROs. These privately organized institutions then devolve standard rules of exchange that substantially lower transaction costs. This achieves the same purpose as state-created liability rules. The difference is that the individual right holders, rather than the state, set the standard terms of exchange. This process of contracting into liability rules significantly reduces state involvement in the creation of efficient entitlements. Given this advantage, I suggest in the conclusion that property rule entitlements may be superior in other situations where right holders encounter each other frequently....

Traditional intellectual property rights theories, those that take a utilitarian (incentive) approach and those adopting a natural rights approach, despite their disagreements, assume that IPRs cover a single, discrete market product. They pay no systematic attention to the role of IPRs as inputs into multi-component products. They are therefore not helpful in understanding the transactional role of IPRs. In order to understand the role of intellectual property rules when economic agents must obtain multiple IPRs before introducing a product to the market, we must turn to other bodies of literature not normally associated with intellectual property: entitlements theory, the new institutionalism, and public choice literature.

* * *

Calabresi and Melamed advance a polarized approach to the initial assignment of rights. Their framework posits a world with only two scenarios: either the legislature issues property rights, or it establishes a liability rule (through what the authors call "collective valuation"). They do not, however, discuss the many non-legislative forms of "collective valuation" that a property rule can call forth. The institutions studied in this Article are examples of a host of such private forums for valuation and transfer of property rights that do not rely directly on the state to carry out their coordinating function. In theoretical terms, this Article seeks to integrate the insights of the modern literature on economic institutions into the Calabresi–Melamed framework by looking for ways in which initial entitlements might be used to channel post-assignment behavior. I also examine a few institutional arrangements to determine whether formal rights are needed at all.

The active investment in creation of collective institutions highlights another gap in our understanding of entitlements. Most writing on property rights theory treats enforcement techniques and technologies as either exogenously determined or subject to only minor optimization. These techniques and technologies are not necessarily considered static, but rather just as more or less given. My point is twofold: institutions are enforcement technologies too, and they are often generated intentionally to reduce transaction costs and to increase the value of assets. To the extent institution-building investment is pervasive, we in the legal academy need to incorporate the possibility of endogenous enforcement "technologies"—including institutions—into our analysis of property rights.

Only repeated transactions among right holders will give rise to the private institutions discussed in this Article. One-shot or sporadic interactions do not justify investments in exchange institutions. Numerous scholars have been fascinated with the tendency of repeated interactions to coalesce into various forms of private ordering. Robert Ellickson has described how informal (i.e., non-legal) behavioral norms can emerge out of repeated interactions among members of close-knit communities. Of course, the communities Ellickson studied differ from the IPR institutions, which are embedded in an industrial milieu and are therefore more concerned with shorter-term self-interest. Because of this difference, Ellickson's principal finding—that community members disregard formal legal entitlements in favor of informal norms—is not duplicated in the institutions studied in this Article.

Even so, similar forces lead community members to develop cooperative norms and push firms into collective IPR institutions. Repeat interaction is the most significant. In some institutions, such as ASCAP, the need for many dealings with copyright licensees (and infringers) brought right holders together. Internal governance rules and economies of scale in enforcement combined to lower drastically the transaction costs of administering these rights. Patent pools facilitate licensing and royalty splitting, and also extensive cross-licensing among members. These centralized institutions both bundle rights and settle accounts among members.

Initial legal entitlements matter very much. But the pressure of numerous transactions produces norms that in effect modify the initial entitlements. In his study, Ellickson concluded that informal norms were paramount. This Article concludes in similar fashion that semi-formal arrangements (or re-arrangements) dominate in the IPR arena. In both cases, repeat interactions drive these arrangements.

While Ellickson is one of the few legal scholars to focus on cooperative norms, an important group of economists has been hard at work in recent years studying the closely related phenomenon of institutions. This "new institutional economics" furnishes a useful set of concepts for helping to understand IPR institutions. In particular, I provide a detailed discussion of Elinor Ostrom's work, one of the best examples of this inductive branch of social science. Her research documents the incremental evolution of private institutions from origins often no more complex than simple bilateral contracts. The "new institutional" approach will help us understand our later discussion of the emergence of private IPR institutions.

The new institutional economics seeks to describe the formation and function of private institutions. The accounts provide detailed descriptions of specific schemes designed to overcome the crucial triad of transaction costs: valuation, monitoring, and enforcement. Although valuation is important in the Calabresi–Melamed Framework, the rubric of "collective valuation" assigns complex group valuation (and hence, implicitly, monitoring and enforcement) to government agencies working off-stage. The institutional literature, in its discussion of valuation, monitoring, and enforcement, fleshes out this aspect of the bare bones Calabresi–Melamed Framework.

Collective rights organizations devise general rules that replicate contracting terms between two parties. Usually, these CROs establish at least a few distinct classes of rights. After setting up the basic categories of rights, CROs then assign each right to one of the classes.

This is hardly the same as the detailed negotiations that accompany an everyday licensing deal. But everyday licensing involves only two parties: a right holder and a single licensee. Each licensing contract, though similar to others in some respects, is unique. A CRO cannot draft individual contracts, but it can assign works to categories based on the members' knowledge and experience. CROs produce an intermediate level of contract detail, reflecting collective industry expertise and the need for efficiency in carrying out a high volume of transactions. They might be called organizations for "bulk contracting, by committee."

One of the central functions of CROs is to set a price for the rights in the portfolio: both a price for the entire portfolio, sometimes referred to as a blanket royalty rate, and prices for the individual rights within the portfolio. In both cases, the price(s) are the same for all takers, or at least for all similarly-situated licensees. By setting collectively-determined prices, CROs create something closely akin to a compulsory license. Essentially all market participants are welcome to use the right(s), so long as they pay the pre-established price.

There is one crucial difference, however, between private collectives and statutory compulsory licenses: in these organizations, the members, and not Congress or a court, set the price. Price setting by CROs almost always involves extensive negotiations; sometimes, ongoing adjustments are carried out via a permanent administrative structure. CROs present a simple, coherent menu of prices and other terms to licensees—and they do so after extensive internal consultation.

This Part describes some of the most significant CROs that have developed thus far in the intellectual property area. These institutions emerged from a background of strong property rights that created potential roadblocks to the health and development of important industries.

Performing Rights Societies

Public performances—on radio and television, and in live entertainment outlets, to name the largest classes—flood our culture at an ever-increasing pace. Imagine the enormous cost if discrete bargains between each "buyer" of a performance right and each copyright owner were required. Yet, the public performance right is one component of copyright, which, like the other branches of intellectual property, protects rights with a strong property rule. Given the enormous number of bilateral bargains called for by the copyright entitlement, collective rights administration of some sort is the only sensible solution.

Performing rights societies have emerged to perform this collective rights administration. ASCAP, the American Society of Composers, Authors, and Publishers, which was formed in 1914, is one of the largest performing rights societies. Like the other institutions of its kind, ASCAP acts as a central depository that allows members to control public performances of their works. ASCAP issues "blanket licenses" covering the relevant copyrights of all members of the Society to radio and television stations and other entertainment outlets. It then monitors the songs played and divides up the total receipts among all members on the basis of a complex pro rata formula. Monitoring and enforcement activities with respect to licensees and infringers are also an important part of ASCAP's function. A rival organization, Broadcast Music Incorporated (BMI), which was founded in 1941 expressly to compete with ASCAP, operates similarly.

The origins of ASCAP fit a characteristic pattern for successful appropriation institutions: it started small and grew incrementally, adjusting its internal governance structure along the way. ASCAP was formed when nine prominent participants in the New York music industry banded together to take concerted action against flagrant, uncompensated public performances of musical works. It appears that no single composer had enough capital single-handedly to fight the restaurant and nightclub owners, who threatened a concerted boycott of any composer who challenged their practices. To meet the threat, ASCAP's founders chose as president George Maxwell, a music publishing executive, and as vice president Victor Herbert, a prominent composer of popular and serious music who was the music director of the Philadelphia Orchestra.

In the beginning, ASCAP was little more than a cost-spreading club for copyright litigation. In this respect, Herbert proved to be a good plaintiff as well as vice president, lending his name to the foundational case written by Oliver Wendell Holmes that established that restaurants which performed music must compensate composers even if patrons are not charged separately for the musical entertainment. ASCAP's second president, Gene Buck, vigorously enforced the public performance rights of ASCAP members; he initiated cases in the far corners of the country, going after such disparate users as dance hall operators, hotels, movie theaters, and eventually radio broadcasters.

After some early procedural setbacks related to membership structure and policing tactics, ASCAP achieved an impressive string of legal victories. In each case, the court found for the copyright holder, over the objections of defendants who often complained about the practical difficulties of policing multiple performances. Significantly, in none of the cases did a court excuse infringement due to the expense of locating and bargaining with copyright holders; and in every case, an injunction was granted.

Despite the swelling ranks, ASCAP's finances crept along a modest expansion path. The group divided what little net royalties there were equally among publishers and composers. Nor were ASCAP employees benefitting personally; the General Counsel, Nathan Burkan, reportedly went entirely without pay for ASCAP's first seven years, a period of almost frantic litigation, judging by how often Burkan's name appears in reported cases involving ASCAP and its members.

ASCAP's big break came with the advent of radio technology in the early 1920s. At first, ASCAP allowed radio stations free use of members' compositions. By 1925, however, the "free sample" era ended and a series of lawsuits began. These were directed at early commercial users of radio—mostly large retail stores and hotels—and helped ASCAP establish the right for compensation to all music played over the radio. By 1940, the radio broadcasting industry had gross revenues of close to $200,000,000. Of this amount, ASCAP collected a reported $4,000,000, which represented two-thirds of ASCAP's gross revenue.

ASCAP's rise paralleled the growth of radio, and later television. From its original nine members, the membership grew to 1,000 composers in 1941, 3,000 in 1958, 17,800 composers and 4,800 publishers in 1977, and over 31,000 composers and approximately 24,000 publishers today. The current membership has now licensed performance rights to over two and a half million compositions.

Despite the meteoric rise of ASCAP, its original organizational design has remained remarkably stable. The first two executives in the organization were drawn from the two major parts of the musical composition industry—composers and publishers. As the institution expanded with the growth of radio, this basic governance structure was maintained. After a very early adjustment in royalty arrangement, the current fifty-fifty split between publishers and composers was agreed upon; it has not changed since. Since 1921, the board has numbered twenty-four members: twelve composers and twelve representatives from the publishing industry. Each group is at least roughly represented by this arrangement, making for a stable institution.

ASCAP's chief competition, BMI, was founded in 1940 by radio stations trying to obtain some leverage against ASCAP. The creation of BMI followed a number of failed attempts to limit ASCAP's effectiveness through legislation. BMI today represents approximately 150,000 U.S. songwriters and composers and approximately 50,000 U.S. publishers.

As ASCAP has grown, it has devised ever more sophisticated techniques for determining (1) the appropriate royalty rate for each industry that makes use of performances, and (2) a fair division of royalty income among members. Currently, tremendous effort goes into structuring a royalty arrangement with each industry that reflects the value of music in that industry and includes realistic collection techniques. Royalty division among members is done on the basis of a combination of self-reporting by licensees and sophisticated sampling techniques. ASCAP's reporting forms require very detailed data regarding the licensee's total revenues, adjustments thereto, and total blanket license royalty calculations. In addition, each radio and television licensee is required to provide a detailed "Program Log" listing all ASCAP-licensed compositions performed in a given period.

Patent Pools

As an illustration of unadorned private liability rules, few institutions compare to the patent pool. In a patent pool, multiple patent holders assign or license their individual rights to a central entity, which in turn exploits the collective rights by licensing, manufacturing, or both. Most importantly, the pool regularizes the valuation of individual patents—making, as the United States Supreme Court put it, "a division of royalties according to the value attributed by the parties to their respective patent claims...."

Thus patent pools, like collective rights organizations in copyright, serve to regularize technology transactions. Indeed, at least one court has noted the similarity between ASCAP and patent pools. Like ASCAP, patent pools serve a needed economic function: they significantly reduce the transaction costs of exchanging rights. When they are not being used as a cover for a cartel, they add significantly to the efficient operation of the patent system, as many industries have discovered over time.

In many cases, pools are creatures of necessity. For example, where different firms hold patents on the basic building blocks of the industry's products, they will have to cross-license to produce at all. This problem affected both the sewing machine industry in the 1850s and the aircraft industry in the early twentieth century. Even where no single patent or set of patents is essential, however, firms in an industry often find that they engage in such frequent negotiations that a regularized institution with formal rules, or even general guidelines, is helpful in reducing transaction costs. The economic literature on institutions explains this quite well: repeat-play makes it easier to reach agreement on any particular issue, because disparities tend to balance out over many transactions.

Patent pools function according to liability rules. Typically, firms are required to license into the pool all patents covering technology of use to the industry. In exchange, pool members are permitted to use any other member's technology for a set fee. Often these fees are calibrated to reflect the significance of the technology being licensed. The first licensing pool was among members of the sewing machine industry beginning in 1856. It operated under these sorts of rules, as have many others, including the aircraft and automobile pools.

All patent pools share one fundamental characteristic: they provide a regularized transactional mechanism that takes the place of the statutory property rule baseline requiring an individual bargain for each transaction. But in most other respects, their characteristics vary. They range from huge, industry-wide institutions with dozens of members and hundreds of patents, to relatively simple arrangements that look like nothing more than multilateral relational contracts. The latter may border on terrain outside the scope of this paper—being not so much liability rules as elaborate installment contracts.

The most well-documented industry-wide pools arose in the automobile and aircraft industries around the turn of the twentieth century. Through the use of pooling, representatives of the various members participate in the valuation of the patented technology. A pool committee determines the royalty that each licensee of pooled technology is charged. This basic structure also served the sewing machine, bathtub, door part, seeded-raisin, coaster brake, and other industries.

The rationale for pools with these sophisticated administrative structures is well described in this passage from the 1935 congressional patent pooling hearings:

> These various institutions have differed materially in the type
> of organization created by the agreements. Perhaps the loosest
> of all is the automobile manufacturers agreement, and obvious
> [sic] the most severe restrictions are imposed where the patents
> pass into the hands of a single owner, yet all these agreements
> have in common the principle that within the industry, the
> individual monopoly created by patents is abolished in the form

> it is provided by statute and a different system is substituted more in harmony with the needs of that industry.
>
> [I]n the airplane cross-licensing agreement, after completely abolishing the monopoly of the individual inventor and opening every patent to every member of the association, it provides that a board of arbitrators may decide in any case what reward should be paid to individual patent owners and this is based not upon the official determination of patentability by the Patent Office, but upon the unofficial determination of the importance of the invention by a board of arbitrators.

Actually, the aircraft pool did not "arbitrate" all patent licensing requests. In its earliest incarnation, the pool aimed to eliminate ruinous litigation and divide royalties on patents existing at the time of the pool's formation according to a set formula. Apart from the "foundational" patents of Glenn Curtiss and the Wright Brothers, which earned millions of dollars in royalties for their holders under the pooling agreement, most licensing was conducted on a royalty-free basis, with mutual forbearance from infringement suits as the real payment for the exchange.

Patents added to the pool after its formation were divided into two classes. Normal patents were licensed into the pool for all to use, with no special royalty payout going to the inventor or firm. Exceptional patents earned ongoing royalties, in an amount determined by a formal arbitration procedure. Under the original contract creating the pool, known as the Manufacturers Aircraft Association (MAA), members agreed:

> To submit claims for compensation in respect to airplane patents or patent rights hereafter acquired to a board of arbitrators consisting of one member appointed by the board of directors of the Association (Inc.), another by the subscriber making the claim, and a third by the other two, who shall determine the total amount of compensation, if any, to be paid for the same, and the rate of royalty to be paid toward such compensation by any subscriber desiring to take a license under such patent. (Art. V, pp. 4–5.)
>
> To waive all claims as against each other for infringements prior to July 1, 1917 (Art. XIV, p. 13); to make various reports and to keep various accounts, etc.

Since compensation requests were in practice limited to exceptional patents, arbitrated valuations were by definition rare. The pool's two-tiered approach created the danger of imprecise valuation, but the repeat-play nature of exchange allowed discrepancies to even out over time. Although one member might make out well on one technology by getting free access to a very valuable invention, the member on the short end of the deal would make up the difference in future transactions. Some measure of the transaction cost savings engendered by the pool may be reflected in the fact that the major patent holders, Wright and Curtiss, lowered their royalty rates after formation of the pool.

The internal structure of the MAA looked surprisingly like that of ASCAP. Voting was weighted by the economic value of the patents contributed by the founding members. This was so, according to the

Attorney General's report which cleared the MAA of antitrust problems, because

> [i]f all the manufacturers had been given equal voice in the Association (Inc.) the smaller manufacturers together would have been enabled to control the Association (Inc.), to wit, the agent of the parties in whose responsibility and vigilance the Wright–Martin and Curtiss corporations are so vitally interested. This conflict of interest accounts for the adoption of the voting trust agreement under which the Wright–Martin and Curtiss corporations named one trustee, the smaller manufacturers another trustee, and a party not favorable to either interest, namely, a member of the Advisory Committee, was selected for the third trustee.

A corresponding governance structure, weighted to reflect the respective patent holdings of the founding members, was built into the auto industry patent pool when it was formed in the early twentieth century. But the similarities do not stop there: the two institutions also shared a massive scale (the auto pool had 79 members and 350 patents when formed, over 200 members and 1,000 patents in 1932); a two-tiered patent classification scheme; an arbitration procedure for exceptional patents; and an institutionalized end to ubiquitous litigation.

As with the MAA, most members of the automobile pool seemed content to rely on the blanket, royalty-free cross licensing that was also available under the pool. What arbitration there was took place in a committee of knowledgeable industry participants. The arrangement was lauded far and wide as a success, even by no less an opponent of the patent system than Walton Hamilton.

Hamilton spoke of the success of the automobile pool as proof of the creaky substructure of the patent system. "A heterodox chapter," he concluded, "challenges the whole theology of the patent system." It was as if the need to reconstitute the property rights by contract—the need to create an administrative apparatus to deal with the rights—proved the irrelevance or inadequacy of those rights.

This Article takes a more optimistic view of the relationship between the patent system and patent pools. Without the property rights—backed by the threat of production-choking injunctions—the advantages conveyed by the pool would never have been realized. These advantages extended far beyond a cessation of patent hostilities. They included the institutionalized exchange of all manner of unpatented technical information, and the creation of a framework for the crucial task of standardizing sizes and configurations for car parts. All this followed from the industry's establishment of the contractual liability rule, or institution. A recognition of these advantages lies behind the language of a 1935 congressional report on patent pools:

> Each of these [patent pooling] agreements therefore represents the perhaps unformulated, but nonetheless definite and considered judgment of the leaders in that industry that it cannot exist under the patent law in the form in which that law was designed, and that progress demands a substitution for the law

> as created by statute and the substitution of a new system of
> law by contract.

It is hard to improve on this formulation: patent pools as a form of contractual governance that "substitutes" for life under property rule entitlements, or "patent law in the form in which that law was designed."

In the pioneering entitlements framework of Calabresi and Melamed, liability rules entail "collective valuation": court-determined compensation to an owner when a right has been violated. Property rules are the opposite: strictly individual valuation with prices set by the right holder alone. The IPR institutions studied here show that this is a false dichotomy. These institutions represent intermediate forms of collective valuation. Firms work together to establish a collective price charged to licensees for use of the members' IPRs. They agree on rules for splitting licensing fees among members. They often participate in the ongoing administration of the collective institution, by adjusting prices due to changing conditions, arbitrating disputes, and the like.

Intellectual property rights, consummate property rule entitlements, are often fragmented among many firms in an industry. Marketable products require many IPR inputs and therefore many IPR transactions. Because IPRs are property rule entitlements, using them requires separate bargains with individual right holders. Where firms are involved in such transactions repeatedly, institutions for regularized IPR exchange tend to emerge. Because they grow out of repeated dealings by knowledgeable industry insiders, and because their internal governance allows for ongoing administrative adjustments, they are more efficient than the compulsory licenses (legislative liability rules) found in parts of intellectual property law. We might call these superior institutions "private liability rules," and the process of creating them "contracting into liability rules," labels that suggest their intermediate nature somewhere between pure individual property rights and pure government-determined liability rules.

Property rule entitlements push right holders together to found these institutions. Thus we end with what seems like a paradox. To encourage effective collective valuation mechanisms—liability rules—one should start with a property rule. The pressure of high transaction costs in an industry where repeat dealings are the norm will produce a better transactional mechanism than a legislature could create in advance.

Notes and Questions

1. Biographical information for the author is found on page 163.

2. One increasingly important form of patent pool is the standard-setting organization. SSOs, as they are known, often (though not always) pool intellectual property rights so as to set technological standards—such as interface protocols and interconnection schemes—that are shared among industry participants. For a detailed account of the functioning of SSOs, and the role that IPRs play in them, see Mark Lemley, "Intellectual Property Rights and Standard-Setting Organizations," 90 *Cal. L. Rev.* 1889, 1891–92 (2002) ("SSOs are a species of private ordering ... [that] may serve to ameliorate the problems of overlapping IP rights in those industries in which IP is most problematic for innovation, particularly in the semiconductor, software, and telecommunications fields."). For a critique of some features of a patent pool involving "third generation" wireless technology, see Michael R. Franzinger, Comment, "Latent Dangers In a Patent Pool: The European Commission's Approval Of The 3G Wireless Technology Licensing Agreements," 91 *Cal. L. Rev.* 1693 (2003).

3. The excerpt above states at one point that "institutions are enforcement technologies too, and they are often generated intentionally to reduce transaction costs and to increase the value of assets." Recent theory has become more sophisticated about the ways in which governance mechanisms such as the CROs studied here interact with and in some ways substitute for purely exclusionary property rights. See Henry E. Smith, "Exclusion Versus Governance: Two Strategies For Delineating Property Rights," 31 *J. Legal Stud.* 453 (2002).

4. Do you think the author is too optimistic about the ability of disparate rightholders to come together to form CROs? When is this likely to occur, and when not? Should legal doctrine or policy take account of the likelihood that rightholders will create a collective solution to a rights "thicket" or bottleneck? For more on "patent thickets," see Carl Shapiro, "Navigating the Patent Thicket: Cross Licenses, Patent Pools, and Standard Setting," in Innovation Policy and the Economy 119 (Adam B. Jaffe et al. eds.) (Cambridge, MA: MIT Press, 2001).

Property Rights in Emerging Platform Technologies*

DOUGLAS LICHTMAN

I. Introduction

Ever since Apple lost to IBM, technology firms have recognized the important role third-party innovation plays in the development of emerging "platform" technologies. The story is by now well known. Apple designed its first desktop computers with easy-access hardware ports and an accessible operating system, the purpose being to facilitate third-party development of compatible hardware and software accessories. But when IBM entered the home computer market, Apple decided that its best strategy was to offer a more integrated product. Thus, the same year IBM unveiled the IBM PC, a machine with built-in expansion slots for hardware and well-publicized hardware and software specifications, Apple introduced the Macintosh, a unit that had some advantages over the IBM PC out of the box but was markedly less accessible to third-party development. Within a few years, hundreds of available hardware and software add-ons (including dozens of applications and accessories that IBM itself had not anticipated) made the IBM PC the dominant home computing platform.

* Reprinted with permission from 29 *J. Legal Stud.* 615 (2000), © 2000, the University of Chicago and Douglas Lichtman.

The IBM approach—what is today referred to as "open architecture"—has been a popular one in recent years. In the market for handheld computers, for example, both Palm and Handspring have adopted variants of the strategy, making available at no charge and to all comers the interface specifications for their respective computing platforms. The motivation in each of these instances is the same: open-architecture strategies allow platform developers to decentralize the innovative process. Firms like IBM, Palm, and Handspring do not need to themselves bear the full responsibility of both identifying the most compelling applications for their platforms and then either developing or contracting with others to develop the necessary peripherals; instead, under an open-architecture approach, they can share that responsibility with third-party innovators. The platform developers earn their profits on sales of the platforms; the third-party entrepreneurs earn theirs on sales of associated hardware, software, and service peripherals.

The open-architecture strategy has a problem, however, in that it creates a market structure fraught with externalities. Think, for example, about peripheral prices. Early in the development of any platform/peripheral ecosystem, peripheral developers enjoy significant discretion to set their prices instead of being forced by competitive pressures to charge marginal cost. This is true in large part because the first firm to identify any add-on category is a monopolist until other firms create comparable goods. Such discretion alone would not be troubling except for the fact that each firm's pricing decision affects every other firm's sales. If a given firm were to charge a lower price, consumers would be more likely to purchase the relevant platform and, hence, more likely to then purchase other firms' peripherals. This is an externality: it is a consequence of each firm's pricing decision that is ignored when each firm sets its price.

What this means—and here let us continue to focus on the pricing externality although parallel arguments can be made with respect to decisions regarding product quality, advertising investments, and so on—is that in markets based on emerging platform technologies, third-party developers as a group will charge prices that are too high. That is, if these firms could internalize the externality, they would (a) charge lower prices, a result that would benefit consumers in a distributional sense and also increase efficiency by lessening the gap between price and marginal cost, and (b) earn greater profits, since under reasonable assumptions each firm would lose money as a result of its own price drop but gain much more thanks to the increase in sales brought on by other firms' reciprocal price reductions. Price coordination would also increase the pace of innovation, since higher profits ex post would mean greater incentives to enter the market ex ante, and, through both lower prices and faster innovation, it would increase the rate of platform adoption as well.

Price coordination is possible in most peripheral markets. Firms can contract, for example, or integrate. But coordination is virtually impossible in markets based on still-emerging technologies. The problem is that there is never an opportunity to bring all or nearly all of the affected firms together to negotiate a mutually beneficial price reduction. At these early stages, firms are constantly entering and exiting the market. Obviously a firm currently in the market cannot coordinate with one that has yet to enter; but in this setting such negotiations are of critical importance since a consumer's decision as to whether to purchase an emerging platform technology is often as much based on the consumer's expectations with respect to the price, quality, and availability of future peripherals as it is based on the price and quality of peripherals already available for purchase.

Negotiations among the subset of firms in the market at any given time are still an option; but, by themselves, negotiations of this sort will likely prove ineffective. After all, current firms will always be reluctant to lower their prices for fear that any price concessions they achieve will be offset by price increases from future firms. This is in fact the externality itself at work: lower prices for current peripherals lead to increased demand for the platform, which, in turn, leads to increased demand for future peripherals; that increased demand tempts future firms to raise their prices, and those higher prices undermine the benefits of the original price reductions. Note that this same problem also makes vertical integration unworkable. The platform owner could in theory buy out current peripheral sellers and lower the prices of their peripherals; but when new peripheral sellers would enter the market, those sellers would charge correspondingly higher prices, eliminating or reducing the benefits of the original integration.

Where does this leave us? The above arguments combine to suggest that in markets based on relatively new platform technologies, pure open-architecture strategies are decidedly second best. The best way for a platform owner to introduce a new platform technology might indeed be to make it profitable for a large number of unidentified firms to develop compatible hardware and software accessories, but accomplishing that goal by making publicly available the platform's technical specifications invites inefficiency. Every time, consumers will face prices that are unnecessarily high. Every time, peripheral sellers will earn profits that are unnecessarily low.

Platform owners choose the open-architecture approach, however, because under current legal rules they have no better alternative. Instead of giving away interface information, these firms should be using that information as leverage, sharing it with all interested third-party developers, but only on the condition that the firms participate in some sort of a price-reduction or profit-sharing program. But intellectual property law gets in the way. Completely insensitive to the peculiar dynamics of the platform/peripheral market structure, the modern intellectual property regime undermines platform owners' influence by allowing unauthorized firms to reverse engineer the platform and, in that way, develop compatible peripherals without the platform owner's permission. Worse, every time platform owners attempt to compensate— say, requiring that platform purchasers agree to use the platform only in conjunction with authorized peripherals—courts interpret one or another intellectual property doctrine so as to block the adjustment, again without even considering the possibility that broader intellectual property rights might facilitate a beneficial form of price coordination.

The argument in this article, then, is not that intellectual property law should recognize in all platform owners absolute control over which firms, if any, develop peripherals compatible with their respective platforms. Nor is it that platform owners should always enjoy absolute control with respect to emerging platform technologies—that is, absolute control over the first generation of some handheld computer or the first release of a new operating system. The point, instead, is that when courts interpret the intellectual property rights recognized in platform technologies, they should consider the possibility that broader readings would facilitate price coordination that, in turn, might lead to lower prices for consumers and higher profits for producers. For the reasons sketched above, that possibility is especially strong in markets based on emerging platform technologies—although there are surely exceptions to that rule and, conversely, settings involving more established technologies where this same logic might hold.

This argument has implications for a number of specific patent and copyright doctrines; those are considered later in the article. As readers familiar with the intellectual property literature will recognize, however, it also has implications for an important debate in intellectual property law, a debate that began with a famous article by Edmund Kitch and concerns the wisdom of allowing original inventors to coordinate the process through which later firms improve and develop their inventions. That debate has, up until now, focused on only one type of coordination: coordination designed to reduce the resources wasted when rival firms either inadvertently duplicate one another's research or race to be first to complete some incremental step. This paper introduces to the debate a second type of coordination: coordination designed to capture demand-side interdependencies. The shift in emphasis is important since, as others have pointed out, given transaction costs and uncertainty, downstream coordination as it is traditionally conceived is virtually impossible for an original inventor to bring about. After all, original inventors hoping to lessen the risk of duplicative follow-on investment face the Herculean task of negotiating detailed contracts with every incremental innovator, avoiding overlap by specifying exactly which research path each is authorized to pursue. The type of coordination considered here, by contrast, can be significantly achieved through more manageable means. For example, the original innovator can impose price caps keyed to rough peripheral categories or develop a profit-sharing plan where the percentage each firm contributes is constant across all firms. Thus, the argument presented here supports what was Kitch's original claim: intellectual property law should, in certain cases, empower original inventors to coordinate the behavior of follow-on inventors.

[In Part II, the author models the effects of noncoordination among platform and peripheral sellers, demonstrating that under plausible conditions uncoordinated prices are 33% higher than they would be if coordinated, and that generally the lack of peripheral coordination has a "sizeable effect" on pricing.]

III. Implications

The externality identified in the preceding section likely affects a wide variety of platform/peripheral markets. It probably affects markets where consumers purchase video game consoles separately from compatible cartridges and markets where consumers purchase computer hardware separately from niche or locked-in software. In cases like these, however, affected firms can mitigate the externality's implications by coordinating prices through contract, integration, or some other formal or informal mechanism. This, for example, might be one reason why Microsoft bundles a word processor, spreadsheet, and database together in its Office product and, further, why Microsoft then tries to sell the Office product together with the Windows operating system. Markets of this general form are not of particular interest here, then, because, even if it is significant, any externality in these markets can be addressed through conventional means.

In markets based on emerging platform technologies, however, voluntary coordination is likely unworkable. As was explained in the Introduction, this is because of the dynamic nature of still-maturing markets. With firms constantly entering and exiting the market, it is almost impossible to bring all affected firms together for a single negotiation. And negotiations among any subset of the firms are unlikely to result in a significant price reduction since involved firms will be hesitant to lower their prices for fear that any price concessions they achieve will be offset by corresponding price increases from uninvolved firms. Of course, the platform owner itself might be able to partially solve the problem by, for example, paying subsidies to firms that lower their prices; but any such solution is significantly limited. When new peripheral sellers enter the market, after all, those sellers either will charge correspondingly higher prices or will themselves demand a significant subsidy, in both cases significantly undermining either the platform owner's objectives or its profitability.

In emerging technology cases, then, the most promising way to internalize the peripheral/peripheral externality is to empower one party—the obvious choice being the platform owner—to coordinate the behavior of all the other firms. The issue is thus an issue for intellectual property law. Patent, copyright, trademark, and trade secret protection combine to give platform owners a certain degree of influence over every would-be peripheral developer. But that influence has traditionally been constrained; courts have in general been unwilling to recognize too much influence for fear that platform owners would use it to exclude firms from the peripheral market. That, of course, misses the insight of open-architecture strategies: many platform owners in fact rely on third-party innovation both to develop their platforms quickly and to identify new applications. These platform owners would use additional influence not to exclude peripheral firms from the market but instead to make the peripheral market more profitable. Thus, there is another factor for courts to consider when applying any of the various doctrines that determine the scope of a platform owner's intellectual property rights: the possibility that broader rights will be used to facilitate downstream coordination to the benefit of consumers, third-party developers, and also the platform owner....

[This article next] considers discretionary rights courts at their option recognize on a case-by-case basis. The subsection is organized around four main inquiries—in patent law, the distinction between repair and reconstruction, and the doctrine of patent misuse; and, in copyright law, the definition of the term "derivative work" and the doctrine of fair use—and argues that each of these inquiries should be guided in part by the arguments presented earlier in the paper. The third and final subsection considers two possible objections to this proposal: that courts might not have the expertise required to engage in the analysis endorsed here and that, even with broader rights, as a practical matter platform owners will not be able to coordinate follow-on innovation.

* * *

The text below surveys four discretionary inquiries in intellectual property law that, in different settings, determine the relative rights of platform owners and peripheral developers. It is in the context of these inquiries that the analysis presented in this article could most easily be brought to bear. . . .

1. Repair/Reconstruction (Patent Law).

[We begin with] the distinction between the repair and reconstruction of a patented combination. The issue arises in instances where a peripheral is listed as an element of a patent claim. The patent holder argues that, by replacing the listed element, users infringe the combination patent. . . .

The distinction between repair and reconstruction is thus a question of patent scope—a question that in this context determines whether peripheral developers need the platform owner's permission to sell compatible peripherals. To the extent that replacing the peripheral is deemed reconstruction, it is under the patent holder's exclusive purview; to the extent that those replacements are deemed repair, the patent holder has no exclusive right. This is a judicially developed distinction, and courts today consider the "totality of the circumstances" when determining whether a given act infringes. One implication of the current paper is thus to suggest that one factor courts should consider as part of this inquiry is how each result would affect the structure and existence of the market for replaceable components.

2. Patent Misuse. Platform owners have from time to time attempted to control peripheral developers by imposing restrictive licenses on purchasers of the platform. For example, in Motion Picture Patents Company v. Universal Film Manufacturing Company,[1] plaintiff-patentee conditioned each sale of its patented film projector on the stipulation that the purchaser rent films only from distributors approved by the patentee. . . .

Patent misuse is traditionally an affirmative defense to a charge of patent infringement. It is an equitable doctrine, the notion being that a court should not use its power to assist a patent holder where, in this or any other interaction, the patent holder is exercising its rights in a

---

1. 243 U.S. 502 (1917).

manner against public policy. The defense can be invoked in any case.
An alleged infringer, for example, can argue that a given patent should
not be enforced because, in some entirely unrelated instance, the patentee has impermissibly used its patent power. A patent holder whose
actions are found to constitute misuse loses all rights vis-à-vis all parties
until the practice is discontinued and its effects on the market are "fully
dissipated."

Why is this troubling? As a practical matter, [it] ... means that
patent holders cannot even attempt to use restrictive licenses for this
purpose. The stakes are too high; one misstep and the patent holder in
essence forfeits patent protection on the platform. Because the arguments presented in this paper would favor, in certain circumstances, the
enforcement of restrictive licenses of this sort, the draconian penalties of
patent misuse seem unnecessarily chilling. Courts would better serve
equity by in these instances narrowing the maximum patent misuse
penalty and thus enabling firms to attempt what might turn out to be
permissible and socially beneficial licensing regimes.

[The author then argues that the benefits of platform-peripheral
coordination should also factor into the analysis of fair use and the
definition of derivative works, both copyright law issues.]

IV. Conclusion

Recent enthusiasm for legal rules that constrain the behavior of
platform owners has to some degree crowded out conversations regarding legal reform of the sort discussed here. That is unfortunate. Just as
traditional network economics related to lock-in and network effects
suggest that legal intervention limiting platform owner control might in
some cases improve societal welfare, the network economics introduced
in this paper suggest conversely that legal intervention supportive of
owner control can at times increase societal welfare as well.

Notes and Questions

1. Douglas Lichtman received a B.S.E. degree from Duke University
and a J.D. from Yale Law School. He teaches at the University of
Chicago School of Law.

2. Lichtman states that the earlier literature on patent scope issues
was restricted to a discussion of "coordination designed to reduce the
resources wasted when rival firms either inadvertently duplicate one
another's research or race to be first to complete some incremental
step." In light of earlier excerpts by Kitch and Merges and Nelson, do
you agree? In particular, what would Merges and Nelson have to say
about a proposal that gave price-setting coordination power to a single
firm? The key question here boils down to this: Is the pricing externality
emphasized by Lichtman worth the cost of a greater concentration of
economic power in the hands of a central platform/peripheral "ecosystem" coordinator? Is the concentration issue diluted in any way by the
fact that Lichtman envisions coordination among independent firms, as
opposed to integration in a single firm?

3. Lichtman specifically limits his prescription to situations in which new platform technologies are *emerging*. How would a court know when this is the case? What harm would follow if a court "got it wrong," and adopted Lichtman's recommendations in the context of a mature, stable platform? Would the resultant harm to competition be large or small? (Lichtman addresses some of these "judicial competence" arguments in an omitted section, where he argues that the platform coordination issue is no more complex than the analysis required by various antitrust doctrines.) Recall in this respect that challenges to platform dominance often come from firms that begin as "peripheral" suppliers—the case of Microsoft, which gained entry to the PC market as the hand-picked supplier of operating systems for the original IBM PC, comes to mind.

C. Patent–Antitrust

Patent and Antitrust Law*

WARD BOWMAN

Introduction

The principal subject of this book is the agreements that owners of patents make with others who wish to use them. The title, *Patent and Antitrust Law*, reflects the importance of antitrust law, a general law favoring competition, in determining the permissible conditions which patentees with limited monopoly, long exempt from rules applicable to nonpatented products or processes, may include in agreements with their licensees. What constitutes patent misuse has been interpreted by courts so as to severely contract the permissible use of patents in resolving supposed conflicts between patent and antitrust law. The central purpose of this study is to assess this conflict by evaluating the various forms of licensing.

A principal conclusion is that the antitrust/patent conflict, as courts have assessed it, is to a large extent illusory. It is based on a long-accepted but mistaken notion that a legal monopoly, a patent, may be used as a lever to monopolize the unpatented. In addition, courts seem oblivious, whether or not patents are involved, to the consumer-benefiting efficiencies derivable from agreements sellers make with buyers concerning how, when, where, and under what conditions a licensee may use information.

Included among those licensing arrangements that will be found *not* to be means of creating new and broader monopoly are: agreements requiring that products used with a patented product be purchased from the patentee (tie-ins); sale or resale at a stipulated price (price-restrictive licensing); sale or use confined to a particular area (territorial licensing); use for a particular purpose (functional division of use); pricing of a final product in which only one of the essential components is patented (end-

* Reprinted by permission from Patent and Antitrust Law (Chicago: Univ. of Chicago Press, 1973), © 1973 The University of Chicago.

product pricing); and licensing multiple patents in blocks (all-or-none offers).

To evaluate the foregoing examples of patentee-licensee contracts in terms of whether they "extend monopoly" is to apply a test that assumes the propriety of allowing a patentee to use any method of charging what the traffic will bear if, but only if, the reward to the patentee arising from the conditional use measures the patented product's competitive superiority over substitutes. Profit maximization—charging what the traffic will bear—it will be shown, is consistent with the patent law and is the main test the courts have assigned themselves. . . .

Chapter 1: The Compatibility of Antitrust and Patent Law Goals

Antitrust law and patent law are frequently viewed as standing in diametric opposition. How can there be compatibility between antitrust law, which promotes competition, and patent law, which promotes monopoly? In terms of the economic goals sought, the supposed opposition between these laws is lacking. Both antitrust law and patent law have a common central economic goal: *to maximize wealth by producing what consumers want at the lowest cost.* In serving this common goal, reconciliation between patent and antitrust law involves serious problems of assessing effects, but not conflicting purposes. Antitrust law does not demand competition under all circumstances. Quite properly, it permits monopoly when monopoly makes for greater output than would the alternative of an artificially fragmented (inefficient) industry. The patent monopoly fits directly into this scheme insofar as its central aim is achieved. It is designed to provide something which consumers value and which they could not have at all or have as abundantly were no patent protection afforded.

Antitrust Law

Under the Sherman Act agreements in restraint of trade (section 1) and monopolization or an attempt to monopolize (section 2) are condemned as illegal. The economic rationale for this condemnation is that monopoly makes it possible to restrict output and raise prices so that consumers pay more for and get less of the things they want most. The output restriction made possible by monopoly idles, or transfers to less urgent uses, those resources which but for the monopolistic restriction would be more efficiently employed. Conversely, a competitive market process allocates scarce resources to those uses the community values most highly. Insofar as the antitrust laws are successful, they promote a market-oriented, profit-incentive process unimpeded by artificial roadblocks to efficiency. Such is the rationale of market competition and the antitrust laws that support it.

Patent Law

Patent law, thought by some to be an exception to a general rule in favor of competition, shares with antitrust law its central purpose—efficiently providing those things consumers value. But the means are different. Patent law pursues this goal by encouraging the invention of new and better products. Invention, like other forms of productive activity, is not costless. Those who undertake it, therefore, must be rewarded. And so elusive a commodity as an idea which qualifies as invention is peculiarly susceptible to being freely appropriated by others. A patent is a legal device to insure that there can be a property right in certain ideas. Thus the temporary right of a patentee to exclude others is a means of preventing "free riding" so that the employment of useful private resources may be remunerated. Without a patent system, prevention of "free riding" would be severely limited. Ability to keep secrets and to enforce private "know-how" contracts would, without patent law, provide inventors very limited protection from rapid and widespread copying by others. Central to the economic justification of a patent system is the presumption that without the patent right, too few resources would be devoted to invention.

The "exclusive right to make, use and vend the invention or discovery," which Congress has long granted patentees, is thus a legal monopoly exempt from the more general proscription of trade restraints and monopolization under early common law and more recent antitrust statutes....

* * *

Chapter 5: More Efficient Use of Patent Monopoly through Use Restriction

If the conclusion is accepted that patentees cannot use the monopoly the law grants them to achieve additional monopoly not ascribable to the competitive superiority which the patent affords, the propriety of allowing patentees to extract the full differential value of the patent is still, for some critics if not for the courts, a problem deserving more careful attention. In this chapter and in the following chapter various forms of restriction on use—profit-maximizing devices—which patentees make with licensees will be analyzed in terms of their effect upon resource allocation. Many, if not most, will be shown to be efficient—not only efficient privately in terms of increasing patent revenue, but efficient socially, in terms of consumer interest when compared with the monopoly alternative where use restriction is outlawed and where a single uniform royalty rate is insisted upon for all prospective licensees.... Here monopoly maximization will be analyzed in broader terms and limited to special forms of price restriction. Successively more complicated situations will be discussed, beginning with a simple end-product patent monopoly.

Exploiting the full value a patent provides over substitutes involves a profit-maximizing process entailing (1) differentiating more urgent from less urgent uses, (2) having the patent utilized most efficiently (lowest cost production of the end products in which the patent is utilized), and (3) provision for the pricing of essential commodities or services jointly required for use with the patent.

For those familiar with the rudiments of traditional monopoly price theory, these conditions will be recognized as involving (1) price discrimination, including both market segregation of customers with different demand elasticities and control over quantities available to individual customers when decreasing demand elasticity for successive units used by each can be exploited (the all-or-none offer case);[1] (2) the uniform interest of both competitors and monopolists in reducing costs (the most economical provision of the product and its essential complements);[2] and (3) the advantages of setting more than a single price when two products must be used together and the price of one affects the sales of the other (cross-elasticity of demand).[3]

Understanding how and why these various monopoly pricing principles apply to patent examples is essential in determining whether specific practices should be permissible under patent or antitrust law.

Beginning then, with the single-market end-product monopoly case, for the purpose of setting the stage for the more complicated cases which derive from it, various kinds of patent-licensing contracts will be examined, including, specifically, patents on input factors used in fixed and variable proportions, joint demands for complements and substitutes, and various aspects of price discrimination. These will successively be reviewed as examples of how and why patentees employ these methods efficiently to extract the maximum return from their patents.

1. Market segregation by a patentee might involve a patented product, say a plastic with two uses. Suppose in one use close substitutes are available, for example, in containers where relatively inexpensive glass and metal are available, but that in the other use, say dentures, the alternative material is very expensive. In such a case charging denture users higher royalties than container users, if cross-selling by users could be avoided, would increase net returns to the patentee. Similarly, even if there were only a single use for a patented product, even by a single user, if this user valued successive increments of the product differently, a patentee would like to be able to exploit this demand pattern. Suppose, for example, the customer would pay 25¢ for the first unit, but only 20¢ for the second after he had the first, and 10¢ for the third after he had the second, but would pay nothing for a fourth after he had the third. Under these circumstances this customer, rather than do without the product, would buy three, paying 25¢, plus 20¢ plus 10¢ (55¢). Charging 55¢ for three units (thus the designation "all-or-none") would give the patentee more revenue than setting a single price and allowing the customer to take as much as he might then choose.

2. If, for example, a patented product could not be marketed except through retailers who by means of resale price maintenance agreements insisted upon markups substantially greater than those prevailing under competitive retailing, it would clearly be in the interest of the patentee to lower the cost of the retailing "complement" so that his patented product would have greater sales. And for similar reasons, if this patented product were manufactured either by the patentee or by licensees, the patent reward would be greater the more efficiently (less costly) this manufacturing could be done.

3. This kind of relationship might be exemplified by a "bacon and eggs" example. These two products can either be substitutes (higher egg prices making for more consumption of bacon) or complements (higher egg prices making for less bacon consumed). In either case, depending upon the relative prices of bacon and eggs, they can be expected to be used in variable proportions. It is also conceivable that the cross-effect of the price of eggs on bacon demand is not the same as the cross-effect of the price of bacon on eggs demand. Suppose, therefore, that bacon is a patented product sold competitively. If the owner of the bacon patent were to discover that raising the price of bacon (eggs remaining at the competitive price) had the effect of greatly reducing the proportions of bacon to eggs, whereas raising the price of eggs (while bacon prices were maintained or lowered to cost) had a much smaller cross-effect on the demand for bacon, then, it would follow that the patentee could gain revenue from "bacon and egg" customers by tying their purchases of bacon to sale of eggs from the patentee. The patentee would then raise the price of these eggs above the formerly competitive price and lower the price of bacon below that which he would charge if eggs were priced competitively, while at that same time substantially increasing his revenue. Moreover, it is notable that this form of patent "exploitation" does *not* provide an equivalent of an additional egg monopoly. It is useful to the patentee only with those customers who demand bacon with their eggs, and but for the "bacon invention" there would be no such customers.

Single-Market End–Product Monopoly

The basis for understanding any monopoly is, of course, the fact that monopolists take conscious account of the influence of output on price. The ability to affect price by varying output defines monopoly power. A valuable end-product patent monopoly is a monopoly prototype. It exemplifies the textbook model in which the monopolist, facing by definition a declining demand curve, increases his output only by lowering price; and effects of the lower price, being borne by him and not, as under competition, largely by rivals, makes marginal revenue (the additional revenue from selling one more unit) less than the price.[4]

The monopoly seller can therefore be described as a price searcher. Given the incomes, the tastes, and the prices of complementary and substitute products available to potential buyers of his product, and given the costs of producing and distributing the varying amounts of his product that these customers require, the monopolist searches for that price, or that amount of output, which will maximize the difference between his total cost and his total revenue. Achieving this result when all output is sold at the same price is the equivalent of selling that amount of product at which the marginal revenue (MR) from additional sales is equated with the marginal cost (MC) of these sales.[5]

Maximum profits are obtained when an increment of output adds as much to revenue as to cost. (Nobody is presumed to purposely spend an additional dollar to get an additional ninety cents.) This incremental method of analyzing the wealth-maximizing position of a monopolist can be shown graphically by plotting prices or costs on a vertical axis and output or sales on the horizontal axis (each for the same relevant period). The demand curve, sloping downward to the right, reflecting the inverse relationship between the selling price and the amount of sales which can be made, can also be read as an average revenue curve (AR). It shows, for any amount of output or sales (on the horizontal axis), what revenue can be obtained per unit of sales (AR). This is the price (P) for that amount. Once this demand curve, or average revenue curve, is established for various prices, or equivalent amounts of sales or output, there is derivable from it a curve which shows for each of these amounts the additional revenue obtainable from one additional unit of output. This is the marginal revenue (MR). It must be below and to the left of a downward-sloping average revenue curve.

Marginal cost (MC) bears the same kind of relationship to average cost (AC) as marginal revenue does to average revenue. If average costs increase with output, marginal cost is above and to the left of average cost for any output. If average costs are declining, marginal cost is below and to the left of average cost. And if, as is usually the case, costs first

4. See, for example, Stigler, *The Theory of Price*, 3d ed. (New York: Macmillan Co., 1966), p. 195.

5. This formulation is general. It is as true for a competitive producer (a price-taker) as it is for a monopolist (a price-searcher). In the former case, however, the output of the single firm is presumed to be so insignificant as to have no effect upon the market price. That price represents the competitor's marginal revenue (**MR**) for any of his outputs, and he produces to the point where his marginal cost equals the price (**P=MR**).

decline and then rise with increasing outputs, the marginal cost curve will intersect the average cost curve at the latter's lowest point.[6]

An example of these relationships is depicted in figure 1.

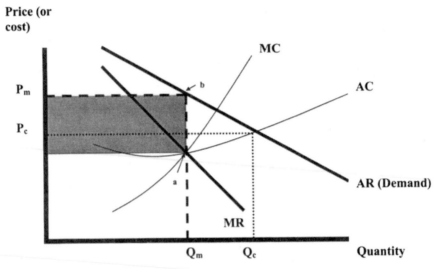

Fig. 1. Monopoly pricing of an end product in a single market.

Given the demand curve (the average revenue curve) in figure 1, and given the costs shown (the lowest available to the patentee whether he made the product himself or had it made by others), there is one price (P_M) and one quantity (Q_M) which will provide more net revenue to the patentee than any other single price or quantity. The "maximizing" quantity (Q_M) is shown by the intersection of the marginal cost curve (MC) and the marginal revenue curve (MR). With quantity (Q_M) customers will pay up to price P_M. The extracompetitive return available to the patentee, the difference between total revenue and total cost, is shown by the shaded area in figure 1.

Were the product, the demand curve for which is shown by AR in figure 1, unpatented, and were the supply curve shown by MC in the figure the same as for the monopoly seller, the competitive price and quantity sold would then be indicated by the intersection of the marginal cost curve, MC, and the demand curve, AR.* The dotted lines on the diagram indicate the lower price, P_C, and the larger quantity, Q_C. Given these competitive supply and demand conditions we can see from the

6. This point of intersection between marginal cost and average cost at the latter's lowest point is equally relevant for average total cost and for average variable cost (fixed cost excluded). A decision about whether to produce, and how much to produce, involves only variable costs. In the long run all costs are variable (AC in fig. 1). In successively shorter runs relatively more costs are "fixed" and therefore irrelevant for current output decisions. And because variable costs are avoidable, unless they can be recovered no output at all is predictable. Thus, in figure 1 the applicability of AC to output decisions requires AC to be read as average *variable* cost.

* [The dotted lines in the graph above are as in the original, showing intersection of AC (not MC) and AR. Note that the price derived from the intersection of MC and AR would still be lower than the monopoly price, and the quantity would be higher than the monopoly quantity.—Eds.]

diagram that if the product patent were awarded to a nonproducing patentee, he could achieve the precise equivalent of setting monopoly-product price at P_M, by charging a flat nondiscriminatory, nonexclusive royalty per unit of the patented product produced. This royalty equivalent to setting the price at P_M would be a royalty rate identified in figure 1 by the vertical distance between point a (the intersection of MC and MR) and point b (the corresponding output on the AR curve).

This equivalence, a uniform royalty rate in lieu of fixing the price of the product, however, rests upon "other things equal" assumptions which diagramming (as in fig. 1) has assumed in a rather heroic manner. Patentee price-searchers, or any other price-searchers, do not have the precise demand schedules economists draw for illustration. They must estimate or guess, on the basis of experience, about demand conditions. Knowledge about demand is not costless, therefore, and these costs may vary under differing licensing arrangements.

It is also most unlikely that the costs incurred in a "do-it-yourself" production scheme will be identical to those incurred when production is under license by others. The differences in the size or in the manner of operations are bound to introduce either economies or diseconomies. Moreover, the cost to a firm, especially one whose output affects price, are significantly related to the firm's estimation of demand and its variability as well as to estimation of the alternative production of any product, being related to rates of output in turn with longer forecast periods. Long-run costs of the type depicted in figure 1, in which the maximizing output occurs at minimum cost, represent an equilibrium monopoly adjustment akin to perfect forecasting—that is, both demand and costs have been drawn in such manner that the maximizing output (Q_M) is achieved at that precise point where average cost is at a minimum. Forecasting is not precise. Only if demand and cost were precisely predictable would the optimum profits depicted in figure 1 be possible.[7]

The decision whether to manufacture or sell or to license others to manufacture or sell a patented end product will, of course, depend upon whether the cost of producing and distributing the product through the patentee's firm is higher than the cost of having these tasks performed as efficiently and cheaply as possible. Higher manufacturing or distribution costs lower the net value to the patentee. A patent is more valuable the less expensive its complements are. A patentee's potential reward depends upon how efficiently (and therefore inexpensively) the products and services with which it must be used are provided. A patentee, to achieve efficient manufacture or distribution, may, in addition to licensing others, improve efficiency by imposing conditions of use upon licensees.

7. Similarly, were the monopoly to be eliminated and the production subject to competition it is clear that costs are not minimized for this larger output. As the dotted lines in figure 1 indicate, the marginal costs are substantially higher than average minimum cost and consequently a rearrangement of production is signaled.

Price Discrimination

The first example (fig. 1) demonstrated how the owner of an end-product patent maximizes the net returns achievable from his patent monopoly. One of the assumptions necessary to the conclusion reached was that all sales were made in a single market at a single price. The demand curve in that example revealed the revenue obtainable for differing amounts of *total* sales; the possibility of charging different prices to different customers was assumed not to exist. A demand schedule showing amounts salable at various prices is typically the summation of the demands of a number of different potential buyers, some of whom, or some groups of whom, may be willing to pay considerably more or less for the product than others. Differing tastes, differing incomes, or differing access to close substitutes for, or complements to, the monopolized product may bring this about. Sometimes these differences can be exploited by a patentee and sometimes they cannot.

"The essence of discrimination is to separate buyers into two or more classes whose elasticities of demand differ appreciably, and this usually requires that the product sold to the various classes differ[s] in time, place, or appearance to keep buyers from shifting."[8] Neither the creation nor the maintenance of separate markets is a costless operation. For discrimination to be practicable it must be achievable at costs which are reasonable in light of the potential profits. The most likely product candidates for discrimination, therefore, are those which do not lend themselves readily to resale from low-price buyers to high-price buyers. The existence of a patent provides no automatic means of overcoming these difficulties; but certain kinds of licensing arrangements in particular circumstances do provide means which make price discrimination economically feasible. Thus, when demand conditions vary in different territories, varying license rates by territory may be feasible; similarly, if a patented product has several end-product uses in which the economic proximity of close substitutes differs substantially, licensing the different uses at differing rates may be practicable. Similarly, if a patented machine were useful to both intensive and extensive users but worth more to the former than to the latter, leasing the machine at rates related to machine output might be a means of increasing patent revenue by discriminatory charges.

All of these price discrimination examples describe means by which a patentee maximizes the return ascribable to the differential advantage the patent affords. Leveraging to new monopoly is not involved. The only difference between the price discrimination case and the single market-one price monopoly case is divisibility of use on the basis of different degrees of unique usefulness (elasticity of demand). And for this condition to apply (differing demand elasticities), these markets are often noncompeting. But it is differing demand elasticity that is crucial; otherwise a single price would be profit maximizing. A discriminatory patent license contract, in the absence of provision or understanding for the elimination of competition with patent substitutes, is an economically explicable means of exploiting this absence of competition between markets, but not creating it.

8. Stigler, *Theory of Price*, p. 209.

Once the appropriate output division is made in the manner indicated, the separate prices are determined in each market exactly as they were in the single-market case depicted in figure 1. The two profit areas are then, of course, summed.

The two separate demand curves appropriately describe (as did figure 1 for the single-product case) market-use subdivision of end-product patents, intermediate-product patents, or process patents. In any of these markets it is differing demand elasticity which makes the price discrimination process profitable. Means of accomplishing discrimination vary under different circumstances. Patent-tying contracts, for example, which the courts condemn almost automatically, may be used to separate users whose demands differ. . . .

An early (1895) case provides an apt example.[9] A machine was invented for stapling buttons to high-button shoes, an operation formerly done by hand at higher cost. The patentee had a number of prospective customers for his machine, some of whom made a great many shoes, others only a few. The invention saved each user a fixed amount on each button attached. Thus the machine was worth more to the more intensive users. An attempt to charge different prices to the different users, however, would have encountered two problems. First, advance knowledge of how intensively each buyer would use the machine would be difficult to come by. Second, preventing those who paid a low price from reselling to those who paid a high price might have proved impossible. A tie-in would resolve the difficulties. The machine might be sold at cost, on condition that the unpatented staples used in the machine be bought from the patentee. Through staple sales, the patentee could measure the intensity with which his customers used the machines. Hence by charging a higher than competitive price for the staples the patentee could receive the equivalent of a royalty from his patented machines.[10]

A tying sale may thus be used as a "counting device" for setting discriminatory prices on the tying product, and as such creates no new and additional monopoly over the tied product. Exactly the same result might be achieved by attaching a meter to the button-stapling machine to measure the intensity of use, then leasing the machine and charging a meter rate.[11] Such other devices, however, might well be more costly.

9. The case is Heaton–Peninsular Button–Fastener Co. v. Eureka Specialty Co., 65 Fed. 619 (C.C.W.D. Mich. 1895). The example is from Bowman, "Tying Arrangements and the Leverage Problem," 67 *Yale L. Rev.* 19 (Nov. 1957).

10. The same "discrimination" result could conceivably have been achieved by giving the machine away and charging a still higher price for staples, except that the machine might be provided to infrequent users. Under these circumstances the patentee might not even secure a return which would cover the cost of supplying the machine.

11. Although each user of a patented button-fastening machine pays the same rate per pair of shoes manufactured, use of the tying device or of a meter has the effect of a different sales price for the machine according to intensity of use. This is discrimination if the large user pays a higher price relative to cost than small users. Whether the machine manufacturer's royalty comes from the sale or lease of the machine or from the sale of the staples or the buttons, the maximum that can be charged is fixed by the amount the machine saves the users. If those to whom the machine is "worth" more can be charged more for the machine, either in the form of a machine charge or indirectly by compulsory purchase of a tied product, the patentee is being rewarded for his machine patent. Interestingly enough, Judge Lurton used almost precisely this reasoning in deciding both

Tying here is used simply as an efficient means of insuring the full monopoly return on the tying product where a monopoly already existed. No leverage can be found; and the output of the tied product, staples, is exactly the same when machine payment is charged directly and staples are sold competitively as when the staples are tied to the machine. So far as staples used for shoes are concerned, the outputs under the two equivalent methods of discrimination are identical.

Although the use of a tie-in sale as a counting device is consistent with the facts of a large number of tying cases—for example, the tying of ink to mimeographs, punch cards to computers, or rivets to riveting guns—it does not provide the only rational explanation of tying practice when variable proportions are involved. The example suggests a means by which a monopolist can separate markets to achieve the maximum return from each of the various markets in which the single product can be sold. In this instance, the higher price charged for the tied product is in lieu of the proper pricing of the tying product without tie-ins. We must remember that profit maximization on only a single product is involved. The example takes no account of the possible effect that the price or the quantity sold of the tying product may have on sales of the tied product, or of the effect that the price or quantity sold of the tied product may have on the sales of the tying product when the demands for the two are related.

Notes and Questions

1. Ward Bowman received an A.B. from the University of Washington in 1933. He worked for government agencies, then became a Research Associate at the University of Chicago School of Law, where he participated with others in the emergence of law and economics as a distinct subdiscipline in U.S. law schools. He was later a Professor of Law and Economics at Yale Law School. He died in 1991. [Thanks to Professor Edmund Kitch and the Honorable Judge Guido Calabresi for this information.]

2. Bowman's analysis of the patent-antitrust "interface" was the standard treatment of the subject from an economic perspective throughout the 1970s and early 1980s. In more recent years, commentators have begun to question some of its basic assumptions, and to explore more complex and nuanced features of the interaction between patent and antitrust law. See the following excerpt from Louis Kaplow, and accompanying notes.

3. Bowman's analysis is in many respects a response to earlier articles explaining tie-ins as illegal attempts to "leverage" a monopoly in one market into another, related market. See, e.g., Donald Turner, "The Validity of Tying Arrangements Under the Antitrust Laws," 72 *Harv. L. Rev.* 50, 62 (1958). Proponents of this "leverage school" sought to ban all tie-ins as per se antitrust violations. See Carl Kaysen & Donald F. Turner, Antitrust Policy: An Economic and Legal Analysis 159 (Cambridge, MA: Harvard University Press, 1959) ("[A] flat rule against tying

Heaton–Peninsular Button–Fastener Co. v. Eureka Specialty Co., 77 Fed. 288 (6th Cir. 1896), and Henry v. A.B. Dick Co., 224 U.S. 1 (1912).

arrangements, regardless of whether or not they serve a useful purpose, appears justified."). See generally Alan J. Meese, "Tying Meets the New Institutional Economics: Farewell to the Chimera of Forcing," 146 *U. Pa. L. Rev.* 1, 5 n.22 (1997) (collecting articles and books espousing this view). Bowman's analysis formed part of the "Chicago School" critique of Leverage Theory. See, e.g., Richard A. Posner, Antitrust Law 198–99 (2d ed. 2001). And because the Chicago School now has several powerful voices on the bench, the Chicago School view is often reflected in actual cases as well. See, e.g., See USM Corp. v. SPS Techs., Inc., 694 F.2d 505, 510–11 (7th Cir. 1982) (Posner, J.) ("The patentee who insists on limiting the freedom of his purchaser or licensee—whether to price, to use complementary inputs of the purchaser's choice, or to make competing items—will have to compensate the purchaser for the restriction by charging a lower price for the use of the patent.").

Several scholars have attempted to move beyond the Leverage–Chicago debate in the analysis of tie-ins. Alan J. Meese, for example, argues that both of these traditional approaches to tie-ins share the assumption—which is often wrong—that sellers/licensors "force" tie-ins on buyers/licensees. Meese argues that in fact many tie-in arrangements are adopted because they favor both the seller and the buyer, and they are often used as a way to overcome market failures that accompany sale of tying and tied products as independent, freestanding products:

> In many cases, tying can be viewed as partial vertical integration designed to eliminate or attenuate market failure. By vesting control over the selection of the tied product in the seller of the tying product, a tying contract can eliminate the transaction costs that can result from reliance on the market (that is, the buyer's unfettered discretion) for choice of the tied product....
>
> [For example,] consider the case of a manufacturer of a complex machine who, in the process of maintaining the machine after it is sold, might gain valuable knowledge about its workings. By requiring purchasers of the machine also to purchase post-sale maintenance services from it, the manufacturer can ensure that it is in a position to gather this sort of information. Absent such a requirement, purchasers—who do not internalize the benefits of the information generated by the seller during the maintenance process—may turn elsewhere for such service, with the result that a suboptimal amount of information about the working of the machine will be generated. Here again, tying can eliminate the market failure that would result from leaving the buyer to choose, on its own, the proper service provider. This justification, it seems, will have increasing relevance in this era of rapidly changing technology, as indicated by the several recent cases involving attempts by manufacturers to require purchasers also to buy repair service from them.

Alan J. Meese, "Tying Meets the New Institutional Economics: Farewell to the Chimera of Forcing," 146 *U. Pa. L. Rev.* 1, 61, 65 (1997) (footnotes omitted). See also Christopher R. Leslie, "Cutting Through Tying Theo-

ry with Occam's Razor: A Simple Explanation of Tying Arrangements,"
78 *Tul. L. Rev.* 727, 730 (2004) (hypothesizing that "some sellers with
market power over the tying product require consumers to buy the tied
product simply to sell more of the tied product at the prevailing market
price.... Unlike the Leverage School and Chicago School, Volume Tying
Theory [espoused in this article].... defines a middle ground that can
explain the existence of certain tie-ins that other tying theories cannot...."). Leslie's Volume Tying Theory demonstrates, according to the
author, that the business practice at issue in the celebrated case of
International Salt Co. v. United States, 332 U.S. 392 (1947)—requiring
purchasers of canning machines to purchase salt from the machine's
seller—can be explained by the economics of the salt industry: high fixed
cost investments required large sales volumes for sellers of salt to break
even, so the tie-in had nothing to do with indirectly charging more for
the patented machines, and everything to do with insuring a large, stable
market for salt.

The Patent–Antitrust Intersection: A Reap-
praisal*

LOUIS KAPLOW

.... Approaches to the patent-antitrust conflict fall into three general
categories. The first sidesteps the conflict by pretending in one way or
another that one half of the problem does not exist. Courts and commentators vary regarding which half they emphasize and generally do not
explain why they effectively ignore the other half. The second approach
resolves the conflict by invoking formalistic constructions that are indeterminate and only superficially address the issues at stake. The third
approach focuses on the relationship between the reward a patentee
receives and the value of the patent. This approach has much in common
with the first in that it emphasizes patent policy at the expense of
antitrust policy, and with the second in that it is often justified by
appeals to many of the more popular formalisms.... [T]his Article
describes the patent-antitrust conflict in a manner that indicates the
weaknesses of the prevalent approaches, and shows that the conflict runs
even deeper than has generally been recognized.

[This article] develops and analyzes a conceptual solution to the
patent-antitrust puzzle. The proposed test examines the ratio between
the reward the patentee receives when permitted to use a particular
restrictive practice and the monopoly loss that results from such exploitation of the patent. Because reward is assumed to induce inventive
activity and thus to produce social benefits, this ratio indirectly reflects a
relationship between social benefit and social cost (monopoly loss). Thus,
generally speaking, the greater the ratio, the stronger is the case for
permitting the practice.... [T]he conclusions [of this article] ... call
into question much of the previous analysis of these issues.

* Reprinted with permission from 97 Harv. L. Rev. 1913 (1984), Copyright © 1984 by
the Harvard Law Review Association and Louis Kaplow.

The ratio test is conceptually simple, yet its practical application is quite complex for a number of reasons. First, coherent practical conclusions about patent-antitrust doctrine can be reached only if similar conclusions have already been made concerning patent policy as a whole, and it is well known that the empirical foundations for current patent policy are shaky at best. Second, even given a developed patent policy, one faces the difficult task of ascertaining the economic effects of a wide variety of patentee practices. This task not only raises most of the ongoing disputes concerning the appropriate contours of antitrust policy generally, but is also subject to several additional sources of uncertainty peculiar to the patent-antitrust context. This Article is an attempt to clarify the issues, but its revelation of the unavoidable complexity of the problem indicates that, in practice, the untangling of the myriad strands in the patent-antitrust conflict might prove impossibly difficult.

I. The Directness of the Patent–Antitrust Conflict and Some Implications

Although the conflict between the patent statute and the antitrust laws has long been thought troublesome, it is in fact even more deep-seated than is generally perceived. Consider a patentee that intends to employ a particular restriction, practice, or strategy in exploiting its patent. Limiting the analysis to the antitrust issues, which is the intended scope of this Article, one might initially conclude that the practice should be held permissible only if it does not violate the antitrust laws. . . .

Most formulations that seek to mediate the patent-antitrust conflict begin by asking whether the restrictive practice in question results in excessive profits to the patentee or merely permits the patentee to realize part of the reward appropriate to the patent. Thus, although the premise has never been fully explicit, courts and commentators appear to have thought that patent-antitrust doctrine should be determined by reference to a specific level of aggregate reward. The following discussion demonstrates how even this slightly refined formulation leads to conclusions quite different from those that courts and commentators might expect. These conclusions motivate the alternative framework that is constructed [below].

In considering the implications of making a particular level of reward the policy goal of patent-antitrust doctrine, it is useful to consider two extreme doctrinal regimes:

1. Antitrust laws reign supreme: A patentee's practice is deemed illegal if it violates any aspect of antitrust law; no privilege is accorded to patentees.

2. Patent statute reigns supreme: The antitrust laws cannot render the patentee's practice illegal; the patentee has an absolute privilege to violate the antitrust laws.

From the perspective of antitrust and patent policy, consider how these two regimes differ. Under regime 1, the patentee would not be allowed, for example, to use price-restricted licenses or to enter into certain patent pools, but would still be permitted to exploit the patent on its own, to sell all rights under the patent to another entity, or to enter into various intermediate arrangements that do not violate any provisions of the antitrust laws. Under regime 2, however, the patentee would be permitted to engage in all of the practices barred under regime 1. Assume that the typical expected reward to the patentee under regime 1 is x. Presumably x is not trivial, though it is less than the reward under regime 2, which I will assume to be x + 10.

Which regime is preferable depends upon how much reward is deemed appropriate. If patent policy dictated an outcome less than or equal to x we would prefer regime 1; if greater than or equal to x + 10, regime 2. (Outcomes between x and x + 10 will be considered momentarily.) But one might ask why legislators would care which regime courts selected, because the legislature could simply adjust the underlying grant. For example, the legislature need only increase or decrease the patent life to compensate for the prohibition or authorization of anticompetitive practices. Therefore, one could argue that it is irrelevant which regime—or which point in between—is adopted by the courts.

There are at least two reservations one might have about such an argument. First, our patent policymaker, Congress, is noted for in-action and has not changed the patent life in over a century. This suggests that Congress is not making such ongoing adjustments. Second, perhaps Congress has chosen to set the patent life only approximately, leaving to the courts the task of fine-tuning the amount of reward in response to changes in technology and the structure of the nation's economy. Although this second point might not seem very plausible, it is instructive to accept this view of the courts' role for a moment to see what conclusions it suggests.

Suppose, for example, that the courts were to determine that the appropriate reward is x + 5. The resulting patent-antitrust doctrine would thus be a compromise between regimes 1 and 2; neither the patentee nor the government would always be the victor. But how should a court decide any particular case? As is often true in the law, the decision in one case will depend upon the decisions in related cases. Yet in this context, the interdependence is extreme: in general, it is wholly indeterminate how any individual case or, similarly, any single component of patent-antitrust doctrine should be decided, because the question is whether the totality of the courts' patent-antitrust decisions leads to the appropriate reward of x + 5. A court could just as easily permit a prohibited restriction, as long as it prohibited some other previously permitted restriction (or group of restrictions) yielding the same aggregate reward. Any pattern of doctrine yielding a total reward of x + 5 would be acceptable. For example, reversing all the rules of a given pattern that yields x + 5—that is, permitting what was previously prohibited and prohibiting what was previously permitted—might also yield the same total. Thus, a focus on aggregate reward produces the conclusion that patent-antitrust doctrine is indeterminate both in the context of individual cases and when one considers the area as a whole.

Given the startling implications of this indeterminacy, one might wonder why courts and commentators have not expressed greater concern in resolving patent-antitrust cases. This problem has never fully emerged because neither courts nor commentators have explicitly considered the consequences of tacitly relying on aggregate reward as a criterion for decision. Legal materials on this subject reveal that efforts have been directed only toward deciding each case on its own facts, in a manner that bears no resemblance to a policy approach focused on aggregate reward in the manner just described. Once one recognizes and understands this indeterminacy problem, however, one must undertake a deeper critique of legal discourse in this area and its relation to the questions and policies at stake.

II. A Framework for Approaching the Patent–Antitrust Conflict

This Part offers partial relief from Part I's discouraging conclusion that patent-antitrust doctrine, although it addresses important concerns in the aggregate, has a largely indeterminate content in the context of individual cases. This relief derives in part from relaxing certain simplifying assumptions implicit in the preceding analysis—assumptions that have not been expressly articulated in prior attempts to address this issue. An analysis that moves beyond such simplifying assumptions yields a far more complicated perspective on the patent-antitrust conflict, but one that is unavoidable if there is to be any hope of clarifying the formidable problems that the conflict raises.

The indeterminacy problem described in Part I rests upon the unstated assumption that the various patentee practices that clash with the antitrust laws are fungible. Part I assumed that the only factor relevant in assessing various practices is the amount of reward to the patentee that results from permitting the practice—two practices providing the same reward were considered equivalent and thus interchangeable. But equal reward is not a sufficient condition for fungibility; for two practices to be equivalent, it is also necessary that they cause equal detriment. In other words, the result of Part I depended on the assumption that restrictive practices that are equally good as rewards to the patentee are also equally bad in terms of the monopolistic harms they cause. More precisely, as will be demonstrated implicitly in the derivation of the ratio test in Section B, it was assumed that the ratio of good to bad was the same for each practice.

On its face, this assumption may seem reasonable. The patentee's reward is made possible through monopolistic restrictions, and one might expect that the reward and the monopoly loss would each be roughly proportional to the extent of the restrictions and thus roughly proportional to each other. Although such a tendency will often be observed, it does not hold as a general proposition. It is simply not true that all activities generating equal profits impose equal damages upon society.

Although much of antitrust commentary (outside the patent-antitrust context) has consisted of debate over which practices should be prohibited by the antitrust laws and which should not, little attention has been given to the question of how much profit the antitrust defendant derives from a given practice in proportion to the harm caused. It is not surprising that this issue has been neglected, because antitrust intervention is predicated upon the mere existence of a net harm to society. The magnitude of the harm is irrelevant, except perhaps in determining enforcement priorities. The amount of the defendant's profit is likewise of no special concern, except to the extent its profit is deemed to be a component in determining the total social cost of a practice. But when patent policy is also implicated, profit plays a central role, because it serves as a reward—and, in turn, an incentive—for the inventive activity that produces the benefits of the patent system.

When monopoly loss is viewed as part of the price society pays to stimulate inventive activity, the natural economic question is how society can purchase a given level of inventive output—which requires a given level of incentive—for the least cost, or, equivalently, how much inventive output society can purchase per unit of monopoly loss that it must bear. This question is intimately related to two policy decisions: first, how society should determine which antitrust prohibitions to apply to patentees, and second, how society should determine the time period over which patentees may exploit their patents. These two decisions— articulating patent-antitrust doctrine and setting the patent life—are interrelated. Part I has already suggested that patent-antitrust doctrine is dependent on the length of the patent life. The opposite connection exists as well: the amount of reward provided and the monopoly loss arising in each additional year in which exploitation is permitted (and thus the appropriate length of the patent life) depend upon what practices patentees may employ during that time period.

To untangle this interrelationship and thus clarify the factors relevant to resolving the patent-antitrust conflict, it is necessary to return to first principles. Section A begins this process by analyzing how the optimal patent life should be determined, taking as given the existence of a set of rules defining the permissible means of exploiting the patent during that time period. Section B examines how a given set of rules governing exploitation should be adjusted—that is, how patent-antitrust doctrine should be articulated—taking as given the optimal patent life derived in Section A. But as previously suggested, adjustments to the patent-antitrust rules generally make it necessary to revise the length of the patent life. [This Article then] explores this feedback effect and demonstrates the need in theory to solve simultaneously the problems of articulating patent-antitrust doctrine and of determining the optimal patent life. The analysis presents a number of considerations, including the derivation of the ratio test, that are directly relevant to the debate over the patent-antitrust conflict. . . .

A. *Deriving the Optimal Patent Life*

1. The Costs and Benefits of Varying the Patent Life.—Determining the optimal patent life from an economic point of view is straightforward once one has defined the functional relationships between the patent life and the costs and benefits of the patent system. To perform this task, however, one must know the range of permissible means of patent exploitation, including the content of patent-antitrust doctrine. Therefore, for the remainder of this Section, I shall assume that some such legal regime is in place.

(a) Benefits of the Patent System.—There are three links in the logical chain connecting the patent life and the benefits of the patent system. A longer patent life increases reward to the patentee, which in turn encourages inventive activity, which in turn produces social benefits. Consider these links in sequence. First, lengthening the patent life presumably increases the reward to the patentee by enhancing the opportunity for monopolistic exploitation. The amount that the reward will increase depends upon a number of factors, including the market value of the invention, the structure of the market involving the patented process or product, and the attributes of the patentee (such as marketing and production capacities) that determine its range of options within the market. Second, the increase in reward is designed to stimulate inventive activity. Determining the extent and types of increased activity is a complex process whose outcome will vary substantially from case to case. Relevant factors include the potential return from further research and development, the risk involved in the undertaking, the nature of rivalry among firms, and the degree to which the enhanced reward to successful patentees is anticipated by inventors. Third, the increase in inventive activity may contribute to social welfare. To the extent that valuable new inventions are discovered that otherwise would have been developed more slowly or not at all, social welfare might be increased.

Although each of these three connections has received substantial attention in the past, our knowledge of the functional relationships between the separate links in the chain connecting patent life to social benefits remains quite limited. I make no systematic attempt here to remedy that deficiency in understanding, although much of the rest of the Article does offer insights into the first connection—that between patent life and reward. Rather, I assume for the moment that we have already made our best attempt, in light of existing information, to define the functional relationship between patent life and the social benefits generated by the patent system.

(b) Costs of the Patent System.—The costs of the patent system go beyond the direct costs of research and development, because the patentee's reward for inventing the patented item arises from allowing monopoly. Like the magnitude of the reward, the magnitude of the loss arising from the legally authorized monopoly depends upon the particular invention, market structure, and attributes of the patentee, as well as the legal rules regulating patent exploitation. The longer the patent life, the greater these costs. Moreover, lengthening the patent life in order to induce further inventive activity increases the period of monopolistic exploitation for those inventions that would have been created even without lengthening the patent life. In regard to these inventions, prolonging the patent life results in a social cost not offset by any social benefit. For present purposes it is assumed that the functional relationship between patent life and the social costs generated by the patent system is known. Later analysis will address in greater detail how monopoly cost varies in different circumstances.

Finally, in defining social costs and benefits, this Article does not address the merits of transferring wealth from consumers to producers in general, or to patentees in particular. These distributional considerations bear directly on the construction of the social cost and benefit functions, and would be taken into account in that process. Only after considering all such factors and deciding that some patentee reward is socially desirable does one undertake further analysis such as that offered in this Article.

2. Determining the Optimum.—The optimal patent life is that length of time at which the marginal social cost of lengthening or shortening the patent life equals the marginal social benefit. If the patent life were shorter than the optimum indicated by this rule, the marginal benefit of lengthening the patent life would presumably exceed the marginal cost; increasing such a patent life would induce further inventive activity that would produce benefits in excess of the accompanying social costs. Similarly, for patent lives longer than the optimum, the marginal cost presumably would exceed the marginal benefit; decreasing such a patent life would then reduce costs by more than the reduction in benefits.

Notice that equating costs and benefits at the margin does not result in equating total costs and benefits. In fact, equating total costs and benefits would be irrational because the result would be a patent system that yielded zero net gain in social welfare. The optimum is attained when the total social benefits exceed the total social costs by the greatest possible amount. Thus, all that can be known about the relationship between total benefits and costs at the optimal patent life is that total benefits exceed total costs; if this were not true, the optimization process would have indicated that there should be no patent system at all.

3. Limitations of the Proportionality Test.—A careful analysis of the steps for determining the optimal patent life reveals the fallacy underlying the common view that patent restrictions should reward the patentee in proportion to the value of its patent. This view has superficial appeal in two respects. First, as between two patentees, the one with the more valuable patent generally should receive the greater reward, because the more valuable invention should be encouraged even if it entails greater cost. But this unrefined notion of proportionality provides no information about what the specific proportion between reward and value should be; rather, it merely suggests that this proportion should be roughly similar for all patents. Moreover, even given a particular proportion, this notion of proportionality does not help us to decide which restrictive practices to authorize or to prohibit. In some circumstances, one patentee might be unable to exploit its patent in the manner that others employ without resorting to a prohibited practice; permitting the practice would then promote this sort of proportionality. In other instances, only some patentees would be able to obtain most of the rewards made possible by a particular restrictive practice; prohibiting the practice would then enhance this type of proportionality.

A more important reason one might favor linking the patentee's reward to the patent's social value is that such a link corrects the market in a manner that induces private actors to develop the appropriate inventions. Absent patent protection, an inventor might capture only a small portion of the value of its inventive activity. As a result, the inventor in many cases could not expect to receive rewards sufficient to cover its costs, even if those costs did not exceed the social value of the invention. The appropriate policy would thus be to permit the patentee to receive reward equal to the full value of its patent. All reward up to that point induces inventive activity only as long as the inventor's expected reward, which equals the expected value of the invention, exceeds (or at least equals) the inventor's expected cost in developing the patented item.

This proportionality argument, however, has a simple but fatal flaw: it overlooks the costs of providing the reward. The argument suggests, for example, that the optimal policy is to permit an unlimited patent life with no restrictions upon practices of exploitation, as long as such practices do not result in reward that exceeds the total value of the patent. Such a view incorrectly focuses on total social benefits, rather than net social benefits (the excess of total benefits over total costs). Taking into account the costs of the patent system leads to the more accurate intuitive view that the optimal patent life combined with the optimal set of antitrust restrictions would provide less reward than indicated by the full value of the patent. Thus, the rule that the reward must not exceed the value of the patent is only a necessary condition for the desirability of a restrictive patentee practice. It is not a sufficient condition not only for the reasons suggested in Section B, but also because the reward would still be excessive if it were not as much less than the full value of the patent as the optimization process suggests it should be.

Once one realizes that the proper level of reward is determined not by simple deduction premised on the value of the patent, but implicitly from a process that seeks to maximize net social benefits, it becomes obvious that the legal system must regulate not only the total reward a patentee receives, but also the means by which that total is realized. This observation is generalized in Section B.

B. *Patent–Antitrust Doctrine and the Ratio Test*

1. Derivation and Interpretation of the Ratio Test.—In deriving the optimal patent life, Section A took as given the existence of a patent-antitrust doctrine indicating the scope of permissible patent exploitation. This Section considers how to optimize that doctrinal configuration, taking as given the patent life derived in Section A.

(a) Deriving the Ratio Test.—One can assess the desirability of permitting a currently forbidden practice by comparing the costs it imposes upon society with the costs of adjusting the patent life to achieve an equivalent reward. The method proceeds in two steps. First, one determines whether permitting the practice would impose more cost per unit of incremental reward than would result from lengthening the patent life to provide the same reward. If so, the practice should remain prohibited because it would be costlier to provide additional reward by permitting the practice than by lengthening the patent life, and if one began with a patent life that was determined to be optimal, lengthening the patent life is itself necessarily undesirable.

For example, suppose that the optimal patent life has been calculated to be seventeen years. Next, suppose that the patent life would have to be lengthened to eighteen years in order to produce the same additional reward that the practice in question can offer for the given seventeen-year patent life. If permitting the practice would entail more loss than would lengthening the patent life to eighteen years, the practice should not be permitted—permitting the practice would be costlier than extending the patent life to eighteen years, and the conclusion that a seventeen-year patent life was optimal implies that extending the patent life to eighteen years is itself undesirable.

If the practice in question would produce the same incremental reward as would extending the patent life one year, but at a lower cost, one proceeds to step two. A second step is necessary because extending the patent life was itself found to be undesirable. In the second step, one must determine whether permitting the practice would impose less cost per unit of incremental reward than would be saved by shortening the patent life to diminish the total reward by an offsetting amount. If so, the practice should be permitted because it is a less costly way of providing reward than was adding the final increment in the patent life. There is, however, a qualification: the conclusion that the practice should be permitted rests on the assumption that the patent life will be correspondingly reduced. This reduction is necessary if we are to maintain the total reward at the level implicit in the original optimal patent life. It should be noted, however, that this result runs counter to a basic assumption of this Section: that the patent life was to be taken as given. Thus, the implications of this qualification require a separate and thorough examination—an examination provided [later in this Article].

The preceding analysis can be cast in terms of a ratio test, with the ratio defined as:

Patentee Reward/Monopoly Loss

In this ratio, "patentee reward" and "monopoly loss" refer, respectively, to the incremental reward and loss resulting from the practice in question. In general, the higher the ratio, the more desirable the practice. In addition, the ratio test may be used to determine the desirability not only of restrictive practices, which are the subject of patent-antitrust doctrine, but also of changes in the patent life itself. Every patent life implies a specific ratio. The ratio implicit in a given patent life simply refers to the ratio of incremental reward to incremental loss that results from a marginal adjustment in the patent life.

The components of the ratio test should be contrasted with the central factors used in Section A. The ratio here compares marginal patentee reward to marginal cost (marginal monopoly loss) rather than marginal social benefit to marginal cost. The latter pair of factors was used in Section A to determine the optimal patent life. The focus in this Section is on patentee reward rather than social benefit primarily because the analysis here takes the optimal patent life as given and asks whether the total reward to the patentee implicit in the optimal patent life can be achieved at a lower cost.

(b) *Applying the Ratio Test.*—The technique for assessing the desirability of restrictive practices can be recast in terms of this simple ratio as follows. One first determines the ratio implicit in the optimal patent life derived in Section A. If that patent life were seventeen years, for example, one could determine the amounts of incremental patentee reward and monopoly loss that would result from extending the patent life to eighteen years and thus compute the ratio of reward to loss for the eighteenth year. This patent-life ratio could then be compared to the ratio for any given restrictive practice. Practices with ratios lower than that for the eighteenth year should be prohibited, and those with higher ratios should—subject to the requirements of the second step—be permitted.

This method of analysis is important for determining the desirability of various restrictive practices because the ratio will not be the same for all restrictions. Two examples, to be discussed at length later in this Article, illustrate this point. At one extreme, consider a patentee that, having invented a minor process improvement, arranges price-restricted licenses covering the entire industry and sets prices substantially above those prevailing before the licensing agreement. Assume further that, because the significance of the patent is rather limited, the royalty charged by the patentee is rather small. In this case, the patentee's incremental reward will consist of the modest royalty payments and a share, in proportion to the patentee's share of the market, of the excess profit resulting from the cartel prices. Unless the patentee has a very high market share, its reward from being permitted to use this scheme will be moderate in comparison to the total loss imposed. Thus, the resulting ratio will be rather small.

In contrast, consider a patentee that charges higher royalties to firms in industries in which the patent is more valuable, rather than charging a uniform royalty at some average level. The use of such discriminatory royalties has two effects. First, it increases total reward by transferring surplus to the patentee from those industries in which the patent is valued more highly. Second, it decreases output in industries charged an above-average royalty and increases output in industries charged a below-average royalty. Even if the output effects produce a net monopoly loss, it might be quite small because the output effects tend to be offsetting. Thus, the denominator of the reward/cost ratio will be relatively small. But because all the reward goes to the patentee, the numerator will be undiluted. Therefore, the ratio in this example might well be substantially higher than that in the first.

(c) *Cost–Effectiveness Analysis: A Practical Restatement of the Ratio Test.*—One practical limitation in applying the preceding analysis is that even if one ascertains the ratios for all relevant practices—in itself a most formidable and controversial endeavor—there is still insufficient information to determine any component of patent-antitrust doctrine unless one also knows the ratio implicit in the optimal patent life. Yet our knowledge is inadequate to inspire great confidence even in the desirability of having a patent system at all, much less in the ability to make the subtle measurements of marginal effects that determine the ratio implicit in the optimal patent life.

Even if this patent-life ratio cannot be readily determined, however, some cost-effectiveness analysis is still possible. In principle, one could derive the ratio for all possible restrictions and order them from highest to lowest. Regardless of the implicit patent-life ratio, improvements clearly might be made possible by shuffling the extant pattern of restrictions. For example, a currently permitted practice with a low ratio might be exchanged for a currently prohibited practice with a high ratio. If the total reward remained approximately the same after such exchanges, one could unambiguously conclude that the changes as a whole were beneficial, even though it might be impossible to know whether any single change was desirable. This process essentially amounts to cost-minimization—the changes in patent-antitrust doctrine would provide the given amount of reward at the least possible cost.

* * *

VII.   Applications: Patentee Control of Unpatented End Products

A frequent issue in patent-antitrust litigation involves the degree to which restrictions imposed by the patentee may be related to unpatented processes, products, or services. For example, the patentee might attempt to tie unpatented products to the sale of its patented product or to control the unpatented output produced by its patented process. The most typical arguments offered are either that such restrictions should be prohibited because they go beyond the scope of the patent—a view that has prevailed in some contexts—or that they should be permitted because they allow the patentee merely to receive the full reward attributable to its invention. This Part focuses upon one particular arrangement: the charging of royalties based upon sales of an unpatented end product when the patent covers only one particular input. This arrangement is described more fully in Section A. I emphasize this example primarily because it has been the subject of extensive commentary. The analysis, however, is directly applicable to the use of other restrictions that are employed for the same purposes. The arguments for and against the prohibition of such restrictions are associated with [William] Baxter and [Ward] Bowman, respectively. Sections B and C consider their justifications in turn and show how each has concentrated primarily on one portion of the ratio. Section D shows that when the numerator and denominator are considered simultaneously, the problem is clarified, although its resolution becomes more complex.

A.   The Example: Royalties Based on Sales of an Unpatented End Product

Consider a situation in which a patentee's invention is used by its licensees in the manufacture of one or more end products that are not themselves subject to patent protection. If the patented input can be used only in a fixed proportion to output—for example, one and only one patented bottom can be attached to each bucket produced—the choice between an input-based and an output-based royalty is immaterial because there is a one-to-one relationship between the two. The analysis therefore focuses on the more frequent case in which there is some potential for varying the amount of the patented input. For example, if the royalty for use of a patented fertilizer were increased, farmers might be able to substitute additional land, other fertilizers, different crop-rotation practices, or increased pesticide use for some of the patented fertilizer.

The potential for substitution by users of the patent gives the patentee an incentive to base royalties directly on the sales of the end product. When the royalty is based upon use of the patented input, the user of the input can decrease royalty payments by changing its production mix to decrease reliance on the input. If, however, the royalty is based upon the amount of output produced, regardless of how much or how little of the patented input is used, the producer will determine its input mix based upon the actual cost of each input and avoid the possible distortion resulting from the royalty charged for the input. Thus, an output-based royalty avoids inefficient substitution away from the patented input and generally permits the patentee to derive more profit from the transaction, just as any firm's market power increases if substitution is not an option for buyers. Furthermore, the producer using the patented product produces with a more efficient input mix. On the other hand, it is possible that an end-product royalty will result in a greater net restriction of output of the end product. The dispute between Baxter and Bowman centers largely on how one should evaluate this set of effects.

B. Baxter's Argument[1]

Baxter characterizes end-product restriction as a situation in which the patentee has extended its monopoly of the patented input to the unpatented end product. Baxter believes that permitting the end-product royalty will further restrict output and thus produce a net monopoly loss. He also believes that, because all inputs are under-utilized when output is diminished, this loss in efficiency will outweigh any benefit arising from a more efficient input mix. He therefore concludes that end-product restrictions should be prohibited.

Baxter's analysis of the economic effects of end-product restrictions is questionable. But even if the analysis is accepted, his argument is troubling because ... he focuses only on the ratio's denominator. His point is simply that the monopoly loss will be greater if royalties are based on end products rather than on inputs. Yet because Baxter concedes that the reward to the patentee will also be greater, his perspective does not rule out the possibility that the ratio will be greater, or at least about the same, if the restriction is permitted.

C. Bowman's Argument[2]

Bowman's analysis emphasizes that permitting the patentee to base its royalty on the end product avoids the inefficient use of inputs by licensees. In addition, he explicitly notes—and proves through examples—that the output under an output-based royalty might be either higher or lower than when royalties can be based only upon use of the patented input. Of course, if output were higher, Baxter's argument

[1. In William Baxter, "Legal Restrictions on Exploitation of the Patent Monopoly," 76 Yale L.J. 267, 302–303, 353 (1966).—Eds.]

[2. In Ward Bowman, Patent and Antitrust Law 76–88 (1973). An excerpt from this book appears elsewhere in this volume.—Eds.]

based upon net inefficiency would turn against him, and Bowman's position would be strengthened. Yet for those cases in which output would indeed be curtailed, Bowman does not attempt to contradict Baxter's claim that the net effect on economic efficiency would be adverse when the input and output effects are compared.

Bowman's attack on Baxter comes from a somewhat different angle. He emphasizes that "no payment can be extracted by the patentee which is not ascribable to the competitive superiority afforded by the patented resources without which the consumers would be even worse off." But this application of Bowman's competitive superiority approach is subject to the same criticisms developed [elsewhere in this article]—the argument focuses solely on the numerator, patentee reward. Although Bowman's other arguments do bear on the magnitude of the denominator, he does not advance any argument that would support the inference that the denominator generally would be small enough to make one confident that the overall ratio would be high. Moreover, Bowman is making the wrong comparison. The quoted argument demonstrates only that allowing the patentee to base royalties on the end product is preferable to the situation in which the patentee had never developed the invention in the first place, not that allowing end-product royalties is better than prohibiting such royalties and allowing input-based royalties instead.

Bowman's argument is, however, responsive to some of the spirit of Baxter's critique. Bowman's analysis demonstrates that the patentee has not really gained a monopoly over the unpatented end product, for the patentee cannot charge royalties that are higher than the value its invention contributes. If the patentee attempted to set its royalties above this level, producers would simply manufacture the end product without the patented input.

D. Applying the Ratio Test

The examination of end-product royalties well illustrates the analysis developed in [this Article].

            * * *

Much of the analysis necessary for applying the ratio test to output-based royalties has already been provided. Section VII.C noted that, if output-based royalties increased output, there would be an unambiguously positive effect. Yet the more frequent result of direct output-based royalties will probably be that the price paid by consumers will increase and output will fall. In that event, the net effect on economic efficiency depends upon the particular circumstances. Despite the uncertainty over whether the denominator of the ratio increases or decreases, however, the fact that end-product royalties unambiguously lead to an increase in the numerator (patentee reward) makes it more plausible that the ratio would increase if such royalty schemes were permitted. Although one can neither state with certainty that permitting end-product royalty schemes improves the ratio, nor confidently identify the range of circumstances under which it might not, the argument for permitting them does seem stronger than that for disallowing them. Of course, as previously noted, there is the additional question whether the overall increase in reward would provide a disproportionately large incentive in such instances.

Notes and Questions

1. Louis Kaplow received a B.A. from Northwestern University, and then M.A., Ph.D., and J.D. degrees from Harvard University. He teaches at Harvard Law School.

2. Near the beginning of the excerpt, Kaplow writes of "Congressional inaction" in the area of patent law revision. A great deal has changed in the roughly twenty years since this was written. In their recent book, William Landes and Richard Posner discuss the "significant expansion" of intellectual property rights beginning in roughly 1976. See William M. Landes and Richard A. Posner, The Economic Structure of Intellectual Property Law 403 (Cambridge, MA: Belknap Press, 2003). Patent law in particular has been the focus of extensive Congressional interest and legislative activity since the 1980s. See Robert P. Merges and John F. Duffy, Patent Law and Policy 56–64 (3d ed.) (New York: Matthew Bender, 2002).

3. Kaplow notes the improbability of Congressional "fine tuning" of the amount of reward to a given patentee via adjustment in the patent term. Several points are in order here. First of all, there has been a major change in the term of U.S. patents since the time Kaplow was writing; patents now expire twenty years after filing, versus seventeen years after issuance when Kaplow was writing. Second, various patent term adjustment mechanisms are now in place. The most important of these stem from the Hatch–Waxman Act, formally known as the Drug Price Competition and Patent Term Restoration Act of 1984, Pub. L. No. 98–417, 98 Stat. 1585 (codified at 15, 21, 28, and 35 U.S.C.). This statute contains complex provisions that add extra periods of protection on the end of pharmaceutical patents, to make up for lengthy regulatory delays in the drug approval process by the Food and Drug Administration (FDA).

Second, subsequent to the Kaplow article, a literature emerged pointing out that patent scope (or breadth) presented an alternative mechanism by which the overall reward value of a patent could be adjusted. See, e.g., Robert P. Merges and Richard R. Nelson, "On the Complex Economics of Patent Scope," 90 *Colum. L. Rev.* 890 (1990) (excerpted earlier in this volume); Richard Gilbert and Carl Shapiro, "Optimal Patent Length and Breadth," 21 *Rand J. Econ.* 106–112 (1990). While this literature in some ways supports one of Kaplow's main points—the sheer complexity of adjusting aggregate patentee reward, due to the multifaceted nature of patent protection—it demonstrated that the legal system not only could but in fact does make micro-adjustments in the overall protection afforded by individual patents. For a recent contribution in this vein, applying the idea of reward tailoring on an industry-by-industry basis, see Dan L. Burk and Mark A. Lemley, "Policy Levers in the Patent System," 89 *Va.L.Rev.* 1575 (2003). For a critique of some aspects of the Burk–Lemley project, see R. Polk Wagner,

"On Patents and Path Dependence: A Comment on Burk and Lemley,"
18 *Berkeley Tech. L. J.* 1341 (2003).

4. Are you convinced of Kaplow's arguments regarding the need to
consider both patentee reward and social cost in choosing the proper
combination of rules to govern patents? Do you agree with his suggested
alternative, the "ratio test"? The force of Kaplow's arguments established this as the definitive academic approach to the patent-antitrust
interface. See Michael A. Carrier, "Unraveling the Patent–Antitrust
Paradox," 150 *U. Pa. L. Rev.* 761, 797 (2002). In the courts, however, the
test has not caught on to date, perhaps because its clarity comes at the
expense of considerable rigor. Id., at 798 (no court has yet applied
Kaplow ratio test). And so the seemingly endless oscillation of patent-
antitrust doctrine continues. Compare In re Independent Service Organizations Antitrust Litigation (Xerox), 203 F.3d 1322 (Fed. Cir. 2000)
(patent-oriented court approves use of service tie-in in connection with
patent license; court's focus is almost exclusively on formalistic "numerator" analysis) with Image Technical Services, Inc. v. Eastman Kodak
Co., 125 F.3d 1195 (1997) (condemning service tie-in on basis that patent
license was a sham, and emphasizing social cost, i.e., "denominator"
analysis). For criticism of the Federal Circuit opinion in the Independent
Service Organization case, see Robert Pitofsky, "Challenges of the New
Economy: Issues at the Intersection of Antitrust and Intellectual Property," 68 *Antitrust L.J.* 913, 919 (2001).

5. Kaplow's statement that "distributional" issues will receive no attention in his analysis is characteristic of one line of law and economics
scholarship, which emphasizes that legal rules should be concerned with
aggregate social welfare, and not concern themselves with the fair
distribution of resources. See Louis Kaplow & Steven Shavell, "Why the
Legal System Is Less Efficient than the Income Tax in Redistributing
Income," 23 *J. Legal Stud.* 667 (1994). This is not to suggest that
Kaplow (or his co-author, Steven Shavell) are anti-redistribution; they
favor redistribution through direct means such as the tax system,
instead of via legal rules. For a recent book-length discussion of these
issues, which argues that "fairness" ought not to figure in the design of
legal rules at all, see Louis Kaplow & Steven Shavell, Fairness Versus
Welfare (Cambridge, MA: Harvard Univ. Press, 2002). For critiques, see
Jeremy Waldron, "Locating Distribution," 32 *J. Legal Stud.* 277 (2003);
Michael Dorff, "Why Welfare Depends on Fairness: A Reply to Kaplow
and Shavell," 75 *S. Cal. L. Rev.* 847 (2002). What do you think—does it
matter that the rules of patent law leave many hardworking inventors
with no reward, even when their inventions make significant contributions? See, e.g., Simon H. Rifkind, "The Romance Discoverable in Patent
Cases," 16 F.R.D. 253, 258–260 (1954), reprinted in 37 J. Pat. Off. Soc'y
319 (1955) (describing the case of Jungersen v. Baden, 69 F.Supp. 922
(S.D.N.Y. 1947) (Rifkind, J.) (invalidating patent on method of jewelry
manufacture that had become very successful commercially, after three
other courts had found patent valid). Does it matter that these cases
probably have little effect on the incentive of future inventors? If it could
be shown that total inventiveness would not decline under a rule that

saved consumers money by randomly invalidating one out of every ten patents, would you support that rule?

6. The final portion of the excerpt looks at the specific practice of output-based royalties. In particular, Kaplow is concerned with the situation where a patent licensee has some ability to vary the mix of components or ingredients (generically, the "inputs") that go into the making of a final product (or "output"). As Kaplow notes, there is some evidence that licensees may in some cases inefficiently vary the mix of inputs to lower the patent royalties they are required to pay. See F.M. Scherer and David Ross, Industrial Market Structure and Economic Performance 522–527 (3d ed.) (Boston, MA: Houghton Mifflin Co., 1990). This was an issue in one early round of the Microsoft antitrust enforcement action. See United States v. Microsoft Corp., 56 F.3d 1448 (D.C. Cir. 1995) (reversing district court ruling refusing to approve consent decree requiring Microsoft to no longer charge licensees on a "per computer" basis regardless of whether licensees included copies of Microsoft's operating system on each individual computer). The consent decree to this effect was approved on remand in 1995. See Michelle Quinn, "Judge OKs Pact Settling Microsoft Antitrust Case," The San Francisco Chronicle, Aug. 22, 1995, at A–1.

7. Ian Ayres and Paul Klemperer make an argument very much in the spirit of Kaplow in their article, "Limiting Patentees' Market Power Without Reducing Innovation Incentives: The Perverse Benefits of Uncertainty And Non–Injunctive Remedies," 97 *Mich. L. Rev.* 985 (1999). Ayres and Klemperer point out that the last small increment of price increase charged by a monopolist may benefit the patentee far less than it costs consumers overall. They thus advocate a patent regime that is considerably more tolerant of long delays in patent enforcement than is conventionally considered wise. (Adjustments to the patent term can be made, they argue, to offset any harm to patentees' incentives.) This is quite consistent with Kaplow's ratio test, as the authors point out:

> Our approach is consistent with the "ratio test" developed by Louis Kaplow. Kaplow suggested that in "assessing the desirability of retaining a currently permitted practice" it is useful to compare the patentee's incremental reward to the incremental social loss resulting from the practice in question, because "[i]n general, the higher the ratio, the more desirable the practice." When applying Kaplow's test to patent pricing itself, one finds that allowing patentees to exploit full monopoly power produces an extremely low and hence undesirable ratio—indicating that giving patentees the ability to raise price all the way to the monopoly level is not cost justified. The ratio test suggests that policymakers should analyze the incremental profits per dollar of social loss on various dimensions of scope. If one margin of protection produces lower patentee profits per dollar of social loss than another margin, it makes sense to reduce the patentee's entitlement where the ratio is low and to expand the patent entitlement where the ratio is high. Doing so can reduce the deadweight loss of patents without reducing the patentee's expected profits.

Id., 97 *Mich. L. Rev.* at 992–993.

D.   Patent Institutions

Addressing the Patent Gold Rush: The Role of Deference to PTO Patent Denials*

ARTI RAI

The proliferation of high-technology patents directly implicates the two institutions that are primarily responsible for administering the patent system—the United States Patent and Trademark Office (PTO), which grants patents, and the Court of Appeals for the Federal Circuit (CAFC), which hears all patent appeals. Thus far, however, commentators have tended to focus not on the institutional actors but rather on change in the substantive patent law. * * *

The absence of attention to the proper role of the CAFC in reviewing PTO decisions denying patentability reflects a larger tendency among patent law scholars to ignore the application of administrative law principles to patent law. Similarly, the CAFC itself has refused to apply administrative law principles to its review of PTO decisions denying patentability. The recent explosion of patent filings in biotechnology and computer software highlights the importance of determining how administrative law principles such as deference should apply to the relationship between the CAFC and the PTO. Deference implicates considerations of institutional competence, and such considerations should figure prominently in any inquiry regarding how the law should engage technologically complex, rapidly expanding industries.

This Article analyzes the CAFC and PTO as an integrated institution.... [T]he CAFC should be wary of reviewing independently PTO's decisions denying patentability. The CAFC's review should be particularly deferential when the denial is based on a determination that the invention is "obvious"—that is, not truly new. Deference to patent denials is warranted moreover, even if the PTO continues to have skewed incentives as well as limitations on its own resources and expertise: these limitations will tend systematically to produce errors in patent grants, not patent denials. Indeed, as a consequence, PTO reform will be much more important for ensuring valid PTO patent grants than for ensuring valid PTO patent denials.

II.   Addressing the Race to Patent

[T]he biotechnology patent race differs in some important respects from the race in computer technology. Responsibility for the biotechnology race rests squarely with the CAFC. Despite its limited understanding of DNA-based technology, the CAFC has refused to defer to the technical expertise of the PTO. By contrast, in the context of computer programs, the differences between the PTO and CAFC have both technical and

* Reprinted with permission from 2 Wash. U. J. L. & Pol'y 199 (2000). © 2000 Arti Rai and Washington University.

legal aspects. Moreover, the PTO's issuance of obvious business method patents has contributed to the race. In both cases, however, there is a serious concern that obvious patents are being issued. Thus, the key to addressing the race to patent will be developing and implementing a cost-effective sorting mechanism for segregating obvious material not worthy of a patent from other material.

* * * In the context of the hundreds of thousands of patent applications that are filed annually, only administrative agencies like the PTO, which can call upon thousands of highly specialized personnel, have the institutional resources to make the complex factual determinations underlying nonobviousness. In contrast, the CAFC (like appellate courts generally) operates under resource constraints that constrain its ability to see more than a small fraction of the technological innovations on which patents are sought. Moreover, because of limited resources, the amount of technical knowledge that can be wielded by any appellate court—including a specialized court like the CAFC—is quite limited. While the CAFC has a number of judges who are technically trained, they are not (and, indeed, could not be) trained in every area of science in which any given patent dispute may arise. As Professor Rochelle Dreyfuss has noted, in cases like nonobviousness "[w]here the law is clear but difficult to apply to complex factual situations," expertise is most usefully deployed not at the appellate level but at the administrative or trial level.[1]

For these reasons, those who have acknowledged the central role of nonobviousness, particularly in the context of computer programs, have argued for various reforms to make the PTO more capable of distinguishing obvious inventions from nonobvious ones. Although these reforms would necessarily cost money, such costs should be relatively small compared to the costs created by invalid patents. One relatively straightforward reform would involve an increase in the number and quality of patent examiners. Another reform might involve changing the incentive structure of the PTO so that examiners are no longer encouraged to issue patents. Currently, examiners are compensated in part based on the number of final dispositions of patents that they accumulate. Because it is easier and faster to achieve a final disposition by allowing a patent than by denying one, there is an incentive to allow applications.

Finally, perhaps the most effective reform would involve instituting an opposition proceeding that allowed interested private parties to challenge the validity of particular patent applications. * * *

PTO reform is clearly necessary. It is, however, by no means sufficient. . . . PTO reform will be for naught if the CAFC continues its current practice of refusing to defer. Indeed, even absent PTO reform (or with incomplete PTO reform), deference to PTO denials of patentability is merited. This is because the PTO's deficiencies, in terms of incentive structure and lack of expertise will lead it systematically to err on the side of granting patents. These deficiencies show that there is no institutional reason for the PTO to err when it denies patents. Similarly,

---

1. [Quoting from Rochelle Dreyfuss in the article excerpted later in this section.— Eds.]

any agency bias in favor of industries that regularly seek patents before the PTO will lead in the direction of erroneous patent grants, not erroneous patent denials. . . .

III.   Deference to PTO Patent Denials: The Doctrinal Analysis

From an administrative law perspective, the issue of how much deference an agency decision should receive turns on where the decision falls on the law/fact spectrum. As was discussed above, nonobviousness—the single key determinant of whether particular biotechnology or computer software will be patentable—represents a mixed question of law and fact. For mixed questions of law and fact (as for "pure" questions of law), the starting point for deference analysis is the Supreme Court's seminal decision in Chevron v. Natural Resources Defense Council.[2]

Because nonobviousness is a mixed question of law and fact to which Congress could not have spoken directly, application of Chevron would require . . . examining whether the PTO's determination regarding nonobviousness was a reasonable one. For example, under the Chevron standard the PTO's determination that DNA sequences could be rendered obvious through the existence of prior art methods (and not simply through the existence of structurally similar DNA) would probably have survived review. . . .

Chevron's emphasis on technical expertise and democratic accountability applies squarely to the PTO. Technical expertise is particularly relevant to nonobviousness determinations, which rely heavily on highly specialized fact-finding. Moreover, as a doctrinal matter, any argument that the technical competence of an agency becomes less important when its decisions are being reviewed by a specialized court has been laid to rest by the recent Supreme Court decision in United States v. Haggar Apparel.[3] Haggar makes it abundantly clear that Chevron analysis applies not only to courts of general jurisdiction that review agency decisions but also to specialized courts that conduct such review.

. . . Although critics of Chevron raise significant constitutional and statutory objections, these objections apply most squarely to "pure" questions of statutory construction, not mixed questions of law and fact.

. . . The Federal Circuit is unlikely, of its own accord, to apply Chevron deference to the PTO's decisions concerning patentability. It is likely, however, that the Supreme Court will mandate that it do so. Recent Supreme Court decision making at the intersection of administrative and patent law makes it clear that the Court considers the PTO an agency to which the ordinary terms of the APA apply. Specifically, the Court's decision in Dickinson v. Zurko[4] held that the APA, which provides that agency factfinding shall only be set aside if it is "arbitrary, capricious, an abuse of discretion or . . . unsupported by substantial evidence" applies squarely to the PTO. Thus, to the extent the CAFC is reviewing a nonobviousness decision in which the PTO made a specific factual determination (e.g., a determination regarding the difference

2.   467 U.S. 837 (1984). . . .

3.   526 U.S. 380 (1999).

4.   119 S. Ct. 1816 (1999).

between the invention at issue and the prior art), the CAFC is already required to show APA-level deference. Even more importantly, the Zurko case strongly suggests that the Supreme Court, if presented with a question regarding what level of deference the PTO should receive on mixed questions of law and fact, would mandate that Chevron apply.

Notes and Questions

1. Arti Rai received both A.B. and J.D. degrees from Harvard University. She has taught at the University of San Diego and University of Pennsylvania Schools of Law, and now teaches at Duke University School of Law.

2. To someone not familiar with the history of the patent system, it might seem quite apparent that the PTO is an executive agency like any other and ought to have its actions reviewed by the same standards other agencies are subjected to. But this notion has only recently become commonplace, for essentially two reasons: (1) the long history of the PTO, and (2) the special nature of patent examination as an administrative function. Point (2) is discussed in the Duffy excerpt, infra, and the notes that follow.

As for its long history, it is important to keep in mind that the PTO is a very old administrative agency—one of the first, in actuality. It was born of an era quite different from the period that most scholars think of as the origin of the "regulatory state"—the early twentieth century. The modern PTO came into existence with the 1836 Act, which required for the first time a regularized administrative apparatus to review each patent application. This took place long before the modern era of administrative law, ushered in by the Administrative Procedure Act (APA) of 1946. The PTO still bears remnants of its origin in the Jacksonian era, a far different period from the Progressive era that gave birth to the modern administrative state. For an enlightening treatment of these issues, see John F. Duffy, "The FCC and the Patent System: Progressive Ideals, Jacksonian Realism, and the Technology of Regulation," 71 *Colo. L. Rev.* 1071, 1124 (2000) (calling the PTO "a system of public regulation that nonetheless exalted the private over the public."). According to Duffy,

> Unlike the sweeping delegations conferred in the Progressive and New Deal eras, the delegations of governmental power for the patent system were, and still are, extraordinarily narrow. The constitutional grant of legislative authority was itself kept very narrow. The clause includes not only the goal to be served—"to promote the Progress of Science and useful Arts"— but also the specific means to achieve the goal—"by securing for limited Times to Authors and Inventors the exclusive Right to their respective Writings and Discoveries." The specificity of the constitutional delegation is particularly striking because the convention was committed to drafting the constitution with "general propositions" and "essential principles" to avoid "clog[ging]" government with "provisions permanent and unal-

terable, which ought to be accommodated by time and events...."

The narrow delegation in the Constitution established a pattern that would be followed in the congressional approach to the regulation of innovation. While the patent act passed in the first Congress did create a Patent Board consisting of three high government officers, the Board's function was limited to determining whether the applicant had created an invention "sufficiently useful and important" to warrant a patent. That discretionary authority, modest by twentieth-century standards, was eliminated within three years as Congress opted for a registration system. When, forty-three years later, the 1836 Patent Act restored some discretionary power to the Executive Branch, the power was limited: unlike agencies in the twentieth century, the Patent Office was given no power to issue substantive regulations—a limitation that continues to have significant legal implications. The power was checked further by an administrative appeal process and by judicial review

Thus, in 1836, when Congress conferred a limited administrative power to the Patent Office, it consciously designed institutional constraints—including an administrative appeals process and judicial review—so that granting patents would itself "be regulated and guarded, to prevent injustice through mistake of judgment or otherwise." Such institutional constraints would be rediscovered in the pessimistic Renaissance [in administrative law] of the 1960s, but they were part of the "technical checks" that the Progressives were loath to impose on their masterful agencies.

In contrast to the late eighteenth and early nineteenth centuries, the Progressive era seems hopelessly naive in believing that long-tenured administrators with broadly delegated powers could be trusted to pursue "the public interest." For example, Jackson's view on personal integrity—that it can protect better against overt improprieties than against more subtle abuses—is far more nuanced and accurate than [the Progressive] view, which relied on personal integrity to protect even against the subtle temptations that an industry could present to its supervising agency. Similarly, the pre-Jacksonian era, while accepting long tenure, restricted delegations of administrative authority for a reason similar to Jackson's for limiting tenure. It was a fear that even long-tenured administrators with good intentions might begin to pursue other goals—particularly, aggrandizement of their own power—rather than public interests. The political philosophy of the late eighteenth and early nineteenth century demanded that the creators of regulatory institutions give thought to, and provide concrete measures to regulate the institution itself. The Progressives lost sight of that tradition.

71 *Colo. L. Rev.* 1071, at 1133–34, 1138–39.

If Duffy is correct about the PTO, what does this suggest about the stringency of judicial review of patentability decisions? Does it support Rai's argument that greater deference to the PTO on the part of the Federal Circuit is appropriate? If so, why? If the PTO long predated the APA and the Progressive-era agencies it was designed to govern, why not craft special rules to govern judicial review in this instance? What might those look like?

3. For more on the proper standard of review in patent-related cases, see Lawrence M. Sung, "Echoes of Scientific Truth in the Halls of Justice: The Standards of Review Applied by the United States Court of Appeals for The Federal Circuit in Patent–Related Matters," 48 *Am. U.L. Rev.* 1233 (1999).

Rethinking Reexamination: Toward a Viable Administrative Revocation System for U.S. Patent Law*

MARK D. JANIS

* * * Those who have advocated the creation of administrative mechanisms for reviewing patent validity have traditionally sought to justify the mechanisms in three primary ways. First, an administrative revocation system might serve as a curative mechanism by which the patent office can correct its own mistakes, reducing the likelihood that a court in any given case will have to reverse the patent office's determination of patentability. Second, at least in U.S. patent policy debates, an administrative review mechanism could constitute an element of the patent law harmonization agenda, given that the patent laws of most other industrialized nations have long contained provisions for administrative review of patent validity. Third, administrative review might provide an alternative forum for resolving patent validity disputes, largely supplanting litigation as the primary mechanism for reviewing patent validity. The relative importance of these considerations has shifted quite dramatically since the creation of the Court of Appeals for the Federal Circuit, with strong implications for the ultimate design of an appropriate administrative revocation procedure.

[The author recounts the historical role of patent reissues as a "curative" mechanism.] Given the long experience with reissue proceedings, it is not surprising that reformers turned to reissue to provide a basic conceptual framework that might be adapted to operate as a curative mechanism. In 1977, the PTO substantially reformulated existing regulations governing reissue procedures. The new regulations, commonly referred to as the Dann amendments, after the then-presiding Patent Commissioner, allowed reissue applicants to obtain advisory rulings on patentability via a reissue proceeding without admitting the existence of any defect. A patentee could initiate a reissue simply by calling the PTO's attention to "prior art or other information relevant to

* Reprinted with permission from 11 Harv. J. L. & Tech. 1 (1997). © 1997 Mark Janis, Harvard University.

patentability, not previously considered by the Office, which might cause an examiner to deem the original patent ... invalid." ...

The Dann Amendments and subsequently-issued guidelines ... also allowed unprecedented opportunities for public participation in reissue procedures. Reissue application files became open to the public, and ... members of the public could file papers for consideration by the reissue examiner, request to participate in interviews, file a brief before the Board of Appeals, and appear at oral argument. Astute practitioners quickly identified a wide range of opportunities presented by this liberal invitation to participate in the reissue process.

The PTO quickly realized that the no-defect reissue procedures were not working as originally envisioned. Significantly more protestor participation than originally anticipated was permitted, giving rise to concerns about delay and harassment. . . .

In 1982, the PTO abolished the no-defect reissue practice and severely limited the public's opportunity to protest pending applications and reissues. According to the PTO, the procedures had become unnecessary due to enactment of the reexamination legislation [in 1980], and placed an undue burden on the PTO. By abolishing no-defect reissues, the PTO made a critical observation about examiner-centered procedures that generally has been overlooked in the current debate over reexamination: patent examiners "are not trained as hearing examiners and have no substantial experience in handling inter partes matters."

3.   Reexamination as a Potential Curative Mechanism

By the mid-twentieth century it was plain that the U.S. patent system needed an antidote to judicial skepticism; it was equally plain that existing administrative review mechanisms could not provide the needed cure. Reexamination was presented as an administrative alternative for arresting the erosion of the presumption of validity.

Legislative support for a reexamination process for administrative review began to build in the late 1960s. . . . [and] finally passed into law in 1980.

Close scrutiny of this legislative history, against the backdrop of then-existing administrative review mechanisms, clarifies [that] a primary purpose of reexamination was to provide the desired antidote to judicial erosion of the presumption of validity. . . .

* * * For much of the twentieth century, foreign patent systems featured a two-tiered hierarchy for the administrative review of patent validity, comprised of an opposition proceeding coupled with a revocation or "nullity" proceeding. The opposition proceeding was designed to afford members of the public an opportunity to challenge the patentability of patent claims prior to patent issuance, and operated on a fairly simple model:

> When the Patent Office has finished its examination and determined that it will allow the patent, a notice is published in the official patent journal of the country. At this time the application becomes open to public inspection and obtaining of copies; in a few countries the entire specification is available in printed

form. Within a specified period members of the public may oppose the grant of the patent. . . . The grounds upon which an application can be opposed are in general the same as the grounds upon which a patent can be refused or invalidated.

Revocation proceedings operated very similarly. A revocation provided the public an opportunity to contest patent validity after patent issuance, typically within a predetermined time limit, and on the same grounds that could be raised in an opposition proceeding. * * *

When proposals for incorporating some form of the two-tiered hierarchy into United States patent law did begin to emerge, they did not become the subject of serious legislative consideration until the harmonization agenda had taken hold. An important proposal of this nature appears in the 1966 Commission Report, in retrospect a truly remarkable document. The report explicitly recommends pursuit of the international harmonization of patent practice toward the ultimate goal of a unified world patent system capable of issuing a "universal" patent.

The report also expressly proposed that the United States adopt a form of the two-tiered hierarchy by implementing mandatory publication of pending applications, a limited opposition procedure (denominated a "citation period"), and an ex parte cancellation procedure. The Report emphasized the curative aspect of the proposed opposition procedure but characterized the cancellation procedure as an alternative to court adjudication of validity. . . .

Congress, in ultimately enacting the reexamination provisions, rejected (at least in part) the recommendations of the 1966 Commission Report. Reexamination must be understood as a rejection of the two-tiered hierarchy that then dominated world patent systems, and the embracing of a completely new conceptual model for the administrative review of patent validity.

One of the major sponsors of reexamination legislation, Senator Fogg, carefully contrasted reexamination proposals with proposals for a pre-issuance opposition procedure. Pre-issuance opposition was disfavored because opposers could unduly delay patent issuance by repeated citations of prior art against the pending application, burdening the applicant with added cost. Moreover, the publication scheme—necessary to the implementation of an opposition procedure—was unacceptable because it would have allowed third parties to infringe freely during the opposition period with no risk of injunction until patent issuance. These are standard, and well-founded, criticisms of pre-issuance opposition, but they do not necessarily explain why reexamination—as opposed to inter partes cancellation procedures—was worthy of enactment.

* * * Perhaps the most common rationale for creating a system of administrative adjudication is to provide a specialized tribunal to resolve disputes in lieu of traditional court adjudication. The litigation-avoidance rationale has long been associated with proposals for administrative review of patent validity issues. For example, in congressional hearings on proposed legislation that would have implemented many of the recommendations of the 1966 Commission Report, a member of the commission testified that the proposed cancellation procedure would

make "a very important contribution" toward reducing the expenses associated with challenging patent validity.[1] Indeed, the cancellation procedure was characterized as a "poor man's declaratory judgment."[2]

When legislative attention turned to reexamination proposals, rhetoric about reexamination as an alternative to litigation was prominent. * * *

III.   Reexamination as an Anachronistic Conceptual Model

Reexamination, according to many, has failed. A number of commentators have sought to explain the failure by assessing selected features of the existing reexamination scheme against general notions of fairness and administrative efficiency. Another way to analyze reexamination's performance is to ask first whether the critical features that define reexamination as a distinct conceptual model for administrative revocation advance any identifiable policy vision, and then to ask whether that policy vision facilitates advancement of the modern American patent system.

Congress originally envisioned reexamination as providing (1) a means for restoring credibility to the patent system by providing a curative mechanism, and (2) a viable alternative to validity litigation.... [This article] argues that Congressional and administrative choices in the implementation of reexamination consistently favored the former policy goal over the latter.

* * * Towards a Viable Administrative Revocation System

Reexamination, although partially justifiable in its initial incarnation as a curative measure, has largely proven to be a failure. Second-generation reexamination, for the reasons discussed, also seems destined to fail as an adequate litigation alternative. This makes plain the proposition that the concept of reexamination should be discarded, but leaves unanswered the question of what should be the PTO's role in resolving validity disputes.

* * * The existing trademark inter partes proceedings supply a good deal of the procedural framework for a viable patent validity inter partes review proceeding. Importantly, trademark inter partes procedures dispense with elaborate threshold requirements and establish an expert panel to hear disputes. They track the substantive scope of validity defenses that would be available in court and allow registrants to retain procedural advantages on validity. Finally, they seek to provide abbreviated procedures that appropriately balance the need to control cost and

---

1.   Patent Law Revision:Hearings on S. 2, 1042, 1377, and 1691 Before the Subcomm. on Patents, Trademarks, and Copyrights of the Senate Comm. on the Judiciary pt. 1, 90th Cong. 95 (1967) (testimony of Simon Rifkind, member of 1966 Commission).

2.   Id. Simon Rifkind testified that

today a prospective infringer may bring an action for declaratory judgment to declare and [sic] issued patent invalid. That proceeds by the same rules and exactly by the same method as if it were an infringement suit in which the patent owner sued the infringer. That is a costly, elaborate, full-fledged courtroom procedure, with all of the pretrial proceedings and expensive depositions, and so forth. A cancellation procedure is a much more limited business.

Id.

complexity against the need to provide adequate opportunities for inter partes challenges. . . .

Major patent jurisdictions in Europe have had long experience with administrative review procedures—oppositions, revocations, and "nullity" proceedings—for adjudicating patent validity. While that experience led most U.S. observers in the mid-twentieth century to reject European systems as too costly and complicated, that assessment should be revisited in view of the escalating costs of patent litigation and the increasingly urgent need to find a mechanism outside the traditional court system for resolving patent validity disputes. First, the experience with so-called "oppositions" under the European Patent Convention ("EPC") should be studied for its possible relevance to a new U.S. administrative review proceeding. Second, patent revocation and nullity proceedings in national jurisdictions, especially the United Kingdom and Germany, should be examined.

European oppositions . . . may be initiated only after grant, within a limited time. . . .

Any person can file an opposition against a European patent without any showing of interest. Significantly, the EPC imposes no true analog to the "substantial new question of patentability" threshold showing [under U.S. reexamination law], although there is some indication that the grounds for opposition must be new. It is necessary, however, for the opposer to include in the statement of opposition the "extent of the opposition" (that is, the patent claims being opposed) and the grounds for the opposition. . . .

The European opposition practice amply demonstrates the viability of administrative revocation proceedings whose substantive scope extends beyond documentary prior art challenges. Under the EPC, an opposer is virtually unrestricted in his or her choice of grounds for opposition: any ground concerning "patentability" or adequacy of disclosure can be pled. . . .

. . . The European Opposition practice provides ample evidence that many of the features already extant in U.S. trademark inter partes practice could be incorporated into a U.S. inter partes patent proceeding. At a minimum, the European experience teaches that inter partes patent proceedings must be heard initially by an expert panel, not by individual examiners; that the substantive scope of the proceedings should include not only validity challenges based upon documentary prior art, but also should include validity challenges requiring non-documentary proofs; and that the presumption of validity should be respected in the administrative proceedings as it would be in the court.

* * * Domestically, the ever-increasing pressures on the federal court system, coupled with the notoriously cumbersome nature of patent validity litigation, make plain the urgent need for a viable administrative alternative for patent validity adjudication. . . .

The United States should take concrete steps to fashion a viable administrative patent revocation system that takes as its primary mission the channeling of patent validity disputes away from the federal court system. With both reexamination reform and pre-issuance publication firmly ensconced in the legislative agenda for patent reform, the time is ripe for a coordinated review of administrative mechanisms for patent review. . . .

Important issues would still remain even if the United States were to [adopt these proposals.]

[Among other problems,] the United States must take into account emerging Seventh Amendment jurisprudence in designing an administrative revocation scheme. The better view is that Congress has the authority to remove patent validity altogether from Article III tribunals and could create, in effect, a mandatory administrative revocation system if it so desired. At some point in the future, it may become desirable for Congress to exercise this authority to its fullest extent, but only after experience demonstrates the advantages of an administrative revocation system. For now, Congress should fashion administrative patent revocation as an alternative to patent validity litigation, allowing the U.S. patent system to build up experience with true administrative revocation before establishing the administrative system as the exclusive forum for patent validity adjudication.

. . . Domestic and international factors, in confluence, present an attractive and compelling opportunity for Congress finally to enact a genuine administrative patent revocation system. Congress should set reexamination reform aside and seize the initiative to make bold and durable reforms to enhance patent validity adjudication.

Notes and Questions

1. Mark Janis received a B.S. from Purdue University and a J.D. from the University of Indiana. He teaches at the University of Iowa College of Law.

2. More recent comprehensive reform proposals have called for either fixing the shortcomings in the current reexamination system or implementing an entirely new administrative patent revocation mechanism. See Federal Trade Commission, To Promote Innovation: The Proper Balance of Competition and Patent Law and Policy (October 2003), avail. at http://www.ftc.gov/opa/2003/10/cpreport.htm; Committee on Intellectual Property Rights in the Knowledge–Based Economy, National Research Council, A Patent System for the 21st Century (Washington, D.C.: National Academies Press, 2004) (Stephen A. Merrill, Richard C. Levin, and Mark B. Myers, eds.). One attempt at reexamination reform that has been widely criticized is the 2002 "Inter partes" reexamination system; one major criticism is that reexamination requestors are prohibited from raising during later litigation any grounds for invalidity asserted during the reexamination. See, e.g., Mark D. Janis, "Inter Partes Patent Reexamination," 10 *Fordham Intell. Prop. Media & Ent. L.J.* 481, 498 (2000) (criticizing this feature of reexaminations, among others). For an argument that this system has not been given a fair trial, see Kenneth L. Cage and Lawrence T. Cullen, "An Overview of Inter Partes Reexamination," 85 *J. Pat. & Trademark Off. Soc'y* 931 (2003).

3. At least one commentator argues that the problem sought to be solved by reexamination (and other attempts to improve patent "quality" through administrative mechanisms) is best left to patent litigation:

> [S]ociety ought to resign itself to the fact that bad patents will issue, and attempt to deal with the problem ex post, if the patent is asserted in litigation. This result is admittedly counterintuitive. It depends crucially on the fact that very few patents are ever the subject of litigation, or even licensing. Because of this, money spent improving the PTO examination procedures will largely be wasted on examining the ninety-five percent of patents that will either never be used, or will be used in circumstances that don't crucially rely on the determination of validity.

Mark A. Lemley, "Rational Ignorance at the Patent Office," 95 *Nw. U.L. Rev.* 1495, at 1510–1511 (2001).

On Improving the Legal Process of Claim Interpretation: Administrative Alternatives*

JOHN F. DUFFY

Claims are the most important part of the modern patent document. They are the "metes and bounds" of patent rights; they "define[] the scope of the patentee's rights." Their proper interpretation is frequently the central issue in infringement litigation.

It was not always so. Two hundred years ago, patent law and practice knew of nothing resembling a modern claim, with all its intricacies and formalities of drafting. The patent claim evolved during the nineteenth century and assumed its place as the central textual definition of the rights conferred by the patent. In those hundred years, the claim's remarkable evolution was so far completed that a claim drafted at the very beginning of the twentieth century could easily serve as an examination question for law students at the end of the century. The success of the modern patent claim is demonstrated by its universal adoption in the patent law of all major industrialized countries....

Examining the legal process of claim interpretation requires attention to institutional development and innovation. Unfortunately, as Professor Williamson notes, "the study of organizational innovation has never been more than a poor second cousin to the study of technological innovation."[1] Any scholar of the patent system should reject that bias, for the history of patent law shows that the technological progress so valued in our culture is inextricably intertwined with the advancement of the legal and social norms by which society organizes itself and provides incentives for productive activity.

---

* Reprinted with permission from 2 Wash. U. J.L. & Pol'y 109 (2000), © 2000 Washington University and John Duffy.

1. Oliver E. Williamson, The Economic Institutions of Capitalism 404 (1985).

Innovation and progress begin with a thorough understanding of both the current technology and its shortcomings. Thus, ... [this] article introduces the existing law governing the institutional allocation of the power to interpret patent claims.... By treating claim construction as a pure issue of law subject to de novo review on appeal, the case law has centralized claim interpretation in the Federal Circuit. While such centralization can produce a desirable uniformity in claim interpretation, it can also lead to dramatic procedural inefficiencies. For example, a significant number of infringement trials may be wasted if, as is likely, institutional differences create frequent divergence between trial and appellate interpretations. The challenge of reform is to eliminate procedural inefficiency without sacrificing uniformity.

* * * In developing more coherent doctrine to govern review of administrative claim constructions, the courts should resort to general administrative law governing judicial review of agency decisions. That law almost certainly dictates a deferential standard of review. The key point is that, unlike appellate review of lower court decisions on mixed questions of law and fact, judicial review of agency decisions on such questions is ordinarily subject to a rule of deference. This is not to say that the administrative law governing review of mixed questions is free from uncertainty; it is not. Throughout the entire twentieth century, courts and commentators endlessly debated the proper approach to judicial review of administrative determinations on mixed questions. Yet though uncertainty reigns in verbal forms and analytic approaches to the issue, the results of the cases—and the terms of the relevant statutory law—show that reviewing courts will afford, and should afford, much greater deference to administrative agencies on mixed questions of fact and law than to lower courts. * * *

... [C]onventional principles of administrative law almost certainly require the courts to defer to the PTO's expertise in interpreting patent claims. Unlike deference to a decentralized system of trial courts, deference to an administrative agency does not undermine national uniformity in claim interpretation. Indeed, a traditional reason for resorting to administrative processes is to achieve national uniformity quickly and inexpensively.... [A] standard doctrine of administrative law—the primary jurisdiction doctrine—permits and sometimes even requires that courts seek administrative opinions in circumstances quite analogous to those present in infringement trials.... [Also, in many other countries,] statutory law already expressly provides for patent infringement courts to obtain advisory opinions from national or international patent offices....

The primary jurisdiction doctrine in administrative law governs situations where a court has jurisdiction over a case but an administrative decision on some issue may be helpful, or necessary, for the judicial resolution of the case.[2]

---

2. See United States v. Western Pac. R.R. Co., 352 U.S. 59, 63–64 (1956) (" 'Primary jurisdiction' ... applies where a claim is originally cognizable in the courts, and comes into play whenever enforcement of the claim requires the resolution of issues which, under a regulatory scheme, have been placed within the special competence of an administrative body...."); see also Reiter v. Cooper, 507 U.S. 258, 268 (1993) (noting that primary

The general procedures associated with the doctrine are easily described. Once it decides to invoke the doctrine, a court "enable[s] a 'referral' to the agency" by giving the parties a "reasonable opportunity to seek an administrative ruling" on an issue relevant to the case before the court.[3] Such a "reasonable opportunity" can be afforded by granting a stay of proceedings or, in the court's discretion, by other means. Importantly, "referral of the issue to the administrative agency does not deprive the court of jurisdiction."[4] The court retains power to regulate all aspects of the doctrine and may even establish a time limit beyond which the court will proceed without the agency's ruling. . . .

* * * Applying a traditional version of the primary jurisdiction doctrine would not require a wholesale transfer of authority from the courts to the agency. . . . [M]any issues of patent claim interpretation may require no specialized technical knowledge or may not be difficult enough to justify the referral to the agency. An example might be found in Markman, which presented an interpretive issue that was both relatively straightforward (none of the judges who interpreted the claims disagreed with the result) and . . . likely to be unique to the case. Where claim construction presents more technical questions, courts should refer the issue to the agency, but the agency's claim construction, like all agency action, would still be subject to judicial review pursuant to the APA.

Successful application of the primary jurisdiction doctrine would, of course, require that the PTO be amenable to interpreting claims upon referral from the courts. This is, however, no different than the ordinary case of primary jurisdiction. . . . [A]dministrative cooperation has been the norm. There is no reason to suspect that the PTO would be less willing to cooperate than other agencies. The agency could insure claim interpretations of high quality by assigning the task to panels of examiners-in-chief or administrative patent judges from the Board of Patent Appeals and Interferences. Indeed, such a process might have important collateral benefits for the agency and for the patent system as a whole. Opining on ambiguities in claims may improve the PTO's ability to detect and eliminate such ambiguity prior to the issuance of a patent, which, in turn, would improve the certainty and reliability of patent rights generally.

Curiously, application of primary jurisdiction to patent infringement cases would be consistent with the historical origins of the doctrine. In the early part of the twentieth century, when primary jurisdiction was first being formulated in rail tariff cases, one prominent commentator— Adolf Berle, whose later fame on corporate law matters overshadowed his earlier work in administrative law—justified and explained the developing doctrine by analogy to the requirement in patent law that parties first seek administrative action in the form of an issued patent

jurisdiction "is a doctrine specifically applicable to claims properly cognizable in court that contain some issue within the special competence of an administrative agency").

   3. Reiter v. Cooper, 507 U.S. 258, 268 (1993).

   4. Id. at 268.

prior to suit in court.[5] Applying the now mature law of primary jurisdiction to patent cases brings the doctrine full circle. . . .

The primary jurisdiction doctrine shows that domestic administrative law contains familiar mechanisms by which courts could obtain administrative assistance in claim interpretation. Similarly, the law of other jurisdictions demonstrates that such mechanisms are not alien to the patent law. The European Patent Convention (EPC), German law, and Japanese law, among others, provide devices by which courts can obtain administrative assistance on claim interpretation. Even in England, where centralization of infringement litigation in a specialized court makes administrative assistance less necessary, the patent agency has authority not only to interpret claims but also to apply those interpretations in ruling on infringement issues. The administrative role in claim interpretation is already expanding in Japan and is destined to increase throughout European countries if the Community Patent Convention is ratified or if the European Union adopts a similar system conferring a truly transnational patent right.

Administrative assistance concerning patents granted by the European Patent Office (EPO) is available to the courts of every EPC country pursuant article 25 of the EPC, which provides:

> At the request of the competent national court trying an infringement or revocation action, the European Patent Office shall be obliged, against payment of an appropriate fee, to give a technical opinion concerning the European patent which is the subject of the action. The Examining Divisions shall be responsible for the issue of such opinions. . . .

Although article 25 was "intended to contribute towards the consistency in the interpretation of European patents," its usefulness has been limited by the EPO's implementing regulations, and the procedure has not been invoked frequently. The regulations require the requesting national court to formulate its request "clearly and precisely" and "where possible to separate clearly the legal aspects from the technical aspects upon which it seeks the opinion of the EPO." Moreover, the rules bar the agency from "giv[ing] any opinion on the extent of protection (article 69 and accompanying Protocol)." Since article 69 of the EPC states that the extent of patent protection is "determined by the terms of the claims" and the accompanying Protocol supplies principles for interpreting claims, the regulations restrict the agency's authority under article 25 to opine on the ultimate issues of claim interpretation. The regulations do indicate that the agency may answer questions having "a legal, as well as technical, aspect." Thus, the EPO probably can issue opinions on subsidiary questions, such as how persons skilled in the relevant art would understand the terms used in claims, without violating the prohibition on opinions concerning extent of patent protection.

The theory underlying the American primary jurisdiction doctrine helps to explain the EPO's reluctance to interpret claims. One of the

5. A. A. Berle, Jr., The Expansion of American Administrative Law, 30 Harv. L. Rev. 430, 445 (1917).

central goals of the primary jurisdiction doctrine—furthering uniformity of result (here, a transnational uniformity)—is simply not an unqualified goal of the European Patent Convention. The EPC is intended to provide a unified examination process but not a unified patent right. Instead, an EPC patent is a "bundle" patent—once granted, it functions as a bundle of national patents from the signatory nations. The patent rights conferred are governed by each nation's own domestic laws and need not be identical. Within such a legal framework, the limitations on the EPO's article 25 power make sense: The agency can provide courts with a central source of technical assistance, including assistance that might implicate claim interpretation. However, deciding the ultimate scope of protection is left to the courts of member states, which may, consistent with the EPC, afford somewhat different levels of protection. * * *

Standard economic analysis posits that "[t]he objective of any procedural system . . . is to minimize the sum of two types of cost"—the cost of erroneous decisions and the cost of operating the procedural system. Applying the doctrine of primary jurisdiction to claim interpretation would shift some interpretive power from the courts to the responsible administrative agency. The principal benefit from the proposal can be predicted with relatively high confidence: It would reduce the cost of operating the procedural system. In large part, this is definitional. Evaluating any proposed substitution of administrative for judicial processes must assume particular conceptions of the "administrative" and "judicial" processes. Those assumed conceptions are the existing administrative and judicial processes in the American patent system. The patent agency is a centralized, expert body that acts through informal procedures, while the courts are a combination of decentralized, nonexpert tribunals and a centralized, expert appellate body, both of which operate with elaborate, formal procedures. To propose substituting administrative for judicial process within such a system is to propose reducing the formality and expense of the legal process.

Other considerations also suggest that administrative processes could reduce the expense of claim interpretation. Allocating decisional authority to an administrative agency substitutes, to some extent, decisionmakers who are familiar with claim construction for district judges who, generally, are not. At a minimum, such a substitution should reduce the costs of acquainting the nonspecialist district judge with the intricacies and formalities of claim drafting. Furthermore, rough estimates of the cost of administrative claim interpretations are possible, and the estimates demonstrate the magnitude of possible savings on litigation expenditures. For example, the cost of a technical opinion from the EPO is merely three thousand dollars, and the process is so streamlined that the parties need not submit briefs or make an appearance before the agency. Three thousand dollars is, perhaps, equivalent to ten hours of a patent attorney's time. If such an expenditure has even a five percent probability of eliminating the need for a retrial (i.e., if one in twenty administrative opinions prevents a divergence in claim interpretation between the Federal Circuit and the district court), then the expenditure would reduce the expense of claim interpretation provided that a retrial would require at least two hundred hours of attorney time, which is approximately equal to the work of five attorneys in one week.

The principal cost of shifting toward administrative claim interpretation is the risk that administrative interpretations might be inferior to judicial interpretations, but this risk should not be large. One point is relatively straightforward: The quality of an authoritative claim interpretation depends not on its fidelity to some abstract ideal of interpretation, but on its predictability. If patent attorneys advising their clients can reliably predict how particular claim language will be interpreted in enforcement proceedings, then the claim has served its purpose. Thus, if administrative and judicial claim interpretations systematically differ but each is as predictable as the other, neither should be viewed as superior to the other.

Beyond this initial point, further progress in the analysis is complicated by the absence of empirical data measuring the predictability or certainty of either judicial or administrative claim interpretations. There is, nonetheless, some reason to think that the quality or predictability of claim interpretations under the proposed system would not be significantly inferior, and may even be superior, to predictability under the current system. Shifting some interpretive responsibility from generalist district courts to the agency would increase specialization within the patent system, and the history of patent administration suggests that specialized institutions advance predictability. The most important increases in centralization of the United States patent system occurred in 1836 and 1982, with the creation of, respectively, the examination system within the Patent Office and the Federal Circuit. In each case, greater specialization was prompted by a perceived need to increase the predictability of the system and, in each case, the change was believed to have achieved that goal.

Notes and Questions

1. John Fitzgerald Duffy received a B.A. from Harvard University and a J.D. from The University of Chicago School of Law. He has taught at Cardozo Law School and William and Mary Law School, and now teaches at George Washington University School of Law.

2. Professor Duffy's proposal to apply the doctrine of primary jurisdiction to patent claim interpretation is one example of the growing application of conventional administrative law concepts and techniques to patent law. For a brief description of the historical origins of the Patent and Trademark Office, and the recent academic literature describing appropriate treatment of the PTO under contemporary administrative law, see the earlier except by Rai and the notes that follow it.

3. Duffy states that predictability is the key to claim interpretation, but laments the "absence of empirical data" on the subject. That is beginning to change. See Polk Wagner and Lee Petherbridge, "Is the Federal Circuit Succeeding? An Empirical Assessment of Judicial Performance," 152 *U. Pa. L. Rev.* 1105 (2004). Wagner and Petherbridge divide Federal Circuit claim interpretation opinions over a seven year period into two distinct methodologies: (1) "proceduralist," which emphasizes plain meaning (especially dictionaries) and a consistent hierarchy of interpretive sources, and (2) "holistic," which employs a more context-specific approach which can vary with the language of the claims, the wording of the patent specification, and the like. According to the authors,

> Institutionally, the Federal Circuit appears to be a court in the midst of broad transition, especially in terms of personnel. The "new" Federal Circuit that is now emerging—a court that is more rules-based and consistent—is already having a measurable impact on patent jurisprudence.

> The findings also suggest a number of policy implications for the court's efforts to meet its mandate. We recommend that the court recognize the importance of methodology and move to standardize the procedural methodological approach—the evidence suggests that the procedural approach is inherently more consistent than holistic analyses....

> In our view, whether the Federal Circuit is succeeding is a question that remains remarkably open. Little in these results would lead one to conclude that the court has been an unqualified success in bringing additional consistency, uniformity, and predictability to the patent law. But at the same time, many findings are unquestionably encouraging, suggesting that the court's effort to meet its mandate is both well underway and moving in the right direction.

152 U.Pa. L. Rev. at 1112–1113.

The Federal Circuit: A Case Study in Specialized Courts*

ROCHELLE COOPER DREYFUSS

* * *

The CAFC partially owes its origin to proposals made by the Hruska Commission in the course of its study of the caseload crisis of the federal courts.[1] Although the major recommendation of the Commission—the creation of an appellate court to handle cases referred by the Supreme Court—was rejected, Congress took note of a secondary finding that there was a special problem in patent law. Perhaps because of its own docket problems and its lack of expertise, the Supreme Court rarely reviewed the patent law decisions of the regional circuits. The resulting lack of national guidance created a microcosm of the difficulties identified by the Commission in the larger universe of the federal court system.

---

* Reprinted with permission from 64 NYU L. Rev. 1 (1989), © 1989 New York University Law Review and Rochelle Dreyfuss.

1. "Recommendations for Change," ... 67 *F.R.D.* 195 (1975). For a description of the work of the Hruska Commission, see J. Sexton & S. Estreicher, "Redefining the Supreme Court's Role" 18–23 (1986)....

First, the PTO, charged with initial determinations of patentability, was left largely to its own devices. Since it—along with its reviewing court, the Court of Customs and Patent Appeals (CCPA)—was free to develop its own notions of patentability but could not impose them on other federal courts, its decisions did not command the respect of the judiciary. As the presumption of validity was eroded by the regional courts, the research community considered the value of patents to be in decline. And because patents were so often held invalid, the public perceived unchallenged patents to be a drain on the economy. It was thought that patentees were setting monopoly prices for inventions that, when properly viewed, were already in the public domain.

Second, the law diverged among regions of the county. Some circuits imposed difficult burdens on patentees, or light ones on infringers. Statistics demonstrate that in the period 1945–1957, a patent was twice as likely to be held valid and infringed in the Fifth Circuit than in the Seventh Circuit, and almost four times more likely to be enforced in the Seventh Circuit than in the Second Circuit.[2] It is no wonder that forum shopping was rampant, and that a request to transfer a patent infringement action from Texas, in the Fifth Circuit, to Illinois, in the Seventh Circuit, would be bitterly fought in both circuits and, ultimately, in the Supreme Court.[3] Furthermore, without knowing where a patent would be litigated, it became impossible to adequately counsel technology developers or users. In such a legal environment, the promise of a patent could hardly be considered sufficient incentive to invest in research and development.

The [Federal Courts Improvement Act of 1982, or "FCIA"] offered a solution to these problems by creating a single forum to hear appeals for most patent disputes. According to proponents of the legislation, channeling patent cases into a single appellate forum would create a stable, uniform law and would eliminate forum shopping. Greater certainty and predictability would foster technological growth and industrial innovation and would facilitate business planning. In addition, proponents hoped that the new court would alleviate the workload crisis, at least at the appellate level, where the technical nature of patent disputes required a disproportionate amount of time from the generalist judges of the regional circuits.

On the whole, the empirical data fulfill the expectations of the Federal Circuit's founders concerning both the precision and accuracy of patent law. As a general matter, the court has articulated rules that are consistent with the underlying philosophy of patent law and that are easy for the lower courts and the research community to apply. The court has been cognizant of the needs of inventors and has made strides toward shaping the law in a manner that resonates with the practicalities of technology development. One unforeseen benefit has been the

    2. Cooch, "The Standard of Invention in the Courts," in Dynamics of the Patent System, 34, 56–59 (W. Ball ed. 1960).

    3. See Hoffman v. Blaski, 363 *U.S.* 335 (1960) (infringer could not transfer case under 28 U.S.C. § 1404 (1982), which permits transfers in the interests of justice, to district that lacked personal jurisdiction over him even though he was willing to waive his objection).

court's synthesis of patent law principles in a manner that had escaped the regional circuits.

A. *Precision*

Precision, as used here, means the extent to which the law produces horizontal equity. The best measure of precision would be to see whether two courts deciding the same case reach the same result. Before the CAFC, this was actually possible since patents sometimes were challenged in more than one forum. However, with the establishment of the new court, repetitive litigation has diminished. A feel for precision, though, may be obtained in another manner—by looking at the way that the CAFC formulates legal principles. Bright line rules, objective criteria, and minimal exceptions may not make for accurate adjudication (the 'right' result in every case), but they create a body of law that is easier to apply uniformly and to predict with certainty. The decisions of the CAFC to date demonstrate that the court has taken seriously the duty to make the law precise, and has made strides in that direction.

The best example of imprecision within pre-CAFC patent law involved the issue of inventiveness. To be patented, an invention must be both new—not previously invented—and nonobvious—not such a small progression that a person having ordinary skill in the art would have been able to construct the invention based on what was previously know in the field. The latter provision historically caused confusion because it essentially asked the trier of fact to decide, with hindsight, whether the invention was a truly significant advance. Since the most sophisticated inventions sometimes appear to be simple, and since it can require comprehensive understanding of the art to know what was originally thought impossible, the requirement of nonobviousness often led to surprising and unpredictable results. Many considered the chaos generated by the nonobviousness requirement to be, almost in itself, a reason to change the administration of the patent law.

As far as precision is concerned, the CAFC has done an excellent job with obviousness. Recognizing that so long as the determination of obviousness rested upon the subjective opinion of the court, it would remain fraught with inconsistency, the CAFC has required the lower courts to review a series of objective elements before concluding that an invention is unpatentable for obviousness. For example, the CAFC now requires evidence concerning the commercial success of patented invention, on the theory that the willingness of others to buy it demonstrates the extent to which it contributes to the field. The court also will consider long felt, but unmet, need as a signal that others had been motivated to make the discovery, but were unable simply to extend prior knowledge to do so. That others in the industry generally acquiesce in [a] license rather than contest the validity of the patent, is also regarded as evidence that those in a position to assess inventiveness think that the discovery meets the standard of patentability.

This use of secondary considerations is not new to the CAFC. Rather, these considerations were previously accorded little weight because their appearance can sometimes be attributed to factors other than nonobviousness. For instance, commercial success may be due to the dominant market position of the patentee before the introduction of the new invention; the sudden ability to meet long felt need could derive from other technological advances, unrelated to the inventor's contribution; acquiescence may be attributed to the relative cost of obtaining a license, as opposed to challenging the patent. Rather than reject these considerations entirely, the CAFC has recognized their importance in making the law precise and instead has sought to minimize the extent to which they can be misused. Thus, the court has elaborated a 'nexus' requirement, which requires that before secondary considerations can be used to demonstrate nonobviousness, a showing must be made that their appearance is attributable to the inventive characteristics of the discovery as claimed in the patent.

Secondary considerations do not constitute a complete answer to the problem posed by obviousness. It is, for instance, possible for a nonobvious invention to fail to present secondary considerations. Nonetheless, it is now less probable that a lower court will declare invalid [a] patent on an invention that, because of the insight of its inventor, met long felt need, enjoyed commercial success, or displayed other objective indicia of having made an important social contribution. Since it is likely that the inconsistent treatment of such inventions was the most destabilizing element of the system, the CAFC has, in this area, made strides in achieving the appearance of precision.

Equally important to patentees, the availability of remedies has been substantially improved. The court has scrupulously followed the Patent Act's mandate that damages be 'adequate to compensate the infringement' by allowing patentees to include in lost profits the drain on human and financial resources. For example, it has awarded patentees lost profits from the sale of related goods. In addition, the court has at times relaxed the burden of proving causation. Patentees have also been permitted to introduce evidence showing that contracts with other licensees should not be dispositive of the royalty that the infringer should pay. In some cases, district courts have been required to compound the prejudgment interest awarded.

The CAFC also has revitalized the role of preliminary injunctive relief in patent disputes. In most areas of the law, courts issue preliminary injunctions upon a showing of irreparable harm and substantial likelihood of success on the merits. In copyright, the showing is reduced because harm is often presumed. Patentees, in contrast, were generally regarded as having an adequate remedy at law, and so courts denied preliminary relief unless they could prove that the patent was valid 'beyond question' and that the infringement was clear. As a result, patentees were placed in a difficult position. Infringers were not deterred from competing with the patentee and its licensees since at the worst, they would have to pay damages set by the court, and their liability might not accrue for many years. Meanwhile, patentees were deprived of royalties, competed at a disadvantage against those who had not financed development of the invention, and were therefore less able to bear the expense of litigation. In the end, they might never be fully compensated.

The CAFC has attempted to bring the right of patentees to preliminary relief into line with that of holders of other intellectual property. It has eliminated the requirement that validity be demonstrated 'beyond question,' holding that 'the burden upon the movant should be no different in a patent case than for other kinds of intellectual property where, generally, only a "clear showing" is required.' Recognizing that continued infringement 'may have market effects never fully compensable in money,' it has held that irreparable injury can be presumed.

* * *

In sum, the CAFC's jurisprudence reveals that the court has begun to make patent law more accurate, precise, and coherent. Its ability to accomplish this task derives largely from the high volume of patent appeals that it hears, which gives the court an overview of the full range of issues and forces it to construct an integrated picture of the law as a whole. In addition, the benefits of specialization appear to lie primarily in giving the court the right mix of cases, not in giving the cases the right kind of judges. The court makes no attempt to compose panels especially to hear patent appeals, and many distinguished opinions have been authored by the judges with the least technical training.

II. The Cost of Specialization: Jurisprudential and Managerial Problems within the CAFC

The idea of a patent court was not without its critics. Even before the Hruska Commission's recommendation, commentators had warned that specialization would produce substantively inferior law. The repetitious nature of the docket might lead to greater coherency but it would take patents out of the mainstream of legal thought, expose the court to a one-sided view of the issues, and discourage qualified people from serving as judges. There are similar concerns with the benefits thought to devolve from monopolization: efficiency may be the result, but channeling cases to a single forum also would deprive patent law of the collective wisdom of the circuit courts. Losing the tension produced by the percolation of ideas within the judiciary would, in addition, reduce the court's incentive to reason clearly or to write persuasively ...

* * *

The experience of the CAFC demonstrates that to some extent, the critics were correct. The CAFC has taken on a decidedly pro-patent bias, though for reasons somewhat different from those which were predicted. Administratively, there are difficult issues that have not been adequately resolved. Some, such as jurisdictional conflicts, were foreseen; others, such as conflicts questions, were not. But none are insurmountable, and they point towards ways to reorganize the court to better employ the benefits of specialization.

A. *Bias*

The anecdotal evidence suggests that the CAFC is a good court for patentees. That this should be the perception is not surprising. The court made its public mark when it upheld Polaroid's patent against an attack by Kodak,[4] and the conclusions reached in the popular press are to some extent substantiated by the CAFC's case law.[5]

The change is evident even when we confine the class of issues to those already discussed. As we have seen, defending patentability is now much easier. The presumption of validity has been invigorated, making the challenger's case harder to sustain. Even if the burden of proof had remained the same, the court's new rules, such as the required use of secondary considerations and the need to show that references disclose a relationship to each other, pose fresh obstacles for challengers. On the enforcement side, the greater availability of injunctive relief, coupled with flexible methods to compute damages, mean that it is now riskier to infringe.

At the same time, it is not clear that these changes are of the type to which the critics were referring. First, the court may be influenced by something more than capture. The last decade has seen a major reorientation of national competitive policy and increased appreciation of the role of high technology in the nation's economy. These changes can be seen in antitrust enforcement policy, in federal laws that encourage private research and development projects, and in the Supreme Court's new sympathy towards state protection of intellectual property. Although the Patent Act has not changed dramatically in that time, it should not be surprising that the CAFC has geared its interpretation of the Act to the current climate. That it might have taken longer for these national trends to influence the regional circuits is no reason to condemn the CAFC as biased. Indeed, the rhetoric that surrounded the court's founding explicitly referred to its ability to 'foster technological growth and industrial innovation.'[6] If anything, the ability of the Federal Circuit to analyze patent questions in a manner congruent to thinking in other areas indicates that the court is not isolated by its special jurisdiction. Rather, it has used its unique position to keep itself within the mainstream.

Second, it is not clear that the CAFC's new rules function as favorably to patentees as is generally thought. The emphasis on objective criteria in obviousness determinations may, for example, hurt patentees who cannot muster the evidence necessary to make an objective case. In addition, the new emphasis on the presumption of validity should not be assessed without noting the new avenue Congress provided for re-examining patents in the PTO. Since the CAFC has announced that the presumption of validity does not apply during re-examination, the system actually retains much the same capacity to invalidate patents.

It may even be wrong to think of the CAFC as the type of court that is in danger of becoming captive to special interest groups, at least with regard to its patent jurisprudence. In this respect, a distinction must be

4. See Polaroid Corp. v. Eastman Kodak Co., 789 F.2d 1156 (Fed. Cir.), cert. denied, 479 *U.S.* 850 (1986).

5. See, e.g., Schmitt, "Business and the Law: Judicial Shift in Patent Cases," *N.Y. Times,* Jan. 21, 1986, at D2 (citing Kodak–Polaroid dispute as the 'most prominent example of an increasingly pro-patent sentiment in American courts').

6. See, e.g., "The Ninth Annual Judicial Conference," 94 *F.R.D.* 350, 358 (1982) (remarks of Rep. Kastenmeier).

drawn between 'balanced' specialized courts that hear cases among evenly matched litigants, such as large, identifiable, well-represented, and allied groups, and 'imbalanced' courts that hear cases pitting a single litigant (such as the United States) or a small, tightly-knit group of litigants against poorly represented, loosely-allied groups, such as users of social services. In the case of courts that entertain actions between well-matched adversaries, there is little reason to suspect that the court will favor any particular group's interests. Where adversaries are imbalanced, however, judges may become more easily swayed by those who appear before them frequently, and by the policy arguments that they hear most often. In addition, frequent litigants who share common goals may have important strategic advantages. Familiarity with the thought processes of the judges may enable litigants to make arguments more closely attuned to the court's concerns. They can also afford to be patient, to choose when and where to press the positions they favor, and to move the court slowly toward a desired goal. One-time litigants cannot pick their cases so carefully, and therefore may not be as able to frame the issues to their advantage.

With regard to its patent jurisdiction, the CAFC is a fairly balanced court. Well-heeled groups appear on both sides of the issues. Moreover, litigants with the greatest power probably are vertically integrated companies. These firms cannot usually forecast which side of a patent issue will favor their interests, as they encompass not only research arms that develop patented innovations, but also manufacturing arms that operate under licenses for inventions patented by others. Thus, to the extent that skepticism towards specialized courts has been bred by the experience of the Tax Court (which is sometimes viewed as the government's court) or the Commerce Court (which was doomed by its perceived disposition in favor of railway owners), this skepticism may be misdirected when leveled at the CAFC. * * *

IV. The Future for Specialization

This brings us to the question of where specialization ought to be headed. This Article has presented a fairly optimistic view, for the Federal Circuit appears to be functioning well. My concluding thoughts are, however, loss hopeful. Before the findings made in this Article can be generalized, it is necessary to examine whether the CAFC's success is due to specialization, or to factors unique to patent law or to the court itself. This Part approaches this inquiry from two perspectives: the first section sets out those elements that are distinctive about the FCIA experiment; the second section uses the findings of the study to reflect upon other suggestions that have been made by advocates of specialization. Both approaches counsel caution. Although the CAFC has, for the most part, accomplished its goals, further resort to specialization may be less productive than this study might otherwise suggest. It may be that if specialization has a future, it is one that requires the development of fresh implementation strategies. The final section looks at this possibility.

A. The Unique Features of the Federal Circuit Experiment

This Article has so far assumed that any benefits to patent law generated through the establishment of the CAFC are attributable to specialization. In fact, there were many deficiencies in the preceding system. To the extent that the CAFC merely compensated for these flaws, its achievements cannot be expected to accrue every time a new specialized court is founded.

Accuracy and precision are cases in point. Prior to the CAFC, there was no authoritative body capable of creating a coherent, uniform body of patent law. The Supreme Court had not reviewed patent matters on a regular basis,[7] and the lower courts of general jurisdiction could not function as substitutes. They could not be expected to produce precision because they were not hierarchically related and did not maintain a practice of deference. Nor could they generate accuracy because no single court heard enough patent cases to allow (or motivate) its judges to develop the kind of expertise required to develop a sophisticated body of law.

Moreover, the PTO could not be expected to perform these functions. Because it must act quickly, inter parties proceedings in the PTO are rare. As a result, the Office hears only from those interested in a lenient standard of patentability. This one-sided view is unsuitable for developing sound patent policy. Nor can the PTO's decisions in individual cases be aggregated to produce a coherent body of law. The asymmetry between the knowledge of the examiner and that of the applicant means that applications are not always decided correctly—or elegantly. For the most part, plenary consideration of applications is not even cost effective because most patented inventions turn out to have no commercial significance.

Not every body of law suffers from such lack of guidance. In particular, areas subject to administrative control have the advantage of an authority capable of using its expertise to develop law that is responsive to its consumers and attuned to the will of Congress. When courts defer to these expert agencies, the law tends to remain both accurate and precise. Similarly, areas that attract greater attention from the legislature or the Supreme Court may not require a specialized court to produce the benefits conferred by the CAFC on patent law.

An analogous point can be made about synthesis. It could be argued that the benefit of integration should not count as an advantage of specialized adjudication because its appearance in connection with the CAFC was partially caused by the peculiar way that patent law was administered prior to the court's establishment. With responsibility over the PTO largely in the hands of the CCPA, and with enforcement questions adjudicated by the regional circuits, no law-making body had the motivation to knit doctrinal strands together. Because most areas of the law are not administered in this piecemeal fashion, specialized adjudication is not always needed to produce this outcome.

The unique structure of patent cases, the patent bar, and patent law consumers also calls into question the transferability of the lessons

_____

7. See, e.g., Graham v. John Deere Co., 383 *U.S.* 1, 34 (1966) (first time in 15 years Court considered issue of invention and first time it interpreted § 103 of Patent Act).

learned in this study. Because both patent law and the facts to which the law applies are technically abstruse, expertise is particularly desirable. Consequently, a benefit—relief of docket pressures—was obtained when these cases were removed from the regional circuits, where they were rare, yet difficult, and another advantage—the development of expertise—accrued when they were gathered into a critical mass. But not all uncommon questions are difficult. Removing relatively easy cases from the circuit courts and funneling them into a specialized tribunal will probably not be so advantageous.

Patent law is also unique in that its primary—if not exclusive—objective is to motivate future behavior. This goal is frustrated if the producers and consumers of patentable information, who are largely intercircuit actors, cannot predict with some degree of confidence what the law will be across the nation. For these actors, the uniformity produced by deciding all cases in a single tribunal may be a more substantial benefit than it would be if patent law had a larger backward-looking component, or if its consumers were localized.

Of course, specialization poses the risk of bias, and without public confidence in the court's neutrality, its ability to exploit the benefits of specialization will be compromised. If the substance of the specialized court's decisions could be monitored to determine whether capture has occurred, this problem could be contained. It is, however, difficult to distinguish between doctrinal changes that occur because a court is biased, and changes that occur because that court possesses special knowledge. To compensate for this inability to test for neutrality, there must be structural reasons for trusting the court. I have argued that the CAFC's neutrality derives from the nature of the bar that practices before it. It is also possible that neutrality comes from the diversity of its docket, which exposes the court to a variety of issues and makes the appointment process less vulnerable to influence by interest groups. In areas where structural safeguards cannot be built into the system, the public confidence that the CAFC enjoys may never be recreated.

Finally, consider that the CAFC is currently one of very few specialized courts in the federal system. Were such courts to proliferate, new problems would emerge. For example, I have suggested several changes in both substantive and procedural law that would make the CAFC function more effectively. But it is not unlikely that other specialized courts will pose different problems, and each court will require solutions tailored to its special needs. The costs of such an eventuality would be high. Issues long regarded as settled would have to be rethought in connection with each new court. The bar would require re-education, possibly leading to overspecialization of attorneys. The final result might be a return to something akin to the writ system, with all of its attendant burdens. Furthermore, balkanization of the law could not be prevented, as it can be in the CAFC context, by the dialogue between specialized and general courts in areas of jurisdictional overlap. * * *

Notes and Questions

1. Rochelle Dreyfuss received a B.A. from Wellesley College, an M.S. from the University of California at Berkeley, and a J.D. from Columbia

Law School. She teaches at NYU School of Law, where she is the Pauline Newman Professor of Law.

2. This article has been called "the seminal work considering the formation of the Federal Circuit and its theoretical basis." R. Polk Wagner and Lee Petherbridge, "Is the Federal Circuit Succeeding? An Empirical Assessment of Judicial Performance," 152 *U. Pa. L. Rev.* 1105, 1108 n.6 (2004). See also Michael P. Van Alstine, "Treaty Law and Legal Transition Costs," 77 *Chi.-Kent L. Rev.* 1303, 1324 n. 61 (2002) ("one of the leading examinations of this [specialized court] experiment").

3. Judge Richard Posner has argued that specialized courts such as the Federal Circuit approach statutory interpretation in a different manner than ordinary courts:

> Specialized judges can be expected to be loose constructionists. Having a stronger sense than generalists of how the issues in cases within their jurisdiction should be decided, they are more likely to see themselves as helping the legislature achieve the goals of a program than as being obliged to stop with the legislative text; this is a notable characteristic of the patent jurisprudence of the United States Court of Appeals for the Federal Circuit.

Richard A. Posner, "Reply: The Institutional Dimension of Statutory and Constitutional Interpretation," 101 *Mich. L. Rev.* 952, 964 (2003) (footnotes omitted; citing excerpted article).

4. The article was cited by the Supreme Court in Holmes Group, Inc. v. Vornado Air Circulation Systems, Inc., 535 U.S. 826, 834, 838–839 (2002) (Stevens, J., concurring) (footnote omitted; citing the excerpted article):

> There is, of course, a countervailing interest in directing appeals in patent cases to the specialized court that was created, in part, to promote uniformity in the development of this area of the law. But we have already decided that the Federal Circuit does not have exclusive jurisdiction over all cases raising patent issues. Necessarily, therefore, other circuits will have some role to play in the development of this area of the law. An occasional conflict in decisions may be useful in identifying questions that merit this Court's attention. Moreover, occasional decisions by courts with broader jurisdiction will provide an antidote to the risk that the specialized court may develop an institutional bias.

For general commentary on the relationship between the Federal Circuit and the Supreme Court, see Mark D. Janis, "Patent Law in the Age of the Invisible Supreme Court," 2001 *U. Ill. L. Rev.* 387 (2001) (arguing for a still-limited but slightly more activist oversight role for the Supreme Court in patent-related matters).

5. To some observers of the Federal Circuit, the notion that the patent bar might "capture" the Federal Circuit would now seem fanciful. Judging from reactions to controversial opinions, many patent lawyers (and even some objective observers) would no doubt argue that the Federal Circuit needs a *closer* connection with the bar and the issues its clients face. See, e.g., Conrad J. DeWitte, Jr., "Festo Change–O? No Way! Why the Supreme Court Should Reverse the Federal Circuit's Attack on the Doctrine of Equivalents," 51 *Cath. U.L. Rev.* 1323 (2002);

Russell B. Hill and Frank P. Cote, "Ending The Federal Circuit Crap-
shoot: Emphasizing Plain Meaning In Patent Claim Interpretation," 42
IDEA 1 (2002); Gerald Sobel, "Patent Scope and Competition: Is the
Federal Circuit's Approach Correct?," 7 *Va. J.L. & Tech.* 3 (2002)
(basically, no); Laurence H. Pretty, "The Recline And Fall Of Mechanical
Genus Claim Scope Under 'Written Description' In The Sofa Case," 80 J.
Pat. & Trademark Off. Soc'y 469 (1998) (criticizing "written descrip-
tion" case law).

Empirical Evidence on the Validity of Litigated Patents*

JOHN R. ALLISON and MARK A. LEMLEY

All patent lawyers have their own ideas about how patent litigation
works. Juries are better than judges for certain types of cases, they
might think. Courts are reputed to be tougher on patents in one district
than in another, or in one area of technology than another. The Federal
Circuit is pro-patent, according to some views, or anti-patent according
to others. All of this "common knowledge" is anecdotal. It is based on
the lawyer's personal experience, or stories she has heard. It may be
true, or it may be a myth.

Because patent litigation tends to be exceptionally costly, with legal
expenses often exceeding one million dollars per party, lawyers and
clients should be eager for more systematic data and fewer anecdotes
about how patents actually fare in the courts and why. In the present
study, our hope is to contribute both to the scholarly empirical literature
on the patent system at work and to offer patent practitioners harder
evidence either to confirm, or to contradict, their assumptions about the
courts' decisionmaking in patent cases. To do this, we have produced a
database of all written, final validity decisions by either district courts or
the Federal Circuit reported in the *United States Patents Quarterly*
("U.S.P.Q.") during an almost eight-year period from early 1989
through 1996. We use this database to develop many descriptive statistics about these patent validity decisions, to test a number of hypotheses
about what accounts for the success or failure of challenges to patent
validity, and to produce a regression model to determine the predictive
power of our findings. Throughout the study we examine a greater
number of variables than in any modern study of patent litigation.

It is also worth noting what we do not do. This is a study confined to
the final results of patent litigation, and to validity litigation at that. It is
therefore a subset of the much larger universes of cases that are filed, of
patents that are issued, and of inventions that are made.

III.   Description of Study

A.   *Population*

* * * Our defined population contains 299 patents litigated in 239
different cases. . . .

* Reprinted with permission from 26 AIPLA Q. J. 185 (1998), © 1998 American
Intellectual Property Law Association.

The population consists only of *final* decisions that resulted in written opinions. Where there is more than one decision in a case, we have reported the last final decision ruling on the validity of that patent. For example, final Federal Circuit decisions supersede trial court decisions in the population. In such a case, the "final" validity decision we have reported is the Federal Circuit ruling. Where the Federal Circuit remands a case, and there is subsequently a final trial court decision on the validity of the patent that is reported in the specified volumes of the *U.S.P.Q.*, we have included the trial court rather than the Federal Circuit decision in the population. Where there is no final decision on a patent—for example in rulings denying summary judgment or motions to dismiss, or appeals that result in a remand for further decision-making that is not subsequently reported—we have not included the case in the population. Similarly, a case is not included if it settles before a final decision on validity. Cases that settle after a final decision that is not vacated remain in the population. Finally, although the definition of the population includes final decisions rendered from early 1989 through 1996, we have replaced district court rulings in this time frame with later, Federal Circuit decisions where appropriate.

The population is defined in terms of patents, not cases. Many of the cases we studied produced final decisions on a number of different patents. We treat each of those patents as a separate unit for purposes of our analysis, just as it would be under patent law.

Our population consists of reported written decisions. This is broader than "published" decisions, as that term is used in local court rules. The population includes cases denominated "not for publication" by the Federal Circuit, as well as district court opinions that are not included in the Federal Supplement. At the same time, it is not as comprehensive as "all decisions" in patent validity cases. Some decisions consist only of jury verdicts or unwritten conclusions on the validity of a patent by a district court judge. We have excluded these decisions from the population, both because they do not produce intelligible data for most of the hypotheses we test, and because any effort to include all such cases necessarily would involve very unsystematic collection, which would produce only a haphazard subset of the cases and almost certainly would introduce various instances of data incomparability. * * *

We use three different statistical approaches to evaluate the data we have produced. Because we have defined a population and included all the members of that population in our data set, the normal tests designed to evaluate the statistical significance of the data do not apply. Within the population, all the numbers we reproduce are by definition "statistically significant." Thus, some of the data we produce are descriptive statistics about the population, such as what percentage of patents were invalid and how many patents were challenged on enablement grounds. These descriptive statistics also include data relating one variable to another, for example, comparing the percentage of jury decisions finding a patent valid with the percentage of bench trial decisions finding a patent valid. These statistics are interesting for what they reveal about the population of judicial validity decisions during a recent eight-year period. As a matter of pure statistics, however, they do not *predict* anything about future litigation.

Because one of our interests is the predictive significance of the data we have collected, we also have evaluated the data set in a second way, as noted earlier. This approach defines our population as a subset of an indeterminate "superpopulation" consisting of final reported validity decisions across a range of time. We then apply the techniques of statistical inference to the population to test a number of hypotheses about the relationship between validity and other factors in the superpopulation....

Finally, we combine a number of these hypotheses into a logistic regression model designed to determine how well the factors we have identified predict the outcome of patent cases....

Results

We have evaluated a number of characteristics of these cases in order to identify possible predictors of patent validity. We will discuss each of these factors separately, and then in the context of the logistic regression model.

A.   Overall Validity

Of the 300 final validity decisions in the data set, 162 (54%) found the patent valid, and 138 (46%) found the patent invalid....

This result is broadly consistent with other recent work on overall patent validity, which has generally found that courts determining the validity of patents since creation of the Federal Circuit adjudge approximately 55% of them to be valid.[1] As those prior studies have noted, this validity rate is significantly higher than it was before the Federal Circuit was created.[2]

For predictive purposes, we tested the following hypothesis:

Hypothesis 1: Issued patents are not more likely to be held valid than invalid.

We set $H[o]$ $q = 0.5$, where q is the probability of final invalidity. The observed probability was $q = 0.46$. The G-square p-value for the test was greater than 0.1, however, indicating that we cannot predict with confidence that patents in general are more likely to be held valid than invalid. From the perspective of an outsider to the patent system, it may

---

1.   See, e.g., Donald R. Dunner, The United States Court of Appeals for the Federal Circuit: Its First Three Years, 13 AIPLA Q.J. 185, 186–87 (1985); Mark A. Lemley, An Empirical Study of the Twenty–Year Patent Term, 22 AIPLA Q.J. 369, 420 (1994) (finding 56% of all litigated patents held valid during the period 1989–1994); Robert P. Merges, Commercial Success and Patent Standards: Economic Perspectives on Innovation, 76 Cal. L. Rev. 803, 822 (1988).

2.   Before creation of the Federal Circuit, studies had found that only about 35% of litigated patents were held valid on average. The percentages were similar in the district courts and the courts of appeal. See [Gloria K. Koenig, Patent Invalidity: A Statistical and Substantive Analysis (Rev. ed. 1980)] at 4–18 to 4–19, 4–22 to 4–23. At the court of appeals level, validity rates varied widely among circuits, ranging from around 10% to over 55%. See id. at 4–32. Koenig's data covered the 1953–1978 period....

be surprising that once a patent has been issued, the chance that a court will hold it valid is only slightly better than even.

Of the 138 patents held invalid in the population, the majority of the grounds for invalidity were rooted in the prior art. . . .

By far the largest number of invalidity determinations were made on the basis of obviousness (58, or 42.0% of all cases finding invalidity), which comports with the results of earlier studies. The second largest number were made on the basis of section 102 non-prior art (43, or 31.1%). Together, sections 102 and 103 accounted for 138 out of 191 total determinations of invalidity. Section 112 accounts for virtually all of the remaining grounds; 45 out of 191 determinations were made on the basis of enablement, written description, claim indefiniteness, or best mode. The remaining grounds for attacking validity resulted in very few invalidity findings.

C. *Judge Versus Jury*

* * * The role of jury trials in patent cases has increased dramatically over the past twenty years. Federal Judicial Center statistics indicate that in 1978, only 8.3% of all patent cases were tried to a jury, while in 1994, the last year for which statistics are available, fully 70% of all patent trials were held before juries. This represents a fundamental change in the nature of patent litigation. Apparently somebody—presumably patentees—thinks trial by jury will benefit them.

The data bear out this assumption. There are significant differences between the validity rates reported by different triers of fact. Of the 298 patents litigated in the population, juries decided the validity of 73 (24.5%), judges decided 143 (48.0%) during a bench trial, and judges decided 82 (27.5%) during pre-trial motions. . . . It is worth noting that because of the population definition, these numbers may actually underestimate the number of patent validity cases tried to a jury. We suspect that jury verdicts are less likely than bench trials to result in reported written opinions, unless the opinion is written in the context of denying a post-trial motion.

The differences between the pre-trial, bench, and jury decisions are striking. . . .

Juries held valid more than two-thirds of the patents tried before them (49 of 73, or 67.1%). By contrast, just over one quarter of the cases decided on pre-trial motion were decided in favor of the patentee (23 of 82, or 28.1%). Although some of this reflects the procedural nature of pre-trial motions—the better cases are more likely to make it to trial, and the weaker cases to be dismissed early—that is not the whole explanation. Given that patents receive a strong presumption of validity, it is reasonable to expect that patentees would be entitled to pre-trial judgment of validity with some frequency. Instead, it appears that pre-trial rulings disposing of validity issues largely favor the defendant, and jury verdicts favor the patentee. There is also a lesser, but still notable, difference between the 57.3% validity rate in bench trials and the 67.1% validity rate in jury trials. . . .

The differences between pre-trial, bench, and jury decisions also carry over to the type of invalidity argument each is likely to find persuasive. . . . [J]uries are largely receptive to arguments based on prior art; 62.5% of the jury findings of invalidity were premised on obviousness, and 37.5% were premised at least in part on section 102 prior art arguments. Only in one case (4.2%) did a jury find invalidity on the basis of enablement or written description violations. By contrast, judges in bench trials were much more receptive to enablement and written description arguments; 19.7% of all invalidity determinations in bench trials were made on this basis. Judges in bench trials were somewhat less likely to find invalidity on the basis of prior art; only 42.6% of judicial findings of invalidity were made on the basis of obviousness, and 19.7% on the basis of section 102 prior art.

D. Subject Matter of the Invention

* * * We also tested the inventions litigated in the population by subject matter. We divided them into several categories. The first three categories—general, chemical, and electrical patents—are mutually exclusive and track the classification scheme used by the PTO. In addition, we categorized certain patents as pharmaceutical or biotech (both overlapping subsets of the chemical group), or as software or computer-related (both overlapping subsets of the electrical group) based on our own evaluation of the subject matter.

The first thing that is striking about these statistics is the nature of the patents that were litigated during this period. The majority of the patents litigated (173, or 57.7%) were classed as general inventions; only a much smaller number were chemical (69, or 23.0%) or electrical (57, or 19.0%) inventions. Contrast this with the number of patents issued. There, the evidence indicates that general patents are significantly less than half of the total number of patents issued. It is evident that litigation most commonly involves run-of-the-mill mechanical inventions, not chemical or electrical inventions.

The numbers of specialized inventions we have identified bear out this conclusion. Biotechnology, pharmaceuticals, computer, and software patents are "hot" areas in patent law. Firms, practitioners, and scholars spend a great deal of time thinking about these types of patents. Our population includes relatively few litigated patents in these areas: only eleven pharmaceutical patents (3.7% of the total), nine biotech patents (3.0% of the total), twenty-six computer-related patents (8.7% of the total), and three software patents (1.0% of the total). Even these small numbers are overstated because many of these categories overlap.

H. Cited Versus Uncited Art

Another issue of significance relates not to prior art cited in the patent, but to prior art upon which defendants rely in litigation. It is received wisdom among patent lawyers that it is much easier to invalidate a patent on the basis of "uncited" prior art, i.e., art that the Examiner did not consider during prosecution. The rationale is that the trier of fact will be reluctant to second-guess the Examiner about an art reference that the Examiner has already considered, but that the trier of fact may be willing to invalidate a patent based on information that was not available to the Examiner.

To test this assumption, we compared the validity determinations made primarily on the basis of cited art and those made primarily on the basis of uncited art. . . .

The first thing worth noting is that most prior art attacks ultimately rely on a relatively small number of references (2.8, on average). Furthermore, most of the references that are argued at trial are uncited references; indeed, in the majority of prior art-related cases, no cited art is relied upon at all. In the cases where patents were actually held invalid, defendants disproportionately relied upon uncited prior art (1.9 uncited references on average, compared with 0.9 cited references).

Statistical tests in the superpopulation indicate with a fair degree of confidence that reliance on uncited art was more likely to lead to a finding of invalidity than reliance on cited art.

I.   *Elapsed Time From Application To Final Judgment*

We evaluated several measures of elapsed time before the final judgment in the case, in an effort to determine whether any of these measures had any relationship to validity. Our collection of these data was motivated by several factors. First, the length and importance of the time a patent spends in prosecution has been hotly debated because beginning in 1995 the expiration date of a patent is measured from the date the original application is filed, not the date the patent issues. . . . Second, information about a technology changes over time, making it reasonable to assume that factfinders might look less favorably upon old patents than upon newer ones.

We define three measures to test various hypotheses about elapsed time. The first is "time in prosecution," meaning the total time elapsed from the earliest filing of a patent application (or parent or grandparent application upon which the current application relies for priority) to the issuance of the patent. The second is "delay," meaning the total elapsed time between the date the patent issues and the date the validity of the patent is finally decided in litigation. The final measure is "lag," meaning the total elapsed time between the filing of a patent application and the final validity decision. Lag is simply "time in prosecution" plus "delay." . . .

The average time in prosecution for litigated patents in the population is 3.6 years, although the lower median (2.7 years) indicates that a few patents spent a great deal of time in prosecution, raising the mean. The average delay after issuance is 8.6 years, and the average lag between filing and resolution is 12.3 years.

The lag and delay statistics are quite interesting, because it appears that most patents litigated to judgment involve fairly old technology. This may be of some significance in the debate over what the patent system contributes to innovation. Litigation does not appear to provide early, certain protection to inventors. In fact, it appears that most patent litigation involves inventions that not only are fairly old, but also have been patented for several years before enforcement. One possible explanation for this finding is that many firms may build patent portfolios over time to give them more freedom of action in their markets, resorting to litigation only when that freedom is subsequently challenged, either by a patent suit by a rival or by a shifting marketplace. In other words, many firms obtain patents with no immediate purpose or early need to enforce them, but rather to fence out competitors and potential competitors.

The fact that most patents are quite old by the time they are litigated to judgment also highlights the importance of careful claim drafting. Claims that are broadly drafted, i.e., that lack unnecessary limitations and are not overly tied to the current implementation of an invention, are more likely to stand the test of time. And it is precisely those patents that turn out to be important in litigation.

Model

We developed a logistic regression model using most of the variables we have tested here in an effort to find reliable predictors of patent invalidity over time. In the model, we considered numerous factors that may serve as predictors of validity.

The results were disappointing, although perhaps not surprising. Of all the factors we tested as possible predictors of invalidity, only one set showed any significant predictive value. That one set was the choice of finder of fact. Compared to pre-trial disposition, trial to either a jury or the bench were significant predictors of the validity of a patent. The exponent coefficients for jury trial and bench trial were 0.359 and 0.389 respectively.

The failure of most other factors as predictors of invalidity suggests that most of the variables that determine invalidity are things that our study cannot measure. Some obvious, but untested, variables include the skill of the lawyers, the amount of money each side is willing to spend on the litigation, the "hometown advantage," the skill, character, and demeanor of fact and expert witnesses, and the abilities of the patent prosecutor. There are clearly relationships of interest to lawyers between validity and many of the factors we have described, but it is also evident that we have uncovered at most only a small part of the story.

Notes and Questions

1. John R. Allison received a B.B.A. from Texas A & M University and a J.D. from Baylor Law School. He is now the Spence Centennial Professor of Business Administration at the University of Texas. Mark A. Lemley received a B.A. from Stanford and a J.D. degree from the University of California, Berkeley (Boalt Hall) School of Law. He has taught at the University of Texas and Boalt Hall Schools of Law, and now teaches at Stanford Law School.

2. The statistical evidence seems to put to rest the debate over whether the Federal Circuit has had a substantive impact on patent law; the increase in validity rates from roughly 35% to 55% is clear evidence of a major impact. But is the 55% rate the "right" one? Is it too high now, or perhaps too low? What effect do you think this higher validity rate will

have on patentee decisions to litigate? On defendants' decisions to license or litigate? On decisions to file patent applications? On overall R & D expenditures by firms and individuals?

Judges, Juries, and Patent Cases—An Empirical Peek Inside the Black Box*

KIMBERLY A. MOORE

The frequency with which juries participate in patent litigation has skyrocketed recently. At the same time, there is a popular perception that the increasing complexity of technology being patented (especially in the electronic, computer software, biological and chemical fields) has made patent trials extremely difficult for lay juries to understand. These developments have sparked extensive scholarly debate and increasing skepticism regarding the role of juries in patent cases.

Juries have participated in some aspects of patent litigation since the enactment of the first patent statute in 1790, which provided for "such damages as shall be assessed by a jury." The enactment of the Patent Act of 1870, however, which gave equity courts the power to award common law damages, spawned an era in which patent cases were almost exclusively decided by the bench. This pattern has changed only recently—and the change has been dramatic. In 1940, 2.5% of all patent cases tried in district court were heard by juries. From 1968 to 1970, the figure was almost unchanged at 2.8%. By contrast, from 1997 to 1999, 59% of all patent trials were tried to juries. This surge in jury requests has prompted a flurry of recent litigation over the right to a jury trial in patent litigation. . . .

Despite extensive debate over the role of the jury in patent cases, no comprehensive empirical research has been done to ascertain, to the extent possible, the differences between jury and judge resolution of patent cases and the cause of the increased demand for jury trials in recent years. Given that patent litigation is an expensive endeavor—it routinely costs each party in excess of a million dollars—there is an urgent need for empirical evidence on patent litigation. This Article undertakes that task by providing the first large-scale comparison of patent-holder win rates and recoveries in cases tried before juries and judges. The data include all patent cases that went to trial in the period from 1983 through 1999 (seventeen years of data). This time period was selected in order to analyze, among other things, the impact the creation of the Federal Circuit may have had on the resolution of patent trials in the district courts. . . .

At first blush, the results of the study suggest that complaints about jury bias and incompetency are unfounded. Judges and juries decide some issues differently. For example, juries are significantly more likely to find patents valid, infringed, and willfully infringed than judges. The differences, however, are not as profound or pervasive as one might

* Reprinted with permission from 99 Mich. L. Rev. 365 (2000), © 2000 Michigan Law Review and Kimberly Moore.

expect. Judges and juries find patents enforceable with similar frequency. Additionally, juries seem as "accurate" in their decisionmaking as judges are, as measured by appellate affirmance rate.

And yet, despite similar affirmance rates for judge and jury trials, there is some ground for concern with jury resolution of patent cases. To a greater degree than judges, juries tend to decide whole suits rather than delineate individual issues, even when separate issues are presented to them via special verdict forms or interrogatories. This finding suggests that judges are subtler at managing the complex nature of patent cases and the technical distinctions between patents and products. It may also affirm the popular perception that juries are unduly swayed by tangential factors.

In addition, who filed the suit is a significant predictor of win rate in jury trials. Juries are significantly pro-patentee in suits for infringement (68% patentee win rate); but when a possible infringer initiates a declaratory judgment action, the patentee only has a 38% win rate. If the same were true of judges, then one could attribute the difference in win rate to the strength of the cases—namely, that alleged infringers only bring declaratory judgment suits when they have strong cases. But patentee win rates are substantially uniform in bench trials, regardless of who initiated the suit.

These data suggest that there may be some problems with juror adjudication of patent suits, though the system masks them. Deferential standards of review leave the Federal Circuit with little ability to disturb potentially flawed jury decisions. Moreover, the system lacks sufficient transparency to ascertain flaws in jury verdicts. The "black box" nature of jury verdicts leaves the Federal Circuit unable to correct inaccuracy or bias on the part of jurors. This reality—particularly in light of the increase in jury adjudication of patent disputes and the potential for jury error where increasingly technical inventions are involved—highlights the value of a peek inside the black box. . . .

I sought to verify the . . . [the Administrative Office of the U.S. Courts] data and to fill in the missing data by researching each of the decisions reported to the Administrative Office. These data were obtained by locating opinions related to the case or news reports, special verdict forms, district court orders and judgments, complaints, and docket sheets from the district courts. When reported district court or appellate decisions detailing the trial court proceedings could not be located, I contacted the courts, the parties, or the attorneys who represented the parties and obtained judgment sheets, courts orders, and verdict forms. In the small number of instances in which verification of whether a particular issue was tried was not possible, it was excluded from the data set. * * *

The vast majority of suits are resolved in advance of trial either by the court on dispositive motion or by the parties themselves through settlement. Increasingly, the patent cases that do progress to trial have been tried to a jury rather than to a judge.

[O]f the 1209 patent trial decisions in the data set, the patentee won 58% of all suits (706 cases) and the alleged infringer prevailed in 42%

(503 cases). These data indicate a statistically significant difference in overall win rate for the patentee and infringer. * * *

The seventeen-year time line for judge resolution of patent trials shows a relatively steady patent-holder win rate over the years. This indicates that judges' behavior in adjudicating patent disputes has followed expected patterns. Such predictability allows for more accurate outcome estimation by parties, which will result in an outcome rate closer to the decisional standard (50%). However, with jury resolution of patent trials being considerably less predictable during the seventeen-year time line (due in part to the relatively small number of jury trials that traditionally occurred), parties are less capable of accurately estimating outcome. If, however, the parties realize that the jury is less predictable and that their outcome estimations are less accurate, one would expect the settlement range for both sides to increase and thereby reduce the number of cases going to trial. Moreover, there is no reason to believe error would be systematically skewed in one direction.

The phenomenon of jury resolution of patent cases is relatively new. As the parties and their attorneys become more experienced with jury resolution of patent cases, outcome estimation error will likely diminish, and there should be a progressive convergence toward an observable 50% outcome. Estimation error decreases with experience under a legal standard because the legal standard becomes more defined over time with experience; it becomes more predictable and more certain. A jury may never be like a legal standard, because juries are one-time players in the litigation game and have no opportunity to learn from or build on past juror experiences or reasoning. If popular perception holds true, juries may be biased in ways that defy predictability. One can predict jury biases in favor of the patent holder, but it is more difficult to quantify juror incompetence to resolve technical matters or juries being swayed by emotional or tangential issues in a case. * * *

These findings suggest that the patent holder has an edge on almost every issue in front of any adjudicator. Patent holders tend to succeed on the same types of issues before judges and juries, with the exception of willfulness where the jury is much more pro-patentee than the judge. The empirical results suggest that the evidentiary burden of proof is more meaningful when judges are adjudicating. When judges adjudicate validity and enforceability, infringers are only successful 36% and 28% of the time, respectively. Juries conclude patents are invalid or unenforceable 29% and 25% of the time, respectively. Patent holders' success rate in proving willful infringement, which also has the higher evidentiary burden, is 53% when judges are adjudicating the issue. When juries decide willfulness, patent holders are successful in 71% of the cases. On the issue of infringement, judges find infringement in 59% of the cases, reflecting this issue's lower evidentiary burden of preponderance of the evidence. Juries find infringement in 71% of the cases, which, considering the difference in evidentiary standards, is remarkably close to juries' findings of willfulness. This contrast with judges' tendencies suggests that juries may be swayed by bias and may not be giving the evidentiary burden much significance. * * *

Although adjudicator (judge or jury) is a statistically significant predictor for damages ... the perception that juries are much more likely to award multimillion dollar damages seems unfounded. Judges make damage awards in excess of $5 million in 17% of the cases, and juries award them in 21%. Jury awards ... are higher than judge awards, but the magnitude of the discrepancy is lower than popularly predicted. This may be attributed in part to the fact that many parties who fear large jury verdicts settle their cases rather than take a chance on a runaway verdict.

[With respect to appeals,] the Federal Circuit affirms judge factfindings in 78% of all judge issues appealed and affirms jury factfindings in 78% of all jury issues appealed. These data indicate that the Federal Circuit upholds the findings of both types of adjudicators at the same rate, suggesting that jury factfindings are no less "accurate" than judge factfindings, as measured by appellate affirmance rate....

Many believe that juries vote for parties rather than decide issues, and that tangential issues sway decisionmaking. In order to test this idea, I looked at how many patent claims get decided all for a single party, and how many produce mixed results on validity and infringement, and what happens when there are multiple patents being tried.... [J]uries are much more likely than are judges to find for the same party when multiple issues need to be resolved. Juries find for the same party in 86% of all instances where they resolve both validity and infringement. Judges find for the same party only 74% of the time. This difference in how judges and juries resolve multiple issues regarding a single patent claim is statistically significant....

In 301 of the 1209 suits in the data set (25%), the trial involved two or more patents or alleged infringement by two or more distinct products. I expected a correlation in outcome of multiple claims, because generally when multiple patents are asserted, they are related patents with similar limitations and similar infringement analysis. This expected correlation did not, however, predict the difference between judge and jury resolution of multiple claim cases which the data revealed.

Judges reached mixed results with significantly greater frequency than juries, which decided cases in an all-or-nothing fashion. When the jury resolved multiple claims, in 87% of the cases it would resolve all the claims for the same party, while judges resolved all claims for the same party 72% of the time ...

Who files the suit (patentee or alleged infringer) is a statistically significant predictor of who wins patent claims. It is also a statistically significant predictor of validity, enforceability, and infringement, but not willfulness.

When these results are broken down by adjudicator, there are significant differences. Who filed the suit is a statistically significant predictor of who wins patent claims in jury trials, but not in bench trials. The difference for jury trials may occur because: (1) there is some advantage gained by the choice of forum; (2) the infringer benefits from determining when the lawsuit begins; or (3) the jury is less likely to be biased in favor of the patentee when the infringer brings suit rather than the patentee. If popular perception is accurate, juries are more likely to find for the patent holder when they perceive her as the injured party seeking vindication. When the infringer brings suit, the patent holder may appear to be less of a victim and the infringer less of a villain.

* * * The most plausible explanation of the data is that there are some differences in judge and jury resolution of patent cases. Because the database of tried cases is not a random or representative sampling of all patent disputes, however, it is impossible to quantify these differences beyond the results disclosed. It may be that the biases implicated by the outcome data can be identified because there has been a dramatic rise in demand for jury trials of patent cases. The parties' outcome estimations have a higher error rate because of the sudden increased demand for juror resolution of patent cases. If this explanation is correct, jury outcome data should tend towards 50% as parties get better at predicting outcome when juries are involved. This, of course, presumes that jury decisionmaking will become more predictable over time. Only time will tell.

Notes and Questions

1. Kimberly Moore received B.S. and M.S. degrees from the Massachusetts Institute of Technology, and a J.D. from Georgetown Law School. She teaches at George Mason University School of Law.

2. The author's judgment that juries decide "whole cases," whereas judges proceed issue-by-issue, certainly comports with conventional wisdom among those with extensive trial experience, including patent lawyers. See, e.g., Simon H. Rifkind, "The Romance Discoverable in Patent Cases," 16 F.R.D. 253, 258–260 (1954), reprinted in 37 J. Pat. Off. Soc'y 319 (1955) (describing importance of telling a story—thus the "romance" of the title—while litigating a patent case). See generally Reid Hastie, "The Role of 'Stories' in Civil Jury Judgments," 32 *U. Mich. J.L. Ref.* 227, 229 (1999) ("Our theory of juror decision processes ... [w]e call ... the 'Story Model' because we claim the central cognitive process in juror decision making is story construction—the creation of a narrative summary of the events under dispute."). Does this suggest the need for any particular forms of "jury control," for example, in the area of willful infringement which, though meant to be an extraordinary finding, finds its way into over 70% of jury verdicts in favor of patentees? Notice also the disparity between jury verdicts in cases where the patentee is the plaintiff, versus those where he or she is the defendant, i.e., declaratory judgment (DJ) suits. Does this suggest that prospective defendants ought to be quick to file DJ suits where they expect to be sued for infringement? In what ways does this allow the defendant to "set the story" for presentation to the jury?

3. George Priest wrote in 1986 that "The ratio of empirical demonstration to assumption in [the intellectual property] literature must be very close to zero...." George L. Priest, "What Economists Can Tell Lawyers About Intellectual Property," 8 Res. L. & Econ. 19, 20 (John Palmer & Richard O. Zerbe, eds., 1986). The last two excerpts demonstrate that this is finally changing. How valuable do you find these insights compared to the other contributions in this volume? What sorts of questions can empirical work answer fruitfully? What questions do you expect to be unresolved even after this literature has grown into a robust enterprise?

II

Copyright

I. History and Basic Concepts

A. History

1. Anglo–American Copyright

European Origins

BRUCE W. BUGBEE*

[T]he Statute of Anne, passed in 1710, has been generally regarded as the earliest copyright legislation. Traditional beliefs in this respect, however, are in need of drastic revision in the light of evidence placing the origin of state protection of intellectual property in Renaissance Italy.

The legal safeguarding of rights in the products of creative thought was virtually ignored in ancient times. . . .

If inventive property was essentially defenseless in classical times, literary property seems to have been equally so. No copyright protection is known to have existed—even under Roman law—and it must be assumed that ancient authors and poets, who sought out wealthy patrons for financial support, were forced to rely upon public opinion as a feeble obstacle to imitators. Among the references to literary and intellectual piracy to be found in classical writings, the accusations of the first-century (A.D.) Roman epigrammatist Martial are particularly prominent. In one of his sallies against those whom he charged with purloining his verses, he suggested a property right in his own works which was valuable and could be sold. Martial, incidentally, is credited with the first use of the term *plagium*, which had previously denoted kidnaping or manstealing, to include literary piracy, and from this originated the word "plagiarize."

Since inventors and authors were apparently neglected by the law even under the unified Roman Empire, it is not surprising to find the early Middle Ages, a period of political fragmentation, equally lacking in

---

* In GENESIS OF AMERICAN PATENT AND COPYRIGHT LAW, 12–13, 43–48 (1967).

known legal protection for intellectual property. Although by no means absent during this period, technological and literary creativity command-ed little prestige or even general interest, and neither was active enough to secure protection. The nearest approach to such protection was a form of local control exercised by certain monasteries over the copying of texts in their libraries or *scriptoria* by representatives of other institutions. Permission to transcribe a well-authenticated manuscript could be grant-ed or withheld by its owner, but this was not true copyright in the modern sense. . . .

The Emergence of Copyright in Venice

Rights of literary property remained legally unprotected until the fifteenth century, when the introduction of the printing press to Europe made the rewards of publishing—or plagiarism—far greater than ever before. Like the earliest patents, the first known copyrights appeared in Renaissance Italy.

The first recorded printing press in Italy was established in 1464 at Subiaco, east of Rome, by the German clergymen Arnold Pannartz and Conrad Schweinheim. After printing editions of Donatus, Cicero, and Lactantius (all 1465) they transferred their operations to Rome in 1467. Soon afterward this craft was introduced into Venice, possibly by Nich-olas Jenson or John of Speyer, and this city quickly assumed the lead in Italian printing.

As it had encouraged the development of other industries by extend-ing benefits, so the Venetian government sought to promote this new trade. Between 1469 and 1517 it issued, without special statutory basis or regulation, a series of *privilegii* (privileges) relating to books and printing. Conferred most often by the Cabinet (but sometimes by the Senate or by the leaders of the other legislative organ, the Council of Ten), these *privileqii* included importation franchises, monopolies, exclu-sion of foreign competition, patents, and copyrights. Of these awards the patents, which were issued for improvements in printing and typogra-phy, were undoubtedly derived from the contemporary Venetian patent system. The monopolies in their unalloyed form usually embodied an exclusive license to print or sell an entire class of books for a specified term. The question of rights of authorship was disregarded; generally the authors were long since dead.

The first of these *privilegii* known to have been issued was that awarded to John of Speyer in 1469. As already seen, he received what may have been an importation franchise, but because it was an exclusive privilege to conduct all printing in Venice for five years this grant had much of the character of a monopoly. Other printers seem to have been in Venice in 1469, and therefore the Venetian printing trade might have been retarded, rather than stimulated, by this overzealously awarded license had the latter not been voided by the grantee's death the following year. The protectionist Venetian government, it may be re-membered, included in this grant a clause barring external competition as well: no books printed abroad were to be imported. This established a precedent, for a regular feature of succeeding *privilegii* was the exclusion of foreign editions of the works encompassed in each grant.

More representative of the Venetian printing monopolies than the 1469 award was Terracina's twenty-five-year privilege for printing all books in the Arabic, Syriac, Armenian, Barbary, Moorish, and Indian languages (1498). Nevertheless, the Venetian practice of extending to patentees who had advanced printing technology a monopoly of all works printed with the new invention resulted in grants of a mixed character. The famous scholar-printer Aldus Manutius, for example, received in 1495–96 a twenty-year monopoly of all works printed by him in Greek, combined with a patent for two of his printing developments—one of them a form of Greek type. Five years later (1500–01) Manutius received a similar award: a ten-year monopoly of all works printed in his italic type.

Particularly significant, however, were those *privilegii* awarded for the protection of authors themselves. On September 1, 1486, the Cabinet granted to Marc' Antonio Sabellico what may be described as the first known copyright in Venice and Italy, and perhaps in the world....

Under this award the grantee, who was historiographer to the Republic, was to exercise exclusive control over the publication of his Decades rerum Venetarum, and anyone who printed this work without his authorization was to be fined 500 ducats. Although this grant did not specifically state that the book was the property of Sabellico, the author's rights of exclusion which it recognized were largely equivalent to property rights. Thus this award can probably qualify as a true copyright, and would therefore represent a major advance in the law of literary property.

Similar in form to Sabellico's copyright was that issued to Petrus Franciscus de Ravenna for his *Foenix* in January, 1491–92. Again the author's proprietary rights were recognized: no one was to print his work without his permission. In 1493 such rights were likewise upheld by the Cabinet in an exclusive, ten-year grant to one Daniele Barbaro concerning the *Castigationes Plinji* of his late brother Hermolao. Other awards followed.

More numerous than true copyrights to authors were the so-called copyrights issued to editors and publishers for individual works written largely or wholly by others. Actually the grants of this type were generally monopolies on a small scale, but they were patterned after the authors' copyrights: no one could print the work concerned without the permission of the grantee. The two earliest examples of this type of privilege, one to an editor and one to a publisher, were conferred in 1492. Awards of this nature quickly became popular, and abuses arose as publishers flocked to the government to reserve well-known titles for themselves. These they hoped to publish at some time in the future—or not at all, if the monopoly of a commercially valuable work could be sold to another printer at a good price. The resulting shortage of available titles soon threatened to stifle the Venetian printing industry, and in 1517 the Senate enacted a statute generally revoking the previously issued *privilegii* concerning books and printing, with only those issued by the Senate itself to be valid thereafter. Future *privilegii* emanating from that body were to pass by a two-thirds vote, and were to be confined to new and previously unprinted works (*atque solum pro libris et operibus novis, nunquam antea impressis, et non pro aliis*)....

In 1537 a law alleging that the quality of Venetian printing had declined attached a 100–ducat fine to the use of paper which blotted when inscribed with marginal notes. More ominous was another form of regulation: an order of the Council of Ten (1515) establishing a censorship of works in the Humanities was followed by a law of 1526–27 for State censorship of all books to be printed, and an enactment of 1542–43 provided for the harsher enforcement of its predecessors. In 1544, moreover, the Council of Ten vested in the three Commissioners of the University at Padua the function of examining all books printed or sold in Venice to determine whether they should receive the Council's *imprimatur*; three years later, in an apparent concession to the Church (the Council of Trent had convened in the meantime), three Commissioners on Heresy were associated with the Council. Both quality and censorship regulations appear to have been widely evaded, but in this era of Protestant Reformation and Catholic Counter–Reformation censorial control by State and Church—including the Inquisition—came to bedevil the Venetian press increasingly....

Prior to 1560 copyrights and publishing grants carried terms with an average length of ten years. After this time the average gradually increased to about nineteen years near the end of the century, although individual terms varied from one to thirty years in length, and occasionally extended for life. Fines imposed for infringement varied in amount, but only one grant carried a penalty of withdrawal of an infringing printer's license (for ten years), in addition to fines. The number of applications per year ranged from one hundred and seventeen in 1561 to seven in 1597 and again in 1599, the Plague and publication of the Clementine Index (1596) being largely responsible for this decrease. Although outnumbered by grants to publishers, copyrights to authors increased in quantity in the latter half of the sixteenth century. Among those who received them were such literary figures as Ariosto and Tasso, and in 1521 Moyse del Castelazzo secured a copyright for his engraved illustrations for the *Pentateuch*. Maps and charts, prominent in the Age of Exploration, were also protected.

A further step toward the more complete regulation of the important publishing industry by the State was a Council decree of 1548–49 ordering the establishment of a gild into which the printers and booksellers of Venice were to be organized. Aside from its aim to improve the Venetian printing trade, the only major industry then unorganized, this measure was intended to assist the suppression of heretical literature. The guild which resulted thus bore some resemblance to the Stationers' Company chartered a few years later in England. Continued attempts to control the press in Venice, particularly those made by the Church and its Inquisition, hastened the eclipse of Venetian printing, and the same was true for Italian publishing in general. George Haven Putnam (himself a publisher) writes: "While other causes ... contributed to the extinction of the prestige of the Venetian Press, and to the very great decline in its business, the chief responsibility for such decline must rest with the Church for its persistent hostility to the smallest measure of freedom of the Press, and for its insistence upon restrictive measures of censorship which were absolutely incompatible with publishing activity and with literary production." The zeal of the Church in extending its control over the press, it should be noted, brought it into a long conflict with the Venetian State.

Other Italian cities enacted legislation to promote their publishing trade, but Venice was foremost in this respect. Although she supported rights of literary proprietorship in the world's first known copyrights and produced a crude form of copyright law in the decree of 1544–45, her regulatory statutes did not affirm that an author has an inherent property right in his works—a right which would not require the issue of a formal copyright to give it birth. The existence of this right, which would be merely secured by the award of a copyright, seems to have been assumed. Thus Venetian grants and enactments sought to protect rights of literary property without fully identifying those rights. Yet after millennia of neglect, this was indeed an advance.

The Origin of Copyright
AUGUSTINE BIRRELL*

... That books were dear in the eleventh century and are (some of them) cheap at the end of the nineteenth is certain enough, but that there were books bought, books read, and books collected before the movable types were invented is also certain, and ought not to be forgotten when the origin of copyright is the subject under consideration.

The trade in manuscripts increased in bulk, and under the protection of the Universities, those great medieval institutions, of powerful ecclesiastics, and cultivated monarchs, developed into a vast industry. You may read in M. Renouard's authoritative book, *Des Droits d'Auteurs* (Paris, 1838), how at the date of the invention of printing there were in Paris and Orleans alone ten thousand copyists....

It is therefore a fact of great significance that at no time during the manuscript period was any claim for author's copyright made or asserted. It is useless to say there was no need for such a claim. True it is that the books reproduced by the copyists were, for the most part, old books—either of devotion, psalters, homilies, and the like, or the classical authors; but the same is largely true at the present day; and there are no members of the *genus irritabile* more jealous of their rights and more envious of each other's reputations than rival editors, annotators, and compilers. With ten thousand copyists at work in Paris and...Orleans alone,...the exclusive rights of living writers, if such rights existed, must have been infringed by the busy pens of the transcribers. The invention of printing, had it stood alone, was nothing more than a clever labour-saving device for multiplying copies more quickly and cheaply than by hand, nor did it involve the birth of a new property-right. Were it lawful to make fifty copies of a book by hand, it were equally lawful to make five hundred by means of a printing press. The new printers pursued precisely the same plan as the old copyists. They had never heard of an author's copyright. When Frobenius of Basle was minded to

* In LECTURES ON COPYRIGHT IN BOOKS, 47–49, 51–54, 68 (1899).

print an edition of the *Adagia* of Erasmus, he never thought of asking
"by your leave," and Erasmus, so far from being angry with a piratical
publisher, sought out Frobenius and lived for some years in his house
and at his charges. Printing by itself was not the mother of author's
copyright.

In considering the origin of copyright, two things must never be
forgotten. First, the Church and her priesthood, frightened—and who
dare say unreasonably frightened?—at the New Learning, and at the
independence and lawlessness of mind and enthusiasm that accompanied
the New Learning; and, second, the guilds or trade unions, jealous of
their privileges, ever at war one with another, and making their appeal
to the Crown for protection against outside interference with their
strictly defined domains of business. . . .

[We come] face to face with the censorship of the Press and the
monopoly of the booksellers, and from these two independent and
occasionally clashing interests sprang copyright.

As to the censorship of the Press, nobody either on the Continent of
Europe or here at home thought of disputing it. In Paris, in London, in
Geneva, it was applied with equal vigour, though to different subject
matter. It is impossible to have any acquaintance with the publications
of the 15th and 16th centuries without amazement at the recklessness,
the scurrility, the foul-mouthedness, as well as the mental disturbance
and moral laxity displayed by too many of them. ... A free Press in
those days was an idea not to be tolerated. Even at a later date and a
quieter time, our own John Milton, a solitary pamphleteer, a non-
church-goer, and a most unrepresentative man, retained "the fire and
the executioner" as the most effectual remedy for those books which he
found "mischievous and libellous." Did Milton mean found by a jury? I
think not.

It would be out of place to attempt here a sketch of the history of
the censorship. What I want to emphasise is the distinctive but cooperative effect of the licensing of books and the licensing of booksellers—imprimaturs and privileges. . . .

The proud spirit of Milton, condemned as rebellious both by Dr.
Johnson and Cardinal Newman, had to submit to the indignity of an
imprimatur for "Paradise Lost" itself. . . .

The most noticeable difference between censorship in France and in
England is that with us the authority has always been centralised and
derived from the royal prerogative. In France there were originally as
many censors as there were ecclesiastics, whilst the Universities and the
Parliaments all had their say in the matter. Ultimately, and in obedience
to the general course of French history, the king became the universal
custodian of every kind of authority, and garotted the Press as and when
he chose. . . .

To conclude this lecture, it is only necessary to remind you that the
Licensing Act of Charles II expired in 1679, and the next statute relating
to books and printing was the unfortunately conceived and unhappily
expressed statute of Queen Anne, which, however, has the honour of

being the first copyright statute at law to be found in the *Corpus Juris* of any State, either of ancient or modern times.

Notes and Questions

1. Bruce Willis Bugbee was born in 1927 in Indianapolis, Indiana, and received an A.B. from the College of William and Mary in 1951 and a M.A. (1952) and PhD (1961) from the University of Michigan. He specialized in Colonial and Revolutionary America, and was an instructor in History at Gettysburg College from 1958 until 1991. He died in 1994.

2. Augustine Birrell was an English scholar and statesman who lived from 1850 to 1933. Educated at Trinity Hall, Cambridge, he was professor of law at University College from 1896 to 1899. He spent much of the remainder of his life in the public sector, serving, among other posts, as minister of education and Chief Secretary of Ireland. He wrote numerous volumes of essays, including *Obiter Dicta* (1884, 1887) and *Res Judicatae* (1892).

3. Bugbee and Birrell offer contrasting accounts of copyright history. As Bugbee explores, early forms of intellectual property protection were designed to promote industry and the dissemination of ancient authors. Birrell situates the birth of copyright amidst government censorship and market control by the Stationers Guild. As you read the material selected for this book, consider whether one or both of these versions of history may have influenced the proponent of a particular theory about the nature of copyright law.

4. The printing press was introduced to Europe in the mid-fifteenth century. Birrell suggests that the printing press was not central to the emergence of copyright law, since scribes were readily available to copy texts. Is this a plausible contention? Is there a difference between hiring 50 scribes to copy a text and printing 500 or 5000 copies on a press?

The First Three Hundred Fifty Years
BENJAMIN KAPLAN*

... How does all this [thinking of the stationer's company] relate to copyright? To mangle Sir Henry Maine's aphorism, Copyright has the look of being gradually secreted in the interstices of the censorship. The patents for books, in that they conferred exclusive rights, bear some family resemblances to the later legal institution of copyright. They did not, however, stand on any notion of original composition, for they might be granted for ancient as well as new works. In the end a large number of patents came into the hands of the major stationers. Besides the patented books, books could be published if they were licensed by the official licensers and printed by an authorized press. A stationer before proceeding to print must in the usual course of Company practice obtain allowance from officers of the Company, and note of the allowance— called entry—was to be made on the Company's Register. At least among

* In AN UNHURRIED VIEW OF COPYRIGHT, 4–6, 7–9 (1967). Columbia University Press.

members of the Company the entry came to betoken ownership of the "copy" of the book, the exclusive right to print and publish it; in general, priority of entry spelled priority of right. Some such scheme of allocation to members was needed for the practical distribution, so to speak, of the authority to print vested in the Company as a community. Again, as between this right of copy by means of entry and a modern copyright the resemblances are merely familial: entries were made not only of new but of old books. How far a search of the Register was initially made to see whether a proposed entry would infringe on one previously made, we do not know. Various claims of infringement were heard by the Court of Assistants of the Company, and scattered accounts appear in the incomplete records of that court, but the tendency to compromise was so strong that we get little impression of any prevailing notions of piracy or plagiarism. We can, however, surmise that the question would have been viewed with printer's or publisher's not author's eyes. . . .

Right of copy was the stationer's not the author's. Living authors furnished some of the material for the printing mills, and increasingly these manuscripts had to be purchased in a business way (usually payment was made in a lump sum); but upon entry the author dropped away and it was the stationer who had the right of multiplication of copies against others of the Company, which is to say, speaking imprecisely, against all those eligible to print. . . .

I shall forbear an account of the gradual decay of the Company, and merely make the point that the Company's strength was dependent in large part upon its alliance with the official censorship. When, after the Restoration, Parliament in 1662 passed a Printing Act duly restricting printing and reinstalling licensing, the stationers must dearly have hoped that the system would stick. It did not. It wobbled and expired through nonrenewal in 1695. Macaulay, writing deliciously of the demise of the censorship, shows that it was due to general disgust at the variable stupidity of the censors.

Three cheers for freedom of the press; but what, now, was to become of the stationers? Anarchical publication lay ahead which the stationers, habituated to protection, were not equipped to meet. So, as Lord Camden later said, "They"—the stationers, whose property by that time "consisted of all the literature of the Kingdom; for they had contrived to get all the copies into their own hands"—"came up to Parliament in the form of petitioners, with tears in their eyes, hopeless and forlorn; they brought with them their wives and children to excite compassion, and induce Parliament to grant them a statutory security." Whence came the Statute of Anne. . . .

I doubt that the statute was any more grounded on a thoughtful review of policy than the defeat of official licensing had been. The stationers made the case that they could not produce the fragile commodities called books, and thus encourage learned men to write them, without protection against piracy; but no one, we can be sure, deliberated what strange results might follow if the same logic were applied to other fragile ventures outside the book field. It is hard to know how far the interests of authors were considered in distinction from those of publishers. There is an apparent tracing of rights to an ultimate source in the fact of authorship, but before attaching large importance to this we have to note that if printing as a trade was not to be put back into the hands of a few as a subject of monopoly—if the statute was indeed to be a kind of "universal patent"—a draftsman would naturally be led to express himself in terms of rights in books and hence of initial rights in authors. A draftsman would anyway be aware that rights would usually pass immediately to publishers by assignment, that is, by purchase of the manuscripts as in the past. . . . Although references in the text of the statute to authors, together with dubious intimations in later cases that Swift, Addison, and Steele took some significant part in the drafting, have lent color to the notion that authors were themselves intended beneficiaries of the parliamentary grace, I think it nearer the truth to say that publishers saw the tactical advantage of putting forward authors' interests together with their own, and this tactic produced some effect on the tone of the statute. . . .

The History of an Idea
PAUL GOLDSTEIN*

. . . After years of failed efforts to extend their censorship, the Stationers shifted their legislative strategy. In place of their own lost profits, they now put the interests of writers and readers at the fore. Beginning in 1706, the Stationers petitioned Parliament that authors would not write new works without the security of an easily enforced property right. Out of three years of intense lobbying came the world's first copyright act, the Statute of Anne, "An Act for the Encouragement of Learning, by vesting the Copies of Printed Books in the Authors or Purchasers of such Copies, during the Times therein mentioned." The Statute dramatically changed the allocation of entitlements among authors, publishers, and readers. Severing the enforcement of literary property rights from the Stationers' monopoly, the Statute unleashed a free market for literature and for ideas.

The Statute of Anne confirmed the Stationers' copyrights and gave them, the coercive remedies they sought. In return, it redistributed some of the publishers' earlier perquisites to the public and to authors. In place of the formerly perpetual monopoly, the term of copyright protection now ended twenty-eight years after a work's publication; after twenty-eight years, anyone could copy the work and, presumably, sell it to the public. Parliament also split the twenty-eight-year copyright into two fourteen-year terms, so that, even in cases where the author had assigned full copyright in a given work to a publisher, the law returned the copyright to the author at the end of its initial fourteen-year term to enjoy for the second fourteen-year term. The Statute's great revolution was to separate copyright from membership in the Stationers' Company. Anyone in the realm, writers as well as publishers, could get copyright in a work simply by enrolling it on the Company's register.

Parliament made one stinting concession to the Stationers' plea to keep a perpetual monopoly in the works to which they held copyright,

* In CopyRIGHT's HIGHWAY 43–45, 46–55 (1994).

giving them a one-time-only twenty-one-year copyright in works that had first been published before the Statute was passed. In the late 1720s, as the end of protection for these books approached, the booksellers once again petitioned Parliament, seeking a return to the comforts of perpetual monopoly. Rebuffed by Parliament, they turned to the English courts, mounting an ingenious legal argument that would frame the terms of copyright debate in England, and later in the United States, right down to the present.

In court, as before in Parliament, the Stationers pitched their argument on the moral claims of authors—claims, they argued, that could not be cabined by the Statute's limited term of protection. The common law of England gave farmers perpetual rights in their real property on the theory that they had mixed their labor with the soil. Why, the Stationers contended, shouldn't the common law also give a perpetual right to authors, whose labor is mixed forever in the texts that embody their ideas? When an author sells a manuscript to a publisher, he is selling not just the tangible manuscript but also a separate and perpetual right to publish the manuscript's contents—a morally compelled natural right with a life entirely apart from the Statute of Anne.

The publishers had more than a theory. They also had a strategy. The strategy was for one of them to bring an action claiming infringement of the common law copyright in Chancery, the arm of the English judiciary empowered to grant injunctions. The publisher would claim that it owned the common law copyright in a work through a transfer from the author, and would allege that the defendant's unauthorized copies of it infringed this right, entirely apart from the Statute of Anne. If this strategy succeeded, Chancery would temporarily enjoin the defendant, pending determination of the facts and governing law. If the Chancery judge had any doubt as to the applicable law—and he surely would, for the Stationers' argument was innovative at best—he would refer the case to the common law courts. . . .

A decade later, the London Stationers obtained in *Millar v. Taylor* the judgment they had sought. . . . The work in issue was The Seasons, a popular epic poem by James Thomson, who had in 1729 sold the copyright to Andrew Millar, a London bookseller. By 1767, the statutory copyright in the poem had expired, and Robert Taylor, a bookseller outside the Stationers' Company, issued a cheap rival edition. Millar sued, claiming infringement of the purportedly perpetual common law right that Thomson had sold him. The questions before the Court of King's Bench went to the very heart of copyright: Should society give authors an exclusive right to their works? If so, should the author's right be perpetual, or should it last just long enough to give him sufficient revenues to induce continued literary efforts, but allow the public to enjoy unlimited editions of his work once the copyright term had ended?

The Justices of King's Bench were no strangers to the claim of perpetual copyright. As a barrister, Lord Mansfield had been counsel to the London booksellers in two of their early Chancery cases. . . . A strong debater and brilliant legal mind, Mansfield was the most intimidating presence on King's Bench; in his twelve years on the court, no justice had dared dissent from his views. Perhaps equally talented but less flamboyant, Justice Joseph Yates had as a barrister represented ... the alleged pirate, in [an earlier] argument before Lord Mansfield.

Since he was Chief Justice, Mansfield delivered his opinion last. To no one's surprise, he agreed with his side justices, Aston and Willes, that a perpetual copyright existed at common law and that the Statute of Anne had neither displaced the right nor limited its term. Mansfield rested his opinion on the theory of natural rights that underlay both real and personal property. "It is *just* that an author should reap the pecuniary profits of his own ingenuity and labor. It is *just* that another should not use his name without his consent. It is *fit* that he should judge when to publish, or whether he even will publish. It is *fit* he should not only choose the time but the manner of publication, how many, what volume, what print. It is *fit* he should choose to whose care he will trust the accuracy and correctness of the impression, in whose honesty he will confide not to foist in additions with other reasoning of the same effect." For Mansfield, the rationale for a property right in unpublished written works applied with equal force to published works such as *The Seasons*; he abruptly dismissed the argument that the Statute of Anne had supplanted the common law.

Justice Yates dissented—the first dissent ever from Chief Justice Mansfield's views—taking three hours to elaborate his position. Yates centered on the claim that ownership can attach to something so fugitive, so entirely outside the claimant's physical possession, as a literary work—an expression, a sentiment—that, once turned loose, is available to all. Common law rights may be secured by possession of a parcel of land or pages of manuscript. But, since the thoughts expressed in the manuscript have no physical dimension, they cannot be possessed nor can they secure common law rights. A writer can choose not to publish his work. But once published, the work becomes as free as air. "Can he complain of losing the bird he has himself voluntarily turned out?" Why should authors have any greater rights in their thoughts than inventors have in their inventions? Everyone would concede, said Yates, that inventions such as the printing press are not protected outside the scope of the patent statute.

Yates did not dispute the essential merit of Millar's entitlement. "The labours of an author have certainly a right to a reward; but it does not from thence follow, that his reward is to be infinite, and never to have an end." Parliament had passed a law determining the extent of the author's property, and the author had little cause to complain of injustice "after he has enjoyed a monopoly for twenty-eight years, and the manuscript still remains his own property." Yates then upended Mansfield's natural rights argument. Would not a perpetual right for writers encroach on the natural rights of the public? "It is every man's natural right, to follow a lawful employment for the support of himself and his family. Printing and bookselling are lawful employments. And therefore every monopoly that would intrench upon these lawful employments is a strain upon the liberty of the subject."

In 1770, Chancery followed the King's Bench decision for Millar and enjoined Taylor's copies. Taylor filed an appeal to the House of Lords, but the booksellers promptly settled with him to end the case. Millar had not lived to see his ultimate victory, and in 1769 his estate sold his newly established perpetual right in *The Seasons* to a group of printers; in turn, they were soon forced to undertake a battle of their own.

Alexander Donaldson, a prosperous Scottish bookseller, had already twice been sued by the English booksellers. Now, undeterred by the decisions of King's Bench and Chancery, with an eye to an authoritative decision from the House of Lords and with the resources to obtain it, Donaldson published an unauthorized edition of *The Seasons*. Thomas Becket, the *Seasons'* authorized publisher, went to Chancery for relief; since *Millar v. Taylor* had already established the perpetual common law right, Lord Chancellor Bathurst granted an injunction. Donaldson appealed to the House of Lords. Here at last was the forum that the booksellers had feared, the prospect that had shaped their litigation strategy from the beginning. The House of Lords heard argument in *Donaldson v. Becket* for three weeks, beginning on February 4, proceedings that attracted tremendous interest. The February 5 issue of the *Morning Chronicle* reported that the "House below the bar...was exceedingly crowded," and that "Mr. Edmund Burke, Dr. Goldsmith, David Garrick Esq.; and other literary figures were among the hearers."

Although the Lords' decision in *Donaldson v. Becket* was to be their own, it was customary for them in taking judicial appeals to request advisory opinions from the twelve leading common law judges. The Lords posed five questions to the judges, one of which was central: If England's common law gave authors an exclusive right in their literary works, and if they did not lose this right on publication, did the Statute of Anne abolish that right and limit authors to the Statute's remedies, conditions, and term?

The judges divided on the question, six stating that the statute preempted the common law, five that it did not. Lord Mansfield, who presumably would have tied the vote, declined to give an opinion, "it being very unusual (from reasons of delicacy) for a peer to support his own judgment, upon an appeal to the House of Lords." The reporter of decisions may have miscounted the judges' vote, for there is some evidence that the justices had in fact voted 6–5, or even 7–4, that common law copyright survived the Statute of Anne. In any event, the vote was only advisory It was ultimately the vote of the House of Lords, 22–11 in Donaldson's favor, Lord Mansfield abstaining once again, that became the decision in the case, overturning the Chancery injunction....

The final outcome of the Stationers' maneuverings would doubtless have pleased Joseph Yates, who resigned from King's Bench less than a year after *Millar v. Taylor* to accept appointment to a lower court and died a few months later. He might have been pleased, too, by Justice Mansfield's last observations on copyright, indicating that the great advocate of natural rights had come around to the view that copyright in fact entails a delicate balance between private and public interests. "We must take care," Lord Mansfield wrote, "to guard against two extremes equally prejudicial; the one, that men of ability, who have employed their time for the service of the community, may not be deprived of their just merits, and the reward of their ingenuity and labour; the other, that the world may not be deprived nor the progress of the arts retarded."

The early years of copyright in the United States paralleled the development of copyright in England in two respects: a copyright act modeled after the Statute of Anne, and a high court case addressing the question whether a natural, common law right survived the Statute. But distinctive forces shaped American copyright law. Writers, not booksellers, led the drive for copyright in the United States. And while colonial printing presses were subject to Crown licensing, no institution in the colonies even approached the Stationers' monopoly over the book trade. Finally, it was a conflict between national and local power, not one between London monopolists and provincial pirates, that dominated the early controversy over copyright in the United States....

As the Constitutional Convention drew near, it became clear to many, including James Madison, that the national interest required a national copyright. Lamenting the Confederation's "want of concert in matters where common interest requires it," Madison noted as an instance "of inferior moment" the lack of uniformity in the laws concerning literary property. The Convention did not have to revisit the question of the need for copyright, for many of the delegates, George Washington among them, had been present at the debates over the state copyright acts.

On September 5, 1787, less than two weeks before the Constitutional Convention ended, David Brearly of New Jersey presented the proposal of the Committee of Detail for a clause in the Constitution empowering Congress to enact a national copyright law. The clause, which passed unanimously and evidently without debate, linked copyrights to patents: "The Congress shall have Power...to promote the Progress of Science and useful Arts, by securing for limited Times to Authors and Inventors the exclusive Right to their respective Writings and Discoveries." (Under usage of the time, "Science" was the subject matter of copyright, "useful Arts" the subject matter of patents.) On May 17, 1790, Congress, exercising the power granted it in this constitutional phrase, passed "An act for the encouragement of learning" that reflected the very practical concerns of a new republic whose geography must have seemed unlimited. The Act gave a fourteen-year copyright not only to "books" but also to maps and charts. President Washington signed the bill into law on May 31, 1790.

That the Constitution empowered Congress to grant copyright for only "limited times" might appear to have answered the great question, whether authors have a perpetual right at common law, that had earlier confronted the English courts. But the constitutional clause constrained only Congress, not the states, and it is the states, not the federal, national government, that are the repositories of common law in the United States. Thus, when a lawsuit first arose questioning whether a common law copyright survived the federal statutes the battle was

between state powers and those of the federal government. The case was
Wheaton v. Peters.

Henry Wheaton was the third Reporter of Decisions of the Supreme
Court of the United States; Richard Peters was the fourth. It was the job
of the Reporter of Decisions, appointed by the Court, to record, index,
abstract, and comment upon the Court's opinions and to arrange for
their publication. Wheaton spent twelve exhausting, financially unre-
warding years improving the accuracy and timeliness of the Court's
reports, all the time embroidering the reports with his own scholarly
annotations. He finally resigned and, failing in his efforts to obtain a
judicial appointment, accepted a diplomatic post in Denmark. (Foreign
service paid better than reporting Supreme Court decisions. As Reporter,
Wheaton never earned more than $1,800 a year; his new position paid
him $4,500.)

Wheaton's successor, Peters, had actively sought the Reporter's job
with help from Wheaton's former publisher. Although Peters lacked
Wheaton's scholarly inclinations, he possessed something far more valuable in a young editor—a strong entrepreneurial instinct. Scholarly
disquisitions on the reported cases consumed costly paper and print;
Peters knew that, at $7.50 per volume, Wheaton's reports had been
beyond the reach of many lawyers. He also understood that busy lawyers
preferred summary and synthesis to learned annotation. He figured that
by trimming the size of the reports he could lower their price and sell
more copies.

If condensed versions could sell more copies of current reports, they
could also help sell past reports. Peters embarked on a condensed six-
volume edition of his predecessors' twenty-four volumes, entitling it
*Condensed Reports of Cases in the Supreme Court of the United States,
Containing the Whole Series of the Decisions of the Court from its
Organization to the Commencement of Peters' Reports at January Term
1827*. He priced the abridged volumes almost 75 percent below Wheaton's volumes.

The *Condensed Reports* enjoyed great commercial success. But Peters's profit was Wheaton's loss, and with the market for his own
volumes shrinking, Wheaton turned to his former law partner, Elijah
Paine, to file suit against Peters. The suit alleged copyright infringement
and sought an injunction and accounting of profits from Peters. After a
two-year standoff between the court's two judges, the case went against
Wheaton. Wheaton then promptly retained—via Paine—his old friend
Daniel Webster to argue the appeal. In late September 1833, Wheaton
sailed back to America from Liverpool to assist in the case.

Wheaton's complaint asserted rights under both the Copyright Act
and the common law. Although the statutory period of protection for
Wheaton's Reports had not yet expired, he pleaded the common law
count as a precaution against a ruling that he had failed to comply with
all the Act's formal requirements for protection, including the deposit of
copies of his reports with the Secretary of State within six months of
publication. Strictly speaking, the Supreme Court did not have to ad-

dress the common law count, but the Justices found the prospect of harrowing the ground already plowed in *Millar* and *Donaldson* too tempting to be lost for small technical reasons.

The Supreme Court delivered its decision on March 19, 1834. As dutifully reported in Volume 8 of *Peters' Reports*, the Court ruled that, once a book is published, the Copyright Act displaces the common law and becomes the exclusive source of rights in a published work. Writing for the majority, Justice John McLean echoed Justice Yates's dissent in *Millar v. Taylor*: "The argument that a literary man is as much entitled to the product of his labor as any other member of society, cannot be controverted. And the answer is, that he realizes this product by the transfer of his manuscripts, or in the sale of his works when first published." Justice Smith Thompson, dissenting, invoked Justice Mansfield: "Every one should enjoy the reward of his labor, the harvest where he has sown, or the fruit of the tree which he has planted...." However much it voiced the English discourse, *Wheaton v. Peters* was at bottom a distinctively American decision, representing a victory for federal over state power.

Wheaton v. Peters ultimately went off on a technicality. The trial court had held that the Copyright Act's deposit requirement was mandatory and that Wheaton's failure to make a timely deposit of his reports in the local district court had forfeited his copyright. Since it was not clear to the Supreme Court Justices that Wheaton had in fact failed to comply with the deposit requirement, they reversed the trial court's decision and remanded the case for another trial on the question. Wheaton prevailed at the retrial, and Peters appealed. Wheaton died while the second appeal was pending; Peters died less than a month later. Peters's estate settled the lawsuit by paying $400 to Wheaton's estate....

Notes and Questions

1. Benjamin Kaplan, the Royall Professor of Law, Emeritus, at Harvard Law School, is a Distinguished Professor of Law at Suffolk University. A 1933 graduate of Columbia Law School, he was a Justice of the Massachusetts Supreme Judicial Court and of the Massachusetts Appeals Court. With Professor Ralph Brown, he co-edited the first U.S. casebook on copyright and unfair competition, "Cases on Copyright, Unfair Competition and Other Topics" (1960).

2. Paul Goldstein is the Stella W. and Ira S. Lillick Professor of Law at Stanford Law School. Born in 1943, Professor Goldstein earned his J.D. from Columbia Law School in 1967. In addition to *Copyright's Highway*, he is the author of the four-volume treatise, *Copyright* (2003), and of the one-volume treatise *International Copyright: Principles, Law and Practice* (2001), as well as of Foundation Press casebooks on copyright and on international intellectual property law.

3. As noted above, the English stationers' monopoly urged the legislation that became the Statute of Anne. Does it follow that the newly-fledged United States, in enacting a similar statute, was catering to the interests of powerful publishers? Consider the following analysis by Professor Thomas Nachbar:

> The contention that the Copyright Clause's limits were designed to limit the power of publishers has some intuitive appeal today, in a world in which increasingly concentrated industry of publishers routinely own the copyright for a work outright and therefore have an incentive to lobby for ever-expanding copyright terms. But when applied to the structure of the publishing industry in 18th-and 19th-century America, the veil of plausibility falls away.
>
> As an initial matter, there was not even a rough analog to the Stationers' Company on the horizon at the time of the framing. Rather, in 1798 the fledgling republic had more than 200 publishers, printers, and booksellers spread through [five states], and they were intensely competitive . . .
>
> Nor did the early American market for copyrighted works operate to give publishers the incentive to seek ever-increasing copyright terms. Instead . . . publishers often had an incentive to reduce the duration of copyright.

Thomas B. Nachbar, *Constructing Copyright's Mythology*, 6 Green Bag 2d 37, 44–45 (2002). See also L. Ray Patterson & Stanley Lindberg, THE NATURE OF COPYRIGHT: A LAW OF USER'S RIGHTS, 47–55 (1991) (doubting historical materials relevant to stationers' copyright were available to Framers and identifying four policies specific to the Copyright Clause: "promotion of learning," "preservation of the public domain," "protection of the author," and "implied right of access"). For a survey of copyright statutes promulgated by the colonies, see Francine Crawford, *Pre-Constitutional Copyright Statutes*, 23 Bull. Copyright Soc'y U.S.A. 11 (1975).

4. Whether by the Stationers' Guild or by the RIAA, tactical litigation has been a central feature in the evolution of copyright law. Courts are not always receptive to these suits, particularly where copyright owners are perceived to be attempting to suppress new technologies. See e.g. Paul Goldstein, COPYRIGHT'S HIGHWAY, 51–54 (revised ed. 2003) (describing the concerns of the pianola and phonograph manufacturers in the litigation challenging pianola sheet music in *White–Smith Music Publ'g Co. v. Apollo Co.*, 209 U.S. 1 (1908)); James Lardner, FAST FORWARD: HOLLYWOOD, THE JAPANESE, AND THE ONSLAUGHT OF THE VCR (revised ed. 2002) (describing the business and legal aspects of the litigation challenging betamax technology in *Sony Corp. of Am. v. Universal City Studios*, 464 U.S. 417 (1984)); Jane C. Ginsburg, *Copyright and Control Over New Technologies of Dissemination*, 101 Col. L. Rev. 1613 (2001) (analyzing several decisions providing strained interpretations of Copyright Act as attempts to restrain copyright owners from acting like "unseemly monopolists" trying to kill off rivals upon emergence of new technologies).

2. Comparative and International Copyright

A Tale of Two Copyrights: Literary Property in Revolutionary France and America

JANE GINSBURG*

Introduction

The French and US copyright systems are well known as opposites. The product of the French Revolution, French copyright law is said to enshrine the author: exclusive rights flow from one's (preferred) status as a creator. For example, a leading French copyright scholar labels one of the 'fundamental ideas' of the French Revolutionary copyright laws of 1791 and 1793 the principle that 'an exclusive right is conferred on authors because their property is the most justified since it flows from their intellectual creation.' By contrast, the 1787 US Constitution's copyright clause, echoing the 1710 English Statute of Anne, makes the public's interest equal, if not superior, to the author's. This clause authorizes the establishment of exclusive rights of authors as a means to maximize production of, and access to, intellectual creations . . .

Conceptions of French copyright law as author-oriented and of Anglo–American copyright law as society-oriented carry certain corollaries. In general, one may anticipate that the more author-centered the system, the more protective the copyright regime will be. . . .

Another consequence of different copyright conceptions pertains to the role of formalities. Formalities are State-imposed conditions on the existence or exercise of copyright. If copyright is essentially a governmental incentive-programme, many formal prerequisites may accompany the grant. For example, requiring the author to affix a notice of copyright, or to register and deposit copies of the work with a government agency, before the right will be recognized or enforced, is fully consistent with a public-benefit view of copyright. Imposition of formalities results from the premise that creating the work does not alone justify protection: it is the author's burden to assert her rights; should she fail to do so, the innocent public should not be liable for unauthorized publication. In effect, the law favours free copying; that initial position should not vary unless the author undertakes to warn the world of her claims. Clearly, formalities clash with a characterization of copyright as springing from the creative act. If copyright is born with the work, then no further action should be necessary to confer the right; the sole relevant act is the work's creation. Hence, an author-oriented system should in theory be formality-free.

Despite these paradigms, the differences between the US and French copyright systems are neither as extensive nor as venerable as typically described. In particular, despite the conventional portrayal, the French Revolutionary laws did not articulate or implement a conception

* In Sherman and Strowel Eds., Of Authors and Origins: Essays on Copyright Law, 131, 132, 133–35, 137–42, 143–45, 146, 149, 151–53 (1994).

of copyright substantially divergent from that of the regimes across the
Channel and across the Atlantic. The French Revolutionary sources
themselves cast doubt upon the assumed author-centrism of the initial
French copyright legislation. The speeches in the Revolutionary assem-
blies, the text of the laws, and the court decisions construing the laws,
all indicate at the least a strong instrumentalist undercurrent to the
French decrees of 1791 and 1793. Similarly, while the law of US letters
predominantly reflects and implements utilitarian policies, US law was
not impervious to authors' claims of personal right. Indeed, some of the
earliest state copyright laws in the USA set forth author-oriented rationales of which any modern Frenchman would be proud—and from which
some Revolutionary legislators may have drawn considerable inspiration. . . .

The Late Eighteenth–Century US Copyright System

The United States Constitution, drafted in 1787, and available in
France in Philip Mazzei's French translation by at least 1790, authorizes
a national copyright regime . . . While records from the Constitutional
Convention concerning the copyright clause are extremely sparse, a
document dated 18 August 1787 notes that the proposed legislative
powers were submitted to the Committee of Detail: 'To secure to literary
authors their copy rights for a limited time. To encourage by proper
premiums and provisions the advancement of useful knowledge and
discoveries.' The referral to the Committee of Detail thus sets forth the
authors' property interest ('their copy rights') and the public interest in
advancement of knowledge as separate considerations of equal weight.'
Similarly, in the *Federalist Papers*, Madison endorsed the copyright
clause, asserting, 'The public good fully coincides in both cases [patents
and copyrights] with the claims of individuals.'

Sources immediately pre-dating the Constitution also indicate American acknowledgement of authors' personal claims, in addition to utilitarian motivations. Before enactment of the Constitution, protection of
literary property was a matter for the states. In his essay *Origin of the
Copy-Right Laws in the United States*, Noah Webster recounted the dire
state of American education in 1782 and his resulting efforts to persuade
state legislatures to protect publications. '[S]chool-books were scarce and
hardly obtainable,' Webster recalled. Having himself 'compiled two small
elementary books for teaching the English language,' he set off to New
Jersey and Pennsylvania to seek copyright protection. The legislatures
were not then in session, but Webster enlisted prominent local academic
figures in his cause. A letter signed by professors at the predecessor
universities to Princeton and the University of Pennsylvania sets the
tone of the arguments in favour of copyright. After praising Webster's
two works as 'very proper for young persons in the country,' the letter
urges:

> Every attempt of this nature undoubtedly merits the encouragement of
> the public; because it is by such attempts that systems of education are
> gradually perfected in every country, and the elements of knowledge
> rendered more easy to be acquired. Men of industry or of talents in any
> way, have a right to the property of their productions; and it encourages
> invention and improvement to secure it to them by certain laws, as has

been practiced in European countries with advantage and success. And it is my opinion that it can be of no evil consequence to the state, and may be of benefit to it, to vest, by a law, the sole right of publishing and vending such works in the authors of them.

While stressing the manifold benefits to public instruction flowing from protecting authors, Webster's fellow copyright-lobbyists also invoked, on behalf of authors, the general Lockean principle that a property right arises out of one's labours. This mixed argumentation also emerges in the state copyright statutes that followed both from Webster's efforts and from the next year's Continental Congress resolution encouraging the thirteen states to pass copyright laws. For example, the preamble to the Massachusetts Act of 17 March 1783 first announced a public-benefit rationale drawn from the English precedent, but then stated:

> As the principal encouragement such persons can have to make great and beneficial exertions of this nature, must exist in the legal security of the fruits of their study and industry to themselves; and as such security is one of the natural rights of all men, there being no property more peculiarly a man's own than that which is procured by the labor of his mind. . . .

For What Kinds of Works was American Copyright Sought or Litigated?

The works generating the subject-matter of copyright deposits and claims reflect the general universe of late eighteenth-century American publications. Perhaps not suprisingly for a young republic, instructive, civics-oriented works dominate the publishing catalogues. For example, examination of the 5,368 publications (including newspapers and pamphlets) listed in the 1790–2 and 1798–9 volumes of Charles Evans's *American Bibliography* indicates that republican publishing habits corresponded to the 'new republican ideology [which] defin[ed] the virtuous citizen as one who was broadly informed about political doctrine and public affairs'. Evans's records for these years show 540 newspapers, 441 titles in political science, 302 titles in history, 270 titles in social science and 61 Fourth of July (Independence Day) orations for 1798–9. By contrast, the publication of novels appears fairly modest: 43 titles for 1790–92 and 119 for 1798–99. This relative paucity of fiction may well also reflect republican values. Thomas Jefferson is reputed to have said that 'A great obstacle to good education is the inordinate passion prevalent for novels, and the time lost in that reading which should be instructively employed.'

A review of the copyright records casts light on the smaller universe of works of actual or perceived economic value and allows comparison of government policy in enacting the copyright incentive to the kinds of works for which authors and publishers in fact accepted the government's offer. Copyright practice apparently met policy goals—copyright was sought for the socially useful, instructive works which Congress had intended to encourage.

Petitions to Congress before enactment of the first copyright statute sought exclusive privileges for works overwhelmingly instructional in character. For example, on 12 May 1789, Jedediah Morse petitioned for exclusive rights in *The American Geography, or a View of the present Situation of the United States of America embellished and illustrated with two original maps*, and on 8 June 1789, one Nicholas Pike, of Massachusetts, sought a privilege for *A new and complete System of Arithmetic*. A recent comprehensive study of copyright-deposit records covering the first ten years of the federal copyright system discloses a preponderance of useful, instructional texts in deposits made pursuant to the first federal copyright statute....

One scholar of publishing history attributes the dominance of textbooks in copyright registers in part to Noah Webster's efforts, and in part to national pride: 'In the post-Revolution textbook boom, the demand for primers, geographies and arithmetics, in both German and English, was high, as American books patriotically replaced the British texts that had been used before.' ...

US copyright litigation, albeit sparse, appears also to have been reserved to quarrels over informational and similar works. A leading study has cited no copyright decisions before 1791, and only two lower-court decisions between that time and the US Supreme Court's first copyright decision, *Wheaton v. Peters*, in 1834. Both lower-court cases concerned compliance with federal copyright formalities. Both also concerned works more of utility and of laborious compilation than of imagination—in one, a 'federal calculator', and in the other, a *Pharmacopoeia of the United States of America*.

The French Enactments Of 1791 To 1793

Revolutionary Copyright Politics: Critical Discussion of the Legal Texts and Their Legislative History

While traditional comparisons of French and Anglo–American copyright law assert that France rejected instrumentalist theories in favour of copyright as the just and fair prerogative of creators, research in primary sources prompts a different conclusion. The various legislative texts reveal a hesitating and uneven progress towards protection of authors' rights. In neither the 1791 law, conferring a public-performance right in dramatic works, nor in the 1793 law, conferring a reproduction right in writings of all kinds, are authors securely at the core of the new literary property regime. Rather, in both texts, broader public concerns divide, or even overshadow, the legislators' attentions. The 1791 text is preoccupied with the recognition and enlargement of the public domain. The committee report in favour of the 1793 law emphasizes that the protection of authors will not prove detrimental to society.

In the 1791 decree, the author's concerns do not occupy centre stage. ...

... The reporter, Le Chapelier, is often quoted as a great exponent of author-oriented rationales for copyright. Almost invariably, the passage quoted is taken out of context. Le Chapelier did declare that 'the most sacred, the most legitimate, the most inviolable, and ... the most personal of all properties, is the work which is the fruit of a writer's thoughts'. But his remark concerned *unpublished* works. Once disseminated, Le Chapelier went on to assert, the manuscript is 'give[n] over to the public ... by the nature of things, everything is finished for the author and the publisher when the public has in this way [through publication] acquired the work.' According to Le Chapelier, the main principle is the public domain, to which authors' rights are an exception. He stressed that the new French law must put the principle and its exception in the right place; were the exception to replace the principle that 'a published work is by its nature a public property' then 'you will no longer have any basis for your law'. Indeed, he criticized the English copyright law for setting up a strongly protected right rather than appreciating the principle of the public domain. This observation is all the more notable when one recalls the Statute of Anne's implicit suspicion of authors' claims, as evidenced by that law's imposition of formalities to avoid public 'ignorance' of the copyright. Le Chapelier's suggestion that the English law lacked proper solicitude for the public domain is difficult to reconcile with the later popular view of Le Chapelier as an ardent advocate of authors' literary-property rights....

By 1793, however, the Revolutionary legislators' copyright rhetoric had shifted away from Le Chapelier's public-domain principle towards recognizing a property right in authors' works even after publication. But this shift did not markedly amend the prior reserved characterization of authors' rights, much less break with it. In the new formulation, authors would still not receive protection primarily for their own sake; rather, recognition of their rights would serve to promote public welfare. Indeed, jurisdiction over elaboration of a copyright law had been transferred from the Committees on the Constitution and on Agriculture and Commerce, to the Committee on Public Instruction. Enacting a copyright law formed part of a grander scheme of public education.

The report of Lakanal, on behalf of the Committee of Public Instruction, at first signalled a more favourable attitude towards authors' rights. This document (which, like Le Chapelier's report, is often quoted selectively) announced in its first sentence a property right in works of authorship. Lakanal also dubbed the proposed law the 'Declaration of the Rights of Genius'—thus stressing copyright's kinship to other great Rights of Man. But other aspects of the report reveal ambiguities. For example, Lakanal's pronouncement of an author's property-right is guarded. Unlike *ancien régime* advocates of literary property, Lakanal did not assert that 'the author is the master of his work, or no one in society is master of his property.' Indeed, unlike Le Chapelier, Lakanal did not even affirm 'the most sacred ... the most personal of properties'. Rather, he proclaimed that this right is '[o]f all rights the least subject to criticism, a right whose increase can neither harm republican equality, nor offend liberty'. The rhetoric here displays a looking-over-the-shoulder quality inconsistent with a firm conviction of the centrality of authors' personal claims....

The text of the 1793 decree also undercuts arguments that this law protects authors primarily because they are authors. Although the version of the decree reported by Lakanal on 21 July contained no formalities, the final text incorporated the requirement of deposit as a prerequisite to suit. As discussed earlier, conditioning the exercise of copyright upon compliance with formalities undercuts the notion of a right inherent in the author. Several early decisions by the courts under the 1793 law held that deposit of copies, rather than simply meeting a procedural requirement, gave rise to the copyright. That is, without deposit, no copyright protection attached to the work. At the least, failure to deposit the work could result in an initially protected work's falling into the public domain. These rulings suggest a judicial view that the act of authorship does not itself afford a basis for recognizing or maintaining protection of authors' rights. . . .

This examination of the legislative sources of the first French copyright laws reveals that these framers did not greet the concept of authors' property rights with the enthusiasm that later writers ascribed to them. . . .

I do not mean to suggest that French Revolutionary legislators perceived copyright solely as a vehicle to foster public welfare. Sympathy for authors' claims of moral entitlement to rights in their works surely influenced enactment of the 1791 and 1793 decrees as well. After all, the Revolutionary copyright laws were drafted and voted in a general climate formally recognizing natural rights, including the 'sacred' right to property enunciated in the Declaration of the Rights of Man. My point is that mixed motives underlay the French Revolutionary copyright laws (as well as their US counterparts) and that the parliamentary speeches and the texts of the laws themselves attest to a certain tension between authors' personal claims of right and the public interest in access to works of authorship. Thus, without denying the presence of a strong authors' rights current in the Revolutionary laws, I would suggest that the Revolutionary legislators generally resolved that public-versus-private tension by casting copyright primarily as an aid to the advancement of public instruction. . . .

Revolutionary Copyright Practice: For What Kinds of Works Was French Copyright Litigated? What Kinds of Arguments Did the Advocates Press?

If the motivations for enacting the first French and US copyright laws were similar, what of the works they yielded? Comparison of the subject-matter the two laws covered might suggest that the two nations sought to promote dissemination of different kinds of works. The US Constitution authorized Congress to create a copyright system to 'promote the progress' of knowledge. Congress adopted a rather pragmatic view of the kinds of works that achieved that objective: the first copyright law protected maps, charts, and books—in that order. The great majority of works for which authors or publishers sought copyright protection under that first statute were highly useful productions.

The first French copyright law conferring a right of reproduction extended not merely to 'writings of all kinds' but to 'all productions of the *beaux arts*'. Putting the two texts side by side, one might conclude that one law promoted Utility while the other sought Beauty. In fact, reports of French copyright-infringement cases up to 1814 indicate that, as in the United States and England, works of information or instruction were most often the subject-matter of copyright litigation.

Moreover, even when the complaint of the French copyright-owner concerned works of higher arts and letters, the arguments of the advocates would none the less sound familiar to an Anglo–American copyright litigant: incentive rationales loom large in the reasoning of lawyers and courts. The French copyright law may have protected a broader range of subject-matter, but in both French and American cases, the subject-matter advanced State interests. If the US framers feared that art might distract hard-working citizens from useful achievements, the French Revolutionaries saw art, or at least some kinds of art, in the service of utility.

Art glorified the French Revolution and spread its ideals. A criminal copyright-infringement affair from Year 7 of the Republic illustrates the point. The work at issue was a play. Theatrical works were among those creations the Revolution sought to encourage. The pleading stressed the utility of dramatic works in disseminating the Enlightenment and the Revolution. The prosecutor, complaining of inadequate enforcement of dramatists' rights in the provinces, declared:

> Shall literary properties be less sacred in the eyes of the republican judge than other properties? It is to the wise men, to dramatic authors, to all literary authors that we principally owe the uncontested superiority of the French language over all the languages of Europe. It is they who render all nations tributaries to our arts, tastes, genius, glory; it is through them that the principles and rules of a wise and generous liberty penetrate beyond our borders and sphere of activity. . . .

The Birth of the Berne Union

SAM RICKETSON*

. . . Literary and artistic works and musical compositions recognize no national boundaries, even where translation into another language is required for a work to be fully appreciated in a particular country. Thus it was that after the need for protection of authors by national laws had been recognized, the works of these authors still remained vulnerable to copying and exploitation abroad. These activities, commonly referred to as "piracy", had been a long-established feature of European social and cultural life, and this continued to be the case for a considerable time after the enactment of national copyright laws. The attitudes of many countries to these practices were highly anomalous: whilst prepared to protect their own authors, they did not always regard the piracy of foreign authors' works as unfair or immoral. Some countries, in fact, openly countenanced piracy as contributing to their educational and social needs and as reducing the prices of books for their citizens. The particular victims of these practices were the United Kingdom and France. During the eighteenth century English authors suffered from the activities of Irish pirates who could flood both the English and other markets with cheap reprints; after the Act of Union with Ireland in 1800, the chief threat came from the publishing houses of the United States and this continued to be a major problem for the rest of the century. French authors, in turn, suffered from the activities of pirates located in Switzerland, Germany, Holland, and in particular, Belgium.

---

* 11 Colum.-V.L.A. J.L. & ARTS 9, 12–21 (1986).

By the early nineteenth century, Brussels was a major center for the piracy of French books, and this led to considerable strains in the relations between France and Belgium. Piracy was likewise rampant between the different German and Italian states.

This widespread piracy of foreign works was the principal reason for the development of international copyright relations in the mid-nineteenth century. The arguments that raged both for and against the protection of foreign authors at this time have a surprisingly modern ring to them. On the one hand, it could be said that the activities of the pirates resulted in cheaper copies and the greater availability of the work in question. In countries hungry for knowledge and enlightenment, this could only be to the advantage of the public interest; and this, indeed, was the reason for the persistent refusal of the United States to protect foreign works throughout the nineteenth century. On the other hand, the moral and practical arguments in the author's favor were obvious: not only was he being robbed of the fruits of his creativity, but this would discourage him from continuing to create, with resultant loss to his own, and other, countries.

It is hard to identify the point at which a country no longer sees advantage in the piracy of foreign works, and decides to extend protection to the authors of such works. It may be that the activities of its own authors have increased, and that the latter now desire protection for their own works abroad. It may also be that, after a while, a country wishes to obtain some kind of international respectability, and to avoid the opprobrium of being labeled as a nation of pirates. Another factor may be that countries with large literary and artistic outputs bring pressure to bear on their more recalcitrant neighbors, promising various forms of trade advantage in return for copyright protection for their authors. Finally, a pirate nation may come to recognize that the rights of authors in their works are of a proprietary nature, and that they should therefore be protected internationally in the same way as other property of foreigners. All these factors were certainly applicable in the case of Belgium, which, in the mid-nineteenth century, switched suddenly from being the chief center of piracy for French works to being one of the most zealous defenders of authors' rights. The same factors applied to many other countries as they began to enter into international copyright relations with each other....

Many European countries ... began to take more formal steps to secure the protection of their authors abroad. In a bold move in 1852, France passed a decree extending the protection of its laws to all works published abroad, irrespective of whether the law of the country in question accorded corresponding protection to the works of French authors. This measure was consistent with the philosophical basis of French copyright law, according to which authors' rights, being natural rights of property, should not be subject to artificial restraints such as nationality and political boundaries. Nevertheless, a practical motivation also lay behind the decree. Up to this time, France had found other nations reluctant to enter agreements for the protection of French works on a reciprocal basis. She therefore hoped that the unilateral grant of protection to authors from these countries in France would "shame" them into responding in like manner. Whether or not there is a causal connection is hard to say, but the fact remains that after 1852 the blockage cleared, and France entered agreements with a large number of their nations under which each agreed to accord protection to the works of the other.

Bilateral copyright agreements of this kind had, in fact, become quite common by the middle of the century. . . .

The basis of the majority of these conventions was national treatment, but, as stated above, they also contained a number of common rules which each country undertook to apply in its protection of works from the other country. There was usually a statement of the categories of works covered by the agreement, and specific provision was generally made for the protection of translation and performing rights. Restrictions in respect of particular kinds of use were also often allowed relating, for example, to education or the reproduction of newspaper articles. The scope and detail of these provisions differed considerably from one convention to another, but the most "advanced", in terms of protection of authors' interest, were to be found in the conventions made by France, Germany and Italy in the early 1880s. With regard to duration of protection, most of the pre–1886 conventions required material reciprocity, providing that country A was not obliged to protect the works of country B for any longer period than that accorded by state B to its own works, and in any event for no longer than country A protected its own nationals.

There were wider discrepancies with respect to formalities: under some conventions, compliance with the formalities of the country of origin of the work was sufficient to obtain protection in the other state; in other conventions, it was necessary for an author to comply with the formalities of both states. Matters were further complicated by the fact that the duration of many conventions was uncertain, in that they were linked to some wider treaty of trade or commerce between the countries in question and might suddenly fall to the ground if the latter was revoked or renegotiated. Another source of uncertainty arose from the insertion of "most favored nation" clauses in many copyright conventions. The effect of these was that the contracting parties agreed to admit each other to the benefits that might be accorded to a third state under another treaty that was made by one of them with that state. The effect of such clauses was that a copyright convention between countries A and B might be abrogated, in whole or in part, by the terms of another convention made by either country A or B with country C if this agreement contained additional measures for the protection of copyright. While these clauses did not mean any loss of protection for authors, they obviously made it difficult for an author from country A to know, at any one time, what level of protection he was entitled to in country B, and vice versa.

It will be clear that this network of bilateral agreements meant that there was little uniformity in the protection that an author might expect to receive in countries other than his own. As far as Europe was concerned, the threat posed by international piracy earlier in the century had largely disappeared by 1886, but quite a number of European states still remained reluctant to enter bilateral agreements on copyright. These included the Scandinavian countries, the Netherlands, Greece, the newly independent Balkan states, and, most importantly, the Russian and Austro–Hungarian empires. Outside Europe, much of the world's surface was then controlled by one of the chief European colonial powers. Of those states which were independent, very few had entered any international copyright agreements, and many, in fact, had no internal copyright laws. The most important of these countries was the United States, which throughout the nineteenth century continued to be a major center for pirated works and resisted efforts by other countries, in particular the United Kingdom, to draw it into bilateral agreements. Several such attempts were made, but the vested interests of publishers and printers, on the one hand, and the voracious appetite for cheap books from the rapidly growing American population, on the other, doomed them to failure.

In light of the above, it was not surprising that moves for a more widely based and uniform kind of international copyright protection began in the middle of the nineteenth century. Several schools of thought can be seen at work here. The first favored a universal codification of copyright law under which literary and artistic works would receive equal protection in every country. This was, of course, an idealist conception, which was based firmly on the natural law view of authors' rights according to which these rights should be protected universally without artificial constraints of time, nationality or territoriality. The precise mechanisms by which this state of affairs was to be brought about was never entirely clear, but presumably it would require some kind of international arrangement under which each nation would agree to adopt a common set of provisions guaranteeing protection to authors. In contrast to this was a more pragmatic approach that recognized the need for more uniform international protection of authors' rights, but advocated more limited means for achieving this, mainly through the replacement of the numerous existing bilateral agreements with a single multilateral instrument. At the start, it was the first of these views that predominated. As early as 1839, support for a universal law of copyright was expressed by Viscount Siméon speaking in the French Chamber of Peers, and two years later by Lamartine in the Chamber of Deputies. However, the first organized expression of opinion is to be found in the resolutions of a Congress on Literary and Artistic Property that met in Brussels in 1858.... There was a general consensus among the participants on the need for uniform international copyright protection, and a number of resolutions were passed. ...

The resolutions of the 1858 Congress, with their strong universalist flavor, foreshadowed many of the provisions that were to be embodied in national laws and bilateral conventions over the next three decades, and, of course, in the Berne Convention itself....

More definite progress came about in another way. In 1878, a major international literary congress was held in Paris at the time of the Universal Exhibition in that city. This was organized by the French *Société des gens de lettres*, and drew together some of the most distinguished authors, lawyers and public figures of the day from three continents. Presided over by no less a personage than Victor Hugo, the congress concerned itself with fundamental questions of principle concerning the protection of authors. After lengthy debates, a number of resolutions acknowledging the natural and perpetual rights of authors were passed, and a call was addressed to the French government to summon an international conference to formulate a "uniform convention for the regulation of the use of literary property." A similar call for the constitution of a general union of states for the adoption of a uniform law for the protection of artistic property was made by an international artistic congress that was held in Paris later that year. The French government, for reasons that are unclear, failed to respond to either call for action, but a more practical development flowing from the 1878 literary congress was its decision to establish the International Literary Association. This was to be open to literary societies and to writers of all nations, and had the following objects:

1. The protection of the principles of literary property.

2. The organization of regular relations between the literary societies and writers of all nations.

3. The initiation of all enterprises possessing an international literary character.

The first president of the Association was Victor Hugo, and its initial membership was extremely wide, being drawn from nearly twenty countries. Since this time, it has played a significant and catalytic role in the majority of international copyright developments. Although it has always had a strong French orientation, its annual congresses have been held in many different cities, beginning with London in 1879. Five years after this, its membership was expanded to include artists, and its name was changed to its present title, the International Literary and Artistic Association (usually known as "ALAI" which is the abbreviation of its French title, *"l'Association littéraire et artistique internationale"*). To ALAI belongs the credit for being the initiator of the meetings and negotiations that led to the formation of the Berne Union. From the very start of its existence, it concerned itself with the legal questions relating to the international protection of authors. Strong universalist views were expressed at several of its early congresses, but at its congress in Rome in 1882 a more practical proposal for a limited multilateral convention was adopted. This was based on a cannily conceived motion prepared by Dr. Paul Schmidt of the German Publishers' Association. It began by saying that this was not the time or place to begin discussion of a new international instrument on copyright. Widespread discussions and consultations were needed before this could be done, but, with a view to beginning this process, the motion charged the office of ALAI with the task of undertaking:

> the necessary measures for initiating, in the press of all countries, as extensive and profound discussion as possible on the question of the formation of a Union of literary property, and for arranging at a date to be subsequently fixed, a conference composed of the organs and repre-

sentatives of interested groups, to meet to discuss and settle a scheme for the creation of a Union of literary property.

The meeting place chosen for the conference was Berne, in neutral Switzerland. This was fitting, as Berne had already been the venue for a number of important international meetings on various matters and the headquarters of several international organizations, such as the Universal Postal Union and the International Telegraph Union, were situated there. . . .

After three days of intensive discussions, the ALAI conference produced a compact convention of 10 articles. Its basic aim was stated to be the "constitution of a general Union for the protection of the rights of authors in their literary works and manuscripts." The fundamental principle of protection was national treatment, which was accorded on the criterion of place of publication or performance of the work rather than the nationality of the author claiming protection. This was subject to the condition that authors claiming protection had complied with the formalities required by the law of the country where such publication or performance had taken place. Protection was also extended to manuscripts and unpublished works, and the expression "literary and artistic works" was defined as including:

> books, brochures or all other writings; dramatic or dramatico-musical works, musical compositions with or without words, and musical arrangements; works of design, painting, sculpture, engraving, lithography, maps, plans, scientific sketches and in general any literary, scientific and artistic work whatsoever, which may be published by any method of printing or reproduction.

As for the rights protected under the Convention, these essentially remained a matter for national treatment. This was a long way removed from the universal codification of copyright principles which had been advocated by the earlier literary and artistic congresses. Nevertheless, it was clear that the ALAI draft was seen as a "progressive" text, which should be revised and augmented with time and the addition of new member states.

The Berne Convention And The Universal Copyright Convention: The American Experience

HAMISH SANDISON*

Early History of U.S. International Copyright Relations

[Former Register of Copyrights] Barbara Ringer has stated: "Until the Second World War the United States had little reason to take pride in its international copyright relations; in fact, it had a great deal to be ashamed of. With few exceptions its role in international copyright was marked by short-sightedness, political isolationism, and narrow economic self-interest."

The grounds for this American self-criticism are twofold: in the first place, up to 1891, the United States denied copyright protection alto-

* 11 COLUM.-V.L.A. J.L. & ARTS 89, 90–95 (1986).

gether to published works by nonresident foreigners; secondly, up to 1955 [when the United States joined the Universal Copyright Convention], the United States refused to enter into multilateral copyright relations outside the Western Hemisphere. Thus, for almost 200 years, it is fair to describe the American approach to international copyright relations as essentially isolationist.

The roots of American isolationism are clearly evident in the U.S. Copyright Act of 1790, which afforded protection to published works only if their authors were citizens or residents of the United States. In this respect, the first federal copyright statute merely mirrored antecedent state copyright statutes enacted by all but one of the 13 newly independent states between 1783 and 1786, which limited their protection to the works of U.S. residents. Of course, the United States was not alone in denying copyright protection to nonresident foreigners at that time: it was not until the first half of the 19th century that such protection was allowed, first by Denmark in 1828 and then by the other major nations of Europe. However, subsequent revisions of the U.S. copyright statute in 1802, 1831, 1856, 1865 and 1870, while greatly expanding the subject matter of protection, still left published works by nonresident foreigners unprotected.

In the absence of copyright protection under U.S. law, literary piracy of foreign—and particularly British—works grew dramatically in the 19th century. Not surprisingly, this produced great resentment among British authors, and none was more vociferous in his condemnation of U.S. law than Charles Dickens. Reporting on a visit to North America in 1842, Dickens wrote to his future biographer:

> I spoke, as you know, of international copyright, at Boston; and I spoke of it again at Hartford. My friends were paralysed with wonder at such audacious daring. The notion that I, a man alone by himself, in America, should venture to suggest to the Americans that there was one point on which they were neither just to their own countrymen nor to us, actually struck the boldest dumb! Washington Irving, Prescott, Hoffman, Bryant, Haileck, Dana, Washington Aliston—every man who writes in this country is devoted to the question, and not one of them dares to raise his voice and complain of the atrocious state of the law. It is nothing that of all men living I am the greatest loser by it. It is nothing that I have a claim to speak and be heard. The wonder is that a breathing man can be found with temerity enough to suggest to the Americans the possibility of their having done wrong. I wish you could have seen the faces that I saw, down both sides of the table at Hartford, when I began to talk about Scott. I wish you could have heard how I gave it out. My blood so boiled as I thought of the monstrous injustice that I felt as if I were twelve feet high when I thrust it down their throats.

Unsuccessful attempts to establish copyright treaty relations with Great Britain were made in 1837, in 1853, and again in 1880–81, foundering each time on the opposition of American publishers who believed that their financial success depended upon being able to sell cheap reprints of British books....

Notwithstanding the opposition of the "book-selling leviathans" [as Anthony Trollope branded American publishers] and their friends in Congress, the movement for international copyright protection continued to gain ground in the United States in the second half of the 19th century, supported by a majority of American authors as well as a growing number of publishers. Most American authors favored copyright protection for foreign works, not only as a matter of principle, but also on economic grounds: without international copyright protection, they faced unfair competition from unauthorized reprints of British books which were cheaper because their British authors received no royalties. As Max Kampelman has noted, "American readers were less inclined to read the novels of Cooper or Hawthorne for a dollar when they could buy a novel of Scott or Dickens for a quarter." American authors were also hurt by the lack of reciprocal protection abroad. Longfellow, for example, complained that, although he had twenty-two publishers in England and Scotland, "only four of them took the slightest notice of my existence, even so far as to send me a copy of the book." American publishers, too, increasingly felt that action was needed to combat widespread literary piracy of foreign works, although they qualified their position by insisting that a foreign work should not be protected unless it was domestically manufactured.

One Hundred and Two Years Later: The U.S. Joins the Berne Convention

JANE C. GINSBURG & JOHN M. KERNOCHAN*

U.S. Efforts to Join Berne

U.S. ratification came one hundred and two years after the United States' official observer at the initial international conference from which the Convention emerged recommended U.S. participation in the Berne Union. At that time, the U.S. had no international copyright relations. We were, and had long been, a "pirate nation" for whom protection abroad offered fewer attractions than free copying at home of foreign, particularly British, works. There was no general provision protecting foreign works until the Chace Act of 1891. Over the intervening century, the U.S. politics of intellectual property changed. From a user and importer of copyrighted works, the U.S. became a producer and leading exporter. The appeal of international protection became correspondingly manifest. There followed a proliferation of bilateral copyright agreements, but, until the 1950s, no participation in a major multilateral copyright convention.

When the U.S. finally joined a major international convention in 1955, it was not the Berne Convention. At that time, U.S. law fell below many of the substantive minima of protection imposed by the Berne Convention. For example, Berne sets forth a minimum duration of copyright of [life plus] fifty years, but U.S. copyright protection endured for only 28 years, unless the proprietor renewed the registration for a second 28–year term. Berne prohibits imposition of formalities conditioning the enjoyment or exercise of copyright, but U.S. law at the time

* 13 Colum.-V.L.A. J.L. & Arts 1, 1–6 (1988).

required a notice of copyright on published copies and omission of the notice resulted in loss of protection. Moreover, U.S. law required registration and deposit of works as a prerequisite to a suit for copyright infringement. Beginning in 1928, Berne provided for the author's "moral rights" to "claim attribution for his work, and to prevent its alteration or mutilation," but the U.S. did not recognize such rights. Rather than amend its law to resolve these and other differences to permit Berne adherence, the U.S. actively promoted the creation of the Universal Copyright Convention (UCC), a new international copyright treaty largely tailored to the peculiarities of U.S. law.

By the late 1980s, however, many U.S. officials and copyright proprietors perceived that remaining outside the Berne Union was at the least inconvenient, and moreover was proving increasingly embarrassing and even detrimental to U.S. copyright interests. Non membership was inconvenient because many U.S. copyright industries found the commonly used indirect method of achieving Berne protection costly and onerous. This method involved manipulating the work's country of origin by effecting "simultaneous" publication in a Berne country (usually Canada), thus obtaining "back door" Berne protection. It was also possible to achieve Berne-level protection in those UCC countries also signatory to the Berne Convention which had merged Berne standards with their domestic law, for the rule of national treatment (according UCC authors the same treatment as nationals) would accord U.S. copyright owners protection coextensive with Berne minima. However, U.S. resort to the UCC and to the "back door" to achieve Berne-level protection without assuming Berne's responsibilities produced considerable resentment, and even threats of retaliation. Moreover, despite occasionally benefiting from Berne, the U.S. had no role in the evolution and management of this premier international pact. In an era of rapid technological change and doctrinal development, the U.S. continued to stand on the outside looking in.

Non membership in the Berne Convention was embarrassing not only because the U.S. was the only non-Unionist Western country, but also because non membership offered one ground of resistance to U.S. trade negotiators seeking to encourage greater respect for U.S. copyrights abroad. If the U.S. so strongly advocated a high level of copyright protection and enforcement by its trading partners, why was the U.S. not a member of the most protective multilateral copyright treaty? Other political considerations also enhanced the attractions of Berne adherence: not only was the UCC less protective than Berne, it was administered by UNESCO, an international agency from which the U.S. had recently withdrawn its support. Moreover, adherence would secure copyright relations with twenty-four additional nations, and would bolster U.S. endeavors to include intellectual property in the General Agreement on Tariffs and Trade (GATT) . . .

The approach common to virtually all the legislation governing the omissions from it, was the "minimalist approach" supported by a preponderance of the interests favoring Berne adherence. In recognition of the ease with which even minority opposing interests can block legislation from passage through the intricate Congressional processes, this approach called for making only those changes in existing U.S. law essential to achieve a plausible level of Berne compatibility. In retrospect, and considering how close the whole effort came to being derailed in its closing stages, it would seem the proponents of this approach were right. The price paid was arguably a less than full embracing of the "Spirit of Berne" in its broadest sense. But adherence, the principal goal, was in fact attained. New battles to move U.S. law further toward a fuller acceptance of Berne's wider implications will certainly be fought in the future . . .

Notes and Questions

1. Jane C. Ginsburg is the Morton L. Janklow Professor of Literary and Artistic Property Law at Columbia Law School. Born in 1955, she received her J.D. from Harvard in 1980, and a Doctor of Laws from the University of Paris II in 1995.

2. Professor Sam Ricketson was born in 1950 and received his LLB from the University of Melbourne, and his LLM and LLD from the University of London. A fellow of the Academy of the Social Sciences in Australia, and a member of the Victorian Law Reform Commission, and a former member of the Commonwealth Copyright Tribunal, he is Professor of Law at the University of Melbourne, Australia. He is the author of the leading treatise on international copyright law, *The Berne Convention 1886–1986* (1987) (2d edition forthcoming 2005, titled *The Berne Convention and Beyond: International Copyright and Neighbouring Rights Agreements from 1886 to the Present*), as well as of many works on Australian intellectual property law.

3. Hamish Sandison is a partner in the English law firm of Bird & Bird, where he specializes in intellectual property and telecommunications. He was educated at Cambridge University (1974 MA) and the University of California, Berkeley (1978 Ll.M.).

4. John M. Kernochan is the Nash Professor Emeritus of Law at Columbia Law School, and the founder and co-director of the Kernochan Center for Law and the Arts at Columbia. Born in 1919, he earned his LLB from Columbia in 1948. For many years, he was also the president of Galaxy Music Corp., whose roster of composers included Jean Sibelius, Ralph Vaughn Williams, Gustav Holst, George Perle and George Rochberg.

5. To what extent could compliance with international obligations shift constitutional analysis of the Copyright Clause? Since the United States began as "a pirate nation," wouldn't an originalist approach to the Constitution recognize that the framers were isolationists with regard to international copyright protection, and accordingly reject internationally harmonizing interpretations? Contra, Graeme W. Austin, *Does The Copyright Clause Mandate Isolationism?* 26 Colum.-V.L.A. J.L. & Arts 17, 50 (2003) ("For contemporary copyright law, the network of international copyright relations within which it is situated means that any meaningful confrontation of copyright bargains and 'give and take' between authors and the public cannot easily be analyzed in terms of a single society.").

6. Similarly, how does compliance with international obligations shift the congressionally calibrated balance of statutory rights? See Rochelle Cooper Dreyfuss, *TRIPS-ROUND II: Should Users Strike Back?* 71 U. Chi. L. Rev. 21 (2004) (arguing for addition of explicit user rights in forthcoming round of WTO negotiations).

7. Despite the goals of international conventions to harmonize and raise the worldwide level of intellectual property protection, does international copyright protection in fact ultimately devolve to a "lowest common denominator" level of protection? See Pamela Samuelson, *Intellectual Property Arbitrage: How Foreign Rules Can Affect Domestic Protections*, 71 U. Chi. L. Rev. 223 (2004) (low protection rules in foreign jurisdictions undermine force of intellectual property protected at higher levels domestically).

B. Basic Concepts

Copyright

PAUL GOLDSTEIN*

What is copyright? A policymaker in the United States will tell you that copyright is an instrument of consumer welfare, stimulating the production of the widest possible array of literary and artistic works at the lowest possible price. But ask the question of a practitioner on the European continent, and he will tell you that copyright is at best a watered-down version of author's right—that grand civil law tradition that places the author, not the consumer, at the center of protection. A low protectionist will tell you that copyright is a monopoly that undesirably drives up the price of goods in the marketplace. A high protectionist will tell you that copyright is a property right—no more, no less—and one without which we would have very few creative works in the marketplace.

Ask the question of a United States trade official and she will tell you that copyright is one of the strongest net contributors to the nation's balance of trade. Ask the question of a school teacher in Thailand and he will tell you that copyright is what stands in the way of getting textbooks into the hands of his students. Ask the question of an anthropologist digging through the remains of the 1976 Copyright Act a century from now and she might tell you that copyright is the symbol of a nation's cultural aspirations. Ask the same question today of a manufacturer of novelty nicknacks and he will tell you that copyright is simply what enables him to meet his payroll at the end of the week.

Confronting this welter of competing perspectives, it is tempting to agree with Professor Lyman Ray Patterson that "the basic and continuing weakness of copyright law in this country" is "the absence of fundamental principles for copyright." No one interested in copyright can afford to overlook Ray Patterson's masterful history of Anglo-American copyright law. But on this point I think Ray is wrong. I believe that there does in fact exist a cohering view of copyright, a view that

---

* 38 J. COPYRIGHT SOC'Y 109, 109–111 (1991).

reconciles most if not all of the competing antiphonies, and one that offers a sound prescription for public policy as well.

Under the view that I propose, copyright is not about protecting authors or publishers, nor is copyright singularly about securing authors' welfare or consumers' welfare. Copyright is not about bolstering international trade balances, nor is it about protecting art, high or low. Copyright is about none of these things; and copyright is about all of them.

Copyright, in a word, is about authorship. Copyright is about sustaining the conditions of creativity that enable an individual to craft out of thin air, and intense, devouring labor, an *Appalachian Spring*, a *Sun Also Rises,* a *Citizen Kane.* Copyright is as much about the pages of deleted text, the scenes that lie on the cutting room floor, as it is about the refined work, the final cut, that ultimately reaches the author's public. But copyright—and authorship—are only in part about the act of creation. If creation is all there was to authorship, copyright could comfortably leave the author scribbling alone in his far-off garret. Authorship in its contemporary sense implies not just an author, but an audience; not just words spoken, but individuals spoken to.

By "authorship" I mean authors communicating as directly as circumstance allows with their intended audiences. Copyright sustains the very heart and essence of authorship by enabling this communication, this connection. It is copyright that makes it possible for audiences—markets—to form for an author's work, and it is copyright that makes it possible for publishers to bring these works to market. (As should by now be evident, when I speak of "publishers" I mean the whole range of intermediaries—book publishers, music publishers, motion picture producers, record producers—whose business it is to bring works to market.)

To be sure, copyright law and policy in different places may emphasize one particular object over another. An emphasis on consumer welfare is the hallmark of copyright jurisprudence in the United States, just as an emphasis on author's right is the hallmark of the continental regimes. But viewed globally, and in the round, it is authorship that provides the cohering theme.

I believe that the historical materials support the view that copyright is at heart a vehicle of authorship, a means for connecting an author to his audience and enabling audiences to repay the author's effort. Contemporary decisions of the United States Congress and courts also support this view of copyright. But my aim today is as much to prescribe as it is to describe. I hope to show not only that copyright is about authorship, but also that authorship offers a helpful benchmark for copyright reform.

Authorship presupposes autonomy. For authorship to flourish, authors must enjoy autonomy in their work. Authors must be protected from the influence of anyone other than their intended audience. Authors must also have the elbow room needed to ply their craft, freeing them to create those works that they believe their audience desires. Both requirements have a legal dimension. Copyright law must protect authors from any influence other than their audience; it must not judge authors' efforts by too exacting a standard; and it must not impose too severe a prohibition against authors' borrowing from others.

Eligibility for Copyright Protection: A Search for Principled Standards

RALPH S. BROWN*

Three Approaches to Copyright

One morally principled approach exalts authors. Authors—using the Constitution's word to include writers, composers, artists, and many others—are the bearers and creators of our culture, both high and popular. Except for a fortunate and highly gifted few, they are not richly rewarded. Their works are easily appropriated by persons who need not compensate them. Further, these works are intellectual creations that bear the creative and personal stamp of their authors. According to this approach, the author should be able to decide when and how to publish his or her personal creation, both as a matter of respect and as a matter of allowing the author to win material rewards as best she can.

It is easy for proponents of this 'exaltation of authorship' approach to slip into bathos about the lofty and lonely position of the author. It is as easy to slip into cynicism, and to observe that, the way the system is organized, those we idealize as lonely authors are often in fact the well-paid henchmen of monster multinational conglomerates that grind out— whatever the cynic despises. Less formidable entrepreneurs are currently obtaining copyrights of catalogs, dolls, and plastic flowers, not exactly the stuff of culture high or low. Cynicism aside, there is probably a substantial consensus in support of Justice Reed's concluding affirmation in Mazer v. Stein that 'sacrificial days devoted to ... creative activities deserve rewards commensurate with the services rendered.'

Unfortunately, such vague rhetoric does little more than adorn the stage on which actual choices must be played out. A measurably more focused statement of the exaltation of authorship approach can be found in the views of the former Register of Copyrights, David Ladd. Ladd takes strong issue with what he perceives to be the basic approach taken in Sony Corp. of America v. Universal City Studios, that is, "allocating to the copyright owner only that portion of compensation, however determined, which would avoid 'harm.' " Believing that such determination is bound to be arbitrary, Ladd asserts 'that the public is best served by regarding copyright as an instrument of property operating in a free market economy,' and he refuses to 'enter into the debate about how much—either by exemptions, limitations, or compulsory licenses—this right and the value of this right should be compromised.'

This is strong medicine, especially when a second dose is proffered. Ladd endorses the idea that when an author has created something and an entrepreneur has incurred the risk and expense in bringing the author's work to the public 'there should be compensation for the use of that work based upon what the public is willing to pay. In other words,

* 70 MINN. L. REV. 579, 589–96 (1985).

reasonable compensation for every use of the work just as with other property, whether it be car rental, lease, or admission to a theater.' Note that this bold position, doubtless acclaimed by copyright owners, seems to call for property rights in 'every use' of a work, held in check only by market forces. In some cases, Ladd would accept 'collective administration' necessitated to transaction costs, for example, when many copyright owners ask some return from a multitude of users making home tapes....

Exaltation of authorship, whatever its emotional appeal, is not, in itself, enough to justify extending existing rights, even if it is likely that creating a new property right will in fact shift resources in the authors' direction. That is the message of the second principled approach, which stems from the Supreme Court's interpretation of the Constitution's copyright clause.

The Supreme Court regularly intones that '[t]he copyright law ... makes reward to the owner a secondary consideration.' As recently as last year the Court restated its view of the purpose of the copyright law:

> The monopoly privileges that Congress may authorize are neither unlimited nor primarily designed to provide a special private benefit. Rather, the limited grant is a means by which an important public purpose may be achieved. It is intended to motivate the creative activity of authors and inventors by the provision of a special reward, and to allow the public access to the products of their genius after the limited period of exclusive control has expired.

The constitutional approach focuses on copyright as a way of promoting the general public good, an approach mandated by the copyright-patent clause itself. The copyright-patent clause is the only one of the enumerated powers of Congress that is prefaced by a statement of purpose: 'to promote the Progress of Science and useful Arts.' The clause does not say 'to maximize the returns to authors and inventors.' Concededly, Congress is not effectively constrained by the declaration of purpose. But when one considers the solemnity of the clause, the Supreme Court's continuing concern for the public good, and the deeply rooted understanding that copyright flows from acts of Congress and not from natural right, one thing seems clear. When Congress legislates and courts fill in the blank spaces, both branches need ways to assess and balance the expected public good and private rewards.

Congress, more overtly than the courts, sometimes does no more than respond to pressure groups. Congress has created a number of exemptions from copyright liability, some of which have been studied, policy-based decisions while others have been decidedly less principled. A kind of copyright pork-barrel has existed, with exemptions from liability being granted to favored constituents. Thus, after having created a public performance right, Congress created a bundle of full and partial exemptions from liability in section 110, the public performance pork-barrel. This section exempts hymn singing at religious services, band music at agricultural fairs, and dances held by organizations such as the American Legion or the Elks Club....

Invocation of the magic word 'market' means that the time has come to examine the usefulness of the economic approach to copyright. Economists tell us that intellectual productions are a form of public good. That is, their quantity is not diminished by consumption. There is as much Hamlet today as there was when it was first created almost four hundred years ago. Furthermore, intellectual productions are not readily 'appropriable' because they are so easily copied or performed. Therefore, they cannot be monopolized unless the state steps in and permits authors and publishers to exclude others from copying or performing. They will demand payment, and the need to pay means that a smaller quantity will be consumed. It diminishes consumer welfare to limit consumption of public goods. However, it may be necessary to accept higher prices and lower consumption in order to induce authors to write and publishers to publish. There are of course other inducements to write—or paint, or compose—such as prestige, prizes, and patronage. Our society, however, depends only in part on these three lures and so creates copyright. Even without subsidies or copyright, there are still inducements for publishers to publish. It is clear that they can and do make money by publishing Hamlet.

The hard part, even for an economist, is to decide just how much legitimation of exclusive rights in intellectual property is needed to induce the optimal flow of writings and of inventions. . . .

Free Speech, Copyright, and Fair Use
L. RAY PATTERSON*

While courts have tended to view copyright as primarily proprietary in nature, Congress has treated it as regulatory.

Copyright's basis as a proprietary concept is that it enables one to protect his or her own creations. Its regulatory basis is that when these creations constitute the expression of ideas presented to the public, they become part of the stream of information whose unimpeded flow is critical to a free society. The right to control access to one's own expressions before publication does not engender free speech concerns, but publishers' control of access after publication does. This explains why historically copyright was deemed a monopoly to be strictly construed and to be shaped to serve the public interest over that of the copyright owner. The public interest to be served was reasonable access to the copyrighted work.

Despite the regulatory nature of copyright statutes, courts tend to treat copyright as proprietary in nature, presumably because they are concerned with equity as between the litigants and the equity is most often in favor of the copyright owner. The statutory limitations on copyright, however, enable courts to avoid the fundamental issue of copyright law. That issue is whether copyright is a right of the author by reason of his creation or whether it is a right created and limited by statute for the public benefit. The 1976 Act has caused the issue to surface. The unresolved question is whether copyright is essentially a proprietary or a regulatory concept. . . .

* 40 VAND. L. REV. 1, 3–13, 57–63 (1987).

The law of copyright can be viewed most usefully as statutory unfair competition based on the misappropriation rationale. The law's function is to protect the copyrighted work against predatory competitive practices. Its purpose, however, is somewhat ambiguous. While copyright's constitutional purpose—the promotion of learning—is clear, it is not clear whether this purpose is better served by encouraging the creation or by encouraging the distribution of works. One's choice of the means by which copyright's constitutional purpose is attained is important, because that choice is determined by, or determines, one's view of copyright as proprietary or regulatory in nature. If one chooses to attain this constitutional purpose by encouraging the creation of works, the proprietary view of copyright follows logically because people commonly are deemed to own what they create. If, on the other hand, one chooses to attain this purpose by encouraging distribution, the regulatory nature of copyright follows logically because distribution requires regulation.

My argument is that copyright's constitutional purpose is best served by encouraging the distribution of works. Learning requires access to the work in which the ideas to be learned are embodied. Because there can be no access without distribution, encouraging distribution is vitally important. The fact that creation is also necessary to the learning process does not alter this conclusion for two reasons. First, if copyright encourages creation, it does so only for the purpose of profit. Profit, however, cannot be obtained without distribution. Second, in creating a work an author harvests his ideas from the public domain. Copyright, which protects the expression of these ideas, is an encroachment on the public domain and can be justified only if it provides the public with some form of compensation. The public can be compensated most effectively by making the author's efforts accessible. Copyright, therefore, can be viewed as being in the nature of a bargain and sale. In return for providing public access to his efforts, the author is given limited protection for a limited period of time. The proprietary view of copyright, however, emphasizes the bargain and minimizes the sale. Thus, the history of statutory copyright in this country reveals that limitations on both the scope and duration of copyright protection have been continually enlarged. Yet, given the function of copyright—protection of the distributed work against predatory competition—it follows that the basic constitutional purpose of copyright—promotion of learning—is best served by encouraging distribution.

This conclusion is contrary to the traditional view that the constitutional purpose of copyright is best served by encouraging the creation of works, but it is well supported by reason and history. First, creativity is not a process amenable to statutory incentives. Second, copyright did not come into existence until the printing press facilitated the reproduction and widespread distribution of books. To protect the right to exclusive distribution, publishers created copyright. From this protection the author who created the work gained at best a reward secondary to that of the publisher. Copyright, therefore, originally functioned to encourage not creation, but distribution. In this regard, copyright's function is essentially the same today.

Notes and Questions

1. Professor Ralph Brown was born in 1913 and received an LL.B from Yale Law School in 1939. A nationally recognized expert in copyright and unfair competition, defamation, and privacy and publicity issues, Professor Brown taught at Yale for over four decades. After reaching emeritus status in 1984, he was a visiting professor at New York Law School. With Professor Benjamin Kaplan, Professor Brown co-edited the first U.S. casebook on copyright and unfair competition, "Cases on Copyright, Unfair Competition and Other Topics" (1960). He passed away in 1998.

2. Born in 1929, L. Ray Patterson became the Pope F. Brock Professor of Professional Responsibility at the University of Georgia School of Law in 1986 after serving as a faculty member and the dean of the Emory University School of Law. He also taught at the University of Texas as well as at Duke, Mercer and Vanderbilt. The author of many works on copyright and its history, including *Copyright in Historical Perspective* (1968), Professor Patterson died in 2003.

3. Consider whether the following remarks of David Ladd, Register of Copyrights from 1980–1985, fairly bear out Ralph Brown's charge of "author exaltation:"

> ... The purpose of copyright is to reward authors as a matter of justice, yes; but only as a beginning. Copyright also is intended to support a system, a macrocosm, in which authors and publishers complete for the attention and favor of the public, independent of the political will of the majority, the powerful, and above all the government, no matter how unorthodox, disturbing, or revolutionary their experience, views, or visions.

> The argument for copyright here, to be sure, is an argument of utility—but not mere economic utility. Utility is found in the fostering of a pluralism of opinion, experience, vision, and utterance within the world of authors.... [O]ur freedom depends not only on freedom for a few, but also on variety, regardless of the ultimate commingling of truth and error. Copyright fosters that variety.

> The marketplace of ideas which the First Amendment nurtures is, then, and must be more widely understood to be, essentially a *copyright* marketplace.... Just as we are best served by many visions and visionaries speaking from and to the breadth of human experience, so also do we require a vibrant, heterogeneous, and dissonant community of publishers. The greater their number and variety, the more likely is any author to find a publisher. And while this is of special importance in the areas of thought and political opinion, it is likewise crucial in the fine arts. Joyce and Proust, Beethoven and Stravinsky were all at one time scorned for works for which they later became immortal, but each found the publisher he needed. Those who pioneer, and thereby often disturb, cannot be silenced by anyone if publishers are numerous and the mail delivers the royalty checks....

By limiting potential rewards in the copyright market—whether
by capping them with a compulsory license, or barring them
with a complete exemption, or refusing to extend copyright to
new uses, or curtailing them in any way under arguments of
"harm"—the entrepreneurial calculus which precedes risk-taking in authorship and publishing is shifted in the direction of
not taking a chance, i.e., not writing or publishing a "risky"
work, whether ideologically or economically risky. Every limitation on copyright is a kind of rate-setting. And however high-
minded, every person who thus sets rates applies a value-
judgment: how much the author or publisher should receive.
Whoever makes this judgment regulates—i.e., controls—how
successful a class of authors, works, or publishers shall be. This
control of idea-laden copyrighted works is more wisely left with
the people than vested in a government tribunal, a statutory
license fee, or even a sincere judge searching a record for
undefined harm. . . .

David Ladd, *The Harm of the Concept of Harm in Copyright*, 30 J.
Copyright Soc'y U.S.A 421, 427–28, 431–32 (1983). For further development of the political independence theme sounded in the first paragraph
quoted from David Ladd, see Neil Netanel, *Copyright and a Democratic
Civil Society*, 106 Yale L. J. 283 (1996), excerpted infra at page 315.

4. Does David Ladd adequately account for the costs borne by publishers in disseminating works? Consider Professor Zechariah Chafee's analysis:

> Although the development expense is not so huge for a book as
> for a machine or a process, it does cost a good deal to print a
> book and to attract buyers. Even if an author could afford to
> publish his own book, he would not do the job well. And if the
> publishers did not get the benefit of the copyright monopoly, it
> would be hard for an author to find a publisher to bring out the
> book . . .
>
> One reason, therefore, for protecting the copyright in the hands
> of the publisher is to give an indirect benefit to authors by
> enabling them to get royalties or to sell the manuscript outright
> for a higher price. A second reason is, that it is only equitable
> that the publisher should obtain a return on his investment . . .
> But we mustn't concentrate our gaze on this one book. Publish-
> ing is close to gambling. Many of the same publisher's books
> never pay back his original outlay. Only an occasional killing
> makes it possible for us to read a number of less popular but
> perhaps more valuable books. . . . If we look at the rate of
> return on *all* books published by any firm, it does not seem
> excessive. Few publishers become millionaires. Thus copyright
> is necessary to make good publishers possible.

Zechariah Chafee, *Reflections on the Law of Copyright*, 45 Col. L. Rev.
503, 506–11 (1945).

5. Professor Patterson suggests that authorship supplies no rationale for U.S. copyright. Other students of copyright history have seconded this contention, at least as far as the Framers are concerned:

> The scope of copyright protection existing at the time of the framing is inconsistent with claims that copyright "must promote 'creative activity' " in order to be valid. The requirement that a work even be creative was not settled until the 1990s. Any attempt to locate with the Framers the proposition that copyright may be given only as a reward for creativity is an exercise in revisionist history; the central place that creativity occupies in copyright is a feature of modern copyright law ...

Thomas B. Nachbar, *Constructing Copyright's Mythology*, 6 Green Bag 2d 37, 44 (2002).

6. Professor Patterson poses the question "whether copyright is a right of the author by reason of his creation or whether it is a right created and limited by statute for the public benefit." Recognizing that "the 1976 Act has caused the issue to surface," he resolves the question by asserting that copyright "originally functioned to encourage not creation, but distribution. In this regard, copyright's function is essentially the same today." But the 1976 Act made a fundamental shift away from its predecessors, for it vested copyright in authors at the moment of creation and fixation of the work, rather than upon publication with notice of copyright. With the 1976 Act, public disclosure of the work is no longer the prerequisite to federal protection, nor are stake-claiming acts such as notice and registration. If copyright now arises out of the act of creation, does that not make it a "right of the author by reason of his creation"? Does that change the "function" of copyright law as well?

A Speech Delivered in the House of Commons on the 5th of February, 1841

THOMAS BABINGTON MACAULAY

[EDITORS' NOTE: Macaulay made the following speech in parliamentary debate on a bill to extend the term of copyright to the life of the author plus sixty years. The then-current term of copyright was twenty-eight years, renewable if the author was still living, for a term concluding with the author's death.]

... The question of copyright, Sir, like most questions of civil prudence, is neither black nor white, but grey. The system of copyright has great advantages and great disadvantages; and it is our business to ascertain what these are, and then to make an arrangement under which the advantages may be as far as possible secured, and the disadvantages as far as possible excluded. The charge which I bring against my honourable and learned friend's bill is this, that it leaves the advantages nearly what they are at present, and increases the disadvantages at least fourfold.

The advantages arising from a system of copyright are obvious. It is desirable that we should have a supply of good books; we cannot have such a supply unless men of letters are liberally remunerated; and the least objectionable way of remunerating them is by means of copyright. You cannot depend for literary instruction and amusement on the leisure of men occupied in the pursuits of active life. Such men may occasionally produce compositions of great merit. But you must not look to such men for works which require deep meditation and long research. Works of that kind you can expect only from persons who make literature the business of their lives. Of these persons few will be found among the rich and the noble. The rich and the noble are not impelled to intellectual exertion by necessity. They may be impelled to intellectual exertion by the desire of distinguishing themselves, or by the desire of benefiting the community. But it is generally within these walls that they seek to signalise themselves and to serve their fellow-creatures. Both their ambition and their public spirit, in a country like this, naturally take a political turn. It is then on men whose profession is literature, and whose private means are not ample, that you must rely for a supply of valuable books. Such men must be remunerated for their literary labour. And there are only two ways in which they can be remunerated. One of those ways is patronage; the other is copyright.

There have been times in which men of letters looked, not to the public, but to the government, or to a few great men, for the reward of their exertions. It was thus in the time of Maecenas and Pollio at Rome, of the Medici at Florence, of Louis the Fourteenth in France, of Lord Halifax and Lord Oxford in this country. Now, Sir, I well know that there are cases in which it is fit and graceful, nay, in which it is a sacred duty to reward the merits or to relieve the distresses of men of genius by the exercise of this species of liberality. But these cases are exceptions. I can conceive no system more fatal to the integrity and independence of literary men than one under which they should be taught to look for their daily bread to the favour of ministers and nobles. I can conceive no system more certain to turn those minds which are formed by nature to be the blessings and ornaments of our species into public scandals and pests.

We have, then, only one resource left. We must betake ourselves to copyright, be the inconveniences of copyright what they may. Those inconveniences, in truth, are neither few nor small. Copyright is monopoly, and produces all the effects which the general voice of mankind attributes to monopoly.... It is good that authors should be remunerated; and the least exceptionable way of remunerating them is by a monopoly. Yet monopoly is an evil. For the sake of the good we must submit to the evil; but the evil ought not to last a day longer than is necessary for the purpose of securing the good.

Now, I will not affirm that the existing law is perfect, that it exactly hits the point at which the monopoly ought to cease; but this I confidently say, that the existing law is very much nearer that point than the law proposed by my honourable and learned friend. For consider this; the evil effects of the monopoly are proportioned to the length of its duration. But the good effects for the sake of which we bear with the evil effects are by no means proportioned to the length of its duration. A monopoly of sixty years produces twice as much evil as a monopoly of thirty years, and thrice as much evil as a monopoly of twenty years. But it is by no means the fact that a posthumous monopoly of sixty years gives to an author thrice as much pleasure and thrice as strong a motive as a posthumous monopoly of twenty years. On the contrary, the difference is so small as to be hardly perceptible. We all know how faintly we are affected by the prospect of very distant advantages, even when they are advantages which we may reasonably hope that we shall ourselves enjoy. But an advantage that is to be enjoyed more than half a century after we are dead, by somebody, we know not by whom, perhaps by somebody unborn, by somebody utterly unconnected with us, is really no motive at all to action. . . .

The principle of copyright is this. It is a tax on readers for the purpose of giving a bounty to writers. The tax is an exceedingly bad one; it is a tax on one of the most innocent and most salutary of human pleasures; and never let us forget, that a tax on innocent pleasures is a premium on vicious pleasures. I admit, however, the necessity of giving a bounty to genius and learning. In order to give such a bounty, I willingly submit even to this severe and burdensome tax. Nay, I am ready to increase the tax, if it can be shown that by so doing I should proportionally increase the bounty. . . .

. . . [I]f the measure before us should pass, and should produce one-tenth part of the evil which it is calculated to produce, and which I fully expect it to produce, there will soon be a remedy, though of a very objectionable kind. Just as the absurd acts which prohibited the sale of game were virtually repealed by the poacher, just as many absurd revenue acts have been virtually repealed by the smuggler, so will this law be virtually repealed by piratical booksellers. At present the holder of copyright has the public feeling on his side. Those who invade copyright are regarded as knaves who take the bread out of the mouths of deserving men. Everybody is well pleased to see them restrained by the law, and compelled to refund their ill-gotten gains. No tradesman of good repute will have anything to do with such disgraceful transactions. Pass this law: and that feeling is at an end. Men very different from the present race of piratical booksellers will soon infringe this intolerable monopoly. Great masses of capital will be constantly employed in the violation of the law. Every art will be employed to evade legal pursuit; and the whole nation will be in the plot. On which side indeed should the public sympathy be when the question is whether some book as popular as *Robinson Crusoe*, or the *Pilgrim's Progress*, shall be in every cottage, or whether it shall be confined to the libraries of the rich for the advantage of the great-grandson of a bookseller who, a hundred years before, drove a hard bargain for the copyright with the author when in great distress? Remember too that, when once it ceases to be considered as wrong and discreditable to invade literary property, no person can say where the invasion will stop. The public seldom makes nice distinctions. The wholesome copyright which now exists will share in the disgrace and danger of the new copyright which you are about to create. And you will find that, in attempting to impose unreasonable restraints on the reprinting of the works of the dead, you have, to a great extent, annulled those restraints which now prevent men from pillaging and defrauding the living. . . .

Notes and Questions

1. Born in 1800 in England, and educated at Cambridge, Lord Thomas Babington Macaulay was a noted historian and member of parliament. He published numerous works, including *Lays of Ancient Rome* (1842), and *History of England* (5 vols. 1849–61). Macaulay died in 1859 and is buried in Westminster Abbey.

2. Some quotations from Macaulay's first speech in Parliament on the term of copyright may portray him as opposed to any increase in protection or extension of term. In fact, as Macaulay's second speech, delivered on April 6, 1842 reveals, Macaulay in fact supported a longer period of copyright, but urged basing the extension on a fixed term of years from publication rather than a term of years to follow the uncertain date of an author's death.

> . . . Sir, I have no objection to the principle of my noble friend's bill. Indeed, I had no objection to the principle of the bill of last year. I have long thought that the term of copyright ought to be extended. . . . My noble friend's bill is not at present a good bill; but it may be improved into a very good bill . . . We are equally desirous to extend the protection now enjoyed by writers. In what way it may be extended with most benefit to them and with least inconvenience to the public, is the question. . . .
>
> What I recommend is that the certain term, reckoned from the date of publication, shall be forty-two years instead of twenty-eight years. In this arrangement there is no uncertainty, no inequality. The advantage which I propose to give will be the same to every book. No work will have so long a copyright as my noble friend gives to some books, or so short a copyright as he gives to others. No copyright will last ninety years. No copyright will end in twenty-eight years. To every book published in the course of the last seventeen years of a writer's life I give a longer term of copyright than my noble friend gives; and I am confident that no person versed in literary history will deny this,—that in general the most valuable works of an author are published in the course of the last seventeen years of his life. . . . I have shown that the protection which he proposes to give to letters is unequal, and unequal in the worst way. I have shown that his plan is to give protection to books in inverse proportion to their merit. I shall move when we come to the third clause of the bill to omit the words "twenty-five years," and in a subsequent part of the same clause I shall move to substitute for the words "twenty-eight years" the words "forty-two years." . . . I feel the firmest conviction that my noble friend's bill, so amended, will confer a great boon on men of letters with the smallest possible inconvenience to the public.

Macaulay's position, however intuitively appealing, ultimately failed both at home and abroad. Although both the U.K. and the U.S. at one time calculated copyright based on a fixed term of years from publication, the international norm set out in the Berne Convention, to which both the U.K. and the U.S. adhere, is the life of the author plus fifty years. In 1993, the European Union (of which the U.K. is a part) added an additional twenty years to the copyright term. The U.S. followed the E.U. in 1998. The current copyright term is therefore ten years longer than the term that Macaulay successfully opposed in 1841.

3. For another expression of skepticism of the ability of patronage to foster authorship, see Paul Goldstein, *Copyright,* 38 J. Copyright Soc'y 109, 113 (1991) ("Consider for a moment the effects of patronage— whether from the Renaissance princes or the United States Congress' modern Medicis. Patronage supports only those authors whose creative efforts meet the patron's taste. Patronage depresses authorship by shutting the author off from the wider audience that he might hope to reach."). See also Neil Netanel, *Copyright and a Democratic Civil Society*, 106 Yale L. J. 283 (1996), excerpted below.

4. The closing paragraph of the excerpt of Lord Macaulay's 1841 address may seem extraordinarily prescient in light of the present ill-will toward copyright often expressed in the popular and academic press. Does overprotection breed contempt for copyright law in general? Consider the following:

> [It] is not that the aims of copyright are flawed. Or that authors should not be paid for their work. Or that music should be given away "for free." The point is that some of the ways in which we might protect authors will have unintended consequences for the cultural environment, much like DDT had for the natural environment. And just as criticism of DDT is not an endorsement of malaria or an attack on farmers, so, too, is criticism of one particular set of regulations protecting copyright not an endorsement of anarchy or an attack on authors. It is an environment of creativity that we seek, and we should be aware of our actions' effects on the environment.

> ... No doubt the technology of the Internet has had a dramatic effect on the ability of copyright owners to protect their content. But there should also be little doubt that when you add together the changes in copyright law overtime, plus the change in technology that the Internet is undergoing just now, the net effect of these changes will not only be that copyrighted work is effectively protected. Also, and generally missed, the net effect of this massive increase in protection will be devastating to the environment of creativity.

> In a line: To kill a gnat, we are spraying DDT with consequences for free culture that will be far more devastating than that this gnat will be lost.

Lawrence Lessig, FREE CULTURE: HOW BIG MEDIA USES TECHNOLOGY AND THE LAW TO LOCK DOWN CULTURE AND CONTROL CREATIVITY 129–30 (2004) (developing theme proposed by Professor James Boyle). Later in his book, Professor Lessig wields different metaphors:

> Think about the amazing things your kid could do or make with digital technology—the film, the music, the Web page, the blog. Or think about the amazing things your community could facilitate with digital technology—a wiki, a barn raising, activism to change something. Think about all those creative things, and then imagine cold molasses poured onto the machines. This is what any regime that requires permission produces. . . . [T]his is the reality of Brezhnev's Russia.

LESSIG, supra, at 305. See also, James Boyle, *Forward: The Opposite of Property?* 66 Law & Contemp. Probs. 1, 17 (2003) "intellectual property is a layer of shellac over expressive content, sealing it off and separating the world into active artists (or content companies) on one side and passive consumers on the other"). Professor James Boyle has further compared changes in patent, copyright, trademark, and database protection to the English "enclosure movement" that, beginning in the fifteenth century, converted common land to private property for the wealthy:

> [A] rapacious, state-aided "privatization," a conversion into private property of something that had formerly been common property, or, perhaps, had been outside of the property system altogether . . .
>
> We are in the middle of a second enclosure movement. It sounds grandiloquent to call it "the enclosure of the intangible commons of the mind," but in a very real sense that is just what it is. True, the new state created property rights may be "intellectual" rather than "real," but once again things that were formerly thought of as either common property or uncommodifiable are being covered with new, or newly extended, property rights.

James Boyle, *The Second Enclosure Movement and the Construction of the Public Domain*, 66 Law & Contemp. Probs. 33, 34, 37–38 (2003). When popular rhetoric pairs copyright owners with biological polluters, Brezhnev's Russia, industrial fixatives, and rapacious enclosers, these metaphors for the current regime copyright bear out Macaulay's predictions. See Robert S. Boynton, *The Tyranny of Copyright?*, N.Y. Times, Jan. 25, 2004 (Magazine), § 6 at 40 (describing advent of "Copy Left" a "protest" movement lacking "coherent political ideology" but sharing the belief that "[w]hile the American copyright system was designed to encourage innovation, it is now, they contend, being used to squelch it"). Macaulay also foresaw that the public opprobrium that follows overprotection could provoke civil disobedience as well. Should this concern for public acceptance restrain policy-makers and legislators when technology poses new challenges? See infra, Jessica Litman, *Copyright Non–Compliance (or Why We Can't 'Just Say Yes' to Licensing)*, 29 N.Y.U.J. Int'l L. & Pol. 237 (1997), excerpted infra at page 425.

5. From the Statute of Anne to the present, duration of copyright term has always generated controversy. For an account of *Donaldson v. Becket* and the Stationers' Guild failed litigation strategy to secure a ruling on perpetual duration, see Paul Goldstein, COPYRIGHT'S HIGHWAY 46–51 (1994), excerpted supra. In France, Victor Hugo unsuccessfully advocated a *domaine public payant* that would have terminated the right to control the work's exploitation at the author's death but would also have granted the author's heirs a perpetual right to compensation. See Victor Hugo, *Address to Congrès littéraire international de Paris 1878*, 216–18 (Société des Gens de Lettres de France, 1879). In a recent proposed variation on perpetual duration, Professor William Landes and Judge Richard Posner proposed a relatively short initial term, followed by a right of indefinitely renewable terms. William M. Landes & Richard A. Posner, *Indefinitely Renewable Copyright*, 70 U. Chi. L. Rev. 471 (2003). At the opposite extreme, Professor Lessig has proposed a cap of seventy five years, renewable in five year increments; authors who fail to renew would neither control works fallen into the public domain nor receive compensation. Lawrence Lessig, THE FUTURE OF IDEAS 251–52 (2001). Other scholars have suggested making older works more susceptible to fair use in order to alleviate the ill effects of overly long copyrights. Joseph Liu, *Copyright and Time: A Proposal*, 101 Mich. L. Rev. 409 (2002); Justin Hughes, *Fair Use Across Time*, 50 UCLA L. Rev. 775 (2003).

Copyright and a Democratic Civil Society
NEIL WEINSTOCK NETANEL*

IV. The Democratic Paradigm

Copyright plays a central role in promoting public education and expressive diversity. But both the neoclassicist approach, with its treatment of creative expression as a "vendible commodity," and the minimalist critics' approach, with its vitiation of the copyright incentive, threaten to diminish that role. This Part lays the foundations for an alternative approach, one that better comports with copyright's appellation as an "engine of free expression." It offers a theoretical framework that seeks to articulate more precisely and more directly than have other commentators the ways in which copyright supports a democratic civil society. The democratic paradigm is hostile neither to economic analysis nor to neoclassicist insights regarding the operation of copyright markets. But the democratic paradigm makes clear that while copyright may operate in the market, copyright's fundamental goals are not of the market. In providing a theoretical framework for a strong, but limited copyright, the democratic paradigm aims to reinvigorate copyright's role in the "preservation of a free Constitution." . . .

A. Democratic Governance and Civil Society

The emergence of democratic institutions in Eastern Europe, coupled with our acute uncertainty regarding the continued vitality and viability of our own, has brought renewed attention to the centuries old concept of "civil society." Civil society is the sphere of voluntary,

* 106 YALE L. J. 283, 341–44, 347, 352–64 (1996).

nongovernmental association in which individuals determine their shared purposes and norms. It may include unions, churches, political and social movements, civic and neighborhood associations, schools of thought, educational institutions, and certain forms of economic organization. It incorporates formal and informal organizations, group identities and the shared purposes, histories, and discursive norms that hold groups together. As such, civil society also comprises the realm of public communication and discourse. This realm, which encompasses numerous forms of cultural expression, the mass media, and, increasingly, the proliferating welter of Internet user groups, bulletin boards, and Web sites, serves both as a fount of organizational life and as an independent manifestation of civic association, the space in which political, social, and aesthetic norms are debated and determined.

Contemporary theorists see a robust, pluralist civil society as a necessary, proactive foundation for democratic governance in a complex modern state. Civil society bolsters representative democracy in a number of ways. First, a robust, participatory, and pluralist civil society is the wellspring of what Robert Dahl, building on Alexis de Tocqueville's observations of antebellum America, has called a "democratic culture," a belief in and understanding of the democratic process that becomes embedded in the minds, habits, and character of a people. A democratic order depends upon a domain in which citizens develop the independent spirit, self-direction, social responsibility, discursive skill, political awareness, and mutual recognition. A state whose citizenry has not internalized these skills and values will rule through fiat and obedience, without any sense, so vital to our understanding of democracy, that its laws and social norms originate in the commitments of a self-governing polity.

. . .

C.   Copyright and a Democratic Civil Society

Copyright is a limited proprietary entitlement through which the state deliberately and selectively employs market institutions to support a democratic civil society. Copyright law provides this support in two fundamental ways. First, through its production function, copyright encourages creative expression on a wide array of political, social, and aesthetic issues. The activity of creating and communicating such expression and the expression itself constitute vital components of a democratic civil society. Second, through its structural function, copyright serves to further the democratic character of public discourse. By according authors and their assigns a proprietary entitlement, copyright fosters the development of an independent sector for the creation and dissemination of original expression, a sector composed of creators and publishers who earn financial support for their activities by reaching paying audiences rather than by depending on state or elite largess. No less importantly, by limiting the scope of that proprietary entitlement, copyright constrains owner control over expression, seeking to preserve rich possibilities for critical exchange and diverse reformulation of existing works. . . .

2. Copyright's Structural Function

In addition to encouraging the production and dissemination of much of the expressive underpinning of civil society, copyright promotes the democratic character of public discourse. Copyright serves this end in two basic ways: It undergirds a sector of expressive activity that is independent from state and elite patronage and it sets limits on private control of creative expression.

a. An Independent Expressive Sector

The public communication of fixed original expression will support a democratic civil society only if such expression is autonomous and diverse. A regime in which government administrators exert broad control over the content and dissemination of tangible expression will be unlikely to maintain viable civil institutions. A civil society in which private elites exert such control will be characterized by hierarchical domination, not democratic participation.

Copyright is vital to maintaining the democratic character of public discourse in civil society. By supporting a market-based sector of authors and publishers, copyright achieves considerable independence from government administrators and private patrons who would otherwise meddle in expressive content. Though not dispositive, it will be helpful, first, to anchor this claim in the early historical development of modern copyright. In so doing, I hope to underscore both the print market's instrumental role in the development of a sphere of democratic public discourse and the Framers' understanding of that role in providing for federal copyright protection. I then discuss copyright's continuing part in promoting expressive plurality in the dawn of digitization, including the problem of market-generated hierarchical domination of public discourse.

Prior to the first modern copyright statutes in the eighteenth century, writers and artists were heavily dependent on royal, feudal, and church patronage for their livelihoods. This dependency undermined expressive autonomy and thwarted the development of a vital, freethinking intelligentsia. As Voltaire described it: "Every philosopher at court becomes as much a slave as the first official of the crown."

The patronage system also served to embed public discourse firmly within the hierarchical order of medieval and early modern Europe. During the Middle Ages, literature and art were commonly commissioned and controlled for purposes of public mystification. They were designed to impress upon their audience the dominant status of the patron, whether it be king, noble, or church. Later, within the framework of late Renaissance neoclassicism, the patronage system fostered a view of the arts as a "gentleman's calling," tailored to aristocratic tastes and far removed from common social experience and creative sensibility.

It was not until the eighteenth century that there emerged a comprehensive sphere of public communication that was both independent of monarchy, aristocracy, and church, and capable of challenging their political and social dominance. That sphere was largely made up of printed materials—newspapers, pamphlets, and books—that received their primary financial support not from official patronage, but from readers and audiences. Freed from capricious and overbearing patrons, writers enjoyed a new, broad latitude to choose their own subject matter and find their own voice. The rapidly expanding reading public gradually shook off the influence of those who had used their control of art and literature to reinforce their positions of power. As it moved from patronage to market support, this sphere of communicative exchange generated, for the first time, a sense of "public opinion," the set of beliefs and norms elaborated in debate and discussion that citizens recognize as something they hold in common.

The notion of public opinion, mediated by printed materials and emerging from autonomous citizen interaction outside of official, hierarchical organs, was central to early understandings of democratic civil society. It emerged with particular force in early eighteenth-century America, where this print-mediated public space, outside any established political structure, defined the goals of the people and called government officials to account for deviating from them. In so doing, it centered the ultimate power of democratic rule in the autonomous institutions of civil society, which would direct and maintain a vigilant watch on elected representatives. Within democratic theory, it shifted the locus of citizen deliberation from the sovereign assembly of classical republicanism to the rough and tumble of the pen and the press.

Modern copyright arose with and contributed to the emergence of this democratic, print-mediated public square. Prior to the enactment of the Statute of Anne of 1710, the printing privileges that the Crown granted to members of the London Stationers Company had served as an instrument of centralized control and censorship. With the expiration of the notorious Licensing Act and the advent of modern copyright, however, authors gained a limited exclusive right to print copies of their works, with the express purpose of encouraging learning through the widespread dissemination of original expression. For the first time, authors could hope to earn their bread from the sale of their work to the public, and to do so through independent publishers who stood apart from the censorial arm of the state and the intermeddling of aristocratic and ecclesiastic patrons. As Oliver Goldsmith declared in 1760: "[Writers] have now no other patrons but the public, and the public collectively considered, is a good and a generous master."

The emergence of a broad market in printed expression encouraged authors to challenge civic and religious authority, in part because rebelliousness and irreverence attracted paying readers. It also greatly enhanced print's democratic character and democratizing influence. The noncommercial literature of letters and political pamphlets in colonial America was ordinarily addressed to a small, educated elite and was composed in a florid style punctuated with classical references that had meaning only for a few. But the establishment of markets for literary works encouraged authors to write for a broader audience. Thus, the unprecedented best-seller success of Thomas Paine's pamphlet Common Sense in 1776 was due, in Paine's own estimation, in large part to his calculated effort to reach the common republican reader by using "language as plain as the alphabet" and by replacing classical references with Biblical references. This "descent" of literature "from the closets of philosophers, and the shelves of polite scholars" to the community at large, while a source of despair for some, was generally viewed as a necessary predicate for representative democracy, the health of which was seen to depend on an educated and informed citizenry.

When the Framers drafted the Copyright Clause and the Copyright Act of 1790, they took as self-evident that the diffusion of knowledge and exchange of view through a market for printed matter was a pillar of public liberty. They were fully immersed in a culture that identified print with republican government and resistance to tyranny. The Framers believed that a copyright-supported national market for authors' writings was vital to maintaining public vigilance against government encroachment, as well as fostering a democratic culture. As President Washington declaimed in his address to Congress in support of the first federal copyright statute, the promotion of science and literature would help to secure a

> free constitution ... by convincing those who are entrusted with public administration that every valuable end of government is best answered by the enlightened confidence of the public; and by teaching the people themselves to know and value their own rights; to discern and provide against invasions of them; to distinguish between oppression and the necessary exercise of lawful authority.

Part and parcel of this vision was an understanding that democratic governance requires not simply the diffusion of knowledge per se, but also an autonomous sphere of print-mediated citizen deliberation and public education. The Framers well understood the dangers of patronage. They had seen first hand the transformation of the American print industry as it emerged, in the mid-eighteenth century, from its servile dependency on colonial government and church largess to become, with the support of a broad-based readership, a powerful and highly combative force in public affairs. It was only by maintaining their fiscal independence that authors and publishers could continue to guard public liberty. For the Framers, therefore, copyright's importance lay in its structural, as well as production, function. By underwriting a flourishing national market in authors' writings, copyright would help to secure authors' and printers' freedom from the corruptive influence of state, church, and aristocratic patronage.

The Framers' basic premises remain at the heart of copyright today. Without legal protection against ruinous copying, authors and publishers would be unduly dependent on state or private beneficence, with its attendant vitiation of critical autonomy and expressive diversity. While circumscribed government subsidies for the creation and dissemination of creative expression may be a valuable, democracy-enhancing measure of a modern democratic state, the widespread, systematic reliance of authors and publishers on such subsidies would ultimately bring the sphere of public communication within the web of state bureaucracy, stifling free expression. Alternatively, in a world with neither copyright nor massive state subsidy, authors would likely rely heavily on private patronage, forcing them to cater to the tastes, interests, and political agenda of the wealthy, rather than seeking a broader, more varied consumer audience. Copyright thus serves to support a robust, pluralist, and independent sector devoted to the creation and dissemination of works of authorship. As such, copyright constitutes an integral part of a system of collective self-rule in which the norms that permeate our social relations and undergird state policy are determined in the space of broad-based citizen debate, rather than by government or private fiat.

This is not to say that the Framers' understandings are directly applicable to late twentieth-century political, cultural, and economic conditions. Our public discourse is far more dissonant and eclectic than that envisioned by the Framers. The political elite of the early Republic abhorred expressions of ideological faction and generally disdained fiction and "light" entertainment. Such works, however, form a major part of our copyright-supported discursive universe. From our perspective, the Framers' watchdog view of literature and the press also seems somewhat simplistic. Today's media conglomerates have attained an agenda-setting power that rivals that of state officials and, in the view of some commentators, undermines the democratic character of public discourse by skewing it towards those with the financial wherewithal to obtain access or buy advertised products.

But this certain disjunction between Framers' suppositions and current conditions in no way contradicts my basic premise that copyright, at its core, continues to underwrite an independent expressive sector that is critical to democratic governance. With regard to the nature and content of public discourse, as the civil society model attests, our conception of democratic governance has come to accept, and indeed celebrate, a diversity of outlook and interest that comports fully with the cacophonous outpouring of expression that makes up our symbolic realm. As discussed above, we have also come to appreciate the sociopolitical valency of much expression that is designed largely for audience enjoyment and appeal. It must be remembered, moreover, that even during what some contemporary commentators regard as the apex of eighteenth-century republican deliberation, editors routinely pledged to make their newspapers "entertaining" as well as "useful." Although we must recognize the vital importance of considered deliberation on issues of public policy, many copyright-protected works of so-called "pure" art, fiction, and entertainment also make a substantial contribution to the "democratic culture" that is central to a viable system of representative democracy. Accordingly, while our copyright market may encompass a wealth and diversity of expression not contemplated by the Framers, the basic principle is the same: To systematically subject authors' expression to the stifling grip of patronage would be inimical to a "free Constitution."

The problems of media concentration and market-based hierarchy are more troublesome, but these, too, do not belie the importance of copyright's structural function for a democratic civil society. My claim is not that copyright, by itself, constitutes a sufficient condition for expressive pluralism and diversity. Indeed, the democratic character of public discourse may well depend upon some measure of state subsidy and regulation to disseminate information and give a voice to persons and views that might otherwise receive insufficient attention in an unregulated media market. But even to the extent that other forms of state involvement may be necessary and desirable, copyright remains a vital component of our system of free expression. Most basically, whatever the limitations of the market for cultivating expressive diversity, an all-encompassing state-supported regime would ultimately be far worse. Even in a representative democracy, massive state involvement would undoubtedly present a serious impediment to expressive autonomy and freedom of information. Indeed, even limited state intervention may be used to further government officials' narrowly conceived political agenda and institutional goals—and given the ubiquity of government in modern life, the dangers of government indoctrination, favoritism, and suppression are certainly no less today than at copyright's birth. Accordingly, even if some state intervention is a necessary counterweight to market-based hierarchy, a strong, self-reliant expressive sector whose roots are outside the state still constitutes an indispensable ingredient of representative democracy. It is that expressive sector—both a watchdog and an independent, nongovernmental site for collective self-rule—that copyright serves to support.

A copyright-supported market would also enhance expressive pluralism and diversity to a greater extent than an expressive sector that relied heavily on corporate patronage. Like their aristocratic and ecclesiastic antecedents, corporate patrons are notorious for supporting expression that furthers their own objectives at the expense of artistic autonomy and diversity. As numerous studies have concluded, corporations regularly eschew avant-garde or controversial expression, tending rather to support cultural production that reflects mainstream interests and tastes, as befits a vehicle of public relations. Indeed, given their inherent conservatism, corporate patrons prefer to support art that has already been evaluated and approved for funding by the federal government, thus augmenting the danger of an official, government-established art that leaves little room for nonconforming views. . . .

b. Imposition of Limits

A copyright constructed in accordance with the democratic paradigm would enhance expressive pluralism and diversity, not only by supporting an independent expressive sector, but also by imposing limits on the proprietary control over cultural works. That imposition of limits must be seen as a vital and integral part of copyright's structural function. No less than substituting paying audiences for patrons and service vendors, it is an important means by which the state may diversify communicative power structures without undue involvement in expressive content.

. . .

Importantly, under the democratic paradigm this diversification aspect of copyright's structural function implements the view that the public domain is no less vital to a democratic civil society than is copyright's protection of original expression. The limits that copyright law imposes on copyright owner prerogatives are thus not simply a neutral ending point where copyright protection ends and some other proprietary right may begin. Rather, they are an affirmative manifestation of copyright's democracy-enhancing principles. They are a statement that, where necessary to further those principles, ideas and expression should be free for all to use.

Under the democratic paradigm, therefore, the limits to copyright's duration and scope represent the outer bounds not only of copyright protection, but also of other forms of private control over publicly disseminated expression. Copyright should serve to circumscribe the propertization of publicly disseminated expression, even as it grants a limited monopoly over the use of expression. . . .

3. Summary

Copyright, in sum, is a state measure that uses market institutions to enhance the democratic character of civil society. Copyright law accords a limited proprietary entitlement that underwrites democratic culture and citizenship in three ways. First, it promotes the creation and distribution of information and educational resources. In supporting a market for creative expression, copyright aims to increase and make widely available the store of knowledge required for effective citizenship and civic association. Second, it enhances civil society's participatory character. Through economic incentives and a careful balance between exclusivity and access, copyright seeks to foster widespread citizen participation in public deliberation. Third, it supports the plurality, independence, and vitality of civil society's communicative sphere. By according authors a carefully tailored proprietary entitlement, copyright frees them from reliance on patronage and cultural hierarchy, while opposing market-based hierarchy and encouraging transformative uses of existing works. In that way copyright law hopes to generate diverse and autonomous contributions to our common discourse.

Significantly, the neoclassicist economic view of creative expression as a commodity and of copyright as a mechanism to further allocative efficiency, fails to account for copyright's role in democratic governance. The activities and transactions that copyright encourages are in, but not of, the market. Copyright's fundamental purpose is to underwrite political competency, with allocative efficiency a secondary consideration. Copyright employs a quasi-proprietary regime to achieve its constitutive goals, but the exclusive rights that copyright law accords are meant to be defined and delimited as required to further copyright's democratic purpose. Too thin a copyright would diminish the incentive for autonomous creative contribution, but a copyright of bloated scope, and one that would treat creative expression as simply another commodity, would stifle expressive diversity and undermine copyright's potential for furthering citizen participation in democratic self-rule.

Notes and Questions

1. Neil Netanel is a professor of law at U.C.L.A. Before that, he taught law at the University of Texas. Born in 1954, Professor Netanel earned his J.D. from University of California, Berkeley, in 1980, and his JSD from Stanford in 1998.

2. Both Lord Macaulay and Professor Netanel reject a patronage-based model of author remuneration, but with different emphases. While Lord Macaulay focuses on the deleterious influence of patronage on authors ("I can conceive no system more fatal to the integrity and independence of literary men than one under which they should be taught to look for their daily bread to the favour of ministers and nobles."). Professor Netanel draws the consequences of compromised authorship to admonish against patronage's propensity to narrow the range of works available to the polity.

3. What is the difference between government patronage and "some measure of state subsidy and regulation to disseminate information and give a voice to persons and views that might otherwise receive insufficient attention in an unregulated media market"?

4. The neoclassicist economic view that Professor Netanel deplores is characteristically expressed in the following excerpt.

An Economic Analysis of Copyright
WILLIAM M. LANDES & RICHARD A. POSNER*

. . . A distinguishing characteristic of intellectual property is its "public good" aspect. While the cost of creating a work subject to copyright protection—for example, a book, movie, song, ballet, lithograph, map, business directory, or computer software program—is often high, the cost of reproducing the work, whether by the creator or by those to whom he has made it available, is often low. And once copies are available to others, it is often inexpensive for these users to make additional copies. If the copies made by the creator of the work are priced at or close to marginal cost, others may be discouraged from making copies, but the creator's total revenues may not be sufficient to cover the cost of creating the work. Copyright protection—the right of the copyright's owner to prevent others from making copies—trades off the costs of limiting access to a work against the benefits of providing the incentives to create the work in the first place. Striking the correct balance between access and incentives is the central problem in copyright law. For copyright law to promote economic efficiency, its principal legal doctrines must, at least approximately, maximize the benefits from creating additional works minus both the losses from limiting access and the costs of administering copyright protection. . . .

I.   THE BASIC ECONOMICS OF COPYRIGHT

A.   *Number of Works as a Function of Copyright and Other Factors*

1.   General Considerations

The cost of producing a book or other copyrightable work (we start by talking just about books and later branch out to other forms of expression) has two components. The first is the cost of creating the work. We assume that it does not vary with the number of copies produced or sold, since it consists primarily of the author's time and effort plus the cost to the publisher of soliciting and editing the manuscript and setting it in type. Consistent with copyright usage we call the sum of these costs the "cost of expression."

* 18 J. LEGAL STUD. 325, 325–333 (1989).

To simplify the analysis, we ignore any distinction between costs incurred by authors and by publishers, and therefore use the term "author" (or "creator") to mean both author and publisher. . . .

The second component of the cost of producing a work increases with the number of copies produced, for it is the cost of printing, binding, and distributing individual copies. The cost of expression does not enter into the making of copies because, once the work is created, the author's efforts can be incorporated into another copy virtually without cost.

For a new work to be created, the expected return—typically, and we shall assume exclusively, from the sales of copies—must exceed the expected cost. . . . Since the decision to create the work must be made before the demand for copies is known, the work will be created only if the difference between expected revenues and the cost of making copies equals or exceeds the cost of expression. . . .

This description of the market for copies and the number of works created assumes the existence of copyright protection. In its absence anyone can buy a copy of the book when it first appears and make and sell copies of it. The market price of the book will eventually be bid down to the marginal cost of copying, with the unfortunate result that the book probably will not be produced in the first place, because the author and publisher will not be able to recover their costs of creating the work. The problem is magnified by the fact that the author's cost of creating the work, and many publishing costs (for example, editing costs), are incurred before it is known what the demand for the work will be. Uncertainty about demand is a particularly serious problem with respect to artistic works, such as books, plays, movies, and recordings. Even with copyright protection, sales may be insufficient to cover the cost of expression and may not even cover the variable cost of making copies. Thus, the difference between the price and marginal cost of the successful work must not only cover the cost of expression but also compensate for the risk of failure. If a copier can defer making copies until he knows whether the work is a success, the potential gains from free riding on expression will be even greater, because the difference between the price and marginal cost of the original work will rise to compensate for the uncertainty of demand, thus creating a bigger profit potential for copies. So uncertainty generates an additional disincentive to create works in the absence of copyright protection.

Practical obstacles limit copying the original works of others even in the absence of any copyright protection. But these obstacles, while serious in some cases, can easily be exaggerated. When fully analyzed, they do not make a persuasive case for eliminating copyright protection.

1. *The copy may be of inferior quality, and hence not a perfect substitute for the original.* In the case of books and other printed matter, the copier may not be able to match the quality of paper or binding of the original or the crispness of the printing, and there may be errors in transcription. None of these is an important impediment to good copies any longer, but in the case of works of art—such as a painting by a famous artist—a copy, however accurate, may be such a poor substitute

in the market that it will have no negative effects on the price of the artist's work. Indeed, the copy may have a positive effect on that price, by serving as advertising for his works. On the other hand, it may also deprive him of income from selling derivative works—the copies of his paintings—himself. (More on derivative works shortly.) To generalize, when either the cost of making equivalent copies is higher for the copier than for the creator or the copier's product is a poor substitute for the original, the originator will be able to charge a price greater than his marginal cost, even without legal protection. And obviously, the greater the difference in the costs of making copies and in the quality of copies between creator and copier (assuming the latter's cost is higher or quality lower), the less need there is for copyright protection.

2. *Copying may involve some original expression—as when the copy is not a literal copy but involves paraphrasing, deletions, marginal notes, and so on—and so a positive cost of expression.* The copier may incur fixed costs as well, for example costs of rekeying the words from the copy he bought or of photographing them. Still, we would expect the copier's average cost to be lower than the creator's because it will not include the author's time or the cost of soliciting and editing the original manuscript. Nevertheless, when the copier cannot take a complete free ride on the creator's investment in expression and his other fixed costs, the need for copyright protection is reduced....

3. *Copying takes time, so there will be an interval during which the original publisher will not face competition.* This point, which is related to the first because generally the cost of production is inverse to time, has two implications for the analysis of copyright law. First, because modern technology has reduced the time it takes to make copies as well as enabled more perfect copies to be made at low cost, the need for copyright protection has increased over time. Second, for works that are faddish—where demand is initially strong but falls sharply after a brief period—copyright protection may not be as necessary in order to give the creator of the work a fully compensatory return.

4. *There are contractual alternatives to copyright protection for limiting copying.* One is licensing the original work on condition that the licensee not make copies of it or disclose it to others in a way that would enable them to make copies. But contractual prohibitions on copying may, like trade secrets, be costly to enforce and feasible only if there are few licensees. Where widespread distribution is necessary to generate an adequate return to the author or where the work is resold or publicly performed, contractual prohibitions may not prevent widespread copying. Thus, the greater the potential market for a work, the greater the need for copyright protection. The development of radio, television, and the phonograph has expanded the market for copies and thereby increased the value of copyright protection.

5. *Since a copier normally must have access to a copy in order to make copies, the creator may be able to capture some of the value of copies made by charging a high price for the copies he makes and sells.* For example, a publisher of academic journals may be able to capture part of the value that individuals obtain from copying articles by charging a

higher price for the journal—especially to libraries; or a record company may be able to charge a higher price because of home taping. Although this possibility limits the need for copyright protection, it does not eliminate it. If one can make many copies of the first copy, and many copies of subsequent copies, the price of copies will be driven down to marginal cost and the creator will not be able to charge a sufficiently higher price for his copy to capture its value in allowing others to make more copies; no one (except the first copier and the most impatient readers) will buy from him rather than from a copier.

6. *Many authors derive substantial benefits from publication that are over and beyond any royalties.* This is true not only in terms of prestige and other nonpecuniary income but also pecuniary income in such forms as a higher salary for a professor who publishes than for one who does not, or greater consulting income. Publishing is an effective method of self-advertisement and self-promotion. The norms against plagiarism (that is, against copying without giving the author credit) reinforce the conferral of prestige by publishing; to the extent that those norms are effective, they ensure that the author will obtain recognition, if not always royalties, from the works he publishes.

Such points have convinced some students of copyright law that there is no need for copyright protection. Legal rights are costly to enforce—rights in intangibles especially so—and the costs may outweigh the social gains in particular settings. Perhaps copyright in books is one of them. After all, the first copyright law in England dates from 1710 (and gave much less protection than modern copyright law), yet publishing had flourished for hundreds of years in England despite censorship and widespread illiteracy. The point is a little misleading, however, In the old days, the costs of making copies were a higher fraction of total cost than they are today, so the problem of appropriability was less acute. Also, there were alternative institutions for internalizing the benefits of expression. And before freedom of expression became generally applauded, publishing was often believed to impose negative externalities—so there was less, sometimes no, desire to encourage it. Finally, while it may be difficult to determine whether, on balance, copyright is a good thing, it is easy to note particular distortions that a copyright law corrects. Without copyright protection, authors, publishers, and copiers would have inefficient incentives with regard to the timing of various decisions. Publishers, to lengthen their head start, would have a disincentive to engage in prepublication advertising and even to announce publication dates in advance, and copiers would have an incentive to install excessively speedy production lines. There would be increased incentives to create faddish, ephemeral, and otherwise transitory works because the gains from being first in the market for such works would be likely to exceed the losses from absence of copyright protection. There would be a shift toward the production of works that are difficult to copy; authors would be more likely to circulate their works privately rather than widely, to lessen the risk of copying; and contractual restrictions on copying would multiply.

A neglected consideration—one that shows not that copyright protection may be unnecessary but that beyond some level copyright protection may actually be counterproductive by raising the cost of expression—will play an important role both in our model and in our efforts to explain the salient features of copyright law. Creating a new work typically involves borrowing or building on material from a prior body of works, as well as adding original expression to it. A new work of fiction, for example, will contain the author's expressive contribution but also characters, situations, plot details, and so on, invented by previous authors. Similarly, a new work of music may borrow tempo changes and chord progressions from earlier works. The less extensive copyright protection is, the more an author, composer, or other creator can borrow from previous works without infringing copyright and the lower, therefore, the costs of creating a new work. Of course, even if copyright protection effectively prevented all unauthorized copying from a copyrighted work, authors would still copy. But they would copy works whose copyright protection had run out, or they would disguise their copying, engage in costly searches to avoid copying protected works, or incur licensing and other transaction costs to obtain permission to copy such works. The effect would be to raise the cost of creating new works—the cost of expression, broadly defined—and thus, paradoxically, perhaps lower the number of works created.

Copyright holders might, therefore, find it in their self-interest, ex ante, to limit copyright protection. To the extent that a later author is free to borrow material from an earlier one, the later author's cost of expression is reduced; and, from an ex ante viewpoint, every author is both an earlier author from whom a later author might want to borrow material and the later author himself. In the former role, he desires maximum copyright protection for works he creates; in the latter, he prefers minimum protection for works created earlier by others. In principle, there is a level of copyright protection that balances these two competing interests optimally—although notice that the first generation of authors, having no one to borrow from, will have less incentive to strike the optimal balance than later ones. We shall see in Section II that various doctrines of copyright law, such as the distinction between idea and expression and the fair use doctrine, can be understood as attempts to promote economic efficiency by balancing the effect of greater copyright protection—in encouraging the creation of new works by reducing copying—against the effect of less protection—in encouraging the creation of new works by reducing the cost of creating them....

Notes and Questions

1. William Landes is the Clifton R. Musser Professor of Law and Economics at the University of Chicago Law School. Born in 1939, Dr. Landes received his Ph.D. in Economics from Columbia University in 1966. Before joining the law faculty of the University of Chicago, he taught in the Economics Departments of Stanford University, Columbia University, the Graduate Center of the City University of New York, and The University of Chicago.

Judge Richard Posner, also born in 1939, received his LL.B from Harvard Law School in 1962. He sits on the Seventh Circuit U.S. Court of Appeals, where he served as Chief Judge from 1993–2000. Judge Posner is also a Senior Lecturer-in-Law at the University of Chicago Law School, where, before going on the federal bench, he was a Professor of Law. He is the author of numerous books on law and economics.

2. Professor Landes and Judge Posner suggest that the purpose of copyright law is to "promote economic efficiency." Is this rationale for copyright protection complete? Is the analysis better suited to corporate rather than to individual copyright holders? Is a high level of copyright protection likely to serve as a greater incentive to a motion picture company's decision to aggregate the capital resources to create audiovisual works than to an author's determination to write a novel that might someday be adapted for film? What considerations might make this comparison spurious?

3. Another rationale for copyright protection stresses a "quid pro quo" between authors and society: authors receive a limited monopoly over the exploitation of their works, in return for which they create works which will ultimately enrich the public domain. For example, recall Professor Patterson's contention that copyright "is an encroachment on the public domain and can be justified only if it provides the public with some form of compensation. The public can be compensated most effectively by making the author's efforts accessible. Copyright, therefore, can be viewed as being in the nature of a bargain and sale."

Quid pro quo rationales invite assessment of the fairness of the exchange: is the public getting enough "quo" for the author's "quid"? Consider the following contention, advanced in connection with the 1998 20-year extension of the copyright term:

> The public gets no new quid pro quo from extending copyright protection for works already created. Removing these works from the public domain works a huge uncompensated wealth transfer from ordinary citizens to Disney, Time Warner and other holders, corporate and individual, of preexisting copyrighted material. It also produces a net social loss by restricting overall level use of this material.

Richard A. Epstein, *Congress's Copyright Giveaway*, Wall St. J., Dec. 21, 1998, at A19 (criticizing the 1998 Copyright Term Extension Act for giving billions of dollars to lobbyists by extending the copyright term at the expense of the public domain bargain of a limited monopoly). Professor William Landes and Judge Richard Posner also question term extensions:

> A fundamental task of copyright law viewed economically is to determine the terms of this hypothetical contract, or in other words to strike the optimal balance between the effect of copyright protection in encouraging the creation of new works by reducing copying and its effect in discouraging the creation of new works by raising the cost of creating them.

> A further complication should be noted. Although in the short run broadening copyright protection shrinks the public domain, in the long run it may expand it. To the extent that broader protection elicits more expressive works by increasing their

profitability, then, given the limited duration of the copyright term, the additional works, though copyrighted, will become a part of the public domain when their copyright term expires. The future public domain is nourished by copyright. However, this consideration has only limited significance when the copyright term is very long, as it is by virtue of the Copyright Act of 1976 and the further lengthening of the term by the Sonny Bono Copyright Term Extension Act.... Because of discounting to present value, extensions of copyright term beyond twenty or twenty-five years have little incentive effect (and thus do not bring forth a significant number of additional expressive works to enrich the public domain when the copyright on those works expires), but greatly diminish the size of the public domain, especially since all extensions of the copyright term have been applied to existing as well as new works.

William M. Landes & Richard A. Posner, THE ECONOMIC STRUCTURE OF INTELLECTUAL PROPERTY LAW 69–70 (2003). The same authors, however, have also proposed "indefinitely renewable" copyrights, see Notes and Questions (5) supra, page 315. Can you reconcile this proposal with the observation that, beyond 25 years, copyright does not generate enough "quo" for the lengthy "quid"?

4. While economic justifications for intellectual property protection typically are presented "ex ante" (the availability of protection provides the incentive to create new works), "ex post" justifications may also be advanced to support continued investment in disseminating or maintaining already-created works. While "ex post" arguments may be historically justified—after all, until the 1976 Act, federal copyright applied essentially only to already-created works, because it did not attach until publication (with notice)—they have also drawn recent fire. Consider the following observations by Professor Lemley on two kinds of "ex post" justifications:

> One form of the new justifications argues that intellectual property protection is necessary to encourage the intellectual property owner to make some further investment in the improvement, maintenance, or commercialization of the product. Another strand argues that such protection is necessary to prevent a sort of "tragedy of the commons" in which the new idea will be overused ...

> The new ex post justifications ... endorse a greater and perhaps unlimited duration and scope of intellectual property rights....

> While the two arguments are somewhat different, both rely on a misleading appeal to a well-established but inapplicable principle, both depend on unproven (or sometimes disproven) empirical claims, and both are in the end strikingly anti-market ... both arguments reflect a fundamental misunderstanding of the economics of private ordering.

Mark A. Lemley, *Ex Ante versus Ex Post Justifications for Intellectual Property*, 71 U. Chi. L. Rev. 129, 130–32 (2004).

5.   Consider yet another review of the justifications for copyright:

> Let us suppose that "in the beginning was the Reader." And the Reader, in a Pirandello-esque flash of insight, went in search of an Author, for the Reader realized that without an Author, there could be no Readers. But when the Reader met an Author, the Author, anticipating Dr. Johnson, scowled, "No man but a blockhead ever wrote except for money."
>
> And the Reader calculated the worth of a free supply of blockhead-written works against the value of recognizing the Author's economic self-interest. She concluded that the author's interest is also her interest, that the "public interest" encompasses both that of authors and of readers. So she looked upon copyright, and saw that it was good.
>
> This, in essence, is the philosophy that informs the 1787 U.S. Constitution's copyright clause ... The means to advance learning is by securing authors' exclusive rights....
>
> [But] the incentive rationale for copyright invites its own rebuttal. For one thing, we may have an ample supply of "blockheads"—poets who burn with inner fire, for whom creation is its own reward, or for whom other gainful employment permits authorial altruism. These creators do not need the incentive of exclusive rights in order to produce works of authorship. As to this group of authors, then, copyright is a wasteful windfall. Moreover, even if the incentive rationale justified some copyright protection, we may be allowing too much. That is, the scope of copyright protection—particularly the derivative works right—may be more generous than is needed to spur initial creativity.
>
> In the abstract, this approach may have some appeal, but it also has considerable practical disadvantages. For example, the scope of a work's protection could not be known *ex ante* (thus permitting predictability in licensing), but would only be discovered in the course of an infringement proceeding, in which the court would address the question whether this incentive was necessary to create this work. Obviously, it also is rather difficult to project how one would show whether or not copyright was a necessary incentive in a given case. Then-Professor (now Justice) Stephen Breyer famously wrote that the case for the copyright incentive rationale has not really been made—but neither, I would suggest, has the case against it. It depends who has the burden of proof: authors to justify copyright, or users to justify non-protection.
>
> If the incentive rationale fails to persuade, let us consider supplemental rationales for authors' rights. A principal alternative, the misappropriation or unjust enrichment rationale, also has shortcomings. Here the argument would be: Regardless of the incentive that copyright may or may not have provided this author, this user is getting something for nothing, and therefore

has misappropriated something of value. The problem here, as
before, is the argument's circularity. Getting something for
nothing is wrongful only if the "something" was subject to
claims of private right. In effect, this contention "proves" the
existence of the property right by pointing to third parties'
desire to "steal" it. But, of course, there's no theft if there's no
property.

Jane C. Ginsburg, *Copyright and Intermediate Users' Rights*, 23 Colum.-
VLA J. L. & Arts 67, 68–69 (1999).

The Philosophy of Intellectual Property
JUSTIN HUGHES*

A Lockean Justification

    ... Locke's theory of property is itself subject to slightly different
interpretations. One interpretation is that society rewards labor with
property purely on the instrumental grounds that we must provide
rewards to get labor. In contrast, a normative interpretation of this labor
theory says that labor should be rewarded....

    We can justify propertizing ideas under Locke's approach with three
propositions: first, that the production of ideas requires a person's labor;
second, that these ideas are appropriated from a 'common' which is not
significantly devalued by the idea's removal; and third, that ideas can be
made property without breaching the non-waste condition. Many people
implicitly accept these propositions. Indeed, the Lockean explanation of
intellectual property has immediate, intuitive appeal: it seems as though
people do work to produce ideas and that the value of these ideas—
especially since there is no physical component—depends solely upon the
individual's mental 'work.' ...

B.   Labor and the Production of Ideas

    A society that believes ideas come to people as manna from heaven
must look somewhere other than Locke to justify the establishment of
intellectual property. The labor theory of property does not work if one
subscribes to a pure 'eureka' theory of ideas. Therefore, the initial
question might be framed in two different ways. First, one would want
to determine if society believes that the production of ideas requires
labor. Second, one might want to know whether or not, regardless of
society's beliefs, the production of ideas actually does require labor. This
second question is the metaphysical one; in its shadow, society's belief
may appear superficial. It is not. We are concerned with a justification of
intellectual property, and social attitudes—'understandings' as Justice
Stewart said—may be the only place to start....

1.   The 'Avoidance' View of Labor

    If we surveyed people on their attitudes toward idea-making, what
might we find? First, we would probably find that many people who
spend time producing ideas prefer this activity to manual labor. It

* 77 Geo. L.J. 287, 296–314 (1988).

probably also is true that many manual laborers would rather spend time producing ideas than performing manual labor. That an idea-maker prefers idea-making to farming, roofing, or putting screws in widgets suggests that idea-making may not be viewed as labor in the same way that the latter activities are. It may share this distinction with such professions as competitive sports. Yet at least at some level of desires, the idea-maker probably prefers to be on vacation than to be in his office or laboratory. For most people creation is less fun than recreation. Although 'idea work' is often exhilarating and wonderful, it is something we generally have to discipline ourselves to do, like forcing oneself to till the fields or work the assembly lines.

This discussion depicts labor in one particular way: something which people avoid or want to avoid, something they don't like, an activity they engage in because they must. Lawrence Becker aptly has described Locke's view of labor as a 'proposal that labor is something unpleasant enough so that people do it only in the expectation of benefits.' In fact, Locke himself refers to labor as 'pains.'

One commentator has observed that this concept of labor is more likely the product of experience than logical rigor:

> [Comparing labor and property] is complicated by an equivocation about the idea of labor, which is dominated by the metaphor of sweat on the brow. Hence it is that the least imaginative work counts most securely as labor. The squires and merchants of the seventeenth century were far from idle men, but administration and entrepreneurship do not so obviously qualify for the title of labor as the felling of trees and the planting of corn.

In an understanding of labor based on the notion of 'avoidance,' labor is defined as an unpleasant activity not desirable in and of itself and even painful to some degree.

At this point we can separate the normative proposition of the labor theory from the instrumental argument with which it is usually identified. The normative proposition states: the unpleasantness of labor should be rewarded with property. In this proposition, the 'should' is a moral or ethical imperative, which is not based on any consideration of the effects of creating property rights. In comparison, the instrumental argument is directly concerned with those effects. It proposes that the unpleasantness of labor should be rewarded with property because people must be motivated to perform labor. In principle, the two propositions can coexist but neither requires acceptance of the other. In practice, however, the two not only coexist, but the instrumental argument often seems to be treated as a 'proof' of the normative argument. The instrumental claim has a utilitarian foundation: we want to promote labor because labor promotes the public good. Once we recognize that property is needed to motivate work for the public good, we may transform the reward into a right just as we often convert systematically granted benefits into rights deserved by the recipients. Perhaps we do this because it would be inconsistent and disconcerting to say that some systematically granted benefit is not deserved. Perhaps we just make the transition from instrumental to normative propositions through lack of attention. For example, in the 1954 case *Mazer v. Stein*, the Court said:

The economic philosophy behind the clause empowering Congress to grant patents and copyrights is the conviction that encouragement of individual effort by personal gain is the best way to advance public welfare through the talents of authors and inventors.... Sacrificial days devoted to such creative activities deserve rewards commensurate with the services rendered.'

As *Mazer* demonstrates, it is strikingly easy to move from an instrumental discussion of consequences to an assumption of just rewards.

Indeed, when the normative proposition emerges in court opinions it is usually used as an adjunct to the instrumental argument. The instrumental argument clearly has dominated official pronouncements on American copyrights and patents. Even the Constitution's copyright and patent clause is cast in instrumental terms. Congress is granted the power to create intellectual property rights in order '[t]o promote the Progress of Science and useful Arts.' As President Lincoln remarked, 'the inventor had no special advantage from his invention under English law prior to 1624. The patent system changed this.... It added the fuel of interest to the fire of genius in discovery and production of new and useful things.' In almost all of its decisions on patents, the Supreme Court has opined that property rights are needed to motivate idea-makers. This instrumental justification is the heart of what Judge Easterbrook has called the Supreme Court's 'Ex Ante Perspective on Intellectual Property.'

The wide acceptance of the instrumental argument suggests wide acceptance of the premise that idea-making is a sufficiently unpleasant activity to count as labor that requires the inducement of reward. Admittedly, this hardly is a tight argument. Idea-making just as easily could be a neutral activity or even a pleasant activity whose pursuit individuals covet.

The issue is not whether idea-making is an absolutely unpleasant activity, but whether it is comparatively less pleasant and less desirable than other activities. As Peter Rosenberg writes in his treatise on patent law, 'while necessity may be the mother of invention, the quest for new products and technologies must fiercely compete against the demands for current consumption.' The judgments we make about most forms of labor are not that they are absolutely unpleasant, but that they are relatively unpleasant. For most people, raking leaves is relatively unpleasant compared to sitting and watching them fall. Similarly, there is a widespread attitude that idea-making is not such a pleasant activity that people will choose it, by itself, over recreation. At least, people will not choose it in sufficient numbers to meet our collective needs. This same characterization applies to labor in the fields, the forests, and the factories. That is our best grounds for assuming that idea-making is a form of labor.

If we believe that an avoidance theory of labor justifies intellectual property, we are left with two categories of ideas: those whose production required unpleasant labor and those produced by enjoyable labor.

Are the latter to be denied protection? This strange result applies to all fruits of labor, not just intellectual property.

2.   The 'Value–Added' Labor Theory

Another interpretation of Locke's labor justification can be called the 'labor-desert' or 'value-added' theory. This position 'holds that when labor produces something of value to others—something beyond what morality requires the laborer to produce—then the laborer deserves some benefit for it.' This understanding of property does not require an analysis of the idea of labor. Labor is not necessarily a process that produces value to others. It is counterintuitive to say labor exists only when others value the thing produced. It also would be counter to Locke's example of the individual laboring and appropriating goods for himself alone. The 'labor-desert' theory asserts that labor often creates social value, and it is this production of social value that 'deserves' reward, not the labor that produced it.

The legal history of intellectual property contains many allusions to the value-added theory. The legislative histories of intellectual property statutes refer repeatedly to the value added to society by inventors, writers, and artists. Indeed those judicial or legislative statements that appear to fuse the normative and instrumental propositions of the labor justification are perhaps based, unknowingly, on the value-added theory. In Mazer v. Stein the Court appeared to be saying that the enhancement of the public good through the efforts of intellectual laborers made the creators of intellectual property worthy of reward. In other words, their contribution to the public good justified the reward of property rights. Earlier I noted that the Constitution's copyright and patent clause is an instrumental provision. More precisely, it is an instrumentalist provision aimed at rewarding people who bring added value to the society. Little else could have been meant by giving people 'the exclusive Right to their respective Writing and Discoveries' in order 'to promote the Progress of Science and useful arts.'

The value-added theory usually is understood as an instrumentalist or consequentialist argument that people will add value to the common if some of the added value accrues to them personally. Paralleling the discussion of the avoidance theory of labor, it is possible also to treat the value-added theory as a normative proposition: people should be rewarded for how much value they add to other people's lives, regardless of whether they are motivated by such rewards.

Some kinds of intellectual property have appeared only in contexts in which the property represents a value added to the society. International News Service v. Associated Press inaugurated 'quasi-property' protection for gathered information. The opinion merged unfair competition doctrine and property arguments to prohibit one party's appropriation of the product of another party's labor. Such appropriations occur only when the party taking the product believes it to have some value. To state the proposition differently, one could not argue that it is unfair competition to take away someone's worthless labor.

Unfair competition is the purloining of another's competitive edge— an 'edge' that has social value. Insofar as protection of gathered information rests on an unfair competition model, it necessarily relies on the value-added justification. If the fruits of labor have no prospective value, stealing those fruits may be socially unkind, but not competitively unfair. Similarly, trade secret infringement cases result from claimed losses of social value by the petitioner. No court has ever had to face a test case of a vigorously defended but worthless trade secret.

There is a very simple reason why the legal doctrines of unfair competition and trade secret protection are inherently oriented toward the value-added theory: they are court-created doctrines and people rarely go to court unless something valuable is at stake. When intellectual property is created more systematically, such as through legislation, the resulting property doctrines seem less singularly oriented toward rewarding social value . . .

Copyright law also seems to defy value-added reasoning. As with patents, one can register a writing for copyright protection without ever planning to publish the work. For copyrighted works, no statutory provision demands 'value.' Indeed, thousands of worthless works are probably copyrighted every month. Bad poetry, box office failures, and redundant scholarly articles are not denied copyright protection because they are worthless or, arguably, a net loss to society.

The interesting issue of proportional contributions further evinces the degree to which the value-added justification underpins intellectual property law. Modern industry depends on equipment and machines utilizing multiple patents to carry out a single activity. Through patent-licensing schemes, patent owners share proportionally in the aggregate value of the intellectual property in such machines. However, the same ability to distribute value has eluded the copyright system.

A modest copyright apportionment doctrine was established in Sheldon v. Metro–Goldwyn Pictures. In Sheldon, both Judge Hand and Justice Hughes upheld the apportionment of only twenty percent of the profits to the plaintiff when the defendant's infringing film used only a small part of the plaintiff's play and expert testimony attributed the movie's success to its popular stars, not the script. But even while making the award, Hand wrote of apportionment that, 'strictly and literally, it is true that the problem is insoluble.' The common wisdom, with some scholarly debate, has been to follow the Sheldon dictum instead of attempting its result.

That the apportionment system has appeared as an ideal in copyright is homage to people's belief in the value-added theory as a normative standard: social value contributed should be rewarded. The fact that an apportionment system in copyright has remained only an ideal is explicable for several reasons. Certainly apportionment could produce uncertain shifts in incentives. It might encourage infringements and discourage originality by lowering the awards against infringers. On the other hand, it might strengthen enforcement by tempting judges to find infringements more often.

Apportionment may remain impractical in copyright for the same reason it would be impractical to have any value-added requirement in copyright law. The 'insoluble' problem for apportionment is measuring the value of a copyrighted work when it forms part of a larger work whose value can be measured by objective criteria, such as box office receipts or number of copies sold. The corresponding problem for a preliminary value requirement in copyright is that it is much harder to predict whether a writing will have value than to do so for an invention. It is often startling to see what copyrighted workers are ultimately judged valuable by society. Before the precocious judgment of history, a 'step forward' in literature or in the arts is easily confused with a step sideways or backwards.

A value-added interpretation of intellectual property laws is easier to support by moving away from particular legal doctrines. Probably the best support for the value-added theory is an argument based upon 'net gain.' This rule-utilitarian argument for granting intellectual property rights finds it unnecessary that individual cases of copyright or patents be of social value. A very high percentage of protected works could be worthless so long as the system of property protection results in a net increase in social value beyond what would be produced without the system.

Notes and Questions

1. Justin Hughes teaches at the Benjamin N. Cardozo School of Law. Born in 1960, Professor Hughes earned his J.D. from Harvard Law School in 1986, and was an attorney-advisor at the U.S. Patent and Trademark Office. As a Henry Luce Scholar, he clerked for the Lord President of the Supreme Court of Malaysia in 1988–89.

2. Does a Lockean analysis of intellectual property adequately account for the intangibility of intellectual property? For a discussion of how copyright law supplies analogous boundaries of 'thingness' around the intangibles, see Wendy J. Gordon, *An Inquiry Into the Merits of Copyright: The Challenges of Consistency, Consent, and Encouragement Theory*, 41 Stan. L. Rev. 1343, 1345–84 (1989).

From Authors to Copiers: Individual Rights and Social Values In Intellectual Property

JEREMY WALDRON*

From the point of view of moral justification, the most important thing about any property right is what it prohibits people from doing: if you own Blackacre, then I may not encroach on that land without your permission. This applies to intellectual property as much as to property in material resources. If you have made a fortune out of popularizing the cheerful scrubbed faces of Mickey and Minnie Mouse, I may not depict them in my underground comic books as "active members of a free thinking, promiscuous, drug-ingesting counterculture." Intellectual property like all other property places limits on what individuals are allowed to do.

* 68 CHI.-KENT L. REV. 841, 842, 862–68 (1993).

Our tendency of course is to focus on authors when we think about intellectual property. Many of us are authors ourselves: reading a case about copyright we can empathize readily with a plaintiff's feeling for the effort he has put in, his need to control his work, and his natural desire to reap the fruits of his own labor.... Clearly our concept of the author and this concept of the copier are two sides of the same coin. If we think of an author as having a natural right to profit from his work, then we will think of the copier as some sort of thief; whereas if we think of the author as beneficiary of a statutory monopoly, it may be easier to see the copier as an embodiment of free enterprise values....

VII. Social Utility and the "No Hardship" Argument

[I]f we are seriously interested in the moral justification of copyright and other forms of intellectual property, we should consider them from the perspective of those whose behavior they constrain. The perspective of the person constrained is particularly important when we are dealing, as we are in the case of intellectual property, with a practice that claims justification on utilitarian grounds. We say glibly that we are conferring rights as a means to the greater public good, and that sounds fine and socially respectable. Intellectual property rights are rewards or incentives, and they serve the excellent purpose of encouraging authors. But the rewards here are not just medals or Nobel prizes; the incentives we dole out amount literally to restrictions on others' freedom that may be exploited for authors' benefits. It sounds a lot less pleasant if, instead of saying we are rewarding authors, we turn the matter around and say we are imposing duties, restricting freedom, and inflicting burdens on certain individuals for the sake of the greater social good. In moral philosophy, where suspicion of utilitarian arguments is rampant, that rings alarm bells. To say that rights are a means to an end is one thing; but the correlative proposition that some should be forced to bear sacrifices for the greater social good smacks dangerously of throwing Christians to the lions for the delectation of Roman society....

[W]hen we impose duties on certain people in order to provide incentives for others for the sake of the general good, are the interests of those who bear the duties also served by the overall good we are promoting. Are they "ends" in this process as well as "means?" The answer is sometimes "no" in the case of utilitarian calculations. If we execute a murderer purely in order to deter later acts of murder, we may promote the general good (if the deterrence theory works), but we will not benefit the person who was executed. He will not have a greater security against homicide as a result. So, absent some other justification for punishing him in this way, he is being used merely as a means to others' ends. Probably this is not true, however, of those who bear the burdens of copyright. The theory of the Constitution seems to be that everyone benefits from "the Progress of Science and useful Arts." The benefits will be widely diffused—as widely as the culture itself—and there is no reason why the beneficiaries will not include those whose copying activities have had to be restrained in order to provide an incentive to authors....

How much of a hardship, then, is it to be prevented from copying or using another's work of authorship without his permission? At first sight, the burdens seem relatively trivial. Justice Stevens' image of millions of people being prevented from taping their favorite television show seems about as serious as it gets. As I said earlier, we are seldom dealing here—as we are, sometimes, in the case of material property—with matters of life and death.

It would be wrong, however, to leave the matter there. People do not pursue costly litigation for the sake of trivia. Usually, of course, the issue is a matter of profits. Let's take an example, this time from the music industry. A singer and a music publisher make millions by recording a song that embodies a feature that musicologists call an "evaded resolution," a feature which just happens to have been copied (along with various other phrases) from a tune composed by somebody else. The original composer sues for infringement of copyright. If his complaint is sustained, the defendant may have to pay all his profits from the second song to the plaintiff in damages or restitution. Surely it can be said that this is a serious burden. The response—from the side of the original composer—will be that it only seems a burden from an ex post perspective. Suppose, ex ante, that the second composer is contemplating the use of the first composer's evaded resolution. He has a hunch that he could make millions from a song incorporating the device, but reluctantly he refrains out of respect for intellectual property (and because he foresees the costly law suit that did in fact ensue). If he now draws attention to the hardship of this self-denial, is there anything in his complaint that we should take seriously? John Locke, for one, would say there is not: " 'tis plain he desired the benefits of another's Pains, which he had no right to." Unfortunately, however, the Lockean rhetoric settles nothing in the context of our discussion, because whether or not the second composer has "no right" to benefit from the musical phrases of the first is precisely the point at issue....

Notes and Questions

1. Born in 1953, Jeremy Waldron is the Maurice and Hilda Friedman Professor of Law at Columbia Law School, as well as Director, Center for Law and Philosophy. Educated at Otago, New Zealand, (B.A. 1974; LL.B.1978) and Oxford (D.Phil. 1986), Professor Waldron has taught at the University of Otago, New Zealand; Lincoln College, Oxford; University of Edinburgh, Scotland; and the University of California (Berkeley) School of Law. From 1996 to 1997, he was the Laurence S. Rockefeller University Professor of Politics and director of the Program in Ethics and Public Affairs at Princeton.

2. Copyright constrains the free circulation of works of authorship, which, absent the statutory monopoly, would form part of the freely appropriable "common." Thus, among the "hardships" copyright protection may cause is suppression of forms of communication that reiterate part or all of prior works. Imposition of a limiting norm extrinsic to copyright law may address this concern, as we will see in a later section on the relationship of copyright and the first amendment (Part III.B, infra). But arguments from within copyright law and theory may also reconcile the interests of first and second communicators.

> [F]irst amendment concerns have a place in a Lockean theory. In a Lockean framework, first amendment freedom manifests a problem with the 'common.' Stated simply, some ideas and facts cannot be removed from the common because there would not be the slightest chance of there being 'enough and as good' afterwards. Imagine the absurdity of a political debate in which some people held copyrights over certain 'new ideas.' This leads to the second element of a Lockean theory of intellectual property: the common. . . .

Justin Hughes, *The Philosophy of Intellectual Property*, 77 Geo. L.J. 287, 314 (1988).

The Public Domain

JESSICA LITMAN*

Our copyright law is based on the charming notion that authors create something from nothing, that works owe their origin to the authors who produce them. Arguments for strengthening copyright protection, whether predicated on a theory of moral deserts or expressed in terms of economic incentives, often begin with the premise that copyright should adjust the balance between the creative individuals who bring new works into being and the greedy public who would steal the fruits of their genius.

The process of authorship, however, is more equivocal than that romantic model admits. To say that every new work is in some sense based on the works that preceded it is such a truism that it has long been a cliché, invoked but not examined. But the very act of authorship in any medium is more akin to translation and recombination than it is to creating Aphrodite from the foam of the sea. Composers recombine sounds they have heard before; playwrights base their characters on bits and pieces drawn from real human beings and other playwrights' characters; novelists draw their plots from lives and other plots within their experience; software writers use the logic they find in other software; lawyers transform old arguments to fit new facts; cinematographers, actors, choreographers, architects, and sculptors all engage in the process of adapting, transforming, and recombining what is already "out there' " in some other form. This is not parasitism: it is the essence of authorship. And, in the absence of a vigorous public domain, much of it would be illegal.

Because copyright's paradigm of authorship credits the author with bringing something wholly new into the world, it sometimes fails to account for the raw material that all authors use. This tendency can distort our understanding of the interaction between copyright law and authorship. Specifically, it can lead us to give short shrift to the public

* 39 EMORY L.J. 965, 966–69, 1012–1023 (1990).

domain by failing to appreciate that the public domain is the law's primary safeguard of the raw material that makes authorship possible.

Commentary on the public domain has tended to portray it either as the public's toll for conferring private property rights in works of authorship or as the realm of material undeserving of property rights. The current trend is to characterize material in the public domain as unprotectible or uncopyrightable. This description has important implications, for it inspires the question "Why not?" Proponents of strong copyright protection have challenged the rationales for refusing copyright protection to authors' creations and have called for property rights to be given in material as yet unprotected by copyright law.

To characterize the public domain as a quid pro quo for copyright or as the sphere of insignificant contributions, however, is to neglect its central importance in promoting the enterprise of authorship. The public domain should be understood not as the realm of material that is undeserving of protection, but as a device that permits the rest of the system to work by leaving the raw material of authorship available for authors to use. . . .

The purpose of copyright law is to encourage authorship. When we embody that encouragement in property rights for authors, we can lose sight of a crucial distinction: Nurturing authorship is not necessarily the same thing as nurturing authors. When individual authors claim that they are entitled to incentives that would impoverish the milieu in which other authors must also work, we must guard against protecting authors at the expense of the enterprise of authorship. . . .

V. EXPLORING THE COMMONS

The historical development of the public domain began as a straightforward problem in statutory construction and proceeded through ad hoc articulation in series of cases decided under successive statutes. Traditional explanations of the public domain have failed to justify the cases on principled grounds. When the public domain is viewed as a commons that rescues us from our choice to grant fuzzy and overlapping property rights in unascertainable material, however, some of the apparent contradictions in lines of cases become more transparent.

One traditional justification for the public domain is that the public domain is the public's price for the grant of a copyright. The public is said to grant the copyright as an incentive to persuade the author to create and publish original works that will enrich the public domain. Thus, copyright endures only for limited times. Some aspects of copyrighted works are thought to be so important to the public that society demands unrestricted access to them immediately, without waiting for the copyright to expire. Ideas and works of the federal government are said to possess these qualities.

This reasoning explains the systems cases well. Systems are important—so important that the public is reluctant to grant a fuzzy property right in systems to anyone claiming an interest. Instead, we have the patent statute under which a claimant can obtain a firmer property right, but only after making a significantly more specific showing of the basis for her claim. In the absence of such a showing, the public claims even original systems as its own. . . .

This quid pro quo justification, however, cannot explain the cases denying protection to scenes à faire. Moreover, it cannot account for the line of cases granting protection to facts in directories and catalogs while denying protection to facts in other sorts of works. Indeed, under traditional justifications for the public domain, the directory case law makes no sense. If we decline to protect information because the law assimilates facts to ideas and systems, then the cases should rigorously dissect the information in directories and catalogs from the form in which the information is expressed. If protection is denied to information because facts are not original, then works conveying information in unoriginal form (alphabetical, for example) should receive little or no protection under the copyright law.

Had the cases denying copyright protection for facts begun from a firm consensus that facts belonged to the public domain, they would likely have developed along precisely those lines. Most of the cases defining the public domain, however, involved courts carving out exceptions to authors' claimed property rights in order to alleviate pressure exerted by the breadth of plaintiffs' claims. That pressure, which strained the integrity of copyright law, was imposed not by plaintiffs' greed but by the inherent limits of the concept of originality. To illustrate how originality generates this pressure and how the courts' resort to the public domain helps to dissipate it, I propose to look again at the public domain case law from the viewpoints of potential defendants, potential plaintiffs, and the system of copyright law as a whole.

A. Protecting Potential Defendants

The dangers of overbroad and overlapping property rights in works of authorship seem most obvious when considering the plight of inadvertent infringers. Ideas, systems, themes, and plots are not easily traced. It is difficult to ascertain the source of an idea and impossible to prove its provenance in any meaningful sense. A court cannot unzip an author's head in order to trace the genealogy of her motifs; indeed, the author herself usually cannot pin down the root of her inspiration. Giving an author a copyright in something that is a basic building block of her art thus risks denying that basic building block to all other authors who come into even fleeting contact with the first author's work. It is our inability to trace or verify the lineage of ideas that makes it essential that they be preserved in the public domain.

Facts seem more verifiable. To the extent that they are drawn from preexisting sources, the sources may be checked. The question "Where is that fact from?" is a question that often seems to have an answer. Nonetheless, protecting facts can pose a separate problem. We often learn the facts we encounter and incorporate them into our views of the world in which we live. Once they have taken residence, they will color the things we believe that we see, and we are helpless to pry them out again in order to sit down and create works of authorship. A rule requiring authors effectively to forget the facts learned from other authors would be destructive and impossible to enforce.

[T]he chief threat of defining the borders of property in works of authorship is that it will penalize defendants for inadvertent or inevitable use of common building blocks, . . .

[W]e [should] understand the principle of seepage: Some aspects of works of authorship are easily absorbed, and once we have absorbed them, we are likely to make them our own and lose sight of their origins. Ideas, information, short phrases, simple plots, themes, stock scenes, and utilitarian solutions to concrete problems all share this characteristic. It makes them difficult to trace. That difficulty should make us leery of granting exclusive property rights in such things without requiring the claimant to offer significant proof in support of her claim of ownership. We have, however, elected to adopt a system that confers property rights without requiring any concrete proof of ownership, because we value the property rights and recognize that in many cases such proof would be impossible to obtain. To keep such a system from defeating its ends, we leave the elements subject to such absorption free from private claims, even in cases in which we could determine their initial source. But we do not concern ourselves with this problem in situations in which the works in question seem unlikely to be absorbed. In such cases, there seems to be no imperative reason for separating protectible from unprotectible elements.

Despite its intuitive appeal, however, th[is] picture of the public domain that emerges from the distinctions among the fact cases is too limited. It emphasizes defendants' motives, supporting a vision of the public domain as a commons that exists chiefly for the benefit of the defendant copying unintentionally and in good faith. The danger of such a view is that it tempts us to abandon the commons whenever proof of copying seems less circumstantial. But here it is useful to recall that many of the cases defining the borders of the public domain involve no such ambiguous situation.

Indeed, if we look only at the interest of potential defendants in avoiding liability for copying that they would be powerless to prevent, then the film cases make no sense at all. In some of the film cases, defendants had provisionally admitted copying for the purpose of a motion to dismiss. In others, the evidence of intentional copying was compelling. Yet courts carved out a commons that immediately benefited parties who had apparently made deliberate use of others' works. The solution to this apparent paradox is the realization that the public domain is not merely a haven for well-meaning potential defendants. It benefits potential plaintiffs as well.

B.   Protecting Potential Plaintiffs

The commons provides significant advantages for parties plaintiff. Because we can rely on the commons, we do not require plaintiffs to prove the originality of their works. We could take another approach, of course: We could insist that plaintiffs bear the burden of demonstrating their works' originality before enforcing their claims. As we currently define originality, however, most plaintiffs would be unable to muster the evidence required, and few would recover.

The principle of seepage is not limited to such material as will inevitably seep from the works of potential plaintiffs into the works of potential defendants. It is equally likely that such material seeped into the works of the potential plaintiffs themselves. To the extent that such elements seeped into plaintiffs' works from other prior works, any property rights in these elements will overlap the claims of others significantly. To resolve the overlap, it would be necessary to require plaintiffs to prove the bases for their claims. If we permit them to do so, we invite the introduction of evidence purporting to prove—or disprove—actual originality. Even raising the possibility that such elements could be protected if plaintiff could only prove their provenance would effectively impose that test on all such cases. A plaintiff required to prove originality of all aspects of her work in order to recover for copyright infringement would be well advised to decline to bring suit.

The absence of a public domain would make copyright meaningless for most plaintiffs if we were to require them to bear the burden of proof on the originality of their works, at least as long as proving originality remained impossible as a practical matter. A second implication is more subtle: Even if proving originality were not impossible, it would be exceedingly unpleasant. It would take the magic away. Authors could no longer safely give free rein to their subconscious minds, and their muses would need to be available for deposition. Many would discover that creations they believed were their own were, at least in the eyes of the law, mere copies of the works of others.

Such a system would probably not endure for long. Forced to face the flaws of a system based on actual proof of originality, we would undoubtedly abandon the concept. But, to the extent that the idea of originality embodies things that we would like to believe, the presence of the public domain has made it possible for us to do so.

The essence of my argument is this: Originality is a conceit, but we like it. To the extent that we are tempted to forget that originality is a conceit, it can be a dangerous principle on which to base a system of property. Most authors would agree in the abstract that the raw material that authors use in their work must be left free for all authors to use. Individual authors can nonetheless dispute the applicability of this abstract principle to a situation in which they see something that they think of as their own in a later author's work. We could force each copyright owner to demonstrate her right to claim such aspects of her work by requiring her to prove their originality, but we would have to accept that she would often be unable to do so in any meaningful way. We could instead tolerate a world in which all authors must seek permission from each of their predecessors, but few new works of authorship would be likely to appear in such a system. Instead, we rely on a commons, and we draw the boundaries of that commons by recalling the fact that the concept of originality we purport to rely on is a mere apparition that we cannot afford to test.

C.   Rescuing the System

There is a third set of interests threatened by the phantasm of originality: the copyright system's interests in preserving its own integri-

ty. The problem of overlapping claims, alluded to above, invites gridlock
in the courts as parties request judicial resolution of insoluble disputes.
This set of interests, I think, best explains the recent impulses of some
courts to expand the borders of the commons. To illustrate this problem,
I offer a final parable.

Imagine the familiar plot of a novel for children. You remember this
book: Our heroine (hero) is an unpopular, bookish sort, small for her age
and, typically, bullied by her more popular classmates. One day in the
public library she finds a book she has never seen before: worn, plump,
and red. (For some reason, the book always seems to be red.) It is a
magic book. Indeed, it seems to be written especially for our heroine
(hero). She reads the book, certain at first that it is some sort of joke,
but then discovers that the magic in the book really works. It takes her
to strange alternate universes, where she meets alien creatures and
ultimately performs brave deeds that save at least a small part of the
world. The class bullies no longer trouble her.

Imagine as well a contemporary author of books for children who
has just finished a manuscript along these lines. Her lawyer remarks in
passing that she recalls reading something of this ilk to her son. (The
son was entranced.) Indeed, now that she thinks of it, she has a vague
recollection of enjoying a similar book borrowed from the library some
thirty years ago. Our author becomes concerned.

A dedicated paralegal spends two days in the municipal public
library and turns up twelve versions of this plot. In each, the book is red.
The author, who cannot recall having read any of them, but is unable to
rule out the possibility, asks her lawyer to explore the question whether
any of these twelve authors would object to publication of her book.
When contacted, the first of them assures the lawyer that he has no
objection, as long as the novel's hero is a young fellow, with a large dog,
getting over his parent's recent divorce. The second author is similarly
obliging, on the condition that the book's central character be a young
Hispanic woman with a part-time job in a diner. The third demands a
Native American, the fourth a Jew, the fifth a WASP.

At this point, our author and her lawyer would like to file an action
to determine with whose conditions she must comply. Imagine now that
they file an interpleader suit, depositing the plot of the novel with the
court and joining the dozen prior authors as defendants. Each of the
dozen files a counterclaim to quiet title in the plot; five other authors of
similar stories seek to intervene.

The court before which this suit is brought faces a quandary. There
is no rule of decision that can resolve the issues in dispute. Theoretically,
each of the authors before the court may be entitled to claim ownership
of the plot on the ground that she originated it; it is, after all, the sort of
plot that any bookish child with a taste for fantasy might have thought
up on her own. On the other hand, any or all of the authors may have
consciously or subconsciously copied the plot from some prior source.
The question cannot be determined directly, and the presumptions and
procedural devices that usually make this determination unnecessary are
of no assistance here, because the court has no basis on which to

apportion the benefits and burdens of the procedural devices among the parties before it.

When we are confronted with an insoluble problem in overlapping deeds, pragmatic concerns may outweigh doctrinal ones. It ceases to matter why this plot is claimed by so many authors; the important thing is that it is. The court could dismiss the case on procedural grounds—the plot of a novel is after all an unfamiliar res. This rescues the court from the spectre of having to make any decision, but it leaves the children's book industry in disarray. Next week, some composers are sure to show up with a dispute over chord progressions. The court could instead award exclusive rights in the plot to one particular author—perhaps the one who bakes the best cherry pie. This solution would seriously inconvenience the other authors, who would presumably incur liability for their use of the plot unless they could disprove access to that author's book. The court could avoid that particular difficulty by awarding the plot to all of the authors before it. This answer would, of course, hinder the authors of the future, but perhaps the world has enough literature about magic books already. Finally, the court could decide that without some principle on which to base a decision, the plot must belong to the commons. This decision relieves the parties of having to produce inconclusive evidence of originality, relieves the court of having to reach a decision with no basis for doing so, and relieves the law of having a predicament posed by overlapping deeds.

My parable is about plots, of course, but it is also a metaphor for scenes a faire. Scenes a faire are common; they are the property shared among the overlapping deeds. Some scenes a faire are common because they are trite; some become trite because they are common; for others it is hard to figure out why they appear so frequently. There is no particular reason why a magic book should be red; if the book is always red or even often red, however, that is a scene a faire. When we grant deeds without doing title searches, we risk significant overlap. We can often fashion rules to permit us to decide between two or three competing claimants, if not necessarily on strictly doctrinal grounds. At some point, however, the frequency of overlapping claims to something in particular will itself become the problem. Assigning that something to the commons is the copyright law's most practical defense.

This leads me to an observation about some recent cases. Some courts have been increasing their resort to the scenes a faire doctrine during the last decade. These courts have been responding to a real and troubling trend. If access to a prior work is the basis for presuming that similarities represent actionable copying, then one would expect a marked increase in everybody's access to everything to carry with it increasing inferences of infringement. The copyright law has defined access as "reasonable opportunity to view'" since before the development of modern methods of mass dissemination. Disproving access is, in most cases, no longer possible. It is not surprising, then, that the pressure of overlapping claims to common material has increased and that the courts have felt it necessary to rely on the public domain in ever more sorts of cases. We may be approaching an era in which familiar solutions to the chimera of originality become insufficient; there may soon come a day when we have to give the notion up.

Conclusion

Copyright law purports to define the nature and scope of the property rights that it confers by relying on the concept of originality. In fact, originality is an apparition; it does not, and cannot, provide a basis for deciding copyright cases. The vision of authorship on which it is based—portraying authorship as ineffable creation from nothing—is both flawed and misleading, disserving the authors it seeks to extol. If we took that vision seriously, we could not grant authors copyright rights without first dissecting their creative process to pare elements adapted from the works of others from the later authors' recasting of them. That dissection would be both impossible and unwelcome. If we eschewed that vision but nonetheless adhered unswervingly to the concept of originality, we would oblige each author to solicit the permission of her predecessors. In such a world, most works of authorship would find themselves enjoined by the owners of other copyrights.

The public domain rescues us from this dilemma. It permits us to continue to exalt originality without acknowledging that our claims to take originality seriously are mostly pretense. It furnishes a crucial device to an otherwise unworkable system by reserving the raw material of authorship to the commons, thus leaving that raw material available for other authors to use. The public domain thus permits the law of copyright to avoid a confrontation with the poverty of some of the assumptions on which it is based.

Notes and Questions

1. Born in 1953, Professor Jessica Litman teaches at Wayne State University and is a 1983 graduate of the Columbia Law School. She has also taught at the University of Michigan Law School and New York University Law School. Her numerous writings in the copyright and trademarks fields include co-authorship of the Foundation Press casebook, *Trademarks and Unfair Competition Law*.

2. Professor Litman emphasizes the "central importance [of the public domain] in promoting the enterprise of authorship." For a more politically-tinged expression, see, e.g., David Lange, *Recognizing the Public Domain*, 44 Law & Contemp. Probs. 147 (Autumn 1981); David Lange, *The Public Domain: Reimagining the Public Domain*, 66 Law & Contemp. Probs. 463, 475 (2003) ("I suggest in turn that thinking of the public domain as conferring a status akin to citizenship—but now a citizenship of the creative imagination—is little more than a step away from civic republicanism toward a clearer understanding of the recognition and protection that exercises of creativity require and should beget.")

3. Does the metaphor or philosophy one chooses to justify copyright dictate one's assessment of the appropriate level of control that copyright owners should exercise? R. Polk Wagner challenges a central tenet of "control criticism"—the claim that control will reduce the availability of information in the public domain:

The core contention here is that the critics understate—perhaps dramatically—the contribution that even "perfect" control of intellectual creations makes to the public domain, just as they overstate the current and potential effectiveness of this control. Combining this understanding with the dynamic incentive—effects of intellectual property rights suggest that such rights (even in strong forms) are likely to increase the content of the public domain rather than decrease it . . .

R. Polk Wagner, *Information Wants to Be Free: Intellectual Property and the Mythologies of Control*, 103 Colum. L. Rev. 995, 997 (2003). See also Jessica Litman, *Digital Copyright*, 77–86 (2000) (describing changing metaphors for copyright since its inception).

II. *Works and Rights Protected*

A. Works

Copyright

PAUL GOLDSTEIN*

Authors and Their Works.

Authorship not only requires authors to have direct access to their audience. Authorship also requires that authors enjoy some not inconsiderable margins—some copyright elbow room—in working within the legal system. Copyright must be quick to protect any work that bears the impress of an author's personality, and careful when prohibiting one author's borrowings from another.

The question of elbow room arises any time a court must determine whether the product of an author's labors evinces sufficient original expression to qualify for copyright. In the United States, the judicially-evolved rules on protectible subject matter reflect the belief that authorship is more likely to flourish if Congress, the courts and the Copyright Office are not too exacting in the demands they make on works seeking admission into copyright. "E.T. Phone Home" may not rise to the level even of the minimally expressive, "Euclid alone has looked on Beauty bare," the line from Edna St. Vincent Millay that Judge Frank told us would qualify for copyright. A circus poster may not rise to the artistic level of a Mary Cassatt. But for authorship to flourish, those who seek to be authors must receive the same welcome as those who succeed as authors. Justice Holmes' perception in *Bleistein v. Donaldson Lithographing Co.*, the circus poster case, that copyright law should not allow the tastes of one generation to control the works available to the next, similarly argues for substantial elbow room at the threshold of protection.

---

* 38 J. Copyright Soc'y 109, 115–17 (1991).

Authorship also requires copyright law to give authors some freedom of movement in drawing on the works of other authors for theme, inspiration and ideas, even though—copyright being evenhanded—this means that their works will be subject to the same sort of borrowing by others. The principle at work here is the commonplace that all works of authorship build on the works and traditions that precede them. Copyright gives a limited property right that at once promises an author protection for the product of her mind, and ensures her the freedom to borrow unprotected elements from the copyrighted works of others. Learned Hand's "abstractions" test and Zechariah Chafees' "patterns" test leave no doubt that this is the most delicate balance in all of copyright.

These two points—that copyright should give authors elbow room when seeking protection for their own works, and when drawing on the works of others—are connected. The connection is particularly evident in a comparison of copyright protection for works of creative authorship— works clearly reflecting the impress of an author's personality—and utilitarian works—fact works and functional works—in which an author's personality leaves only the faintest, if any, trace. The connection, roughly speaking, is that the thinner is a work's creative content, the thinner will be its protection.

The first Copyright Act protected "maps, charts and books." Maps and charts are by nature utilitarian products, reflecting little if anything of an author's personality. The third class of works—books—could certainly encompass works of creative authorship. But, in the early years of United States copyright, the exigencies of practical life in a new nation filled this class with works of low personal creativity as well—spellers, grammars, dictionaries. Courts gave these utilitarian works only the narrowest scope of protection, protecting them against literal copying— what we would today call piracy. The result was fitting. Works of fact and function can efficiently be expressed in only a limited number of ways; it is hard—or at least socially costly—to recast them while retaining their utility. Also, in an age of improvement, there was a perceived public interest in having improved versions from competitors. It was thus natural for courts to emphasize what the competitor contributed to a work over what the copyright owner lost. Copyright's term of protection was correspondingly modest—fourteen years, with a renewal term of equal duration.

This remained pretty much the story through the middle of the nineteenth century: a predominance of utilitarian works and a low-level copyright statute aimed at ensuring competition in the dissemination of fact and function in the marketplace. With the emergence of an American tradition of creative authorship in the mid-nineteenth century—with the works of James Fenimore Cooper, Washington Irving and Nathaniel Hawthorne joining the more humble spellers, grammars and dictionaries—the copyright situation changed dramatically. Increasingly it became evident that personality and creativity resided not in language alone, but that creativity lay also in a work's deeper text, in the vision that the author sought to communicate to her audience. An author's vision could transcend a particular language—English, German, French—and a particular medium—novel, play or abridgement.

In 1870 Congress expanded the scope of copyright by adding an exclusive right against translations and an exclusive right against dramatizations. Courts, too, recognized that creative authorship resides in more than the surface language of a text. In the mid–1800's courts began to replace literal similarity as the test for infringement with a more vexing—but altogether appropriate—test of substantial similarity. It was at about this time, then, that copyright in the United States took on its double aspect: protecting not only utilitarian products, but also works of creative authorship. . . .

Notes and Questions

1. Although artistic merit is not supposed to be a condition of copyright, Professor Robert Gorman has demonstrated that judges too often yield to the temptation to evaluate a work's aesthetic qualities. Consider his critique:

> I would urge that there must be very strong reasons to withhold copyright protection from a work on account of its lack of creativity. As Holmes reminds us, copyright judges are not well-equipped by virtue of their legal training and life experience to make these kinds of subjective determinations, and making such judgments based on content may inhibit the constitutional objective of promoting learning and culture through a supportive legal and economic environment. Even so, there are extraordinary situations in which the copyright claimant has failed the test that was memorably formulated by Professor Benjamin Kaplan in his lectures here [at Columbia Law School] nearly 35 years ago, as published in his book *An Unhurried View of Copyright*: "To make the copyright turnstile revolve, the author should have to deposit more than a penny in the box." Kaplan's concern was about attempts to "fence off small quanta of works or other collocations; these pass quickly into the idiom; to allow them copyright, particularly if aided by a doctrine of 'unconscious' plagiarism, could set up untoward barriers to expression." This view has long been reflected as well in Copyright Office regulations, which declare ineligible for copyright simple phrases and commonplace graphic symbols. Granting exclusive rights in the thoroughly familiar and trite will inhibit rather than promote the progress of learning by chilling new works that often must freely borrow from earlier ones.

> But circumstances that invite an aesthetic veto by a copyright court are, I suggest, extremely rare. As the *Feist* decision itself states: "To be sure, the required level of creativity is extremely low; even a slight amount will suffice. The vast majority of works make the grade quite easily, as they possess some creative spark, 'no matter how crude, humble or obvious' it might be." Some fifteen years before *Feist*, the 1976 House of Representatives Committee Report, generally recognized as the

key to understanding the then new Copyright Act, reminded us
that "the phrase 'original works of authorship' ... does not
include requirements of novelty, ingenuity, or aesthetic merit."
This caution seems particularly warranted in light of the constitutional basis of the *Feist* decision, unless we would wish to
have routine and highly subjective disputes converted too readily into issues of constitutional moment. I strongly share the
view expressed in a more recent directory case by Judge Pierre
Leval of the Second Circuit Court of Appeals, one of our premier
copyright jurists, that:

> the thrust of the Supreme Court's ruling in *Feist* was
> not to erect a high barrier of originality require-
> ment.... To the contrary, such a requirement would
> be counterproductive. The policy embodied into law is
> to encourage authors to publish innovations for the
> common good—not to threaten them with loss of their
> livelihood if their works of authorship are found insuf-
> ficiently imaginative.

... [The cases I have examined nonetheless] delineate
several representative matters and show a common trend. That
trend is for courts to enlarge the scope of the judiciary's
aesthetic discretion in the face of legislative and constitutional
ambiguity—and sometimes in the face of relatively clear language suggesting the contrary....

These developments are not uniformly to be criticized.
Some are all but a necessity ... given the statutory ambiguities
and the play of important copyright policies....

I therefore have some modest prescriptions. First, *Feist*
should be viewed as setting an extremely modest baseline for
creativity; perhaps an ember rather than a spark is the apt
metaphor. In addition, in determining creativity, courts should
avoid divining and evaluating the subjective motivation of the
artist or author, and the same for the amount of time devoted to
the enterprise. Moreover, if the creativity is indeed thought to
be at a low level, the better response in most cases is not for the
court to deny copyright altogether but rather to grant a "thin"
copyright, as we routinely do with maps and functional works;
this will afford deserved protection against the literal copier ...
without unduly inhibiting later creative work by others. When
issues of artistic status ... arise, courts should rely not on their
own aesthetic intuition and preferences but rather on the opinions of art professionals; even if those cannot always agree, the
court's judgment will be better informed and focused....

These prescriptions will help move the courts toward a
more predictable jurisprudence and one that better honors the
admonitions set forth by Justice Holmes a century ago and still
worthy of heed today.

Robert Gorman, *Copyright Courts and Aesthetic Judgments: Abuse or Necessity?*, Annual Horace S. Manges Lecture, 25 Colum. J. Law & the Arts, 1, 3–4, 18–19 (2001).

2. Three years later in the same forum, Professor Diane Zimmerman rejoined:

> [J]ust what is so terrible about having to distinguish works based on qualitative or equivalent norms? A rigorous standard for copyright, I would suggest, actually comports better with our common sense understanding of why we think this form of economic protection is important. No one defends copyright because it so important to us that the mundane design and layout of a mailing envelope is protected. The Berne Convention does not seem on its face to preclude the experiment ... precedent for selectivity does exist. Judgment calls were hardly foreign to federal Courts in the nineteenth century. German courts have used a heightened threshold to weed out coverage for what is sometimes referred to as "small change."
>
> Perhaps one reason the thought of making value judgments about communicative works offends our sense of propriety is that we are conditioned against it by our traditions of protecting free speech. But in truth, qualitative judgments are not always inimical to first amendment principles, particularly where the government has a noninvidious reason to encourage speech activities, rather than an interest in restricting some of them. NEA grants, for example, require selection, and it can be based on legitimate criteria chosen to serve the government's objectives. Public libraries don't have to buy every book that is published. They can select, as long as their criteria are acceptable.
>
> It would be challenging to develop the right standards for copyrightability, I agree, although presumably the burden would at least be shared between Congress and the courts. I recognize that critics have called the German standard romantic and unworkable. Perhaps reserving copyright for works that matter in educational or cultural terms and denying it to small change and to things we'd get even without it (say, labels) would also turn out to be impractical and unfair. But I don't think the case against it has really been made ...

Diane Zimmerman, *It's an Original! (?): In Pursuit of Copyright Law's Elusive Essence*, Annual Horace S. Manges Lecture, forthcoming, 28 Colum. J. Law & Arts—(2005). What kind of standards could be developed to calibrate levels of protection to levels of originality? How often are works of significance identified at the time of their creation?

3. For post-modernist visions of copyright law that challenge the traditional concept of authorship, see David Lange, *At Play in the Fields of the Word: Copyright and the Construction of Authorship in the Post Literate Millennium*, 55 Law & Contemp. Probs. 139 (1992); Peter Jaszi, *On the Author Effect: Contemporary Copyright and Collective Creativity*, 10 Cardozo Arts & Ent. L. J. 293 (1992) (discussing treatment of collective creativity under Copyright Act); David Nimmer, *Brains and Other Paraphernalia of the Digital Age*, 10 Harv. J. Law & Tech. 1 (1996).

Fact or Fancy: The Implications for Copyright
ROBERT A. GORMAN*

Our copyright law, as does the Copyright Clause of the Constitution, reflects a tension of two policies: To promote the progress of science and the useful arts in the long run, we permit the author for a limited time (not so limited any more) to stop others from copying or embellishing upon his work. We permit, indeed encourage, later authors and artists to build upon the copyrighted works of their predecessors, while holding out the threat that if they use too many such "bricks" in their building they may be branded infringers.

Since the avowed purpose for granting the exclusive right is to disseminate and add to knowledge in the public domain, Congress and the courts have devised doctrines to limit during the copyright term the author's control over the use of his work by others. Some of those doctrines deal with copyrightability. For example, copyright is said to protect only the author's expression, or word sequence, and not the underlying ideas, facts, or systems. . . .

The tension between author control and public dissemination is particularly keenly felt in a category of artistic and literary works which might be called "fact works," works which compile and communicate factual information about our society and the world about us, past and present. Examples are maps, directories and works of history and biography. These may be contrasted with what may be called works of imagination or fancy, such as music, sculpture and dance. Our law, as reflected in the terms of our copyright statutes and the language of our courts, emphasizes the greater need to disseminate the contents of fact works in contrast to the contents of artistic or literary fancy. . . . When Professor Chafee quoted the phrase "a dwarf standing on the shoulders of a giant can see farther than the giant himself," in his classic article on the fundamental issues of copyright, he was drawing no distinction between works of fact and works of fancy, but this aphorism has surely been given more of a place of honor in the developing law concerning copyright of fact works. The reasons for this warrant brief summary.

1. There is more of a public interest in access to facts about ourselves, the world about us, and our history and future. (While this may be true, it is a reason which actually "cuts both ways," for dissemination of fact works must not be so freely permitted as to destroy the incentive to research, compile and write such works, so important to the progress of society.)

2. More than with works of fancy, in many fact works the literary or artistic expression is dictated by and inseparable from the underlying information; maps and directories are the best exam-

* 29 J Copyr. Soc. 560, 560–63, 585–91 (1982).

ples. Courts are torn between on the one hand protecting the expression and as an incident curbing dissemination of the facts, or on the other hand disseminating the facts and as an incident permitting copying of expression. The tension here is thus keener than in works of fancy, where congruence of fact and form is not as pervasive.

3. Precisely because many fact works do not permit of varieties of expression by their authors, similarity in appearance between their works and those of their predecessors is sometimes written off as a product of coincidence and not of copying, or as allowable copying in view of the expressive limits of the genre.

4. A fourth reason why the dissemination impulse is greater in fact works than in works of fancy is because the policies of the First Amendment and of fair use are explicitly designed with a view toward commentary concerning political, social and historical phenomena.

5. Finally, in many fact works, the author's principal contribution comes from expense, time and effort—sometimes picturesquely described in the cases as "sweat of the brow"—rather than the kind of literary or artistic expression normally the concern of copyright. Courts may therefore believe that copyright is an inapt vehicle for rationalizing the monopoly of fact works.

Having thus generalized about differences between fact works and works of fancy, one must caution that even within the field of fact works, there are gradations as to the relative proportion of fact and fancy. One may move from sparsely embellished maps and directories to elegantly written biography. The extent to which one must permit expressive language to be copied, in order to assure dissemination of the underlying facts, will thus vary from case to case and genre to genre. But the basic distinction between fact works and works of fancy is, I believe, valid and of significance for copyright analysis. . . .

Most of the major fact-work cases in the past twenty years have involved works of history and biography, with such colourful dramatis personae as Howard Hughes, Ezra Pound, Julius and Ethel Rosenberg, Alex Haley and his forebears, Bugsy Siegel, John Wayne and the Hindenburg dirigible. These cases are very many which state that there is a greater public interest in the unpermitted dissemination of these kinds of works than of works of fancy, and the brooding omnipresence of thee First Amendment seems to give this contention enhanced credibility. Although it generally goes unchallenged, several arguments might be made to the contrary.

First, the societal importance of generating historical and biographical research and writing warrants a stronger monopoly as an incentive, not a lesser one. Second, at least in comparison with other fact works where there is a close congruence between fact or idea and the author's expression (such as maps, directories and printed forms), the variety of ways in which historical and biographical fact can be formulated makes it possible to satisfy the dissemination impulse by throwing the facts into the public domain while giving the expression as much protection as with works of fancy. Third, one might even plausibly argue that there should be yet greater protection of expression in works of fact than in works of fancy; the author of a fact work must cling to expression-protection as his only incentive to produce, because the underlying facts are in the public domain, while the author of a fanciful work can in any event rely upon copyright of the underlying fictional story line as incentive enough.

To help explore the range of copyright protection for works of history and biography, one might conjure up a fanciful case of a scholar of American history whose readings lead him to develop the hypothesis that President Lincoln was shot not by John Wilkes Booth but by an impecunious actor and former slaveowner named Jesse Jones. He concludes that Jones, motivated by a desire to preserve slavery and acquire a plantation once more, bound and gagged Booth, assumed his identify, murdered the President, and somehow after removing his own make-up saw to it that the police were led to Booth, whom they killed before asking any questions. Jones lived on for a while, unable to own slaves (and still unable to get an acting job), and a few years later, driven to insanity by guilt and remorse,, he took his own life. Our historian sets forth his work in a 400–page book, and one day he finds that a forty-page version has appeared in Reader's Digest, without attribution. He also finds that his work has been converted into a one-hour television "docu-drama." ... Does our historian have any legal recourse ... ?

Copyright law will afford our historian rather little solace.... Let us examine each of his activities and contributions, keeping in mind the proscription in section 102(b) of copyright protection for any "idea, ... concept, principle, or discovery, regardless of the form in which it is described [or] explained."

1. The idea of researching and writing about Jones is surely unprotectible against copying, The idea may be brilliant, but the first person to regard an historical figure as research-worthy cannot bar others from writing about that person, any more than the first person to explore a country or river can prevent others from doing the same. The inhibition upon the "progress of science and useful arts" would be intolerable. Of pertinence here and later are the eloquent words of Justice Brandeis in *International News Service v. Associated Press*:

> "the general rule of law is, that the noblest of human productions—knowledge, truths ascertained, conceptions, and ideas—become, after voluntary communication to others, free as the air to common use."

...

2. Nor will federal copyright law afford our historian a monopoly over newly unearthed facts about Jones, Booth and Lincoln. Although facts have instinctively been deemed uncopyrightable, typically by virtue of a reference to the progress of science and the useful arts, one can adduce several more specific reasons: facts are not "authored" by human beings; section 109(b) bars copyright protection for "discoveries"; and no doubt one could also rely upon fair use and First Amendment analysis. Although the research may have been prodigious and imaginative, and despite the protectionist impulse for such "sweat of the brow," a number

of recent and thoroughly reasoned cases have clearly stated that such research and its fruits are in the public domain....

3. Our historian cannot prevail when Reader's Digest or the teleplay copies from him the quotations of other persons articulated in their conversations or letters. Although the word sequence may be protected by copyright ... enforcement rests with the copyright owner, which our historian is not (barring a formal transfer of copyright to him). Nor will it do to argue that the quotations of others become "engrossed" into our client's historical writing so as to become part of a derivative work owned by him, since such incorporation does not affect the ownership of period of protection of those quotations. Such is the lesson of section 103(b) of the Copyright Act....

4. While our historian might reluctantly concede that he ought not to be permitted to exact a royalty for the unauthorized dissemination of material that does not "belong" to him, he will surely be more possessive about the intellectual contributions that are truly original with him. Can he claim that he is the author (and copyright owner) of certain historical speculations that are not objectively demonstrable, such as Jones forcibly confining Booth, and Jones' psychological motivation? These insights and hypotheses are not manifested in earlier documents, and are thus not merely "original" in the sense normally contemplated by our copyright law (i.e., they have not been copied from the work of another) but are also "novel" within the much more rigorous requirement of the patent system that the work must not have been thought of and put to use by anyone else before. These represent a different level of historical contribution from that of unearthing an object of significance, and bear much more of the individual stamp of the historian's own wit and imagination.

Even so, these various inferences and hypotheses should not be copyrightable. The hypothesis about the confinement of John Wilkes Booth purports to be an inference about an actual historical event; whether rooted in circumstantial or direct historical evidence, it is essentially a "discovery" which section 102(b) declares to fall outside the protection of copyright....

Indeed, even if the so-called factual incident (such as the confinement of Booth by Jones) proves to be totally incorrect, and no more than a product of our historian's fancy, there is no wrong in republishing it....

A Manifesto Concerning the Legal Protection of Computer Programs

PAMELA SAMUELSON, RANDALL DAVIS, MITCHELL D. KAPOR, J.H. REICHMAN*

Introduction

Virtually all of the voluminous published literature and public debate about the legal protection of computer programs has focused on

* In Symposium: Toward a Third Intellectual Property Paradigm, 94 Colum. L. Rev. 2307, 2310–12, 2315–2319; 2327–32, 2347–53 (1994).

how existing laws can or should apply to computer programs (e.g., whether copyright protects program user interfaces, whether algorithms are patentable, etc.). As the Office of Technology Assessment recently observed, there has been little normative analysis of the kind of legal protection that would be socially desirable for software and how it might best be accomplished. Such an analysis could articulate what aspects of programs are valuable, to what extent legal protection is needed for different loci of value, and how legal protection of software should be tailored to promote consumer welfare. Four years ago the authors of this Article—two technologists and two lawyers—undertook such a normative analysis. This article reports the results of our collaboration.

In brief, we have concluded that while copyright law can provide appropriate protection for some aspects of computer programs, other valuable aspects of programs, such as the useful behavior generated when programs are in operation and the industrial design responsible for producing this behavior, are vulnerable to rapid imitation that, left unchecked, would undermine incentives to invest in software development. These aspects may need some legal protection against cloning that existing legal regimes cannot provide. Most of the considerable controversy about software protection, within the software industry and the legal community, has arisen when software developers have tried to use existing legal regimes to protect these kinds of program innovations. The authors have been among those who have opposed efforts to stretch the bounds of existing legal regimes to protect these aspects of programs. In this Article, we argue that the software controversy has focused on the right problem, but has raised it in the wrong legal milieu. The problem is that behavior and other industrial design elements of programs are often expensive to develop and inexpensive to copy. This makes it possible for an imitator to produce a functionally indistinguishable program—a clone—that the imitator can sell at a lower price. Competition from these clones can destroy incentives to invest in software innovation. None of the existing legal regimes is well-suited to solving this problem. . . .

1 Important Characteristics of Computer Programs

Computer programs have a number of important characteristics that have been difficult for legal commentators and decisionmakers to perceive. First, the primary source of value in a program is its behavior, not its text. Second, program text and behavior are independent in the sense that a functionally indistinguishable imitation can be written by a programmer who has never seen the text of the original program. Third, programs are, in fact, machines (entities that bring about useful results, i.e., behavior) that have been constructed in the medium of text (source and object code). The engineering designs embodied in programs could as easily be implemented in hardware as in software, and the user would be unable to distinguish between the two. Fourth, the industrial designs embodied in programs are typically incremental in character, the result of software engineering techniques and a large body of practical knowhow.

1.1 Programs Behave

1.1.1 Computer Programs Are Not Only Texts; They Also Behave

At first glance, a program appears to be a textual work. Source code is clearly some form of text, even if in a strange language not easily read by the casual observer. The view of programs as texts has been widely adopted in the legal community.

While conceiving of programs as texts is not incorrect, it is seriously incomplete. A crucially important characteristic of programs is that they behave; programs exist to make computers perform tasks. Program behavior consists of all the actions that a computer can perform by executing program instructions. Among the behaviors commonly found in word processing programs, for example, are copying text, deleting text, moving text from one place to another, and aligning margins. Program manuals typically contain a good description of much of a program's behavior. Programs often compete on the basis of behavior; advertisements routinely list the capabilities (i.e., "features" which are discrete units of behavior) a program has that its competitors do not. Advertisements for tax preparation programs, for example, may emphasize the variety of tax forms they can handle (that is, the variety of tax-preparation behaviors the program is capable of producing).

Behavior is not a secondary by-product of a program, but rather an essential part of what programs are. To put the point starkly: No one would want to buy a program that did not behave, i.e., that did nothing, no matter how elegant the source code "prose" expressing that nothing.

Hence, every sensible program behaves. This is true even though the program has neither a user interface, nor any other behavior evident to the user. When someone sends electronic mail, for example, she will interact with a program that initiates transmission of the mail. This program hands the message off to a sequence of other programs that see to its delivery in a manner that is invisible to the user. The transmission programs have neither user interfaces nor visible behavior. Nonetheless, each behaves in ways important to the user.

1.1.2 Text and Behavior Are Largely Independent

Although the text of a program is designed to produce certain behaviors, program text and behavior are more independent than might be readily apparent. That is, two programs with different texts—e.g., VP–Planner and Lotus 1–2–3—can have completely equivalent behavior.

A second comer can develop a program having identical behavior, but completely different text through a process sometimes referred to as "black box" testing. This involves having a programmer run the program through a variety of situations, with different inputs, making careful notes about its behavior. A second programmer can use this description to develop a new program that produces the specified behavior (i.e., functionally identical to the first program) without having access to the text of the first program, let alone copying anything from it. A skilled programmer can, in other words, copy the behavior of a program exactly, without appropriating any of its text.

The independence of text and behavior is one important respect in which programs differ from other copyrighted works. Imagine trying to create two pieces of music that have different notes, but that sound indistinguishable. Imagine trying to create two plays with different dialogue and characters, but that appear indistinguishable to the audience. Yet, two programs with different texts can be indistinguishable to users.

1.1.3 Behavior is Valuable

Behavior is not the only source of value in a program, but it is the most important. People pay substantial sums of money for a program not because they have any intrinsic interest in what its text says, but because they value what it does and how well it does it (its behavior). The primary proof that consumers buy behavior, rather than text is that in acquiring a program, they almost never get a readable instance of the program text. They acquire object code not source code, a text that is, at best, quite obscure. Even so, shrink-wrap licenses purport to prohibit all sensible ways of examining that text (i.e., disassembling or decompiling the object code). Hence, when buying software in the retail market, consumers buy behavior and nothing more. There is, by explicit arrangement, nothing else in the package.

Not only do consumers not value the text that programmers write (source code), they do not value any form of program text, not even object code. Computer science has long observed that software and hardware are interchangeable: Any behavior that can be accomplished with one can also be accomplished with the other. In principle, then, it would be possible for a purchaser of, say, a word processor to get a piece of electronic hardware that plugged into her computer, instead of a disk containing object code. When using that word processor, the purchaser would be unable to determine whether she was using the software or the hardware implementation.

Thus, to the user of a word processor, it is immaterial whether the program is implemented in hardware or software. The user would just as willingly buy the hardware as the software version, as long as it exhibited the desired behavior. When buying the hardware version, there would be no text in the package at all (not even the obscure text of object code). Yet the value to the user would be unchanged.

All this stands in sharp contrast to traditional literary works which are valued because of their expression (i.e., what they say and how well they say it). Programs have almost no value to users as texts. Rather, their value lies in behavior....

1.4.2 Programs Are Compilations of Useful Behavior

... [P]rograms are not just compilations of behavior, they are compilations of useful behavior, a carefully selected collection of utilitarian components working together.

1.4.3 Constructing Programs Is an Industrial Design Process

Once one understands that programs are machines that happen to have been constructed in the medium of text, it becomes easier to understand that writing programs is an industrial design process akin to the design of physical machines. Each stage of the development process requires industrial design work: from identifying the constraints under which the program will operate, to listing the tasks to be performed (i.e., determining what behavior it should have), to deciding what component parts to utilize in bringing about this behavior (which in the case of software, includes algorithms and data structures), to integrating the component utilitarian elements in an efficient way.

A substantial amount of the skilled effort of program development goes into the design and implementation of behavior. Designing behavior involves a skilled effort to decompose the overall, complex task (e.g., word processing) into a set of simpler sub-tasks requiring simpler behaviors (e.g., deleting a character). Constructing the interaction of these sub-tasks to produce useful behaviors (e.g., deciding whether the "delete word" command should be implemented as a sequence of delete character commands) also requires design skill. Knowing how and where to break up a complicated task and how to get the simpler components to work together is, in itself, an important form of the engineering design skill of programmers.

The goal of a programmer designing software is to achieve functional results in an efficient way. While there may be elements of individual style present in program design, even those style elements concern issues of industrial design, e.g., the choice of one or another programming technique or the clarity (or obscurity) of the functional purpose of a portion of the program....

1.5 Innovation in Programs is Largely Incremental and Cumulative in Character

Innovation in software development is typically incremental. Programmers commonly adopt software design elements—ideas about how to do particular things in software—by looking around for examples or remembering what worked in other programs. These elements are sometimes adopted wholesale, but often they are adapted to a new context or set of tasks. In this way, programmers both contribute to and benefit from a cumulative innovation process. While innovation in program design occasionally rises to the level of invention, most often it does not. Rather, it is the product of the skilled use of know-how to solve industrial design tasks.

Even the conceptual metaphors embodied in software are typically incremental in character. Word processing paper is an extension of traditional paper; the automated spreadsheet is an extension of the traditional paper spreadsheet. Both products are innovative, but both also derive from an existing idea: a manual version. Put more generally, software development typically involves the automation of known tasks, which, almost by definition, involves an incremental innovation. Many extensions of functionality that are built upon a program's core conceptual metaphors (such as cutting and pasting with word processing software) also involve incremental innovation, applying human factors engineering to the design task.

The technical community has recognized the cumulative and incremental nature of software development, and has welcomed efforts to direct the process of software development away from the custom-crafting that typified its early stages and toward a more methodical, engineering approach. The creation of a software engineering discipline reflects an awareness that program development requires skilled effort and applied know-how comparable to other engineering disciplines.

The products of software engineering almost invariably contain admixtures of old and new elements. Some consist almost entirely of old elements. The innovation in such programs may lie in the manner in which the known elements have been combined in a new and efficient manner. Or it may come from combining some new elements with well-known elements in order to achieve the same result in a new way. When we speak of programs as "industrial compilations of applied know-how," it is in recognition of the frequency with which software engineering involves the reuse of known elements. Use of skilled efforts to construct programs brings about cumulative, incremental innovation characteristic of engineering disciplines. A well-designed program is thus akin to the work of a talented engineer whose skilled efforts in applying know-how, accumulated from years of experience and training, yields a successful design for a bridge or other useful product. . . .

2.2.3 Why Copyright Law Is Ill–Suited to Protecting Software Innovations

The dual nature of programs has also created conceptual difficulties for copyright law. For a time, copyright officials were unsure that computer programs in machine-readable form were copyrightable subject matter. Copyright law has traditionally excluded machines and technological processes from its domain, leaving their protection to patent law.

Even after Congress decided to make copyright protection available to programs, their utilitarian character has made it difficult for courts to apply traditional copyright doctrines to computer programs and to make distinctions that are legally as well as technically meaningful. Courts have also frequently found the traditional tests for copyright infringement to be unsatisfactory or unworkable as applied to computer programs, and have consequently undertaken to develop new (and often inconsistent) tests for judging infringement in software cases. However, copyright has no ready answers to many questions posed in software cases because it has never before regulated competition in technological fields. The very vocabulary and metaphorical structure of copyright law makes it difficult to talk about programs in a meaningful way.

Copyright law is mismatched to software, in part, because it does not focus on the principal source of value in a program (its useful behavior). As explained above, program text and behavior are largely independent, so that protecting program texts does not prevent second comers from copying valuable program behavior. The ability to copy valuable behavior legally would sharply reduce incentives for innovation, and thus thwart the policy behind legal protection. As we explain below, the right way out of this bind is not to conceive of behavior as a nonliteral element of the program's text, as some courts have done, but instead to regard it as the entity that an appropriate legal regime should protect.

Once one recognizes that computer programs are machines whose medium of construction is text, it becomes obvious why copyright is an inappropriate vehicle for protecting most program behavior. Copyright law does not protect the behavior of physical machines (nor their internal construction), no matter how much originality they may embody. Historically, innovations in the design of machine behavior have been left to the rigors of patent law.

. . .

That program behavior, in general, is unprotectable by copyright law on account of its functionality does not mean that behavior can never be protected by copyright law. Sometimes program behavior is "expressive" in a traditional copyright sense; when it is, copyright applies. Recall that program text is a medium in which it is possible to construct both useful and expressive behaviors. Just as it is possible to construct both useful devices (such as chairs or screwdrivers) and expressive devices (such as sculptures or music boxes) out of media such as steel and plastic, it is possible to construct both useful behaviors and expressive behaviors out of software.

United States law has devised imperfect, yet nonetheless workable, ways to distinguish between a copyrightable sculpture and an uncopyrightable tool when dealing with artifacts made of steel or plastic. It can make similar distinctions between the expressive and functional behavior of computer programs. That it may occasionally be difficult to distinguish between a useful artifact and an expressive artifact (e.g., a kinetic sculpture) does not make easy cases impossible to recognize. Nor does it undermine the usefulness of a general distinguishing principle of this sort.

When the execution of program instructions results in the display of pictures or text that qualify as an original work of authorship separate from the program that generated it, copyright protection for the picture or text is appropriate. When the execution of program instructions results in a series of pictorial images combined with text and sounds, program behavior can be part of a copyrightable audiovisual work.

When program behavior has both functional and expressive components, it should generally be easy to distinguish between them for copyright purposes. The primary function of screen-saver programs, for example, is to produce behavior that protects computer screens from burnout. Screen-saver behavior may also include moving pictures of flying toasters. If a second comer copies the flying toaster graphics, copyright infringement is likely. Courts should not, however, find copyright infringement if a second comer develops a program that protects computer screens from burnout in a manner that is functionally indistinguishable from the first program.

. . .

Notes and Questions

1. Robert A. Gorman, Kenneth Gemill Professor Emeritus, University of Pennsylvania School of Law, and Professor of Law at Arizona State University, was born in 1937 and received his LLB from Harvard in 1962. A leading authority in copyright law and labor law, he is the co-author of Foundation Press casebooks in both fields, as well as of a labor law treatise. A past president of the AALS (Association of American Law Schools) and the AAUP (American Association of University Professors), he is a member of the World Bank Administrative Tribunal and of the Asian Development Bank Administrative Tribunal.

2. For a biographical note on Professor Pamela Samuelson, see supra, Chapter 1 at page 85.

Randall Davis is a Professor of Computer Science and Engineering at the Massachusetts Institute of Technology. He was Chair of the National Research Council Committee on Intellectual Property Rights and the Emerging Information Infrastructure, whose study, *The Digital Dilemma: Intellectual Property in the Information Age*, was published in 2000.

Mitchell Kapor is the founder of Lotus Development Corporation and the designer of Lotus 1–2–3. Mr. Kapor was born in 1950 in New York, and received a B.A. from Yale College in 1971. In 1990, Mr. Kapor co-founded the Electronic Frontier Foundation.

Jerome H. Reichman is the Bunyan S. Womble Professor of Law at Duke University Before coming to Duke, he taught at Vanderbilt, Michigan, Florida and Ohio State Universities and at the University of Rome, and was a Fulbright Scholar to Madras University in India. Born in 1936, Professor Reichman earned his J.D. from Yale Law School in 1979.

3. Professor Gorman's scholarship on fact works emphasizes the distinction between fact works and works of fancy. The distinction, however, is one of outcomes, not of legal rules. In fact, application of a unitary standard of originality leads to the lesser treatment of fact works. Is a unitary regime of copyright protection, in which different kinds of works receive the same basic types of protections, more intellectually coherent, more practically workable, than a regime in which the statutory scope of protection depends on the type of work? Does a unitary regime adequately protect works like databases and software? Are the interests of the author and the public identical for each kind of intellectual creation? Consider these observations from Professor Gorman's earlier foray into the fact work field (observations made long before the Supreme Court's *Feist* decision interred the "sweat of the brow" rationale for protection):

> The plodding industry of the directory maker, the enterprise of the news-gatherer, the heroism of the map-making explorer, the comic inspiration of the cartoonist and the mental agony of the creative writer are lumped together for legal purposes, although the social interest in protecting their work and the social risks in allowing a limited monopoly in the reproduction of their products is different in each case.

> In literary or artistic works, the three components of the intellectual product—the ideas, their patterning, and their ultimate expression—are generally all originated by the author. While the author's broad ideas must be left in the public domain free for all to use, his patterning of those ideas and mode of

expression are copyrightable. As distinguished from literary or artistic works, there is a class of publication which involves only the gathering of facts or their representation in language or picture. Included in that class—which will be denoted "fact works"—are maps, news and historical accounts, directories, advertising art, photographs, and a closely related type of production, legal and business forms. In these works the author's raw materials are objective data, and his unique contribution is to gather these facts and to express them in language or visual images so ordered as to be intelligible and useful to others. The pattern and expression are basically mechanical and do not reflect the personality of the author. In maps, for example, they are lines and shapes the relations of which are determined by geographical configuration; in directories, they are terse entries simply organized. What the copyright monopoly here protects is not a product whose social value is its mark of personality or individuality, but the effort, time, expense, and, in certain cases, the skill employed in performing a task which does not require special intellectual competence.

Robert Gorman, *Copyright Protection for the Collection and Representation of Facts*, 76 Harv. L. Rev. 1569, 569–70 (1963).

B. Rights

Individuality and Authorship [and the expansion of rights protected]

JANE C. GINSBURG*

If late eighteenth and early nineteenth century Anglo–American courts tended to view original authorship as original labor, writers themselves were beginning to characterize original authorship as an expression of each author's individual personality. . . .

Justice Holmes set forth the most celebrated American judicial espousal of the "copyright as personality" approach in Bleistein v. Donaldson Lithographing Co., in which the Court rejected a challenge to the copyrightability of commercial art (a circus poster). The defendant had contended that a copyrightable work must rise to some level of aesthetic merit. Holmes found the source of authors' claims to protection in each creator's unique individuality:

> [The work] is the personal reaction of an individual upon nature. Personality always contains something unique. It expresses its singularity even in handwriting, and a very modest grade of art has in it something irreducible, which is one man's alone. That something he may copyright unless there is a restriction in the words of the act.

The work may embody the author's persona, but how does it follow from determining that the work is "him" that it is also his? The

* From *Creation and Commercial Value: Copyright Protection for Works of Information*, 90 Colum. L. Rev. 1865, 1881–88 (1990).

personality approach enunciated by literary figures and judges appears to assume that the presence of authorial spirit in a work suffices to confer ownership rights in it. In a sense this approach begins from the same premise as the labor view of copyright. According to Locke, one owns the fruits of one's efforts because they are the "labour of his body, and the work of his hands"; hands and body are parts of oneself, and "every man has a property in his own person." If every man owns himself, then Locke's "bodily continuity" concept would also support the conclusion that the author owns those things in which his self may be found.

The notion of the possessive personality received vigorous articulation in United States legal theory shortly before Justice Holmes's Bleistein opinion. Samuel Warren and Louis Brandeis's 1890 article, The Right to Privacy, argued that common law copyright, and its new corollary, privacy, found their source in rights of personality. Reviewing English common law copyright decisions protecting writers of letters and other unpublished works against their unauthorized public disclosure, Warren and Brandeis contended that vindication of literary property rights did not adequately explain the courts' results. The prevailing concept of literary property as encompassing rights to profit by one's writings did not respond to the claimants' actual concern "to be let alone," whatever the commercial value of their writings. Rather, copyright and privacy should both be seen "as a part of the more general right to the immunity of the person—the right to one's personality." For Warren and Brandeis, the "right to one's personality" both transcends property, and, perhaps somewhat contradictorily, is embraced within the "right of property in its widest sense."

Logically, the property-in-personality notion can be extended beyond the privacy right, which controls disclosures about oneself contained in one's unpublished writings, to the literary property right, which controls published manifestations of oneself as revealed in one's writings. The self-revelatory character of literary creation justifies the creator's assertion of private property rights in the work when published as well as in the work before it is disclosed. Warren and Brandeis's quotation from Drone's copyright treatise favors this proposition: "The very meaning of the word 'property' in its legal sense is 'that which is peculiar or proper to any person; that which belongs exclusively to one.' The first meaning of the word from which it is derived—proprius—is 'one's own.'" Justice Holmes may well have been echoing these ideas when he stated that the "something irreducible which is one man's alone" and that is present within even the most "modest grade of art" is the "something" to which the property rights of copyright attach.

One should next consider whether this change in the rhetoric and rationale for copyright protection corresponded to a change in the scope of protection. Arguably, the property rights arising from the presence of the creator's personality within the work should allow a depth of coverage that is no greater than the scope associated with the labor concept of authorship (as understood in the eighteenth and nineteenth centuries). After all, just as the labor approach would deny the status of infringement to laboriously produced variations upon prior works, so the personality approach might exculpate variations that manifested the second comer's personality. Under Justice Holmes's generous formulation, the variations need not be extensive to capture the second comer's persona. Indeed, the personality view might find more authorship in a lesser degree of variation than would the labor approach. As a result, one might expect that a personality basis of copyright would not expand the scope of copyright protection, and in particular, would not permit the author to control variations made upon her works.

In fact, however, in the course of the nineteenth century, the scope of copyright protection embraced an increasing range of activities. A review of the first hundred years of United States copyright enactments, from 1790 to 1891, shows a progression from rights simply in "printing, reprinting, publishing and vending," to the additional rights of "completing, copying, executing, finishing, and vending . . . and in the case of a dramatic composition, of publicly performing. . . . [a]nd authors may reserve the right to dramatize or to translate their own works."

Former Justice Kaplan has suggested that the changing status of authors in the nineteenth century, from imitative craftsmen to professionals conscious of their unique individuality, led in the nineteenth century both to increasing intolerance of copying and to disapproval of composition heavily dependent on predecessors' works. This evolution in literary circles in turn produced an evolution in the scope of copyright protection toward coverage of abridgments, translations, and similar variations.

Arguably, the expansion of copyright scope had at least as much, if not more, to do with contemporary economic pressures. If the first copyright statute was limited to "printing, publishing and vending" when it was enacted in 1790, the English-language book trade perhaps defined the relevant market for works of authorship. Subsequent statutory expansions would reflect, then, the recognition that substantial markets for translations and dramatizations also existed, or had developed. The reason for statutory expansion would derive to some extent from the labor theory of protection: having realized that the first authors' labors bear fruit through others' translations and dramatizations as well as through reproductions, Congress would have determined that these fruits should be reaped by the authors, rather than by third parties. But this rationale does not explain why third party translators and dramatists, who also labored, owe tribute to the initial authors. Some additional concept of the nature of initial authorship may be needed to fill the gap between protecting the first author's own labors, and prohibiting others from adding their labors to the first work. The personality concept of authorship may supply the link from reproduction rights to derivative work rights.

While a causal link between a personality perspective on authorship and a broader scope of rights may be difficult to prove, one at least can observe that contemporaneously with the rise and judicial acceptance of the personality approach came a different concept of what constituted the author's protectable creation. This concept pointed the way to extension of the scope of copyright protection from mere security against reproduction to control over derivative works as well. In an 1899 decision concerning Oliver Wendell Holmes, Sr.'s, The Autocrat of the Breakfast Table, the Supreme Court announced:

> It is the intellectual production of the author which the copyright protects and not the particular form which such production ultimately takes, and the word 'book' ... is not to be understood in its technical sense of a bound volume, but any species of publication which the author selects to embody his literary product.

The Court thus enunciated a conception of authorial creation in which the "intellectual production" exists independently of the medium of expression. This deincorporealizing conception—well understood in modern copyright law—ultimately affected the scope of protection. If the author's "product" would no longer be confined to any particular print manifestation of the work, and instead would be perceived as capable of inhabiting any of many forms, it followed that the copyright can cover any and all of the varying habitats, from bound volumes to pamphlets. It also followed that if the copyright protects the "intellectual production," regardless of the form of its embodiment, then a pamphlet version can infringe the bound volume.

The idealization of the intellectual production facilitates acceptance of the notion of dependent (and thus infringing) derivative works. Indeed, a few years later, in 1911, the Supreme Court, per Justice Holmes, took the next step toward bringing derivative works within the bounds of the author's copyright, holding that a film based on the novel Ben Hur was an infringement of the statutorily recognized right to dramatize.

The path from The Autocrat of the Breakfast Table to Ben Hur in fact traversed more ground than might initially appear. In the earlier decision, the Court supplied a conception of a "literary product" that permitted a broader scope of protection, but did not draw all the implicit conclusions. Rather, the Court held that the copyright might extend to the various formats in which the work might be presented, but it also indicated its view that the "literary product" encompassed no more than the author's choice and ordering of words. Hence, the copyright would not cover substantive alterations to the work. With respect to Ben Hur, by contrast, the Court detached the "literary product" even further from its formal moorings. The Court confronted the defendant's argument that the prior decision would not permit extension of the copyright to film versions because the film did not reproduce the novel's words, but merely proceeded from the novel's ideas. The Court's invocation of the statutory dramatization right permitted it to stretch the reach of the rights in the "literary product" beyond the realm of literature to other forms of expression of the author's elaborated ideas. . . .

Derivative Rights and Derivative Works in Copyright
PAUL GOLDSTEIN*

B. INFRINGEMENT OF DERIVATIVE RIGHTS

The English and American history reflects both a growing commitment to derivative rights and a clear sense that the proper measure for

* 30 J. Copyright Soc'y 209, [PIN cite] (1982).

their infringement will often necessarily differ from the measure employed in cases involving the narrower reproduction right. Yet virtually none of the decisions has drawn a principled line capable of separating derivative rights from reproduction rights, and only a few have systematically addressed the distinction's full implications: How, specifically, must infringement tests be reshaped to meet the peculiar needs of derivative rights? Must fair use and the originality requirement be recast? And what of remedies?

Copyright's underlying economic principles offer a helpful starting point for answering these questions. The purpose of copyright is to attract private investment to the production of original expression. Copyright seeks to achieve this purpose by giving copyright owners the exclusive right to reap the profits taken from reproductions, performances and other specifically prohibited uses of their original expression. This method implies a floor for investment by requiring that, to be protected, a work be original with the author and not copied from some other source. The method also implies a ceiling on investment by protecting expressions but not their underlying ideas, thus giving copyright investors no incentive to invest in the production of new ideas. In sum, the general incentive structure of copyright is to channel investment to the production of expression that is sufficiently original to qualify for copyright protection and to avoid infringing other copyrighted works.

Copyright's seminal design for regulating the production of copies provides the clearest example of this incentive structure at work. Section 106(1)'s grant of the exclusive reproduction right and section 102(a)'s declaration that copyright subsists in original works of authorship together establish one set of upper and lower limits to copyright investment. Margaret Mitchell and her publisher will invest time and money in writing, editing, producing and promoting the popular novel, Gone With the Wind, knowing that no one may copy the work's expressive content without their consent. They are also presumably aware of the floor and ceiling to their protection. They know that others will be free to use any of the novel's underlying ideas—basic plot, theme and character elements—just as they themselves were free in producing the novel to borrow ideas from other works.

The incentive structure of the Act's provisions respecting derivative rights and derivative works differs in two ways. First, section 106(2)'s grant of the exclusive right 'to prepare derivative works based upon the copyrighted work' enables prospective copyright owners to proportion their investment in a work's expression to the returns expected not only from the market in which the copyrighted work is first published, but from other, derivative markets as well. The copyright owners of Gone With the Wind can hope to monopolize not only the sale of the novel's hardcover and paperback editions, but also the use of the novel's expressive elements in translations, motion pictures and countless other derivative formats. Second, just as these owners had a copyright incentive to originate the expression for the novel, Gone With the Wind,

section 103—which extends copyright protection to the original elements
of derivative works—gives them and their licensees an incentive to add
original expression to each derivative work in order to qualify it for
copyright protection of its own.

Taken together, sections 102(a) and 103, and sections 106(1) and
106(2), give a prospective copyright owner the incentive to make an
original, underlying work, the exclusive right to make new, successive
works incorporating expressive elements from the underlying work, and
the incentive and exclusive right to make still newer, successive works
based on these. The continuum may stretch from an underlying novel or
story to the work's adaptation into a motion picture, its transformation
into a television series, and the eventual embodiment of its characters in
dolls, games and other merchandise. The works at the outer reaches of
this continuum, and some intermediate works as well, will frequently
bear scant resemblance to the expression or the ideas of the seminal
work and will often be connected only by a license authorizing use of a
title or character name.

This analysis offers some help in identifying the point at which the
right 'to reproduce the copyrighted work in copies' leaves off and the
right 'to prepare derivative works based upon the copyrighted work'
begins: It is that point at which the contribution of independent expression to an existing work effectively creates a new work for a different
market. The infringer who copies a novel verbatim violates only the
right to reproduce, for he has created neither independent expression
nor a new market. An infringing novel that borrows expressive elements
from the original, but adds new expressive elements of its own, also
violates the right to reproduce since, treating two novels with overlapping expression and essentially the same themes and characters as
close substitutes, no new market has been created. A paperback edition
of a hardcover novel will also violate the right to reproduce since, though
aimed at an arguably different market, it adds nothing expressively
different to the original. By contrast, motion pictures, translations and
comic strips based on the novel will all infringe the derivative right
because they add new expressive elements and serve markets that differ
from the market in which the original was first introduced.

Having determined that a derivative right is in issue, it is far more
difficult and consequential to draw the line that separates infringing
from non-infringing derivative uses. The central problem is that all
works are to some extent based on works that precede them. Ravel's
orchestration for Pictures at an Exhibition clearly derived from Moussorgsky's Suite for Piano. But it is no less true that Moussorgsky derived
the inspiration for his work from Victor Hartmann's sketches and
drawings displayed in 1874 in the rooms of the St. Petersburg Society of
Architects, and that Hartmann's sketches and drawings derived from
subjects and from compositional, stylistic and thematic elements appearing in earlier works. The example, admittedly stretched, should at least
suggest the nature of the problem.

Judicial guidance has been uncertain at best. Copyright's main
infringement measure, the idea-expression distinction, has been applied

unevenly to derivative rights, bouncing between the high level of protection given against such uses as motion pictures and television productions and the low level of protection given against certain nonliterary uses such as accounting or legal forms. Decisions at both extremes are flawed—the first for using copyright to regulate conduct that is more properly the subject of state unfair competition law, the second for applying copyright in a way that directly contradicts the statute. Another problem is that courts have not always appreciated the special constraints that arise when the fair use defense is applied to derivative uses. And copyright remedies, originally shaped with the case of literal copies and directly competing markets in mind, are sometimes misapplied to cases involving derivative works in noncompeting markets.

1. Ideas and Expressions

According to copyright gospel, infringement will be found only if defendant's work copies from plaintiff's, and only if the copying produces substantial similarities between the expression, and not just the underlying ideas, of the two works. Courts applying the idea-expression distinction to claims of literary infringement hold that themes and bare plots are no more than unprotectable ideas, but protection will be given against surface paraphrasing. As to the area between, courts generally treat the question as one of degree—the degree to which the copyright owner has developed theme and plot through setting, scenes, incidents, dialogue, characterizations and other detail, and the degree to which the alleged infringer has borrowed these details.

The rules on copyright infringement were shaped in the years before derivative rights were added to the statute, when the only question for decision was whether defendant's work constituted a copy of plaintiff's. The easiest case for substantial similarity arose when defendant had made a verbatim copy of plaintiff's entire copyrighted work. But courts were also prepared in the early abridgment cases to prohibit copiers from borrowing long, verbatim passages from the copyrighted work or publishing their works with only colorable variations from the original. And, eventually, with the addition of the performance right, courts following Daly v. Palmer found infringement even if there was no literal similarity at all between the two works, but only substantial similarity in protectable elements of incident and characterization.

The idea-expression distinction is far more difficult to apply across different formats, between an underlying work such as a novel and a work such as a motion picture alleged to derive from the novel. Although motion picture producers pay substantial sums to acquire literary properties, the elements that they ultimately employ sometimes bear only scant resemblance to the original. The first step "in adapting a book for the screen is to pare it down, cut it back to the basics and distill it into what movie people call its 'filmable elements.' Although the film's producers will try not to make too many changes in well known novels, they make take considerable liberties with lesser known works. Sometimes a single incident in the novel will form the entire movie—'we cut out everything else—the adult characters, the romantic interests, the outside problems and all the rest—to get to that little chunk.' "

As a book is transformed into a movie or television series, descriptive passages drop out and the actors' and set designers' skills substitute for the novelist's detailed characterization and scenic descriptions. Screenplays, it has been noted, are "barely readable conglomerations of dialogue, camera directions, setting descriptions, and character analysis." The standard form of literary agreement typically gives the producer the unquestioned right to alter the property at will. The first draft screenplay will invariably be rewritten in the course of filming and editing. Sometimes all that will be left of the original work is little more than the title. The result may be a motion picture that is truer to the novel than any more literal, plodding imitation could possibly be. But has expression been taken and not just ideas?

Benjamin Kaplan has astutely observed that it "is surely wrong to assume that what Hollywood is content to call a dramatization or screen treatment of a novel or play would necessarily be an infringing copy if not licensed."

Why, then, do firms negotiate and pay for elements whose use will not constitute copyright infringement? One answer is that they are buying the use of elements—primarily titles and character names—that, though not protected by copyright, may be protected under unfair competition or trademark law. More important, the license is the key to their participation in the overall commercial enterprise based on the underlying work, an enterprise that may consist of a multitude of carefully orchestrated elements including hardcover publication, mass market paperback publication, novelization of the motion picture, television sales and sales of merchandising rights, and in which each element enhances the value of the others. And these firms are buying time. Timing often requires that licenses be executed well before the licensee knows whether its work will incorporate copyrighted elements of the underlying work. Indeed, rights are sometimes licensed at a point when the literary property is hardly more than a twenty-page outline prepared by a well-known author. A license at this early stage assures the producer of the freedom to use copyrighted elements if it later so chooses.

These practical considerations suggest that it is mistaken to confuse the scope of an executed license with the substance of the work produced under it. Courts, unfortunately, have repeatedly made the mistake. It is no coincidence that the principal cases establishing broad rights against infringement by derivative works characteristically involve situations in which the alleged infringer had at some earlier point sought a license. The tendency in these cases, always unarticulated because legally irrelevant, is to take the earlier quest for a copyright license as evidence that one was needed, and to bar defendants from asserting that the rights they once tried to acquire do not now exist. For the reasons given, the emphasis is clearly misplaced. Prior negotiations may have motives that are completely irrelevant to the question of copyright infringement and should be given no weight in infringement determinations other than as evidence of access. . . .

2.   The Calculus of Rights.

Disregard for copyright's incentive structure has not been all in the direction of expanding the scope of derivative rights. Indifference to copyright economics has also occasionally produced improper curbs on derivative rights, most notably in cases perceived to involve utilitarian uses and fair uses of underlying works. The mistake in both contexts stems from a failure to distinguish between derivative rights and reproduction rights, and to recognize that the investment effects of section 106(2)'s exclusive right to prepare derivative works differ markedly from the investment effects of section 106(1)'s exclusive right to reproduce copies.

Derivative rights affect the level of investment in copyrighted works by enabling the copyright owner to proportion its investment to the level of expected returns from all markets, not just the market in which the work first appears, as is generally the case with reproduction rights. The publisher who knows that it can license, and obtain payment for, the translation, serialization, condensation and motion picture rights for a novel will invest more in purchasing, producing and marketing the novel than it would if its returns were limited to revenues from book sales in the English language.

Derivative rights also affect the direction of investment in copyrighted works. By spreading the duty to pay over different markets, section 106(2) tends to perfect the information available to the copyright owner respecting the value of its works to different groups of users. It also enables choices in light of that information. Knowing that the French and German language markets belong exclusively to it, a publisher of English language works may decide to invest in works that, once translated, will appeal to these audiences as well. The publisher can acquire a work because of its motion picture potential and can comfortably invest in the work's development and marketing to increase that potential. The publisher may choose either direction, both, or neither; and it can seek returns in other derivative markets, or only in the original market. The important point is that, by securing exclusive rights to all derivative markets, the statute enables the copyright proprietor to select those toward which it will direct investment.

The Economics of Improvement in Intellectual Property Law

MARK A. LEMLEY*

... I have a colleague in practice who claims that as a trade secrets lawyer, his job is to "prosecute thieves and defend entrepreneurs." For a lawyer in private practice, determining which is which may not be that difficult on a case-by-case basis: the answer may depend largely on who is paying the bills. Courts hearing intellectual property cases are not so fortunate, however. They must find a way to distinguish between improvement—which is thought to be a noble task, a necessary part of innovation, and generally to be encouraged—and imitation, which is generally considered both illegal and even immoral. This distinction is not easy to make, but it is critical to achieving the proper balance of

* 75 TEX. L. REV. 989, 990–92, 1015–24, 1029 (1997).

intellectual property rights. Allow too much imitation, and you will stifle the incentives for development and commercialization of new products. Discourage improvements too strongly, and you will freeze development at the first generation of products.

This problem is not new. Even before the United States adopted its patent and copyright laws, Lord Mansfield said the following in an English case involving a copyright claim against improved navigational charts:

> The rule of decision in this case is a matter of great consequence to the country. In deciding it we must take care to guard against two extremes equally prejudicial; the one, that men of ability, who have employed their time for the service of the community, may not be deprived of their just merits, and the reward of their ingenuity and labor; the other, that the world may not be deprived of improvements, nor the progress of the arts be retarded.

Unfortunately, there has not been much improvement in the law of improvements since 1785.

A number of doctrines in modern copyright and patent law attempt to strike some balance between the rights of original developers and the rights of subsequent improvers. Both patents and copyrights are limited in duration and in scope. Each of these limitations provides some freedom of action to subsequent improvers. Improvers are free to use material that is in the public domain because the copyright or patent has expired. They are free to skirt the edges of existing intellectual property rights, for example by taking the ideas but not the expression from a copyrighted work, or by "designing around" the claims of a patent. However, improvers cannot always avoid the intellectual property rights of the basic work on which they wish to improve. Some improvements fall within the scope of the preexisting intellectual property right, either because of an expansive definition of that right or because economic or technical necessity requires that the improver hew closely to the work of the original creator in some basic respect. Here, the improver is at the mercy of the original intellectual property owner, unless there is some separate right that expressly allows copying for the sake of improvement.

Patent and copyright law differ in how they treat improvements that fall within the scope of the original intellectual property right. Patent doctrines such as the rule of blocking patents.... offer some protection to the developers of significant or radical improvements. Improvers are therefore in a position to bargain with original patent owners to allocate the gains from their respective invention, and in some circumstances may even be free to use that invention without payment. By contrast, copyright doctrine currently offers little or no protection to improvers. Rather, the exclusive rights granted to the copyright owner in section 106 extend to cover any "copy" or adaptation or alteration of the original that is nonetheless "substantially similar" to the original work. So improvers—even radical improvers—have no power to bargain with copyright owners to divide the value of the improved work. If the work is substantially similar to the underlying copyrighted work, the original copyright owner has the right to exclude it from the market entirely. Further, because the rule is that improvers cannot even copyright their original contributions to what is on balance an infringing work, there is no way for the improver to capture even part of the value of her contribution. To be sure, improvers may be protected under copyright's "fair use" doctrine. But application of that doctrine is fraught with uncertainty, and historically has emphasized market harm to the original copyright owner. The result is a rule which in some respects gives broader protection to copyright owners than that given to patentees, and arguably provides insufficient incentive to improve upon copyrighted works....

B.   Evaluating Infringement by Improvers

Unlike patents, copyrights do not have claims. Infringement is tested by comparing the accused work to the copyrighted work to determine whether substantial copying has occurred. The simplest case is one in which the entire copyrighted work has been copied verbatim. This of course constitutes infringement, just as copying the patent owner's invention infringes the patent. Beyond this point, however, the patent and copyright infringement tests diverge. For one thing, it is possible to infringe a copyright by copying only a small portion of the copyright owner's work. Copying even a few hundred words from a book, or a few seconds of music from a song, may be enough to infringe the copyright in the entire work. By contrast, copying part but not all of a claimed invention is not patent infringement, since every element of the claimed invention (or an equivalent) must be present in the accused device. Thus, improvers may be liable for copying even a relatively small portion of the original work.

Further, copyright infringement is not limited to cases of verbatim copying. The courts long ago recognized that such a limitation would render copyright protection ineffective, allowing "plagiarist[s] [to] escape by immaterial variations." Defendants may infringe the copyright by taking only the "nonliteral" elements of a work, such as the plot outline of a movie, the structure, sequence and organization of a computer program, or even the "total concept and feel" of a song, a television show, or a greeting card. While one might analogize this protection against nonliteral infringement to patent law's doctrine of equivalents, the animating principle is somewhat different. Nonliteral copyright infringement involves the copying of elements of a work which, while not literally contained in the physical manifestation of the work, nonetheless constitute part of the original expression of the work, as distinguished from its idea or its functional attributes. Thus, improvements in the text of a work which keep the structure identical likely will not escape the web of nonliteral copyright infringement. On the other hand, the fact that two different plot devices for a mystery novel are functionally equivalent does not mean that one will infringe the copyright of the other. By contrast, the test for the doctrine of equivalents in patent law—insubstantial differences, as measured by factors such as reasonable interchangeability—allows the law to reach different works that operate on similar functional principles.

C.   Mechanisms for Protecting Improvers

One thing that the derivative works right does do is make it clear that copyright law is intended to reach improvers as well as counterfeiters. The copyright owner's control over works in markets other than the one he entered is no accident, but part of the scheme of copyright protection. Nonetheless, there are a few legal rules that function to protect improvers in copyright law. To compare these rules to analogous doctrines in patent law, let us once again hypothesize three types of improvers: minor improvers, significant improvers, and radical improvers.

1.   Minor Improvers—In Part II, I defined a minor patent improver as one who advances social utility by adding to the basic invention, but who does not contribute enough to justify receiving a patent in her own right on the improvement. For consistency, I will adopt the same definition here. Because copyright protection is so much easier to obtain than patent protection, however, the effect of this rule is to make the group of "minor improvers" very small. Most improvements will be sufficiently original that they would ordinarily qualify for copyright protection in their own right, and will therefore fall into the category of "significant" improvements. Nonetheless, certain improvements to an original work can be classified as "minor" even under this restrictive definition. Editorial corrections or revisions that do not themselves contribute copyrightable material fall into this category, as do factual corrections to a database or certain types of restoration efforts to works of art.

Minor improvers receive no special protection under copyright law. They are subject to the same rules of copyright infringement as any other copier, notwithstanding their improvements. Thus, it is possible that minor improvements will qualify as a fair use, particularly if they are done in the context of copies made for a public benefit and do not harm the market for the original work. But most copies that contain only minor improvements will not qualify as fair uses. And while it is theoretically possible that the changes made to the original work by the minor improver will cause the improved work to be noninfringing, in practice the likelihood of a change being both sufficiently minor as not to qualify for copyright protection and sufficiently major as to preclude a finding of substantial copying (or infringement of the derivative works right) is minimal. Minor improvers are therefore likely to be guilty of copyright infringement. As with minor improvements that infringe patents, improvements that infringe copyrights are effectively captured by the copyright owner, since anyone copying the new work would similarly be guilty of infringing the copyright on the original work.

2.   Significant Improvers—This class of improvers is quite broad, encompassing any improvement to a copyrighted work that itself contains original, creative expression, up to some arbitrary limit separating significant from radical improvements. Virtually any work that qualifies as a "derivative work" under the definition in section 101 will qualify as at least a significant improvement, since the additional effort involved in adapting the original work to a new market will almost always include original expression contributed by the improver. Thus, translating an original work into a new language, making a movie from a screenplay,

and even producing stuffed animals based on a movie involve the inclusion of significant new creative elements. Further, nonliteral copies that compete directly with the original will often qualify as significant improvements as well. A novel may copy the detailed plot structure of an original work, for example, but contribute entirely new text and characters. In all of these cases, the improver is guilty of copying from the original work, but has also contributed valuable material to the new work.

In the patent context, we referred to this situation as involving "blocking patents." The improver could not legally use the material covered by the original patent without permission, but the original patent owner similarly could not use the new material contributed by the improver. Perhaps surprisingly, there is no analogous doctrine of "blocking copyrights" granting copyright infringers the rights to their own improvements. Instead, section 103 of the Act provides that original works of authorship contributed as part of the creation of a derivative work are copyrightable only by the original copyright owners or their licensee. This means, for example, that if an improver makes a movie which is later determined to have infringed the copyright on the book on which it was based, the improver may not be entitled to any copyright protection for the movie—even those portions of the movie which were contributed by the improver. Indeed, in one case the fact that a scriptwriter used the "Rocky Balboa" character from a prior film in creating an unauthorized sequel to Rocky caused the court not only to find that the scriptwriter was infringing the copyright in the "Rocky" character, but to invalidate the scriptwriter's derivative work copyright completely.

Because section 103 of the Act denies copyright only in the "part of the work" that incorporates infringing material, some infringing derivative works may nonetheless be copyrightable in part. This is particularly true in the case of compilations, where the infringing material can be separated easily from other parts of the work. Thus, the House Report accompanying the 1976 Act provides that "an unauthorized translation of a novel could not be copyrighted at all, but the owner of copyright in an anthology of poetry could sue someone who infringed the whole anthology, even though the infringer proves that publication of one of the poems was unauthorized." This limitation on section 103 may provide significant improvers with solace in some cases, notably where the copied material is easily separated from the improver's contribution. In other cases, however, where the material is inextricably intertwined, the improver loses the entire value of her contribution. This is the case with regard to movies or plays based on a book. It is also likely to be the case with many improvements in the field of computer software. Finally, the promise of digital information—that it can easily be altered, translated between media, and transformed—now seems to be its peril as well.

The effect of this rule is to allow the original copyright owner to capture the value of even significant improvements made by others. While the improvements themselves are nominally in the public domain, no one can use those improvements in conjunction with the original work without infringing the copyright on that work. Further, the existence of this power of capture may influence license negotiations between copyright owners and potential improvers, tipping the balance in favor of the creators of original works at the expense of improvers. Relative to patent law, then, copyright law provides less encouragement for significant improvements, and gives more power to original copyright owners.

3. Radical Improvers—The final case involves improvers who have made a major contribution to social value, for example a work in which the new material predominates over infringing material.... Radical improvers still infringe the original copyright so long as they have copied any substantial portion of the original work. Thus, the maker of a major motion picture relying on only a small portion of a play, the publisher of a news story which includes three hundred words quoted from a forthcoming biography, and the composer who writes a song which is similar in only a few notes to a previously published song are all subject to suit for copyright infringement notwithstanding the value of their contributions. Infringement under the derivative works right may even extend to complementary goods that do not directly copy any of the underlying work ...

IV. Is Differential Treatment of Improvement Justified?

Comparing the treatment of improvers under patent and copyright law leads to a rather surprising result: copyright law is significantly more hostile to improvements than is patent law. What is surprising is not so much that the rules differ, but the way in which they differ. Copyright is traditionally thought to afford weaker, not stronger, protection than patent law, in part to compensate for the fact that copyrights are so much easier to obtain than patents and last so much longer. But in the context of improvements, the opposite result obtains....

Notes and Questions

1. For a biographical note on Professor Lemley, see supra, Chapter 1, at page 263.

2. Professor Landes and Judge Posner offer an economic rationale for the derivative works right:

> The most compelling reason for vesting the original author with control over derivative works is to minimize transaction costs. Suppose Dostoevsky's heir owned the copyright on the original Russian version of the *The Brothers Karamazov*, but and American owned the copyright on the English translation. A publisher who wanted to bring out a new edition of that translation would have to deal with two copyright holders. Transaction costs would be reduced if one person owned both copyrights. Of course, even if they were separately owned to begin with, one of the owners could buy the other's copyright. But such a transaction, with its attendant costs, can be avoided if the law places the power to obtain both copyrights in the same person to begin with—which in effect is what it does. What is more, there is no reason to stop with two. There could be hundreds of derivative works of a popular original. A popular movie, for example, might give rise to a multitude of ancillary products ranging

from lunch boxes to toy dolls to electronic games, all incorporating characters from the movie. Another derivative work would be unlikely to infringe *all* of them—many of them the author might be unaware of—but to be on the safe side he would have to obtain a license from each copyright owner of a derivative work to which he had or might be claimed to have access. The transaction costs would often be not merely high, but prohibitive.

... And by enabling the author's property right to be subdivided, the copyrightability of derivative works facilitates transactions; compare time-sharing and other subdividings of more conventional property rights. In the case of a movie based on a book, for example, the producer will invariably acquire the copyright on the movie, the derivative work, because he is best able to exploit derivative uses of the movie, for example video cassettes, adaptations for television, posters ... And in cases in which the original is in the public domain, there is no copyright owner to prevent the copying of a translation or other derivative work, and so the incentive to prepare such works would be impaired if derivative works could not be copyrighted.

William M. Landes & Richard A. Posner, THE ECONOMIC STRUCTURE OF INTELLECTUAL PROPERTY LAW 110–11 (2003).

3. The scope of copyright has evolved, and grown, from a series of specifically-drafted rights keyed to particular types of works, as set out in the 1909 Act and its predecessors, to the broader synthesis of rights expressed in the 1976 Act. Professor Litman articulates the problems that beset both techniques:

To solve the dilemma of updating and simplifying a body of law too complicated for legislative revision, Congress and the Copyright Office have settled on a scheme for statutory drafting that features meetings and negotiations among representatives of industries with interests in copyright. ...

The process Congress has relied on for copyright revision, however, has shaped the law in disturbing ways. The inter-industry negotiations that resulted in the 1909 Copyright Act sought to revise a body of law based on an old model in order to enable it to embrace a variety of new media. Industries for whom the old law worked well sought to retain their advantages; industries that found the old law inadequate sought profound changes in the way the copyright statute treated them. Affected interests compromised their disputes by treating different industries in disparate ways. The draft bill that emerged from the conferences among industry representatives defined particular copyright rights with reference to the type of work in which copyright was claimed, and the statute enacted in 1909 retained the draft bill's essential strategy. Authors of particular classes of works were granted specific, enumerated rights; rights differed among the classes of copyrightable works. Thus, the 1909 Act gave the proprietor of the copyright in a dramatic work the exclusive right to present the work publicly, the proprietor of the copyright in a lecture the exclusive right to deliver the work in public for profit, the proprietor of the copyright in a musical composition the exclusive right to perform the work publicly for profit except on coin operated machines, and the proprietor of the copyright in a book no performance or delivery right whatsoever.

The drafters of the 1976 Act pursued similar goals to different conclusions. Congress and the Copyright Office again depended on negotiations among representatives of an assortment of interests affected by copyright to draft a copyright bill. During twenty-one years of inter-industry squabbling, the private parties to the ongoing negotiations settled on a strategy for the future that all of them could support. Copyright owners were to be granted broad, expansive rights, including future as well as currently feasible uses of copyrighted works. Each of the copyright users represented in the negotiations, meanwhile, received the benefit of a privilege or exemption specifically tailored to its requirements, but very narrowly defined. The 1976 Act solved the problem of accommodating future technology by reserving to the copyright owner control over uses of copyrighted works made possible by that technology. Broad, expansive rights were balanced by narrow, stingy exceptions.

A comparison of the immediate futures of the 1909 and the 1976 Acts reveals that they failed the future in similar ways. Narrow provisions became inapplicable or irrelevant as technology developed, while those interests absent from the meetings of industry representatives encountered significant legal barriers to their activities. The inflexibility of specific provisions distorted the balance that the statute's drafters envisioned when it was enacted, and interested groups came running to Congress to plead for quick fixes. This history illustrates that broad rights and broad exceptions swallow up their specific counterparts. Because technological development will change the world that a copyright law seeks to order, the law needs flexible provisions of general application.

Jessica Litman, *Copyright Legislation and Technological Change*, 68 OR. L. REV. 275, 278–82 (1989). More fundamentally, Professor Litman criticizes the premises underlying the current Congressional approach to copyright legislation:

The inquiry relevant to copyright legislation long ago ceased to be "is this a good bill?" Rather, the inquiry has been, and continues to be "is this a bill that current stakeholders agree on?" The two questions are not the same. ... A copyright law cannot make sensible provision for the growth of technology unless it incorporates both the flexibility to make adjustments and the general principles to guide courts in the directions those adjustments should take. The negotiation process that has dominated copyright revision throughout this century, however, is ill adapted to generate that flexibility.

Jessica Litman, *Digital Copyright* 63 (2000).

What's So Fair About Fair Use?

ALEX KOZINSKI AND CHRISTOPHER NEWMAN*

What I would like to call into question is whether the "exclusive Right" of authors to profit from their work need necessarily entail an exclusive right to control the uses to which that work is put ... This begs the question by assuming that without injunction there can be no copyrights. Yet property rights can and do exist even though damages are the only remedy for their loss ...

Framed in this way, the problem is akin to that of deciding whether property should be protected by a liability rule as opposed to a property rule. One of the big advantages of private ownership is that it leads to efficient uses of scarce physical resources. But private property can also be used inefficiently. If Donald Trump offers you a billion to let him tear down your family home and put a casino in its place, you have the right to say no, even though your house is a dump.... As a general rule, we don't override your right to exclude in the name of efficiency. Why? There are a number of reasons. One is that, not being omniscient, we can't go around second guessing every failed transaction to figure out whether it *was* inefficient. It may have been a rational decision to hold out for a better price. So even though individual refusals to sell may sometimes be inefficient, respecting the owner's right to hold out promotes efficiency overall.

Does the same hold true for copyrights? Again, we have a system that generally tends toward utility maximization, this time by encouraging the production of valuable intellectual works. On the other hand, we also have inefficient hold outs, in the form of authors who use their exclusive right to prevent the creation of valuable derivative works. So far the analogy looks pretty good. But there's a very important difference between the two: A piece of land can't serve both as your living room and Trump Towers, but a piece of intellectual property suffers from no such limitation ...

Suppose someone besides J.K. Rowling writes an unauthorized Harry Potter sequel. Assume that everyone knows this sequel is not by Rowling or authorized by her. We can imagine that Rowling might find it disturbing to see her character in someone else's book. But does the ersatz sequel really rob Rowling of the use of her character the same way taking away your car deprives you of its use? The appearance of this

* 46 J. COPYRIGHT SOC'Y U.S.A 513, 520–22, 529 (1999). This article is based on the 1999 Donald C. Brace Memorial Lecture. The footnote accompanying the credit line to the publication in the Journal of the Copyright Society states: "This lecture was delivered by Judge Kozinski. Hence the folksy first person style. However we have it on good authority that all the best parts were put in by Judge Kozinski's law clerk [Mr. Newman]."

sequel certainly doesn't require Rowling to alter her day to day existence. Further, her identity as the creator of Harry Potter is still intact; her reputation is unharmed. She is still just as able to do all the things with her character that she could before, and will be able to continue earning the appreciation of the people who like what she does.... [T]he only thing wrong with this picture is that value has been created from Rowling's work for which she has not been compensated. So long as we make sure she gets her share of the profits ... Rowling has no other "claim or complaint."

One might object that Rowling *will* be robbed of the use of her character ... Even though there is no physical impossibility involved in exploiting the character in numerous ways, an unrestrained glut of knock-off Harry Potter books will cause people to get sick of him, thus dissipating demand. This might destroy the market for future sequels, depriving Rowling of the chance to create any. Such an outcome could harm the progress of the arts, by preventing the creation of authentic works that would have been of higher quality. Such a scenario is conceivable, but in my view unlikely. Cervantes had no power to enjoin unauthorized sequels to his immensely popular *Don Quixote*. He did, however, have the power to provide the real thing—and the world could tell the difference....

The simple fact is that owners of intellectual property tend to be control freaks, and regard anyone who would erode this control as an enemy. "It's my creation," they will say. "What right do others have to tamper with it?" To this I say: It's your creation if you keep it secret. Once you release it to the rest of us, it enters our minds and becomes ours as well ... So long as their right to a share in the profits of derivative uses is enforced, I suspect that copyright holders would actually be better off in a system in which everyone was allowed to exploit the work. When set free to do so, people will find ways to extract value from intellectual properties that original authors, too fearful of sullying their creations, would never dream of.

Notes and Questions

1. Born in 1950 in Bucharest, Romania, Judge Alex Kozinski, a 1975 graduate of the University of California, Los Angeles, School of Law, sits on the Ninth Circuit U.S. Court of Appeals. He is the author of many law review articles, including in the intellectual property field, and has also been "the Nintendo reviewer for the Wall Street Journal," see Alex Kozinski, *Trademarks Unplugged*, 68 NYU L. Rev. 960, 960 & n. 1 (1993). Christopher Newman graduated from the University of Michigan Law School in 1999 and practices law at Irell and Manella in Los Angeles.

2. Neither Professor Lemley, nor Professor Landes and Judge Posner, nor Judge Kozinski address, or at least take seriously, the author's artistic or editorial interest in determining whether or not to authorize the creation of a derivative work, and in selecting the persons to whom to grant authorization. Are these concerns irrelevant to copyright law? Consider the following exploration of authors' non economic interests.

Copyright and the Moral Right: Is an American Marriage Possible?

ROBERTA ROSENTHAL KWALL*

II. ANALYTICAL FRAMEWORK FOR THE MORAL RIGHT

A. Components and Attributes of the Moral Right

The moral right doctrine generally is said to encompass three major components: the right of disclosure, the right of paternity, and the right of integrity. Some formulations of the moral right doctrine also include the right of withdrawal, the right to prevent excessive criticism, and the right to prevent assaults upon one's personality. For purposes of illustration, these components will be explored briefly in the context of the following hypothetical. A playwright, enthralled with the idea of writing a piece poking fun at the evangelical segment of society, suddenly envisions a story line through which she can communicate her ideas. In one day she outlines the plot and sketches some dialogue so that she will have a rough draft which she can develop further when inspiration strikes again. At this point, the playwright's interest in her work would be protected by an aspect of the moral right doctrine known as the right of disclosure or divulgation. Underlying this component of the moral right is the idea that the creator, as the sole judge of when a work is ready for public dissemination, is the only one who can possess any rights in an uncompleted work. Prior to the time the playwright places her work into circulation, therefore, she retains the same right to determine both the form of her play before it is distributed and the timing of public circulation.

Suppose that a few days after the playwright had finished her rough draft, she entered into an agreement with a publisher in which she promised to produce the final publication version of the play within six months. Subsequently, a personal crisis in the playwright's life triggers a deep sense of religious conviction and she no longer wishes to finish the play. In these circumstances her refusal to complete the play would be supported by her right to refuse to disclose, a corollary to the right of disclosure. Application of this right would preclude a judgment ordering the playwright to complete the play, although a court might award the publisher damages for breach of contract.

Some scholars believe that a second component of the moral right doctrine, known as the right of withdrawal, would allow the playwright in our hypothetical situation to recall all existing copies of her work if, following actual publication, she experienced a radical change of the convictions that originally provided the impetus for the play. Other commentators, however, have expressed doubts regarding the viability of the moral right of withdrawal because of the practical inconsistency in assuming that the public will forget works to which it has already been exposed.

To continue the illustration, now assume that the playwright completes her work and subsequently visits a publisher with her manuscript

* 38 VAND. L. REV. 1, 5–16 (1985).

in hand and offers it to the publisher for $1500. The publisher condition-
ally agrees to this arrangement, providing the playwright makes certain
revisions. When the playwright tenders the revised manuscript to the
publisher, the publisher refuses to publish it with the playwright's name,
notwithstanding the appearance of the playwright's name on the original
manuscript. In these circumstances the playwright would be protected
by another component of the moral right, the right of paternity. As its
name suggests, the right of paternity safeguards a creator's right to
compel recognition for his work and prevents others from naming
anyone else as the creator. Therefore, the playwright would be able to
force publication of the work under her name. Additionally, the right of
paternity protects a creator in the event that someone falsely attributes
to him a work that is not his creation.

Two other aspects of the moral right doctrine are the creator's right
to prevent excessive criticism and the creator's right to relief from other
assaults on his personality. To appreciate fully the theoretical basis for
these two rights, one must recall that the moral right doctrine safeguards rights of personality rather than pecuniary rights. The creator
projects his personality into his work, and thus is entitled to be free from
vexatious or malicious criticism and from unwanted assaults upon his
honor and professional standing. By virtue of the prohibition against
attacks on the creator's personality, the creator also is protected against
misuse of his name and work. In the context of our hypothetical
situation, such misuse would occur if an antireligious organization
claimed that the playwright subscribed to antireligious views solely by
virtue of her authorship of the play.

In the hypothetical situation, now suppose the playwright enters
into an agreement with a movie producer authorizing the producer to
write a screenplay based upon her play. The final version of the screenplay, however, distorts considerably the playwright's theme and muti-
lates her story line. The component of the moral right doctrine that
would grant relief to the playwright in this situation is called the right of
integrity. This right lies at the heart of the moral right doctrine. In our
hypothetical case the adaptation process naturally would require certain
modifications in the playwright's manuscript, but the right of integrity
prevents those who make such alterations from destroying the spirit and
character of the author's work. Although adaptations of a work from one
medium to another present the most obvious potential for violations of a
creator's right of integrity, in reality, any modification of a work can be
problematic from an integrity standpoint. Any distortion that misrepre-
sents an artist's expression constitutes a violation of the creator's right
of integrity.

There is, however, one rather incongruous aspect of the right of
integrity. If the artist in our hypothetical situation was a painter rather
than a playwright, the right of integrity probably would not allow her to
prevent the destruction of one of her paintings by its owner. Perhaps the
underlying rationale for this exception is that a work which has been
destroyed completely cannot reflect adversely upon the creator's honor
or reputation. Nevertheless, some commentators have criticized the
destruction exception on the ground that it negates the creator's right of

paternity and frustrates the public's interest in enjoying the artist's work.

To summarize, the moral right doctrine encompasses several discrete components. All nations that have adopted the moral right doctrine statutorily include at least some of the above protections, but the contours of the doctrine vary among the adhering countries. Although a detailed analysis of the doctrine's application in foreign jurisprudence is beyond the scope of this Article, a few general observations are in order.

The 1971 revision of the Berne Convention for the Protection of Literary and Artistic Works contains a moral rights provision, Article 6bis, which recognizes the right of paternity and a limited right of integrity. The right of integrity is violated only by a distortion, alteration, or mutilation of the creator's work that is prejudicial to his honor or reputation. Both of these rights are independent of the creator's economic rights, and continue to exist following the creator's transfer of his economic rights. Despite the general recognition that Article 6bis affords the moral right doctrine, the treaty contemplates that the specific legislation of the respective Union members will govern substantive applications of the right. Some signatories to the Berne Convention are far more protective of a creator's moral rights than are others. France, for example, awards the greatest protection, while Germany and Italy follow closely behind. Several nations that are not members of the Berne Convention provide extensive protection for moral rights as part of their copyright laws. Ecuador, for example, protects an author's rights of paternity, disclosure, integrity, and withdrawal.

No discussion of the moral right doctrine would be complete without addressing how foreign jurisprudence treats three issues that arise in connection with the doctrine's application: alienability of the right, its duration, and its exercise after the creator's death. Although countries that have adopted the moral right do not endorse a uniform position with respect to these matters, neither inalienability nor perpetual duration are critical to the moral right's existence.

Some scholars have argued that moral rights should not be alienable because they protect personal attributes such as personality, honor, and reputation. France and numerous other countries expressly adhere to this position, and so, theoretically, in those countries a creator cannot waive or assign his moral rights. Nevertheless, in adjudicating the validity of waivers as a defense in actions for alleged right of integrity violations, the French judiciary tends to enforce contracts allowing reasonable alterations that do not distort the spirit of the creator's work, particularly with respect to adaptations and contributions to collective works. Indeed, this inclination on the part of French courts, which always have exhibited the utmost regard for the personal rights of creators, illustrates the inherent infeasibility of a truly inalienable moral right. The interests of creators in safeguarding their reputations and professional standing must be balanced against the interests of those who perform adaptations in maintaining creative liberty.

The United States balances these interests somewhat differently than those countries that recognize the moral right. Whereas countries that have adopted the moral right generally will not interpret contracts which do not address moral rights as implying a tacit waiver of the creator's rights, the opposite is true in the United States. Although courts in the United States rely on equitable principles to protect a creator against excessive mutilation of his work, in general the creator has the burden of extracting an agreement regarding modifications from the purchaser. Even when the creator has secured such an agreement, the danger exists that the contract will not bind subsequent purchasers. Waivers of the right of paternity are viewed favorably in this country, as evidenced by the traditional rule that a creator is not entitled to credit, absent a contractual provision to the contrary.

Article 6bis of the Berne Convention does not address the alienability issue, but it does address a second important issue concerning the moral right-duration. The 1971 Conference amended Article 6bis to include a provision calling for the recognition of a creator's moral rights following his death for a minimum period consisting of the duration of his copyright. Article 6bis(2) does afford each member some latitude in this respect, however, by providing that those countries whose laws do not protect all of the moral rights set forth in Article 6bis(1) on a posthumous basis may allow some of these rights to cease following the creator's death.

Countries that recognize the moral right can be divided into two groups with respect to the question of the right's duration. The first group, which includes West Germany and the Netherlands, follows the approach advocated by the Berne Convention and simultaneously terminates a creator's moral rights and copyright. The second group adheres to the French view that moral rights are perpetual. In France a creator's moral or personality rights always have been regarded as a separate body of protections, rather than as a component of the creator's pecuniary rights. Thus, in French theory no logical inconsistency results from protecting a creator's moral rights in perpetuity, despite the limited duration of his copyright.

Two justifications support the survival of moral rights subsequent to the creator's death. First, focusing solely on the interests of the creator, any mutilation or modification of his work that would be detrimental to his reputation during his lifetime is equally, if not more, injurious after his death, when he can no longer defend the integrity of his work. Second, focusing on society's interest in preserving its cultural heritage, when a creator's work is altered after his death, society is the ultimate victim for it can no longer benefit from the creator's original contribution. Adoption of these rationales helps to answer the related question concerning power of enforcement of a creator's moral rights following his death. In many countries moral rights are treated as any other form of property, and therefore, vest in the spouse and next of kin upon the creator's death. This approach, influenced by the first justification, recognizes a creator's family and descendants as the appropriate guardians of his reputation. Some countries, however, cognizant of society's interest in maintaining its cultural heritage, provide more extensive protection by entrusting a deceased creator's moral rights to an official body designated to protect the nation's creative works. . . .

Notes and Questions

1. Born in 1955, Roberta Rosenthal Kwall a 1980 graduate of the University of Pennsylvania Law School, is the Raymond P. Niro Professor of Intellectual Property Law and Director of the Center for Intellectual Property Law & Information Technology at DePaul University College of Law.

2. Judge Kozinski recognizes that his proposal to substitute a compensation regime for the exclusive right to authorize derivative works clashes with the proposed moral right of integrity. Indeed, he welcomes the conflict:

> It seems to me that this [compensation] is all authors can rightfully demand in the name of "moral rights." It would be immoral to alter Rowling's reputation by causing people to attribute my work to her. But why is it immoral simply to build on her ideas in my own name, so long as I compensate and give her credit for the value of whatever I borrow?

Alex Kozinski, *What's So Fair About Fair Use*, 46 J. Copyright Soc'y. 513, 522 n. 22 (1999).

3. Is recognition of moral rights inconsistent with the US copyright regime? Consider the following critique of the proposed legislation ultimately enacted as The Visual Artist's Rights Act [VARA]:

> The principal entertainment and cultural industries of the United States, in summary, are highly collaborative, contemplate and depend upon a wide variety of derivative forms in their distribution to the public, and are historically regulated by individually and collectively negotiated agreements. The introduction into these industries of a right exercisable by any one of a host of collaborative contributors to protest the alleged distortion or modification of a particular literary or artistic contribution is extremely problematic. At best, it introduces an element of instability and uncertainty, as well as the frequent possibility, because of the increased threat of litigation, of delay in public access to and enjoyment of entertainment vehicles. At worst, it threatens to prevent altogether the dissemination to the United States and international public of a host of cultural and entertainment materials in forms that are varied, appealing and affordable. Any significant limit upon the ability of producers and publishers to disseminate works in these secondary markets—dissemination which commonly can mean the difference between a losing and a profitable business venture—runs a substantial risk of chilling investment in the arts and entertainment fields. This may in turn reduce the financial support of innovative creative endeavor—a result that will obviously be harmful to the public interest. Introduction of moral rights into these industries (particularly if these rights are statutorily declared to be non-alienable and non-waivable) will also unsettle the network of contractual agreements that have been devel-

oped over many years in the various industries and that appear on the whole to be working quite successfully and fairly.

Robert Gorman, *Federal Moral Rights Legislation: The Need for Caution*, 14 NOVA L. REV. 421, 423–24 (1990).

4. For a counter argument, at least with respect to the moral right of attribution, consider the following analysis, offered in support of a potential amendment to the copyright act to include a right of attribution of authorship:

> Giving credit where it is due ... is instinctively appropriate because it furthers the interests both of authors and of their public. For the public, the author's name, once known, alerts readers/viewers/listeners to particular characteristics or qualities to expect in the work. For authors, name recognition enhances sales (at least when the work that previously bore the author's name has been well-received). As one Federal Court judge aptly put it:

>> Reputation is critical to a person who follows a vocation dependent on commissions from a variety of clients. Success breeds success, but only if the first success is known to potential clients. To deprive a person of credit to which he was justly entitled is to do him a great wrong. Not only does he lose the general benefit of being associated with a successful production; he loses the chance of using that work to sell his abilities.

> Most national copyright laws guarantee the right of attribution (or "paternity"); the leading international copyright treaty, the Berne Convention, requires that Member States protect other Members' authors' "right to claim authorship." Yet, perhaps to the surprise of many, no such right exists in US copyright law nor in other US laws. (The Federal Court judge just quoted sits on the *Australian* Federal Court, not on any U.S. bench.) ...

> Does the copyright clause's authorization to Congress to secure the exclusive rights of authors in their writings include the power to enact moral as well as economic rights? The constitutional text hardly compels the interpretation that the "exclusive Right" is exclusively pecuniary. Although the first copyright statute and its successors provided only for the economic rights to print, publish and vend, that should not prompt an originalist negative inference that the constitution restricts Congress' power to the rights (and subject matter) selected for coverage in the first copyright statutes. Such an inference would exclude from Congressional prerogative not only moral rights, but also the pecuniary rights, such as translation and public performance rights, that Congress later brought within the statutory grant. "Exclusive Right" implies authors' control over their works; ensuring attribution is one element of that control. In addition, exercise of that kind of control is fully consistent with the constitutional goal of authorizing exclusive rights: to promote the progress of knowledge. In the constitutional scheme, exclu-

sive rights are an impetus to authorship. Name recognition can furnish an important incentive to create and disseminate works: fame may, after all, bring fortune, and if fortune is not forthcoming, glory or notoriety may (at least for a time) console those whom the market has yet to reward. . . .

The U.S. Constitution authorizes Congress to secure for limited times the exclusive right of authors to their writings. Curiously, those rights, as enacted in our copyright laws, have not included the right to be recognized as the author of one's writings. Yet, the interest in being identified with one's work is fundamental, whatever one's conception of the philosophical or policy basis for copyright. That is, whether one sees copyright as a personality right conferring on the author the ownership of the fruits of her labor, or as an economic incentive scheme to promote the production of works of authorship, or as a public works program designed to fill the public domain, (or, most accurately, as a combination of the three), giving credit where it is due is fully compatible with both the author-regarding and the public-regarding aspects of these goals.

Jane C. Ginsburg, *The Right to Claim Authorship in U.S. Copyright and Trademarks Law*, 41 U. Houston L. Rev. 263, 264–65, 286–87, 306–07 (2004).

III.   *Limitations on Copyright*

A.   Fair use

Toward a Fair Use Standard
PIERRE N. LEVAL*

II.   The Nature and Contours of Fair Use

The doctrine of fair use limits the scope of the copyright monopoly in furtherance of its utilitarian objective. As Lord Ellenborough explained in an early dictum, "[W]hile I shall think myself bound to secure every man in the enjoyment of his copyright, one must not put manacles upon science." Thus, the introductory language of our statute explains that fair use may be made for generally educational or illuminating purposes "such as criticism, comment, news reporting, teaching . . . scholarship, or research."

Fair use should not be considered a bizarre, occasionally tolerated departure from the grand conception of the copyright monopoly. To the contrary, it is a necessary part of the overall design. Although no simple definition of fair use can be fashioned, and inevitably disagreement will

* 103 Harv. L. Rev. 1105, 1110–28 (1990).

arise over individual applications, recognition of the function of fair use as integral to copyright's objectives leads to a coherent and useful set of principles. Briefly stated, the use must be of a character that serves the copyright objective of stimulating productive thought and public instruction without excessively diminishing the incentives for creativity. One must assess each of the issues that arise in considering a fair use defense in the light of the governing purpose of copyright law.

A. *The Statutory Factors*

Following Story's articulation, the statute lists four pertinent "factors to be considered" "in determining whether the use made of a work in any particular case is a fair use." They are, in summary, the purpose and character of the use, the nature of the copyrighted work, the quantity and importance of the material used, and the effect of the use upon the potential market or value of the copyrighted work. Each factor directs attention to a different facet of the problem. The factors do not represent a score card that promises victory to the winner of the majority. Rather, they direct courts to examine the issue from every pertinent corner and to ask in each case whether, and how powerfully, a finding of fair use would serve or disserve the objectives of the copyright.

  1. Factor One—The Purpose and Character of the Secondary Use.— Factor One's direction that we "consider[] ... the purpose and character of the use" raises the question of justification. Does the use fulfill the objective of copyright law to stimulate creativity for public illumination? This question is vitally important to the fair use inquiry, and lies at the heart of the fair user's case. Recent judicial opinions have not sufficiently recognized its importance.

In analyzing a fair use defense, it is not sufficient simply to conclude whether or not justification exists. The question remains how powerful, or persuasive, is the justification, because the court must weigh the strength of the secondary user's justification against factors favoring the copyright owner.

I believe the answer to the question of justification turns primarily on whether, and to what extent, the challenged use is *transformative.* The use must be productive and must employ the quoted matter in a different manner or for a different purpose from the original. A quotation of copyrighted material that merely repackages or republishes the original is unlikely to pass the test; in Justice Story's words, it would merely "supersede the objects" of the original. If, on the other hand, the secondary use adds value to the original—if the quoted matter is used as raw material, transformed in the creation of new information, new aesthetics, new insights and understandings—this is the very type of activity that the fair use doctrine intends to protect for the enrichment of society.

Transformative uses may include criticizing the quoted work, exposing the character of the original author, proving a fact, or summarizing an idea argued in the original in order to defend or rebut it. They also may include parody, symbolism, aesthetic declarations, and innumerable other uses.

The existence of any identifiable transformative objective does not, however, guarantee success in claiming fair use. The transformative justification must overcome factors favoring the copyright owner. A biographer or critic of a writer may contend that unlimited quotation enriches the portrait or justifies the criticism. The creator of a derivative work based on the original creation of another may claim absolute entitlement because of the transformation. Nonetheless, extensive takings may impinge on creative incentives. And the secondary user's claim under the first factor is weakened to the extent that her takings exceed the asserted justification. The justification will likely be outweighed if the takings are excessive and other factors favor the copyright owner.

The importance of a transformative use was stressed in the early decisions, which often related to abridgements. For example, *Gyles v. Wilcox* in 1740 stated:

> Where books are colourably shortened only, they are undoubtedly infringement within the meaning of the [Statute of Anne]....
>
> But this must not be carried so far as to restrain persons from making a real and fair abridgment, for abridgments may with great propriety be called a new book, because ... the invention, learning, and judgment of the [secondary] author is shewn in them....

In the United States in 1841, Justice Story wrote in *Folsom:*

> [N]o one can doubt that a reviewer may fairly cite [quote] largely from the original work, if ... [its design be] ... criticism. On the other hand, it is as clear, that if he thus [quotes] the most important parts of the work, with a view, not to criticise, but to supersede the use of the original work, [infringement will be found].

Courts must consider the question of fair use for each challenged passage and not merely for the secondary work overall. This detailed inquiry is particularly important in instances of a biographical or historical work that quotes numerous passages from letters, diaries, or published writings of the subject of the study. Simply to appraise the overall character of the challenged work tells little about whether the various quotations of the original author's writings have a fair use purpose or merely supersede. For example, in the recent cases of biographies of Igor Stravinsky and J. D. Salinger, although each biography overall served a useful, educational, and instructive purpose that tended to favor the defendant, some quotations from the writings of Stravinsky and Salinger were not justified by a strong transformative secondary objective. The biographers took dazzling passages of the original writing because they made good reading, not because such quotation was vital to demonstrate an objective of the biographers. These were takings of protected expression without sufficient transformative justification.

I confess to some error in Salinger's case. Although the majority of the biographer's takings were of unprotected facts or ideas and some displayed transformative value in sketching the character portrait, other takings of highly expressive material exhibited minimal creative, transformative justification. My finding of fair use was based primarily on the overall instructive character of the biography. I failed to recognize that the nontransformative takings provided a weak basis for claiming the benefits of the doctrine and that, unless attention were focused on the individual passages, a favorable appraisal of the constructive purpose of the overall work could conceal unjustified takings of protected expression. The converse can also be true: a low estimation of the overall merit of the secondary work can lead to a finding for the copyright owner in spite of a well-justified, transformative use of the particular quotation that should justify a favorable finding under the first factor.

. . .

... In *New Era,* unlike *Salinger,* various persuasive justifications were proferred as to why quotation was necessary to accomplish the biographer's objective. For example, the biographer sought to support a portrait of his subject as a liar by showing he had lied; as a bigot by showing he had made bigoted pronouncements; as pompous and self-important by quoting self-important statements. The biographer similarly used quotations to show cruelty, paranoia, aggressiveness, scheming. These are points which often cannot be fairly demonstrated without quotation. The Second Circuit's majority opinion rejected the pertinence of even considering the necessity of quotation of unpublished matter to communicate such assessments. Citing *Salinger,* it reasserted that "[unpublished] works normally enjoy complete protection."

I believe the *Salinger/New Era* position accords insufficient recognition to the value of accurate quotation as a necessary tool of the historian or journalist. The biographer who quotes his subject is characterized as a parasite or free rider. If he copies "more than minimal amounts ... he deserves to be enjoined." Nor does this restriction "interfere ... with the process of ... history," the *Salinger* opinion insists, because "[t]he *facts* may be reported" without risk of infringement. Can it be seriously disputed that history, biography, and journalism benefit from accurate quotation of source documents, in preference to a rewriting of the facts, always subject to the risk that the historian alters the "facts" in rewriting them?

As to ideas, the analysis is similar. If the secondary writer has legitimate justification to report the original author's idea, whether for criticism or as a part of a portrait of the subject, she is surely permitted to set it forth accurately. Can ideas be correctly reported, discussed, or challenged if the commentator is obliged to express the idea in her own different words? The subject will, of course, reply, "That's not what I said." Such a requirement would sacrifice clarity, much as a requirement that judges, in passing on the applicability of a statute or contract, describe its provisions in their own words rather than quoting it directly.

Is it not clear, furthermore, as Chief Judge Oakes' separate opinion in *New Era* recognized, that at times the subject's very words are the facts calling for comment? If a newspaper wishes to report that last year a political candidate wrote a personal letter demeaning a race or religion, or proclaiming ideals directly contrary to those now stated in his campaign speeches, how can it fairly do this without quotation from the letter? If a biographer wished to show that her subject was cruel, jealous, vain, or crazy, can we seriously contend she should be limited to giving the reader those adjectives, while withholding the words that support the conclusion? How then may the reader judge whether to accept the biographer's characterization?

The problem was amusingly illustrated in the fall-out of *Salinger*. After the decision, the biographer rewrote his book, this time without quotations. Resorting to adjectives, he described certain of Salinger's youthful letters as "self-promoting ... boastful" and "buzzing with self-admiration." A reviewer, who had access to the letters, disagreed and proclaimed that the letters were in fact "exuberant, self-deprecating and charged with hope." Where does that leave the reader? What should the reader believe? Does this battle of adjectives serve knowledge and the progress of the arts better than allowing readers to judge for themselves by reading revelatory extracts?

. . .

Quoting is not necessarily stealing. Quotation can be vital to the fulfillment of the public-enriching goals of copyright law. The first fair use factor calls for a careful evaluation whether the particular quotation is of the transformative type that advances knowledge and the progress of the arts or whether it merely repackages, free riding on another's creations. If a quotation of copyrighted matter reveals no transformative purpose, fair use should perhaps be rejected without further inquiry into the other factors. Factor One is the soul of fair use. A finding of justification under this factor seems indispensable to a fair use defense. The strength of that justification must be weighed against the remaining factors, which focus on the incentives and entitlements of the copyright owner.

2. Factor Two—The Nature of the Copyrighted Work.—The nature of the copyrighted work is a factor that has been only superficially discussed and little understood. Like the third and fourth factors, it concerns itself with protecting the incentives of authorship. It implies that certain types of copyrighted material are more amenable to fair use than others.

Copyright protection is available to very disparate categories of writings. If it be of original authorship, *i.e.,* not copied from someone else, and recorded in a fixed medium, it is protected by the copyright. Thus, the great American novel, a report prepared as a duty of employment, a shopping list, or a loanshark's note on a debtor's door saying "Pay me by Friday or I'll break your goddamn arms" are all protected by the copyright.

In the early history of copyright, British courts debated whether letters written for private communication should receive any protection at all from the Statute of Anne. The question was soon satisfactorily settled in favor of protection, and I do not seek to reopen it. I do not argue that writings prepared for private motives should be denied copyright protection. In the unlikely event of the publication of the Collected Shopping Lists (or Extortion Notes) of a Renowned Personage, of course only the author should enjoy the author's rights. When it comes to making fair use, however, there is a meaningful difference between writings conceived as artistic or instructive creation, made in contemplation of publication, and documents written for a private purpose, as a message or memo, never intended for publication. One is at the heart of the purpose of copyright—the stimulation of creative endeavor for the public edification. The others are, at best, incidental beneficiaries. Thus, the second factor should favor the original creator more heavily in the case of a work (including superseded drafts) created for publication, than in the case of a document written for reasons having nothing to do with the objectives of copyright law.

The statutory articulation of this factor derives from Justice Story's mention in *Folsom* of the "value of the materials used." Justice Story's word choice is more communicative than our statute's "nature of," as it suggests that some protected matter is more "valued" under copyright law than others. This should not be seen as an invitation to judges to pass on literary quality, but rather to consider whether the protected writing is of the creative or instructive type that the copyright laws value and seek to foster.

The *Nation, Salinger,* and *New Era* opinions discussed the second factor solely in terms of whether the copyrighted work was published or unpublished. The *Nation* opinion observed that the unpublished status of a copyrighted work is a critical element of its nature and a "factor tending to negate the defense of fair use"; "the scope of fair use is narrower with respect to unpublished works."

. . .

The Supreme Court and the Second Circuit justify these positions by the original author's interest in controlling the circumstances of the first public revelation of his work and his right, if he so chooses, not to publish at all. These are indeed legitimate concerns of copyright law. An author who prefers not to publish a work, or wishes to make aesthetic choices about its first public revelation, will generally have the legal right to enforce these wishes. Due recognition of these rights, however, in no way implies an absolute power to bar all quotation, regardless of how persuasive the justification.

A ban on fair use of unpublished documents establishes a new despotic potentate in the politics of intellectual life—the "widow censor." A historian who wishes to quote personal papers of deceased public figures now must satisfy heirs and executors for fifty years after the subject's death. When writers ask permission, the answer will be, "Show me what you write. Then we'll talk about permission." If the manuscript does not exude pure admiration, permission will be denied.

The second factor should not turn solely, nor even primarily, on the published/unpublished dichotomy. At issue is the advancement of the utilitarian goal of copyright—to stimulate authorship for the public edification. Inquiry into the "nature" or "value" of the copyrighted work therefore determines whether the work is the type of material that copyright was designed to stimulate, and whether the secondary use proposed would interfere significantly with the original author's entitlements. Notwithstanding that nearly all writings may benefit from copyright, its central concern is for the protection of material conceived with a view to publication, not of private memos and confidential communications that its authors do not intend to share with the public. The law was not designed to encourage shoppers to make written shopping lists, executives to keep orderly appointment calendars, or lovers to write love letters. Certainly it was not to encourage the writing of extortion notes. To conclude that documents created for purposes outside the concerns of copyright law should receive more vigorous protection than the writings that copyright law was conceived to protect is bizarre and contradictory. To suggest that simply because a written document is unpublished, fair use of that document is forbidden, or even disfavored, has no logical support in the framework of copyright law.

I do not argue that a writer of private documents has no legal entitlement to privacy. He may well have such an entitlement. The law of privacy, however, and not the law of copyright supplies such protection. Placing all unpublished private papers under lock and key, immune from any fair use, for periods of fifty to one hundred years, conflicts with the purposes of the copyright clause. Such a rule would use copyright to further secrecy and concealment instead of public illumination.

. . .

3.   *Factor Three—Amount and Substantiality.*—The third statutory factor instructs us to assess "the amount and substantiality of the portion used in relation to the copyrighted work as a whole." In general, the larger the volume (or the greater the importance) of what is taken, the greater the affront to the interests of the copyright owner, and the less likely that a taking will qualify as a fair use. This factor has further significance in its bearing on two other factors. It plays a role in consideration of justification under the first factor (the purpose and character of the secondary use); and it can assist in the assessment of the likely impact on the market for the copyrighted work under the fourth factor (the effect on the market).

As to the first factor, an important inquiry is whether the selection and quantity of the material taken are reasonable in relation to the purported justification. A solid transformative justification may exist for taking a few sentences that would not, however, justify a taking of larger quantities of material.

In its relation to the market impact factor, the *qualitative* aspect of the third test—"substantiality"—may be more important than the quantitative. In the case of President Ford's memoir, a taking of no more than 400 words constituting " 'the heart of the book' " caused cancellation of the first serialization contract—a serious impairment to the market for the book. As to the relationship of *quantity* to the market, presumptively, of course, the more taken the greater the likely impact on the copyright holder's market, and the more the factor favors the copyright holder. Too mechanical a rule, however, can be dangerously misleading. One can imagine secondary works that quote 100% of the copyrighted work without affecting market potential. Consider, for example, a lengthy critical study analyzing the structure, symbolism and meaning, literary antecedents and influences of a single sonnet. Fragments dispersed throughout the work of criticism may well quote every word of the poem. Such quotation will not displace the market for the poem itself. If there is strong justification and no adverse market impact, even so extensive a taking could be a fair use.

Too rigid a notion of permissible quantity, furthermore, can seriously distort the inquiry for very short memos or communications. If a communication is sufficiently brief, any quotation will necessarily take most or all of it. Consider, for example, the extortion note discussed above. A journalist or historian may have good reason to quote it in full, either for historical accuracy, to show the character of the writer, or to suggest its effect on the recipient. The copyright holder, in seeking to enjoin publication, will argue that the journalist has taken not only the heart but the whole of the protected work. There are three responses, which relate to the first, second, and fourth factors. First, there may be a powerful justification for quotation of the entirety of a short note. Second, because the note was written for private motives and not for publication, quotation will not diminish the inducement to authors to create works for the public benefit. Finally, because the note is most unlikely to be marketed as a work of its author, there is no effect on its market. Courts must then evaluate the significance of the amount and substantiality factor in relation to the copyright objectives; they must consider the justification for the secondary use and the realistic risk of injury to the entitlements of authorship.

4. *Factor Four—Effect on the Market.*—The fourth factor addresses "the effect of the use upon the potential market for the copyrighted work." In the *Nation,* the Supreme Court designated this "the single most important element of fair use." The Court's recognition of the importance of this factor underlines, once again, that the copyright is not a natural right inherent in authorship. If it were, the impact on market values would be irrelevant; any unauthorized taking would be obnoxious. The utilitarian concept underlying the copyright promises authors the opportunity to realize rewards in order to encourage them to create. A secondary use that interferes excessively with an author's incentives subverts the aims of copyright. Hence the importance of the market factor.

Although the market factor is significant, the Supreme Court has somewhat overstated its importance. When the secondary use does substantially interfere with the market for the copyrighted work, as was the case in *Nation,* this factor powerfully opposes a finding of fair use. But the inverse does not follow. The fact that the secondary use does not harm the market for the original gives no assurance that the secondary use is justified. Thus, notwithstanding the importance of the market factor, especially when the market is impaired by the secondary use, it should not overshadow the requirement of justification under the first factor, without which there can be no fair use.

How much market impairment must there be to turn the fourth factor against the secondary user? By definition every fair use involves some loss of royalty revenue because the secondary user has not paid royalties. Therefore, if an insubstantial loss of revenue turned the fourth factor in favor of the copyright holder, this factor would never weigh in favor of the secondary user. And if we then gave serious deference to the proposition that it is "undoubtedly the single most important element of fair use," fair use would become defunct. The market impairment should not turn the fourth factor unless it is reasonably substantial. When the injury to the copyright holder's potential market would substantially impair the incentive to create works for publication, the objectives of the copyright law require that this factor weigh heavily against the secondary user.

Not every type of market impairment opposes fair use. An adverse criticism impairs a book's market. A biography may impair the market for books by the subject if it exposes him as a fraud, or satisfies the public's interest in that person. Such market impairments are not relevant to the fair use determination. The fourth factor disfavors a finding of fair use only when the market is impaired because the quoted material serves the consumer as a substitute, or, in Story's words "supersede[s] the use of the original." Only to that extent are the purposes of copyright implicated.

B. Are There Additional Factors?

I. False Factors.—The language of the Act suggests that there may be additional unnamed factors bearing on the question of fair use. The more I have studied the question, the more I have come to conclude that the pertinent factors are those named in the statute. Additional considerations that I and others have looked to are false factors that divert the inquiry from the goals of copyright. They may have bearing on the appropriate remedy, or on the availability of another cause of action to vindicate a wrong, but not on the fair use defense.

(a) Good Faith.—In all areas of law, judges are tempted to rely on findings of good or bad faith to justify a decision. Such reasoning permits us to avoid rewarding morally questionably conduct. It augments our discretionary power. It provides us with an escape from confronting questions that are difficult to understand. The temptation has been particularly strong in dealing with the difficult issue of fair use. This practice is, however, misguided. It produces anomalies that conflict with the goals of copyright and adds to the confusion surrounding the doctrine.

Copyright seeks to maximize the creation and publication of socially useful material. Copyright is not a privilege reserved for the well-behaved. Copyright protection is not withheld from authors who lie, cheat, or steal to obtain their information. If they have stolen information, they may be prosecuted or sued civilly, but this has no bearing on the applicability of the copyright. Copyright is not a reward for goodness but a protection for the profits of activity that is useful to the public education.

The same considerations govern fair use. The inquiry should focus not on the morality of the secondary user, but on whether her *creation* claiming the benefits of the doctrine is of the type that should receive those benefits. This decision is governed by the factors reviewed above—with a primary focus on whether the secondary use is productive and transformative and whether it causes excessive injury to the market for the original. No justification exists for adding a morality test. This is of course not an argument in favor of immorality. It favors only proper recognition of the scope and goals of a body of law.

A secondary user, like an original author, may be liable to criminal prosecution, or to suit in tort, if she has stolen information or has committed fraud. Furthermore, if she has infringed upon a copyright, morally reprehensible conduct may influence the remedy, including the availability of both an injunction and additional damages for willfulness.

This false morality factor derives from two misunderstandings of early precedent. The first results from the use of words like "piracy" and the Latin phrase *"animus furandi"* in early decisions. In rejecting the defense of fair use, courts sometimes characterized the offending secondary work as having been written *animo furandi* (with intention of stealing). Although this characterization seemed to imply that fair use requires honest intentions, the courts reasoned in the opposite direction. The decisions did not explore the mental state of the secondary user to determine whether fair use was shown. They examined the secondary text to determine whether it made a productive transformative use or merely restated the original. If they found no productive use justifying the taking, judges adorned the conclusion of infringement with words like piracy or *animus furandi*. The morality of the secondary user's conduct played no role in the decision. The irrelevance of the morality of the secondary user's conduct was underlined in decisions like *Folsom v. Marsh*. There Justice Story emphasized not only the good faith and "meritorious labors" of the defendants, but also the usefulness of their work. Finding no "bona fide abridgement" (what I have described as a transformative use), Justice Story nonetheless concluded with "regret" that good faith could not save the secondary work from being "deemed in law a piracy."

A second misleading assumption is that fair use is a creature of equity. From this assumption it would follow that unclean hands and all other equitable considerations are pertinent. Historically this notion is incorrect. Litigation under the Statute of Anne began in the law courts. Although plaintiffs who sought injunctions could sue, and did, in the courts of equity, which exercised parallel jurisdiction, the fair use doctrine did not arise out of equitable considerations. Fair use was a judge-made utilitarian limit on a statutory right. It balances the social benefit of a transformative secondary use against injury to the incentives of authorship.

The temptation to determine fair use by reference to morality also can lead to examination of the conduct and intentions of the plaintiff copyright holder in bringing the suit. The secondary user may contend that the copyright holder is disingenuously invoking copyright remedies as a device to suppress criticism or protect secrecy. Such considerations are also false leads.

Like a proprietor of land or an owner of contract rights, the copyright owner may sue to protect what he owns, regardless of his motivation. His rights, however, extend only to the limits of the copyright. As fair use is not an infringement, he has no power over it. Whether the secondary use is within the protection of the doctrine depends on factors pertinent to the objectives of the copyright law and not on the morality or motives of either the secondary user or the copyright-owning plaintiff. . . .

Fair's Fair: A Comment on the Fair Use Doctrine

LLOYD L. WEINREB*

. . . It is evident that Judge Leval's main conclusions are widely shared. There is broad agreement that a determination of fair use should depend largely, if not exclusively, on answers to two questions about the social utility of the secondary use, which are drawn from utilitarian assumptions about the copyright scheme generally. First, does the use interfere with copyright incentives to creative authorship? Second, does the use itself serve the creative and disseminative purposes of copyright? Those who have discussed the issue differ mostly about the subsidiary questions that they frame, which highlight more or less distinct aspects of the main questions. They give somewhat different weight to the elements that are to be considered, and they assign the burden of proof somewhat differently. Together, their analyses sharpen and clarify the issues that they address and provide a richly informed, subtly inflected basis for applying their common approach.

They all, however, in my view, share a common mistake. Fair use does not exclude consideration of factors not related to the utilitarian justification for copyright—other social values or, more simply, fairness. So far as it is possible in this instance to speak of legislative intent, the fair use provision of the Copyright Act is intended to include such consideration. To do so need not make the determination of fair use an arbitrary and unpredictable exercise of judicial power. On the contrary, giving such factors their appropriate place avoids ad hoc and unpredictable distortions of the argument in other respects to take account of them indirectly.

Copyright is property and has much of the significance of property. If the constitutional clause enabling Congress to confer copyright has a utilitarian cast, nevertheless, the concept of copyright itself does not originate in the Constitution. It is most doubtful that the brief phrase at the beginning of the clause should be understood to exclude all nonutilitarian considerations from a statutory copyright scheme, much less from a subsidiary element of such a scheme. Were it necessary to find a constitutional basis for inclusion of such considerations, reference to the necessary and proper clause would be sufficient. (As noted above, no such question arises in any case with respect to considerations of fairness that favor fair use.) To attend exclusively to utilitarian concerns treats copyright as if it were altogether a social product and had no private aspect. That cannot be done without violence to the understanding that copyright is property at all.

* 103 HARV. L. REV. 1337, 1150–53 (1990).

There is, furthermore, nothing in the Copyright Act to support so restrictive an approach. Section 107, botched job that it is, does not appear to be a utilitarian limitation on the general utilitarian purpose of the Act. Although some of the elements jumbled together may be susceptible to such an interpretation, others are not; and none of them requires it. The very jumble of different approaches in section 107 is an indication that fair use is not cabined in that way. Other sections of the Act do indeed sustain a utilitarian analysis; they provide specific exemptions from liability for infringement for uses the (asserted) social value of which is readily apparent. Section 107, in contrast, refers to uses that are *fair*, as did the judicial doctrine before it. We ought to start there. Ordinarily, the criterion of fairness is not equated with utility (or efficiency and the like) but is distinguished from it.

The four statutory factors that have dominated the analysis of fair use both in the cases and in commentary are related in obvious ways to the overall copyright scheme. The "nature of the copyrighted work," for example, addresses the basic distinction between idea and expression and others related to it, like the distinction between fact and fiction. The amount copied from the copyrighted work and the effect on the market for it have a direct bearing on the original author's reward, which is the engine that drives the whole machine. The four factors may also have other significance, related not to copyright but to other social purposes or not utilitarian in any narrow sense at all. Nothing in the statute suggests that such considerations should be ignored. In some instances, whether or not the purpose of copyright so dictates, it is clear from a consideration of the statutory factors that the use in question exceeds well-established limits of fair use. . . . In other instances, including some of the uses specified in the statute, established practice indicates that the use is fair, even though it may go against the purpose of copyright. Such an understanding may have been developed with an eye to the broader question, on the basis that its uniform application will serve the purpose of copyright overall, even if not in a particular case; but it need not have been. In any event, it is not necessary to look beyond the understanding itself to answer the question of fair use, because whatever its basis, it is dispositive. Even if there is not an understanding applicable to the precise use in question, the significance of the statutory factors from a utilitarian copyright viewpoint is not all there is to consider. Rather, that is one aspect of the issue of fairness, resolution of which then calls for reasoning by analogy, all things considered, to other uses concerning which the question of fair use is more settled. The conclusion may coincide with an assessment strictly along copyright lines, or it may not.

Furthermore, unless one disregards the plain language of the statute, the statutory factors are not exclusive. Although courts and commentators have for the most part not agreed explicitly with Judge Leval's conclusion that the statutory factors are all that count, they usually come out very nearly the same way as a practical matter. They recite the four factors, indicate in which direction each "weighs," add up the respective weights, and reach a conclusion on that basis. Often there is nothing else to consider. But sometimes there is. Fairness is a particularly open concept, on which almost any of the facts in a concrete situation may have a bearing (with the exception, one is tempted to say, of facts about the utility of one outcome or another). The statutory factors, which are focused on elements likely to be significant in any copyright dispute, are central to the question of fair use. But copyright is itself set in a social context, and more general considerations of fairness may come into play. From that larger perspective, it makes a difference whether a user obtained his copy of the original work lawfully or by theft, and if lawfully, by a means that is entirely proper or in some manner underhanded. It makes a difference whether a copyright owner's reason for refusing to give a license for the use is one that the community generally approves, copyright issues aside, or is one that it allows but disapproves. The community's understanding of and attitude toward a practice that directly implicates considerations of copyright may nevertheless transcend that aspect of the matter and dictate a contrary conclusion. That may occur, for example, when a new technology is introduced for which the closest analogies within the area of copyright are inapt, because of an overwhelming difference of scale or scope that transforms the place of the practice in everyday life.

The principal objection to enlarging the inquiry into fair use in this way will be, I think, that fairness is too vague a standard: it gives courts too much power with too little guidance about how to use it and makes it impossible for authors, publishers, and the rest to know what is allowed and what not. It is a mistake to suppose that because fairness is a very open standard and its application highly fact specific, it is without substantial content. In this context (like some others in which claims are made for the definiteness of a strictly utilitarian calculation), fairness has more, and more widely accepted, meaning than notions like productivity, incentive, and injury, which themselves depend on implicit evaluative measures and are easily, even unconsciously, manipulated. The Supreme Court's fractured votes in *Sony* and *Harper & Row,* the majority and dissenting Justices alike purporting to apply the four statutory factors from a utilitarian standpoint, amply demonstrate how little confidence one can have in that approach.

Nor need one fear, from the opposite direction, that a court inquiring about fairness will be obliged simply to validate whatever practices have become accepted as a matter of fact. Particularly in an age of rapid technological change, the community's normative standards may lag behind commercial exploitation of a new product. Once again, however, such practices arise in a context not only of copyright but also of general standards of fairness. If what is accepted is ordinarily a strong indication of what is acceptable, normative considerations also are relevant, not least to the question of whose practices and understandings ought to be considered. In the end, if there is present a strong element of fairness (or, more likely, unfairness), it will probably be taken into account, whether it is openly acknowledged or not. The clarity and predictive value of judicial decisions is considerably enhanced if the courts explain what they do without distortion to conform to a faulty legal formula. . . .

Fair Use as Market Failure: A Structural and Economic Analysis of the Betamax Case and Its Predecessors

WENDY J. GORDON*

2. *Markets in Copyright.* Copyright and patent law create ownership rights in intellectual property, with the primary goal of generating monetary incentives for the production of creative works, thereby "promot[ing] the Progress of Science and useful Arts." If the creators of intellectual productions were given no rights to control the use made of their works, they might receive few revenues and thus would lack an appropriate level of incentive to create. Fewer resources would be devoted to intellectual productions than their social merit would warrant.

Economists ordinarily characterize intellectual property law as an effort to cure a form of market failure stemming from the presence of "public goods" characteristics. A public good is often described as having two defining traits. First, it is virtually inexhaustible once produced, in the sense that supplying additional access to new users would not deplete the supply available to others. Second, and more important for the instant purposes, persons who have not paid for access cannot readily be prevented from using a public good. Because it is difficult or expensive to prevent "free riders" from using such goods, public goods usually will be under-produced if left to the private market. A familiar example of a public good is national defense. Since it is not possible to use a radar early-warning network in a way that discriminates between one person who has paid for defense and his neighbor who has not, a less than optimal amount of national defense will be produced if its purchase is left to the usual consensual market mechanisms of voluntary purchase. Some sort of compulsory payment, such as taxation, and central decision-making may be necessary to eliminate free riders and obtain the socially desirable amount of defense.

Books and inventions exhibit certain public goods characteristics. Once the literary work or the discovery embodied in the invention is made available to the public, the sequence of words or the discovery might be used by countless consumers without exhausting the supply. Any number of persons can simultaneously use the newly invented process or reprint the literature without physically depriving others of its use. Physical control, therefore, does not offer its usual potential as a mode of inexpensive enforcement for excluding free riders.

Though taxation and centralized purchasing might provide a satisfactory solution for some public goods problems, such an approach is inappropriate for much intellectual property. A democratic society demands decentralized and diverse creation in the intellectual sphere; freedom from state control is essential lest freedom of expression be curtailed by fear of governmental reprisal. Thus, for works of expression,

* 82 COLUM. L. REV. 1600, 1610–19, 1627–35, 1657 (1982). Copyright 1982 by Wendy J. Gordon.

the public goods problem is addressed by another method. Statutes create special property rights for authors; they can sell the physical copies of their works and at the same time retain legal control over the reproduction and certain other uses of the work embodied in those copies. In other words by the law provides a means for excluding nonpurchasers. Copyright law therefore allows a market for intellectual property to function.

In addition, the copyright law makes it easy to proceed through consensual market transfer. The requirement that a notice of copyright be placed on all publicly distributed copies facilitates identification of those works that are not in the public domain and cannot be used without purchase of a copyright license, and also facilitates identification of the works' owners. The registration of copyrights in the Copyright Office makes owners relatively easy to locate, and gives further information on the validity and duration of the copyright claimed. To discourage departure from the market system. Congress has made certain copyright violations criminal, and has established statutory damages and other devices to lighten a plaintiff's enforcement task. The copyright statute thus facilitates the functioning of the consensual market in four ways: it creates property rights, lowers transaction costs, provides valuable information, and contains mechanisms for enforcement.

When the market functions, no finding that the defendant acted "unreasonably" or against the public interest is requisite for judging culpability for the tort of copyright infringement. Like the intentional tortfeasors discussed in the preceding section, copiers of creative works ordinarily can identify and bargain with copyright owners. If copies are made without permission, the court will not use a "reasonableness" test to second-guess whether the copyist's production was in the public interest. In the ordinary copyright case, the court assumes that the defendant could have, and therefore should have, proceeded through the market.

Copyright markets will not, however, always function adequately. Though the copyright law has provided a means for excluding nonpurchasers and thus has attempted to cure the public goods problem, and though it has provided mechanisms to facilitate consensual transfers, at times bargaining may be exceedingly expensive or it may be impractical to obtain enforcement against nonpurchaser, or other market flaws might preclude achievement of desirable consensual exchanges. In those cases, the market cannot be relied on to mediate public interests in dissemination and private interests in remuneration. In extreme instances, Congress may correct for market distortions by imposing a regulatory solution such as a compulsory licensing scheme. Thus, to avoid threatened monopolistic control over the manufacture of piano rolls and other mechanical recordings, Congress provided that any person who wished could make and sell recordings of copyrighted music, so long as he paid to the copyright owner an amount determined under the statute. But the broad brush of this regulatory solution is too sweeping for most cases.

Fair use is one label courts use when they approve a user's departure from the market. A useful starting place for analysis of when fair use is appropriate is therefore an identification of when flaws in the market might make reliance on the judiciary's own analysis of social benefit appropriate. By making such an identification, a measure of coherence can be brought to the doctrine of fair use. As will be seen, there are certain "conditions of perfect competition"—or assumptions about how a proper transactional setting should look—whose failure is particularly likely to trigger in the courts an unwillingness to rely on the owner's market right to achieve dissemination.

II. THE THREE PART TEST FOR DETERMINING FAIR USE

Fair use should be awarded to the defendant in a copyright infringement action when (1) market failure is present; (2) transfer of the use to defendant is socially desirable; and (3) an award of fair use would not cause substantial injury to the incentives of the plaintiff copyright owner. The first element of this test ensures that market bypass will not be approved without good cause. The second element of the test ensures that the transfer of a license to use from the copyright holder to the unauthorized user effects a net gain in social value. n88 The third element ensures that the grant of fair use will not undermine the incentive-creating purpose of the copyright law. . . .

III. EVIDENCE OF A MARKET APPROACH IN EXISTING AUTHORITIES

This Article has suggested that a court will ordinarily not grant a defendant fair use treatment unless the facts of the case give reason to mistrust the market. This section will review cases and authorities in which recurring patterns of such mistrust appear to have guided courts in the fair use area. The discussion will show that courts and, in following their lead, Congress, have at times grappled with a market approach, that such an approach is reflected in the traditional fair use factors, and that, were the courts to embrace the market approach more fully, a more effective and consistent use of the traditional factors would result.

A. Inquiries Into Market Breakdown Under the Traditional Fair Use Approach

1. Market Barriers: New Technologies and Other Applications. As previously discussed, the impossibility or difficulty of achieving a market bargain is a factor that may justify a grant of fair use. The relevance of market barriers to fair use is implicitly reflected in the legislative history of section 107 of the Copyright Act. The Senate Report to the new copyright act states that "[a] key, though not necessarily determinative, factor in fair use is whether or not the work is available to the potential user," so that the out-of-print status of a copyrighted work may help to justify fair use. This is consistent with a market approach, since markets cannot form where goods are unavailable. Similarly, the Guidelines for Educational Fair Use in the House Report single out for fair use treatment instances of classroom photocopying in which bargains are particularly unlikely to occur because the teacher's use is spontaneous, individual and unsystematic. One of the prerequisites for making multiple copies under the Guidelines is that "[t]he inspiration and decision to use the work and the moment of its use for maximum teaching effective-

ness are so close in time that it would be unreasonable to expect a timely reply to a request for permission."

A particular type of market barrier is transaction costs. As long as the cost of reaching and enforcing bargains is lower than anticipated benefits from the bargains, markets will form. If transaction costs exceed anticipated benefits, however, no transactions will occur. Thus, the confluence of two variables is likely to produce a market barrier: high transaction costs and low anticipated profits. New technologies are likely to present both high transaction costs and, where uses by individual scholars or in individual homes are at issue, correspondingly low anticipated profits. This may explain why the "personal," "individual" nature of copying has been held relevant to fair use, and why "home use" may be relevant to the reach of copyright law. Consider, for example, the impact of the photocopy machine or the tape recorder. Each makes it possible for individuals to make use of copyrighted works in new and potentially valuable ways. From the point of view of the individual user, the anticipated "profit" is likely to be small, so his use will be easily discouraged by transaction costs. Also, the technology's novelty may mean that the participants have no established market channels to rely on, so that the purchase of permissions is likely to be cumbersome and expensive. High transaction costs and low per-transaction profits will converge. From the point of view of the copyright owner, the costs of enforcement against a diffuse group of individuals might outweigh anticipated receipts. A custom of use without payment will easily arise in such contexts unless the transaction costs of seeking permission or of enforcement are in some way reduced.

In such situations, transaction costs are likely to prevent at least some value-maximizing transfers from occurring if the copyright is enforced. At the extreme, enforcing the owner's rights might eliminate the use, and thus bring no income to the owner and deprive society of the benefit of the technology. For this reason, new technologies may become the subject of fair use treatment.

New technologies do not always involve market barriers, however, and thus do not always merit fair use consideration. In a case where a county educational program was videotaping educational television programs, the systematic and centralized nature of the copying and the various market alternatives that were present made license and purchase agreements quite possible. The court there denied fair use treatment at least in part because of this possibility. Thus it is the absence of a market and the prospect that such a market may form that is important, not the technological nature of the use.

The role of transaction costs also explains those cases that rely on the copyright owner's apparent or likely consent in granting fair use. Where a transfer is likely to be in the mutual interest of both owner and user, the courts appear unwilling to deter such transfers by imposing the costs of obtaining actual consent.

2. Externalities, Nonmonetizable Interest, and Noncommercial Activities. An analysis of the limitations of markets can also illuminate the special status that certain uses, such as scholarship, have in fair use

tradition. The costs and benefits of the parties contracting for the uses often differ from the social costs and benefits at stake, so that transactions leading to an increase in social benefit may not occur. Thus, for example, a critic of the Warren Commission's investigation of the Kennedy Assassination might write a "serious, thoughtful and impressive" book that will further public interest more than the revenues of his book alone would indicate. One might say that publication of his book gives an "external benefit" to persons who might gain knowledge from the public debate sparked by the book without having purchased the book itself. Similarly, teaching and scholarship may yield significant "external benefits"; all of society benefits from having an educated citizenry and from advances in knowledge, yet teacher salaries and revenues from scholarly articles are arguably smaller than such benefit would warrant. When a defendant's works yield such "external benefits," the market cannot be relied upon as a mechanism for facilitating socially desirable transactions.

In cases of externalities, then, the potential user may wish to produce socially meritorious new works by using some of the copyright owner's material, yet be unable to purchase permission because the market structure prevents him from being able to capitalize on the benefits to be realized. Though such inability would not itself justify fair use, it may signal to the court that it should investigate whether the social costs of relying on the market are unacceptably high. It is therefore not surprising that section 107 of the Copyright Act, which addresses fair use, lists several uses that potentially exhibit positive externalities, such as "teaching," "scholarship," and "research," among the uses for which fair use may be given.

Section 107 also directs the courts to consider "the purpose and character of the use, including whether the use is of a commercial nature or is for nonprofit educational purposes." Where the defendant does not seek to earn profits, it may be argued that his willingness and ability to pay for the copyrighted resources he uses will not provide an accurate measure of the public interest served by his use. Distinctions between profit and nonprofit entities or commercial and noncommercial uses must, however, be employed with great caution. Henry Hansmann has suggested that nonprofit organizations can be fully participating members of the market process. Conversely, even commercial uses and face market failure.

Distrust of the market may also be triggered when defendant's activities involve social values that are not easily monetized. When defendant's use contributes something of importance to public knowledge, political debate, or human health, it may be difficult to state the social worth of that contribution as a dollar figure. If the defendant's interest impinges on a first amendment interest, relying upon the market may become particularly inappropriate; constitutional values are rarely well paid in the marketplace and, while the citizenry would no doubt be willing to pay to avoid losing such values, it is awkward at best to try to put a "price" on them. Not surprisingly, it has been suggested that fair use be granted when first amendment issues are involved.

While in all of the cases described in this section—those involving external benefits, noncommercial uses, and nonmonetizable values— reason exists to distrust the market, it may be particularly difficult to determine whether the breakdown is substantial enough to frustrate the purposes for enforcing copyrights. What one deals with here may be not only traditional market failure, in the sense that conditions of perfect competiton have failed, but also a court's perception that the criterion of economic "value" is itself flawed. This concern is not illegitimate, but it should not be extended to make the copyright law an instrument of income redistribution. The courts should thus take care that they do not tax copyright owners to subsidize impecunious but meritorious users under the guise of maximizing value. Only when the public interest to be served is great, and the damage to the owner small, does the need for this caution diminish.

3. Anti–Dissemination Motives. Section 107 places first among the purposes for which fair use is appropriate "criticism" and "comment," uses that a copyright owner might be reluctant to license. Similarly, the treatment of burlesques and satires, which can be considered types of commentary, has been a volatile subject of fair use law. These uses share a type of market failure that helps to explain their fair use treatment and that is particularly important in a field where advancement of knowledge is the ultimate goal. The case law has tended to grant fair use treatment where copyright owners seemed to be using their property right not for economic gain but to control the flow of information.

The usual economic assumption is that the owner of a resource will either exploit that resource himself, or will sell it to someone else who will. The owner of a copyright, however, may not be willing to exploit all of the possible derivative works over which his copyright would ordinarily give him control. Even if money were offered, the owner of a play is unlikely to license a hostile review or a parody of his own drama; a publicity-shy tycoon who owns the copyright on magazine articles discussing his life is unlikely to license a biographer to use these articles; a candidate for governor is unlikely to license his copyrighted campaign music to be utilized in his opponent's televised advertisement; and the publisher of a periodical is unlikely to license his competitor to use his copyrighted magazine covers in comparative advertising. Because the owner's antidissemination motives make licensing unavailable in the consensual market, and because the free flow of information is at stake, a strong case for fair use can be advanced in these cases. Thus, it has often been suggested that burlesques and satires of copyrighted works deserve generous fair use treatment, since the copyright owners are unlikely to produce or license such work themselves.

It might be argued that allowing fair use to criticisms, satires, and other materials that are potentially hostile to the copyrighted work will undermine incentives to produce original work. But while criticisms and the like may indeed reduce an owner's receipts, the goal of copyright is to generate incentives for the production of works that satisfy consumer tastes. If a criticism reveals a work's flaws, it is appropriate that demand for the work should decrease.

Criticism is valuable, inter alia, because the market works to further the social good only when consumers have accurate information about the goods available. As the Supreme Court has written: "So long as we preserve a predominantly free enterprise economy, the allocation of our resources in large measure will be made through numerous private economic decisions. It is a matter of public interest that those decisions, in the aggregate, be ... well informed." A similar public policy argument would encourage the taste-changing functions of burlesque and satire. For these and other forms of criticism, fair use is particularly appropriate when the owner's reluctance to license use of his work is motivated by the desire to restrict the flow of information.

In discussing instances where copyright owners' antidissemination motives trigger a distrust of the market, however, it must be stressed that refusals to grant permission to license should ordinarily be honored. A refusal to license must not automatically justify a right to fair use; markets can function only if owners have a right to say "no" as well as "yes." When an owner refuses to license because he is concerned that defendant's work will substitute for his own work or derivative works, the owner is representing not only his own interest, but also the interest of his potential customers and thus the public interest. Market failure should be found only when the defendant can prove that the copyright owner would refuse to license out of a desire unrelated to the goals of copyright—notably, a desire to keep certain information from the public. Unfortunately, some courts seem to have viewed even some legitimate refusals as justifying fair use treatment. A clearer focus on whether the nature of the reluctance to license involved market failure could help avoid this problem.

Even though the presence of antidissemination motives signals a reason to mistrust the market, a market breakdown is not always the result. Where, for example, a potential satirist plans a remunerative commercial use whose popularity will depend in part on the attractive or dramatic qualities of the original being satirized, he may be willing to offer a substantial payment for the right to use elements of the copyrighted work in a satirical form. The copyright owner might accept such payment in the expectation that it should more than compensate him for any loss he might experience in his primary market as a result of the satirical treatment. If a market bargain would be possible, fair use should be denied unless the court perceives a danger that the owner might use his market right to distort the satiric content.

Several factors already employed by the courts and Congress are relevant to the inquiry into whether a bargain for a use could take place. As mentioned, the commercial nature of the use is important, as is substantiality. The more commercial the nature of the use, and the more the defendant's work will compete with the copyrighted work, the greater the impact of any given quantity of copying is likely to be. Also, anticipated profit—the incentive for a market bargain—is more likely to be high where the taking is extensive. These criteria in turn can have an impact upon the court's assessment of substantiality. If despite the theoretical possibility of an antidissemination motive the court feels that a market bargain could have been reached, or that the defendant is operating in a realm that the copyright owner himself might have been willing to exploit, fair use should be denied. . . .

Conclusion

It is important that a market failure approach to fair use not expanded into a justification for allowing court intervention whenever the market fails to reach "perfect" results, for no market is ever perfect. What emerges from the case law and the copyright statute is a focus on individual types of transactions, not a concern with restructuring an entire set of markets to reach ideal goals, and an identification of those imperfections that will not be tolerated because of their particular impact on dissemination and the ultimate goals of copyright. That transactional emphasis is the proper one. It allows particularly desirable transfers that are blocked by market failure to go forward outside the market, but also allows the courts to impose liability where widespread use of this bypass would cause substantial injury to the copyright owner. This Article has accordingly discussed not only the market failure grounds for fair use, but also the limitations that should be placed on employment of the doctrine. It is submitted that the three-part test presented here is of assistance in analyzing fair use issues and provides a helpful tool for predicting and guiding decisions in this most difficult area of copyright law.

Notes and Questions

1. Born in 1936, Judge Pierre Leval sits on the U.S Court of Appeals for the Second Circuit. He received his LL.B from Harvard Law School in 1963, and served as Assistant United States Attorney, Southern District of New York, (1964–68), as Chief Appellate Attorney, (1967–68); with the firm of Cleary, Gottlieb, Steen & Hamilton, New York, N.Y., (1969–75); as First Assistant, and Chief Assistant, District Attorney's Office, New York County, (1975–77); and as United States District Court Judge, Southern District of New York, (1977–93).

2. Lloyd L. Weinreb is the Dane Professor of Law at Harvard Law School, where he has taught since 1965. Born in 1936, Professor Weinreb received an LL.B from Harvard in 1962 and an M.A. from Oxford in 1963. In addition to copyright and intellectual property, he also teaches and writes in the fields of criminal law and jurisprudence.

3. Wendy Gordon is a professor and the Paul J. Liacos Scholar-in-Law at Boston University Law School. Born in 1949, she earned her J.D. from University of Pennsylvania Law School in 1975. Professor Gordon is also a Fulbright Scholar and was elected to the Visiting Senior Research Fellowship at St. John's College, Oxford.

4. Judge Leval's evocation of laundry lists and extortion note prompts the question whether the fair use doctrine should allow greater copying from works whose creation copyright did not induce. Is this a good idea in theory? In practice?

5. The emergence of performance rights societies, such as ASCAP, in the early twentieth century supports Professor Gordon's analysis of a market failure in rights enforcement. "[U]nlicensed performances went on in cabarets, dance halls, and restaurants in virtually every city, town, and village in the United States. To police each infringing performance and file lawsuits against them would likely cost more than any damages that might be recovered. It would cost fifty dollars to collect ten." Paul Goldstein, Copyright's Highway 54 (revised ed. 2003). Professor Goldstein goes on to trace the beginnings of ASCAP from a handful of composers and music publishers meeting in 1913 to "its present operations in a skyscraping command center that overlooks Manhattan's Lincoln Center, collecting almost $650 million annually for distribution to close to 150,000 writer and publisher members." Id. at 60. Participants in collective licensing societies in effect relinquish their individual rights to control the public performance of their works, in return for assurance of payment pursuant to collectively negotiated licenses. The availability of collective licensing in turn suggests a limit to the transaction costs justification for fair use, as do technological means of lowering transaction costs. The latter proposition is explored further in Tom Bell, *Fair Use vs. Fared Use*, excerpted infra, p. 416.

Reconstructing the Fair Use Doctrine

WILLIAM A. FISHER*

C.   Reconstructing the Fair Use Doctrine

This section considers how a judge who had time on his hands and extensive access to information, who knew that other courts would adhere to his rulings, and who fully shared the utopian vision advanced in this Part might rebuild the fair use doctrine. The following section extracts from that discussion a set of proposals a real federal court might practicably and comfortably adopt.

A quick review is in order. Artists make money by extracting fees from persons who desire access to their works. Part IV showed why in many circumstances, it would be inefficient to empower an artist to demand payment from every person who wished to put her works to one of the uses listed in section 106 of the Copyright Act. Part IV also showed that it matters *which* activities consumers are permitted to engage in for free and which are deemed to require the consent of the artist. The rights prescribed by section 106 vary in the amount of benefit they provide copyright owners per unit of cost to the rest of us. Generally speaking, the economist would like to avoid two situations: one in which artists are accorded entitlements from which they gain little but which cost the public a good deal, and one in which they are denied entitlements from which they could gain much at modest cost to the public. Somewhat more precisely, maximization of allocative efficiency can be achieved by arranging the set of activities putatively reserved to copyright owners by section 106 in order of their incentive/loss ratios, identifying the point in the series at which the benefits secured by holding out monetary incentives to talented persons exceed by the

* 101 Harv. L. Rev. 1659, 1766–79 (1988).

maximum amount the attendant monopoly losses, and declaring all uses above that point fair and all uses below it unfair.

A modified version of this technique could be put to good use by our hypothetical judge. If full exploitation of the rights prescribed by section 106 would afford creators of a particular type of intellectual product more income than they deserve, the judge would be able to promote his goals by declaring fair (and thus encouraging) activities that would contribute to the attainment of the good society and by declaring unfair activities that would not. How, then, should he decide which uses fall into which category? That question reduces to two problems. The first, addressed in subsection 1, is how might the judge go about ranking the putatively infringing uses of a particular sort of copyrighted material in terms of their relative importance to his agenda. The second, addressed in subsection 2, is where in that series he should draw the line between fair and unfair activities.

1. Ranking Entitlements.—Because, other things being equal, the judge would rather that people be better rather than worse off by their own lights, he would have to take into account all of the considerations identified by the portion of the economic analysis directed toward arranging uses in the right order. But sections A and B of this Part have identified a number of goals other than maximizing the satisfaction of current consumers' tastes that the judge would seek to advance. Specifically, sensitivity to the five concerns itemized below could and should affect his determination of the optimal order of entitlements.

(a) Transformative Uses.—Active interaction with one's cultural environment is good for the soul. A person living the good life would be a creator, not just a consumer, of works of the intellect. This is not to say that all passive uses of cultural artifacts are bad; even in utopia, people can be expected to listen to symphonies without playing along, to attend dramatic performances without mounting the stage, even to watch some television. But the proportion of active to passive activities in the lives of most Americans today is too low. Whitman's contention that, to realize the promise of democracy, to create and sustain a society in which people flourish, we must cultivate a new kind of "character"—one not only more "attentive," more capable of appreciating the texture of the surface of life, but also more energetic, more actively engaged in the production and transformation of "Culture"—is even more applicable to the United States of the 1980's than it was to the United States of the 1860's.

What does that have to do with the fair use doctrine? It suggests that uses of copyrighted material that either constitute or facilitate creative engagement with intellectual products should be preferred to uses that neither constitute nor foster such engagement. Our hypothetical judge should thus modify the sequence of uses generated by economic analysis, which takes as given Americans' present tastes, either by shifting transformative uses upward or by shifting passive uses downward. Assume, for example, that he has succeeded in ranking according to their incentive/loss ratios the various ways in which copyrights in feature movies could be violated. Included in the list are home videotaping of the sort at issue in *Sony* and the production of "sequel" movies.

Because the latter is more creative than the former, the latter should be moved up in the series, or the former should be moved down.

For two related reasons, systematic application of this procedure would advance the utopian agenda. First, it would create more opportunities for Americans to become actively involved in shaping their culture, thereby increasing access to the good life. Second, by altering the relative ease with which Americans can engage in different sorts of activities— that is by making creative activities less expensive or more convenient and making noncreative activities more expensive or less convenient— the procedure would modify consumers' habits and eventually their desires, thereby enhancing not just their access to but also their appreciation of the good life.

(b) Education.—During the prolonged debate that resulted in the 1976 comprehensive reform of the Copyright Act, it was often suggested that some sort of special exemption for "educational" uses of copyrighted materials be incorporated into the statute. Only a few of these various proposals found expression in the language of the statute that Congress ultimately adopted. Despite this meager congressional acknowledgment of the special character of education and despite the fact that, in recent litigation, "nonprofit educational users have been singularly unsuccessful in asserting fair use," a suspicion persists among many students of the doctrine that educational activities should stand on a somewhat different footing from other kinds of uses.

The utopian vision advanced in this Part provides a way of giving shape to and justifying that intuition. Recall that one of the important features of the good society would be an extensive system of public education, which would include not just "schooling," but also a variety of institutions designed to enhance people's knowledge of public affairs and appreciation of different kinds of art. Realization of that objective plainly would require a good deal more than reform of copyright law. But until such time as the federal or state governments can be induced to provide an educational regime of the sort envisioned, the fair use doctrine can and should be crafted to implement parts of it. A good way of doing so would be to accord preferential treatment in the fair use calculus to activities that facilitate education—either by enhancing access to information and argument on matters of public importance or by increasing the ability of teachers to design and deliver to students the packages of materials they deem most effective. The more a particular use would advance that end, the more of a boost it should get.

Examples, drawn from the case law, of uses that would qualify on this basis for special protection include: taking from a book defending a woman's right to an abortion portions of interviews of women who had had abortions and publishing them in a book arguing against such a right; reprinting excerpts from an author's copyrighted letters in a critical biography of him; reproducing in a biography of a composer passages from a previously published biography for the purpose of substantiating criticisms of the first biographer's conclusions or use of evidence; and copying, for classroom use, portions of copyrighted materials unavailable in the form deemed most educational by a teacher.

To apply this procedure sensitively, a judge would have to bear in mind that the degree of preferential treatment to which a particular activity is entitled depends on how important use of the copyrighted material is to the activity's educational value. If, for example, much of the credibility and force of a "pro-life" argument derives from the author's ability to quote interviews conducted by an advocate of the right to an abortion, the place of the activity in the sequence of uses should be changed significantly. By contrast, if the reader's capacity to assess one historian's criticism of another is enhanced only marginally by the former's quotation of passages from the latter's work, then sensitivity to the educational value of such criticism does not require adjustment of the sequence of putatively infringing uses.

(c) Diversity.—Closely related to the goal of facilitating education is that of fostering cultural diversity. The objective of producing a society in which people exercise (and thereby develop) their faculties of choice and discrimination will be served by providing the populace as wide a range of cultural artifacts as possible. One way to advance that end is to give special consideration, when deciding which uses of a type of copyrighted material should be deemed fair, to those likely to produce "derivative works" that will add to the variety of intellectual products available to the public.

In most circumstances, this consideration will reinforce the two guidelines just considered. So, for example, parody deserves a boost in the fair use calculus, partly because it is a transformative use, partly because it improves the ability of consumers to assess the merits of the parodied work, and partly because it increases the variegation of the artistic environment.

(d) Protecting the Creative Process.—In his efforts to afford the public opportunities to transform and learn from intellectual products, the judge should be careful not to lose sight of the concerns of producers. In particular, both to ensure that artists (as well as consumers) have maximum opportunities for engaging in meaningful work and to increase the maturity and diversity of the artifacts they generate, he should be loath to privilege activities that threaten the creative process. So, for example, he should disfavor conduct that results in disclosure of works of art before their creators deem them finished, insofar as both premature divulgence itself and fear of such disclosure undercut artists' willingness and ability to take the time they need to refine their works to their satisfaction. The courts' current reluctance to recognize as fair any copying of "unpublished" materials goes a considerable distance toward accommodating this concern. More precise would be a guideline that simply incorporated the concern itself—namely, that disfavored unauthorized uses of materials the creators of which were still considering revising.

(e) Equalizing Public Access.—One of the major conclusions of the argument summarized in section A.3 was that, in the good society, people's lots in life would be much less unequal than they are in the United States today. The bearing of that proposition on the ways in which we compensate artists is considered in the next subsection. A less

apparent but equally important implication of the conclusion is that the law should be adjusted to equalize consumers' access to works of the intellect.

Clearly, the most direct route to the latter goal would be to redistribute wealth and income in American society, thereby providing persons more equal means to purchase access to copyrighted materials. Unfortunately, fundamental reform along those lines does not appear imminent. Until it happens, our hypothetical judge can and should make adjustments in the fair use doctrine to effect, in some small measure, the sort of levelling commended by the utopian vision; other things being equal, activities that would tend to equalize public access to intellectual products should be given priority over activities that would not. So, for example, the fact that the behavior of Bestseller Book Club described in Part IV impedes Plaintiff's ability to engage in price discrimination in the marketing of her work should count against it. Conversely, an activity that facilitates price discrimination should be favored.

2. Compensating Creators.—Like the economic analysis of Part IV, the utopian analysis deployed in this Part is notably less helpful in determining where the line should be drawn between fair and unfair activities than it is in ranking entitlements. Nevertheless, this subsection argues, a few guidelines may be derived from the approach.

Recall that section A.3 isolated two grounds on which the creators of intellectual products might legitimately be accorded lots in life better or worse than average: the proposition that unequal effort warrants unequal rewards; and a modified version of Rawls' difference principle. Unfortunately, the impediments to using the fair use doctrine to implement those ideals are substantial.

As to the unequal-effort criterion, two obstacles seem insurmountable. First, courts cannot obtain the information necessary to apply the principle to particular cases. It may be true that M, who by dint of concentration and effort produces a respectable symphony despite his modest talent, deserves more income than N, who dissipates her enormous talent and produces only a respectable symphony, but accumulation of the data necessary to determine which artists are more like M and which are more like N plainly would be infeasible. Second, even if courts had the requisite information, the importance of enabling both the creators and the users of intellectual products to predict in advance what activities will and will not give rise to liability would counsel against the sort of case-by-case adjudication that tying rewards to effort and not talent would require.

The barriers to accommodation of the modified difference principle at first blush seem nearly as formidable. Remember the difficulties we encountered in giving effect to the formula for the maximization of allocative efficiency that emerged from Part IV. Applied to copyright law, the variant of the difference principle elaborated in section A.3 differs from the economist's formula in two respects, both of which seem to exacerbate rather than reduce those difficulties. First, because it permits increasing the incomes of categories of artists only up to the point beyond which additional rewards would cease to yield net improvement in the life of the least advantaged member of the society, the levels of compensation commended by the difference principle would be both lower and even harder to ascertain than the economist's test. Second, the contribution to each citizen's powers of imagination and communication made by seminal works of literature and art—which the modified difference principle, unlike the economist's test, takes into account—would be extremely difficult to measure and might well more than offset the constraint just mentioned. In short, if drawing the line between fair and unfair uses using economic analysis was difficult, drawing it using the difference principle often would be nearly impossible.

Upon reflection, however, it appears that the proffered theory of distributive justice may not be altogether toothless. In three contexts, itemized below, it could provide our hypothetical judge some assistance.

(a) Superfluous Income.—The most obvious but perhaps most important implication of the theory is that, if the diminution in the incomes available to the creators of a particular type of work caused by shifting the line between fair and unfair uses from point X to point Y would not cause any significant reduction in the quality or quantity of works produced, the judge ought to make the move. In this respect, the utopian analysis leads to precisely the same conclusion as the economic analysis—and both repudiate the labor-desert/entitlement theory advocated by some commentators. For the reasons suggested in Part IV, this guideline may have more real-world applications than one might suspect. Thus, if further empirical research confirmed Judge Breyer's predictions regarding the insignificant impact of a reduction in copyright protection for tradebooks upon their production, a substantial expansion of the set of fair uses of such books would be warranted.

(b) Diversity.—If the choice between point X and point Y *would* make some difference in the future output of works, the judge should be less willing to pick the lower of the two points if consumer demand for intellectual products of the type in question is currently low than if the demand is high. The reason is that the modified difference principle urges us to adopt the system of incentives that (as compared to a regime of strict equality) would yield the greatest net improvement in the quality of life of the least advantaged member of the society, and one important source of her quality of life is diversity in the cultural artifacts to which she is exposed. So, for example, a judge who could simultaneously adjust the fair use doctrine as applied to poetry, sculpture, detective novels, and Broadway musicals should set the lines higher for the first two than for the third and fourth.

(c) *Minimal Compensation.*—One of the major implications of the arguments summarized in section A.3 is that a just society would be a relatively egalitarian society. It may be impossible to predict the schedule of incomes for different types of artists and other workers that the application of the unequal effort and modified difference principles would yield, but it can be said with some confidence that no one's share of resources would fall dramatically below the mean. In this respect, the utopian analysis points in a very different direction from economic analysis. To illustrate, imagine that the producers of a particular type of intellectual product—say, the designers of video games—are passionate about their work and would continue doing it even if paid poorly. Moreover, only those who love the job do it well. Consistent application of the argument developed in Part IV would require expansion of the set of fair uses of video games to the point where their creators were left only enough income to live on. Fidelity to the conceptions of just compensation advanced in this Part, by contrast, would require that the expansion be halted when further movement would leave designers of average talent and diligence incomes substantially below the national average.

Can we offer the judge any further guidance? Two additional potential applications of the utopian analysis to the task of setting artists' incomes do suggest themselves. On balance, however, both seem inadvisable. They—and the reasons for rejecting them—are reviewed briefly below for the purpose of showing the limits of the theory.

(d) Detoxification.—It might be contended that the "diversity" guideline proposed above is too mild. If Americans currently indulge to excess their tastes for certain sorts of intellectual products, should we not undertake more vigorous initiatives to change their behavior? For example, if the amount of time people devote to noncreative, passive pursuits—like watching television—is too great, why not use more drastic measures to help free them from their addiction? One such measure seems at hand: if we expanded radically the set of uses of copyrighted television programs deemed fair, fewer such programs (or poorer quality programs) would be produced. The less attractive the menu of material "on the air," the more time people would probably spend in more active leisure activities.

Unfortunately, to be effective, the reduction in the quantity or quality of television programs would have to be very substantial, which would render the tactic objectionable on two grounds. First, it would entail a functionally "coercive" limitation on consumers' freedom to choose how to spend their free time in a context in which misguided decisions do not do them irreparable harm and in which, arguably, people become thoughtful regulators of their behavior only by making and learning from mistakes. As such, it is vulnerable to especially strong versions of the argument against certain forms of paternalism. Second, it would likely require that the incomes of many of the persons who assist in the production of television programs be reduced to levels well below the national average. As such, the proposal would entail deliberately doing injustice in order to advance the utopian agenda. Even assuming such a tactic is in some contexts justifiable, it is sufficiently troubling to counsel against adoption of the plan.

(e) Rewarding Quality.—Individual works of art surely differ in the degree to which they contribute to our common stock of allusions and insights. Should we not try to stimulate the production of intellectual products that would do so most? Specifically, should we not narrow the scope of the fair use doctrine as applied to those individual copyrighted works that enhance especially noticeably the complexity and resonance of our language? In support of such a proposal, it might be argued that

judges construing the current fair use doctrine already frequently protect covertly works they consider of "high quality" and disfavor original or derivative works they regard as "trash," that they cannot be prevented from making such aesthetic judgments, and that empowering the parties to contest—and requiring judges to defend—those evaluations would improve them. Moreover, the proposed modification of the fair use doctrine would enable us to reduce (at least marginally) the incidence of the phenomenon—all too common in American literary history—of an unusually talented writer, financially strapped or simply discouraged by a meager income, producing less or poorer quality work than he is capable of.

Unfortunately, three considerations require rejecting the proposal. First, although it is possible in retrospect to identify works of art that have made especially large contributions to American culture, determining in advance which works will have such an impact would be extremely difficult. Second, for such a system of incentives to work effectively, it would be essential that persons contemplating either creating or using works of art be able to predict reasonably accurately how federal judges would assess their quality—the chances of which seem slim. Third, though the proposal would not empower judges to engage in censorship, it would entail some degree of governmental control over the definition of good and bad art, and the history of experiments in regulation of that sort should give one pause.

In sum, for the time being, it seems wisest to limit judges' involvement in the compensation of artists to: (i) the avoidance of superfluous income; (ii) the promotion of cultural diversity by favoring types of art for which popular demand currently is low; and (iii) providing artists (to the extent practicable) minimal levels of income. . . .

Notes and Questions

1. William A. Fisher is the Hale & Dorr Professor of Intellectual Property Law at Harvard Law School. Born in 1953, he earned his JD from Harvard in 1982, and his Ph.D. in History from Harvard in 1991.

2. Contrast Judge Leval's, and Professors Weinreb, Fisher and Gordon's approaches to fair use. Filtered through the statutory factors, Judge Leval focuses mainly on "transformative use" by other creators. Professor Weinreb urges a formulation of fair use that centers on elemental notions of fairness in society. Professor Fisher suggests that the judge should be more active in advancing specific societal values through the fair use doctrine. Professor Gordon's analysis of fair use rests on the transaction costs of enforcing a copyright holder's rights. Which formulation of fair use do you find more persuasive? Does that formulation shift depending on the type of copyrighted material at issue? Does that formulation depend on your belief in the purposes and function of copyright? Compare these different formulations of fair use to the variety of concepts used to justify copyright in Part I.B.

3. Does Judge Leval neglect to consider whether there are uses that may be fair but not transformative? Does Professor Weinreb fail to

provide proper guideposts to formulate that which is fair? Does Professor
Fisher place the judge in the position of being an arbiter of taste and
culture? Does Professor Gordon overlook "fair" uses that may already be
monetizable?

[EDITOR'S NOTE: The following two articles by Professor Tom Bell and
Professor Jessica Litman discuss a precursor to the Digital Millennium
Copyright Act (DMCA), the White House Information Infrastructure
Task Force's "White Paper." While the DMCA ultimately differed from
the White Paper in several respects, many of the concerns raised by
Professors Bell and Litman remain applicable.]

Fair Use vs. Fared Use? The Impact of Automated Rights Management on Copyright's Fair Use Doctrine

TOM W. BELL*

I. Introduction

"Information wants to be free," claim those who decry the over-
zealous enforcement of copyrights. But they cannot mean what they say.
Information wants nothing at all. This contemporary epigram instead
reveals, indirectly, what people want. Perhaps it originated as a mere
prediction about the difficulty of enforcing intellectual property rights on
the Internet and in other digital intermedia. Facing newly effective
means of enforcing such rights, however, those who claim "information
wants to be free" increasingly give the slogan a normative spin. Its
meaning then boils down to this: people want information for free.

So restated, the catch-phrase still rings true. All else being equal,
who would not prefer to get information—that increasingly vital good—
at no cost? But, alas, information never comes for free. We can only
account for its costs as fully as possible, try our best to minimize them,
and allocate them fairly.

The information economy balances fixed and variable costs from
several sources. On the one hand, consumers necessarily bear costs when
they search for, interpret, and collect information. This holds true even
when—perhaps especially when—the fair use defense to copyright infringement allows a consumer to avoid paying cash for the right to use
an expressive work. On the other hand, information providers necessarily bear costs when they create, package, and distribute information.
They thus seek remuneration and profit through licensing fees, at least
so far as the countervailing fair use defense and various practical hurdles
will allow.

One method in particular offers information providers a promising
way to increase their licensing opportunities: automated rights manage-

* 76 N.C. L. REV. 557, 557–96 (1998).

ment ("ARM"). ARM enables information providers to enforce standard copyright claims mechanically, without resort to the threat of litigation. It also allows copyright owners and others to create and enforce contracts that specify other sets of rights. Although ARM may give information providers newfound power to control the use of their wares, it does not necessarily justify that control. The proper legal response to ARM thus remains an open—and vital—question.

ARM portends far-reaching and unprecedented effects on rights to information in the new digital intermedia. Specifically, ARM threatens to reduce radically the scope of the fair use defense to copyright infringement. ARM will interact with existing legal doctrines to supplant fair use with an analogous but distinctly different doctrine: fared use. . . .

A.   Automated Rights Management

Owners of conventional sorts of property do not rely on the law alone to protect their assets. They also deploy fences, locks, and guards. Automated rights management provides the owners of intangible assets with similar defensive mechanisms, albeit ones built into computer hardware and software and implemented via firewalls, encryption, and passwords. Although ARM researchers continue to develop and experiment with a variety of approaches, the huge market for intellectual property protection virtually ensures that ARM technology will see increasingly widespread use.

ARM appeals to information providers because it stands to give them the power to accomplish two things that hitherto seemed impossible in digital intermedia. First, ARM will make it possible and cost-effective for information providers to enforce standard copyright or trade secret claims. Second, ARM will empower them to enforce contracts that define different or additional rights. Additionally, ARM promises to perform these functions cleanly and effectively, without resort to uncertain and wasteful litigation. . . .

Subscription services, which charge for access to proprietary databases by the hour or month, currently account for most of the intellectual property sold through digital networks. Although even this sort of electronic tollbooth qualifies as "automated rights management" in a broad sense, most ARM technicians aspire to something more sophisticated. At a minimum, they aim at permitting information providers, and perhaps even individual owners of proprietary data, to sell access on a document-by-document basis.

The simplest such pay-per-use systems offer encrypted documents for sale, or rather the keys to those documents, one at a time. The purchaser of a key gets access to a single locked document. This approach still leaves the purchased information subject to subsequent copying in its original medium, however. More sophisticated ARM systems thus employ methods such as steganography, micropayments, and imbedded applications to give information providers exact and continuous control over proprietary information.

At its most powerful, ARM supports the "superdistribution" of proprietary information. In other words, it allows information providers to market documents that disallow certain types of uses (e.g., copying) and provide continuing revenue (e.g., charging 2 [cents] per access) regardless of who holds the document (e.g., including someone who obtained it post-first sale). Superdistribution thus offers information providers a rather daunting compendium of powers. In practice, of course, no ARM system can guarantee absolute control over information, especially after it escapes digital media. By accident or design, documents inevitably will fall outside the reach of ARM. Even if only partially effective, however, ARM will radically improve the efficiency of licensing practices in the digital intermedia. Consequently, it will have a radical impact on the fair use doctrine. . . .

C.   The Dystopian View

. . .

1.   The End of Unbilled Use in Digital Intermedia

Parties who make frequent appeal to the fair use doctrine fear that they will not enjoy in digital intermedia the sort of immunity from licensing fees that fair use provides in traditional media. Because a copyright does not give its owner the right to require licensing fees for uses falling within the scope of 107, parties availing themselves of fair use typically regard it as free use. The prospect of paying in digital intermedia for what apparently comes free elsewhere thus evokes contempt, if not horror, from those who re-work information for a living. It seems certain, however, that the combination of automated rights management and the legal doctrines set forth in American Geophysical, Princeton University Press, the NII White Paper, and the NIICPA will have just such an effect.

The sort of copyright nightmare that friends of fair use fear unfolds something like this: Imagine that you download some quotes from text on the Church of Technolism's web page, incorporate them in an essay critical of the Church, and publish it on your own web page without seeking the Church's permission. The Church of Technolism objects to your comments and demands that you cease republishing quotes from its online document. You refuse. Although the Church sues for copyright infringement, you rest easy in your faith that the fair use defense will excuse your copying. But it does not.

The court finds not that you have quoted too much, but rather that you have paid too little. Although you quoted no more than what your critique required, you neglected to pay the Church of Technolism for your republication of its copyrighted materials. Citing American Geophysical, Princeton University Press, the NII White Paper, and the recently enacted NIICPA, the court holds that the advent of convenient and cheap means of making licensing payments forecloses your claim that paying for your use would have proven too burdensome. In short, as automated rights management has grown in scope, your fair use defense has shrunk.

As this scenario illustrates, the near future may hold some changes for the fair use doctrine. Whether these changes qualify as beneficial or detrimental will come under consideration in the next Part. The next section will first show, however, that fair use faces something more worrisome than ubiquitous licensing fees. The same events that conspire to end the unbilled use of copyrighted works in digital contexts, together with related factors, threaten to constrain severely the sorts of critical commentary and parodies that copyright owners so often find offensive.

2. Private Censorship by Copyright Owners

Increasingly, consumers in all probability will find that access to information in digital intermedia comes subject to contractual provisions that aim to secure rights more broad than those provided by the Copyright Act. Consumers will find, in particular, that such contracts inhibit or forbid uses that would otherwise arguably fall within the scope of the fair use defense. IBM's entry into the market for ARM services, for example, specifies that consumers signing onto its InfoMarket Service "may not copy, modify, adapt, reproduce, [or] translate ... any information delivered or accessed via the Service." This proposed agreement clearly aims to foreclose appeals to the fair use defense.

Despite their vocal concerns about losing unbilled use in digital contexts, champions of fair use have made comparatively little noise about the potential impact of such contracts. To bring that impact into focus, let us briefly return to the hypothetical nightmare in progress: The court holds not only that you have no right to use the Church of Technolism's copyrighted materials without paying, but that you have no right to use them without permission. The Church has cited not only its rights under copyright law—a claim weakened by the policies underlying the fair use defense—but a contract arising out of your willing use of the particular service that controls access to the Church's web page. That contract gives the Church of Technolism the right to prevent any and all quotations of the text from its web page. Thanks to that contract, you find that you cannot buy your way out of copyright infringement. The Church of Technolism thus wins as its remedy not payment of the lost licensing fees, but rather an injunction on your unauthorized use.

Chilling though this scenario may sound, it remains technically and legally plausible. Copyright owners often evince a desire to prohibit the critical, blasphemous, or satirical reuse of their works. In Campbell v. Acuff–Rose Music, Inc., the Supreme Court forbade employing copyright law to achieve such censorship, of course. It did not, however, expressly rule out using contract law to similar effect.

Though thin-skinned copyright owners might have it otherwise, mass distribution in conventional media does not lend itself to the imposition and enforcement of such anti-criticism contracts. The digital intermedia, in contrast, deliver information through channels ready-made to impose contracts limiting or forbidding fair use. Moreover, automated rights management makes enforcing those contracts wholly viable from a technical point of view.

As discussed more fully below, however, courts will probably hold that the fair use defense gives consumers the right to engage in limited critical reuses. ARM or not. Fair use will thus continue to play a vital role, albeit a diminished one, in a world of otherwise pervasive fared use. Contracts that interfere with the fair use defense might risk federal preemption. Before addressing that particular issue, however, the next Part examines how the fair use doctrine will interact with the pre-contractual self-help measures that ARM will make available to copyright owners in digital intermedia.

III.   The Future Revisited: From "Free Use" to Fared Use

This Part critically evaluates the dystopian future of fair use described above and describes fared use as a better and more likely alternative....

A.   Fair Use Versus "Free Use"

Predictions that consumers will not generally enjoy unbilled access to copyrighted works in digital intermedia appear to assess the future accurately. For reasons set forth above, the advent of sophisticated automated rights management will sharply lower transaction costs for regulating the use of copyrighted materials. The legal doctrine set forth in American Geophysical and Princeton University Press, with or without the NII White Paper's broad interpretation of these cases, will limit the applicability of the fair use doctrine online. New technology and current law will thus end up partially supplanting the fair use defense in the digital intermedia. For reasons set forth below, however, even parties who currently benefit from applying the fair use defense in conventional media should welcome this change.

1.   Fair Use Is Not Free Use

Despite gross misconceptions to the contrary, fair use never comes for free. One way or another, consumers using conventional media must pay to browse magazines at newsstands, to photocopy and distribute newspaper stories for spontaneous classroom use, to search for quotes and type them into articles, and to otherwise avail themselves of the fair use doctrine. Although such acts do not entail paying licensing fees, they inevitably impose a variety of transaction costs—for personal transport, manipulating paper and ink, searching card catalogs, and so on—that follow from the very nature of conventional media. It makes no difference that consumers pay licensing fees in cash whereas they pay fair use's transaction costs in lost opportunities. Economically speaking, a cost is a cost.

The digital intermedia allow consumers to avoid or reduce such transaction costs. Bits flow directly to homes and offices, copy easily into RAM or magnetic storage, forward instantly to destinations worldwide, and submit easily to electronic searches. Transaction costs remain even here, of course. The burgeoning growth of the Internet and other digital intermedia indicates, however, that consuming bits very often costs less than consuming atoms. The increasing reliance of legal academics on commercial online services, CD–ROMs, and the Internet confirms this observation. Those who decry the advent of fared use thus err when they imply that it must impose a net cost on consumers. To the contrary, fared use offers a considerable likelihood of providing more and better verified, organized, and interlinked information, at less cost, than fair use does now.

2. Fixing Market Failure

Scholars have explained fair use in at least three ways: (1) as a proxy for a copyright owner's implied consent; (2) as part of a bargain between authors and the public, struck on their behalf first by courts and then by Congress; and (3) as a response to a market failure in private attempts to protect authors' expressions from undue copying. The first of these three explanations has fallen into disfavor because it does not explain why fair use protects parody and other uses of copyrighted material that owners find disagreeable. The second explanation receives due consideration below. The present subsection addresses the third explanation of fair use and argues that, as a response to market failure, the fair use doctrine can and should give way in the face of the effective enforcement of authors' rights through automated rights management.

Lawmakers enacted the Copyright Act to cure an alleged case of market failure: creating a work can cost authors a good deal, whereas copying a work costs free riders very little. Absent special protection from such copying, the argument goes, authors will underproduce and the public will suffer. Copyright, as Justice Holmes explained, therefore "restrains the spontaneity of men where but for it there would be nothing of any kind to hinder their doing as they saw fit;" namely, copying others' expressions at will. Perhaps in the digital intermedia automated rights management will cure this market failure by protecting authors' works through technological and contractual means. ARM's other curative effects interest us here, though.

Markets, like squeezed balloons, bulge outward where unconstrained. In its attempt to protect authors from the discouraging effects of unfettered copying, copyright law has thus created market failure elsewhere. The costs of avoiding infringement by obtaining permission to use a copyrighted work, and thus avoiding infringement claims, often exceed the benefits of the desired use. Such transaction costs threaten to prevent many socially beneficial uses of copyrighted works from taking place. The doctrine of fair use attempts to cure this particular market failure by excusing as non-infringing a limited (though poorly defined) class of uses of copyrighted works. As Professor Gordon describes it, "courts and Congress have employed fair use to permit uncompensated transfers that are socially desirable but not capable of effectuation through the market."

Understanding fair use as a response to market failure does much to explain the vagaries of its development in the case law. More to the point, it lends support to the holding in American Geophysical. Consistent with the market failure theory of fair use, the court reasoned that "a particular unauthorized use should be considered 'more fair' when there is no ready market or means to pay for the use, while such an unauthorized use should be considered 'less fair' when there is a ready market or means to pay for the use." In other words, the scope of the fair use defense rises and falls with the transaction costs of licensing access to copyrighted works.

Automated rights management radically reduces the transaction costs of licensing access to copyrighted works in digital intermedia.

Indeed, as its name suggests, it makes licensing automatic. Insofar as it responds to market failure, therefore, fair use should have a much reduced scope when ARM takes effect. Should fair use disappear entirely? Were ARM to abolish transaction costs, Coase's theorem would suggest that the market would internalize all costs and permit only value-maximizing transfers. ARM does not wholly negate search and exchange costs, however, thus perhaps leaving contractual gaps for fair use to fill. Furthermore, Congress employs fair use to redistribute rights in accord with its particular notions of equity. The defense thus excuses certain "socially beneficial" uses, such as criticism and parody, that copyright owners might prefer not to license. Fair use thus remains relevant, even given ARM. Exactly how the two will interact to create a fared use system, and how well that system accommodates the concerns that drive fair use, receives consideration below.

First, though, a cautionary reminder: no forecast of the probable impact of ARM can overlook the fact that, just as ARM technology may shape the law, the law will shape the development of ARM. Although robust and sophisticated ARM technology would likely curtail application of the fair use doctrine, unduly aggressive application of the fair use doctrine might thwart creation of the necessary technology. This risk should concern not only computer scientists and information providers, but artists and audiences, too. Stifling ARM would stifle the wide variety of new expressions and experiences that the digital intermedia promise to inspire, promote, and provide.

3. Maintaining Copyright's Quid Pro Quo

As courts and commentators often have noted, the Constitution demands a public benefit as the price for the limited statutory privileges that copyright creates. In contrast to the view that the fair use doctrine represents a second-best response to pervasive market failure, therefore, some commentators regard the doctrine as an integral part of this constitutional quid pro quo. On this view, fair use provides a public benefit—unbilled access to copyrighted works—to balance the State's grant of a limited monopoly.

Automated rights management at first appears to threaten this bargain. It seems as if ARM restricts the public's access to copyrighted works in digital intermedia without offering a benefit in return. As this subsection's consideration of the issue shows, however, friends of fair use should not assume that ARM will leave the public worse off. To the contrary, it appears likely to provide a net benefit to the public.

By reducing transaction costs throughout the market for copyrighted expressions, ARM benefits the public both directly and indirectly. Having emanated from an intentionally vague statute and developed in various, occasionally contradictory cases, the fair use doctrine necessarily blurs the boundary between valid and invalid copyright claims. High risks of "theft"—here, infringement—increase the insecurity of copyright's protection. Though the resultant uncertainty obviously harms producers and sellers of copyrighted works, it also harms consumers. Academics, artists, commentators, and others desirous of reusing copyrighted works without authorization must borrow at their peril, consult experts on fair use, or, sadly, forego such reuse altogether. ARM's clarifying power directly benefits those who would reuse copyrighted works—and through them their public audiences—by creating harbors safe from the threat of copyright litigation.

Moreover, ARM benefits the public indirectly by increasing the transactional efficiency of the market for expressive works. Like other markets, the market for expressive works does not constitute a zero sum game. And, as Coase observed of markets in general, it is obviously desirable that rights should be assigned to those who can use them most productively and with incentives that lead them to do so. It is also desirable that, to discover (and maintain) such a distribution of rights, the costs of their transference should be low, through clarity in the law and by making the legal requirements for such transfers less onerous.

ARM, by its systemic improvement of copyright's transactional efficiency, helps us discover and maintain a distribution of rights to expressive works that will increase net social wealth. ARM thus stands to benefit both producers and consumers.

In particular, because it increases the value of expressive works, ARM will put deflationary pressure on the price of accessing them. In general, an asset's current price internalizes the value of its future income stream. Copyrights therefore commonly lose present value because, with the passage of time and their wider distribution, they prove increasingly vulnerable to uncompensated uses. Because it reduces such risks, ARM tends to increase the value of copyrights. But although this windfall might initially accrue to copyright owners, competition among information providers would force access prices downward, toward the marginal costs of obtaining and distributing expressive works. Directly or indirectly, such price pressure would similarly affect the prices that copyright owners can demand. Gains that ARM provides to copyright owners would thus pass on to consumers in the form of reduced access fees.

Because ARM will increase the value of copyrighted works, moreover, it will encourage their greater production and improved distribution. Consumers will thus benefit from better access to information. Access providers will improve the information itself, too, increasing its quantity and making it better organized, verified, interlinked, diverse, up-to-date, and relevant. Although this cornucopia of information may at first come only for a fee, some of it eventually will fall into the public domain. To judge from current implementations of ARM, copyright owners might very well offer limited free access to their wares in an attempt to draw more extensive (and expensive) uses. Entrepreneurs will undoubtedly create other services, at present utterly and inevitably unforeseen, to attract and satisfy consumers of information.

As such considerations demonstrate, "strict copyright enforcement doesn't necessarily mean people would pay more for viewing copyrighted material." Because automated rights management creates well-defined and readily transferable property rights to information, it puts the power of the market in the service of consumer demand. As Professor Goldstein explains, "there is no better way for the public to indicate what they want than through the price they are willing to pay in the marketplace. Uncompensated use inevitably dilutes these signals." Fared use therefore probably will provide better public access to copyrighted works in digital intermedia than fair use does or could. At any rate, no one can plausibly claim that fared use necessarily would serve the public interest any less well than the existing quid pro quo. . . .

B.   Objectionable Use Remains Fair Use

If ARM can give information providers the power to monitor various uses and reuses of their copyrighted materials for billing purposes, it can also give them the power to bar such uses as they find objectionable. Technical prowess alone does not justify such censorship, however. Public policy and copyright law pose additional hurdles, and, as this Subpart shows, quite high ones. Whether an information provider could overcome those hurdles by supplementing copyright law with contract law remains a distinct possibility, and one that Part IV considers separately.

The prospect of information providers using ARM to track and prohibit objectionable uses of copyrighted works might well alarm free speech advocates. It seems unlikely, however, that the First Amendment's influence over state action would reach such private action. Thanks to the idea-expression distinction, moreover, courts have found that they do not unconstitutionally hinder free speech in using state power to enforce copyright claims against commentators. As the Supreme Court has observed, the idea-expression distinction "strikes a definitional balance between the First Amendment and the Copyright Act by permitting free communication of facts while still protecting an author's expression."

Where the First Amendment proves impotent against ARM-based censorship, however, civil disobedience might have a very real impact. Because ARM's powers would at most reach only cut-and-paste quotations, it would not limit criticism or reportage that merely paraphrases a protected work. Nor, of course, could a copyright owner count on ARM to catch reuses that, innocently or not, include cut-and-paste quotes of works stolen ("liberated," some would say) from ARM protection. . . .

For now, at least, fair use can trump a copyright owner's objections. The American Geophysical court allowed licensing to limit the fair use defense only "when the means for paying for such a use is made easier." The court thus conditioned its holding on the observation that "a particular unauthorized use should be considered 'more fair' when there is no ready market or means to pay for the use.'" In this, it followed the Supreme Court's reasoning in Campbell v. Acuff–Rose Music, Inc.:

> The market for potential derivative uses includes only those that creators of original works would in general develop or license others to develop. Yet the unlikelihood that creators of imaginative works will license critical reviews or lampoons of their own productions removes such uses from the very notion of a potential licensing market.

> Therefore, although information providers might like to stop wags who evade ARM protection and reuse "liberated" works in objectionable

ways, the fair use defense would continue to shield such defendants from copyright infringement claims.

One might well question the economic wisdom of such a policy. Just because an information provider refuses to license a particular use does not mean that no market exists. Rather, it demonstrates that the information provider demands more for that use than anyone wants to pay. Even a flat refusal to deal does not demonstrate market failure. As Professor Gordon has observed, "[a] refusal to license must not automatically justify a right to fair use; markets can function only if owners have a right to say 'no' as well as 'yes.' " Strictly speaking, courts should thus find market failures only when technical barriers—not mere refusals to deal—prevent licensing agreements from taking place.

As the reasoning in the Campbell and American Geophysical decisions on this point demonstrates, however, the fair use doctrine sometimes favors public access over sound economics. Information providers who would prefer to use ARM and copyright law to completely bar objectionable reuses of their work will thus probably find their efforts thwarted by anti-ARM techniques and the fair use doctrine. Here, at least, fair use strikes back at ARM.

Suppose that you defused the ARM protecting a copyrighted expression and reused the work without the owner's authorization. Often such an owner, offended, will disdain to charge you a licensing fee. But some owners will, if able, take your coin (and your apology). Can you count on the fair use defense to excuse not only your objectionable reuse of a copyrighted work but also your refusal to pay for that use? Probably so. Reuses that qualify for the fair use defense do not, under 107 of the Copyright Act, constitute infringement. The Act would thus not obligate you to pay.

Requiring payment in such circumstances arguably makes more sense, for the same reasons that support the spread of licensing generally. Furthermore, excusing non-payment might encourage over-production of reuses that aim, for purely economic reasons, to offend copyright owners. True, parody and other criticism "can provide social benefit, by shedding light on an earlier work, and, in the process, creating a new one." But too much of a good thing is no good at all.

Such theoretical considerations have yet to change copyright law, however. Unless and until they do, it looks as if information providers will have to suffer objectionable uses without remuneration, license them grudgingly, or try to prevent them by means of supplementary contracts....

Copyright Non–Compliance (Or Why We Can't "Just Say Yes" to Licensing)

JESSICA LITMAN*

... I have complained more than once over the past few years that the copyright law is complicated, arcane, and counterintuitive; and that the upshot of that is that people don't believe that the copyright law says

* 29 N.Y.U.J. INT'L L. & POL. 237, 238–42, 244–46, 251–52 (1997).

what it does say. People do seem to buy into copyright norms, but they don't translate those norms into the rules that the copyright statute does; they find it very hard to believe that there's really a law out there that says the stuff the copyright law says.

Of course we have many laws that people don't seem to believe in. Think of the laws prohibiting consensual sodomy, for instance. When I was a child and my father told me about those laws, I had a tough time believing that he wasn't making it up. Or, think about the national fifty-five-miles-per-hour speed limit law. Or the laws that say that minors can't buy cigarettes. These are all laws that people don't believe say what they say. And, since they don't think that familiar sexual activities, or driving at seventy miles per hour, or buying a pack of Marlboros from the cigarette machine in the cafeteria, are really against the law, they don't refrain from doing those things just because some law on the books says they can't.

People don't obey laws that they don't believe in. It isn't necessarily that they behave lawlessly, or that they'll steal whatever they can steal if they think they can get away with it. Most people try to comply, at least substantially, with what they believe the law to say. If they don't believe the law says what it in fact says, though, they won't obey it—not because they are protesting its provisions, but because it doesn't stick in their heads. Governments stop enforcing laws that people don't believe in. Laws that people don't obey and that governments don't enforce get repealed, even if they are good laws in some other sense of the word. The national fifty-five-miles-per-hour speed limit, for instance, (had it been followed) would have conserved fuel and saved lives, but it wasn't, so it didn't, and now it's history; Congress finally repealed it.

People are nonetheless attached to the symbolic significance of some of these laws. "They're good," people say, "because they make a statement. They express the norms of civilized society." You hear that sort of thing often when you are talking about the war on drugs; many people agree that the laws against drugs aren't working; indeed, are doing as much harm as good, but they are unwilling to give up the symbolic force of the prohibitions. That's one good reason to keep a law around even though nobody seems to be obeying it. It can be very expensive to cling to a law that is unenforced and unenforceable, but sometimes, with some laws, some people feel that it is worth the price for the symbolism. Certainly, you hear a lot of that in support of laws that legislate morality.

But laws that we keep around for their symbolic power can only exercise that power to the extent that people know what the laws say. If nobody knew that we had a law against selling cocaine, it wouldn't be serving much of a symbolic function. (To go back to the laws against consensual sodomy for a moment, they stopped performing whatever symbolic function they were supposed to perform once people stopped believing that there were real laws out there that made things like that illegal.) So, the answer to the question "Why is it a problem that people don't believe in the copyright law?" depends on the reason they don't believe in it. The reason people don't believe in the copyright law, I would argue, is that people persist in believing that laws make sense, and the copyright laws don't seem to them to make sense, because they don't make sense, especially from the vantage point of the individual end user.

Copyright law is horribly complicated. Sometime around the turn of the century, we in the United States reached the collective judgment that copyright was too complicated for mere mortals (or indeed for mere senators) to appreciate, and we settled on an approach whereby we assembled all of the copyright experts—that is, the entities whose businesses involved printing, reprinting, publishing and vending—and assigned them the task of sorting out the relationships among them. So, whenever we need a major revision of the copyright law, it has become traditional to assemble all of the current stakeholders in informal negotiations and present whatever they agree on to Congress.

That, today, is common ground. The laws that come out of such a process have both strengths and weaknesses. At least in the short term, they tend to be laws the relevant industries can live with, because the relevant industries wrote them. Those laws can solve the problems posed by different entities' different needs by specifying, so that, e.g., video games can be treated differently from video tapes, or cable television can be treated differently from broadcast television, which can be treated still differently from satellite television. For that reason, though, the differences in treatment may not have much logical appeal. In addition, the negotiating process tends to divide users into discrete interests. Businesses and institutions who are at the bargaining table request and receive specific privileges, and nobody ends up being a proxy for the general public.

The current crisis has been precipitated by the widespread adoption of new digital technology, which enables members of the general public to print, reprint, publish, vend, and communicate with a vast audience without resorting to the traditional intermediaries. Estimates peg the number of current U.S. users of on-line services at anywhere between ten and twenty-four million people, and those numbers are growing all the time. Current stakeholders, who are accustomed to the current rules, would of course prefer that the rules that apply to the general public engaging in these activities be the current rules, or ones that work as much like them as possible. They have been seeking ways to maintain what they see as the appropriate balance in the law, by reinvigorating and extending their version of the current rules. . . .

The trouble with the plan is that the only people who appear to actually believe that the current copyright rules apply as writ to every person on the planet are members of the copyright bar. Representatives of current stakeholders, talking among themselves, have persuaded one another that it must be true, but that's a far cry from persuading the ten or twenty million new printers and reprinters. The good old rules were not written with the millions of new digital publishers in mind, and they don't fit very well with the way end users interact with copyrighted works. If you say to an end user, "you either need permission or a statutory privilege for each appearance, however fleeting, of any work you look at in any computer anywhere," she'll say "There can't really be a law that says that. That would be silly." Even copyright lawyers, who have invested years in getting used to the ways the copyright law seems arbitrary, have had to engage in several pretzels worth of logical contortions to articulate how the good old rules do and should apply to end users without any further exemptions or privileges.

Instead, though, of polling the old guard for its version of good rules to constrain the individual end users who, after all, are now threatening to compete as well as consume, and then foisting those on the public in a "just say yes—to licensing" campaign, it might be worthwhile to step back a step.

I take it that a law that folks complied with voluntarily would be superior on many counts to one that required reeducation campaigns, that depended on technological agents to be our copyright police, and that relied on felony convictions to be our deterrents. Nobody has proposed a law that might meet this description because the members of the copyright bar have all looked around and concluded that consumers will not voluntarily comply with the current collection of copyright rules. Stop and think about that for a minute. We can't rely on voluntary compliance because the great mass of mankind will not comply voluntarily with the current rules.

Well, why not? Is it that consumers are lawless, or ignorant? Is it, in other words, the consumers' fault? Or might there instead be some defect in the current rules—at least from the consumers' standpoint? To recast the question, can we look at the dilemma from the opposite direction? Are there rules that we believe consumers would comply with voluntarily? Do those rules potentially supply sufficient incentives to authors and their printers, publishers, and vendors to create new works and put them on the global information infrastructure, and, if not, can we tweak them so that they do? ...

The other conclusion I draw is this: more than ever before, our copyright policy is becoming our information policy. As technology has transformed the nature of copyright so that it now applies to everybody's everyday behavior, it has become more important, not less, that our copyright rules embody a deal that the public would assent to. The most important reason why we devised and continued to rely on a copyright legislative process whereby the copyright rules were devised by representatives of affected industries to govern interactions among them is that it produced rules that those industries could live with. Now that it is no longer merely the eight major movie studios, or the four television networks, or the 6,000 radio stations, or the 200–some book publishers, or the 57,000 libraries in this country that need to concern themselves with whether what they are doing will result in the creation of a "material object ... in which a work is fixed by any method," but rather millions of ordinary citizens, it is crucial that the rules governing what counts as such an object, and what the implications are of making one, be rules that those citizens can live with.

The White Paper suggests that we invest in citizen reeducation to persuade everyone that the current copyright rules are right, true, and just. I am less distressed by this suggestion than I might be if I thought it were likely to work. There's something profoundly un-American about the campaign, at least as the White Paper describes it. But, instead of trying to change the minds of millions of people, instead of trying to persuade them that a long, complicated, counterintuitive, and often arbitrary code written by a bunch of copyright lawyers is sensible and fair, why don't we just replace this code with a set of new rules that more people than not think are sensible and fair? ...

Notes and Questions

1. Born in 1964, Professor Tom W. Bell teaches at Chapman University School of Law. He received his J.D. from the University of Chicago in 1993. Prior to joining the Chapman faculty, Professor Bell served as Director of Telecommunications and Technology Studies at the Cato Institute, and was on the faculty of the University of Dayton Law School.

2. For an argument that automated rights management of the kind the White Paper proposed to protect (and that the subsequently-passed DMCA does protect) implicates a first amendment right to maintain anonymity in one's reading choices, consider the following:

> For the most part, First Amendment jurisprudence has defined readers' rights only incidentally. Historically, both courts and commentators have been more concerned with protecting speakers than with protecting readers. Protection of speech is, of course, the First Amendment's central, express guarantee. Until recently, however, the technological means to monitor individuals' reading habits did not exist. Thus, the questions whether the First Amendment should be read to establish a right to read and what scope to accord such a right have demanded, and received, comparatively little attention. They merit a great deal of attention now. In light of the new digital monitoring technologies, it is vitally important that we reexamine our understanding of reading, its relationship to speech, and its place in our jurisprudence of speech and speaker's rights.... [T]he close interdependence between receipt and expression of information and between reading and freedom of thought make recognition of such a right sound constitutional policy.
>
> ...
>
> The existence of a right to read anonymously, in the abstract, does little to guarantee individual readers protection against private conduct. The First Amendment affords protection only against governmental conduct that threatens reader anonymity. How, then, is the right to read anonymously triggered by the so-called "copyright management" efforts of private content providers? Quite simply, it is not—but the proposed anti-tampering provisions of the NIICPA are a different story. The proposed Chapter 12 of the Copyright Act would prohibit—and in some cases, criminalize—efforts to "remove or alter" copyright management information or to "avoid, bypass,

remove, deactivate, or otherwise circumvent ... any process, treatment, mechanism, or system" put in place for copyright protection. On their face, these provisions would reach both the conduct of the willful infringer and that of the concerned libertarian who tampers with copyright management software only, and only to the extent necessary, to preserve his or her anonymity. Arguably, enforcement of these provisions supplies the requisite government action. If so, their breadth cannot be justified by any governmental interest.

Julie Cohen, *The Right to Read Anonymously*, 28 Conn L. Rev. 981, 1003–04, 1019–20 (1996).

3. Suppose you purchase a digital file of your favorite songs, and the automated rights management system accompanying the file prohibits retention copying of any kind, instead charging you a fee each time you listen to it. How would this system comport with the different formulations of fair use? How does it comport with your sense of what is fair? Does your response depend on what you paid for the file? Whether the automatic rights system is timed to block access after a certain period? Whether you feel that the recording industry's past pricing policies were extortionate, and conferred no benefits on the recording artists? Whether you feel the rights system intrudes on your privacy? Are any of these concerns relevant to Judge Leval's conception of fair use? To Professor Weinreb's? To Professor Fisher's?

4. For further concerns about the use of state contract law to disrupt the congressionally calibrated balance of rights provided by the copyright statute, see, e.g., David Nimmer, Elliot Brown & Gary N. Frischling, *The Metamorphosis of Contract into Expand*, 87 Cal. L. Rev 17 (1999).

B. Copyright and the First Amendment

Does Copyright Abridge the First Amendment Guarantees of Free Speech and Press?
MELVILLE B. NIMMER*

I. THE NEED TO RECONCILE COPYRIGHT AND THE FIRST AMENDMENT

... Whether more closely aligned with the creators, or with the so-called user groups, copyright practitioners and their clients are likely to place the recognition of a viable and meaningful copyright law high on their scales of value. Further, they are likely to oppose vehemently governmental censorship of literary, musical and artistic works. I would venture to suggest that these two attitudes—favoring copyright and opposing censorship—not only do not appear to be contradictory, but rather are regarded, by most, as mutually supportive. A legal system protective of the creator and those who claim through him will both assure a property right in artistic expression, and will abjure the silencing of that expression through censorship. But most people who

* 17 UCLA L. REV. 1180, 1189–93 (1970).

oppose censorship, including those concerned with copyright, base that opposition not merely on the narrow economic ground that a creator and his assigns should be able to exploit the creator's works, but also, and more fundamentally, on first amendment principles of freedom of expression. It is not just the artist's right to freely express himself that is regarded as important. Freedom of speech for all men, whether or not they can qualify as artistic creators, is the basic principle that underlies the opposition to governmental censorship.

It is here, I would suggest, there lies a largely ignored paradox, requiring exploration. The first amendment tells us that "Congress shall make no law ... abridging the freedom of speech, or of the press." Does not the Copyright Act fly directly in the face of that command? Is it not precisely a "law" made by Congress which abridges the "freedom of speech" and "of the press" in that it punishes expressions by speech and press when such expressions consist of the unauthorized use of material protected by copyright? But surely, many will conclude, the first amendment does not apply to copyright infringers. Yet, is such a conclusion justified? The language of the first amendment does not limit its protection to speech which is original with the speaker, but rather states that Congress shall make "no law" abridging freedom of speech; and Mr. Justice Black has said that this reference to "no law" means no law, "without any 'ifs' or 'buts' or 'whereases.' " If one adopts Justice Black's absolutist approach to the first amendment it is difficult to see how any copyright law can be regarded as constitutional.

It might be contended that copyright laws fall within a built-in exception to first amendment protection, not by the words of the first amendment, but by reason of another passage of the Constitution, namely the copyright clause, expressly authorizing Congress to grant to authors "the exclusive right" to their "writings." However, there are several reasons why refuge for copyright may not be found in this manner. First, if a completely literal reading of the first amendment is to be made, then we must likewise recognize that the first amendment is an amendment, hence superseding anything inconsistent with it which may be found in the main body of the Constitution. This, of course, includes the copyright clause. In any event, even were the original Constitution and the Bill of Rights to be viewed as a single instrument, the copyright clause may not be read as independent of and uncontrolled by the first amendment. Because Congress is granted authority to legislate in a given field, it does not follow that such a grant immunizes Congress from the limitations of the Bill of Rights, including the first amendment....

But if the copyright clause does not render the first amendment inoperative, why does not the contrary conclusion follow? Doesn't the first amendment obliterate the copyright clause and any laws passed pursuant thereto? This returns us to Mr. Justice Black's absolutist approach. It cannot be denied that the copyright laws do in some degree abridge freedom of speech, and if the first amendment were literally construed, copyright would be unconstitutional. But no one (including, one suspects, even Mr. Justice Black) really believes that every law which abridges speech falls before the first amendment.... No one can

responsibly adhere to the position that the first amendment must be
literally construed so as to invalidate all laws which in any degree
abridge speech....

B. *A Balance Based Upon the Idea–Expression Dichotomy*

Does the law of copyright, as we know it today, effectively serve the
interests underlying copyright, while not encroaching upon the interests
underlying freedom of speech? That is to say, is there an acceptable if de
facto definitional balance in the law as it presently exists? To find the
answer we start with the fundamental principle that copyright does not
protect an author's "ideas" per se. If it did, there would certainly be a
serious encroachment upon first amendment values. The market place of
ideas would be utterly bereft, and the democratic dialogue largely stifled
if the only ideas which might be discussed were those original with the
speakers.

But if copyright does not protect "ideas," what does it protect? The
conventional formulation is that while copyright may not be claimed in
an idea, it may be claimed in "the expression of the idea." Does that
mean that only the exact words used by an author are protectible? If
that were the rule, copyright interests would be badly served, indeed.
The economic motivation of creation which underlies copyright would be
almost completely vitiated if anyone could with impunity take an author's work by the device of making a few changes in wording, or even
by closely paraphrasing the entire work. Judge Learned Hand long ago
made clear that copyright "cannot be limited literally to the text, else a
plagiarist would escape by immaterial variations." If the reach of copyright is thus not limited to verbatim repetition, yet does not extend to
ideas per se, how does one draw the line that separates non-protectible
ideas from the protectible "expression of ideas"? Learned Hand had said
that "wherever [the line] is drawn, it will seem arbitrary ..." and that
"the test for infringement of a copyright is of necessity vague." But
Judge Hand vividly described the nature of the quest for "the expression
of an idea" in what I call the "abstractions test":

> Upon any work, and especially upon a play, a great number of
> patterns of increasing generality will fit equally well, as more and more
> of the incident is left out. The last may perhaps be no more than the
> most general statement of what the play is about, and at times might
> consist of only its title; but there is a point in this series of abstractions
> where they are no longer protected, since otherwise the playwright could
> prevent the use of his 'ideas', to which, apart from their expression, his
> property is never extended.

Professor Zechariah Chafee (who, incidentally, is an example par
excellence of one committed to both copyright and free speech) suggested
the level of abstraction which will constitute the copyright line: "No
doubt, the line does lie somewhere between the author's idea and the
precise form in which he wrote it down. I like to say that the protection
covers the 'pattern' of the work ... the sequence of events, and the
development of the interplay of characters." Though Professor Chafee's
"pattern" test is particularly applicable to fictional works, it, together
with Hand's "abstractions test," suggests the general nature of the
dichotomy between non-protected ideas, and the protected "expression of

ideas." It is the particular selection and arrangement of ideas, as well as a given specificity in the form of their expression which warrants protection under the law of copyright.

Here, then, is a definitional balance under which ideas per se fall on the free speech side of the line, while the statement of an idea in specific form, as well as the selection and arrangement of ideas fall on the copyright side of the line. Does this particular balance adequately serve both the interests which underlie copyright, and those which freedom of speech are intended to protect? In general, I would defend this de facto definitional balance.

Does the copyright limitation whereby authors may not prohibit others from copying their abstract ideas serve to discourage creativity, or otherwise retard the "progress of science and useful arts"? Our experience tells us that it does not. Despite the fact that ideas, as distinguished from their "expression," are "free as air," we have witnessed an increasingly immense flow of works emanating from the creative segments of our society. It is true that we have no positive evidence as to whether the flow would have been still greater had ideas per se been legally protectible, but there is reason to believe that idea protection would have in fact been counterproductive. Most, if not all, writers draw from the stock of ideas of their predecessors. Professor Chafee reminded us that "a dwarf standing on the shoulders of a giant can see farther than the giant himself." If writers and other creators could not build upon the ideas of their predecessors, not only would free speech be stifled, but the creative processes themselves—the copyright side of the definitional balance— would also be severely circumscribed. . . .

If on the whole, non-protection for ideas is consistent with the objectives sought under the copyright laws, is the other side of the definitional balance also defensible? That is, does the copyright prohibition on repeating or copying the "expression" of ideas comport with the underlying rationale for freedom of speech? In general, it seems to do so. Take the most important objective that underlies freedom of speech—the maintenance of the democratic dialogue. That process is also known as the marketplace of ideas, and not without reason. It is exposure to ideas, and not to their particular expression, that is vital if self-governing people are to make informed decisions. It is important that we have free access to the ideas of both William F. Buckley, Jr. and Eldridge Cleaver; and everyone should have the right to disseminate Buckley's and Cleaver's ideas, either by way of endorsement or criticism. But that process of enlightenment does not require the freedom to reproduce without permission either Buckley's book *Up From Liberalism*, or Cleaver's *Soul On Ice*. To reproduce the "expression" of their ideas may add flavor, but relatively little substance to the data that must inform the electorate in the decision-making process. Such minimal substance, lost through the copyright prohibition on reproduction of expression, is far out-balanced by the public benefit that accrues through copyright encouragement of creativity.

The other two justifications for free speech likewise are not measurably frustrated by the copyright abridgement of the right to reproduce an author's expression. The safety valve rationale is hardly applicable. It is not likely that men will resort to violence because they lack the legal right to reproduce the expression of another, even though such violence might result if idea dissemination were permitted only for ideas original with the speaker. Similarly, free speech as a function of self-fulfillment does not come into play. One who pirates the expression of another is not engaging in *self*-expression in any meaningful sense.

On the whole, therefore, I would conclude that the idea-expression line represents an acceptable definitional balance as between copyright and free speech interests. In some degree it encroaches upon freedom of speech in that it abridges the right to reproduce the "expression" of others, but this is justified by the greater public good in the copyright encouragement of creative works. In some degree it encroaches upon the author's right to control his works in that it renders his "ideas" per se unprotectible, but this is justified by the greater public need for free access to ideas as a part of the democratic dialogue....

[EDITOR'S NOTE: Professor Nimmer goes on to question whether the idea-expression dichotomy may not represent a proper definitional balance in areas where the dichotomy inadequately protects first amendment speech interests.]

Consider the photographs of the My Lai massacre. Here is an instance where the visual impact of a graphic work made a unique contribution to an enlightened democratic dialogue. No amount of words describing the "idea" of the massacre could substitute for the public insight gained through the photographs. The photographic expression, not merely the idea, became essential if the public was to fully understand what occurred in that tragic episode. It would be intolerable if the public's comprehension of the full meaning of My Lai could be censored by the copyright owner of the photographs. Here I cannot but conclude that the speech interest outweighs the copyright interest. ...

If such photographs are to be treated as outside the scope of copyright protection, will this not tend to diminish, if not eliminate entirely, the news photography industry, thereby defeating the speech interest itself? The answer may lie in an application of the compulsory license approach ...

Copyright and The First Amendment
PAUL GOLDSTEIN*

... Although its censorship function was dissipated with enactment of the Statute of Anne, copyright persists in its potential for conflict with the first amendment. Dispensed by the government, copyright still constitutes the grant of a monopoly over expression....

... The statutory monopoly ... originates from the constitutional grant to Congress of the authority to secure "for limited Times to Authors ... the exclusive Right to their ... Writings...." Congressional exercise of this mandate, in the first copyright act and its subsequent

* 70 COLUM. L. REV. 983, 984, 987–88, 1006–07, 1009–18, 1020, 1022, 1032–34, 1055–56 (1970).

amendments, has effected a gradual widening of authors' rights and a consequent diminution in the public's right to speak and to hear previously unprotected expressions.

. . .

This article will assess the extent to which copyright's statutory . . . monopol[y] presently conflict[s] with the first amendment and will identify methods for reconciling the competing interests involved in these conflicts. Two principles will be relied upon for analysis and accommodation of the conflicting interests in infringement cases. The first of these is termed, simply, the *first accommodative principle*; it requires that copyright infringement be excused if the subject matter of the infringed material is relevant to the public interest and the appropriator's use of the material independently advances the public interest. The *second accommodative principle* requires that only "original" literary property be protected against unauthorized use, that actual damages be demonstrated by the plaintiff, and that the granting of legal, not equitable, relief be the general rule when the plaintiff prevails. The application of these two principles in copyright infringement cases is intended to accommodate the conflicting values of the first amendment and the Copyright Act in a manner which fundamentally advances their respective goals.

. . .

III.   ACCOMMODATION OF THE STATUTORY MONOPOLY

A.   *Preliminary Considerations*

Complete vindication of the creator's economic interest would logically require that the statutory monopoly be absolute. Likewise, the logic of full vindication of the immediate public interest in free access would require that no statutory monopoly at all be permitted. The copyright statute reflects a reasoned compromise between these competing interests.

That the statutory copyright monopoly generally comports with first amendment values is evidenced by the extent to which its actual boundaries fall short of the boundaries theoretically possible for an absolute monopoly over artistic subject matter. An absolute monopoly, clearly abhorrent to first amendment values, could protect (1) in perpetuity (2) all creations of the mind (3) against all possible unauthorized uses of the creation, (4) including uses which merely tend to approximate the creation, and it could grant the creator and his successors in interest (5) absolute control over the marketing of the creation and (6) injunctive, as well as monetary relief as of right.

Compared to this hypothetical monopoly, which would effectively exclude the public from free access, statutory copyright appears pervasively inhibited. These inhibitions derive in part from the constitutional mandate (1) that the period of protection not exceed "limited times" and (2) that protection be accorded only to "writings." Furthermore, though the Constitution's copyright clause authorizes an "exclusive right" in authors, the legislative and judicial method has been to dilute exclusivity by (3) sanctioning many unauthorized uses of copyright subject matter,

(4) premising infringement upon actual copying rather than incidental replication, (5) depriving the copyright owner of control over copies of his work once they have entered the market place, and (6) treating the injunction as a discretionary rather than a mandatory remedy....

... The first accommodative principle, drawn from Supreme Court decisions reviewing state administration of libel and privacy doctrines, has two tenets. It requires that conduct, otherwise constituting copyright infringement, be excused if (1) the subject matter appropriated is relevant to the public's interest in its own cultural, social and political advancement and (2) the use to which the infringed subject matter is put by the appropriator independently conduces to advancement of the public interest. The second accommodative principle, derived from the Supreme Court's innovation of the misappropriation doctrine, also has two tenets. It requires (1) that the protection which the statute provides be elastic, its boundaries extending only in proportion to the originality of the work, and that the judicial administration of the protection be sensitively attuned to measure the originality of the labors of both parties to suit; and (2) that, to be actionable, invasions of the property interest conferred by the statute must inflict economic harm upon the owner, and that, to the extent possible, damages be preferred over the injunctive remedy.

B. *The First Principle: Permitted Uses*

The law permits a variety of unauthorized uses of copyrighted subject matter. The dynamics of this permission correspond generally with those contemplated by the first accommodative principle. They tend to excuse otherwise infringing conduct where the subject matter appropriated is relevant to the public's interest in its own political and cultural advancement and the infringer dedicates the subject matter to a use independently conducive to the public interest.

. . .

1. *Statutory Permission*

To the extent that the aggregate of rights assigned by the Copyright Act to a particular type of work describes less than an entire right to exclude, it may fairly be inferred that Congress rationally distinguished uses which should be excused from those which should not. Thus, while barring the public from printing, reprinting, publishing, copying, vending, translating or making another version of a copyrighted literary work, the Act nowhere proscribes its circulation in a public library, much less its private perusal. Furthermore, while one cannot, without the author's consent, publicly perform a copyrighted dramatic work, private performance is permitted. . . .

. . .

2. *Decisional Permission: The Doctrine of Fair Use*

The mechanics of accommodation, implicit in the Copyright Act's prescription of rights, are explicitly recognized in cases decided on the ground of fair use.... The effect of the fair use defense is to excuse otherwise infringing conduct in circumstances where the public interest compels free access.... Properly construed, the doctrine's purport is to "subordinate the copyright holder's interest in a maximum financial return to the greater public interest in the development of art, science and industry."

. . .

The pending copyright revision bill [now the 1976 Act,—eds.] substantially endorses the . . . approach under which the determination whether a particular use is fair requires consideration of three factors: the extent to which the subject matter copied is the object of a compelling public interest; the extent to which defendant's vehicle of expression is independently capable of advancing the public interest; and the extent to which plaintiff is economically injured by defendant's conduct.

. . .

The first two factors, subject matter and use, coincide in their thrust with the two aspects of the first accommodative principle. The third, or economic, factor is not contained in the first accommodative principle simply because the *Times* and *Hill* line of cases from which the principle is derived accords no weight to a plaintiff's pecuniary loss. The economic factor in fair use doctrine establishes an inverse ratio: the likelihood that defendant's conduct will be excused increases as the consequent economic harm to plaintiff decreases. . . .

. . .

3. *The Dynamics of Permission: Private Standing to Assert the Public Interest*

The first accommodative principle is general in its application. Derived from abstract first amendment theory, it is capable of reconciling any legal interest with the public right to hear. Its generality aside, this first accommodative principle possesses in its second tenet a perspective which is valuable to the analysis . . . of statutory copyright's second accommodative principle . . .

The second tenet of the first accommodative principle requires that otherwise infringing conduct be excused if it independently operates to advance the public interest in broad dissemination of copyrighted works. In the context of an *inter partes* infringement action, advancement of this public interest logically requires that the infringer be exculpated. Piracy's natural effect is to expose a work to an audience wider than the one sought by the copyright owner, either because the infringing work can be obtained at a price lower than that of the authorized copy, or because the infringing material is directed to persons whose interests were not accounted for by the owner's marketing decision. Thus, for example, when a court accredits a fair use defense it only incidentally vindicates the pirate's isolated economic interest; its paramount objective is to broaden public access to expression.

From this perspective, the public interest in access is, in any case, identified with an infringer's conduct. More pointedly, the infringer is given standing to assert the public interest. In the context of the second accommodative principle—which seeks to coordinate property with the public interest—adherence to this perspective requires that the accused infringer be exonerated if he can demonstrate that the property used by him is the object of a compelling public interest and, at the same time, that its sacrifice will not unduly prejudice the copyright owner....

C. *The Second Principle: The Substantive Tenet*

The function of the second accommodative principle is to coordinate property with the public interest. It differs from the first accommodative principle in that it accounts not only for the immediate public interest in access but, also, for the long-range public interest in the cultivation of expressive activity through the award of property incentives. The second principle, though it adopts the perspective of the first, also contains a counterpart to that perspective. While the first accommodative principle, and, in part, the second, identify the accused infringer with the immediate public interest, the second principle also identifies the copyright owner with the long-range public interest in the promotion of expression. The owner's particular request that his property be secured against unauthorized use can be generalized to the basic position that a full monopoly is required to maintain incentive. Under this view, any infringement action contains two disputes, one requiring the resolution of interests *inter partes* and the other requiring the resolution of competing political and economic assumptions.

The second accommodative principle's method is to distinguish in any protected work those components which are the subject of a compelling public interest from those whose protection create economic incentive in the author. This critical distinction is maintained internally by the statutory requirement that only original works may be copyrighted and is externally manifested in the principle's requirement that the copyright interest be thoroughly elastic. Copyright's monopoly boundaries must be susceptible to expansion or contraction according to the relative urgency of the public interest. Elasticity means, then, that as the legitimacy of the public interest in participation increases, so the property interest protected by copyright ought correspondingly to diminish. It also means that as the economic justification for extending copyright protection increases so, correspondingly, ought the public right to participation decrease. In either case, the immediate public interest in participation is asserted by the alleged infringer, and the long-range public interest by the copyright owner.

1. The Framework for Doctrinal Elasticity

Any copyrighted work consists of both ideas and their expressions. Ideas usually take the form of an underlying plot, theme, or conception. Expression may take the form of narrative and dialogue explicating plot, musical elaboration of a basic theme, and the visual details employed to express an initial artistic conception. As between these two components, it may be assumed for introductory purposes that the public interest in free access to a work's ideas is more pressing than the interest in free access to its expression. While ideas can be identified with the public interest, the protection of expressions can be economically justified since they represent a creator's individual departure from what is contained in the common store of knowledge. Copyright's pervasive elasticity and accord with the public interest can best be measured by its treatment of ideas and expressions as separate components of a work. These two components are the concern of copyright's three governing questions: whether a particular work is deserving of protection in the first instance; if so, how to distinguish the work's protectable content from its unprotectable content; and, whether a work accused of infringing the protected work does or does not infringe.

Resolution of the first question, which asks whether a work is to be accorded property status, turns upon the work's originality. To be eligible for copyright protection, a work must be original with its author; copyright status will be extended to a work only if it was created independently by its author and not as a consequence of his copying another work. The fact that the work is similar or even identical to works already published will not debar it from protection so long as it is clear that the similarity is the result of coincidence rather than piracy.

In the event that the first question is answered in the affirmative, the second and third questions require a determination of the extent to which the work is to be protected. Copyright law, reluctant to permit "a monopoly of the ideas expressed," has developed the rule that copyright cannot be accorded to an idea but only to an expression. Yet, as the distinction between idea and expression is one of degree only, the rule governing the answer to the second question is an elastic one. The answer to the third question is derived from the same rule: use of a creator's expressions constitutes infringement, while the use of his ideas does not. In its concern with the accused work's infringing degree, the rule governing the answer to the third question is similarly elastic.

. . .

a.   Administration of the Idea–Expression Distinction.

. . .

The central motive of the idea-expression distinction, from the perspective of either protection or infringement, is to assure the liberation of ideas from all monopoly constraint. . . . Recognizing that expression is no more than an articulated idea or ideas and that the distinction is one of degree only, the law operates by degrees in determining whether a work's content is protectable or has been infringed by another work. From the viewpoint of protection, the more an idea assumes expressive proportions the more extensive is the right accorded to it. Determinations of infringement proceed from a similarly flexible basis: the restatement, or even verbatim copying, of an idea is not actionable; yet, as the restatement or appropriation progressively incorporates the idea's verbal exposition, there is an increasing probability that infringement will be found. The factual determination of the extent to which an idea has graduated into an expression corresponds, then, with the legal determination of the extent to which rights may be said to attach to a work and, conversely, with the determination whether that work has been infringed.

Just as the legal rules of copyright promote elasticity, copyright's rules of evidence governing proof of copying conduce to a similar result. To prevail in an action for infringement, plaintiff must prove, among other things, that defendant has copied his work. . . .

b.   Administration of the Originality Requirement.

. . .

The rules governing administration of the idea-expression distinction
and proof of copying only partially discharge copyright's first amendment function. The operation of these rules, being exclusively concerned
with the immediate inter partes rights of plaintiff and defendant, does
not reflect an historical conscience. Yet, the ideas and expressions used
by a creator are rarely novel with him; he draws, whether consciously or
not, upon a daily increasing inventory of cultural and political statements. The public's right to participate in ideas cannot, then, be defined
by exclusive reference to a single creator's work. It has a more compelling interest in free access to the world's general stock of expression.
First amendment principles require that the grant of a copyright monopoly in no way impede this access. On the other hand, as a matter of
economic incentive, they also require that a creator not be dissuaded
from his efforts by the knowledge that similarity between his work and
that of his predecessors will deprive him of a copyright property. Copyright's requirement of originality, flexibly administered in both its substantive and evidentiary aspects, guarantees this balance through a
method which complements that employed in the context of the idea-
expression distinction. Furthermore, the originality requirement vindicates this generalized public interest by granting defendant standing to
assert it as a defense in an infringement suit.

. . .

The originality requirement operates to invest this premise with a
thoroughly principled rationale. According to its logic, plaintiff's ideas
are free not simply because free trade in ideas is compelled by first
amendment policy, but because the artistic ideas voiced by plaintiff are
rarely, if ever, new. They depend for their vigor upon an accumulation of
thought having a long intellectual history. Thus, to permit any plaintiff a
monopoly in the ideas expressed in his work would not only bar public
access to items of cultural and political value; it would as well grant
plaintiff a property in subject matter which is not his own. . . .

. . .

D.   *The Second Principle: The Economic Tenet*

The economically based tenet of the second accommodative principle
holds that, to be actionable, invasions of the copyright must effect
economic harm and that an award of damages should be preferred to the
injunctive remedy. Since copyright property has economic value only, the
principle would permit any public participation in the property which
does not tend to impair its value. The preference for damages over
injunctive relief is a corollary of the requirement of demonstrable injury.
From a first amendment viewpoint, the effect of an injunction is to
restrain the infringing expression altogether—an effect which goes beyond what is necessary to secure the copyright property. An award of
monetary damages, which permits the infringing expression at a reasonable cost, is more tolerable from a first amendment point of view.

The economic tenet requires that no matter how unscrupulous an infringer's conduct may appear, it will be excused unless it effects economic harm. Whatever justification there is for the position that recovery should be permitted regardless of injury necessarily derives from the position that infringement constitutes an immoral act. The considerations which attend the award of damages—or, in the proper case, injunctive relief—should be stripped of such a moral judgment. The remedial provisions of the Copyright Act, as applied, largely support this proposition. By implicitly endorsing the view of the infringer as an advocate of the public interest, courts in dispensing remedies tend to treat infringements as instances of public participation in private property for which the copyright owner is entitled to reasonable recompense.

. . .

2. *Compulsory Licensing: The Preference for Damages over the Injunctive Remedy.* As the effect of infringement is broader dissemination of a work, the infringer is making marketing decisions which complement the owner's. The infringer can theoretically be treated as the owner's agent, accountable for the profits the owner would have made had he entered those markets himself. If the infringer is also viewed as a representative of the public interest, it is apparent that injunction of his conduct operates to impede public access to the copyrighted work. Thus, from a first amendment viewpoint, an assessment of damages against an infringer is preferable to an injunction terminating his activities. The direct effect of an injunction is to restrain the infringer; its indirect, and more significant, consequence lies in its constriction of the audience which will have access to the copyrighted work. Copyright doctrine should, therefore, conform to the general constitutional rule which restricts use of the injunctive remedy against conduct which is consonant with first amendment rights.

Yet, recourse to injunctive relief in copyright cases is not uncommon, and it is in the administration of this remedy that copyright doctrine departs most notably from the requirements of the second accommodative principle. The test typically applied to determine whether an injunction for the life of a copyright will issue is whether the infringement is likely to continue; the remedy will be denied where "the infringement has come to an end before suit is commenced and there is little likelihood or danger of its renewal at any time in the future."

The ostensible rationale for this test is that the prospect of continuing infringements constitutes the irreparable harm which equity has traditionally required for an injunction to be awarded. Yet, in most cases at least, injury to the copyright property can be fully cured by an award of money damages; where the infringement is a continuing one, an award of permanent damages can be assessed. The test to be employed should, then, presume the sufficiency of damages in the usual case and permit the injunctive remedy only when the harm threatened is irreparable in economic terms. . . .

Reliance upon monetary rather than injunctive relief implicitly endorses a scheme of compulsory licensing. The copyright owner is deprived of choices relative to the marketing of his property, choices, for example, as to price, timing and territory of distribution. In addition to this implicit sanction of the compulsory license concept, American copyright law explicitly provides for compulsory licensing in the case of sound recordings of musical compositions....

Notes and Questions

1. Born in 1923, Professor Melville Nimmer of UCLA Law School published *Treatise on Copyright*, and *Treatise on the Theory of the First Amendment*. He received his LL.B from Harvard in 1950 and joined the faculty of UCLA in 1962. Professor Nimmer died in 1985. For a biographical note on Paul Goldstein, see supra, page 283.

2. Although the first amendment is often invoked as a limitation on the scope of copyright protection, copyright also implements first amendment policies. Consider, for example, the following:

> [I]n the absence of an effective means of communication, the right to speak would ring hollow indeed. And, in recognition of these principles, we have consistently held that the First Amendment embodies, not only the abstract right to be free from censorship, but also the right of an individual to utilize an appropriate and effective medium for the expression of his views.

> At issue is not just the right to use an appropriate and effective medium, but also to make a particular medium appropriate and effective. The goal is to ensure that printed and published materials effectively convey the creator's expression.

Justin Hughes, *The Philosophy of Intellectual Property*, 77 Geo. L. J. 287, 361 (1988)

3. Professor Goldstein's article on copyright and the first amendment queried whether injunctive relief is always appropriate in cases raising important speech interests. Paul Goldstein, *Copyright and the First Amendment*, 70 Colum. L. Rev. 983, 1032–35 (1970). Twenty years later, Judge Leval echoed this concern:

> One of the most unfortunate tendencies in the law surrounding fair use is the notion that rejection of a fair use defense necessarily implicates the grant of an injunction. Many commentators have disparaged the overly automatic tendency of courts to grant injunctive relief. The copyright statute and its predecessors express no preference for injunctive relief. The 1976 Act states only that a court "may ... grant temporary and final injunctions on such terms as it may deem reasonable to prevent or restrain infringement of a copyright." Moreover, the tendency toward the automatic injunction can harm the interests of plaintiff copyright owners, as well as the interests of the public and the secondary user. Courts may instinctively shy away from a justified finding of infringement If they perceive an unjustified injunction as the inevitable consequence...

> It is a venerable maxim that irreparable injury is "presumed" I case of copyright infringement. Injunction thus follows as a matter of course . . . In the vast majority of cases, this remedy is justified because most infringements are simple piracy. . . . These infringers incur no development cost, not advertising expense, and little risk. . . . Allowing this practice to flourish destroys the incentive to create and thus deprives the public of the benefits copyright was designed to secure. . . .
>
> Such cases are worlds apart from many of those raising reasonable contentions of fair use. Historians, biographers, critics, scholars, and journalists regularly quote from copyrighted matter to make points essential to their instructive undertakings. Whether their takings will pass the fair use test is difficult to predict. It depends on widely varying perceptions held by different judges. Yet there may be a strong public interest in the publication of the secondary work. And the copyright owner's interest may be adequately protected by an award of damages for whatever infringement is found.

Pierre N. Leval, *Toward a Fair use Standard,* 103 Harv. L. Rev. 1105, 1130–32 (1990). See also Mark A. Lemley and Eugene Volokh, *Freedom of Speech and Injunctions in Intellectual Property Cases,* 48 Duke L.J. 147, 147 (1998) ("preliminary injunctions in intellectual property cases are often (though not always) unconstitutional").

4. For more on the relationship between copyright and the first amendment, see Neil Weinstock Netanel, *Locating Copyright Within the First Amendment Skein,* 54 Stan. L. Rev. 1 (2001) (arguing that expansion of copyright law in recent decades warrants more aggressive application of first amendment principles copyright cases); Yochai Benkler, *Free as the Air to Common Use: First Amendment Constraints on Enclosure of the Public Domain,* 74 N.Y.U. L. Rev. 354 (1999) (arguing that given emerging methods of production of digital information, copyright promotes neither diversity of information nor free expression); Jack M. Balkin, *Digital Speech and Democratic Culture: A Theory of Freedom of Expression for the Information Society,* 79 N.Y.U. L. Rev. 1, 1–2 (2004) ("[F]ree speech values—interactivity, mass participation, and the ability to modify and transform culture—must be protected through technological design and through administrative and legislative regulation of technology, as well as through the more traditional method of judicial creation and recognition of constitutional rights"). Note that the Supreme Court recently rejected many of these arguments. See Eldred v. Ashcroft, 537 U.S. 186, 221 (2003) (holding that First Amendment poses no obstacle to Congressional extension of copyright terms that defers for twenty years entry of works into the public domain: "The First Amendment securely protects the freedom to make—or decline to make—one's own speech; it bears less heavily when speakers assert the right to make other people's speeches.").

III

Trademarks

I. History

The Historical Development of Trademarks

SIDNEY A. DIAMOND*

2. Antiquity

In all likelihood, the first kind of marking was the branding of cattle and other animals. This began long before reading and writing, so that for many centuries brands took the form of designs only. The English word "brand," incidentally, is derived from the Anglo–Saxon verb meaning "to burn." Note that the word survives, not only in its literal sense, but also in the pertinent expression "brand name."

Wall paintings of ancient Egypt show cattle being branded by field workers. Cave paintings of southwestern Europe, dating from the late Stone Age or early Bronze Age, show cattle branded on their flanks.

The Book of Genesis contains several references to branding. When Cain was expelled from the Garden of Eden after killing Abel, the Lord set a sign upon Cain—and some translations use the word "mark" instead of "sign." This may be the earliest literary reference to branding. Whoever wrote the passage in Genesis evidently was familiar with the practice. . . .

Pottery jars were necessities of daily life in Greece and Rome. The maker's name generally was placed on the handle . . . Porcelain was a Chinese invention . . . It may be considered a refinement of pottery and appeared much later. Early porcelain pieces typically bore date marks, identifying the emperor during whose reign the object was made . . . Sometimes the maker's name also appeared; and occasionally this was accompanied by an indication of the place of manufacture or of the destination specified for the particular piece. Porcelain dated the second year of the reign of Emperor Wu Feng can be checked against other historical sources. That year translates into 57 B.C. in our system. Since this was only about two thousand years ago, it is possible to identify objects from such periods with some degree of confidence.

Bricks and tiles bear an obvious relation to pottery. They probably had their origin also in observations of the characteristics of sun-dried

* 65 TRADEMARK REP. 265, 266–88 (1975).

mud. The earliest identified markings on bricks and tiles come from Mesopotamia and Egypt. Sometimes the inscription was the name or symbol of the monarch, indicating either that it was built for him or during his reign. Sometimes the symbol indicated the particular construction project for which the building materials were intended. Many Roman terra-cotta tiles and bricks have survived. Typically, these bear either the maker's name or a factory mark. In some instances, the source of the clay used for the particular tile or brick is identified. Some of the names inscribed in the material have been identified as the builders of the particular structures who had ordered the fabrication of the tiles or bricks. A number of the early Roman inscriptions, produced by stamps impressed in the moist clay, appear in reverse ... Later, it was realized that the stamps must be prepared in reverse form in order for the inscription to come out correctly ...

Ancient lamps and other articles made of clay have been found with the equivalent of true trademarks, used to indicate source. The apparent reason for this use of marks in ancient times was a response to the expansion of trade. Goods traveled to comparatively distant markets, which represented a substantial change in the customary method of doing business directly with an artisan in his shop. Although the suppliers were individuals rather than enterprises, the need for source identification evidently was recognized because of demands from remote consumers for repeat orders for goods whose quality had proved satisfactory. Quite clearly, such marks performed the same basic functions as the modern trademark.

During the period 1300–1200 B.C., there was substantial trade between India and Asia Minor. The Hindus regularly used marks on their goods.

Somewhat later, the Roman oil lamp became an important article of trade. About one thousand different Roman potters' marks have been identified as in use during the period of approximately three centuries running from 35 B.C. to 265 A.D. The FORTIS brand appears to have been very successful; specimens bearing that mark come not only from Italy but also from places that now are in France, Germany, Holland, England and Spain. One writer states that the FORTIS mark was copied and counterfeited, which would account for the large number of specimens over a wide area. Conceivably, it became the generic designation for a particular type of oil lamp and was used on that basis by competing manufacturers in other areas ...

Some of the Roman potters' marks were rather imaginative in their concepts. For example, a potter named Lupus (the Latin word for "wolf") adopted the design of a wolf's head as his trademark. Markings were used on other types of goods in Roman times. One evidently important export item was ointment for the treatment of the eyes; the name of the Roman doctor who compounded the ointment appeared on the container. Identifying marks also were used on Roman wine and cheese for export.

From marks of this sort, it is only a short step to sign-boards on shops. However, in some cases at least, it seems probable that the sign-boards came first and the designs on them later were reproduced as markings on the goods.

Sign-boards were used by ancient Egyptians, Greeks and Romans. Many have been found in Pompeii and Herculaneum, where the volcanic eruption that destroyed the cities also preserved their ruins. It apparently was common practice to use rebuses (like the design of a wolf's head to represent Lupus the potter) when the names of the individuals permitted this kind of treatment.

3. Mediaeval Times

Beginning about 500 A.D. and continuing for almost a thousand years, western mankind lived through a time known as the Dark Ages, which was characterized by a decline of learning. During this period, the use of marks virtually disappeared. Artisans were unable to read or write even the simplest types of inscriptions. Markings on swords and other weapons seem to have been the only kind that survived at all.

In ... the fourteenth to the sixteenth centuries, there was a revival of learning and also a vast expansion of trade. As a corollary to these developments, there was an increased use of marks of many different kinds. However, much illiteracy continued and accordingly marks tended to be restricted to designs or crude monograms. In the mediaeval period, the use of marks proliferated to such an extent that it becomes possible to identify various types and to categorize them.

First were the personal marks, which identified individuals. These included coats of arms and signets or seals. Another type of personal mark was the house mark, literally affixed to a house, which identified the family living there. If the householder became an innkeeper or a shopkeeper, the house mark naturally found its way on to the sign that was put out to attract customers. And if the householder was an artisan, the house mark also would be applied to his goods, especially when he began to sell them to customers other than his close neighbors.

Second were the proprietary marks, which were used to indicate the ownership of goods. In many instances, the proprietary mark was derived from the house mark; the same symbol that appeared on the house would be applied to tools and other articles to identify them with their owner and permit him to claim them if they were lost or taken away. Similarly, house marks became the basis for cattle brands.

It was common in mediaeval times for a merchant to adopt an identifying mark that appeared on packages or on the goods themselves, especially when they were to be shipped for considerable distances. One frequently mentioned incident involved some balls of wax that were recovered from a shipwreck. The merchants who had shipped the wax were able to establish their ownership of the salvaged property by the proprietary marks that appeared on the goods. ...

Still another kind of mark was the appellation of geographical origin. Typical were the tapestries of continental Europe. These were marked with the place of origin. In addition, tapestries sometimes bore an official stamp of guarantee certifying their quality. And the personal mark of the weaver also is found on some tapestries. The cloth trade in

England provides another example of the use of marks of geographical origin. By the end of the fifteenth century, these marks also became recognized as the means of identifying cloth of superior quality.

During early times, many other kinds of articles were marked. We are not always certain of the reason or the purpose. Artists' signatures became common during the mediaeval period. These, of course, are a kind of indication of the origin of the goods—in a very personal sense. Some artists used monograms as symbols. Bells were among the earliest articles to bear markings. In Switzerland, some have been identified back as far as the twelfth century. . . .

Watermarks on paper started in Italy and France during the thirteenth century. Originally, these probably were merely decorative in nature, as is demonstrated by the fact that the same design was used by various papermakers. In time, they came to indicate origin in a particular manufacturer.

The use of printers' and publishers' marks on books began around 1450. Colophons, as these marks still are called, sometimes derived from the shop signs of the printers. Originally, these too seem to have been decorative rather than proprietary. Since there was no concept of copyright at the time, the book trade was characterized by rivalry among printers for the most accurate version of a particular work. This led to the use of the mark as an identification of origin.

Trademark infringement problems arose early in the publishing business. The preface to the 1518 edition of the works of Livy published by Aldus of Venice warns readers of the use by other printers of imitations of Aldus' dolphin and anchor design. . . .

The great feature of the mediaeval period was the rise of the guilds, starting around the fourteenth century. These organizations were tightly controlled groups of artisans. Typically, the members of the guild were required to use a compulsory production mark, the principal purpose of which was to fix the responsibility for poor quality merchandise. Guild marks also were used to enforce control of the industry, especially territorial trade barriers. Goods appearing on the market outside the approved distribution area could be recognized by their markings. Abuses of these territorial restrictions led to early common-law concepts of unlawful restraint of trade. . . .

What little we know about the penalties imposed for infringement during the middle ages makes an interesting series of anecdotes. [T]he following are arranged chronologically.

A law of Parma dated 1282 applied to knives, swords and other steel or iron articles. It provided that the artisan must not use the same or a similar mark as any other person in the guild. The penalty was ten pounds for each offense.

In the fourteenth century, an innkeeper passed off a low grade of wine for a superior variety known as Rudesheimer. The Elector Palatine ordered hanging forthwith.

In 1512 the Council of Nuremberg took up the complaint of the famous artist Albrecht Durer, who used an "AD" monogram as his identifying mark. The Council issued a decree that "a certain foreigner" (his name was omitted from the public record) must obliterate the Durer monogram. As a sidelight on this decision, it may be noted that the "certain foreigner" evidently was allowed to continue copying Durer's works so long as he did not use the "AD" monogram—the idea of an artist's copyright in his creations had not yet become part of the law.

... One report states that in 1554 ... there was an edict of Charles V concerning Flemish tapestries, which provided that city of origin and maker's marks were compulsory and that infringers were to be punished by cutting off the right hand....

It also should be noted that there is no indication that any infringer's right hand actually was cut off. The edict established that as a penalty, but there does not appear to be any documented instance of its enforcement.

. . .

4. Industrial Revolution

The industrial revolution was characterized by an enormous growth of industry as modern manufacturing methods replaced the handwork of older times. One natural result was the concentration of production capacity in larger units and this in turn required the development of methods of distribution to get the goods to the consumer. Along with the growth of distribution came the use of advertising to acquaint the consuming public with the availability of the goods. And with increasing advertising came the increased use of trademarks in their modern function as identifiers of the source of the goods.

French porcelain provides a familiar example of a product that became known by its trademark. The royal factory at Sevres marked its goods from the eighteenth century on, with the design changing from time to time ... Meissen ware from Germany also was marked ...

Pewter ware also regularly bore identifying marks. In England, William Hogg resisted the temptation to use his own surname as the basis for a design mark and chose a swan instead ...

Silver hallmarks of quality and makers' marks to identify the individual silversmith continued as the industrial revolution developed. One famous American silversmith of the Revolutionary period whose initials are sought by collectors was Paul Revere, the same man who made the famous ride in 1775.

Merchants' marks also were in use around this time. In France, the commercial identification of the seller of silk fabrics seemingly was more important than the manufacturer, for many silk merchants' marks were recorded and have survived ...

One interesting document, turned up not by a lawyer but by a pottery historian, comes from the Herculaneum Pottery Works, founded in Liverpool in 1796. A resolution of the Committee of Management dated August 6, 1822, ordered that:

> ... to give publicity and identity to the china and earthenware manufactured, the words "Herculaneum Pottery" be stamped or

marked on some conspicuous part of all china and earthenware hereafter made at this manufactory....

5. Development of Modern Trademarks

... In the Anglo–American legal system, protection for trademarks was quite late in coming, aside from the old laws prescribing bizarre punishments for violations in specific industries. The beginning of legal protection for trademarks as such generally is traced to a 1783 dictum in an English case, stating that an action for damages would lie based upon fraud. The shift to an equitable remedy based upon the invasion of a property right did not come until the nineteenth century. The first record of an injunction against trademark infringement is an English case decided in 1838. ...

Notes and Questions

1. Sidney A. Diamond served as Commissioner of Patents and Trademarks from 1979–1981. He died in 1983.

2. Consider Sidney Diamond's survey of the historical predecessors of trademarks. Do the uses of markings in antiquity, the middle ages, and the industrial revolution reflect the same mix of concepts at play as in modern trademark law? What did they have to do with fairness or with competition? To what extent did these markings seek to prevent deceit? To prevent "trespass" onto proprietary goodwill?

The Making of Modern Intellectual Property Law

BRAD SHERMAN & LIONEL BENTLY*

Trade marks as a form of intellectual property

When modern intellectual property law first took shape in the 1850s, or thereabouts, trade mark law was not recognised or indeed even considered as a possible candidate for inclusion. This is unsurprising given that modern trade mark law, as we understand it today, did not really exist at the time. Rather the law—which consisted of statutes such as the 1863 Exhibitions Medals Act and offered protection for things such as needle labels and marks for use on cutlery—remained subject specific and reactionary; in short, pre-modern. Moreover, the nature of the law in the middle part of the century was dilatory and chaotic. Indeed as Joseph Travers Smith, a leading trade marks solicitor of the time, said, 'trade marks are not recognised as having any legal validity or effect ... there is no written law on the subject of trade marks, and we have consequently no definition by which we can try what a trade mark is, nor consequently what particular symbol amounts to a trade mark, and ... the existing law gives no remedy against an actual pirate, but only against the person who fraudulently uses a trade mark'.

Despite the uncertain and (at least to our modern eyes) somewhat alien nature of the law in this area, over the second half of the

* 166–72 (CAMBRIDGE U. PRESS 1999).

nineteenth century trade mark law came to take shape as a discrete and
recognised area of law. A number of factors provided the impetus for the
crystallisation of modern trade mark law. In part, growing recognition
and use of marks in commercial practice led to increased specialisation
in this field. In turn this heightened the calls for recognition of trade
marks as a separate area of law and for the introduction of a registration
system for marks. These changes were reinforced by the fact that a
distinct domain for trade marks was slowly carved out at common
law. . . .

At the same time as trade mark law was taking on its now familiar
shape there was growing pressure for it to be included within the
framework of intellectual property law. The pressure for inclusion came
from a number of different sources. For many, factors such as shared
professional bodies (patents and trade mark agents), the nature and
form of international treaties, and the logic of industrial property made
the connection between trade marks and designs and patents an obvious
choice. Indeed, as trade mark law was in the process of formulation,
patents, designs and copyright law provided an important point of
analogy: for the existence of the right; as an aid to interpreting trade
mark doctrine; for the shape the system of registration should take; and
the language and structure to be used in trade mark legislation. Another
point of connection which existed between trade marks and copyright
and design was that they dealt with similar subject matter. At its most
extreme it was suggested that a trade mark, like a work subject to
copyright and design right, embodied the personality of its creator. As
John Smith reported to the 1862 Select Committee on Trade Marks, 'I
consider a trade mark to be equivalent to a man's signature to a letter.
There may be hundreds of John Smiths, but there would be such an
individuality in each man's signature, that you could identify the whole.
I consider that when a man puts a mark upon any article he produces to
identify it as his production, that it is equivalent to his name.'

Another practice which helped to reinforce the association between
trade marks and intellectual property law arose from the pragmatic
actions of trade mark proprietors who, in the absence of a specific, tailor-
made register for marks, utilised the pre-existing arrangements for
copyright and designs. As well as the quasi-official registration of newspaper titles and labels as books at the Stationers' Company, manufacturers also made use of the Design Register to gain protection for their
marks as designs by, for example, registering labels as designs. The
association between trade marks and copyright was reinforced by the
fact that the pictorial nature of the trade mark also suggested a link
with artistic copyright.

While there were many points shared in common between trade
marks and the then existing categories of intellectual property law, there
were a number of objections to trade marks being accepted as a part of
intellectual property law. Indeed, two primary reasons were given as to
why trade marks should not be and for a while were not included within
the remit of intellectual property law.

The first objection to treating trade marks as a species of intellectual property turned on the issue of creativity. While the rights granted by design, patents and copyright could be excused (and justified) because they were only granted for new creations (and as such nothing was therefore being taken away from the public), this was not the case with trade marks which in many cases dealt with pre-existing subject matter. Hindmarch, who drafted the Government Bill in 1862, and who was consistently opposed both to allowing assignment of marks separately from goodwill and to treating trade marks as property, captured the tone of these arguments when he said:

> I have heard persons refer to the law of patents, and the law of design, as parallel cases; but there is nothing parallel there. A man who comes and takes a patent gives a consideration for the grant he obtains, and so with a man who comes and registers a design, he acquires a copyright of a limited character, never exceeding three years; he also gives some consideration; there is something new, which the world knows nothing about, and in consideration of that the copyright is given; but in this case, in which it is proposed to give a copyright in a trade mark, there is no consideration ... it would be to create a ... monopoly totally and entirely unknown to law ... and, as I conceive, contrary to the spirit of the great statute against monopolies.

The upshot of this was, as Hindmarch said in another context, that 'copyright in books and designs is a totally different thing [from that of trade marks] because there is a property created'. With trade marks, however, 'we create nothing new, but provide only a new mode of defending the right that we acknowledge'.

The second reason why trade marks were considered to fall outside the intellectual property rubric was that whereas copyright, patents and designs were primarily concerned with the creation and protection of property, trade marks were more concerned with forgery or fraud. While there were arguments to the contrary, the consensus of opinion was that in 'the existing state of the law a trade mark is clearly no property at all'. Rather, as Macfie said, the object of trade mark legislation 'is to prevent the criminal use of a name or distinguishing indication, in fact to counteract falsification or forgery, which would not only deprive traders of a reputation they have laboured for, but would mislead the public'. Campin was clearer as to the distinction when he said, 'it should be remembered that there was this important difference between patents and trade marks, that copying or infringing the latter was really analogous to forgery, while the infringement of a patent was merely interfering with a private right of property'. Combined together, the facts that trade marks dealt with pre-existing subject matter rather than the creation of new material and that they were more concerned with regulating fraud than property, meant that trade marks were said to fall outside the scope of intellectual property law.

Notes and Questions

1. Brad Sherman is Professor of Law at Griffith University, Brisbane. He is also the director of the Australian Center for Intellectual Property in Agriculture, which is co-hosted by the Australian National University

Faculty of Law. He received his LLB from the University of Queensland, his LLM from the University of London, where he taught at the London School of Economics, and his PhD from Griffith.

Lionel Bently is the Herschel Smith Professor of Intellectual Property Law, University of Cambridge, and a Fellow of Emmanuel College. He received his BA from Cambridge in 1986 and was a Professor of Law at Kings College, University of London.

2. Sherman & Bently describe the reasons why trademarks were not originally considered a form of intellectual property. What has changed since? Given the modern rationales for trademark protection, what kind of intellectual property is a trademark?

Two Hundred Years of American Trademark Law

BEVERLY W. PATTISHALL*

I. Origins

It seems not too much to describe trademark protection as an essential element of the free society we have enjoyed for two centuries. A free commerce, at least, could hardly exist without it. Unless one can be assured of some sanctity for his means of commercial identity, thereby to enjoy the fruits of his own labor, free enterprise and the beneficial competition it engenders is without motivation. As with so much else that characterizes our free society, we inherited the essentials of our law protecting trademarks from our British brethren....

The history of trademarks extends for at least four thousand years, but that of trademark law, hardly four hundred. Little which might be described even loosely as trademark law can be found in recorded British or other law materials of a date prior to four centuries ago. In the United States, my counterpart, reporting at our first centennial celebration, would have been pressed for substance to occupy even the fifteen minutes I have been assigned. He might have begun, however, on a founding father note, for the court records of Fairfax County, Virginia, disclose that:

> In 1772, George Washington, then only a farmer and businessman, went to the court to get a trademark for his brand of flour, which he proposed to name, simply "G. Washington." The presiding justices so ordered.

Likewise involving a founding father is the petition to Congress of the Boston sailcloth maker, Samuel Breck, to be allowed to register his mark. The petition was referred by Congress to Secretary of State Thomas Jefferson, who reported back to Congress on December 9, 1791 as follows:

> The Secretary of State, to whom was referred by the House of Representatives the petition of Samuel Breck and others, proprietors of a sail-cloth manufactory in Boston, praying that they may have the

* 68 TRADEMARK REP. 121, 121–28 (1978).

exclusive privilege of using particular marks for designating the sail-cloth of their manufactory, has had the same under consideration and thereupon

Reports, That it would, in his opinion, contribute to fidelity in the execution of manufacturing, to secure to every manufactory, an exclusive right to some mark on its wares, proper to itself.

That this should be done by general laws, extending equal rights to every case to which the authority of the Legislature should be competent.

That these cases are of divided jurisdiction: Manufactures made and consumed within a State being subject to State legislation, while those which are exported to foreign nations, or to another State, or into the Indian territory are alone within the legislation of the general government.

That it will, therefore, be reasonable for the general government to provide in this behalf by law for those cases of manufacture generally, and those only which relate to commerce with foreign nations, and among the several States, and with the Indian tribes.

And that this may be done by permitting the owner of every manufactory to enter in the record of the court of the district wherein his manufactory is, the name with which he chooses to mark or designate his wares, and rendering it penal to others to put the same mark on any other wares.

Mr. Jefferson's conviction as to the benefits of trademark protection, his recognition of the primary significance of use, his delineation of the jurisdictional boundaries and his recommendation of strong sanctions for trademark violation are extraordinarily prescient examples of his wisdom. His proposed device of registering by entry in the appropriate court's records is intriguing in light of the earlier corresponding colonial practice disclosed by the "G. Washington" flour entry. No doubt the practice was simply another which had devolved to us from similar practices in England.

The history of our trademark law reveals a persistent legislative apathy, or at least a proclivity for being distracted from it by issues more politically charged. Secretary Jefferson's excellent recommendations met the same fate subsequently accorded less precognitive but worthy trademark law proposals, and Congress did not attempt enactment of a trademark law until 1870. Nine years later that law was held unconstitutional as having been wrongly based upon the Constitution's patent and copyright clause. A preliminary review of Mr. Jefferson's 1791 recommendations could have led the Congress correctly to the Commerce Clause and precluded the 1870 abortive effort, for they point directly to that basis.

II. Early Cases and Doctrines

Congress' disinterest in a trademark statute during most of the Republic's first century may be somewhat excused when we note that its constituency likewise seems not to have been greatly concerned with trademark rights during those frontier years. Not until the 1837 decision in Thomson v. Winchester is there any reported American decision that might be described as a trademark case, and Taylor v. Carpenter, decided in 1844, was the first reported case of a trademark character in the federal courts. It involved an English concern's complaint that its name and other distinguishing devices on its spools of thread had been copied. Judge Story held that the case was "one of unmitigated and designed infringement of the rights of the plaintiffs for the purpose of defrauding the public and taking from the plaintiffs the fair earnings of their skill, labor, and enterprise." He also commented: "I do not quote cases to establish the principles above stated. They are very familiar to the profession, and are not now susceptible of any doubt." Yet, twenty-six years later when the Act of 1870 was passed there were only sixty-two reported American trademark cases. Curiously, the six remaining years of our first century raised the total of reported trademark-trade identity cases to one hundred thirty-six, but only seven seem to have involved marks registered under the federal statute....

Amoskeag Mfg. Co. v. Spear, decided in 1849, was an early landmark American case involving label simulation and alleged trademark infringement as well as such ancillary issues as acquiescence, grade marks and the significance of wrongful intent. It held that although plaintiff's trademark was not protectible because it was in fact a quality grade mark, the accused labels were as a whole calculated to deceive. It also held that plaintiff's acquiescence was in the nature of a revocable license and "that an injunction must be granted whenever the public is in fact misled, whether intentionally or otherwise, by imitation or adoption of marks, forms or symbols which the party who first employed them had a right to appropriate ..." Cox comments in his 1892 compilation of cases that:

> This case is justly regarded as the leading American adjudication, especially as defining the doctrine of infringement.

... The 1865 California Supreme Court decision in *Derringer v. Plate* seems to have been our first dealing with the long problematical national trademark rights question. The plaintiff was the famous Philadelphia pistol maker and the defendant a Californian who sold pistols marked "Derringer." The reliability of pistols being a rather serious subject in the West at the time, the court seems not to have hesitated to hold sweepingly that trademark rights are not limited by territorial bounds, that the owner of a trademark in one American state owned it in all states and that plaintiff should be protected in California at common law even though he had not complied with the California registration statute of 1863.

Nearly all of our early reported cases were of a trade identity unfair competition character rather than what we would today describe as trademark cases. One of the first that seems to have been purely trademark, however, was *Burnett v. Phalon*, decided in 1867 by the New York Court of Appeals. It involved hair oil, the plaintiff's product being sold under the mark COCOAINE and the defendant's under COCOINE. Judge Pierrepont held that COCOAINE was a valid mark belonging to plaintiff and that: "Every man had a right to the reward of his skill, his energy and his honest enterprise." Defendant's use of COCOINE or any other mark imitative of plaintiff's was enjoined. Cox describes this as a leading case illustrating that coined words may be protected against others that are *idem sonans*. Significantly disclosing the developmental state of our trademark law even after the close of our first century, he also states that defendant's label was quite unlike plaintiff's and that the chance of deception seemed to be limited to persons purchasing by reliance on the name. He then comments that the decision is important for "the principle, that although an article may have no other name than that which is claimed as a trade-mark, the name may be monopolized."

. . .

The "Desiccated Codfish" case of 1868, *Town v. Stetson*, has a certain nostalgic charm and its rule a contemporary applicability. The plaintiff sold desiccated codfish and defendant began to sell fish under that name and was preliminary enjoined. On defendant's motion the restraint was dissolved and the Court held:

> No manufacturer can acquire a special property in an ordinary term
> or expression, the use of which as an entirety is essential to the correct
> and truthful designation of a particular article or compound.

Trademark assignability as well as confusing similarity were the issues in the Bovilene—Bovina pomade case of 1869. The plaintiffs were assignees of the BOVILENE business and, on defendant's motion to dissolve a preliminary injunction restraining them from infringing plaintiffs' rights, the Court refused and held succinctly: "There is a right of property in a trademark which is capable of being transferred to another."

In 1871, the problem of geographical terms as trademarks was the basic issue of the first trade identity case to be decided by the United States Supreme Court, *Canal Company v. Clark*. The plaintiff claimed the exclusive right to LACKAWANNA for coal mined in the Lackawanna Valley. Defendant claimed the right to use LACKAWANNA for coal likewise mined there. The court considered the authorities at length, . . . It held, after well stating some of the fundamentals of Anglo–American trade identity law, as follows:

> And it is obvious that the same reasons which forbid the exclusive
> appropriation of generic names or of those merely descriptive of the
> article manufactured and which can be employed with truth by other
> manufacturers, apply with equal force to the appropriation of geographi-
> cal names, designating districts of country. Their nature is such that
> they cannot point to the origin (personal origin) or ownership of the
> articles of trade to which they may be applied.

It could be said that for most of our first century there was no such thing in the United States as trademark law in the sense we understand that term today. Walter J. Derenberg points out in his treatise, "Trade-Mark Protection and Unfair Trading," that even as late as 1860 the term "trademark" really denoted only the name of the manufacturer. Even though an article may have become well-known under an arbitrary mark, if that mark did not directly denote the article's source, another was free to use it. . . .

The Lanham Trademark Act—Its Impact Over Four Decades

BEVERLY W. PATTISHALL*

I. HISTORY AND BACKGROUND

A. *The Predecessor Acts*

In 1845, the State of New York enacted the United States' first trademark statute. Eleven other state trademark acts were passed between 1847 and 1866; yet, as our first century ended in 1876 there were only sixty-two reported decisions in actions that could be described as trademark or trade identity cases. Our first federal trademark act was that of 1870, ingenuously entitled "An Act to revise, consolidate and amend the statutes relating to patents and copyrights." It afforded exclusive rights to the marks registered under it, and use was not a prerequisite. Registration was granted to those "who are entitled to the exclusive use of any lawful trade-mark or who intend to adopt and use any trade-mark for exclusive use within the United States...." The Act was amended in 1876 to afford criminal sanctions against trademark infringement and the attendant "evils and injuries to long-suffering commercial and manufacturing interests...." Because of its basic conceptual error of treating the trademark subject matter as though it were a patent or copyright, an error often repeated today, the Act was held unconstitutional in 1879.

On March 3, 1881 another Act was passed which sought to "authorize the registration of trade-marks and protect the same." Perhaps overreacting to the unconstitutionality of the 1870 Act, the scope of the 1881 Act was limited to marks used in commerce with foreign nations and the Indian tribes. Registration under it afforded little other than access to the federal courts and prima facie evidence of ownership, but the Act did prohibit registration to others of marks "likely to cause confusion or mistake in the mind of the public, or to deceive purchasers."

On February 20, 1905 a new trademark act was passed which continued the register of the prior Act and remained our basic trademark statute for over forty-two years. Even though four times as long as the Act of 1881 and containing many more sophisticated provisions such as opposition, cancellation and interference procedures as well as detailed requirements and specifications for registration, it provided hardly more substantive rights than did its 1881 predecessor. The industrial-commercial development then occurring in the United States, and the concomitant interest in trademark protection, resulted, however, in many thousands of trademark registrations. During the course of its enactment, the wording of the new Act was amended to provide our first, albeit cumbersome, statutory recognition of a secondary meaning doctrine. The amendment was called the "ten year proviso," and it enabled registration of marks otherwise unregistrable as being merely surnames, descriptive words or geographical terms if they had been in use since ten years prior to passage of the statute. Also made registrable as a special

* 76 TRADEMARK REP. 193, 193–200 (1986).

exception were the surnames of applicants themselves, no doubt thereby encouraging the prevalent but fallacious notion of an unlimited right to use one's own name as a trademark.

The 1905 Act contained numerous rather detailed inter partes and ex parte registration provisions and procedures, and the 1881 Act's "likely to cause confusion" and "goods of the same descriptive properties" clauses were combined in the new Act as the test for registration over prior marks. The test of infringement, however, did not prescribe likelihood of confusion and remained merely in terms of "counterfeits, copies and colorable imitations" applied to "goods of the same descriptive properties." Also, infringing use was restricted only to marks which were themselves used in interstate commerce.

The 1905 Act was amended on sixteen occasions the most significant being the Act of 1920 which permitted registration of almost anything that could be said to distinguish one's goods if it had been used in commerce for one year previously. The Act was originally passed to cure the problem of valuable marks not registrable under the 1905 Act due to that Act's descriptiveness or surname prohibitions, particularly that problem as it pertained to registrations for such marks in foreign countries where domestic registration by the applicant was a prerequisite. Registrations frequently were sought and granted under the 1920 Act for other purposes such as to obtain the benefits of federal jurisdiction and notice of registration.

B. The Gestation and Birth of the Lanham Act

Commencing in 1920, an American Bar Association Patent, Trademark and Copyright Section committee attempted the drafting of a general revision of the trademark laws. Starting in 1924, Congressman Vestal introduced their draft bill in the 69th Congress and repeatedly through the 72nd, but to no avail. In 1938, Texas Congressman Fritz G. Lanham undertook the task and introduced in the 75th Congress a bill primarily drafted by Edward S. Rogers of Chicago. Progress was delayed by World War II, but the bill was debated in each Congress on into the 79th when it was vigorously attacked by the Justice Department on monopoly grounds. It was amended just before passage to include such compromises as empowering the Federal Trade Commission to bring cancellation actions under certain circumstances, nullifying incontestable rights for marks that had been used to violate the antitrust laws and limiting incontestability in other respects. After some twenty-six years' effort, the Act finally was passed and signed by President Truman on July 5, 1946 to become effective one year later.

By the time of passage of the Lanham Act, many deficiencies of the Act of 1905 had been substantially minimized by able court decisions rendered during the course of that Act's forty-two years. The period was one of burgeoning commercial development and accompanying trademark litigation. During it, most of the prior doubts as to the sufficiency of the commerce clause as a basis for federal trademark legislation were assuaged as well as some of the prior over-emphasis upon descriptive properties of goods and whether they were directly competitive. Similarly, in testing for infringement, the question of whether marks were "counterfeits, copies or colorable imitations" had been largely replaced in fact by a question of market realities as to likelihood of confusion regardless of the Act's artificial prescriptions.

The Lanham Act's development, debate and passage were anomalous in that the Act's basic premise and philosophy were notably discordant with the political and legal tenets of the times. The teachings in vogue during that later part of the "New Deal" era had found and were still finding expression in a host of "monopoly phobia" trademark decisions generally inhospitable to trademark rights and antithetical to the avowed purposes of the new Act. Principal protectionist provisions of the Act were included directly in reaction and as a curb to such attenuating decisions, and the wonder is that the Act ever was passed. Skillful handling by its dedicated proponent, Congressman Lanham, and eleventh hour compromising with anti-monopolists of the Justice Department somehow achieved passage of this "vested interest," protectionist legislation so strikingly at odds with the prevailing political values of the administration that had remained so long in power. The declared protectionist purposes of the Act, so apparent in its operative provisions, were emphatically expressed in its statement of intent:

> Intent of Act. The intent of this Act is to regulate commerce within the control of Congress by making actionable the deceptive and misleading use of marks in such commerce; to protect registered marks used in such commerce from interference by State, or territorial legislation; to protect persons engaged in such commerce against unfair competition; to prevent fraud and deception in such commerce by the use of reproductions, copies, counterfeits, or colorable imitations of registered marks; and to provide rights and remedies stipulated by treaties and conventions respecting trademarks, trade names, and unfair competition entered into between the United States and foreign nations (Amended Oct. 9, 1962, 76 Stat. 769).

Edward S. Rogers wrote of the above in his December, 1946 "Introduction" to Daphne Robert's The New Trade–Mark Manual:

> Here we have a direct statement of a national policy by the Congress. The purpose of the Act is, in brief, to protect trade-marks and to repress unfair competition. And it is heartening that all the implications of the new statute are to encourage the use of trade-marks and thus to recognize their social value.

II. THE LANHAM ACT

A. The Act's Beginning Impact

With high hopes for greatly augmented protection, both business and the bar enthusiastically greeted the passage of the new trademark act some nine months after, and almost as a part of, the optimism that came with the victorious conclusion of World War II. During that first year before the Act took effect, various symposia were held by bar associations enabling those who had recently acquainted themselves with the twenty page statute to lecture those who hoped to learn something about its new and unusual features. Widely discussed were the provisions defining and confining the highly touted new trademark right called "incontestability." How to avail one's clients of that right and the other benefits of the new Act, what indeed were those benefits and whether any negatives were implicit in the Act as might warrant caution or delay in embracing it were the subjects of assorted learned lectures, articles and memoranda to clients. Not only did the professional journals proclaim that the promised land for trademarks lay just ahead, but also the commercial and general news publications.

The United States Patent Office braced itself for the anticipated application onslaught of July 5, 1947 and retained as full time special counsel the eminent authority, Professor Walter J. Derenberg, to aid and advise as to the flood of new questions which were expected and did arise concerning the statute. The registering of such newfangled subject matter as configurations of goods, musical sounds and the like, not to mention service marks, collective marks and certification marks, presented broad new vistas replete with problems, challenges and exciting opportunities. Unfamiliar terms and concepts like "concurrent registration," "Principal Register," "Supplemental Register," "related company," "distinctiveness," section 2(f) applications, section 8(a) affidavits of use, section 12(c) republication, registration, re-registration and renewal under the new Act all had to be studied, comprehended and applied in serving the best interests of trademark owners and users. It was indeed a lively time, both for those in the trademark office and the practice, during the last few years of the "forties." Just to avail trademark owners of the Act's benefits generated something of a boom for practitioners and Examiners. The focus of attention on the subject of trademarks resulting from the publicity given the Act's passage also seemed to stimulate businessmen into more aggressive concern, not just with perfecting their new trademark rights under the Act, but with pursuing infringing violators as well. . . .

Notes and Questions

1. Beverly W. Pattishall was a senior partner in the Chicago law firm of Pattishall, McAuliffe, Newbury, Hilliard & Geraldson before his death in 2002, at the age of 86. Born in 1916, he earned his J.D. from the University of Virginia in 1941, and then fought in World War II. He coauthored a casebook on trademark and unfair competition.

2. Remember that the first Federal Trademark Act was held to be unconstitutional because it treated trademark subject matter as intellectual property comparable to a copyright or a patent. See *The Trade-Mark Cases*, 100 U.S. 82 (1879). Accordingly, protections for trademark have been enacted under the Commerce Clause. Does the Intellectual Property Clause impose any restraints, or "internally preempt" such legislation? Compare Paul J. Heald & Suzanna Sherry, *Implied Limits on the Legislative Power—The Intellectual Property Clause as an Absolute Constraint on Congress*, 2000 U. Ill. L. Rev. 1119, 1167 (2000) (arguing Intellectual Property Clause constrains congressional flexibility, particularly when "Congress effects a grant of exclusive rights that imposes monopoly-like costs on the public") with Thomas B. Nachbar, *Intellectual Property and Constitutional Norms*, 104 Colum. L. Rev. 272 (2004) (arguing Intellectual Property Clause does not embody sufficiently strong constitutional norm warranting application of Clause's limits to Congress's other Article I powers).

II.   Basic Concepts

A Treatise on the Law of Trade Marks, With a Digest and Review of the English and American Authorities (1860)

FRANCIS H. UPTON*

As the true interests of manufacturers and commerce have been more perfectly developed, and more fully understood and appreciated, it has been found, that an exclusive property right in trade marks, and its adequate protection by Courts of Equity, not only imposes no restraint upon the freedom of trade, but that its direct and inevitable tendency is, to promote and encourage that laudable competition, in which lies the true interest of the public—that competition which stimulates effort, and leads to excellence, because of the certainty of protection in the attainment of its adequate reward.

It is now, therefore, the well established doctrine, that the exclusive property of the manufacturer, or merchant, in his trade marks, is of that nature and character, that its adequate security and protection, by the exercise of the highest powers of the courts, is an imperative duty, as well for the safety of the interests of the public, as for the promotion of individual justice—and a duty which cannot be evaded or denied, without a violation of those principles upon which a large portion of equity jurisdiction is founded—and its most important functions are exercised.

When we come to consider the character and extent of the wrong that is committed by an invasion of the right of property in a trade mark, the just and rational grounds upon which this doctrine has now become firmly established, will be made perfectly apparent.

The right of property in trade marks does not partake in any degree of the nature and character of a patent or a copyright, to which it has sometimes been referred—nor is it safe to reason from any supposed analogies existing between them.

The exclusive right of multiplying copies of original productions of the mind, whether in the form of books, maps, engravings, designs or other of the manifold emanations of human thought, expressed by words or symbols—bears no appreciable resemblance to a right of property in a mere name, figure, letter, mark, device or symbol—when used as a designation of a thing,

The former, which is copyright property, is granted by express statute—and, whatever may have been its origin, is controlled by the limitations and conditions of the law of its being; it is a property in the thing itself—the words—letters, designs or symbols, which are the signs of things, and the forms and embodiment of thought. The latter is a property, not in the words, letters, designs or symbols as things—as

* 13–16, 22–23, 95–96.

signs of thought—as productions of mind—but, simply and solely, as a means of designating things—the things thus designated being the productions of human skill, or industry, whether of the mind or the hands or a combination of both: and this property has no existence apart from the thing designated—or separable from its actual use, in accomplishing the present and immediate purpose of its being. It is a right of property, neither created nor controlled by any legislative enactment, but existing at common law, independent of all statute provisions ...

During the current [19th] century, which, beyond all others, has been characterized by a wonderfully increased activity in the multiplication of all conceivable productions to supply the material needs or wants of man—natural or artificial—the right of property in trade marks, has grown to be of immense and incalculable value to the manufacturer—the merchant—and the public.

It is the means, and in many instances, the only means, by which the former are enabled to inspire and retain public confidence in the quality and integrity of things made and sold—and thereby secure for them a permanent and reliable demand—which is the life of manufacturing and mercantile operations.

And it is also in the like instances, the only means, by which the public is protected against the frauds and impositions of the crafty and designing, who are ever on the alert to appropriate to themselves the fruits of the well earned reputation of others, regardless of individual rights or the public interests.

As this peculiar character of property has increased in value and estimation, so, it has become more and more important, that the principles of law should be clearly defined and well understood, which lie at the foundation of its existence—which indicate its true nature and character—which prescribe rules for its acquisition, preservation and transmission—and which define its violation, and provide the means for its protection, as well in the form of preventive, as of retributive justice....

A consideration of the correct legal definition of a trade mark—of the necessity in which its use originated, and of the justice as well as policy of protecting it as property, serves to indicate that class of persons in a mercantile community who become possessed of this species of property and entitled to its protection and enjoyment—for, while ... no one is excluded from the right to acquire, on the other hand, such only do acquire the right, whose possession brings them within the true policy and just intendment of the law.

It is not the abstract right to the exclusive use of a certain, name, letters, mark, device or symbols, which can be acquired and possessed.

It is such use only, in connection with, and as a designation of, the particular property to which it is affixed. It follows, therefore, that the exclusive right to the trade mark, can exist in him only, who, in some form, and to some extent, possesses an exclusive right to the property to which it is appended.

The fundamental policy of the law is, to protect the manufacturer, who by his skill and industry, has produced an article of merchandise, that has found favor with the public, and which he has designated by a particular name or mark. We accordingly find, that in nearly all the reported cases in which the right has been recognized, the complainants have been manufacturers, and, as such, possessed of an exclusive right in the designated commodity. . . .

Firmly established as is the doctrine which recognizes and protects property in trade marks, and resting, as it does, upon the soundest principles of public policy, and a just appreciation of individual right—it should, nevertheless, be borne in mind, that it is a doctrine which maintains the existence of a right in one, to the exclusion of all others— and, therefore, is a doctrine, which, from its very nature, should be applied with the extremest caution, so that its application shall never involve a violation of, or departure from, the principles upon which it is founded.

An incautious application of the doctrine, by which, is intended, such an application as departs from the precise purpose of the law, and the true policy which has induced its provisions—must directly and inevitably lead to a transgression of those limits prescribed by a just regard to personal rights and public interests—and to the creation of monopolies which are alike injurious to individuals, and prejudicial to the community.

The Rational Basis of Trademark Protection

FRANK I. SCHECHTER*

The orthodox definition of "the primary and proper function of a trade-mark" is that given by the Supreme Court of the United States in the leading case of Hanover Star Milling Co. v. Metcalf: "to identify the origin or ownership of the goods to which it is affixed." The "origin or ownership" so designated by a trademark must be the "personal origin or ownership." In order to test the adequacy of this definition, which has been used by the courts practically uniformly, with but the slightest variation of language and none of meaning, it will be necessary to consider very briefly the actual usages of trade as well as certain historical data, with which the present writer has dealt more thoroughly elsewhere. . . .

Four hundred years ago a trademark indicated either the origin or ownership of the goods to which it was affixed. To what extent does the trademark of today really function as either? Actually, not in the least! It has been repeatedly pointed out by the very courts that insist on defining trademarks in terms of ownership or origin that, owing to the ramifications of modern trade and the national and international distribution of goods from the manufacturer through the jobber or importer and the retailer to the consumer, the source or origin of the goods bearing a well-known trademark is seldom known to the consumer. . . .

* 40 Harv. L. Rev. 813, 813–14, 816, 817, 818–22, 825, 830–31 (1927).

Discarding then the idea that a trademark or trade name informs the consumer as to the actual source or origin of goods, what does it indicate and with what result? It indicates, not that the article in question comes from a definite or particular source, the characteristics of which or the personalities connected with which are specifically known to the consumer, but merely that the goods in connection with which it is used emanate from the same—possibly anonymous—source or have reached the consumer through the same channels as certain other goods that have already given the consumer satisfaction, and that bore the same trademark....

Superficially it may appear to be very fine hair-splitting to say that while the consumer does not know the specific source of a trademarked article, he nevertheless knows that two articles, bearing the same mark, emanate from a single source. However, the precise distinction is vital in the present connection, for it brings out clearly the creative and not merely symbolic nature of the modern trademark or trade name....

The true functions of the trademark are, then, to identify a product as satisfactory and thereby to stimulate further purchases by the consuming public. The fact that through his trademark the manufacturer or importer may "reach over the shoulder of the retailer" and across the latter's counter straight to the consumer cannot be overemphasized, for therein lies the key to any effective scheme of trademark protection. To describe a trademark merely as a symbol of good will, without recognizing in it an agency for the actual creation and perpetuation of good will, ignores the most potent aspect of the nature of a trademark and that phase most in need of protection. To say that a trademark "is merely the visible manifestation of the more important business good will, which is the 'property' to be protected against invasion" or that "the good-will is the substance, the trade-mark merely the shadow," does not accurately state the function of a trademark today and obscures the problem of its adequate protection. The signboard of an inn in stage-coach days, when the golden lion or the green cockatoo actually symbolized to the hungry and weary traveler a definite smiling host, a tasty meal from a particular cook, a favorite brew and a comfortable bed, was merely "the visible manifestation" of the good will or probability of custom of the house; but today the trademark is not merely the symbol of good will but often the most effective agent for the creation of good will, imprinting upon the public mind an anonymous and impersonal guaranty of satisfaction, creating a desire for further satisfactions. The mark actually sells the goods. And, self-evidently, the more distinctive the mark, the more effective is its selling power.

II

The protection of trademarks originated as a police measure to prevent "the grievous deceit of the people" by the sale of defective goods, and to safeguard the collective good will and monopoly of the gild. The repression of trademark infringement came into the common law through an action of deceit and, although it is the public rather than the owner of the trademark who is actually deceived, the common law trademark action is still deceit. Equity, on the other hand, acting "in aid of" and "ancillary to" what it deemed to be a "legal right" to have a particular trademark, at first assumed jurisdiction in such cases to protect the plaintiff's "title" to trademarks, regardless of the question of deceit. Thus in the great case of Millington v. Fox, Lord Chancellor Cottenham stated: "Having previously come to the conclusion that there was sufficient in the case to show that the plaintiffs had a title to the marks in question, . . . they undoubtedly had a right to the assistance of a court of equity to enforce that title."

However, subsequent decisions of the equity side indicated a shifting from the proprietary aspect of trademark protection to practically the same basis as that of the common law—as is indicated in the oft-quoted dictum of Lord Langdale, uttered in 1842: "I think that the principle on which both the courts of law and of equity proceed is very well understood. A man is not to sell his own goods under the pretence that they are the goods of another man. . . ." Equity did not continue the unqualified protection of trademarks in aid of a definite legal right of property but acted under the doctrine of "passing off" in England, or of unfair competition in the United States, which was in itself but "a development of the law of fraud. Its aim was simply to prevent the deceitful sale or passing off of goods made by one person or firm for goods made by another." Contemporary professional testimony makes this point quite clear. "The diversion of custom" is the gravamen of the action in either "passing off" or "unfair competition." The Supreme Court has held: "The essence of the wrong consists in the sale of the goods of one manufacturer or vendor for those of another. . . . This essential element is the same in trade-mark cases as in cases of unfair competition unaccompanied with trade-mark infringement."

Recent decisions both in this country and in England have extended the doctrine of "unfair competition" beyond cases where there is an actual "diversion of custom." But the process has been one of making exceptions rather than of frank recognition of the true basis of trademark protection. No necessity or justification for the protection of marks on non-competing goods is seen except (1) where, while there is no actual diversion of trade, there is a likelihood of confusion as to the source of the infringing goods; (2) where the use of the infringing mark or name may work some discredit and financial liability or other similar concrete injury on the plaintiff. Thus, a recent writer states: "Where there are no circumstances that would cause the public to think the products bearing the same name were made by the same party, no wrong is done. The classic example given in Ainsworth v. Walmsley: 'If he does not carry on a trade in iron, but carries on a trade in linen and stamps a lion on his linen, another person may stamp a lion on iron,' is still the law." This conclusion that "no wrong is done" is based upon an archaic notion of the function of a trademark as solely indicating "source or origin." It assumes that "the elementary equitable principle upon which the whole law of this subject is based * * * is that one may not palm off his goods as the goods of another" and that the sole injury resulting from the use of the same "lion" mark on linen and iron might be a confusion as to the source of these two dissimilar products. It ignores the fact that the creation and retention of custom, rather than the designation of source, is the primary purpose of the trademark today, and that the preservation of the uniqueness or individuality of the trademark is of paramount importance to its owner. . . .

Trademark pirates are growing more subtle and refined. They proceed circumspectly, by suggestion and approximation, rather than by direct and exact duplication of their victims' wares and marks. The history of important trademark litigation within recent years shows that the use of similar marks on non-competing goods is perhaps the normal rather than the exceptional case of infringement. In the famous English Kodak case, cameras and bicycles were the articles in question; in the Aunt Jemima's case, pancake flour and syrup; in the Vogue case, fashion magazines and hats; in the Rolls–Royce case, automobiles and radio parts; in the Beech–Nut case, food products and cigarettes. In each instance the defendant was not actually diverting custom from the plaintiff, and where the courts conceded the absence of diversion of custom they were obliged to resort to an exceedingly laborious spelling out of other injury to the plaintiff in order to support their decrees. The real injury in all such cases can only be gauged in the light of what has been said concerning the function of a trademark. It is the gradual whittling away or dispersion of the identity and hold upon the public mind of the mark or name by its use upon non-competing goods. The more distinctive or unique the mark, the deeper is its impress upon the public consciousness, and the greater its need for protection against vitiation or dissociation from the particular product in connection with which it has been used. . . .

IV

From the necessities of modern trademark protection mentioned above, on the one hand, and from the decisions emphasizing the greater degree of protection to be given to coined, rather than to commonplace marks, the following principles necessarily emerge: (1) that the value of the modern trademark lies in its selling power; (2) that this selling power depends for its psychological hold upon the public, not merely upon the merit of the goods upon which it is used, but equally upon its own uniqueness and singularity; (3) that such uniqueness or singularity is vitiated or impaired by its use upon either related or non-related goods; and (4) that the degree of its protection depends in turn upon the extent to which, through the efforts or ingenuity of its owner, it is actually unique and different from other marks. . . .

Notes and Questions

1. Francis Henry Upton was born in 1814 in Salem, Massachusetts, and graduated from Harvard in 1835. He went on to practice law in New York City. During the Civil War, he acted as counsel for captors in prize courts. In addition to this treatise, he published "The Law of Nations affecting Commerce during War, with a Review of the Jurisprudence, Practice, and Proceedings of Prize Courts" in 1863. He died in June, 1876.

2. Frank Schechter's scholarship in the 1920s on the impact of the industrial revolution on trademarks is considered among the most influential works in the field. At the time he wrote this article, he was in-house counsel for the BVD undergarment brand. He lived from 1890–1937.

3. From an Upton-ian perspective, is Schechter advocating "an incautious application of the doctrine"? Articulate the differences in the two authors' rationales for trademark protection; in their expositions of the proper scope of trademark protection.

4. Upton recounts that "in nearly all the reported cases in which the right has been recognized, the complainants have been manufacturers, and, as such, possessed of an exclusive right in the designated commodity." The right to which Upton refers is a chattel right, not an intellectual property right, such as a patent or a copyright. If the trademark owner also initially owned the physical goods to which the mark was affixed, what did that imply about the nature of the trademark owner's business? How does that compare with the activities of today's trademark owners? If trademark law today covers at least most of these activities, what changes in trademark law has its current reach required?

Transcendental Nonsense and the Functional Approach
FELIX COHEN*

What's in a Trade Name?

If courts prevent a man from exploiting certain forms of language which another has already begun to exploit, the second user will be at the economic disadvantage of having to pay the first user for the privilege of using similar language or else of having to use less appealing language (generally) in presenting his commodities to the public.

Courts, then, in establishing inequality in the commercial exploitation of language are creating economic wealth and property, creating property not, of course, *ex nihilo,* but out of the materials of social fact, commercial custom, and popular moral faiths or prejudices. It does not follow, except by the fallacy of composition, that in creating new private property courts are benefiting society. Whether they are benefiting society depends upon a series of questions which courts and scholars dealing with this field of law have not seriously considered. Is there, for practical purposes, an unlimited supply of equally attractive words under which any commodity can be sold, so that the second seller of the commodity is at no commercial disadvantage if he is forced to avoid the word or words chosen by the first seller? If this is not the case, i.e., if peculiar emotional contexts give one word more sales appeal than any other word suitable for the same product, should the peculiar appeal of that word be granted by the state, without payment, to the first occupier? Is this homestead law for the English language necessary in

* 35 Colum. L. Rev. 809, 814–17 (1935).

order to induce the first occupier to use the most attractive word in selling his product? If, on the other hand, all words are originally alike in commercial potentiality, but become differentiated by advertising and other forms of commercial exploitation, is this type of business pressure a good thing, and should it be encouraged by offering legal rewards for the private exploitation of popular linguistic habits and prejudices? To what extent is differentiation of commodities by trade names a help to the consumer in buying wisely? To what extent is the exclusive power to exploit an attractive word, and to alter the quality of the things to which the word is attached, a means of deceiving consumers into purchasing inferior goods?

Without a frank facing of these and similar questions, legal reasoning on the subject of trade names is simply economic prejudice masquerading in the cloak of legal logic. The prejudice that identifies the interests of the plaintiff in unfair competition cases with the interests of business and identifies the interests of business with the interests of society, will not be critically examined by courts and legal scholars until it is recognized and formulated. It will not be recognized or formulated so long as the hypostatization of property rights conceals the circularity of legal reasoning.

Expressive Genericity: Trademarks as Language in the Pepsi Generation
ROCHELLE COOPER DREYFUSS*

One problem with analogizing rights in trademarks to rights in other intellectual property can be seen when comparing the product for which exclusivity is sought with the business of its creator. In patent, copyright, misappropriation, and publicity, the law protects the one and only product that the creator has for sale: the invention, the book, the news story, or the spectacle. If the creator cannot reap a profit from that product, then there is nothing upon which to base a source of pecuniary return. Exclusivity is therefore necessary to assure the creator freedom from those who did not make the creative effort and thus would undercut the price at which the creator could profitably sell the work. In contrast, the owner of a trademark is really in the business of selling a different product-dolls in the case of Mattel. The profit and the incentive to enhance quality comes from the marketing success of this other product, not the trademark. Exclusivity in the trademark is only needed to point consumers in the right direction, and that function is preserved by protecting the mark's signaling function.

Indeed, it is somewhat perverse to encourage the trademark owner's primary activity by facilitating the capture of profits from some other good. In the case of other intellectual property rights, the choice of exclusivity as an incentive mechanism is at least partially justified by the notion that the values captured provide the optimal amount of incentive to produce works of a similar nature in the future. But the public may enjoy the expressive dimensions of a trademark more than it values the underlying product. If so, diverting surplus value to activity in the

* 65 NOTRE DAME L. REV. 397, 408–10 (1990).

product field would lead to over-stimulation of investment in the product.

Even if the public does value trademarks enough to care whether the economy provides enough motivation to produce them, it is not clear that surplus value protection is necessary. The exigencies of the marketplace require its participants to develop signals in order to differentiate their goods from those of their rivals. Nice symbols are more likely to be produced than displeasing ones because the more agreeable the signal, the more easily it will be remembered, and the better the product will sell.

The fallacies in the real property and intellectual property analogies are unsatisfying from more than a theoretical point of view; they have direct impact on the manner in which benefits are distributed as between right-holders and the public. For the traditional rights, this allocation is achieved by asking the question, how much exclusivity is necessary to accomplish the desired goals? Once these goals are realized, surplus can be diverted to consumers. This is not to say it is always easy to find the best balance between access and reward: for the statutory rights, allocation is accomplished somewhat arbitrarily by legislative fiat; for common law rights, case-by-case analysis often leads to unsatisfactory results in individual cases. But although disagreements will be inevitable, the justifications for these rights do provide a framework that makes a discussion of the balance possible.

These quasi-trademark claims stand in sharp contrast. By equating "value" with "right," the decisions fail to create an internal reference point against which to measure the need for exclusivity. Instead of asking a question about how much value the creator needs in order to be optimally motivated, this right simply asks whether value, for every diversion of value is, by definition, too much. Thus, the problems engendered by expanding proprietary rights exist not only for the paradigm cases involving surplus value, but for all other hybrid usages. Furthermore, the rights created apparently endure forever; enforcement decisions are devoid of reference to the illicit motives of other users, to the potential harm to the complainant's activities, or to the inability of the complainant to receive an adequate return on investment. Nor is there room, as there is in copyright and traditional trademark law, to compare the public's need to put the protected work to a particular use with the right holder's claim for control.

Trademark Law: An Economic Perspective

WILLIAM M. LANDES & RICHARD A. POSNER*

II. The Economics of Trademarks

A. *Introduction*

To oversimplify somewhat, a trademark is a word, symbol, or other signifier used to distinguish a good or service produced by one firm from the goods or services of other firms. Thus "Sanka" designates a decaffeinated coffee made by General Foods and "Xerox" the dry copiers made

* XXX J. L. & Econ. 265, 268–70, 273–75 (1987).

by Xerox Corporation. "Bib"—the "Michelin Man"—is the symbol of tires made by the Michelin Company. A stylized penguin is the symbol of a line of paperback books published by Penguin Books; a distinctively shaped green bottle is a trademark of the producer of Perrier bottled water; the color pink is a trademark for residential insulation manufactured by Owens–Corning.

1. Benefits of Trademarks

Suppose you like decaffeinated coffee made by General Foods. If General Foods' brand had no name, then to order it in a restaurant or grocery store you would have to ask for "the decaffeinated coffee made by General Foods." This takes longer to say, requires you to remember more, and requires the waiter or clerk to read and remember more than if you can just ask for "Sanka." The problem would be even more serious if General Foods made more than one brand of decaffeinated coffee, as in fact it does. The benefit of the brand name is analogous to that of designating individuals by last as well as first names, so that, instead of having to say "the Geoffrey who teaches constitutional law at the University of Chicago Law School—not the one who teaches corporations," you can say "Geoffrey Stone—not Geoffrey Miller."

To perform its economizing function a trademark or brand name (these are rough synonyms) must not be duplicated. To allow another maker of decaffeinated coffee to sell its coffee under the name "Sanka" would destroy the benefit of the name in identifying a brand of decaffeinated coffee made by General Foods (whether there might be offsetting benefits is considered later). It would be like allowing a second rancher to graze his cattle on a pasture the optimal use of which required that only one herd be allowed to graze. The failure to enforce trademarks would impose two distinct costs—one in the market for trademarked goods and the other in the distinct (and unconventional) market in language.

a) The Market for Trademarked Goods. The benefits of trademarks in reducing consumer search costs require that the producer of a trademarked good maintain a consistent quality over time and across consumers. Hence trademark protection encourages expenditures on quality. To see this, suppose a consumer has a favorable experience with brand X and wants to buy it again. Or suppose he wants to buy brand X because it has been recommended by a reliable source or because he has had a favorable experience with brand Y, another brand produced by the same producer. Rather than investigating the attributes of all goods to determine which one is brand X or is equivalent to X, the consumer may find it less costly to search by identifying the relevant trademark and purchasing the corresponding brand. For this strategy to be efficient, however, not only must it be cheaper to search for the right trademark than for the desired attributes of the good, but also past experience must be a good predictor of the likely outcome of current consumption choices—that is, the brand must exhibit consistent quality. In short, a trademark conveys information that allows the consumer to say to himself, "I need not investigate the attributes of the brand I am about to purchase because the trademark is a shorthand way of telling me that the attributes are the same as that of the brand I enjoyed earlier."

Less obviously, a firm's incentive to invest resources in developing and maintaining (as through advertising) a strong mark depends on its ability to maintain consistent product quality. In other words, trademarks have a self-enforcing feature. They are valuable because they denote consistent quality, and a firm has an incentive to develop a trademark only if it is able to maintain consistent quality. To see this, consider what happens when a brand's quality is inconsistent. Because consumers will learn that the trademark does not enable them to relate their past to future consumption experiences, the branded product will be like a good without a trademark. The trademark will not lower search costs, so consumers will be unwilling to pay more for the branded than for the unbranded good. As a result, the firm will not earn a sufficient return on its trademark promotional expenditures to justify making them. A similar argument shows that a firm with a valuable trademark would be reluctant to lower the quality of its brand because it would suffer a capital loss on its investment in the trademark.

It should be apparent that the benefits of trademarks in lowering consumer search costs presuppose legal protection of trademarks. The value of a trademark is the saving in search costs made possible by the information or reputation that the trademark conveys or embodies about the brand (or the firm that produces the brand). Creating such a reputation requires expenditures on product quality, service, advertising, and so on. Once the reputation is created, the firm will obtain greater profits because repeat purchases and word-of-mouth references will generate higher sales and because consumers will be willing to pay higher prices for lower search costs and greater assurance of consistent quality. However, the cost of duplicating someone else's trademark is small—the cost of duplicating a label, design, or package where the required inputs are widely available. The incentive to incur this cost (in the absence of legal regulation) will be greater the stronger the trademark. The free-riding competitor will, at little cost, capture some of the profits associated with a strong trademark because some consumers will assume (at least in the short run) that the free rider's and the original trademark holder's brands are identical. If the law does not prevent it, free riding will eventually destroy the information capital embodied in a trademark, and the prospect of free riding may therefore eliminate the incentive to develop a valuable trademark in the first place. . . .

2.   The Costs of Legally Enforceable Trademarks

These costs are modest, at least in the simple case of the "fanciful" mark, such as "Exxon" and "Kodak," which has no information content except to denote a specific producer or brand. Since the mark "goes with" the brand (in a sense explained later), the transfer of the mark is automatically effected by a transfer of the rights to make the branded product, as by a sale, or licensing, of production rights or assets. Rent seeking to stake out a trademark is not much of a problem either. Prior to establishing a trademark, the distinctive yet pronounceable combinations of letters to form words that will serve as a suitable trademark are as a practical matter infinite, implying a high degree of substitutability and hence a slight value in exchange. Finally, the costs of enforcement, though not trivial (especially where there is a danger of a brand name's becoming a generic name), are modest and (again putting aside the generic problem) do not include the cost in inefficient resource allocation from driving a wedge between price and marginal cost. A proper trademark is not a public good; it has social value only when used to designate a single brand.

We may seem to be ignoring the possibility that, by fostering product differentiation, trademarks may create deadweight costs, whether of monopoly or (excessive) competition. We have assumed that a trademark induces its owner to invest in maintaining uniform product quality, but another interpretation is that it induces the owner to spend money on creating, through advertising and promotion, a spurious image of high quality that enables monopoly rents to be obtained by deflecting consumers from lower-price substitutes of equal or even higher quality. In the case of products that are produced according to an identical formula, such as aspirin or household liquid bleach, the ability of name-brand goods (Bayer aspirin, Clorox bleach) to command higher prices than generic (nonbranded) goods has seemed to some economists and more lawyers an example of the power of brand advertising to bamboozle the public and thereby promote monopoly; and brand advertising presupposes trademarks—they are what enable a producer readily to identify his brand to the consumer. Besides the possibility of creating monopoly rents, trademarks may transform rents into costs, as one firm's expenditure on promoting its mark cancels out that of another firm. Although no monopoly profits are created, consumers may pay higher prices, and resources may be wasted in a sterile competition.

The short answer to these arguments is that they have gained no foothold at all in trademark law, as distinct from antitrust law. The implicit economic model of trademarks that is used in that law is our model, in which trademarks lower search costs and foster quality control rather than create social waste and consumer deception. A longer answer, which we shall merely sketch, is that the hostile view of brand advertising has been largely and we think correctly rejected by economists. The fact that two goods have the same chemical formula does not make them of equal quality to even the most coolly rational consumer. That consumer will be interested not in the formula but in the manufactured product and may therefore be willing to pay a premium for greater assurance that the good will actually be manufactured to the specifications of the formula. Trademarks enable the consumer to economize on a real cost because he spends less time searching to get the quality he wants. If this analysis is correct, the rejection by trademark law of a monopoly theory of trademarks is actually a mark in favor of the economic rationality of that law.

Advertising and the Public Interest

RALPH S. BROWN*

The law of trade symbols is of modern development, largely judge-made and only partly codified. Its impetus comes from the demands of modern advertising, a black art whose practitioners are part of the larger army which employs threats, cajolery, emotions, personality, persistence and facts in what is termed aggressive selling. Much aggressive selling involves direct personal relationships; advertising depends on the remote manipulation of symbols, most importantly of symbols directed at a mass audience through mass media, or imprinted on mass-produced goods. The essence of these symbols is distilled in the devices variously called trade-marks, trade names, brand names, or trade symbols. To the courts come frequent claims for protection, made by those who say they have fashioned a valuable symbol, and that no one else should use it. Very recently, for example, the vendors of Sun–Kist oranges lost a court battle to prevent an Illinois baker from selling Sun–Kist bread. The highest court, in its most recent encounter with a like case, upheld the power of a manufacturer of rubber footwear to prevent the use of a red circle mark by a seller of rubber heels, which the plaintiff did not manufacture.

In these cases, a choice of premises and techniques is still open. One set of premises, which seems to subsume Justice Frankfurter's felicitous dictum, recognizes a primary public interest in protecting the seller who asks the court to enjoin "another [who] poaches upon the commercial magnetism of a symbol he has created." This expansive conception merits critical attention. Are all forms of poaching forbidden? Should they be, consistent with another premise? This one asserts, in the words of Judge Frank, "the basic common law policy of encouraging competition, and the fact that the protection of monopolies in names is but a secondary and limiting policy." The legal ties which bind together some apparently inconsistent decisions may be found, but not simply in an indiscriminate prohibition of poaching, nor yet in a presumption in favor of competition, no matter how compelling. Rather, courts move from these and other premises to refinements of doctrine.

It is proposed here to seek, in the milieu in which trade symbols are created and used, for data underlying both premises and dogma. This will require an independent evaluation of the institution of advertising. What do we get for the three billions of current annual outlay? Do we want it? Unfortunately, there is little consensus as to what values advertising serves. Its votaries have poured their most skillful symbols back in the soil from which they sprang. Its detractors, maddened by the success of this propaganda, would purge Radio City with fire and sword. One thing the examination will reveal is that what appear to be private disputes among hucksters almost invariably touch the public welfare. We shall therefore be concerned to ask, when courts protect trade symbols, whether their decisions further public as well as private goals.

The principal reason for advertising is an economic one—to sell goods and services. We can describe this process, and its economic

* 57 Yale L. J. 1165, 1165–69, 1180–84 (1948).

effects, with relative confidence, compared to the obscurity which sur-
rounds the psychological, cultural, or other social consequences of modern advertising. These may turn out to be more portentous than the
affairs of the market-place. But the materials are uncollected or unrefined. In this survey we can only drop a handful of problems into a
footnote. The reader must make his own judgments from his own
observations, remembering, as we turn almost exclusively to economic
discussion, that man does not live by bread alone.

Informative and Persuasive Advertising

The buying public submits to a vast outpouring of words and
pictures from the advertisers, in which, mingled with exhortations to
buy, is a modicum of information about the goods offered. From the
point of view of the economic purist, imparting information is the only
useful function of advertising. A perfect market demands a perfect
enlightenment of those who buy and sell. One of the many imperfections
of the real world is that, absent advertising, most buyers would have to
go to a great deal of trouble to discover that is offered for sale. To the
extent that the blandishments of sellers inform buyers what is to be
bought, and at what price, advertising undoubtedly helps to quicken the
stream of commerce.

Most advertising, however, is designed not to inform, but to persuade and influence. What is the occasion for such tremendous outlays
on persuasion and influence in a well-ordered economic system? If we
consider first the total stream of production and consumption, persuasive advertising seems only to consume resources that might be put to
better use producing more goods and services. It does not increase total
demand, it only increases wants. Effective demand arises, not from what
we would like to have, but from the purchasing power of the community
created by its productive power. We consume what we produce, and no
more. Considering the economic welfare of the community as a whole, to
use up part of the national product persuading people to buy product A
rather than product B appears to be a waste of resources....

The Sovereign Consumer

Defenders of the institution have two additional lines of defense.
The first is that persuasive advertising creates a cluster of values, no less
real because they are intangible. The second, related to the first, argues
that the sovereign consumer has made a free election between those
values and the austerities of price competition.

These considerations bring us to the consumer as an individual. As
an individual, instead of a faceless component of mass purchasing power,
he is a creature of infinite diversity, with, moreover, a soul. To make a
complete analysis of what he gets from advertising, the relations of
material rewards and spiritual values, as affected by advertising, would
have to be considered. That task we must leave to the philosophers and
the psychologists. As was indicated earlier, they have not yet performed
it. The only arena which is at all adequately staked out is that of the
economic conflict between seller and buyer. The agreed goal is the
maximum satisfaction of each consumer, as determined by his free
choice in disposing of his income. In a roundabout way, problems of

aggregate output and investment, already discussed, bear on the same goal. Now we have to consider how persuasive advertising adds to or subtracts from the sum of the individual's satisfied wants.

What are the intangible values? One is said to be the assurance of reliability, because the advertiser wants to build up repeat sales, and cannot afford to sell patently unsatisfactory goods. Admitting, for the sake of getting on, that unadvertised brands offer a greater opportunity for "hit-and-run" frauds, the difficulty with this contention is that the hope of continued custom is quite unrelated to the magnitude of persuasive advertising. Nothing more than information as to source is necessary for the consumer to be able to repeat a satisfactory purchase.

Other values derive from the proposition in that cheapness is not enough. The buyer of an advertised good buys more than a parcel of food or fabric; he buys the pause that refreshes, the hand that has never lost its skill, the priceless ingredient that is the reputation of its maker. All these may be illusions, but they cost money to create, and if the creators can recoup their outlay, who is the poorer? Among the many illusions which advertising can fashion are those of lavishness, refinement, security, and romance. Suppose the monetary cost of compounding a perfume is trivial; of what moment is this if the ads promise, and the buyer believes, that romance, even seduction, will follow its use? The economist, whose dour lexicon defines as irrational any market behavior not dictated by a logical pecuniary calculus, may think it irrational to buy illusions; but there is a degree of that kind of irrationality even in economic man; and consuming man is full of it.

The taint of irrationality may be dispelled by asserting flatly that the utility of a good, that is, its capacity to satisfy wants, is measured exactly by what people will pay for it. If, as is undeniably the case, consumers will pay more for an advertised brand than for its unheralded duplicate, then consumers must get more satisfaction out of the advertised brand. The nature of the satisfaction is of concern only to the moralist. Though this argument can easily be pushed to absurdity— suppose it was to the interest of the advertisers to consume half the national product in persuasion?—it seems plausible if it is based on the dogma of consumer autonomy. Then anyone who questions the untrammeled use of influence by the seller and its uncoerced acceptance by the buyer is at best a Puritan, at worst a Fascist. The debate seems to end in a defense of freedom, for the advertiser as well as for the consumer.

But does the sovereign consumer have real freedom of choice? The first requisite of choice is an adequate presentation of alternatives. The classical economists who enthroned the consumer never dreamed that he would make his decisions under a bombardment of stupefying symbols. He should be informed, and willing to pay the necessary price for information. But the most charitable tabulations reveal relatively little information in advertising directed to consumers outside the classified columns and local announcements. National advertising is dominated by appeals to sex, fear, emulation, and patriotism, regardless of the relevance of those drives to the transaction at hand. The purchase of many advertised articles, then, has a raw emotional origin. Many others are compelled by the endless reiteration of the advertisers' imperative: eat lemons, drink milk, wear hats. Pseudo-information fills any gaps. It takes many forms. There is the bewildering manipulation of comparatives and superlatives: "No other soap washes cleaner"; "The world's most wanted pen." In the atomic age, precise scientific data are helpful. Bayer's Aspirin tells us that the tablet dissolves in two seconds. Whether the analgesic effect is then felt in one hour or two hours will no doubt be explained in time. Buick lists among its features such well-understood engineering terms as "Dynaflow Drive, taper-thru Styling, Vibra–Shielded Ride, Hi–Poised Fire-ball Power." The reader, after ten minutes with a magazine or the radio, can select his own examples of the types of influence that are thought to move the sovereign consumer.

The foundation of free choice, to repeat, is an adequate presentation of alternatives. Admittedly, many choices, for example in politics or religion, are presented under a smoke screen of exaggeration and emotion. But there are usually at least two sides to the argument. The choice between one highly advertised dentifrice and another is, in important respects, no choice at all. It cannot register a decision to support or reject institutional arrangements which, as had been shown, contribute to monopolistic waste of resources; it cannot reflect a preference to get more or less for one's money, to take an illusion or leave it. It is only a choice of between one illusion and another. That advertisers, despite their intramural rivalry, are aware that they stand on common ground, is shown by their united opposition to institutions which enlarge the consumer's alternatives. An instance is the forays and reprisals against the consumers' movement.

The forces which counter advertising propaganda may be listed as follows. First, as an individual protest, is the sentiment described as "sales resistance," a compound of realism, skepticism, and apathy. Second is organized sales resistance, the pressure for reform by the slow-moving consumers' organizations. Third, most important economically, is the still small voice of the lower price tag on an unadvertised substitute. Fourth, the nub of the present discussion, comes the shaping of legal institutions, either to curb the excesses of advertising or to foster the second and third forces just listed. It is intended to discuss in a later article the enforcement of truth in advertising, as an indication that freedom to persuade and influence has its boundaries, and the possible use of antitrust, taxation, or other devices to set new boundaries. The law also has to take a stand when the use or misuse of advertising has created measurable values for the advertiser, and "another poaches upon the commercial magnetism of the symbol." How much protection will be given the advertiser against the poacher? The answer is sought in the law of trade-marks and trade names.

Summary

Before assessing the relevance of that body of doctrine to the good and bad in advertising, it may be desirable to summarize the conclusions reached thus far. Advertising has two main functions, to inform and to persuade. With qualifications that need not be repeated, persuasive advertising is, for the community as a whole, just a luxurious exercise in talking ourselves into spending our incomes. For the individual firm, however, it is a potent device to distinguish a product from its competitors, and to create a partial immunity from the chills and fevers of competition. The result of successful differentiation is higher prices than would otherwise prevail. The aim, not always achieved, is higher profits. Whether persuasive advertising enhances the total flow of goods by promoting cost reductions is disputable. Whether it swells the flow of investment by the lure of monopoly profits is doubtful.

For the consumer who desires to get the most for his money, persuasive advertising displays a solid front of irrelevancy. The alternatives to what the advertisers offer are not adequately presented, and the choice among advertised products is loaded with a panoply of propaganda for which the buyer pays, whether he wants it or not. However, both buyer and seller profit from informative advertising. In a complex society, it is an indispensable adjunct to a free traffic in goods and services. The task before the courts in trade symbol cases, it may therefore be asserted, should be to pick out from the tangle of claims, facts, and doctrines they are set to unravel, the threads of informative advertising, and to ignore the persuasive. The two functions are very much intertwined in trade symbols, how confusingly will appear when we try to separate them. . . .

Breakfast with Batman
JESSICA LITMAN*

III. The New Politics of Merchandising

The expansion of the law of trade symbol protection has tracked two distinct but related trends. First has been an evolution in widely held views of the public interest. Ralph [Brown] argued in Advertising and the Public Interest that just because people paid more for products did not mean there had been any actual increase in productivity and welfare—rather, we had let ourselves be talked into paying more money for the same stuff. That, he insisted, was obviously in the interest of the producers whose advertising had persuaded the public to pay a higher price, but was wasteful for the public at large. Today, that once self-evident point is controversial. Productivity seems to be measured less by what people make than by what people are inclined to buy. What consumers are willing to pay has become synonymous with value. Commodification is the preeminent engine of progress. Transforming ephemeral figments into saleable property is a patriotic act, and the fact, without more, that an offer to sell something will find customers is reason enough to sanction its appropriation from the commons. There has been inexorable pressure to recognize as an axiom the principle that if something appears to have substantial value to someone, the law must and should protect it as property. Recent years have seen an explosion of cases in which courts have relied on trademark-like rubrics to uphold claims to exclusive rights in names, faces, voices, gestures, phrases, artistic style, marketing concepts, locations, and references.

* 108 Yale L. J. 1717, 1725–1731 (1999).

Second, the descriptive proposition that trade symbols have no intrinsic value has come to seem demonstrably inaccurate. The use of trademarks on promotional products has evolved from an advertising device for the underlying product line to an independent justification for bringing a so-called underlying product to market. Elvis Presley's estate has earned more annually in license fees than it did in the late singer's most profitable year. Warner Brothers has brought out a seemingly endless series of lackluster Batman sequels. Critics disliked the sequels, and their box office performances were mediocre, but the sales of Batman toys have more than made up for it. It is hard to maintain a straight face when asserting that the "Batman" mark has value only as an indicator that Batman-branded products are licensed by Warner Brothers. The worth of such valuable trade symbols lies less in their designation of product source than in their power to imbue a product line with desirable atmospherics.

Indeed, in the new orthodoxy, marketing is value. American industry seems to proceed on the assumption that we can make the consumer richer simply by revising a product's packaging, without having to make any changes in the product itself.

Consider the effort and expense that goes into distinguishing a Ford Taurus from a Mercury Sable and persuading customers to buy one rather than the other, when, after all, they're essentially the same car. Buying a truck? Agonize over whether you'd rather drive a Mazda B–Series (Get in. Be moved.), "the official truck of the AMA Motorcross Nationals," or haul your friends to the river, kayaks in tow, in a Ford Ranger (Built Tough. Built To Last.). The only major difference between them is the marketing. Auto companies can pitch their vehicles to specialized, niche markets without needing to redesign anything but the ad campaigns for their cars.

But why not? If the illusion of a vehicle custom-built for a particular sort of buyer is worth a couple of thousand dollars to a couple of million consumers, the customers will be happier, the auto companies will be wealthier, and the American economy will keep chugging along, picking up speed without burning additional coal. Anecdotal evidence suggests that many consumers don't feel duped, or, in any event, don't mind being duped. It isn't as if anyone has tried to conceal that the Sable and the Taurus are twins, that Advil and Motrin and generic ibuprofen are the exact same stuff, or that the reason that Tylenol and not some other brand of acetaminophen is "the pain reliever hospitals use most" is that McNeil sets the hospital price of Tylenol low enough to enable it to make that claim. At some level, most consumers know that; most of them have nonetheless settled on their own favorite advertised brands.

Moreover, there is something more going on than producers and consumers agreeing with each other to pretend that the atmospherics of product advertising are somehow reflected in the advertised products. Ask a child, and he'll persuade you that the difference between a box of Kellogg's Corn Flakes with a picture of Batman on it and some other box without one is real. There is nothing imaginary about it. It has nothing to do with the way the cereal tastes. What kids want isn't a nutritious part of a complete breakfast; they want Batman to have breakfast with them. One box supplies that; the other doesn't.

An important premise underlying Ralph [Brown]'s analysis was that trade symbols themselves had no legitimate intrinsic value except insofar as they symbolized information about the products they accompanied. As a normative proposition, that would strike many consumers today as questionable; as a descriptive one, it is demonstrably untrue. Consumers have come to attach enormous value to trade symbols, and it is no longer uncommon to see the symbols valued far in excess of the worth of the underlying products they identify. In a very real sense, trade symbols are themselves often products: Toys are designed, perfumes are compounded, and breakfast cereals are devised for no better reason than to serve as a vehicle for the trade symbol du jour. If we have come to value the atmospherics embodied in advertising, shouldn't our law be reformed to protect them from unauthorized imitation?

IV.   Protection and Competition

At first glance, the syllogism seems to pack powerful intuitive appeal. Ralph [Brown]'s argument relied on the axiom that what he called the persuasive function of trade symbols was of no value to the public at large; indeed, from the viewpoint of the public interest, the persuasive value of advertising was at best irrelevant and at worst pernicious. Affording it strong legal protection, therefore, seemed perverse. Whether or not that axiom described the U.S. economy in 1948, it seems naive in 1999. In today's world, the public has invested considerable spending dollars and a significant chunk of intangible goodwill in the atmospherics purveyed by advertisers. If society now values the persuasive function of trade symbols more than it used to, then perhaps it ought to protect that persuasive function more powerfully than it used to.

To say that many consumers seem to attach real value to atmospherics, however, doesn't itself demonstrate that those atmospherics should be afforded legal protection. Many things have value. As Ralph Brown reminded us often, the essence of any intellectual property regime is to divide the valuable stuff subject to private appropriation from the valuable stuff that, precisely because of its importance, is reserved for public use. In the law of trade symbols, for instance, it has long been the rule that functional product features may not be protected, because they have too much value, not too little. Value, without more, does not tell us whether a particular item for which protection is sought belongs in the proprietary pile or the public one.

To agree to treat a class of stuff as intellectual property, we normally require a showing that, if protection is not extended, bad things will happen that will outweigh the resulting good things. But it would be difficult to argue that the persuasive values embodied in trade symbols are likely to suffer from underprotection. Indeed, the Mattels, Disneys, and Warner Brothers of the world seem to protect their atmospherics just fine without legal assistance. Not only can their target audiences tell the difference between, say, a Barbie doll and some other thirteen-inch fashion doll, but, regardless of features, they seem well-trained in the art of insisting on the Mattel product. Nor is the phenomenon limited to the junior set. The popularity of Ralph Lauren's Polo brand shirts or Gucci handbags is an obvious example.

To the extent that consumers want to purchase the higher-priced spread, they ought to be able to be sure that they are paying the higher price for the genuine branded article. If the concept of branding is itself legitimate, then we want to ensure consumers' protection against confusion or deception. Conventional trademark law does that. But, to stick with Lauren's Polo for a minute, what about consumers who want to pick up a polo shirt with some design on the chest at a good price? What if, instead, they want to buy this month's issue of Polo magazine (which follows the sport, not the fashion)? It seems obvious why Lauren might want to hinder the first and collect a license fee. There seems, nonetheless, to be no good reason why we should help him.

If competition is still the American way of doing business, then before we give out exclusive control of some coin of competition, we need, or should need, a justification. Protecting consumers from deception is the justification most familiar to trademark law, but it does not support assigning broad rights to prevent competitive or diluting use when no confusion seems likely. Supplying incentives to invest in the item that's getting the protection is another classic justification for intellectual property, and it is equally unavailing here. An argument that we would have an undersupply of good commercials if advertisers were not given plenary control over the elements in their ads cannot be made with a straight face. Finally, there is the perennially popular justification of desert. Producers have invested in their trade symbols, the argument goes; they have earned them, so they're entitled to them.

But so have we. The argument that trade symbols acquire intrinsic value—apart from their usefulness in designating the source—derives from consumers' investing those symbols with value for which they are willing to pay real money. We may want our children to breakfast with Batman. It may well increase the total utils in our society if every time a guy drinks a Budweiser or smokes a Camel, he believes he's a stud. We may all be better off if, each time a woman colors her hair with a L'Oreal product, she murmurs to herself "and I'm worth it." If that's so, however, Warner Brothers, Anheuser–Busch, R.J. Reynolds, and L'Oreal can hardly take all the credit. They built up all that mystique with their customers' money and active collaboration. If the customers want to move on, to get in bed with other products that have similar atmospherics, why shouldn't they? It's not very sporting to try to lock up the atmospherics.

To the extent, moreover, that the impulse to protect something beyond any prevention of consumer confusion derives from the perception that this thing has value, that it is something people want to buy, then giving its purveyor intellectual property protection is the wrong response. If the thing itself is valuable, if it is in some sense itself a product, then we want other purveyors to compete in offering it to consumers in their own forms and on their own terms. Competition is, after all, the premise of the system. Without competition, none of the rest of the rules make any practical sense. . . .

Notes and Questions

1. Felix S. Cohen was born in New York in 1907. He attended The City College of New York, received an M.A. in philosophy from Harvard in 1927 and a Ph.D. from Harvard in 1929. In 1928 Cohen entered Columbia Law School, graduating in 1931. He spent much of his career in public service, with a particular focus on Native American law. He taught legislative drafting and legal philosophy at Yale Law School, and jurisprudence at The City College of New York's Department of Philosophy. Cohen also taught at the New School for School Research and the University of Newark Law School (later Rutgers Law School).

For biographical notes on Rochelle Dreyfuss, William M. Landes, Richard A. Posner, Ralph Brown and Jessica Litman, see supra, Chapters 1 and 2, at pages 255, 327–28, 307, 346.

2. According to Felix Cohen, the underlying rationale of trademark law is circular: "It purports to base legal protection upon economic value, when, as a matter of actual fact, the economic value of a sales device depends upon the extent to which it will be legally protected." How does this reasoning differ from traditional rationales for protecting other kinds of intellectual, or tangible, property? Are you persuaded that this argument is a "vicious circle"? Consider Professor Dreyfuss' critique of the analogy of rights in trademark to rights in other forms of intellectual property. How does her criticism compare with Cohen's? How does her critique compare with the reasons Sherman & Bently, supra, offer for the historical exclusion of trademarks from intellectual property?

3. Compare the economic and competitive rationales for trademark protection as described by Cohen (to promote a "homestead law" of language); Schechter (to "identify a product as satisfactory and thereby to stimulate further purchases by the consuming public"); Landes & Posner (to "reduce consumer search costs" and to "foster quality control"); Brown (to "encourage competition" by disseminating information); and Litman (to allow consumers to "invest . . . symbols with value" and to permit purveyors to compete in offering that perception). How do they differ? Which analysis do you find most persuasive? Does that analysis, in turn, influence your instinct as to the appropriate scope of protection?

4. What public interest is served by persuading or influencing consumers to perceive similar products as significantly distinct from each other? Is trademarks law simply the enforcement of "false consciousness"? What arguments do Landes and Posner bring to bear against the contention that "by fostering product differentiation, trademarks may create deadweight costs"?

III. Scope of Protection

Trade-Marks and Trade Names—An Analysis and Synthesis

MILTON HANDLER & CHARLES PICKETT*

THE MONOPOLY ARGUMENT EXAMINED

There are two implications of the monopoly argument which must be carefully noted because of their far-reaching effect. One is that a monopoly can be and is necessarily acquired upon the appropriation of a fanciful word as a trade-mark. The other is that rights in what are called trade names, i.e., descriptive and generic words, are not as great and the protection accorded such marks is more limited than in the case of trade-marks, since there is and can be no monopoly in them. If, however, no monopoly is obtained in the case of arbitrary marks, or if the monopoly which is acquired is actually no broader than that in descriptive terms, there is obviously no point to the original argument. The accuracy of these implications, therefore, must be immediately considered.

It is important, at this point, to distinguish between two possible uses of word marks, which for convenience we shall call use as a mark, or trade-mark use, as contrasted with descriptive or use in a non-trade-mark sense.

There are two essentials of a trade-mark use within our definition. The word must be employed to denominate or designate a definite species of commodity or a particular business. Affixation of the word to an article, however, is unnecessary. "Kodak" stamped upon a camera, "Kodak" used as the flare-head in an advertisement of the same article, "Kodak" in a price-list enumerating different brands of cameras, are all examples of denominative uses of the term "Kodak." But where the word in its context indicates not the species but the genus "Buy me a black camera or Kodak" or is descriptive of the qualities of a product, rather than indicative of its source "Our cameras are made according to the Kodak principle" the use is non-denominative or descriptive. While we would not say that a word had been used as a mark unless used denominatively as explained, it does not follow that all denominative uses are to be regarded as trade-mark uses. The novelist who writes "Mr. Jones carried a Kodak camera under his arm" is using Kodak, presumably, to indicate a particular species of camera. But the reference is so clearly non-commercial, even though the book is sold for profit, that we would not consider it a trade-mark use. The second requirement, therefore, is that the mark should be used commercially. All uses which are non-commercial or non-denominative, we shall regard as descriptive.

Similarly, with respect to trade names or marks etymologically descriptive or generic, we shall distinguish between such literal usage as "this vest fits snugly" or "this watch is made at Waltham, Massachu-

---

* 30 Colum. L. Rev. 168, 170–71, 175–79 (1930).

setts," and the use of the same words in a secondary or denominative sense, as Snugly–Fit Vests and Waltham Watches.

THE MONOPOLY TESTED

Turning now to the first or negative implication of the monopoly argument, it becomes clear upon reflection that a complete monopoly, in the sense of the right to enjoin any use of a word whatsoever, is never acquired however unique or original the mark may be. Suppose the mark Kodak, an arbitrary collocation of letters, coined by the Eastman Kodak Company, is used in the editorial columns of the New York Times, in the latest novel or in ordinary conversation. While so far as we know there is no authority on the question, it is difficult to conceive of a court, no matter how profoundly impressed by the monopoly argument, issuing an injunction under such circumstances. It will undoubtedly be conceded that such non-commercial usage is privileged, if it can be shown that even certain commercial uses are permissible.

Can a technical mark be commercially used without infringing the rights of the owner? Normally, an invented term such as Lajax or any other groupings of nonsense syllables is incapable of commercial use except as a mark. Consequently the monopoly is quite real since any use *ex hypothesi* would be denominative and hence an infringement. But it frequently happens that such marks, while undoubtedly valid, can be and are used descriptively as above defined. . . .

It may well be contended that in attempting to prove the restricted scope of the monopoly in an arbitrary mark, we have relied entirely, to this point, upon typical cases which were not contemplated or thought of when the monopoly argument was formulated. While we readily concede that the situations discussed above are uncommon, there are two answers to this contention. The propriety of using so broad a term as monopoly is best tested and the scope of the monopoly determined in the border-line cases in which the issue is sharply defined. Moreover, if the monopoly contemplated is merely a monopoly against denominative use by another upon similar goods, we seriously question the aptness of the term to describe the actual rights acquired. Besides, the bugaboo that troubles the courts when trade-mark rights are sought in such descriptive words as Snugly–Fit or Fashionknit is not that exclusive rights will be obtained in the term as a mark but that the monopoly will extend to the literal or primary meanings of the words as well, thus impoverishing the language. If the monopoly is so restricted, even where it is supposed to prevail, the courts have needlessly disturbed themselves with a phantom of their own creation and have failed to face the real issue.

We have shown that the monopoly in arbitrary words at best is limited to trade-mark or denominative use. It is thus apparent that when courts advert to the monopoly argument in holding descriptive words incapable of appropriation as technical trade-marks, it must be assumed that they are not referring to a monopoly of the dictionary meaning of these words (which, by the way, is never sought) since there is no monopoly in the corresponding meaning of technical trade-marks. They must consequently be referring to a monopoly in the secondary meaning or denominative use of such terms. Which raises two questions: (1)

Whyshould it not be possible to acquire such a monopoly, if one can be obtained in fanciful words? (2) Can a monopoly of this sort really be had in fanciful words? We postpone consideration of the first question for the present and turn immediately to the second.

In tracing the limits of this monopoly, two restrictions must be noted at the outset. A uses an arbitrary mark locally in New York, B in Los Angeles, C adopts a mark for kitchen utensils, D takes it for motor boats. While the exact boundaries of the law are yet unclear, the monopoly seems to extend no further than the territorial market and the class of goods upon which the mark has been used, although the trend of the decisions is undoubtedly in the direction of greater and more effective protection. We do not rely overmuch on these cases, which raise peculiar problems of their own.

The more typical situation consists of the use of the same mark upon a competing product sold in the same market. . . .

So far then as denominative use of the mark upon the same class of goods in the same market is concerned, the monopoly would seem to be absolute. But is this always so? Suppose the defendant takes as a mark a word substantially similar to the plaintiff's fanciful brand, but descriptive of the qualities of the article to which it is applied. Will the plaintiff's monopoly yield to the defendant's privilege to use the normal descriptives or appellatives of the language? . . .

[For example], it has been held that an uncooked pudding may be called *Pudding* despite the previous adoption of *Puddine* as a mark for the same dessert. Most of the decisions are in accord with the *Pudding* case[]. On the other hand, injunctions against the use of such descriptive or generic words as *Curative Soap*, *Super-Flash* for gasoline, *Vitalizing Ore*, and *Extract of Coca and Kola*, have been granted at the instance of the respective proprietors of the technical marks, *Cuticura Soap*, *Silver Flash*, *Vitae-Ore* or *V. 0.*, and *Coca-Cola*.

While these cases' seem to represent conflicting tendencies, reconciliation is not impossible. It will be noted that they present contrasting states of fact. In one group of cases, the defendant uses the normal generic designation for the product or words descriptive of commercially significant qualities. It would be a serious hardship if a tradesman were not permitted to indicate that his product was a pudding or a muffler. A contrary rule would necessitate the invention and popularization of new synonyms. While as we shall see later, it may not be necessary that a tradesman take *pudding* as a mark, he must call his preparation *pudding* if it is to be sold at all. Although it may be possible theoretically to distinguish between denominative and non-denominative usage, this nice discrimination is not feasible practically. *Curative Soap* and *Super-Flash* gasoline, however, refer to less important commercial qualities. Adequate reference to the articles can be made without employing these words as marks. The distinction which is not feasible in the case of pudding is perfectly possible here. While the word soap cannot be dispensed with, the curative properties of the article can be sufficiently indicated without calling it Curative Soap. The defendant's privilege to use commercially important generic and descriptive words should be, in the final analysis, the measure of the monopoly in a fanciful word. The plaintiff's monopoly should yield to and be no broader than the defendant's necessity. Much of the confusion in the cases has resulted from a failure fully to realize this obvious truth.

The monopoly in a trade-mark thus turns out to be of rather ghostly constitution. The exceptions tend to become the rule. The monopoly is, as we have seen, not preclusive of non-commercial and non-denominative uses of the identical mark nor of the use of substantially similar descriptive or generic terms.

Dawning Acceptance of the Dilution Rationale for Trademark–Trade Identity Protection

BEVERLY W. PATTISHALL*

I. INTRODUCTION

A. Origins and History

In 1927, the late Frank I. Schechter urged that the only rational basis for trademark protection lay in proscribing the "gradual whittling away or dispersion of the identity and hold upon the public mind of the mark or name by its use upon non-competing goods." Schechter never actually referred to his theory as one protecting against "dilution," but rather as a basis providing "preservation of the uniqueness of a trademark." He argued that "uniqueness or singularity" is the essential trademark right and also that the right to preservation of the trademark's uniqueness or singularity amounted to a property right belonging to the trademark owner, but only in the cases of coined or unique marks.

Prior to Schechter's radical, new rationale for trademark protection, a few decisions had afforded relief, ostensibly under the traditional likelihood of confusion rationale, against what really amounted to diluting rather than confusing use of famous marks on widely diverse goods. The first of a series of the so-called "anti-dilution" statutes espousing Schechter's thesis was not enacted until twenty years later. During the succeeding thirty-six years, there followed a steadily expanding legislative endorsement of the concept by an additional twenty-one states. The courts with a few exceptions, however, failed to follow that lead. Even a half century after Schechter, the statutes, or basic provisions of them, were being widely ignored or curiously misconstrued and emasculated by the courts. . . .

II. A DAWNING

The 1977 New York Court of Appeals decision in *Allied Maintenance Corp. v. Allied Mechanical Trades, Inc.*, [42 N.Y.2d 538 (1978)], appears to have precipitated a change of course in the interpretation of the law of dilution, not only in the state courts of New York, but also in the federal courts of the Second Circuit and in both federal and state courts elsewhere. Such seems to have been *Allied*'s impact, despite the facts

* 74 Trademark Rep. 289, 289–92, 295–97, 299–302, 308–10 (1984).

that the decision was by a 4–to–3 divided court and the majority spoke concerning dilution almost entirely by way of dicta. . . .

III. THE COURTS AND DILUTION POST-ALLIED

A. Interpretation, Definition and the Confusion Error

. . . Many courts now appear quite comfortable with the dilution concept and are lucid in defining it. Leading the list is the sound, if prosaic, definition endorsed by the *Allied* Court: "[T]he whittling away of an established trademark's selling power and value through its unauthorized use by others upon dissimilar products. . . ." Some examples of post-*Allied* definitions are:

> We turn next to the likelihood of dilution, which occurs when the use of a name or mark by a subsequent user will lessen the uniqueness of the prior user's name or mark. The essence of dilution is the watering down of the potency of a mark and the gradual debilitation of its selling power. "Dilution" in this context refers to a loss of distinctiveness, a weakening of a mark's propensity to bring to mind a particular product, service, or source of either. Likelihood of confusion is therefore unnecessary to a finding of dilution. Section 368–d's [New York Anti–Dilution Statute] qualifying clause means exactly what its language denotes. Neither competition between the parties nor confusion about the source of products . . . appears to be necessary to state a cause of action for dilution. . . .

. . . Numerous opinions since *Allied* have noted the prevalent errors of prior opinions, particularly those which required a likelihood of confusion. Unfortunately, that misconception seems to be of a particularly virulent strain for it curiously and repetitively persists, even in the jurisdictions where the dawn of anti-dilution enlightenment currently seems to shine brightest. . . .

B. Differences of Goods, Marks and Names

Dilution occasionally is found unlikely because the accused use involves different goods, although use of the same or a closely similar mark on different goods traditionally has been considered the gravamen of a dilution problem, and in spite of the statutes' express provision for relief "notwithstanding the absence of competition between the parties."
. . .

Differences of goods and marks problems, so familiar in the context of likelihood-of-confusion causes of action, henceforth may be expected to arise frequently in dilution cases. As with confusion issues, they are difficult, nebulous and ephemeral fact questions of state of mind reaction to given stimuli. The likelihood of confusion issues, however, are focused essentially upon evaluating the likelihood of a mistaken state of mind resulting from a particular stimulus. The dilution issue, although entirely one of state of mind, raises no question of mistake, deception or confusion. Quite the contrary, the diluting effect can only occur when confusion as to source or origin is absent. It occurs when an awareness that a particular mark signifies "a single thing coming from a single source" becomes instead an unmistaken, correct awareness that the mark signifies various things from various sources. Of course, a given use—confusing as to source—ordinarily will result also in some dilution.

Usually, not all persons will be likely to be confused by a confusing use. For those not likely to be confused, a dilution reaction usually will result. There may be even a third category, those who consciously may be in doubt as to both possibilities, i.e., the same or a different source.

C. The Extent of Requisite Distinctiveness

... A meaningful dichotomy is developing now between those courts stressing and those deprecating strong distinctiveness as a sine qua non for protectibility against dilution. Some courts have adopted the view corresponding to the *Allied* dissent that any name or mark which in fact identifies its user should be protected against dilution to the extent it actually functions as an identifier. The opposite standard, endorsed by those who hold with the *Allied* majority's strong distinctiveness requirement, or who place greater emphasis upon uniqueness, arbitrariness, fame and celebrity, has even more adherents, among them, the respected treatise author Professor J. Thomas McCarthy.

Apparent in many opinions and discussions of the anti-dilution concept is a reluctance to apply the concept freely to protecting all such names and marks as would be entitled to the traditional type of protection against confusion. This reflects a judicial concern with inhibiting free commercial use of the language, and fear of fostering monopolies were mere ordinary marks and names afforded protection against dilution. Relief against traditional infringement or unfair competition requires a showing of likelihood of confusion which itself provides a pragmatic screen against excessive application. The nebulous, previously unfamiliar nature of the dilution tort, and the lack of any such screen perhaps engender excessive judicial restraint in dilution cases. Helpful as are the recent meaningful definitions of the doctrine, there is a need for more adjudication prescribing the metes and bounds of what should be protected against dilution.

As so often with the law, a middle ground probably is correct....

VI. *SOME OBSERVATIONS*

A. What Is Needed Now?

Much of the prolonged difficulty encountered by the dilution rationale seems to have derived from the sharp difference between its basic concept and that of the confusion of source rationale. The historical or traditional confusion of source torts of trademark infringement and trade identity unfair competition sound in deceit. Their talisman and test is a likelihood of confusion or deception as to source with the goods or services of the prior user. The facts of these cases take many forms, but the unitary rationale for all is the right to protection from confusion of identity. Their essential guideline and limit is that whatever identifies as to source is entitled to protection against a likelihood of confusion, but only to the extent it identifies and only to the extent confusion is likely.

Dilution results when use of a mark by others generates awareness that the mark no longer signifies anything unique, singular or particular, but instead may (or does) denominate several varying items from varying sources. In short, when use of the same or similar marks by others has caused a mark to become less distinctive than before, it has been diluted.

The tort of trademark or trade name dilution sounds not in deceit but in trespass and is a wrong damaging to an incorporeal property right in the sanctity of whatever distinguishing quality may be associated with one's mark or name. The right is to be protected against any trespass likely to diminish or destroy the distinguishing quality of that mark or name. The guideline and limit for protection against dilution is to protect the distinctive quality of that which is distinctive to the extent it is likely to be diluted or threatened with dilution....

B. Evolutionary Events

The market place, where trademarks are in action today, is a multimedia, mass merchandising one. The marketing revolution of the past three decades has permanently shifted consumer product distribution from the "hand to hand" methods that prevailed even into the 1950s to the fast tracks of media motivated, self-service and semi-self-service distribution. This applies not only for small, consumable and portable goods, but also for heavy appliances and similar items, even automobiles. The number of product brands and images now competing for a few instants of awareness by the consumer increases annually.

These pervasive changes have generated a dramatically increased need for realistic, effective and prompt protection of the enormous "commercial magnetism" values rapidly derived from the identifying use of marks and names in the complex and turbulent market place where billions of dollars are involved in purchaser choices every day. The need for the traditional protection against confusion of source remains and, indeed, is increasing. The need for effective protection against dilution, however, seems to have become acute. Happily, the dawn of acceptance for a legal rationale affording such protection also seems to have arrived.

Are the State Antidilution Laws Compatible With the National Protection of Trademarks?
MILTON HANDLER*

There were two theories on which the law of trademarks might have rested. One was the law of fraud and deceit and the other was trespass. In the early years of trademark litigation, patent lawyers who handled both specialties sought to analogize trademarks to patents and to treat the invasion of trademark rights as a trespass. The courts rejected the analogy. Pattishall, who is a leading proponent of dilution, frankly proposes that infringement be treated as a trespass....

He thus would replace what Learned Hand described as the Law and Prophets on the subject, "that one merchant shall not divert customers from another by representing what he sells as emanating from the second," with a trespass theory of protection. This is antithetical to the very origins and course of development of the common and federal statutory law of trademarks and unfair competition. One might question whether this is the direction in which the law of trademarks should

* 75 Trademark Rep. 269, 273–74, 276–82, 285–87 (1985).

proceed. The question, however, is at least in part quite academic since twenty-two states have already enacted antidilution laws. I want to discuss the merits of the dilution approach as a matter of public policy and to probe whether the dilution laws are compatible with the Lanham Act. . . .

The legislative history of neither [the Massachusetts nor the New York] state statutes provides any clear indication as to what marks are to be protected nor the degree of protection to be afforded. The key terms—distinctiveness and dilution—are left at large without even any elementary analysis of the statutory purposes or goals or the relationship of the novel concept of dilution to the traditional principles of the law of trademarks and unfair competition.

As is not unusual in the construction of new legislation, the courts, treating the dilution statutes as "alien intruders" into the law initially gave them little or no effect. . . .

More recently, there has been a one-hundred eighty degree shift in the judicial attitude towards the antidilution legislation. For example, in 1977 the New York Court of Appeals conceded that despite an "absence of judicial enthusiasm for the antidilution statutes," the New York statute extended "the protection afforded trademarks and trade names beyond that provided by actions for infringement and unfair competition." In short, the statute meant exactly what it said and should be applied by the courts in accordance with its plain meaning. An increasing number of courts are now taking a similar view of dilution protection. The shift is significant since it is probably easier for plaintiffs to prove dilution than a likelihood of confusion. But how much easier? The absence of any legislative definition of the key terms of the legislation has made it difficult to develop any judicial consensus on the meaning of "distinctiveness" and "dilution." Some courts have found marks sufficiently "distinctive" if they have acquired secondary meaning, while others have applied stricter standards of commercial celebrity. And, no one seems to know what degree of "whittling away" is necessary to constitute dilution. . . .

An overbroad view of the distinctiveness requirement could result in an undesirable monopolization of language. Schechter minimized any such effect by confining dilution to coined or fanciful marks. Others would limit it to celebrated marks of undeniable commercial magnetism. If all that is required is the existence of secondary meaning and if the theory is applicable even where the products are the same, have not we radically altered the law of trademarks, with trespass superseding deceit as the basis of protection? And if dilution applies to nondenominative and noncommercial usage, then the rights in secondary meaning marks will be on a parity with governmentally granted patents and the monopoly of language will be complete. Does this make sense as a matter of public policy?

The ambiguity of the antidilution legislation allows considerable latitude to the courts in determining what marks possess a distinctive quality warranting antidilution relief. Like Schechter, the courts can restrict this remedy to coined and invented marks. Or they may go further and include within the statute's ambit famous marks whose commercial magnetism is undeniable. They can draw the distinction, as they have done in traditional infringement actions, between strong and weak marks. There are secondary meaning marks that have achieved a high degree of celebrity that have as much if not more selling power than coined marks. Clearly, however, the run-of-the-mill brand names that are devoid of commercial magnetism, despite the existence of secondary meaning, are essentially incapable of being diluted. The broader the construction and application of these statutes, the greater is the likelihood of conflict with existing trademark jurisprudence. Conversely, the narrower the interpretation, the greater the prospect of compatibility and reconciliation.

It is ironic that although the legislation is specific that the absence of competition between the parties should not preclude injunctive relief, thus making it clear that the main thrust of the legislation was to deal, as did Schechter, with the extension of protection against the use of marks on noncompeting and unrelated products, the statute is now being invoked even where the products are the same. The legislation by its very terms responded to what was felt to be a need to extend protection beyond the very product upon which the mark was being used. There is no indication in the sparse legislative history or from the very wording of these laws that dilution or trespass was to be substituted for confusion and deception where the challenged use was on the same product.

Even more difficult than the determination of what categories of trademarks are eligible for antidilution relief, is the ascertainment of the intended meaning of dilution. Is the concept limited to the use of the identical mark? Or as in the law of trademarks proper, does the term embrace mere similarity? In trademark law similarity is qualified by the adjective "confusing." How similar must the marks be to warrant a finding of dilution or trespass? Let us take for example a compound mark consisting of two words or marks with prefixes or suffixes. There are many cases that hold that the common use of one of the words in such compound marks or of a prefix or suffix does not necessarily constitute infringement. The test is whether there is a likelihood of confusion. Does such usage, however, constitute dilution or trespass? Suppose we have a brand name consisting of six letters. The defendant duplicates one, two or three of such letters with or without some transposition. Does this constitute dilution no matter how different the marks in their totality may be? ...

If we choose to base the dilution doctrine on the present vague notions of what marks are distinctive and what constitutes dilution, we run the danger of further encouraging the litigation explosion now engulfing our courts....

Under the *Polaroid* doctrine, the existence of a likelihood of confusion is a function of many interdependent variables, including the strength of the plaintiff's mark, the defendant's good faith, the quality of the defendant's product, etc. In formulating this doctrine, the Second Circuit Court was seeking to protect the plaintiff's good will, both in the fields in which it was operating and the area of likely expansion, without at the same time unfairly burdening the defendant by denying it the use of a mark which was not causing the plaintiff any harm. Thus, in *Pfizer*, where the plaintiff alleged that its "Sportscreme" mark was infringed by the defendant's use of "Ben–Gay Sports Gel," the court applied *Polaroid* where the products were essentially the same, and observed that no one factor, not even the similarity of the marks, was sufficient to prove a likelihood of confusion. It adopted a balanced approach and considered the equities of the defendant's position as well as the claimed rights of the plaintiff. Dilution protection however does not permit of any such balancing—it relies on similarity only. Thus, it is conceivable that defendants, such as Pfizer, could in good faith adopt a mark and spend millions of dollars in advertising its products, yet be enjoined despite no likelihood of confusion or any injury to the plaintiff. Considering the difficulty of anticipating what marks can be diluted, and when they are in fact diluted, I believe such a regime would too often lead to results that are manifestly unfair.

Much of the problem stems from the general orientation of the dilution theory. While it strongly enhances the rights of plaintiffs, it fails to consider those of defendants. This type of approach runs contrary to the historical purposes of trademark law which recognizes the need in every case to weigh the rights of the plaintiff against those of the defendant....

Though they strengthen trademark protection and so further the Lanham Act's goal of affording to trademarks the greatest possible protection, the vice of the antidilution statutes is that they result in a lack of uniformity, producing a checkerboard jurisprudence, thus frustrating a major goal of the federal law....

There appears to be an effort to get Congress to amend the Lanham Act to embrace antidilution as a basis for federal trademark relief. I hope that many of you, realizing the disastrous effect such legislation may have on your clients and on the further development of the law in our chosen specialty, will join me in registering our opposition to any such change in the federal law. Let us strengthen the Lanham Act wherever necessary, so that consistent with our history and traditions, we will effectively protect the valuable brands and good will of our business enterprises without unnecessarily impairing the rights of others to engage in fair competition.

Notes and Questions

1. Columbia Law School Professor Milton Handler was also a founding partner of the law firm Kaye Scholer. Professor Handler graduated from Columbia Law School in 1926 and taught antitrust and trade regulation there for nearly 50 years. He authored one of the country's first textbooks on trade regulation. He died in 1998, at age 95.

2. Charles Pickett received his B.S. from CCNY in 1925 and his J.D. from Columbia University in 1928. He was admitted to the NY Bar in 1931. He was first an associate at the firm Chadbourne, Stanchfield and Levy, and later was an associate at Chadbourne, Wallace, Park and Whiteside.

3. When the Federal Anti–Dilution Statute ultimately passed in 1996, Professor J. Thomas McCarthy characterized it as "a very potent piece of legislation. All who do business in the United States will have to deal with it either as a sword or will be looking for a shield against claims under the new law." J. Thomas McCarthy, *The 1996 Federal Anti–Dilution Statute*, 16 Cardozo Arts & Ent. L.J. 587, 599 (1998). He further predicted that, as judges began to interpret this new legislation, "the difficulty of determining what marks are 'famous,' will, I think, continue and the definitional process will be vague and imprecise." Id.

Five years later, Judge Pierre Leval reiterated this concern, warning:

> It is important that courts take seriously their delegated duty to interpret the [Dilution] Act. ... They must ... ensure that the requirements of fame and distinctiveness are stringently enforced. Words like "fame" and "distinctiveness" are tricky.
> . . .
>
> The legislative history tells us that Congress intended the Act to apply to truly famous marks that are truly distinctive, truly unusual—names like Buick, Dupont or Kodak, and the right cannot reasonably apply to ordinary descriptive marks that have achieved acquired distinctiveness. If it did, the distinctiveness requirement would be nullified. By definition, every mark that has become famous has acquired distinctiveness. Without acquired distinctiveness, it wouldn't be famous. To allow the Act to apply to a weak descriptive mark, on the basis of acquired distinctiveness, would mean that big companies using common descriptive names—American, National, Western, New York, etc.—could preempt those ordinary names, enjoining hundreds of other users in every area of commerce. The weakest marks would enjoy the strongest rights. This was certainly not what Congress intended.

Pierre N. Leval, *Trademark: Champion of Free Speech*, 27 Colum. J. Law & Arts 187, 208–09 (2004). Suppose courts heed Judge Leval's caution against misuse of the statute to benefit marks whose protection Congress did not intend to reinforce. Is there still a problem regarding the scope of protection of those marks Congress *did* intend to cover?

4. Recall the rationales for protection against "dilution" and protection against source confusion. Is the move from deceit to trespass problematic? Is there a danger that trademark can be leveraged to perpetuate intellectual property monopolies that are supposed to endure for only "limited Times?" On the other hand, are trademark protections a legitimate method of filling in gaps in copyright protection? For example, the copyright law does not entitle most authors to name credit; to what extent can or should the trademark law supply a remedy? See, e.g., Roberta Rosenthal Kwall, *The Attribution Right in the United States: Caught in the Crossfire Between Copyright and Section 43(A)*, 77 Wash. L. Rev. 985 (2002); Jane C. Ginsburg, *The Right to Claim Authorship in U.S. Copyright and Trademarks Law*, 41 Hous. L. Rev. 263 (2004).

The Death of Ontology: A Teleological Approach to Trademark Law

GRAEME B. DINWOODIE*

INTRODUCTION

We live in an age of abundant symbolism, which generates a glut of meaning: meaning is everywhere, and everything has meaning. Meaning is constructed not only from verbal communication, but also from sensory experience, personal conduct and physical surroundings. And postmodern scholars tell us that meaning is contingent; it is individuated, contextualized, and unconstrained by the illusory crutches of shared idiom and common understanding. What then is trademark law, the law that governs symbolic meaning in the marketplace, to make of this contemporary perspective? This Article contends that, in order to regulate effectively the present-day marketplace, trademark law must recognize the limitless sources of meaning; it must confront the postmodern reality that meaning arises from context and experience rather than from the intrinsic essence of matter.

This proposition may, to the traditional trademark scholar, appear dangerously indeterminate and unconfined. But this Article also affirms the limited nature of trademark protection. Trademark law regulates only a particular form of meaning. It deals merely with symbols that identify the source of a product and distinguish that product from others, and it extends such symbols protection solely against confusing imitation. This restricted scope of protection enables courts to prevent consumer confusion—trademark's primary purpose—without interfering unduly with the economic climate of free competition.

Historically, the ability of trademark law to obviate consumer confusion without impeding competition was also assisted by restricting the types of symbols to which it would readily accord the fullest protection. Words and two-dimensional pictorial images, which are the most common types of trademark subject-matter, generally possess characteristics that facilitate compliance with trademark's intended limits. Most importantly, their appropriation by a single producer does not affect the capacity of others to produce competing goods. Protecting the right of a solitary producer to label a personal computer with the word "APPLE" or the picture of an apple does not unduly restrict competitors from manufacturing a rival product. It is perhaps unsurprising, therefore, that trademark law traditionally privileged the source-identifying capacity of these classes of subject-matter, and circumscribed protection of other classes such as product color or design features that do not share those comforting characteristics.

Besides, this approach arguably reflected a generalized truth about the respective capacity of words and non-verbal subject-matter to bear meaning for consumers. Words, it was assumed, best identified the source of products, and this assumption may have (for some period of time) been largely consonant with reality. But making these generalized

* 84 Iowa L. Rev. 611, 613–18, 621–24, 624–5, 632–39, 643–44 (1999).

assumptions about the proficiency of particular classes of subject-matter to convey meaning is under attack. The very use of generalized assumptions has been challenged as a matter of philosophical theory, and current social observation suggests that the communicative predominance of linguistic matter is eroding. Postmodern thought challenges the notion that meaning is determined by overarching truths, and instead exalts the theory that individuated meaning ensues from particular contexts. And our semiotic senses are in a state of tumult. Society is becoming more visual, and less lexical. Members of Generation X discard unwanted digital documents by clicking on an icon of a trash-can rather than by typing "delete" or "erase." Moreover, this trend is likely only to increase as the pressures of global commerce and technological advances reduce the barriers of distance and difference. While languages divide, other (non-linguistic) forms of symbols might possess homogenizing capacities that producers may exploit.

In this social context, a broad array of non-traditional symbols are increasingly apt to serve as trademarks (or, as nonverbal matter is called, "trade dress") by identifying a product's source. Trademark protection based upon a symbol's ontological classification as a word, picture, shape, packaging, design, color, or smell, is estranged from reality—whether reality is uncovered by abstract philosophical discourse or more concrete empirical observation of late twentieth century experience. Because protecting source-identifying symbols in the marketplace is the very raison d'être of trademark law, it would be an abdication of responsibility for trademark law to repudiate that presently-constituted and more deeply understood reality. More particularly, it would countenance significant competitive costs that flow from permitting the creation of consumer confusion.

While recognition of this postmodern reality is thus important and appropriate, it is not without its difficulties. Although nontraditional subject-matter may equally identify a product's source and distinguish it from other products, protecting that nontraditional matter as a trademark may give rise to very different consequences than protecting traditional trademark subject-matter. If ontological restrictions upon trademark subject-matter are removed, a new set of limits must prudently be established if trademark protection is not to spawn adverse competitive effects from overprotection. In this Article, I suggest that such limits can be found by tethering trademark law directly to its limited purposes, and by grounding protection not in over-generalized assumptions, but rather in the real present-day impact of particular symbols in society. . . .

[T]rademark protection should depend upon whether the particular symbolic matter identifies the source of a product (i.e., whether the matter is "distinctive"), and upon whether protection of the particular symbol would accord the producer a practical monopoly and prevent effective competition by others (i.e., whether the matter is "functional"). Distinctiveness is a prerequisite for protection, and functionality restricts protection. Together, and applied with particularity, these inquiries into real-life effects—and not reliance upon generalized assumptions—should set the parameters of what protection trademark law should offer. . . .

I. THE DEVELOPMENT OF TRADE DRESS PROTECTION FOR PRODUCT DESIGN

In the early years of the Lanham Act, disputes under the Act largely involved producers claiming rights in words and two-dimensional logos that identified the source of their products and distinguished them from the goods of others. Over time, however, the categories of subject-matter protected as trademarks grew to encompass the packaging or receptacles in which products were contained. This expansion in subject-matter reflected the realization that consumers had come to identify and distinguish products by their packaging. Consumers clearly identified the carbonated soft drink produced by the Coca–Cola Company as much from the shape of the bottle in which it was contained as by the word COKE® emblazoned on the side of the bottle. Eventually, this acceptance of the growing bases for consumer identification led to the acknowledgment that the source o a product could be identified not only by the packaging in which was contained (for example, the appearance of the box in which the new iMac personal computer is sold) but by the design of a product itself (for example, the very appearance of the iMac personal computer). The first recognition of this development at the federal appellate level came in 1976 from the Eighth Circuit in Truck Equipment Service Co. v. Fruehauf Corp., where the court of appeals affirmed a successful infringement claim predicated upon the appearance of the hopper of a truck acting to identify its source. In the following two decades, courts have protected as trade dress the design features of an extensive range of products including kitchen appliances, sporting equipment, candies, bathroom fittings, sports cars, giant gumball machines, furniture, hardware items, fashion accessories, lamps, and even golf holes.

Recognition that a source-identifying product design could be protected under the Lanham Act against confusingly similar designs precipitated an increasingly large number of suits to enjoin product simulation. Indeed, this activity under the federal trademark statute became an integral part of design protection efforts on the part of many producers, largely because designs received inadequate protection under other intellectual property laws (i.e., copyright and design patent) that would appear at first glance more suited to the protection of designs. A decade ago, the late Ralph Brown noted that "[i]f the flow of reported decisions is any guide to the pace of activity in the real world, unfair competition law appears to be overtaking both copyright and design patent as a source of protection for designs." Ten years later, a torrent of cases pursued under the Lanham Act—which embodies both federal unfair competition law and its sibling regime of trademark—has increased rather than abated. These developments have, however, caused significant problems for trademark and unfair competition law.

II. SHAPES ARE NOT WORDS: THE PROBLEMS PRECIPITATED BY TRADE DRESS PROTECTION FOR PRODUCT DESIGN

Three primary difficulties are raised by the expansion in the subject-matter covered by trademark laws to include product design. First, because product design is potentially protected under other intellectual property regimes, addressing design under trademark law challenges the neatness of the traditional intellectual property paradigms whereby art was protected by copyright, functional inventions under patent, and source-identifiers such as words or slogans under trademark law. A product's design is art; it may embody a functional invention; and increasingly it may act as a product's source-identifier. The shape of a classic Ferrari sports car may at once be an artistic work of authorship, embody an aerodynamic advance that enhances a car's acceleration, and serve to inform consumers that the car is made by Ferrari. Trademark law properly deals with product design only in so far as it performs this final role as a source-identifier. But in so doing, it runs the risk of regulating the product as art or as a functional invention, both of which are properly the domain of other intellectual property regimes (specifically, copyright and patent).

Second, the expansion in intellectual property protection that typically accompanies subject-matter moving beyond its traditional regime gives rise to concerns of disrupting the competitive equilibrium carefully embodied in each of the respective regimes. In particular, the patent and copyright statutes contain many detailed limitations and exemptions to balance the rights of creators and inventors, on the one hand, and users and later developers on the other. In contrast, a trademark law that accorded very limited rights against the confusingly similar use of words, of which there are an infinite supply, had less occasion to address that balance.

Finally, the breakdown in the historical treatment of different categories of subject-matter by different intellectual property regimes has strained analytical concepts developed only with reference to the traditional (and hence dominant) subject-matter of the respective regimes. Trademark analysis was developed largely to determine the protectability of words and two-dimensional logos; as applied to shapes, that analysis has proven formalistic and unhelpful. As a result of its grounding in the different premises applicable to words, it fails either to reveal the basis for protecting one design but not another, or to reflect the different social and competitive conditions of a society that is increasingly visual rather than lexical. . . .

B. THE EXCLUSIONARY NATURE OF PROTECTING DESIGNS

Protecting nontraditional subject-matter such as designs under the trademark laws may also affect the competitive balance reflected in that regime. Affording trademark rights in source-identifying words is minimally intrusive upon the competitive capacities of other producers. Although contemporary scholarship suggests that trademark rights in words may be exclusionary in expressive and political terms—and that scholarship offers a useful parallel for addressing the similarly exclusionary effect of product design trade dress rights—trademark protection for words occasions only a slight exclusionary effect if measured in competitive terms. The range of words by which to identify (as opposed to describe) a particular product is infinite, particularly as trademark law generously treats the use of neologisms as source-identifiers, and thus it is easy to adopt an alternative label for a competing product; the part of the lexical commons that is appropriated by the first producer is very small. The grant of trademark rights in a verbal mark typically does not make it significantly more difficult for a competitor to produce a rival product; restricting the words by which the competitor may identify its product does not limit the ways in which the competitor may design its product. And rarely will a word selected to identify a product of itself make the product more desirable to consumers. Finally, the scope of trademark rights excludes only confusingly similar uses of the word by competitors: uses on wholly dissimilar goods may well be noninfringing because they are less likely to cause confusion among consumers.

Although these last two characteristics must be qualified in light of modern merchandising practices, which increasingly treat even verbal trademarks as commodities in and of themselves, and the availability of dilution claims, the non-exclusionary nature of traditional trademark rights has forestalled much criticism of anti-competitiveness to which other intellectual property regimes are increasingly subjected. Aspects of trademark law have episodically attracted adverse comment from a competitive standpoint, but on the whole trademark protection has withstood such malediction because of its merely incidental effect on the costs and opportunities of production and its more limited scope.

Support for trademark law can, however, be stated more positively. By protecting the integrity of consumer understanding, trademark protection affirmatively promotes competitive values. Safeguarding the reliability of informational short-cuts reduces costs ("search costs") to consumers of becoming informed about the benefits of a particular brand. From the producer's perspective, by guarding the market identity of a product, trademark law provides incentives to manufacture goods of distinction and consistent quality, secure in the knowledge that efforts to differentiate them from other products will be protected, and that the goodwill flowing from the quality or distinction will not be appropriated. This in turn enhances diversity of product and thus consumer choice. And protecting alternative and distinguishable products, rather than encouraging competition in a single product of every type, arguably assists smaller enterprises; such enterprises might be swamped by larger competitors (or low quality producers) if the only competitive variable were efficiency of plants and distribution networks (or lowering of cost by reductions in quality) rather than different qualities of product.

These same pro-competitive values are furthered by trade dress protection, which subsists under the same statute for the same purposes. Nevertheless, in contrast to word marks, product design trade dress rights are more likely to be exclusionary in nature. These rights are more likely to afford protection to something that is in and of itself of value to the consumer. And, perhaps more importantly, it is easier to call a product by another name than to make a product work by another design; the supply of shapes by which to design a particular product is more confined. Consumers may recognize the Sunbeam food mixer by its distinctive configuration; but if Sunbeam obtains trade dress rights in the mixer's design features, those rights may curtail the capacity of competitors to produce a rival food mixer that neatly collects diced vegetables in a round salad bowl ready for serving. If the first manufacturer of a frisbee obtained trademark rights in the aerodynamic shape of that product, rival products might be unable to hover. Where trademark rights are granted in product designs, therefore, the restraints imposed upon a competitor's choice of source-identifier may (unlike word marks) effectively act as a constriction of production choices.

In light of the more limited supply of designs, systems with a primary intent to accord intellectual property protection to spatial features include a range of safeguards to prevent the grant of overbroad rights to a single producer. Trademark laws do not possess the same built-in safety-valves. In particular, trademark law does not contain pre-fixed temporal limits; unlike copyright law it contains no express exclusion of protection for ideas; and unlike patent law, it does not require the design to achieve any level of creativity or novelty so as to regulate the appropriation of matter in the public domain. The interpretation of trademark protection as pro-competitive or (at worst) benign is largely premised upon the dominant subject-matter of words and two-dimensional pictorial images; reviews of its competitive effect have been increasingly less sanguine as the subject-matter of trademark protection has expanded to protect designs.

Yet, as noted above, trade dress protection for product designs offers the same competitive advantages as protection for words. To be sure, product design trade dress protection may stock greater potential to generate anti-competitive consequences, but that should not detract from its fundamentally pro-competitive character when properly confined. All overbroad intellectual property rights represent risks to the competitive environment. The potentially different competitive effect of trademark protection for words and shapes should thus be acknowledged but not overstated. The competitive costs of protection must be balanced with its competitive gains.

C. CLASSICAL TRADEMARK ANALYSIS DOES NOT ACCOMMODATE EVOLUTION IN THE RECEPTION AND CREATION OF MEANING

The final difficulty caused by the expansion of trademark subject-matter to include product design reflects a broader concern stemming from an evolution in the ways that society communicates. The roots of trademark law are firmly planted in the protection afforded words—words that identified a product's source, served no other communicative function, and represented the primary means by which the public received short-form information about the source of goods or services. These assumptions have been undermined by a paradox of the late twentieth century: the primacy of words as source-identifiers is eroding while the broader communicative significance of trademarks is growing. . . .

[V]isual communication is different from textual communication. While the visual form may function to identify a product's source and thus equally implicate the purpose of trademark protection, it has a lesser developed idiom, which renders our assessment of it more complex and less intuitive. And a visual medium may provide less freedom for competitors to deviate from standardized norms, although this may recede as we develop a larger and more refined shared "dictionary" (a "pictionary," perhaps) for visual matter. This is not to say that visual symbols are ineffective tools of communication; indeed, they may in a single symbol communicate more effectively and more precisely than words. It is a truism that, sometimes, a picture is worth a thousand words. Rather, because visual symbols pack information and meaning even more intensely into a single unit than words, granting rights in a visual symbol may appropriate to an individual much more of the communicative commons....

Notes and Questions

1. Professor Graeme Dinwoodie teaches at Chicago–Kent College of law, where he is also Associate Dean, Director of the Program in Intellectual Property Law, and Norman and Edna Freehling Scholar. Professor Dinwoodie holds a First Class Honors LL.B. degree in Private Law from the University of Glasgow, an LL.M. from Harvard Law School, and a J.S.D. from Columbia Law School. He was the Burton Fellow in residence at Columbia Law School for 1988–89, working in the field of intellectual property law, and a John F. Kennedy Scholar at Harvard Law School for 1987–88.

2. Consider the doctrine of "aesthetic functionality" in trade dress protection. According to Professor Dinwoodie:

> The aesthetic functionality doctrine as first articulated can be, and was, subjected to telling criticism. In its original form, the doctrine possessed the potential to emasculate trademark protection for designs, particularly for successful designs. It rewarded fruitless designs with unnecessary protection, but exposed successful designs to unchecked imitation. . . .
>
> [One] explanation of the doctrine reveals the presumption that ornamental designs cannot identify source (or will not be recognized as identifying source) in addition to pleasing the consumer's aesthetic tastes. Only a design that does nothing other than identify source can act as a trademark. . . . [This] version of aesthetic functionality is merely a categorical exclusion of design features from trademark protection. . . [I]if trademark law is to retain a doctrine of aesthetic functionality, it must be rooted in some value other than an exclusion of source-identifying design features that serve no other role or that do not primarily serve a source-identifying role.

Graeme B. Dinwoodie, *The Death of Ontology: A Teleological Approach to Trademark Law*, 84 Iowa L. Rev. 611, 690–93 (1999). See also, Jessica Litman, Note, *The Problem of Functional Features: Trade Dress Infringement Under Section 43(a) of the Lanham Act*, 82 Colum. L. Rev. 77 (1982). What value would provide an appropriate theoretical foundation for aesthetic functionality?

Expressive Genericity: Trademarks as Language in the Pepsi Generation

ROCHELLE COOPER DREYFUSS*

Trademarks have come a long way. Originating in the stratified economy of the middle ages as a marketing tool of the merchant class, these symbols have passed into popular culture. During the journey, ideograms that once functioned solely as signals denoting the source, origin, and quality of goods, have become products in their own right, valued as indicators of the status, preferences, and aspirations of those who use them. Some trademarks have worked their way into the English language; others provide bases for vibrant, evocative metaphors. In a sense, trademarks are the emerging lingua franca: with a sufficient command of these terms, one can make oneself understood the world over, and in the process, enjoy the comforts of home.

Trademark law has not kept pace with trademark practice. Concerned initially with maintaining the lines of communication between the mercantile class and its customers, the law encouraged entrepreneurs to invest in quality-producing activities by protecting the goodwill that inhered in their source-identifying marks. Thus, in both state unfair competition cases and federal trademark actions, claims focused on the impact of the mark on purchasing decisions. By the same token, defenses centered on the commercial requirements of the competitive marketplace. The terms that delimited the reach of trademark law-consumer confusion, gap bridging, fair use, genericity, abandonment-were understood strictly by reference to these commercial interests.

But as trademark owners have begun to capitalize on the salience of these symbols in the culture, the justifications that formerly delineated the scope of the law have lost significance. The Mets' right to prevent others from selling banners, caps, and tee shirts marked with its logo could not initially be explained on quality-promotion grounds so long as it was clear that fans are not confused, and that they did not regard the franchise as insuring the quality of anything but a baseball team. Nor does traditional trademark law offer an account for, or limits to, McDonald's claim to control non-food uses of the prefix "Mc," or George Lucas's attempt to exclude public interest groups from utilizing the title of his movie, "Star Wars."

Lacking the traditional analytical tools provided by trademark law, courts have lately attempted to apply first amendment jurisprudence to such claims.... [A]lthough the Constitution supplies a normative principle favoring public access to the tools of expression, the body of law that has developed under the first amendment provides a surprisingly uncongenial framework for analysis. Perhaps this provision is simply too blunt an instrument to parse rights to individual words; perhaps its focus on the communication of ideas makes it an inappropriate way to think about the linguistic material by which ideas are conveyed.... Indeed, the controversy surrounding the burning of an American flag—the

* 65 Notre Dame L. Rev. 397, 397–99, 405–06, 407, 416–18 (1990).

trademark of the United States—demonstrates how little the law under-stands the evocative significance of trademarks and how poorly current jurisprudential techniques deal with conflicting claims to these ideo-grams. . . .

If investment is dispositive of the trademark owner's right to control, then the public's ability to evoke the expressive dimension of marks is in danger of significant restriction. Furthermore, fallacies in the fundamental assumptions made by courts that have approved this "if value, then right" theory mean that the right lacks a coherent limit. Without a principled way to bound the power of control, it is not possible to fashion defenses analogous to the sort commonly found in real property, trademark, copyright, patent, or state-based intellectual prop-erty law.

The point concerning the effect of the new theory on expressive concerns can be demonstrated by considering the use of trademarks in parodies, which have been considered important vehicles for social commentary at least since the time of Chaucer. Others have noted that even modest expansion of the domain of trademark law has threatened such usages, but the problem is now much more severe. Girl Scouts v. Personality Posters Manufacturing, for instance, involved the sale of posters depicting a pregnant girl dressed in a Girl Scout uniform over the motto, "Be Prepared." Before courts began to adopt the new reason-ing, this was analyzed as a Polaroid type of case in which the unlikeli-hood of consumer confusion led the court to conclude that the trademark owner did not require relief. However, once the right to capture all the value in a signal is accepted, it is difficult to see why the Girl Scouts should be unable to control the humorous benefit that comes from contrasting pregnancy with the public perception of Girl Scouts. Since it is the scouting organization that created the perception, it should, under this reasoning, be the one to decide when, where, and if the slogan invoked. . . .

The fallacies in the right/value theory can be revealed in a number of ways, not the least of which is that the choice for assigning surplus value is not between a trademark owner and a trademark user-Mattel and BVD-but between trademark owners and the public-Mattel and tee-shirt consumers. If Mattel is given (through trademark law or another legal regime) the right to exclude others from selling "Barbie" tee shirts, then it can indeed charge a premium over the cost of manufacturing the shirt, which will be paid by those purchasers who value the product at or above the set price. If, on the other hand, no one has an exclusive right to use the word on a shirt, a supracompetitive price will presumably attract rivals, who will compete it down to cost. In that event, the surplus value will go not to BVD or to Mattel, but to purchasers. Since it is they who found uses for "Barbie" in excess of signaling, this does not seem like a case in which parties reap that which they have not sown.

To put this in a larger context, public goods can usually be made into exclusive property by operation of law; the issue in such cases is whether there is a justification for giving private parties wealth that would otherwise accrue to those who use the goods. Outside the signaling context (where trademark rights are protected), increasing the pool of word utilizers does not impose costs on prior users in the way that, say, adding cattle to a pasture detracts from its ability to maintain the first farmer's herd. Accordingly, and contrary to the dissents' implication in Johnson, the rationale that supports exclusive rights in real property has no application here. . . .

Since the process of producing a word is expensive, the real question in requiring substitution through nominal definition is, who should pay the cost. As between members of the public . . . who wish to use trademarks expressively and trademark owners . . . , the latter appears to be the superior choice. First, the cost of developing perfect synonyms for marks could be considered part of the quid pro quo for acquiring control over them. It is, in contrast, difficult to see how a single expressive user could capture enough of the benefits of a new word to compensate for the cost of developing it. Although this user could ask for contributions from the public, which would also benefit from the naming of new conceptualizations, the transaction costs involved in such an enterprise are likely to be prohibitive. Second, trademark owners are already in the business of developing words and advertising their meaning. The marginal cost of developing two words for the same concept is surely lower than the cost that a member of the public would incur in creating only one word. Moreover, words are most readily adopted into language when they fill conceptual voids; indeed, most trademarks that have passed into the language have done so precisely because there was no other word to describe the product they signified. Since trademark owners control timing, they are in the best position to exploit the window of opportunity provided by the existence of empty language slots.

In fact, the notion of imposing this duty on trademark owners is not new, for the doctrine of genericity works exactly this way. It protects the efficacy of communication by recognizing the public's need for a trademark that becomes the common signifier for the set to which the product on which it appears belongs. Such marks are considered generic, and a successful demonstration of genericity is a defense to infringement actions. Not only does the doctrine protect public access to important words, it has a significant side effect. An owner that does not wish to lose its mark will often introduce a second word, which it educates the public to use for the category. The trademark itself can then retain its role as a signal. . . .

If the Court's ability to compartmentalize vocabulary and understand language contextually is a universal facility—and linguistic research indicates that it is—then trademark law could be altered with this capacity in mind. Thus, it should be possible to build upon the defenses that trademark law has constructed for the competitive vocabulary a parallel set of principles to protect expressive speech. In a regime that recognized the facility to compartmentalize, signaling functions would be analysed according to the conventional Polaroid principles [for assessing likelihood of confusion], and the newly developed doctrines would operate to allocate rights when trademarks are used expressively. Proprietary rights to marks would then be protected across the entire signaling spectrum, except in instances in which expressive communication was suppressed by the loss of vocabulary.

Reliance on traditional trademark principles as a framework for expressive speech may appear incongruous in view of the remarks made earlier about the dissonance between the justifications for trademark protection and the motivation that has led to the recognition of rights in hybrid cases. However, trademark law has several properties that make it a useful place to begin developing a jurisprudence that can analyze claims to the expressive vocabulary. This branch of the law is one of the only areas in which the problem of words, as distinguished from ideas, has received systematic analysis. The lack of cases at the antitrust/trademark and first amendment/trademark interface is some indication that the structure it has developed ably protects communicative efficiency within the marketplace of commerce. Accordingly, it holds some promise for the marketplace of ideas. Furthermore, its method of analysis has managed to avoid the need to decide which of its elements are constitutionally compelled. In light of the difficulty in deciding when "symbols [are] sufficiently special to warrant ... unique status" under the first amendment, a prudentially-based scheme, whose doctrines act as a buffer between proprietary and public claims, may be the wisest, and only available avenue for fully safeguarding speech.

Notes and Questions

1. What role does the general public play in the reception and creation of a trademark's meaning? To what extent does trademark law accommodate the popular appropriation of trade-names and symbols? Judge Alex Kozinski observes:

> The originator of a trademark or logo cannot simply assert, "It's mine, I own it, and you have to pay for it any time you use it." Words and images do not worm their way into our discourse by accident; they're generally thrust there by well-orchestrated campaigns intended to burn them into our collective consciousness. Having embarked on that endeavor, the originator of the symbol necessarily—and justly—must give up some measure of control. The originator must understand that the mark or symbol or image is no longer entirely its own, and that in some sense it also belongs to all those other minds who have received and integrated it. This does not imply a total loss of control, however, only that the public's right to make use of the word or image must be considered in the balance as we decide what rights the owner is entitled to assert.

Alex Kozinski, *Trademarks Unplugged*, 84 Trademark Rep. 441, 456–57 (1994).

2. Professor Michael Madow, analysing the right of publicity, provides a contrasting post-modern perspective on the role the public plays in generating the meaning of popular culture:

> [D]espite the dominance of global entertainment conglomerates, popular culture is not simply something that is "fabricated by technicians hired by businessmen" and then imposed

from above upon a passive, atomized, and uncritical populace. ...[T]he consumers of cultural commodities are not all "cultural dopes." Their participation is not "limited to the choice between buying and not buying." Instead, the consumption of cultural commodities can be, and often is, an active, creative practice, in which the "consumer" appropriates the product by investing it with (new) meaning ... [Even within significant] constraints, individuals and groups do participate actively in the process of generating and circulating meanings that constitutes "culture." ...

[T]he so-called "national audience" for mainstream cultural products is in reality composed of a large number of overlapping subgroups and subcultures structured along racial, ethnic, gender, generational, occupational, and other lines. These groups have their own histories, experiences, interests, and cultural competencies, which they bring to bear in the consumption (that is, the reception and appropriation) of cultural commodities. For this reason, popular culture remains what it long has been: a struggle for, and over, meaning. ... It is impossible, I think, for the law to remain neutral in this contest.

Michael Madow, *Private Ownership of Public Image: Popular Culture and Publicity Rights*, 81 Cal. L. Rev. 127, 139–41 (1993). Whose analysis about the public's role in the reception and creation of meaning do you find more persuasive? To what extent do Professor Madow and Judge Kozinski ultimately disagree? Does the scope of trademark protection depend on which theory you apply?

3. To what extent, if at all, does trademark law threaten First Amendment values? Consider Professor Denicola's perspective:

Judicial antipathy toward the enrichment that flows to the copyist has carried trademark owners to a series of triumphs over competing contentions. At some point, however, extensions of the trademark monopoly must be tempered by the realization that unlimited control over the of trade symbols will at times interfere with the exercise of basic first amendment rights.

Trademark law, even if more by chance than design, has generally avoided such constitutional confrontations. Traditional theory, with its reliance on the confusion rationale, poses no threat to freedom of speech. Even the misappropriation and dilution rationales, whatever their substantive merits, do not endanger free speech interests when directed at the decorative or trademark use of another's mark. When the trademark is utilized as a vehicle for the communication of ideas, however, constitutional interests can no longer be ignored.

That the protection of trademarks does not on the whole exceed permissible bounds is no consolation to one whose constitutional rights are jeopardized. Nor is judicial intuition alone, however well educated, a sufficiently secure barrier against the infringement of free speech interests. When substantive standards offer the convenient malleability that characterizes the law of trademarks, nothing short of a candid examination of the constitutional implications of asserted rights can satisfactorily defend constitutional preserves.

Robert C. Denicola, *Trademarks as Speech: Constitutional Implications of the Emerging Rationales for the Protection of Trade Symbols*, 1982 Wis. L. Rev. 158, 206–07 (1982).

4. Evoking perceived judicial antipathy to satiric use of trademarks, Harriette Dorsen echoes Professor Denicola's concerns:

> Many trademark infringement cases involving satire misapply the language of the statutes and impose liability on a theory similar to satiric appropriation—which provides the basis of a remedy for defamation—here for damage to a trademark's 'reputation.' Where the satiric use is viewed as distasteful, the courts may find harm to reputation in the possibility that consumers will assume that the trademark owners were the source of the publication and thus think less of the product, just as a defamatory statement about individuals might lower them in the community's esteem. As one court put it: 'A "trademark" is not what is infringed. What is infringed is the right of the public to be free of confusion and the synonymous right of a trademark owner to control his product's reputation.' Use of the word 'reputation' in this context, however, confuses the issue. Trademark law is not meant to protect reputation in the defamation sense but only in the sense that the mark not lose its ability to distinguish one product from another. . . .
>
> . . . [Granting] relief for what is nothing more than 'satiric appropriation.' Such holdings violate[s] . . . the first amendment. Injunctions granted in such cases threaten to stifle legitimate satiric comment. A proper analysis must recognize that the satiric use of a trademark, while unauthorized and arguably in bad taste, is nevertheless protected by law. Only where likelihood of consumer confusion can be shown should the satirist be liable. Harm to business reputation should not be a factor

Harriette K. Dorsen, *Satiric Appropriation and the Law of Libel, Trademark and Copyright: Remedies Without Wrongs*, 65 B.U.L. Rev. 923, 924, 941–42, 949–52 (1986).

5. Compare Judge Leval's retrospective on a ruling he had made as a district court judge, when he held that the First Amendment blocked a claim of trademark infringement brought against *New York Magazine*'s satiric appropriation of the cover of the *Old Farmer's Almanac*:

> I have no regrets about the ultimate decision but now believe my analysis was flawed. We lawyers learn in kindergarten how important it is to avoid unnecessary constitutional adjudications. Did I need to rely on, even create, constitutional doctrine? Clearly not—for at least two reasons.
>
> First, before making my First Amendment ruling, I had determined that [the defendant's] joking reference to the [plain-

tiff's trademark] was instantly recognizable as a joke. ... It is an essential element of an action for trademark infringement that the defendant have caused a likelihood of confusion—a likelihood that consumers will be confused as to whether the plaintiff is associated with the defendant's product or message. Without likelihood of consumer confusion, the [plaintiff] could not win under the trademark laws. So why make a Constitutional ruling?

The problem goes still deeper. It is a mistake to see the trademark law as a unidirectional rule—a one-way highway of exclusivity eventually blocked off by the First Amendment. To the contrary, the trademark law is a complex, integrated body of rules which is deeply concerned with the protection of free expression. Trademark, like copyright, does indeed place limitations on speech. But, as in the case of copyright, it has always had as a central concern distinguishing between speech that should be suppressed and speech that should not. Merchants need a source-identifying mark; society requires freedom for certain kinds of messages. Trademark law developed as an integrated body of rules to balance the potential conflict ...Where the trademark law, by its own terms, protects the unauthorized use of another's trademark, there is no need to turn to the Constitution to justify a judgment in the alleged infringer's favor.

Pierre N. Leval, *Trademark: Champion of Free Speech*, 27 Colum. J. Law & Arts 187, 188–89 (2004). Do you agree that trademark law by its own terms safeguards free speech values? See, e.g., Stacy Dogan, An Exclusive Right to Evoke, XLIV B.C. L. Rev. 291 (2003) (raising concern that federal and state antidilution laws could give trademark owners control over the cultural associations that their marks evoke).

IV

Design Protection

I. History and Basic Concepts

The borderline between copyright and patent has proven to be a difficult one. Few issues bring out the conflict more clearly than the matter of industrial designs. It is clear that conventional artistic expression that happens to be attached to some useful object, and is easily removed from it—think of a Rodin statue bolted to a desk—is copyrightable. Equally straightforward is the case of a useful item whose shape, though dictated by functionality, just happens to be aesthetically pleasing. For example, the prosaic "carabiner" or metal clasp well-known to serious rock climbers is considered aesthetically pleasing by many non-climbers, who use them as key chains and the like. Beyond these clear examples lie a host of knotty questions.

In the U.S., creative expression is protected by copyright. So long as a work of expression is "separable" from an underlying object, copyright will protect it. The "separability" test, described in the second excerpt below, creates enormous problems in copyright law. On the other extreme, patents are available for all useful items regardless of their aesthetic appeal. For items of "ornamental design," a special design patent statute is available. Designs that are novel and nonobvious are subject to protection under this statute, but many designs fail to meet these requirements.

The first excerpt below describes the evolution of legal regimes to protect industrial designs in Europe and the U.S. The author describes the relationship between copyright protection and special (or "sui generis") design protection statutes. The analysis traces the development of two primary schools of thought: (1) "cumulation," which permits a work's creator to protect the work with copyright and design protection; and (2) "dissociation," which requires the legal system to segregate works into those that are protectible only under copyright and those that are protectible only under design protection law; there is no overlap.

506

Design Protection in Domestic and Foreign Copyright Law: From the Berne Revision of 1948 to the Copyright Act of 1976*

J. H. REICHMAN

The distinctive philosophy of protection that characterizes the laws of literary and artistic property in the Berne Union countries[1] was extended only gradually, and against considerable opposition, to 'works of art applied to industry.'[2] Throughout most of the nineteenth century, the separation of 'beauty' from 'utility' was an axiom rooted in Enlightenment ideals. Reformers who attacked 'art for art's sake' as an elitist slogan found support for functionalism in Greek philosophy of art and pointed to Cellini's saltcellars or Raphael's candelabra as proof that art remained art even when applied to useful objects. But this lofty discourse minimized the economic aims of industrial art, which only came into its own when the industrial revolution had made it possible to reproduce useful articles in series and which then assumed the eminently practical task of increasing sales of goods on the general products market. The Berne Union countries, at the Berlin Revision Conference of 1908, mentioned the category of 'applied art' for the first time, but declined to grant ornamental designs of useful articles full protection in the law of literary and artistic property. The Conference left member states free to deal with this controversial subject matter 'so far as the domestic legislation of each country allows.'

The United States ... appeared to go further toward recognizing applied art under the Copyright Act of 1909 than had the Berne Union countries at the Berlin Revision Conference of 1908. Congress added the phrase 'models or designs of works of art' to the 'works of art' otherwise protected in section 5(g) of the 1909 Act as 'writings of an author.' ...

In December 1948, the United States Copyright Office changed the definition of a 'work of art' in Regulation Section 202.8. The new definition included 'works of artistic craftsmanship, in so far as their form but not their mechanical or utilitarian aspects are concerned, such as artistic jewelry, enamels, glassware and tapestries, as well as all works belonging to the fine arts.' In 1949, the Register published his opinion that mass-produced artistic jewelry could qualify as copyrightable works of art on analogy to Cellini's saltcellars; the Copyright Office accepted for registration many three-dimensional works of applied art in the next few years. By September 6, 1952, when the United States signed the Universal Copyright Convention at Geneva, this country's domestic law

---

* Reprinted with permission from 1983 Duke Law Journal 1143 (1983); © 1983 Jerome Reichman and Duke Law Journal.

1. The Berne Union was created by the Berne Convention for the Protection of Literary and Artistic Works.... The Berne Convention, signed September 9, 1886, appears in 3 COPYRIGHT LAWS, Multilateral Conventions, Berne Copyright Union, item A–1 [hereinafter cited as Berne Convention]; it was revised ... at Paris on July 24, 1971, id. at item H–1, (entered into force July 10, 1974 in accordance with article 28) [hereinafter cited as Paris Revision].

2. S[tephen] Ladas, Patents, Trademarks, And Related Rights: National And International Protection 828–37 (1975) ...

appeared to afford limited recognition to applied art, consistent with treaty obligations and with the future working relations between the Geneva countries and the Berne Union.

When the United States Court of Appeals for the Fourth Circuit heard *Stein v. Mazer*, the Copyright Office intervened with an amicus brief contending that the statuettes of male and female dancing figures were entitled to copyright protection under the 1909 Act despite their commercial use as lamp bases. The Fourth Circuit, relying heavily on this brief, upheld copyrightability. The Supreme Court of the United States affirmed the Fourth Circuit's decision in the landmark case of *Mazer v. Stein* [347 U.S. 201 (1954)], which validated Regulation Section 202.8 and established for the first time the protectibility of applied art in United States copyright law.

The issue for a majority of the Supreme Court was not whether a manufacturer had the right to register a lamp base but rather whether an artist's right to copyright a work of art was compromised by his intention to apply that work of art to mass-produced useful articles. The Court answered in the negative, because the creator of a picture or a statue was an author whose 'writings' fell within the constitutional enabling clause. The Court held that the distinction between 'fine arts' and 'useful works of art' had ended with the 1909 Act's deletion of the fine arts clause of the 1870 Act. Because the statutory authority to protect 'works of art' and 'reproductions of works of art' encompassed the statuettes in question, they could not be excluded by judgments concerning their aesthetic value or by 'a narrow or rigid concept of art.' Moreover, the potential patentability of the statuettes as lamps did not bar their copyrightability as works of art, even though the United Kingdom had reached the opposite result. 'The dichotomy of protection for the aesthetic is not beauty and utility but art for the copyright and the invention of original and ornamental design for design patents.'

The decision in *Mazer v. Stein* had a 'revolutionary impact' that took some time to make itself felt. With *Mazer*, the United States acquiesced in the proposition, formally honored by most of the world, that an ornamental design did not necessarily cease to be artistic when embodied in a useful article. But the *Mazer* Court never addressed the related problem that some, many, or most ornamental designs might not rise to the level of protectible works of applied art. Perhaps the traditional art form of the statues obscured this issue; or perhaps the Court assumed that the nondiscrimination principle of Bleistein dictated a very broad definition of a work of art.

* * *

B. Legitimation of Applied Art in the Berne Union.

1. The Unity of Art Thesis in France. The copyright approach to industrial art rests on the notion that ornamental designs of useful articles should not be denied protection as artistic works merely because of their industrial character. A cultural and political bias in favor of gratuitous art or 'art for art's sake' fueled resistance to this proposition. It is now clear, however, that copyright protection of aesthetic designs affects competition between useful articles whose legal status is other-

wise determined by the laws of industrial property. The laws governing industrial property, including patent, trademark and, since the eighteenth century, sui generis design laws, obey different legal principles that drive most useful articles toward free competition. . . .

[E.] Pouillet's 'theory of the unity of art' gained legislative recognition in both France and Belgium. Viewing attempts to establish a rational line of demarcation between the design law and the copyright law as futile, Pouillet maintained that decorators, painters, sculptors, and fashion designers were all artists whose works uniformly deserved to be governed by the copyright paradigm. Under Pouillet's influence, French copyright law, as amended in 1902, extended protection to 'designers of ornaments, whatever may be the merit and the purpose of the work.' By the 1930's, despite pockets of judicial resistance, French law had rejected every test of aesthetic creation that 'would allow industrial art to be separated from real art.' Consequently, originators of 'all creations of form, even the most modest,' obtain a generous bundle of economic and moral rights for a term of life plus fifty years from creation, and need not comply with any formal prerequisites whatsoever, such as notice, registration, or deposit.

Despite the triumph of the unity of art thesis, the French legislature did not repeal the special design law of 1806. Instead, the legislature passed the design law of July 14, 1909, still in force, which further refined the advantages conferred by sui generis legislation with respect to establishing proof of ownership, facilitating transfers of title, and restricting competition. The unity of art principle, expressly confirmed by the law of 1909 and later by the copyright law of March 11, 1957, gave designers and manufacturers the opportunity to cumulate the advantages of both acts without penalizing them for failing to take one route or the other in any given case. Provided that a design were registered under the design law of 1909, the provisions of this law might fully satisfy the owner's legal needs. If, for one reason or another, his attempt to invoke the design law proved abortive or otherwise insufficient, the owner could simultaneously invoke the protection of copyright law in the very action for infringement under the design law. If, finally, the creator had ignored the design law altogether, his entitlement to copyright protection from the date of creation would not suffer merely because special design protection might have been available had he taken the pains to meet the requirements of registration and deposit.

The unity of art thesis in France produced two results of primary importance from the comparative standpoint. First, it led France to extend copyright protection to all industrial art, including commercial designs 'on the lower frontier of applied art' that 'depend on what is called industrial aesthetics.' Second, it led to gradual integration of the copyright law and the special design law into what is technically described as a regime of absolute or total cumulation. . . .

It should be stressed that countries opposed to the unity of art thesis did not automatically relegate designs excluded from copyright law to the public domain. Both Germany and Italy, while subscribing to different exclusionary criteria, agreed in principle that designs of useful articles should be regulated by sui generis design laws modeled on the French design law of 1806. These sui generis design laws placed ornamental designs within a hybrid legal framework, heavily influenced by patent law, that seemed consistent with the industrial character of the useful articles in which any artistic components were embodied.

The legal status of industrial art thus varied from country to country, despite the broad multilateral conventions that otherwise regulated artistic property on the one hand and industrial property on the other.

* * *

[As these historical examples demonstrate,] [t]he harder a country makes it to obtain copyright protection for industrial art, the more that country's special design law may determine the scope of the design protection actually available within that system. If a country makes it easy for industrial art to qualify for copyright protection as applied art, designers will have less incentive to make use of a special design law and design protection will increasingly be characterized by the copyright approach. The true scope and effectiveness of any given design law will therefore depend on the extent to which the scope of protection it affords, and the conditions it imposes, are undermined by the concurrent availability of copyright protection for industrial art. At the same time, measures needed to limit concurrent protection are likely to derogate from general principles of copyright law.

* * *

Three options—cumulation, noncumulation and partial cumulation—have thus continued to exist in the Berne Union's intellectual property law system after the Brussels Conference of 1948. Some countries have shifted allegiance over the course of time, notably the United Kingdom and the Benelux group. The choices among these options made by different countries reflect more than domestic self-interest; they also reflect fundamental differences of principle concerning both the nature of art and the proper limits of protection for intellectual property, which differences are exacerbated by the hybrid nature of industrial art. Until they are resolved or tempered by compromise, no international system of design protection can fulfill its goals, despite continuing efforts at harmonization and reform.

C. Options for the United States

* * *

This article concentrates on the copyright approach to industrial art in the United States, from the *Mazer* decision of 1954 to the General Revision of Copyright Law enacted in 1976. The subject can be subdivided into two periods. During the first, from 1954 to 1969, the Copyright Office tried to limit the access of industrial art to protection afforded by the Copyright Act of 1909, while pressing Congress for prompt enactment of a sui generis design law intended to resolve many of the problems known to exist abroad. In the second period, from 1969 to 1976, the Copyright Office sought to limit the breaches in defenses erected earlier, while Congress delayed enactment of both the general revision of copyright law and the special design law incorporated within it.

Since 1954, the United States has experimented with each of the basic positions in foreign law and found all of them unsatisfactory.
* * *

2.   An Interim Theory of Dissociation. The unity of art theory asserts that industrial art is art; the theory of dissociation starts from the premise that industrial art is inextricably bound up with industrial products. Industrial products are protected by the laws of industrial property, which, in Italy, treat ornamental features of 'shape, design, and color' as the subject matter of a special design law. The question then arises as to when elements of shape, design, and color used to embellish an industrial product may be considered 'works of art applied to industry' and therefore protectible under copyright law notwithstanding the existence of a special design law. The answer, according to the theory of dissociation, is that copyright protection will be accorded to a work that contains its own message and conserves its artistic value independently of the material support in which it is embodied.

The theory of dissociation was carried to its logical conclusion in the last reform of relevant Italian law. Article 5 of the Italian Design Law of 1940 declared expressly that ornamental designs and models should not be protectible in copyright law.... If a design actually registered under the design law might have qualified for copyright protection instead, the act of registration will normally constitute a renunciation of the protection that copyright law might otherwise have provided....

Dissociation theory subjects 'creations of form,' whose aesthetic character is manifested in the lines and shape of a product, to the design protection law in force. It excludes from copyright law those functional shapes, devoid of ornamentation, that cannot be conceived of separately from the material objects they 'circumscribe in space.' In practice, dissociation theory excludes virtually all three-dimensional designs, because only the design that has been added to the object without losing its autonomous character is ever copyrightable.

3.   Toward an American Regime of Sui Generis Protection.
* * *

[Professor Reichman describes developments in U.S. law in the direction of segregating works into either copyright protection or design protection, and not allowing a single work to be protected by both—i.e., a "dissociation" approach, as opposed to "cumulation."]

Adoption of dissociation theory was merely the first step toward obtaining a major reform of design legislation that the Copyright Office hoped would be even more anticumulationist than the Italian model. The second step would involve both completing the design protection law then under study and strictly defining the new law's relationship to the copyright law so as to exclude designs of useful articles from copyright protection. The third step was to obtain rapid congressional approval of this scheme before the legislative phase of the general revision of copyright law got under way.

* * *

The line of demarcation to be established between the new design law and the Copyright Act of 1909 was crucial to the success of this proposal. Would a manufacturer, offered a choice between soft design protection on soft terms for five years or hard design protection on hard terms for a maximum of fourteen years, also be entitled to claim soft protection on soft terms for up to fifty-six years in copyright law? Could a designer circumvent both components of a dual regime of design protection by asserting that a particular design possessed 'separable' artistic values or that it otherwise constituted a 'work of applied art?'

The group of American experts answered both questions in the negative. They said that the line of demarcation between copyright law and design protection law should be based on the 'usefulness' of the article in which the design or work of art was embodied. A broad definition of a 'useful article' was accordingly drafted to include 'an article normally having an intrinsic function other than merely to portray its own appearance or to convey information.' Under this definition, works of fine art were not useful articles 'because their normal and intrinsic function is to portray their own appearance'; similarly, books, maps or documentary films did not fall within this definition because they 'convey information.'

Design protection attached only after embodiment in the useful article, and normally after disclosure through marketing.

* * *

The decision of the drafters of [the proposed sui generic design protection bill] to use the useful article to demarcate between copyright and design protection law was not rooted in the notion that ornamental designs of useful articles were "less valuable aesthetically or culturally than 'works of fine art,' " whatever the United States position had been in the past. Instead, they chose this line of demarcation primarily because 'the impact of long term statutory protection upon the consuming public and the national economy is much greater in the field of useful commodities than . . . in the area of fine arts' and because 'articles . . . bought for use have much greater economic significance than those . . . bought solely for display.' . . .

The solution proposed by the committee of experts in 1959 suffered from being ahead of its time rather than from the regressive tendencies attributed to it by a powerful lobby. Far from 'maiming' copyright law, the reforms embodied in S. 2075 would have checked the drift toward giving 'too few designs . . . too much protection' that followed *Mazer v. Stein.*

* * *

b. Noncumulation without a design law. The Copyright Office originally used the Italian criterion of separability to thwart the possibility of interpreting Mazer v. Stein so as to adopt the French unity of art doctrine. Although the exclusionary power of the separability criterion had undoubtedly been weakened in the course of time. the Copyright Office had nonetheless managed to avoid a direct test of its legality prior to the 1976 decision in Esquire, Inc. v. Ringer [591 F.2d 796 (D.C. Cir. 1978)]. Enactment of Titles I and II before 1976 would have relieved the pressure on separability and made it both plausible and feasible for the Copyright Office to implement a program of partial cumulation along the lines suggested above. But Esquire, together with other decisions tending to validate a broad reading of Mazer, undermined the criterion of separability before the design law of Title II could be adopted. These cases legitimated an American version of the unity of art thesis on the very eve of final adoption of the General Revision of Copyright Law under way since 1955.

Sometime after May 1976, when the district court decided Esquire, the House Committee on the Judiciary was prompted to amend the Senate's version of the pending revision bill by adding the separability language in section 202.10(c) of the 1959 regulation almost verbatim to the definition of 'pictorial, graphic, and sculptural works' in section 101 of Title I. Under the definition of 'useful articles,' also in section 101, ornamental designs of such articles, however aesthetically pleasing, would normally possess an intrinsic utilitarian function. The amended text thus subjected virtually all industrial art seeking copyright protection under Title I to the separability criterion of sections 101 and 102(a)(5), despite the district court's decision in Esquire. This doctrine of separability could then authorize the denial of copyrightability to modern, functional designs, a practice the Register had unsuccessfully tried to defend at the district court level in Esquire. Such designs would obtain protection for up to ten years under the sui generis regime of Title II, which had already passed the Senate for the fifth time.

The new definition of pictorial, graphic, and sculptural works, combined with Title II of the pending revision bills, amounted to an American version of the Italian noncumulationist model. This scheme, unlike its Italian counterpart, did not provide for the protection of utility models. It sanctioned a dual regime of short-term design protection, below the line of demarcation with copyright law, that would have enabled users to choose between absolute protection under the design patent law and protection against copying under Title II.

[T]he House Judiciary Subcommittee on Courts, Civil Liberties, and the Administration of Justice decided, in a closely divided vote, to strike Title II from the Senate's version of the general revision bill. The Conference Committee did not restore this provision to the Final Act before its enactment in October 1976.

The General Revision of Copyright Law that emerged from the Conference Report was thus a mutilated version of the Register's last proposal. It retained the separability criterion in the new definition of 'pictorial, graphic, and sculptural works,' which reads as follows:

> 'Pictorial, graphic, and sculptural works' include two-dimensional and three-dimensional works of fine, graphic, and applied art, photographs, prints and art reproductions, maps, globes, charts, technical drawings, diagrams, and models. Such works shall include works of artistic craftsmanship insofar as their form but not their mechanical or utilitarian aspects are concerned; the design of a useful article, as defined in this

section, shall be considered a pictorial, graphic, or sculptural work only if, and only to the extent that, such design incorporates pictorial, graphic, or sculptural features that can be identified separately from, and are capable of existing independently of, the utilitarian aspects of the article.

The General Revision also retained the inclusive definition of useful articles: "A 'useful article' is an article having an intrinsic utilitarian function that is not merely to portray the appearance of the article or to convey information. An article that is normally a part of a useful article is considered a 'useful article.'" But the reformed copyright law lacked the special regime of design protection that gave logical coherence to the Italian system. By ... rejecting a special design bill, Congress, in the provisions signed into law on October 19, 1976, ensured continuation in the United States of a system that was fundamentally flawed.

Notes and Questions

1. For a biographical note on Jerome Reichman, see supra, Chapter 2, page 362.

2. Reichman notes that "in Italy, [legislation] treat[s] ornamental features of 'shape, design, and color' as the subject matter of a special design law." Italian designs are famous the world over. See, e.g., http://www.scuoladesign.com (website of the Scuola Politecnica di Design (SPD) in Milan, a famous design academy). Is this a coincidence? Is the strong legal protection for designs a result of Italian interest in industrial design, or a cause of it?

3. In a series of related articles, Reichman has documented that the different approaches to industrial design protection described in the excerpted article are not static. In his view, each country continually cycles among the various approaches:

> And so it goes, round and round across the world's intellectual property system, from one generation to the next without breaking the cyclical pattern. Chronic underprotection in industrial property law leads to chronic overprotection in artistic property law, which in turn inspires further reactive reforms of industrial property law tending to reinstate levels of underprotection that will foster renewed appeals to copyright law.

J.H. Reichman, "Past and Current Trends in the Evolution of Design Protection Law—A Comment," 4 *Fordham Intell. Prop. Media & Ent. L.J.* 387, 389 (1993).

4. The European countries whose design protection regimes Reichman describes recently drafted unifying legal principles for members of the European Union. See E.U. Directive 98/71 ("Design Directive"), O.J. L289/28–25. See also Katrine A. Levin and Monica B. Richman, "A Survey of Industrial Design Protection in the European Union and the United States," [2003] *Euro. Intell. Prop. Rev.* 111 (2003) (describing the European Design Directive requirement of "individual character," required for protection under the European system, and akin to the "novelty" requirement for obtaining a U.S. design patent).

II. Scope of Protection

Applied Art and Industrial Design: A Suggested Approach to Copyright in Useful Articles*

ROBERT C. DENICOLA

The word 'copyright' evokes images of books, movies, or sound recordings. Further reflection might yield visions of paintings, photographs, or sculptural works. Few, however, associate copyright with belt buckles, table lamps, or pencil sharpeners—yet to some unsettled extent, even these items have their place in the copyright scheme.

Copyright law has reluctantly embraced a variety of works embodied in utilitarian objects, while simultaneously purporting to exclude the general province of industrial design. The courts have concluded that a light bulb protruding from Michelangelo's David ought not render the statue unprotectible, while insisting that the overall design of modern street lights lies beyond the scope of copyright protection. The grudging inclusion of selected useful objects has led both Congress and the courts to seek a rationale that could stand fast against the deluge of mass-produced industrial goods. Although the search has not gone well, the decision to exclude the general appearance of commercial products from copyright protection remains unshaken. The result has been a patchwork of ad hoc decisions, united only by their common references to statutory formulations that do little more than restate the dilemma.

The legal status of commercial design, however, is only partially fixed by copyright principles. Design patents long offered the possibility of protection for the ornamental design of a useful product. Their integration into a general patent regime directed primarily at mechanical rather than aesthetic innovation, however, severely undermined their practical utility. Consequently, alternative proposals have become a congressional fixture, spawning a raft of conflicting academic analysis. The failure to win more specialized protection has encouraged efforts to assimilate design protection into the law of copyright. Indeed, even passage of a sui generis design statute would do little to deflect attempts to secure the more expansive monopoly offered by copyright.

This Article examines the current status of useful articles under the Copyright Act of 1976 and proposes an alternative analysis of their copyrightability. Congress, borrowing heavily from prior administrative and judicial formulations, has constructed an elaborate mechanism to differentiate protectible 'applied art' from unprotectible 'industrial design.' Thus, the Act rejects both wholesale inclusion and exclusion of utilitarian objects, leaving it to the courts to define and defend a middle ground. Against the backdrop of Justice Holmes's admonition to avoid judicial determinations of artistic merit or worth,[3] however, few touch-

---

* Reprinted with permission from 67 Minn.L.Rev. 707 (1983); © 1983 Minnesota Law Review and Robert C. Denicola.

3.

It would be a dangerous undertaking for persons trained only to the law to constitute themselves final judges of the worth of pictorial illustrations, outside of the narrowest

stones developed. Yet, a discriminating approach is both defensible and desirable. Industrial design differs in important respects from the traditional subject matters of copyright, and presents a less compelling claim to the statutory monopoly. But it is unwise, if not in fact impossible, to exclude from the scope of copyright all works capable of serving some useful purpose. The attempts of the Congress, the Copyright Office, and the courts to delimit the boundaries of copyright in useful articles have been only partially successful. Their efforts have a transient quality conspicuous even in a legal regime populated by concepts as ephemeral as 'idea,' 'expression,' and 'creativity.' A good portion of the difficulty arises from the tendency to focus exclusively on the results of the creative effort. This Article suggests that it is the process of creation that distinguishes industrial design from applied art and other forms of authorship traditionally recognized by copyright law.

I. INITIAL ENCOUNTERS

Among the items eligible for copyright under the 1909 Act were those specified in section 5(g): 'Works of art; models or designs for works of art.' With the deletion of [the 1870 Act's] reference to the 'fine arts,' a major barrier to copyright in the design of useful objects apparently fell. No logic could demonstrate that crystal wine glasses, pearl rings, or even handsome radio cabinets were not 'works of art.' The Copyright Office, however, quickly moved to exclude useful articles from the scope of copyright by resurrecting the very distinction so recently abandoned by the Congress. In a 1910 regulation defining 'works of art,' the Copyright Office restricted the newly established classification to 'the so-called fine arts,' expressly excluding 'productions of the industrial arts utilitarian in purpose and character.'

The 'industrial arts,' however, proved difficult to contain. . . .

In 1954, the United States Supreme Court considered a copyright infringement claim involving china statuettes of Balinese dancing figures. The contestants in Mazer v. Stein[4] were rival lamp manufacturers. The copyright owner, with the addition of the appropriate hardware, employed the statuettes as bases for table lamps. The statuettes, sans sockets and wiring, were registered with the Copyright Office as 'works of art' and 'reproductions of a work of art.' A competitor copied the figures and put them to a similar use.

The defendants premised their response to the charge of infringement chiefly on the federal design patent law, which protects 'any new, original and ornamental design for an article of manufacturer.' Only

---

and most obvious limits. At the one extreme, some works of genius would be sure to miss appreciation. Their very novelty would make them repulsive until the public had learned the new language in which their author spoke. It may be more than doubted, for instance, whether the etchings of Goya or the paintings of Manet would have been sure of protection when seen for the first time. At the other end, copyright would be denied to pictures which appealed to a public less educated than the judge.

Bleistein v. Donaldson Lithographing Co., 188 U.S. 239, 251–52 (1903) (Holmes, J.). See Mazer v. Stein, 347 U.S. 201, 214 (1954) ('Individual perception of the beautiful is too varied a power to permit a narrow or rigid concept of art.').

   4. 347 U.S. 201 (1954).

design patents, they argued, could monopolize the appearance of mass-produced utilitarian articles. The Court did not agree: 'Neither the Copyright Statute nor any other says that because a thing is patentable it may not be copyrighted. We should not so hold.'[5] The contention that useful articles were beyond the limits of copyright was formally put to rest:

> The dichotomy of protection for the aesthetic is not beauty and utility but art for the copyright and the invention of original and ornamental design for design patents. We find nothing in the copyright statute to support the argument that the intended use or use in industry of an article eligible for copyright bars or invalidates its registration. We do not read such a limitation into the copyright law.[6]

Mazer, however, fell far short of a wholesale endorsement of copyright in the design of useful objects. The Court was quick to point out the narrow issue for decision: 'The case requires an answer, not as to a manufacturer's right to register a lamp base but as to an artist's right to copyright a work of art intended to be reproduced for lamp bases.'[7] The statuettes, as works of art, were entitled to copyright. Neither prior nor subsequent use in utilitarian articles, nor the fact that they were conceived expressly for such an end, jeopardized that status. Utility and art were no longer mutually exclusive, but it was still only the latter that could command copyright. Mazer answered one question, yet wisely eschewed another. The use to which 'works of art' are put is irrelevant, the Court declared, but the bounds of that statutory classification remained uncertain. A dancing figure qualified, but the Court had said nothing of the forms displayed by toasters or automobiles, or the designs of wedding gowns or belt buckles.

* * *

In retrospect, Mazer v. Stein did little to clarify the issue of copyright in the design of commercial products; it merely enjoined the automatic excision of all utilitarian articles. Although the Copyright Office Regulations soon reflected the Court's narrow holding, the administrative response did not end with codification. Determined to close the door that Mazer left ajar, the Copyright Office sought a formulation that would accommodate Mazer, yet exclude the general realm of industrial design. After one aborted attempt, it settled on the 'separability' standard that has come to dominate current analysis: If the sole intrinsic function of an article is its utility, the fact that the article is unique and attractively shaped will not qualify it as a work of art. However, if the shape of a utilitarian article incorporates features, such as artistic sculpture, carving, or pictorial representation, which can be identified separately and are capable of existing independently as a work of art, such features will be eligible for registration.

5. 347 U.S. at 217.

6. Id. at 218. The Copyright Office had by this time registered a variety of utilitarian articles, including 'book ends, clocks, lamps, door knockers, candlesticks, inkstands, chandeliers, piggy banks, sundials, salt and pepper shakers, fish bowls, casseroles, and ash trays.' Id. at 221 (Douglas, J., concurring). Some of these items, however, may not be protected under the more intricate standard currently in effect. . . .

7. 347 U.S. at 205.

Mazer had quickly become the limit of copyright in useful articles.

Even the guarded terms of Mazer and its regulatory progeny, however, brought major change. Overcoming a long-standing exclusion, graphic designs adorning textiles were now securely within the subject matter of copyright. The regulations said as much. Indeed, any two-dimensional graphic work could arguably be 'identified separately' from the utilitarian article to which it was applied, and copyright registrations were issued in connection with graphic designs appearing on products ranging from shoe soles to dinnerware. Yet there were limits. When the graphic elements went beyond mere applique and became more intimately associated with the utilitarian features of the article, protection was denied.

The test of separate identity and independent existence could be particularly troublesome when the copyright claim was directed at three-dimensional aspects of utilitarian articles. Some objects presented little difficulty. The 'Flying Lady' hood ornament could be detached from the accompanying Rolls–Royce, yielding a perfectly independent statuette. With a bit more imagination, gargoyles could be mentally chiseled from pediments, and lamp shades and sockets stripped from dancing figures. The case law, however, presented greater challenges. For example, it seemed natural to extend protection to children's coin banks shaped in forms ranging from dogs to humans, despite the difficulty in identifying features 'capable of existing independently.' The 'work of art' was the bank itself. If the overall shape of a cocker spaniel bank was protectible, could anything more than aesthetic prejudice exclude the overall shapes of tea kettles, home computers, or food processors? Other cases similarly undermined the administrative criterion. Copyright was upheld in a ring box with no mention of separability, and registration issued for a series of molds used in the manufacture of ceramic figures. Yet such objects offered no obviously separable elements; the art lay in the articles themselves.

* * *

Despite the shortcomings of the doctrinal formulations, both the courts and the Copyright Office maintained the conviction that copyright protection for the general design of commercial products was inappropriate. Efforts to achieve a general revision of the copyright law began within a year after the decision in Mazer v. Stein, and throughout the twenty-one years of legislative machinations that preceded the enactment of the current statute, the Copyright Office consistently counseled against the extension of copyright to industrial design.

II. THE COPYRIGHT ACT OF 1976

A. *THE REVISION EFFORT*

The decision to undertake a major revision of United States copyright law provided proponents of protection for industrial design a unique opportunity. Influenced perhaps by the position of the Copyright Office, however, their energies focused not on copyright per se, but rather on a series of companion bills offering sui generis protection for ornamental designs of useful articles....

Bills for the protection of industrial design had been introduced regularly since the turn of the century, and the issue had generated a plethora of conflicting analysis. The Copyright Office itself had developed an extensive bibliography on the subject.

During the 1960's, separate design protection bills passed the Senate on three occasions. In 1969, the Senate formally joined the design proposals with copyright revision. Carried by the momentum of the revision effort, design protection legislation appeared as Title II of the general copyright revision bill when the Senate ultimately forwarded the legislation to the House in 1976. Title II provided protection for the 'original ornamental design of a useful article.' 'Staple or commonplace' designs were excluded, together with those 'dictated solely by a utilization function of the article.' Protection extended for a maximum of ten years, and prohibited the manufacture, importation, or sale of articles 'the design of which has been copied from the protected design, without the consent of the proprietor.' The bill established administrative machinery for the registration of protectible designs, but left to the President the designation of the appropriate governmental office to oversee the scheme. Title I provided that copyright in works utilized in connection with useful articles was unaffected by the protection available under Title II, unless the proprietor actually obtained a Title II registration.

Title II, designated the Design Protection Act of 1975 did not survive consideration in the House. The Judiciary Committee 'chose to delete Title II in part because the new form of design protection provided by Title II could not truly be considered copyright protection and therefore appropriately within the scope of copyright revision.'[8] ...

The legislative energy necessary to grapple with the issue of design protection was apparently exhausted in the formulation of Title II. In the copyright revision bill itself, there was old wine in old bottles. The cornerstone of the revision bill's approach to copyright in useful articles was a narrow codification of Mazer, which Congress read as holding 'that works of art which are incorporated into the design of useful articles, but which are capable of standing by themselves as art works separate from the useful article, are copyrightable.' The 'works of art' classification of the 1909 Act was abandoned and replaced by a reference to 'pictorial, graphic, and sculptural works.' This new category endeavored to supply 'as clear a line as possible between copyrightable works of applied art and uncopyrighted works of industrial design.' The line, however, was neither clear nor new. After declaring that 'pictorial, graphic, and sculptural works' included works of 'applied art,' the definition stated:

> [T]he design of a useful article, as defined in this section, shall be considered a pictorial, graphic, or sculptural work only if, and only to the extent that, such design incorporates pictorial, graphic, or sculptural features that can be identified separately from, and are capable of existing independently of, the utilitarian aspects of the article. * * *

The failure to win protection for industrial design reflects more than the vagaries of the legislative process. Sixty years of unsuccessful lobbying suggests more substantive difficulties. One can appreciate the reluc-

---

8. H.R. REP. NO. 1476, supra note 3, at 50.

tance of Congress to subsume industrial design within the scope of copyright, or to authorize a more specialized monopoly, by considering the basic arguments generally used to support the recognition of proprietary rights in intellectual property.

The most obvious effect of extending copyright or more specialized protection to the design of commercial products would be the exclusion of such designs from the public domain, thus preventing their free use by competing manufacturers. The necessity of such an artificial incentive, however, is hardly clear. In one sense, manufacturers do not have the option of discontinuing the creation of industrial designs, since all products must take on some shape and appearance. Thus the question is not whether manufacturers will design, but rather how large an investment of resources they will devote to the development of designs possessing some particular virtue or appeal. Even without the stimulus provided by the prospect of a statutory monopoly, there appear to be significant incentives to invest in design. If that is indeed the case, restraints on competition may achieve little in the way of increased design activity.

The most obvious incentive to produce appealing designs is the desire to attract customers, since '[b]etween two products equal in price, function, and quality, the better looking will outsell the other.'[9] Even a design that is merely different rather than 'better' may have its advantages, because it may appeal to a desire for diversity or distinctiveness and aid in marketing by differentiating the product from its rivals. By accentuating performance characteristics such as strength, durability, or workmanship, an appropriate design may increase sales even when aesthetic appeal is not a significant consideration. Effort invested in design may also result in enhanced performance or reduced production costs.

Given the obvious advantage of a well conceived product design, the question becomes whether the risk of appropriation by a competitor will nevertheless cause manufacturers to significantly decrease their investment of resources in design activity. For several reasons, the answer may often be 'No.' The cost of creating an appealing design, for example, may represent only a small fraction of total product development and production costs. With so much at stake, a manufacturer is unlikely to forego the substantial benefits of a well designed product merely because a competitor might gain a marginal saving through design piracy. If the design is indeed advantageous, even a relatively short lead time may be sufficient to permit recovery of design costs. In addition, the risk of copying may frequently be overstated. Outside the limited reach of design patent law, no legal barrier currently exists to prevent design piracy. Yet variations in product appearance continue to be the norm. Indeed, there are disincentives to copying. Product differentiation may be as valuable to a competitor as to the design originator. Major competitors may be reluctant to tarnish their image by engaging in design piracy, since consumers frequently associate copies with lower quality and desirability. Copying may sometimes cause consumers to confuse the copy with the original, thus creating potential liability in an

9. R. LOEWY, INDUSTRIAL DESIGN 10 (1979).

action for trademark infringement or unfair competition. Even when copying does occur, its impact may be modest if the utilitarian qualities of the original cannot be duplicated because of mechanical patent or trade secret protection, or because of the copier's less sophisticated production capabilities. * * *

III.   APPLIED ART AND INDUSTRIAL DESIGN

A.   *THE DESIGN PROCESS*

The objective of the separability test, according to its legislative history, is to divide copyrightable 'applied art' from uncopyrightable 'industrial design.' Rational application of the standard thus requires some appreciation of the distinctive nature of industrial design.

In a sense, the origins of industrial design can be traced to the earliest attempts to fashion natural materials into more useful forms. Not until the Industrial Revolution brought the capacity to manufacture unlimited quantities of identical products, however, did a discreet conception of industrial design begin to emerge. Initially, industrial design was little more than a belated attempt to conceal the patent ugliness proliferated by developing technologies. This concept of industrial design as decoration, however, was gradually replaced by a vision premised on a more intimate relationship between the nature of a product and its appearance. In 1894, Frank Lloyd Wright declared that 'the machine is here to stay,' and challenged the designer to 'use this normal tool of civilization to best advantage instead of prostituting it as he has hitherto done in reproducing with murderous ubiquity forms born of other times and other conditions.' The twentieth century soon saw industrial design become an integral aspect of product development.

The dominant feature of modern industrial design is the merger of aesthetic and utilitarian concerns. It is the influence of nonaesthetic factors, the nexus between what the product must do and how it must look, that distinguishes true industrial design from other artistic endeavors. The industrial designer as engineer—a perspective no less valid than industrial designer as artist—is subject to the functional constraints inherent in each undertaking. The designer cannot follow wherever aesthetic interests might lead. Utilitarian concerns influence, and at times dictate, available choices. Indeed, aesthetic success is often measured in terms of the harmony achieved between competing interests. The merger of aesthetics and utility defines the designer's craft, so that 'whatever else he is or isn't—artist, engineer, salesman, planner, management consultant, inventor—the industrial designer is a problem solver.'

The most obvious factor influencing and directing the designer's creativity is the necessity of accommodating the functional operation of the product. At its most fundamental level, this consideration simply excludes any form that significantly interferes with the utility of the article. Modern approaches to industrial design, however, generally seek a relationship between form and function far more intimate than simple compatibility. Raymond Loewy, perhaps the design profession's most celebrated practitioner, speaks of the 'natural form' and 'self-expression of the machine.'[10] The notion of form reflecting function is a basic tenet of contemporary design: 'The best designs are those in which the appearance springs truly from the structure, and is a logical expression of it.'[11] Perusal of any of the multitude of books collecting illustrations of 'modern' design confirms the general acceptance of this fundamental credo. The notion of expressing function through form differs in an important respect from the more primitive requirement that form be compatible with function, since the former is itself a purely aesthetic concern, expressing one conception of 'good' design. In this sense, the principle suggests limitations not unlike those imposed on any artist by internal or external conceptions of artistic merit or worth. When practiced, however, the principle operates to intensify the nexus between form and function. . . .

B. COPYRIGHT IN USEFUL ARTICLES

The legislative history describes the separability test as an attempt 'to draw as clear a line as possible between copyrightable works of applied art and uncopyrightable works of industrial design.' In truth, of course, there is no line, but merely a spectrum of forms and shapes responsive in varying degrees to utilitarian concerns. Only a model appealing directly to the considerations underlying the separability standard can avoid purely arbitrary distinctions.

Taking Mazer as its touchstone, Congress sought to isolate pictorial, graphic, and sculptural works that are 'incorporated into a product,' or 'employed as the design of a useful article.' Congress thus attempted to distinguish artistic works that are merely utilized in the design process from those that result from the process itself. The distinction could, of course, be implemented by excluding all works created with some utilitarian application in view, but this would overturn Mazer, together with a host of other eminently sensible decisions, in favor of an intractable factual inquiry of questionable relevance. Any such categorical approach would also undermine the legislative determination to preserve an artist's ability to exploit utilitarian markets. Alternatively, the statutory directive requires a distinction between works of industrial design and works whose origins lie outside the design process, despite the utilitarian environment in which they appear. Copyrightability, therefore, should turn on the relationship between the proffered work and the process of industrial design. Because the dominant characteristic of industrial design is the influence of nonaesthetic, utilitarian concerns, copyrightability ultimately should depend on the extent to which the work reflects artistic expression uninhibited by functional considerations. Only such a direct assessment of the nature of the claimant's contribution can implement the congressional decision to exclude the general realm of industrial design, while preserving exclusive rights in 'applied art.' . . .

10. R. LOEWY, supra note [9], at 13.

11. W. CAIN, ENGINEERING PRODUCT DESIGN 157 (1969). 'One of the functions of aesthetics in engineering design is to indicate function and purpose.' F. ASHFORD, supra note 154, at 13. 'One might call the process beauty through function and simplification.' R. LOEWY, supra note [9], at 47.

The notion of distinguishing applied art from industrial design by examining the extent to which utilitarian considerations influence artistic expression has rarely surfaced in the case law. A few decisions make passing reference to similar ideas,[12] but the approach has never been used as a general model of the separability criterion. Yet no other model appears capable of successfully implementing the legislative decision to maintain unrestrained competition in the marketing of useful articles, subject only to an artist's exclusive rights in 'incorporated' art.

A model emphasizing the influence of utilitarian factors frees the judicial analysis from its unfortunate fixation on appearance alone. If the ultimate aim is to distinguish applied art from industrial design, theories focusing only on appearances cannot achieve the desired end. It is the process more than the result that gives industrial design its distinctive character. Although the shape of an old-fashioned telephone, for example, would likely be excluded from copyright under any of the alternative interpretations of the separability test, what of the design of a pencil sharpener fashioned to present a similar appearance? The decision in Ted Arnold Ltd. v. Silvercraft Co.[13] to protect such a work may well be correct. Although the appearance of the two products is similar, the creative process is not. In the context of a pencil sharpener, the form represents an essentially arbitrary conception responsive only to aesthetics.

The perspective afforded by this suggested approach to the separability standard may explain the superficial appeal of many competing models. In some instances, for example, physical separability may underscore the unconstrained, artistic nature of a particular product feature. The ability to remove a hood ornament without affecting an automobile's performance evidences its purely aesthetic origins. Art equally divorced from utilitarian influence, however, may often escape such narrow vision. Two-dimensional graphic works are not in reality physically detachable from the objects on which they appear. Three-dimensional shapes, whether coin banks,[14] pajama bags,[15] jewelry,[16] or pencil sharpen-

12.

In the case of costume jewelry, while the overall form is to some extent pre-determined by the use for which it is intended, the creator is free to express his idea of beauty in many ways. Unlike an automobile, a refrigerator or a gas range the design of a necklace or of a bracelet, may take as many forms as the ingenuity of the artist may conceive.

Trifari, Krussman & Fishel, Inc. v. Charel Co., 134 F.Supp. 551, 553 (S.D.N.Y. 1955) (copyright upheld in costume jewelry). 'Plaintiff concedes that the dimensions it designed were limited by the dimensions of the pencil sharpener. But this does not mean that the antique telephone is merely utilitarian. There was still room here for considerable artistic expression.' Ted Arnold Ltd. v. Silvercraft Co., 259 F.Supp. 733, 735–36 (S.D.N.Y. 1966) (copyright upheld in pencil sharpener casing). 'The shapes of the toys and their dimensions and configurations also appear to have been dictated primarily by utilitarian considerations.' Durham Indus., Inc. v. Tomy Corp., 630 F.2d 905, 915 (2d Cir. 1980) (denying copyright in 'sculpture' of mechanical games).

13. 259 F.Supp. 733 (S.D.N.Y. 1966).

14. See, e.g., Goldman–Morgen, Inc. v. Dan Brechner & Co., Inc., 411 F.Supp. 382 (S.D.N.Y. 1976); Royalty Designs, Inc. v. Thrifticheck Serv. Corp., 204 F.Supp. 702 (S.D.N.Y. 1962).

15. See R. Dakin & Co. v. A & L Novelty Co., 444 F.Supp. 1080 (E.D.N.Y. 1978).

16. See, e.g., Boucher v. DuBoyes, Inc., 253 F.2d 948 (2d Cir.), cert. denied, 357 U.S. 936 (1958); Cynthia Designs, Inc. v. Robert Zentall, Inc., 416 F.Supp. 510 (S.D.N.Y. 1976);

ers may also represent essentially arbitrary artistic conceptions, despite the absence of physical separability. Similarly, since utilitarian factors will significantly influence the overall shape of most useful articles, a general rule of exclusion such as that expounded in Esquire [v. Ringer, 591 F.2d 796 (D.C. Cir. 1978)] is not without justification, yet it too sweeps too broadly.[17] Such draconian models can at best only approximate the distinctions pursued in the revision effort. Only direct reference to the legislative conceptions of 'applied art' and 'industrial design' embodied in the separability test can produce more discriminating results.

Emphasis on artistic independence has the additional advantage of neutralizing the arbitrary nature of the 'useful article' characterization. The statutory category comprising articles 'having an intrinsic utilitarian function' may yield too rich a harvest, but works at the margin will generally survive inspection in any event. When utility is peripheral, as in paperweights or bookends, form is generally not significantly constrained by function, and thus the work will retain protection regardless of its characterization.

Attention to functional influences on form and appearance may also alleviate the de facto discrimination against nonrepresentational art that has regrettably accompanied much of the current analysis. It is difficult to quarrel with Judge Gesell's observation in Esquire that copyrightability ought not depend on adherence to particular artistic visions or styles.[18] There is no justification for limiting copyright to works reflecting aesthetic regimes in which the standard of merit is resemblance to external objects, while excluding those which seek virtue in the relationship of forms within the work itself. Yet, since the ordinary observer can more easily recognize a representational work that has been incorporated into a utilitarian object, emphasis on physical separability will frequently cause more abstract forms to be either overlooked or thought too 'integrated' to satisfy the statutory requirement. The general exclusion of overall shapes has a similarly pernicious effect. To avoid a crass or tasteless appearance, a utilitarian article is more likely to be given an abstract rather than representational form, although either may be arbitrary with respect to the underlying utility. Thus a ban on copyright in overall shape will fall heavily on abstract forms, barring works whose origins may lie far from the practical influences of the design process. The discrimination is diminished, however, under a model that places direct emphasis on the relationship between form and function. The shape of a Mickey Mouse telephone is copyrightable because its form is

Trifari, Krussman & Fishel, Inc. v. B. Steinberg–Kaslo Co., 144 F.Supp. 577 (S.D.N.Y. 1956); Trifari, Krussman & Fishel, Inc. v. Charel Co., 134 F.Supp. 551 (S.D.N.Y. 1955).

17. See, e.g., Durham Indus., Inc. v. Tomy Corp., 630 F.2d 905, 913 (2d Cir. 1980) (shape of mechanical games not copyrightable); Eltra Corp. v. Ringer, 579 F.2d 294, 297 (4th Cir. 1978) (typeface designs not copyrightable); Norris Indus. Corp. v. Int'l Tel. & Tel. Corp., 212 U.S.P.Q. (BNA) 754, 755–56 (N.D. Fla. 1981), affd, 696 F.2d 918 (11th Cir. 1983) (hubcaps not copyrightable); SCOA Indus., Inc. v. Famolare, Inc., 192 U.S.P.Q. (BNA) 216, 218 (S.D.N.Y. 1976) (shoe sole not copyrightable). Cf. Jack Odelman, Inc. v. Sonners & Gordon, Inc., 112 F.Supp. 187, 188–89 (S.D.N.Y. 1934) (copyright in drawing of dress gives no monopoly over the manufacture of the garment itself).

18. 414 F.Supp. at 941.

independent of function. A telephone shape owing more to Arp, Brancusi, or Moore than Disney may be equally divorced from utilitarian influence. An abstract shape employed as a lamp base may embody an artistic conception as untainted by utilitarian concerns as the Mazer statuettes. In all instances, unless the legislative distinction between applied art and industrial design is ignored, copyrightability must turn on the extent to which the work reflects either the independent perspective of the artist or the more integrated approach of the designer.

* * *

Notes and Questions

1. Robert C. Denicola received a B.S.E. degree from Princeton, and then J.D. and Ll.M. degrees from Harvard Law School. He has taught at the University of Nebraska School of Law since beginning his teaching career.

2. Denicola proposes to distinguish copyrightable from uncopyrightable in the design context on the basis of the "process of creation"—whether a design grew out of am artistic or industrial setting. This has proven to be an influential test, and has been adopted by several courts. See, e.g., Brandir Intern., Inc. v. Cascade Pacific Lumber Co., 834 F.2d 1142, 1145 (2d Cir. 1987) ("We believe that Professor Denicola's approach provides the best test for conceptual separability and, accordingly, adopt it here. . . ."). See also Celebration Intern., Inc. v. Chosun Intern., Inc., 234 F.Supp.2d 905, 913 (S.D. Ind. 2002) (citing excerpted article on the way to holding costume design is copyrightable).

3. Denicola states: "Even without the stimulus provided by the prospect of a statutory monopoly, there appear to be significant incentives to invest in design. If that is indeed the case, restraints on competition may achieve little in the way of increased design activity." Does this sound familiar from the readings on patent law? Consider the excerpt from Kitch, Graham v. John Deere, earlier in Chapter 1, in which he restates the traditional ideal standard for the nonobviousness requirement in patent law: "[T]he central point is that not every innovation needs the patent system to induce its appearance." The similarity in these arguments may explain why the U.S. continues to insist that only nonobvious designs of useful articles may be protected, and then only under the design patent statute. (The exception is useful designs which satisfy the "separability" test of copyright law.) Do you think there is a need for protection of obvious but nonetheless important designs? For a discussion of these and related issues, see J.H. Reichman, "Of Green Tulips and Legal Kudzu: Repackaging Rights in Subpatentable Innovation," 53 *Vand. L. Rev.* 1743 (2000).

4. As Reichman has described so ably, manufacturers of industrial products continue to explore novel legal theories in the quest for some semblance of design protection. One fruitful development in this direction in recent years has been the law of trade dress, a branch of trademark law. For recent developments in this connection, see Wal–Mart Stores, Inc. v. Samara Bros., Inc., 529 U.S. 205 (2000) (holding that product design is protectable under trade dress law only if it has acquired "secondary meaning" in accordance with trademark law); Traf-Fix Devices, Inc. v. Marketing Displays, Inc., 532 U.S. 23, 33 (2001) (holding that a functional feature is any feature which bestows a competitive advantage on the seller of a product embodying it, or "affects the cost or quality of the device"). See generally, Mark Alan Thurmon, "The Rise and Fall of Trademark Law's Functionality Doctrine," 56 *Fla. L. Rev.* 243 (2004) (criticizing the potential breadth of the Supreme Court's functionality test in *TrafFix*).

†